GLOBAL ASSEMBLAGES

GLOBAL ASSEMBLAGES

Technology, Politics, and Ethics as Anthropological Problems

EDITED BY

AIHWA ONG

AND

STEPHEN J. COLLIER

BLACKWELL PUBLISHING
350 Main Street, Malden, MA 02148-5020, USA
9600 Garsington Road, Oxford OX4 2DQ, UK
550 Swanston Street, Carlton, Victoria 3053, Australia

First published 2005 by Blackwell Publishing Ltd

5   2008

Library of Congress Cataloging-in-Publication Data

Global assemblages : technology, politics, and ethics as anthropological
problems / edited by Aihwa Ong and Stephen J. Collier.
p. cm.
Includes bibliographical references and index.
1. Social change.   2. Globalization–Social aspects.   3. Technological innovations–Social aspects.
4. Discoveries in science–Social aspects.   I. Ong, Aihwa.   II. Collier, Stephen J.
HM831.G49 2005
303.4–dc22   2003026675

ISBN: 978-0-631-23175-2 (cloth : alk. paper)–ISBN: 978-1-4051-2358-7 (pbk. : alk. paper)

A catalogue record for this title is available from the British Library.

Set in 10.5 on 13 pt Dante
by Kolam Information Services Pvt. Ltd, Pondicherry, India
Printed and bound in Singapore
by COS Printers Pte Ltd

For further information on
Blackwell Publishing, visit our website:
www.blackwellpublishing.com

CONTENTS

CONTENTS

NOTES ON CONTRIBUTORS

Geoffrey C. Bowker is Director, Center for Science, Technology, and Society, Santa Clara University. He studies political, organizational, and social factors in the design of scientific cyber-infrastructure, most notably in the domains of biodiversity science and the geosciences. He is author with Leigh Star of *Sorting Things Out: Classification and Practice* and has just completed a manuscript entitled *Memory Practices in the Sciences*.

Teresa Caldeira is Associate Professor of Anthropology at the University of California, Irvine. Her research has focused on the interconnections among urban violence, spatial segregation, and democratization. Currently, she is investigating the re-creation of gender and generational roles among São Paulo youth in the context of increasing urban violence and of unprecedented access to information and to new technologies. Her book *City of Walls: Crime, Segregation, and Citizenship in São Paulo* won the 2001 Senior Book Award of the American Ethnological Society.

Lawrence Cohen is Associate Professor in the Departments of Anthropology and of South and Southeast Asian Studies at the University of California, Berkeley. His work engages rhetorics and practices of life and politics in contemporary India and includes close engagements with topics ranging from senility and same-sex desire to surgical operations, political violence, and the fashion industry. He is the author of the award-winning *No Aging in India: Alzheimer's, the Bad Family and Other Modern Things*.

Stephen J. Collier is a Faculty member in the Graduate Program in International Affairs, The New School University. His interests include neoliberalism, postsocialist transformation, and urban change. He is currently completing a book, *Post Soviet Social*, on contemporary Russia.

Elizabeth C. Dunn is Assistant Professor of Geography and International Affairs, University of Colorado, Boulder. Her interests include standards and standardization, postsocialist eastern Europe, food politics, and the economic and social origins of food-borne disease. Forthcoming publications include "Trojan Pig," "A Steak is an Outcome Space: Traveling Facts, Negotiated Meaning, and the Social Construction of Safe Meat," in *Traveling Facts*, and *Privatizing Poland: Transforming Work and Personhood after Socialism*.

Sarah Franklin is Professor of Social Studies of Biomedicine at the London School of Economics. She is author or coauthor of *Embodied Progress: A Cultural Account of Assisted Conception, Technologies of Procreation: Kinship in the Age of Assisted Conception*, and *Global Nature, Global Culture*, and co-editor of *Off-Centre: Feminism and Cultural Studies, Reproducing Reproduction: Kinship, Power and Technological Innovation, Relative Values: Reconfiguring Kinship Studies*, and *Remaking Life and Death: Towards an Anthropology of the Biosciences*, and is currently completing a book about cloning entitled *Dolly Mixtures*. Her most recent ethnographic research has been based at two pre-implantation genetic diagnosis clinics in London and in Leeds.

Monique Girard is Associate Director of the Center on Organizational Innovation at Columbia University. Her current research addresses the relationship between collaborative organization and interactive technologies with an emphasis on how these new technologies are providing virtual venues for communication between citizens, architects, urban designers, advocacy groups, and decision-makers. Girard is coauthor (with Francesca Polletta and David Stark) of "Policy Made Public: Technologies of Deliberation and Representation in Rebuilding Lower Manhattan."

Susan Greenhalgh is Professor of Anthropology at the University of California, Irvine. Her work examines population as a domain of modern power, the role of modern science and technology in constituting life, and the workings of states and their policies and programs. She is author of *Under the Medical Gaze: Facts and Fictions of Chronic Pain, Governing by Numbers: Population in the Making of Modern China*, and *Population and Power in Post-Deng China: Institutions & Biopolitics* (with Edwin A. Winckler).

Douglas R. Holmes is Professor of Anthropology at Binghamton University. His research focuses on advanced European integration and the challenges of investigating this kind of complex technocratic phenomenon ethnographically. He is the author of *Integral Europe: Fast-Capitalism, Multiculturalism, Neofascism* and *Cultural Disenchantments: Worker Peasants in Northeast Italy*.

James Holston is Associate Professor of Anthropology at the University of California, San Diego. His research focuses on citizenship, democracy, law, violence, architecture and planning, as well as on new religions. He is currently writing a book on the insurgence of democratic citizenship in the urban periphery of São Paulo and its contradiction in violence and misrule of law under political democracy. His publications include *The Modernist City: An Anthropological Critique of Brasília* and the edited volume *Cities and Citizenship.*

Andrew Lakoff is Assistant Professor of Sociology and Science Studies at the University of California, San Diego. His forthcoming book, *Pharmaceutical Reason: Technology and the Human at the Modern Periphery,* examines the role of the global circulation of pharmaceuticals in the spread of biological models of human behavior and thought.

George E. Marcus is Joseph D. Jamail Professor and Chair, Department of Anthropology, Rice University. He is interested in the changing nature of ethnographic methods and writing, and his research has concerned the work and thought of various kinds of elites, experts, and intellectuals operating within changing forms of capitalism and modernity. Recent publications include *Ethnography through Thick and Thin, Critical Anthropology Now,* and the eight volumes of the *Late Editions* series of annuals.

Bill Maurer is Associate Professor of Anthropology, University of California, Irvine. He is currently working on an anthropology of money and finance. He is the author of *Recharting the Caribbean: Land, Law and Citizenship in the British Virgin Islands,* co-editor of *Gender Matters: Re-Reading Michelle Z. Rosaldo,* and co-editor of *Globalization under Construction: Governmentality, Law, and Identity.*

Hirokazu Miyazaki is an Assistant Professor of Anthropology, Cornell University. He has written on the place of hope in knowledge formation drawing on his research in Fiji and Japan. He is the author of *The Method of Hope* and is completing a book entitled *Economy of Dreams: Anthropology, Finance, and Japan.*

Vinh-kim Nguyen is Associate Professor in the Faculty of Medicine at McGill University. He has worked with community-based organizations in West Africa since 1994 on expanding access to treatment for HIV, informing his anthropological research on epidemics and politics. He focuses on emerging forms of therapeutic citizenship, humanitarian intervention, and biopolitics, and is currently writing a book on these themes.

Carlos Novas is a doctoral student in the Department of Sociology at Goldsmiths College, University of London, funded by the Wellcome Trust Programme on Biomedical Ethics. He is studying the practices of the self and the political economy associated with the rise of the new genetics.

Kris Olds is Associate Professor of Geography, University of Wisconsin-Madison. His research focuses on the geographical organization of power and global networks in relation to contemporary urban transformations. Recent publications include (as author) *Globalization and Urban Change: Capital, Culture, and Pacific Rim Mega-Projects,* and (as co-editor) *The Globalization of Chinese Business Firms,* and *Globalization and the Asia-Pacific: Contested Territories.*

Aihwa Ong is Professor of Anthropology and Southeast Asian Studies at the University of California, Berkeley. She has conducted fieldwork in Southeast Asia,

South China, and California, and her current interests concern government, risk, and security in Asian cities. Recent works include the award-winning *Flexible Citizenship*, and *Buddha is Hiding: Refugees, Citizenship, the New America*. Her next book is entitled *Deterritorializing Citizenship*.

Gísli Pálsson is Professor of Anthropology at the University of Iceland and the University of Oslo. His research focuses on the social implications of biotechnology, human–environmental relations, and Inuit genetic history. Pálsson has done anthropological fieldwork in Iceland and The Republic of Cape Verde. Among his books are *The Textual Life of Savants, Nature and Society: Anthropological Perspectives, Images of Contemporary Iceland*, and *Writing on Ice: The Ethnographic Notebooks of Vilhjalmur Stefansson*.

Paul Rabinow is Professor of Anthropology at the University of California, Berkeley. He has done fieldwork in Morocco and in biotechnology companies and genomics laboratories in California and France. His most recent books are *Essays on the Anthropology of Reason, French DNA, Trouble in Purgatory*, and *Anthropos Today*.

Annelise Riles is Professor of Law and Professor of Anthropology at Cornell University. Her research focuses on rationality, expertise, and theory as ethnographic subjects. Her first book, *The Network Inside Out*, concerned knowledge practices within global nongovernmental organizations and at United Nations global conferences. An edited collection, *Documents: Artifacts of Modern Knowledge*, is forthcoming. She is currently completing a book based on fieldwork among regulators of the global economy and legal theorists concerning relations of means to ends.

Janet Roitman is presently at the CNRS-MALD, Paris. Her interests include economic regulation and social transformations in the Chad Basin. Recent publications include *Fiscal Disobedience: An Anthropology of Economic Regulation in Central Africa*, and "Productivity in the Margins: the Reconstitution of State Power in the Chad Basin," in an edited collection entitled *Anthropologies at the Margins of the State*.

Nikolas Rose is Professor of Sociology and Director of the BIOS Centre for the Study of Bioscience, Biomedicine and Biotechnology at the London School of Economics and Political Science. His current research concerns biological and genetic psychiatry and behavioral neuroscience, and its social, ethical, cultural, and legal context and implications. His most recent book is *Powers of Freedom: Reframing Political Thought*, and his next book is entitled *The Politics of Life Itself*.

Nancy Scheper-Hughes is Professor of Medical Anthropology at the University of California, Berkeley, where she directs the graduate program in Critical Studies in Medicine, Science, and the Body. She has conducted research on mother love and child death in Brazil, madness and culture in rural Ireland, AIDS and sexual citizenship in Cuba, Brazil, and the United States; violence and truth in the New South Africa; death squads, democracy, and the execution of Brazilian street children;

and the repatriation of Ishi's brain. Her most recent books are *Commodifying Bodies* (co-edited with Loic Wacquant) and *Violence in War and Peace* (co-edited with Philippe Bourgois). Her next book is entitled *The Ends of the Body: The Global Traffic in Organs*.

David Stark is Arthur Lehman Professor of Sociology and International Affairs at Columbia University and an External Faculty Member of the Santa Fe Institute. He examines organizational innovation and reflexivity as the result of rivalrous frames of worth. Stark's recent publications include: "The Organization of Responsiveness: Innovation and Recovery in the Trading Rooms of Lower Manhattan" (with Daniel Beunza), "Permanently Beta: Responsive Organization in the Internet Age" (with Gina Neff), "Innovative Ambiguities: NGOs' Use of Interactive Technology in Eastern Europe" (with Jonathan Bach); and *Postsocialist Pathways: Transforming Politics and Property in Eastern Europe* (with Laszlo Bruszt).

Marilyn Strathern is Professor of Social Anthropology at the University of Cambridge, and member of the Nuffield Council of Bioethics. She has a longstanding ethnographic interest in gender relations (*Women in Between*) and kinship (*Kinship at the Core*), which led to a critical appraisal of ownership and control in models in Melanesian societies (*The Gender of the Gift*). More recently, she has worked on reproductive technologies (*Reproducing the Future* and the coauthored *Technologies of Procreation*) and property forms (*Property. Substance, and Effect: Anthropological Essays on Persons and Things*), and on developments in intellectual and "cultural" property rights.

Nigel Thrift is Head of the Division of Life and Environmental Sciences and Professor of Geography at the University of Oxford. His main interests are in nonrepresentational theory, international finance, management knowledges, consumption, the history of time, and the intersection between the informational and the biological. Recent publications include *Spatial Formations*, *City A–Z* (co-edited with Steve Pile), *Cities* (with Ash Amin), *The Cultural Geography Handbook* (co-edited with Kay Anderson, Mona Domoshand, and Steve Pile), *Patterned Ground* (co-edited with Stephan Harrison and Steve Pile), and *Knowing Capitalism*.

Caitlin Zaloom is Assistant Professor of Anthropology at the University of Pennsylvania and Faculty Fellow at the International Center for Advanced Studies at New York University. Her forthcoming book, *Out of the Pits: Financial Reason from Chicago to London*, examines the practices of economic rationality, risk-taking, and technological change in the context of global financial transformations.

ACKNOWLEDGMENTS

We wish to express our appreciation to the authors who entrusted their latest work to this volume, giving it the form and quality of an emerging interdisciplinary conversation. The book had its origins in a workshop, "*Oikos* and *Anthropos*: Rationality, Technology and Infrastructure," which met in Prague in April 2002. This forum was an opportunity for scholars to present initial drafts of their papers and to engage in intensive discussion, the substance of which found its way into the book.

Douglas Guthrie, a Professor of Sociology at NYU, provided vital intellectual and logistical support for our meeting in his capacity as Program Director of the Social Science Research Council, and Director of Global Education at New York University. The meeting received support from an Alfred P. Sloan grant from the program on "The Corporation as a Social Institution" of the SSRC. We also thank Thea Favaloro, the Associate Director of NYU-Prague, and Jiri Pehe, the NYU-Prague Director, for their assistance and hospitality.

In Berkeley, we are grateful to Holly Halligan for her help in posting materials on the web. Ryan Centner, a graduate student in sociology, helped us with library materials and research. Shannon May, a graduate student in anthropology, gave us timely and skillful assistance in editing the final manuscript. The Abigail Hodgen Fund at the University of California, Berkeley, provided support for the final preparation of the manuscript.

Aihwa Ong and Stephen J. Collier

PART I

INTRODUCTION

GLOBAL ASSEMBLAGES, ANTHROPOLOGICAL PROBLEMS

STEPHEN J. COLLIER AND AIHWA ONG

The diverse phenomena associated with "globalization" pose curious problems for social scientific observers.[1] There is no agreement about whether globalization is happening or what "globalization" means, to say nothing about whether "it" is a good thing. Yet its recurrence in discussions over the past 10–20 years is striking. The term has been an almost unavoidable marker for heterogeneous and often contradictory transformations – in economic organization, social regulation, political governance, and ethical regimes – that are felt to have profound though uncertain, confusing, or contradictory implications for human life.

The issue cuts to the heart of the modern disciplines. Increasingly, the phenomena that concern social scientists assume spatial forms that are nonisomorphic with standard units of analysis. Various localisms and regionalisms along with "transnational" patterns have been the subject of growing interest. More fundamentally, many observers have argued that we are witnessing a shift in the core dynamics of social, cultural, and economic life.

A range of analytic responses to this situation can be identified. One has been a turn to more or less grand statements about a new order of things or shifting macroprocesses: from modernization to globalization, for instance, or the emergence of global cities, or a network society.[2] A second has examined "localities," however defined, as articulations with, effects of, or dynamic responses and resistances to, global forces.[3] A third has sought to reconstitute the categories of the social sciences in new forms. One thinks, for example, of "global culture," or the more specified concept of technological, cultural, or media "scapes."[4]

All these trajectories of research have been and will continue to be productive. The approach presented in this volume overlaps with them in important ways, but its point of entry, core problems, and mode of analysis are distinct. It does not examine the changes associated with globalization in terms of broad structural transformations or new configurations of society or culture. Rather, it examines a specific range of phenomena that articulate such shifts: technoscience, circuits of licit and illicit exchange, systems of administration or governance, and regimes of ethics or values. These phenomena are distinguished by a particular quality we refer to as *global*. They are abstractable, mobile, and dynamic, moving across and reconstituting "society," "culture," and "economy," those classic social scientific abstractions that, as a range of observers have recently noted, today seem over-vague and under question.[5]

As global forms are articulated in specific situations – or territorialized in *assemblages* – they define new material, collective, and discursive relationships.[6] These "global assemblages" are sites for the formation and reformation of what we will call, following Paul Rabinow, *anthropological problems*. They are domains in which the forms and values of individual and collective existence are problematized or at stake, in the sense that they are subject to technological, political, and ethical reflection and intervention.

The chapters in this volume examine a diversity of such global assemblages, from neoliberal reform of the public sector in Russia and Brazil, to bioscience and pharmaceuticals in Africa and Argentina, to the trade in human organs in Moldova, Israel, and India, to accounting and finance in Tokyo, Chicago, and the Middle East. The contributors enter these politically or morally charged domains through a mode of inquiry that remains close to practices, whether through ethnography or careful technical analysis. The result is a discerning, reflective, and critical approach that we feel is defining an important and exciting trajectory of interdisciplinary inquiry in the human sciences.

Before moving to a more systematic discussion, it will be helpful to illustrate this distinctive approach to anthropological problems through an example. In the chapter that begins part II on "Bioscience and Biological Life," Sara Franklin examines stem cell research as one element of what she calls "the global biological."[7] What here is 'global,' exactly? The apparatus of scientific research and technoscientific production associated with stem cells is organized in a transnational, if not exactly global, space. This apparatus is linked to what is generally called 'global' capital, though its flows are socially, institutionally, and technologically concentrated in important ways.

But stem cell research has a 'global' quality in another sense. In principle, its significance is not delimited by social, cultural, or economic determinations. *Potentially*, stem cell research could be organized in any social context, and findings based on this research would be valid anywhere. *Potentially*, it bears on biological life – every human (and, presumably, nonhuman) being on the planet – and can transform how we understand, intervene in, and, indeed, live human life *qua* biological life.

Franklin's analytic strategy, however, is not to examine stem cells as an ideal-typic 'global' form that is freed of context. Rather, she examines the ensembles of heterogeneous elements – the assemblages – through which stem cell research and its significance are articulated.[8] Thus, the actual scope of stem cell research is determined by a specific distribution of scientific expertise and global capital, which are necessary infrastructural conditions for its spread. Also crucial are regimes of 'ethical' regulation instituted through the political system in various countries. The United Kingdom, Franklin notes, has emerged as an important center of stem cell research thanks to a relatively lenient regulatory regime. The United States, meanwhile, has been pushed to the periphery by limitations on the extraction of stem cells. Notably, the ethical principles in the name of which U.S. restrictions on stem cell research are justified also have a 'global' quality. They invoke a form of humanism that claims to be concerned not with a culture or a particular social group but with human life as such. Yet, like stem cell research itself, this humanism is not all encompassing in its actual scope, and can only be made effective through specific political and technical arrangements.

Franklin's case is also exemplary in its cautious assessment of the 'anthropological' significance of stem cell research. Stem cell research has occupied a space of rancorous moral discord, rife with proclamations of salvation or apocalypse. But it is unlikely, Franklin holds, to usher in a future of biological control or to create a seamless space of technoscience that embraces all of humanity in a virtuous effort to foster life – or, for that matter, in a diabolical effort to technify it – any time soon. And yet, the process of stem cell research is associated with significant changes that deserve careful observation. "If we are not yet in the age of 'biological control,'" Franklin writes, progress in stem cell research means that life "is nonetheless substantially altered."[9] For example, stem cell research may force revision of long-held assumptions concerning the nonreversibility of the aging process of cells and, consequently, of biological organisms. As therapeutics are developed, they will pose problems of political regulation and of ethical reflection and practice for individuals and collectivities.

In this chapter, we develop the various concepts we have introduced. First, we explore what we mean by 'anthropological problems' and examine how the chapters in this volume understand a structure of reflection – involving practical and transformative work – to be central to such problems today. Second, we introduce the 'global assemblage'. Third, and finally, we examine how globalization might be conceived not as a process of secular transformation *per se* but as a problem-space in which contemporary anthropological questions are framed. In presenting these orientations, we also develop the themes around which we have grouped the chapters in the volume: biological life; social technologies and governmentality; reflexivity and calculative action; ethics and values; health and security.

These loose-knit conceptual orientations – along with those presented in the other two chapters in this introductory part, by Stephen Collier and Andrew Lakoff and by Paul Rabinow – do not suggest an overarching theoretical approach. Rather, they suggest a few among many possible orientations to the wealth of exemplars and concepts presented in the chapters that follow.

Anthropological Problems

In defining the theme of this volume as concerned with anthropological problems, we refer to an interest in the constitution of the social and biological existence of human beings as an object of knowledge, technical intervention, politics, and ethical discussion.

As a range of thinkers, including Hannah Arendt, Michel Foucault, and Karl Polanyi, have shown, this understanding of 'anthropological' problems is specific to a limited range of historical situations.[10] In *The Order of Things*, Foucault showed how biological and social life emerged as that order of existence through which human beings were made objects of systematic investigation in what he called the human sciences.[11] In these fields, a series of questions about "the human" that had previously been addressed in philosophical or theological discussions were posed in domains of secular inquiry. Thus, Foucault argued, the 'modern *cogito*' is not the Cartesian "I" that identified her- or himself as the subject and object of a knowledge that was guaranteed through the circuit of a third term: the 'infinite,' God. Rather, the human sciences understand human beings through the 'finitudes' of an individual history and conditions of collective existence.[12] The modern *cogito* concerns work, sickness and health, material conditions, social interaction, and biological being rather than isolated reflection or spiritual life; problems that are 'anthropological' rather than theological or philosophical.

Foucault called the new figure that emerged as the object of these human sciences "modern man." Following Rabinow's usage in Chapter 3, it is preferable to refer to this figure as *anthropos*. *Anthropos* suggests the specific formation of the human sciences: anthropologies, *logoi*, of humans as biological and social beings. It also suggests an analytic orientation to the malleability, specificity, and historicity of the forms of life constituted through these finitudes.

Hannah Arendt made a related argument in *The Human Condition* concerning the *oikos*, referring to collective rather than individual existence.[13] Arendt pointed out that, for the Greeks, questions of collective existence that bore on the biological and social needs of human beings were confined to the household. Such questions were distinct from the concerns of political life. In the modern polity, by contrast, these biological and communal problems were released from the household to displace or interact with an older juridical understanding of political order. In *The Great Transformation*, Karl Polanyi traced this shift through the thought of British liberalism, for which "[t]he biological nature of man appeared as the given foundation of a society that was not of a political order." "Economic society," he noted, "emerged as distinct from the political state."[14] This "society" took the form of a new kind of collective existence – what Arendt called the "national *oikos*."

Many of the chapters in this volume examine forms of biological or social life that are beyond the horizon of what these thinkers could have imagined. For instance, the institutions of the welfare state as we know them today were only just taking form when *The Human Condition* and *The Great Transformation* were written. The anthropological problems associated with the neoliberal attempt to reform and rationalize social welfarism – a problem that is central to many chapters in this volume – could not, consequently, have been within the scope of Polanyi's or Arendt's analysis. Likewise, Foucault's concepts of biopower and biopolitics were not developed with forms of biological life defined by gene sequences or stem cells in mind. In studying such domains, the chapters explore how these classic diagnoses might be directed to contemporary problems.

Reflexive practices – technological, political, and ethical

For Arendt, Foucault, and Polanyi, new awareness of these figures of *oikos* and *anthropos* was linked to new forms of practical and transformative work. Polanyi, thus, examined what he called "social technologies" that intensified control over human activity through new regimes of visibility and discipline – a concern that resonates with important themes in Foucault's work on knowledge/power.[15] Arendt noted that "economic society" was the form through which biological and social life became a preeminent problem for modern politics or, in Foucault's term, biopolitics.

This focus on reflection and on practical and transformative work as central to the forms of *oikos* and *anthropos* today is common to a range of diagnoses of the social condition of the present. The theoretical writings of Ulrich Beck and Anthony Giddens on reflexive modernization provide recent examples.[16] A central feature of these diagnoses is an emphasis on how, in various domains, modern practices subject themselves to critical questioning. David Stark has usefully termed such practices *reflexive practices*.[17] Stark's chapter with Monique Girard in this volume, which examines a new media startup during the Internet boom of the late 1990s, provides one concrete illustration. In a highly uncertain economic, technological, and legal environment, Girard and Stark found managers constantly placing the very organizational model of the firm in question. These managers go so far as to perpetually ask, "What is new media?" making the firm "a project perpetually 'under construction.'"[18]

More generally, we can say that the chapters in this volume consider the forms of individual and collective life as they are reflected upon and valued, constituted and reconstituted, through reflexive practices. In this sense they take up questions that have been richly examined in interdisciplinary work in the social studies of science, which have focused on a particular kind of reflection – technoscientific – and a particular kind of observer engaged in such reflection – scientists.[19] The chapters here examine, on the one hand, a wider range of reflexive practices and, on the other, a wider range of reflexive observers.

We turn first to the diverse forms of reflexive practice examined in this volume. The managers in Girard and Stark's study of a new media firm are engaged in reflexive practices that can be called *technological*. Following a classic social scientific understanding of technology, such reflection concerns first of all not machines or mechanical applications but the problem of choosing the most appropriate means for achieving given ends or goals, whether these are technoscientific, organizational, or administrative.[20] Thus, in Girard and Stark's example, managers raise questions concerning the appropriate organizational form for achieving certain ends, as well as, notably, the appropriateness of the framework within which questions of means and ends are addressed (thus, their question: "What is new media?").

A second kind of reflexive practice examined in a number of chapters in the volume can be called *political*, concerning the appropriate form and scope of juridico-legal institutions in resolving problems of collective life. In Marilyn Strathern's case, a Canadian state commission reflects on the proper role of public opinion in shaping state regulation of reproductive behavior and seeks to operationalize this opinion through a specific technology of political reason – the social audit. In Janet Roitman's study of trafficking in the Chad Basin, bandits and traffickers reflect on the very terms of political legitimacy in defining their formally illegal activities as "work" rather than as "crime." Nikolas Rose and Carlos Novas examine how groups of individuals invent the categories and practices of a "biological citizenship" by seeking to ground claims to resources and protections on shared predispositions to disease.

A third and final type of reflexive practice examined in the volume can be called *ethical*. Ethical reflection may relate to questions of value or morality. But it may equally relate to ethics in the sense in which the term is used in philosophical discussions: reflection on the problem of how one should live. As Collier and Lakoff discuss in detail in Chapter 2, the ethical reflection examined in these chapters is very much wrapped up with political and technological problems, giving a distinctive form to what they call 'regimes of living.'

Two examples can illustrate these dimensions of 'ethical' reflection. In his chapter on the problem of modeling biodiversity, Geoffrey Bowker shows how ecologists committed to conservation grapple with scientific findings that throw into question the "stable ecosystem," a concept that had served as a basic point of reference for those engaged in environmental politics. By developing technoscientific means to assign an "economic" value to ecosystems without reference to their stability, these ecologists seek to constitute a form of conduct that satisfies both ethical and technoscientific ends. Caitlin Zaloom's chapter on bond traders provides an example of ethical reflection concerned with self-formation. Zaloom examines how calculative action emerges as part of a personal ethos that requires control over one's passions and a strict separation between one's personal life and the world of trading. This ethos of technically rational behavior is actively produced through a range of training procedures, institutional routines, and bodily dispositions.

A second important feature of the reflexive practices examined in this volume is that they involve a broad range of observers in diverse social and geographic positions. At one level, those who are able to participate in 'technological' reflection – whether in the domains of economics, science, technoscience, or administration –

are by definition 'elite.' Many of the chapters that follow are, consequently, concerned specifically with elite subjects: Bill Maurer on the debates over Islamic accounting in a transnational network of economists, auditors, and businessmen; Andrew Lakoff on marketers in pharmaceutical companies; Douglas Holmes and George Marcus on Alan Greenspan; Hiro Miyazaki and Annelise Riles on financial analysts in Tokyo; Aihwa Ong or Kris Olds and Nigel Thrift on highly placed planners, educational administrators, and knowledge workers in Singapore and Malaysia.

But the anthropological significance of reflexive practices seems to lie also in their more general importance for, and availability to, individuals and collectivities in a range of positions. Thus, the chapters examine a diversity of relatively 'peripheral' sites and subjects engaged in technological, political, and ethical reflection: Teresa Caldeira and James Holston on activists in Brazilian squatter settlements; Lawrence Cohen on those who sell their organs in India; Janet Roitman on bandits and traffickers in the Chad Basin; Nikolas Rose and Carlos Novas on "biological citizens" in the U.K.; Vinh-kim Nguyen on AIDS patients in the Ivory Coast.

Global Assemblages

A sense that various kinds of reflexive practices are ever more broadly important for individual and collective life has been chronic to modern social theory. Giddens' recent version of this diagnosis resonates with many of the themes we have raised, emphasizing both the pervasive importance of global forms in modern institutions and what he calls the "displacement and reappropriation" of expertise to a range of nonexpert sites. As Giddens argues:

> The global experiment of modernity intersects with, and influences as it is influenced by, the penetration of modern institutions into the tissue of day-to-day life. Not just the local community, but intimate features of personal life and the self become intertwined with relations of indefinite time-space extension. We are all caught up in everyday experiments whose outcomes, in a generic sense, are as open as those affecting humanity as a whole. Everyday experiments reflect the changing role of tradition and, as is also true of the global level, should be seen in the context of the *displacement and reappropriation of expertise*, under the impact of the intrusiveness of abstract systems. Technology, in the general meaning of 'technique,' plays the leading role here, in the shape both of material technology and of specialized social expertise.[21]

Giddens' passage raises a range of questions. Some he addresses in largely theoretical terms. All deserve further reflection. In what sense is the "experiment" of modernity "global"? What is the nature of this "penetration of modern institutions"? Which "we" is in question in the claim "we are all caught up in everyday experiments"? When are these "abstract systems" intrusive, and when liberatory? Are these processes general to an age we want to call modernity?

In the next section of this chapter, we turn to the final question, which concerns the temporal specificity of the processes under discussion. Here, we further explore the character of those phenomena Giddens associates with "modern institutions" – paradigmatically "material technology" and "specialized social expertise."

As suggested above, we propose to refer to these phenomena as having a "global" quality. In doing so, we mean to emphasize a peculiar characteristic of their foundations or conditions of possibility. Our point of reference is classic: Max Weber's *The Protestant Ethic and the Spirit of Capitalism*. The immediate topic of *The Protestant Ethic* is the relationship of modern capitalism to the distinctive this-worldly asceticism found in Protestantism. Its *problem*, however, concerns the significance for human life of the "specific and peculiar rationalism" that, Weber claimed, initially emerged in "Western civilization."[22] The theme is set out in a late Preface, whose famous and cryptic first sentence reads: "A product of modern European civilization, studying any problem of universal history, is bound to ask himself to what combination of circumstances the fact should be attributed that in Western civilization and in Western civilization only, phenomena have appeared which (as we like to think) lie in a line of development having universal significance and validity."[23] The passage jars relativistic sensibilities. Some close reading is required.

In this famous passage, the word "universal" appears twice. As Tobias Rees has explained to us, the two occurrences translate two distinct German words that have very different meanings.[24] In its first usage – "universal history" – "universal" means "all-encompassing." "Universal history," thus, covers all times and places. In its second usage – which refers to a "specific and peculiar rationalism" – universal refers to phenomena whose significance and validity are not dependent on the 'props' of a 'culture' or a 'society.' They are rather, to repeat Giddens' phrase cited above, "based on impersonal principles, which can be set out and developed without regard to context." In calling the "specific and peculiar rationalism" that interests him "universal," Weber does not deny its specificity, but also emphasizes this unusual feature of its "validity" or "foundations." Thus, on the one hand, Weber traces economic rationalism through the norms and dicta of the Protestant ethic. On the other hand, this rationalism does not depend on these cultural origins: "Today the spirit of religion asceticism ... has escaped from the cage. But victorious capitalism, since it rests on mechanical foundations, needs its support no longer."[25]

It also bears noting that in speaking of a "universal" quality of this rationalism, Weber did not imply a positive value judgment. The parenthetical "(as we like to think)" suggests a critical stance, though one that should be understood in precise terms. It involves neither a sociological reduction to "structure" or a logic of power nor a cultural reduction or relativization of such "universal" phenomena. Rather, it suggests a careful technical analysis – a *technical criticism*.[26] Such a technical criticism would examine both the "mechanical" foundations of these phenomena and the actual processes and structures that define their scope and significance. Its goal is to understand how they function as a source of tension and dynamism for the forms and values of human life; that is, to grasp how they structure a certain class of anthropological problems.

Global forms

This second sense of 'universal' captures what we mean by 'global.' Our definition might be clarified through an illustrative contrast. In the anthropological tradition, kinship systems or circuits of ritual exchange are "cultural" or "social" phenomena in that they are only intelligible in relation to a common set of meanings, understandings, or societal structures. Their validity is "conventional." It is dependent on being "held" or "accepted."[27]

Global phenomena are not unrelated to social and cultural problems. But they have a distinctive capacity for decontextualization and recontextualization, abstractability and movement, across diverse social and cultural situations and spheres of life.[28] Global forms are able to assimilate themselves to new environments, to code heterogeneous contexts and objects in terms that are amenable to control and valuation. At the same time, the conditions of possibility of this movement are complex. Global forms are limited or delimited by specific technical infrastructures, administrative apparatuses, or value regimes, not by the vagaries of a social or cultural field.

Two examples from the volume can illustrate this point. Elizabeth Dunn examines ISO standards as a global form through the lens of the Polish meatpacking industry. To function, standards require substantial changes in work routines, in the physical organization of production processes, and in record-keeping procedures to allow the production of a vast quantity of information that is 'legible' to health inspectors, regulators, or investors in diverse sites.[29] A standards regime, in this case, functions as an example of what Bruno Latour has called an "immutable mobile."[30] It is a technoscientific form that can be decontextualized and recontextualized, abstracted, transported, and reterritorialized, and is designed to produce functionally comparable results in disparate domains.

Another example can be taken from two contributions on the organ trade. In their respective chapters, Lawrence Cohen and Nancy Scheper-Hughes note a series of technical improvements in extraction, transport, and donor matching that has allowed traded or gifted organs to cross lines of caste, kinship, and social standing. Through this process, remote sites are brought into intimate interaction as organs themselves attain an increasingly 'global' quality. This space of interaction can be conceived as what Andrew Barry has called a "technological zone."[31] It is delimited by specific technological forms, material or transport infrastructures, circuits of interaction, and situated values.

Technoscience – whether material technology or specialized social expertise – may be exemplary of global forms. We will also use the term to describe forms of politics and ethics structured around collectivities to the extent that they are not defined culturally (like the nation as a community of common history, language, and experience) or socially (like an economic class, defined in terms of a structural relationship to production). Novas and Rose's analysis of biological citizenship based on a common genetic sequence variation in otherwise unrelated individuals suggests one example. Such 'global' forms also emerge in transnational collectivities, as Nguyen shows in his chapter on what he calls "antiretroviral globalism." Nguyen examines a biosocial "vanguard" of individuals being treated for AIDS in Africa that is not defined first of all "socially" but biomedically: in terms of a complex of symptoms that constitutes a disease and in terms of therapeutic technologies – namely AIDS drugs. These biomedical definitions of 'identity,' Nguyen points out, may form a "rallying point for transnational activism in a neoliberal world in which illness claims carry more weight than those based on poverty, injustice, or structural violence."[32]

Ethical problems related to biological life (health and disease, malnutrition and water) and to social life (access to goods and services, abstract freedoms to organization and belief) may also assume a global form. They may apply to biological life; they may be organized through institutions that define humanity as a single political collectivity; and they may be attached to 'global' ethical technologies. Strathern provides one example in showing how the values of liberality and democracy are operationalized through the "flexible" ethical form of the social audit, and made to operate in a diversity of environments.[33] In other cases, different ethical regimes compete for "global" status. Susan Greenhalgh examines such a case in her study of the regulation of reproduction in China. The Chinese government justifies its interventions in relationship to one 'global' ethical form – the imperative for all governments to manage population growth – and is criticized from the perspective of another – the claim that women have a right to control their reproductive decisions.

The actual global

The analytic terms suggested by observers like Barry ("technological zones") and Latour ("immutable mobiles") suggest powerful concepts for understanding the complex infrastructural conditions that allow global forms to function. But the chapters that follow focus equally on how global forms interact with other elements, occupying a common field in contingent, uneasy, unstable interrelationships. The product of these interactions might be called the *actual* global, or the global in the space of assemblage. In relationship to "the global," the assemblage is not a "locality" to which broader forces are counterposed. Nor is it the structural effect of such forces.[34] An assemblage is the product of multiple determinations that are not reducible to a single logic. The temporality of an assemblage is emergent. It does not always involve new forms, but forms that are shifting, in formation, or at stake. As a composite concept, the term *"global* assemblage" suggests inherent tensions: global implies broadly encompassing, seamless, and mobile; assemblage implies heterogeneous, contingent, unstable, partial, and situated.

Thus, a central argument of Dunn's chapter is that although some Polish producers are integrated into global or European markets through the imposition of standards, others, who lack the resources to comply, are driven into the black market. For the latter group, the imposition of standards creates "a kind of personhood that evokes responses developed under socialism and impelling people to seek out ways to circumvent discipline."[35] This circumvention and its effects are as much part of the assemblage as is the global form itself. Scheper-Hughes' and Cohen's chapters show that although scientific advance and marketization have resulted in the vast extension of the organ trade, distinctive limitations are imposed by national and international 'ethical' and political regulation, and by continuing limitations on the technical capacity to abstract organs from one context to another. The significance of the organ trade for individuals and collectivities – sellers, donors, recipients, buyers, doctors, and brokers – is determined by their respective positioning in relation to this assemblage of elements.

In conceptualizing the form taken by the actual global in these cases we might draw on another image, that of a 'global variable' in a computer program. A global variable is not part of a step in a sequence in any given module but is executed independently. It is used by various parts or modules of a program, and has a common value across modules,[36] acting as a point of communication or interaction among them. However, a global variable does not produce similar effects every- where, and its function may be limited by direct conflicts with other variables in specific sub-modules of a program. Its operation and significance, thus, are defined as much by these exclusions or conflicts in particular modules as by the variable's global character.[37]

Another series of illustrations can be drawn from chapters that examine the distinctive form of calculative rationality associated with a market environment. Market calculation is an ideal-typic global form. It rests, in principle, on the most "mechanical" foundations imaginable. It can incorporate and allocate anything that is assigned a market value – that is, a value that is expressed in monetary, quantitative, commensurable, and, thus, calculable terms. In this specific, limited, and ideal-typic sense, market calculation is freed of *any* social or cultural considerations, responding only to the global logic of supply and effective demand.

But to examine formal rationalization and calculation in the space of assemblage is to examine their interaction with specific substantive or value orders. Various chapters dealing with neoliberal reform provide examples. Neoliberalism, as Nikolas Rose has defined it, is a political rationality that seeks to govern not through command and control operations but through the calculative choice of formally free actors.[38] It operates, in other words, according to a rationality of a market *type*. As such, it has proven highly expansive and mobile. But neoliberalism's actual shape and significance for the forms of individual and collective life can only be understood as it enters into assemblages with other elements. Thus, in his chapter on neoliber- alism and biopolitics in post-Soviet Russia, Collier examines budgetary reforms that seek to rationalize the system of public-sector provisioning by constituting local governments as nodes of decision-making and calculation. The aim of such reforms is not to 'marketize' the public sector but to subtly reengineer the values, procedures, and substantive forms of the Soviet social, producing one variety of what Neil Brenner and Nik Theodore call "actually existing neoliberalism."[39]

Another function of the study of assemblages is to gain analytical and critical insight into global forms by examining how actors reflect upon them or call them into question. For example, a number of chapters examine situations in which it becomes necessary for actors to shift between modes of reflection and intervention; when, for instance, technical modes of reflection and action break down, and ethical or political reflection – or alternative frames of technical response – emerge in their stead. Vivid examples of such breakdown are found in two contributions on financial prognostication and economic policy-making. Miyazaki and Riles examine how some Japanese financial analysts vacillate between attempts to overcome the failures of stock predictions through ever-more complex techniques of prognostication and an acceptance of such failures as an "endpoint." In the latter case, failure is recognized as an unavoidable condition within which actors must find corresponding modes of rational action, such as real-time response to market data as opposed to prognostication. Douglas Holmes and George Marcus examine decision-making by Alan Greenspan at the Federal Reserve. In an environment of massive complexity and uncertainty, in which policy choice cannot be simply data-driven, a series of highly personalistic factors, ethical dispositions, and bodily states – "hunches," "intuitions," "feelings," stomach aches – come to assume a central role in actual decisions.[40] In examining such elements the authors draw attention to the "*de facto* and self-conscious critical faculty that operates in any expert domain."[41] Examination of this "self-conscious critical faculty" – which Holmes and Marcus call a "para-ethno-graphic" feature of domains of expertise – points to an understanding of the "social realm not in alignment with the representations generated by the application of the reigning statistical mode of analysis."[42]

Another critical function of the study of assemblages is that it brings to light, in Gísli Pálsson and Paul Rabinow's phrase, "a specific historical, political, and economic conjuncture in which an issue becomes a problem," and, perhaps, allows us to question whether the problems posed about "global" phenomena are the right ones.[43] Thus, in their chapter on human genome projects in the U.K., Estonia, Sweden, and Iceland, Pálsson and Rabinow propose a critique of professional ethics that asks why "the social-scientific and ethical gaze"[44] has focused its attention so firmly on the Icelandic case and ignored others. Maurer, meanwhile, engages debates around the question of whether an "Islamic spirit of capitalism" is in conflict with the underlying task of Western accounting – to provide "decision-useful" information – which presumes a specific universal form of the human: the maximizing individual. He asks whether it is really so obvious that there is a *specific* problem with Islamic banking.

Globalization as Problem-Space

The situations examined in the chapters that follow are indisputably contemporary. But are the problems new? As Giddens has noted, 'modernity' has inherently 'globalizing' tendencies, and the 'global' qualities of technology, politics, and ethics examined in these chapters are hardly novel. How, then, is one to think about the temporal specificity of these processes? And how do they inform a critical engagement with the present?

One set of discussions around globalization has been quick to offer grand diagnoses of contemporary changes both in celebratory proclamations (of capitalism or democracy triumphant, of a new transnational consensus on values) and in visions of cataclysm (the spread of a global monoculture, the hegemony of markets or capital). Another has sought, in a more sober mode, to sort out claims and counter-claims by asking to what extent specific processes associated with globalization are actually 'new'.[45]

The contributions here seem to be engaged in a somewhat different project. They frame 'the present' in terms of specific trajectories of change: of techniques for compiling species databases (Bowker); of transplant technologies (Scheper-Hughes and Cohen); of state budgetary institutions through the 20th century (Collier); of stem cell research (Franklin); of management consultancy (Olds and Thrift); or of shifts in birth policy in China (Greenhalgh). These trajectories of change do not add up to the grand structural transformations of Schumpeter's "thunder of world history."[46] Rather, they inscribe what Deleuze has called "little lines of mutation," minor histories that address themselves to the 'big' questions of globalizations in a careful and limited manner.[47]

To illustrate, we may consider a set of chapters that deal with the modern 'social.' Here, "the social" refers not to the framework of sociological analysis ("society") but to a specific range of knowledge forms, modes of technical intervention, and institutional arrangements. These include mechanisms of economic coordination or regulation and institutions of social citizenship that defined the norms and forms of collective life for most residents of urbanizing and industrializing countries over the course of the 20th century.[48]

Discussions of globalization have been filled with broad diagnoses of the transformation of the modern social: claims and counter-claims about the collapse of national economic coordination, the end of social citizenship, or the erosion of social welfare regimes. The chapters that follow do not address the modern social by sorting out these claims in a general way. Rather, through a focus on technologies, infrastructures, and institutions, they seek to understand more subtle transformations in these fields and the specific problems these transformations pose.

Examples can be drawn from two chapters on Latin America and two chapters on Southeast and East Asia. Taking the Latin American cases first, chapters by Lakoff and by Caldeira and Holston address the transformation of modern social welfare in the contexts of neoliberal reform and democratization, processes whose coupling forged key dynamics of structural change in the region in the 1990s. Lakoff examines the transmutation of epidemiological techniques originally developed in a project of social medicine. In the context of the modern social, such techniques were meant to yield information about disease patterns in a general population. These data would, in turn, imply a 'public' response in the form of policy. Today, as the project of social medicine has broken down, these techniques are abstracted, transported, and reter-ritorialized, as the private sector has adopted epidemiological models to build databases that record prescription rates of psychiatric specialists in Argentina. These models are deployed not in the name of a 'public' project of social medicine but of a private strategy of transnational corporations to increase drug sales by rewarding physicians who prescribe them, bringing private corporations, afflicted patients, and state regulation into new alignments. Caldeira and Holston examine shifting technologies of modern urbanism in Brazil. As the political franchise has been expanded through constitutional reforms, previously excluded groups are now appearing in the political sphere through claims on core benefits of social citizenship such as access to basic utilities and social services. But neoliberalism has undermined the bases of social citizenship by either rolling back or privatizing social services. Resulting shifts in social welfare, marketization, administration, and political franchise are reconfiguring the field of biopolitics.

Two chapters on East and Southeast Asian cases examine tensions between national identity and new citizenship regimes that are oriented to incorporating those who can most effectively participate in and promote contemporary knowledge economies. Ong's chapter examines neoliberal strategies for developing knowledge-driven economies in Malaysia and Singapore. Technocrats have sought to create new "ecologies of expertise" by extending social and citizenship rights to expatriate scientists. Such efforts create tensions between those who consider themselves proper members of the 'nation' and the institutions through which the state assigns certain rights and privileges. What is more, a relaxed approach to global research standards has sparked debates by actual citizens as to the proper avenues for curbing potential abuses by foreign experts.

Olds and Thrift, finally, examine elite business education institutions in Singapore that are used to promote a newly intensified form of citizenship that emerges in a context where "ideal citizens" are centers of calculation. In contrast to the passive citizenship of post-World War II projects of social modernity these institutions are defining forms of citizenship through which "accumulation becomes the very stuff of life, through persuading the population to become its own prime asset – a kind of people mine . . . of reflexive knowledgeability."[49]

Assemblage, reassemblage

In the past few years, a series of significant shifts – which should not be presumptively understood to follow a single logic – have led some observers to speculate about the end of the moment when 'globalization' seemed to capture something essential about the present. The collapse of the stock bubble focused on internet, communication, and energy stocks and the collapse of corporate spending in the United States have not only had an immediate economic impact but may affect the rate of technological change as major corporations reign in investment on research and development. At the same time, a series of reactions to neoliberalism – whether manifest in privatization, capital market liberalization, or social-sector reform – have also gained momentum. These include the response to the Asian financial crisis and more recent developments in Latin America, where democratic elections have brought to power populists whose platforms include anti-globalization positions. Finally, the events of September 11, 2001, and the succession of conflicts and policy shifts that followed them have broadly changed the tenor of world affairs. The period from roughly the end of the cold war to 9/11 was a decade in which many technological, political, and ethical problems seemed to be organized around the insistent spread of global forms; the 1990s were, to borrow a technical term from Michel Foucault, a governmentality decade. The dynamic changes were occurring along the axis of governmentality and biopower. Today, security and sovereignty are increasingly active sites of problematization, yielding new tensions and problems.[50]

This emerging state of affairs has provoked another spate of epochal and totalizing proclamations about the present. Triumphal visions abound, although the specifics of these visions have shifted. On the other hand, the anti-globalization movement seems to have shifted its analysis – unblinking, unperturbed, and unaltered – from largely political–economic claims to the global war on terrorism. Millennial themes and grand diagnoses have been deftly redirected from globalization to a post-globalization era.

As we have tried to show in this chapter, the contributions to this volume suggest a different approach. They are engaged in a form of inquiry that stays close to practices. Their mode of diagnosing the anthropological significance of these practices stays close to specific problems. They may give up, thereby, some generality, politics, and pathos. But for that, perhaps, the approach they suggest remains more acute, adroit, and mobile than grand diagnoses. It does not suggest an absence of a critical stance. Indeed, each chapter presents an analytic or critical response to changes that are at the center of political and ethical debates. But in these politically and morally freighted domains, relations of power – or, for that matter, relations of virtue – and appropriate avenues of response are not always immediately obvious. Indeed, these chapters share a sense that the fields of moral, ethical, or political valuation and activity are shifting, and that, consequently, these fields should themselves be a central object of inquiry.

Accordingly, it remains important today to reflectively cultivate more partial and cautious positions of observation that nonetheless grapple with "big" questions. It may be helpful, in this light, to ask how the tools and examples presented in this volume can be relevant to understanding contemporary shifts, and what new sites of research might be opened by an approach such as the one we have outlined.

Neoliberalism today remains a pervasive form of political rationality whose formal and 'global' character is allowing it to enter into novel relationships with diverse value orientations and political positions. Thus, in Latin America, the election of populist leaders in Brazil and Argentina has not meant the immediate backlash against 'globalization' that some observers – and "financial markets" – expected. Consequently, we should seek to understand the anthropological significance of what will certainly prove to be novel accommodations between new populist policies of social welfare or job creation and neoliberal technologies of reform that use 'economic' strategies of formal rationalization. We might also expect readjustments in the balance between neoliberalism and security as guiding orientations in world affairs. Many parts of the world that seemed, as Manuel Castells has written, "structurally irrelevant" during the 1990s have come to the focus of attention. With growing awareness of the role of parts of Africa, the Caucuses, Afghanistan and Pakistan, Indonesia, and the Philippines as logistical bases for international terrorism, the problem of bringing these areas into grids of security is increasingly vexing for the richest and most powerful countries in the world. Security, economy, and sovereignty are in motion.

The biosciences and information technology will also remain a site of dynamic change in this new context. As Donna Haraway long ago pointed out, the generation of information technology that boomed during the 1980s and 1990s, largely in the private sector, was the product of state intervention and, specifically, the military–industrial complex.[51] Today, the military is increasingly reliant on private companies for technology in everything from GPS systems to remote satellite imaging to identification technology to warfare simulations to biodefense research. In this context, questions are being raised concerning the maintenance of proprietary access to strategic information and to technology that is now being disseminated in part through market logics.[52] Related problems may emerge in the biosciences. Private research is newly significant for the 'public' goals of security today, and would become dramatically more so in the event of a bioterrorism attack. Continuing debates around the distribution of AIDS drugs in poor parts of the world and new diseases such as SARS impose political, ethical, and technological pressures on the relations among science, market mechanism of distribution, and the actual geography of afflicted or threatened populations.[53] These shifts trace little lines of mutation that disarticulate and rearticulate elements, forming new assemblages that will be the sites, objects, and tools of future reflection.

Notes

1   We acknowledge the comments and suggestions of Jennifer Collier, Ruth Collier, Talia Dan-Cohen, Andrew Lakoff, Shannon May, Tobias Rees, and Antina von Schintzler. We also thank the contributors to this volume for their input on various formulations of the ideas in this chapter.

2   Ulrich Beck, Anthony Giddens, and Scott Lash, *Reflexive Modernization: Politics, Tradition, and Aesthetics in the Modern Social Order* (Cambridge: Polity, 1994); Manuel Castells, *The Rise of Network Society* (Oxford: Blackwell, 1996); J. Timmons Roberts and Amy Hite, eds., *From Modernization to Globalization: Perspectives on Development and Social Change* (Oxford: Blackwell, 1999); Saskia Sassen, *The Global City: New York, London, Tokyo* (Princeton: Princeton University Press, 1991).

3   Michael Burawoy, ed., *Global Ethnographies* (Berkeley: University of California Press, 2000); Jean Comaroff and John Comaroff, *Millennial Capitalism and the Culture of Neoliberalism* (Durham, NC: Duke University Press, 2001).

4   Arjun Appadurai, "Disjuncture and Difference in the Global Cultural Economy," in *The Anthropology of Globalization: A Reader*, Jonathan Inda and Renato Rosaldo, eds. (Oxford: Blackwell, 2002); Mike Featherstone, *Global Culture* (London: Sage, 1991); Fredric Jameson and Masao Miyoshi, *The Cultures of Globalization* (Durham, NC: Duke University Press, 1998); Karen Fog Olwig and Kirsten Hastrun, eds., *Siting Culture: The Shifting Anthropological Object* (London: Routledge, 1997).

5   See, for example, Bruno Latour, *We Have Never Been Modern* (Cambridge, MA: Harvard University Press, 1993), and "When Things Strike Back: A Possible Contribution of 'Science Studies' to the Social Sciences," *British Journal of Sociology* 51(1), January/March 2000, pp. 107–123; Timothy Mitchell, *Rule of Experts: Egypt, Techno-Politics, Modernity* (Berkeley: University of California Press, 2002); Paul Rabinow, *Anthropos Today: Reflections on Modern Equipment* (Princeton, NJ: Princeton University Press, 2003); David Stark, "For a Sociology of Worth," Department of Sociology, Columbia University, unpublished MS.

6   See the first chapter of Latour, *We Have Never Been Modern*.

7   See also Sarah Franklin, Celia Lury, and Jackie Stacey, *Global Nature, Global Culture* (London: Sage, 2000).

8   For example, Gilles Deleuze and Feix Guattari, *A Thousand Plateaus* (Minneapolis: University of Minnesota Press, 1987); Gilles Deleuze, *Foucault* (Minneapolis: University of Minnesota Press, 1986), particularly the chapter "A New Cartographer."

9   Sarah Franklin, "Stem Cells R Us: Emergent Life Forms and the Global Biological," Chapter 4, this volume, p. 67.

10 Giorgio Agamben has pointed to the relationship between Foucault and Arendt in his *Homo Sacer: Sovereign Power and Bare Life* (Stanford: Stanford University Press, 1998). The relationship between Foucault and Polanyi is, so far as we know, largely unexplored.

11 Michel Foucault, *The Order of Things: An Archaeology of the Human Sciences* (New York: Pantheon, 1971).

12 Biology, society, and culture are Hubert Dreyfus and Paul Rabinow's gloss on Foucault's triadic "finitudes" of life, labor, and language, in *Michel Foucault: Beyond Structuralism and Hermeneutics* (Chicago: University of Chicago Press, 1982).

13 Hannah Arendt, *The Human Condition* (Chicago: University of Chicago Press, 1958).

14 Karl Polanyi, *The Great Transformation* (Boston: Beacon, 1957), pp. 120–121.

15 Thus, Jeremy Bentham's social technologies were of central interest to both thinkers, although Polanyi seems to have thought more deeply about the relationship of such technologies to liberal thought.

16 Beck et al., *Reflexive Modernization*.

17 David Stark used this term at the workshop "*Oikos* and *Anthropos*: Rationality, Technology, Infrastructure," Prague, The Czech Republic, April 2002.

18 Monique Girard and David Stark, "Heterarchies of Value: Distributing Intelligence and Organizing Diversity in a New Media Startup," Chapter 16, this volume, p. 294.

19 See, for example, Bruno Latour, *Science in Action: How to Follow Scientists and Engineers through Society* (Cambridge, MA: Harvard University Press, 1988).

20 For basic definitions, see Max Weber, *Economy and Society* (Berkeley: University of California Press, 1978); and Niklas Luhmann, *Observations on Modernity* (Stanford: Stanford University Press, 1998).

21 Giddens, "Living in a Post-Traditional Society," pp. 58–59.

22 Max Weber, *The Protestant Ethic and the Spirit of Capitalism* (London: Routledge, 1992), p. xxxviii.

23 We have adopted two changes to Talcott Parsons' standard 1930 translation that were suggested and explained to us by Tobias Rees. First, "significance and validity" are substituted for "meaning and value" in the original. "Meaning" could be understood as "significance" in English, but the latter is less ambiguous, since it cannot be confused with "sense." "Value" can be assumed to be a mis-translation, or in any case an imprecise translation, based on Weber's later admonitions in this text that science cannot ground value judgments. Validity refers to standards of proof or demonstration of adequacy or instrumental effectiveness, not to value in the sense of a normative judgment. Second, "cultural," which in the original modifies "phenomena," is omitted. As Rees explains, the German root *Kultur* would in this case have implied a contrast with "natural." Thus, "cultural phenomena" are best understood simply as "human" phenomena. The omission of "cultural" avoids confusion with the American anthropological "culture" (Tobias Rees, personal communication). The first amendment can also be found in the recent translation by Peter Baehr and Gordon Wells (New York: Penguin, 2002).

24 Rees suggested the following interpretation of the distinction between *Universalgeschichte* (universal history) and *Universelle* (universal significance and validity).

25 Weber, *The Protestant Ethic*, p. 181.

26 For the original usage, see Max Weber, *The Methodology of the Social Sciences* (New York: Free Press, 1949). The concept is also developed in Stephen J. Collier, "Post-Socialist City: The Government of Society in Neoliberal Times," Ph.D. dissertation, University of California, Berkeley, December 2001.

27 Leo Strauss makes the distinction in these terms in "On Aristotle's Politics," in *The City and Man* (Chicago: University of Chicago Press, 1964), pp. 14–15.

28 Franklin et al., *Global Nature, Global Culture*.

29 Charles Sable Prokop, Jane E. and Charles F. Sabel, "Stabilization Through Reorganization? Some Preliminary Implications of Russia's Entry into World Markets in the Age of Discursive Quality Standards," in *Corporate Governance in Central Europe and Russia*, R. Frydman, A. Rapaczynski and Carol Gray, eds. (Budapest: CEU Press, 1996).

30 Latour, *Science in Action*, p. 227.

31 Andrew Barry, *Political Machines: Governing a Technological Society* (New York: Athlone Press, 2001).

32 Vinh-kim Nguyen, "Antiretroviral Globalism, Biopolitics, and Therapeutic Citizenship," Chapter, 8, this volume, p. 143.

33 See Lawrence Cohen, "Where it Hurts: Indian Material for an Ethics of Organ Transplantation," *Daedalus* 128(4), 1999, pp. 135–165.

34 See Kris Olds and Nigel Thrift, "Cultures on the Brink: Reengineering the Soul of Capitalism – On a Global Scale," Chapter 15, this volume.

35 Elizabeth C. Dunn, "Standards and Person-Making in East Central Europe," Chapter 10, this volume, p. 175.

36 Oxford English Dictionary Online; http://www.oed.com, 2003.

37 We acknowledge the help of Christopher Kelty in thinking through this image.

38 Nikolas Rose, "Governing 'Advanced' Liberal Democracies," in *Foucault and Political Reason: Liberalism, Neo-liberalism, and Rationalities of Government*, Nikolas Rose, Andrew Barry, and Thomas Osborne, eds. (London: UCL Press, 1996).

39 Neil Brenner and Nik Theodore, "Cities and the Geographies of 'Actually Existing Neoliberalism,'" in *Spaces of Neoliberalism: Urban Restructuring in North America and Western Europe*, Neil Brenner and Nik Theodor, eds. (Oxford: Blackwell, 2002).

40 Douglas R. Holmes and George E. Marcus, "Cultures of Expertise and the Management of Globalization: Toward the Re-Functioning of Ethnography," Chapter 13, this volume, pp. 236–237.

41 Ibid., p. 237.

42 Idem.

43 Gísli Pálsson and Paul Rabinow, "The Iceland Controversies: Reflections on the Transnational Market of Civic Virtue," Chapter 6, this volume, p. 94.

44 Pálsson and Rabinow, "The Iceland Controversies," p. 92.

45 See, for example, the chapters in David Held and Anthony McGrew, eds., *The Global Transformations Reader: An Introduction to the Globalization Debate* (Malden, MA: Polity Press, 2000).

46 Joseph Schumpeter, "The Crisis of the Tax State," *International Economic Papers* 4(7), 1954.

47 Gilles Deleuze, "Foreword: The Rise of the Social," in Jacques Donzelot, *The Policing of Families* (New York: Pantheon, 1979).

48 Deleuze, "The Rise of the Social."

49 Olds and Thrift, "Cultures on the Brink," p. 272.

50 For one perspective on sovereignty and biopolitics, see Aihwa Ong, "Graduated Sovereignty in South-East Asia," *Theory, Culture and Society* 17(4), August 2000, pp. 55–75.

51 Donna Haraway, *Cyborgs, Simians, and Women: The Re-Invention of Nature* (New York: Routledge, 1991).

52 For work on neoliberal technologies of administration and remote satellite imaging, see Lyle Fearnley, "The Global Market and Technologies of Security: Shifting Strategies within U.S. Remote Sensing Satellite Programs," Columbia University, unpublished MS; Ryan Bishop and John Phillips, "Sighted Weapons and Modernist Opacity: Aesthetics, Poetics, Prosthetics," *Boundary 2* 5(13), 2002, pp. 161–191; Ryan Bishop and John Phillips, "Unmanning the Homeland," *International Journal of Urban and Regional Research* 26(3), September 2002, pp. 620–625.

53 Aihwa Ong, "Assembling around SARS: Technology, Body Heat, and Political Fever in Risk Society," in *Ulrich Beck und Zweite Moderne*, Natan Sznaider and Angelika Poferl, eds. (Dusseldorf: Nomos Press, 2005).

2

ON REGIMES OF LIVING

STEPHEN J. COLLIER
AND ANDREW LAKOFF

The chapters in this volume examine practices in technical domains ranging from the life sciences, to urban planning, to social administration, to finance.[1] But it is clear that their goal is not to understand technical operations *per se*. What, then, draws them together? In what follows, we suggest that despite the diversity of objects and sites that these chapters consider, they are linked by a common interest in examining processes of reflection and action in situations in which "living" has been rendered problematic. These situations provoke reflection on questions such as: What is human life becoming? What conventions define virtuous conduct in different contexts? We propose the concept of 'regimes of living' as a tool for investigating how such situations are structured today.

In the first part of this chapter, we suggest that these situations can be fruitfully analyzed by engaging a set of discussions on ethics in philosophy and critical theory. Here the term "ethics" refers not to the adjudication of values but, as Bernard Williams puts it, to the question "How should one live?"[2] Ethical problems, in this sense, involve a certain idea of practice ("how"), a notion of the subject of ethical reflection ("one"), and questions of norms or values ("should") related to a certain form of life in a given domain of living. This engagement with philosophical discussions helps to frame ethical questions in terms of techniques, practices, and rationality. Moreover, it identifies two elements of contemporary social life – biopolitics and technology – that feature centrally in the problematic situations we examine here.

However, our goal is different from that of the moral philosophers we discuss. The philosophical discourse on ethics is often oriented to explaining the inadequacies of contemporary ethics through reference to the loss of a past in which ethics was coherent, based on a common tradition and a shared vision of human nature. This diagnosis of the pathologies of the present is part of a quest to define a more coherent ethics. In contrast, as interpretive social scientists, our purpose is to analyze how ethical problems are configured today. We hope to contribute to an *analytics* of contemporary ethics, rather than a diagnosis of their incoherence. Following Michel Foucault's method in his genealogy of ethics, this approach seeks to identify the elements – techniques, subjects, norms – through which the question of 'how to live' is posed.[3]

In the second part of this chapter we introduce the concept of the regime of living as a tool for mapping specific sites of ethical problematization. By 'regime of living' we refer to a tentative and situated configuration of normative, technical, and political elements that are brought into alignment in situations that present ethical problems – that is, situations in which the question of how to live is at stake. Here the word *regime* suggests a "manner, method, or system of rule or government,"[4] including principles of reasoning, valuation, and practice that have a provisional consistency or coherence. To say that such regimes relate to questions of *living* means: first, that they concern reasoning about and acting with respect to an understanding of the good; and second, that they are involved in processes of ethical formation – that is, in the constitution of subjects, both individual and collective.

We explore the operation of regimes of living through a number of exemplars drawn from the volume – these include cases described by Marilyn Strathern on ethical regulation in Canada, Teresa Caldeira and James Holston on development and urbanism in Brazil, Janet Roitman on the "garrison–entrepôt" in the Chad Basin, and Lawrence Cohen on the organ trade in India. These exemplars illustrate the dynamic process through which a situated form of moral reasoning – a regime of living – is invoked and reworked in a problematic situation to provide a possible guide to action. They also illustrate the centrality of biopolitics and technology to contemporary ethical problems. In diverse sites, one finds forms of moral reasoning that are not linked by a common culture but whose shared characteristics can be analyzed in terms of intersections of technology, politics, and values.

The analytic mode of this chapter is methodological rather than theoretical or strictly empirical. Its purpose is neither to put forward an over-arching description of ethical problems in the present nor to multiply instances of local specificity. Rather, we seek to clarify a form of inquiry common to the chapters that follow and to make explicit some strategies for defining shared objects and problems.[5]

Technological Reason and Biopolitics as 'Ethical' Problems

As an initial illustration of how the chapters in this volume critically engage 'ethical' problems, we turn to Marilyn Strathern's chapter, "Robust Knowledge and Fragile Futures." This chapter describes the work of the Canadian Royal Commission on New Reproductive Technologies, formed to make policy recommendations to the Canadian Government. Strathern's account begins from a problematic situation: the invention of new technologies poses questions concerning the regulation of human reproduction. Notably, it is the state, and specifically this Royal Commission, that is identified as the appropriate agent to respond. The Commission employs a distinctive form of reasoning that rests on the 'liberal' principle that it should act on behalf of the values of "Canadian society as a whole."[6] This principle, in turn, presents a technical challenge: how to make 'society' register its opinion – how, as Strathern puts it, to "set in motion social processes that would yield information attributable to [this] society."[7] The Commission's answer is the appropriation and deployment of an 'ethical' technology – a survey – that aims to capture the diversity of opinion of Canadian society. This procedure constitutes a *social audit*, whose purpose is to analyze not financial values and flows but the values of society. These values are supposed to form the basis of policy, allowing the Canadian Government to claim that its action reflects and is accountable to the "will" of the Canadian people.

The Commission understands the 'problem' in this situation as involving competing values about the morality of the use of reproductive technologies.[8] Accordingly, it sees its task as the resolution of conflicts among these values through an appeal to a *universal* value – liberality. This approach places the Commission's activities within the domain of 'ethics' in the term's narrow contemporary usage, indicating the application of values or moral rules to specific situations. But we might also see the work of the Commission in terms of a regime of living – that is, as part of a more contingent assemblage of values and of political and technical elements.[9] In the case that Strathern describes, the social audit crystallizes a form of reflection and practice on the question of how a peculiar kind of ethical subject – society – should live.

An important claim of Strathern's chapter is that the activity of the Commission on Reproductive Choice is inadequate to the challenge of reflecting upon the 'ethical' problems raised by new reproductive technologies. Ultimately, she suggests, the point of the exercise was simply to *have gone through* the process of the audit, to *have recorded* society's opinion. This opinion was not meaningfully reflected in policy and, indeed, the recommendations that resulted from the social audit seem to have been determined in advance by the very value upon which the Committee's work was premised: liberality. Would the recommendations have been different, Strathern asks provocatively, if 'society' was deemed to be illiberal?

Strathern's analysis recalls the concern of some contemporary moral philosophers and critical analysts that, as ethical discourses have proliferated, they are increasingly inadequate to the problems with which they grapple.[10] As Alasdair MacIntyre argues in his important book on Western moral philosophy, *After Virtue*, "moral countenance can now be given to far too many causes...the form of moral utterance provides a possible mask for almost any face."[11] MacIntyre's diagnosis of this situation proceeds from the suggestion that contemporary ethical discourse "can only be understood as a series of fragmented survivals from an older past" when ethics was "at home in larger totalities of theory and practice in which they enjoyed a role and function supplied by contexts of which they have now been deprived."[12] The "older past" MacIntyre has in mind is that of classical Greece, which serves as a model of coherence in comparison to what he sees as the disorder of contemporary ethical discourse. In his reading of the classical tradition, practical reason, the institution of citizenship, and conceptions of the virtues were rationally organized on the basis of a common understanding of human ends and a stable cosmos or tradition. In this context, individuals could conduct their lives with respect to a stable understanding of the good. For MacIntyre, contemporary ethical discourse lacks such a stable cosmos or a teleological understanding of human nature to guide ethical reasoning. Consequently, he argues, contemporary ethics has devolved into empty debates about incommensurable values that are not amenable to rational resolution.

In contrast to MacIntyre, however, our goal is not to diagnose the malaise of contemporary ethics; nor is it to propose a means of rectifying our ethics. Nonetheless, the contrastive comparison between contemporary and classical ethics that MacIntyre and others have undertaken proves useful for the present analysis. Whatever one makes of his account of the classical tradition, MacIntyre's discussion brings into view distinguishing features of the way the question of "how one should live" is posed today.

Thus, in the case of the Canadian Commission, the "how" includes technical means – reproductive technology, the survey, focus groups – that stand in uncertain relationship to values or ethical principles. The "should" does not refer to virtues derived from an understanding of human nature or to a common tradition – indeed, the ethical norm is in formation: the very phenomenon that the Commission seeks to reflect is the 'diversity' of Canadian society. And the ethical subject – the "one" – is not an individual reflecting on the conduct of life but a collection of experts adjudicating among values. Their charge, moreover, is to act in the name of an entity that would have been foreign to the classical ethical formation – society. The life in question is collective, and it is not only the life of citizens but of biological and social beings, insofar as they are engaged in reproductive behavior.

These distinctive features of contemporary ethics can be understood through two broad contrasts highlighted by MacIntyre and others. The first is between the "practical reason" of the classical tradition and modern "technological reason." The second is between the classical account of the *polis* as a domain in which reasoning citizens meet as equals and a key dimension of the modern polity – biopolitics. For a range of critical observers the rise of biopolitics and technology are key moments in a narrative about the loss of coherence of ethical reason in modernity. However, we read the centrality of biopolitics and technology to modern social life in a different light. From an anthropological vantage, they can be understood as sources of dynamism that are critical to understanding how the constitution of ethical subjects, forms of ethical reasoning, and practices of living with respect to the good are at stake today.

Moral philosophy's "classical tradition"

In MacIntyre's account, the key feature of classical ethics was that it rested upon a shared view of human nature – what Charles Taylor calls a "specific anthropology."[13] As MacIntyre describes this ethical configuration, "human beings, like the members of all other species, have a specific nature; and that nature is such that they have certain aims and goals, such that they move by nature toward a specific *telos*."[14] Living life with respect to one's *telos* was the central task of ethical self-formation.[15] From this starting point, MacIntyre paints a picture of a coherent ethical configuration that rests on two key elements: practical wisdom as a basis for rational action and the *polis* as a context of ethical reasoning. As we will see, both are central to his understanding of the disarray of contemporary ethics.

According to this account of ethical action in the classical tradition, to live a good life an individual had to possess a certain kind of discernment in determining what actions were appropriate, 'good,' or virtuous.[16] Such discernment did not involve knowledge of a fixed set of moral rules, nor was it a purely abstract form of rationality. It was, rather, a capacity for reasoned choice – a practical wisdom – that allowed an individual to act on the basis of "the requirements of virtue in each fresh context."[17] The ability to make such practical choices was an excellence of character that was itself the product of work on the self or a process of ethical self-formation. As MacIntyre summarizes it: "The education of the passions into conformity with pursuit of what theoretical reasoning identifies as the *telos* and practical reasoning as the right action to do in each particular time and place is what ethics is all about."[18] Practical wisdom, thus, was always linked to the character of the person who was engaged in reasoning. In contrast to the modern situation, MacIntyre argues, practical wisdom could only be exercised by a good person; and conversely, goodness required intelligence.

A second important feature of this philosophical engagement with the classical tradition relates to the context in which practical wisdom could be exercised and the good life pursued. Classical ethics was necessarily pursued in the distinctive space of the *polis* and through the conduct of a political life.[19] Correspondingly, the contemporary absence of a structured domain like the *polis* frames many philosophers' analysis of the inadequacies of ethics today.

For example, Hannah Arendt, in a manner that resonates with MacIntyre, describes the classical *polis* as a space of freedom in which an ethics based on speech and action of citizens was possible. In analyzing this space she draws a critical distinction between the *polis* – the space of politics in which citizens met as equals – and the *oikos* or household – the space of mutual interdependence for the sake of sheer life.[20] It was only upon entering the *polis* and leaving behind the cares of the *oikos*, upon freeing oneself from the cares of sheer life, that the citizen could pursue the good life. As Arendt notes, "[t]he 'good life,' as Aristotle called the life of the citizen, therefore was not merely better, more carefree or nobler than ordinary life, but of an altogether different quality. It was 'good' to the extent that by having mastered the necessities of sheer life, by being freed from labor and work, and by overcoming the innate urge of all living creatures for their own survival, it was no longer bound to the biological life process."[21] "Ordinary life," as Taylor calls "the life of production and reproduction, or economic and family life" – was for Aristotle "simply of infrastructural significance ... a goal of association, because you need it in order to carry on the good life."[22] As we will see, Arendt contrasts this configuration to the centrality of "the biological life process" in modern politics.

For MacIntyre, the context of the *polis* is significant in another respect that is crucial to his diagnosis of contemporary ethics – namely, that it provided a common tradition in relation to which ethical problems were posed. Answers to such problems were not to be discovered through moral rules that applied everywhere to all human beings. Rather, the good could be understood only in relation to the context-dependent and always embedded problems, mores, and conventions – the *nomos* – of a given human community.[23] The *polis* defined the horizon or common tradition of such a community. The preoccupation of practical wisdom was to grasp the requirements of virtue, not as strict rules or moral laws but as a relatively flexible and critical engagement with a tradition.[24] Thus, in MacIntyre's reconstruction, classical ethics assumed both an embeddedness in a certain tradition and a critical distance from the tradition's specific dictates.[25]

How does MacIntyre's reconstruction of the classical tradition inform his diagnosis of the malaise of contemporary ethics? And what elements of his diagnosis might be usefully redirected toward an analytics of the dynamism of current ethical, technical, and political configurations?

Technological reason

For MacIntyre, a key problem with contemporary moral philosophy is that it assumes a separation between ethics and rationality. In this sense it precludes a structure of practical wisdom akin to that of classical ethics. Modern thinkers, he argues, have emphasized a view of reason that, as Taylor puts it, is not "defined substantively, in terms of a vision of the cosmic order, but formally, in terms of the procedures that thought ought to follow, and especially those involved in fitting means to ends, instrumental reason."[26] This instrumental or *technological* reason has a disembedded character: it is not wedded to a specific social or cultural context, to an understanding of the good, or to a stable understanding of a human nature that grounds action.[27] Questions of fact are de-coupled from questions of value. The result, MacIntyre argues, is an incapacity to conceive 'ethics' as a form of reasoned action, and a tendency to frame ethical problems in terms of "irrational" values that cannot be rationally debated.

Moreover, MacIntyre argues, in modernity the exercise of reason is dissociated from ethical self-formation and from a specific subject of reason. "For Kant," he notes, "one can be both good and stupid; but for Aristotle stupidity of a certain kind precludes goodness."[28] Thus, a number of problematic 'ethical' figures in modernity – the technocratic expert who is concerned only with facts and not with values, or, we might add, the contemporary ethicist, whose 'expertise' or authority lies purely in questions of value rather than in questions of fact – would not have been conceivable for classical ethics.[29] Modern reason raises the possibility that one can be both good and stupid; or, for that matter, bad and smart.

For MacIntyre, the disjuncture between ethics and rationality in modernity is the product of an historical process through which the moral subject has been deprived of a social milieu and *telos* that could rationally ground moral judgments. But the emergence and spread of modern forms of rationality need not be seen solely in terms of the 'decline' of an ethical cosmos and the eclipse of a coherent ethics. As Max Weber and others have argued, the techniques of instrumental reason – are of increasingly broad ethical significance across the life worlds[30]. The extension of such techniques can be understood as constantly provoking new 'ethical' questions as concrete forms of technological reason enter into dynamic, productive, and often problematic relations with values.[31] Moreover, technological reason is continually involved in constituting "human nature" and diverse ethical subjects. Vivid examples can be found in the debates swirling around reproductive technology and associated questions concerning definitions of the beginning of life – and, thus, the definition of life itself – or in political battles over technologies of administration in domains such as welfare reform that redefine human collectivities.

Biopolitics

Parallel to their analysis of the distinction between practical wisdom and a disembedded technological reason, MacIntyre and Arendt use a contrast between the classical *polis* and the modern polity to criticize contemporary ethical reasoning. As we have seen, in Arendt's understanding of the classical tradition, citizens could only constitute themselves as ethical subjects in a space of freedom from the mundane concerns of biological and social existence.[32] In the modern polity, by contrast, biological and social processes for sustaining and reproducing human life are central problems. Arendt associates this feature of the modern polity with the domain of 'society.' Society here is neither the state nor the individual household – the two spaces whose opposition organized classical ethics – but a third term: a "national *oikos*," or national household, in which "the fact of mutual dependence for the sake of life and nothing else assumes public significance and where the activities connected with sheer survival are permitted to appear in public."[33] Relatedly, fostering the "ordinary life" of a population is a central basis for the legitimacy of modern states and a primary goal of regulating collective life.[34]

For Arendt, one implication of the rise of the social is the erosion of the *polis* as a context for a coherent and rational ethics.[35] The emergence of life itself as the central problem of the modern polity is linked to the rise of a mass society geared to the satisfaction of the basic wants of the population rather than the political life of citizens. In turn, she argues, the mass character of contemporary politics means that behavior displaces action in the public sphere, which is not a space of reason and freedom but a space of conformity and statistical regularity. In a distinct but parallel fashion, MacIntyre argues that contemporary politics does not constitute the horizon of a common tradition in relation to which rational citizens can fashion an ethical way of living.

But the centrality of social and biological life in the modern polity – leading to a situation we might call, following Foucault, 'biopolitical' – need not be seen only in terms of a loss of a common point of reference for ethical reasoning. As Strathern's case and the exemplars we consider below demonstrate, 'society' emerges as a central ethical subject in modernity. At the same time, 'politics' is reconfigured in more partial and provisional forms around problems of collective existence related to life itself.

Counter-politics of sheer life

This point is persuasively demonstrated in Teresa Caldeira and James Holston's chapter "State and Urban Space in Brazil: From Modernist Planning to Democratic Interventions," which examines neoliberalism, social welfare, and popular politics in São Paulo squatter settlements. The authors' point of departure is the emergence of modern urbanism in the post-World War II project of state-led developmentalism in Brazil. This form of urbanism, which defined the totality of social relationships as a possible object of state intervention, constituted society as a field of technical manipulation and as an ethical substance through which certain ideals – equality, modernity – could be realized for the entire Brazilian nation. In so doing, it created a political space in which Brazilians appeared not only as holders of juridical rights but as members of a population with social and biological needs.

However, as Caldeira and Holston note, the actual operation of "total planning" contradicted the core principles of Brazilian social modernity in important ways. Large portions of the urban population that were incorporated into plans as laborers were excluded from the basic institutions of social and political citizenship, and could only inhabit modern cities by means of illegal or irregular settlements. However, this disenfranchisement did not prevent the formation of expectations among the residents of such settlements that the state would deliver core social goods and services. The resulting clash between an inclusive national ideology and the actual facts of exclusion from Brazilian social modernity led these marginal subjects to craft a distinctive strategy for making claims on the state. This strategy did not reject the project of social modernity; rather, it was a "counter-politics" that articulated claims to inclusion or citizenship in the Brazilian 'nation' precisely on the basis of demands for service delivery, infrastructure provision, and participation in planning decisions.[36] A type of citizenship, a certain set of technologies related to the satisfaction of daily needs, and a set of values concerning expectations of state administration crystallized in a regime of living that we can call a *counter-politics of sheer life*. This form of situated moral reasoning involves a claim to state resources that is articulated by individuals and collectivities in terms of their needs as living beings.[37]

As we have seen, the philosophical engagement with classical ethics is useful in understanding ethical problems not in terms of moral rules or values but as configurations of reason, technique, and institutions of collective life. This discussion also points us toward technological reason and biopolitics as dynamic sites of ethical problematization. For social scientific observers, these insights suggest that it is unsatisfactory to limit discussion of contemporary "ethical" problems to the self-forming individual or to the quest to find a rational form of acting with respect to the good. In these cases the elements that compose contemporary problems of living stand in flexible, provisional, and tense interrelationship. Just as fundamentally, these cases indicate that the range of situations in which problems of living arise is much broader than what moral philosophy and critical theory have conceived as the proper domain of ethics. These situations shape partial and provisional reconfigurations of "ethical" reflection and action – what might be called minor traditions.

Banditry

To illustrate this point, we turn to Janet Roitman's chapter on practices of wealth creation among bandits and traffickers in the Chad Basin. As in Caldeira and Holston's example, Roitman's case does not involve "ethics" in any conventional sense; it is perhaps even more remote from the scene of classical ethics as conceived by moral philosophers than Caldeira and Holston's counter-politics of sheer life. Nonetheless, it examines a site in which the question of "how to live" is posed in relationship to technology and biopolitics.

Roitman's analysis centers on what she calls a distinctive "military–commercial nexus"[38] – the garrison–entrepôt – characterized by a range of "unregulated economic activities and violent methods of extraction," such as banditry and trafficking. Various political and economic transformations interact dynamically with the formation of the garrison–entrepôt. These include structural adjustment policies, fiscal crisis, privatization, the erosion of the state monopoly on violence, and the increasing marginalization of the Chad Basin from the global economy. In this context, Roitman's insight is to understand the garrison–entrepôt not in terms of absence – of law, civility, or a coherent grounds for ethical reasoning – but as a distinct domain, with its own norms, technologies, and sites of practice. Despite its problematic legal status, Roitman argues, the garrison–entrepôt constitutes a mode of regulating economic activity that is also "fundamental to the workings of the various national states of the Chad Basin."[39]

Moreover, participants in the garrison–entrepôt engage in forms of situated action and reflection on questions of living that enable them to forge 'ethical' orientations to their work. Roitman describes how actors operating in the garrison–entrepôt – such as bandits, traffickers, and "fighting customs officials" – reflect on the tension between the "licit" and the "legal." Terms and values that are typically associated with the functioning of the modern state – such as security, employment, and the redistribution of wealth – are part of a language for making ethical distinctions among various formally illegal activities. For example, illegal and sometimes violent appropriation is understood as a kind of tax collection, since it is linked to what are seen as licit practices of redistribution or forms of 'work.' As Roitman writes, the "idea that theft and highway robbery constitute work is more than just a rationalization of illicit practice; it is a reflection that is grounded in particular notions about what constitutes wealth, what constitutes licit or proper manners of appropriation, and how one governs both wealth and economic relations."[40] "Banditry," in this case, emerges as a regime of living that actively reworks existing forms of regulation, governing, and ethical action.

In Roitman's case, as in the others we have described, technological reason and biopolitics are sites of dynamism. They shape uncertain situations in which the very terms of ethical activity – the subject in the name of whom action takes place, the values that guide ethics, and the relevant forms of ethical reason and practice – are in question. The point is not to argue that the necessary elements of a coherent ethics – a common tradition, a telos of ethical self-formation, or a stable anthropology – are lacking in these sites of ethical problematization. Rather, it is to repose the question for a contemporary investigation of problems of living: how, today, is our anthropology at stake in our ethics?

Regimes of Living in Operation

In the remainder of this chapter, we examine the dynamics of regimes of living as they take shape in diverse situations. We also consider how, as a methodological tool, the concept of regimes of living may help draw diverse projects into a field of common problems by establishing interconnections among sites of analysis and by pointing to a shared ethos of inquiry.

Regimes of living, as we have noted, are situated configurations of normative, technical, and political elements that are brought into alignment in problematic or uncertain situations. A given regime provides one possible means, and always only one among various possible means, for organizing, reasoning about, and living 'ethically' – that is, with respect to a specific understanding of the good. Regimes of living have a certain systematicity or regularity – like a diet, a medical regimen, or a set of exercises – that give them a provisional consistency or coherence. But they do not necessarily have the stability or concrete institutionalization of a political regime. Rather, they may be conceived as abstract congeries of ethical reasoning and practice that are incited by or reworked in problematic situations, taking diverse actual forms.

To illustrate the operations of regimes of living, we draw on a familiar and classic example – Max Weber's description of Benjamin Franklin's ethic of self-conduct. Weber showed that this ethic was organized around a strange and unprecedented principle: the duty to accumulate rather than consume capital. It endowed a range of practices crucial to the development of modern capitalism that had no intrinsic value with "ethical sanction." Weber traces the formation of the Protestant ethic by examining Franklin's dicta on how to live a good life: "a penny saved is a penny earned"; "*time* is money"; "*credit* is money"; "*the good paymaster is lord of another man's purse.*"[41]

The significance of these dicta for Weber is that they describe underlying norms of action in a diversity of circumstances, some of which are remote from the site of their initial formation – from Protestant doctrine, to Franklin's reflections on the virtues of economic living, to transparent capital accounting in a large industrial enterprise. They suggest important elements of how such situations are organized ethically through a process that combines principles of ethical reasoning with concrete practices in specific contexts. The activities identified by these maxims are not only 'ethical' in the sense of morally correct. They also suggest techniques for working on the self, for constituting the self – whether that 'self' is a Protestant, a virtuous early post-Revolutionary American, or a capitalist enterprise – as a certain kind of subject. Thus, when combined with various norms of conduct and forms of practice, the Protestant ethic can be seen to provide a "foundation and justification" for related but distinct regimes of living in diverse sites.[42]

One important quality of regimes of living is a certain capacity for extension or abstraction. Once they have taken shape, they can be flexibly invoked by actors (whether individual or collective) in problematic or uncertain situations – situations that are characterized by a perceived gap between the real and the ideal, that are in search of norms and forms to guide action. Thus, on the one hand, regimes of living give problematic situations a certain moral or ethical structure for a particular, situated, ethical subject. On the other hand, a regime of living assumes concrete, substantive form only in relation to the exigencies of a given situation, and may even be reshaped, or reworked in a given situation. The relation between a problematic situation and a regime of living can, thus, be understood as one of *co-constitution* or *co-actualization*.

Operability

As an illustration of the co-constitution of regimes of living and problematic situations, we turn to a fourth exemplar, Lawrence Cohen's chapter, "Operability, Bioavailability, and Exception," which examines contemporary regulation of the organ trade in India. The backdrop to Cohen's case is the combination of developments in the life sciences (in organ extraction, grafting, donor screening and matching, and in immunosuppressant drugs), advances in communications and transport technology, and changing conceptions of the "end of life" that together have vastly expanded the "bioavailable" population; that is, the population whose biomatter – here kidneys – is "available for...selective disaggregation."[43]

Following scandals in Bombay and Bangalore in 1994, the Parliament of India passed the Transplantation of Human Organs Act (THOA), whose provisions were imitated in similar acts at the local level in many Indian states. The Act drew a distinction between sold and 'gifted' organs, deeming transplantation from living donors ethical only when spurred by familial love. But the law also allowed 'exceptions' to be granted by medical–bureaucratic structures called "Authorization Committees." The resulting situation reflects a complex ethical logic: "The sovereign state protects persons from practices deemed exploitative and uncivilized. Out of love, family members and friends may desire to give a kidney to one who needs it. To prevent the moral economy of the latter from degenerating into the uncivil economy of the former, only four permitted classes of kin are constituted as *normal* donors. To prevent state protection from shutting down other life-saving circuits of love and flesh, the formal logic of exception is set up." After a period of strict prohibition, Cohen notes, most Authorization Committees tended to allow the 'exception' to become the 'rule,' placing organ sales in a structure of formal legality. The "ethics of the exception," thus, is a regime of living forged through a specific relationship between state practice, biomedicine, transplant doctors, and the committees that regulate them.

But frequently buried in the noisy 'public' and 'political' discussions around the organ trade, as Cohen shows, a different regime of living is shaped by those who decide to sell an organ. These sellers may act 'out of love,' felt not for the recipient of the organ but for the beneficiary of money gained from its sale. For such individuals, the problem of how to act in this uncertain situation is structured in part by the twin technopolitical situations of "bioavailability" and the exception in the national law on organ transplant. Cohen discovered another element of this regime of living almost accidentally, when he found that *all* of the 30 women he interviewed concerning organ sales had undergone previous sterilization surgeries. The surgeries were connected to state-based developmental strategies that sought to control population growth among the "lower classes," whose 'unruly' passions could not, it was presumed, be tamed by other means. Cohen suggests that in this context sterilization surgeries became one "form through which constitutively marginal, pre-modern subjects can secure some form of modern participation in the nation-state."[44] The result is the crystallization of a regime of living, *operability*, through which invasive surgery becomes part of a repertoire of ethical possibilities that are weighed in making a decision about selling one's kidney.

Cohen's case also underscores a point made earlier concerning the kind of 'life' that is at stake in the mutual constitution of regimes of living and problematic situations. In contrast to classical ethics, the operation of regimes of living does not necessarily involve an individual's capacity for insightful understanding; and the 'life' in question is not necessarily that of a reasoning citizen. Rather, the life at stake in a given regime of living may be collective as well as individual; and problems of 'ordinary life' – mutual existence for the sake of sheer life and biological life itself – are central to regimes of living. What is more, the life in question is not characterized by an internal logic or higher coherence that could be derived through abstract reflection. And regimes of living do not provide definitive resolutions to problematic situations by recourse to a politics, a space of universal rationality, or a tradition. They do not produce, as Taylor summarizes the Aristotelian position, "a kind of awareness of order, the correct order of ends in my life, which integrates all my goals and desires into a unified whole in which each has its proper weight."[45]

Indeed, as we see in the exemplars we have considered, the invocation of a regime of living may raise as many ethical "problems" as it resolves; its relation to a 'good life' is strained. Consider: Strathern's note concerning the possible 'illiberality' of society's values that threatens to undermine the very principle in the name of which social audit emerged and was deployed; Weber's gloomy conclusion that the Protestant ethic may turn out to be an iron cage; the unstable 'ethical' space in Roitman's characterization of the garrison–entrepôt, which emerges as a troubling product of transformations in the exercise of economic regulatory authority; or, in Cohen's case, the Pyrrhic victory of a form of citizenship based on an ethos that brings the sale of body parts into a desperate calculation concerning basic survival. These are not, certainly, 'identities' to be celebrated, and the situated and provisional understanding of the good established in them does not provide an integrated, consistent, and rationally justifiable ground for the good life. And yet, the regimes of living we have discussed provide, in uncertain situations, contingent means for organizing, reasoning about, and living 'ethically.' They define situated understandings of the good, modes of possible action, and techniques for working on or forming subjects.

A field of common problems

Our use of the concept of the 'regime of living' exemplifies a mode of analytic work that is neither theoretical nor strictly empirical but "methodological." This analytic stance contains an implicit critique of attempts in moral philosophy to theorize a generalized 'ethical' condition of the present. But the aim of this exercise has not been simply to deny the universality of normative philosophical claims by reaching to detailed knowledge of local specificity and a cogent understanding of actors' contexts and motives. At one level, the contributions to the volume are exemplary of a classic 'ethnographic' imperative: to avoid universal generalization, to attend to practices, local histories, and contexts, and to actors' own understandings of what they are doing. But the concept of the regime of living points to a set of more substantive characteristics shared by these chapters. As such, it can serve as a tool to map a field of inquiry by grasping both empirical connections among sites and conceptual interconnections among problems.[46]

One type of such connection results from the movement of technological or biopolitical forms that are "global" – in the sense that they are not attached to a social or cultural context – through the efforts of concrete individuals or through institutional or organizational relationships. For example, the technologies of social audit that Strathern describes circulate in global expert communities, shaping distinctive ethical and technical responses in disparate sites.[47] Regulation of the circulation of human organs presents another instance of this kind of connection. Here, an object that technological change has made increasingly abstractable and mobile – the transplantable human organ – draws donors, buyers, doctors, and brokers into comparable problematic situations.[48]

A second type of connection among sites can be identified in the case of structurally similar sociohistorical or technopolitical situations. For instance, we can compare Roitman's "trafficking" to other situations in which questions concerning the legitimacy of the state have emerged in the context of the decline of state power and the broad expansion of criminal activity. Thus, the anthropologist Carolyn Humphrey notes in her analysis of Russian bandit gangs that the "category of people who engage in activities defined by the state as illegal do not necessarily define themselves as criminals."[49] Rather, echoing Roitman, they have an elaborate understanding of legitimate work defined specifically in contrast to the illegitimacy of the institutions of formal legality. The notion of "counter-politics" provides another example of connections between sites that result from similar structural situations. In Caldeira and Holston's case, residents of squatter settlements constitute themselves as active citizens through a "strategic reversal" that appropriates precisely the values of the biopolitical regime from which they were excluded.[50] Akhil Gupta has examined a similar situation in which rural social movements have mobilized against the "urban bias" of post-World War II developmental strategies by making claims on precisely those ends promised by, but not delivered to, much of rural India. As in Brazil, a counter-politics emerges as a kind of second-wave reaction to the exclusions of state-led projects of social modernity, and a certain regime of living orients collective aspirations that are articulated in political space.

Notably, the connections among these sites do not rest on a common cultural field or a common social logic. Actors in Europe and the Chad Basin do not face the same issues, or have recourse to the same range of responses. The space of inquiry defined by a regime of living is not delimited by boundaries of territory, political structure, language group, or common experience. Rather, it points to more heterogeneous and provisional linkages that structure common problems of living for actors – and common problems of inquiry for critical observers.

The position of the observer

As we have noted, the analytic framework we have proposed here is inspired by a critical engagement with two approaches that examine biopolitics and technological reason as central to contemporary ethical problematizations. One, based in moral and political philosophy, has returned to the classical tradition to diagnose the incoherence of contemporary ethics. The other, from interpretive social science, tends to use ethnographic analysis to emphasize particularization and specificity, underlining the diversity of sites and subject positions from which "ethical" problems are posed.

In contrast to the philosophical position, the approach we have outlined does not support an attempt to establish a firmer ground for ethics through reference to a common tradition or a common *telos*. Indeed, one implication that might be drawn from the preceding argument is that such efforts are based on a mistaken conception of the structure of contemporary ethical problematizations. Such efforts take for granted precisely what is under question in a study of regimes of living: the anthropological forms that are at stake – in formation – in our ethics.

Investigation into technical practices, as exemplified by the contributors to this volume, suggests a different critical point of entry. The function of the exemplars we have considered here – and the methodological purpose of the regime of living – is not to explore the conditions for a rational ethics; nor is it to reject, as such, the terms and values of ethical discourse today. Rather, it is to sort out some of the concrete implications of these situations for the politics and practice of living.

Thus, Strathern's concern is not that we put "liberality" as a value into question any more than it is that we take it as an unquestioned good, but that, rather, we evaluate specific programs organized in the name of liberality by examining concrete technopolitical arrangements. The result is an incisive technical critique of attempts to operationalize ethics in this particular domain. Cohen's point is not to denounce the "ethics of the exception" in general but to sort out ethical problems around the structure of the exception, and to show how attention to a particular value – familial love – might be used to destabilize taken-for-granted ethical judgments about organ sales. Roitman neither celebrates nor condemns the life of banditry so much as she uses its analysis to inquire into the structure of ethical positionings around the legality or illegality of failed states. Finally, Caldeira and Holston cautiously treat the substantial gains of squatter movements in the democratization of the 1990s, examining the tensions between the extension of political franchise and the erosion of public space that has resulted from deregulation and neoliberal reform. What these analyses suggest, in any case, is that the analysis of contemporary sites of ethical problematization involves an 'anthropological' investigation into how the nature and practice of human life and the *telos* of living are constituted and reconstituted.

Notes

1 We acknowledge the helpful comments of Mireille Abelin, Talia Dan-Cohen, Rebecca Herzig, Frederic Keck, Paul Rabinow, Tobias Rees, Aihwa Ong, and Natasha Schull.

2 Bernard Williams, *Ethics and the Limits of Philosophy* (Cambridge, MA: Harvard University Press, 1985).

3 In his later work on classical and Christian techniques of the self, Foucault showed how empirical investigation into the history of ethical reflection could be a way of engaging ethics without relying on abstract, transhistorical formulations. Central to this genealogy of ethics was the technique of locating ethical "problematizations," moments when previously taken for granted forms became problems for thought. Foucault's move to ethics has sometimes been seen as a "retreat" to the question of the subject, away from questions of power. It seems, rather, to have been an attempt to reimagine the possible relationships between ethics, technology, and politics, by genealogically decoupling techniques of the self from normalization processes. He created a typology of ethical action – which included ethical substance, mode of subjectivation, techniques, and *telos* – in order to map some of the shifting configurations of ethical action from the classical period, to the Christian era, to modernity. See Michel Foucault, "On the Genealogy of Ethics: An Overview of Work in Progress," in *Ethics, Subjectivity and Truth: Essential Works of Foucault*, vol. I, Paul Rabinow, ed. (New York: The New Press, 1997). For a discussion of the term "problematization" see Paul Rabinow, *Anthropos Today* (Princeton, NJ: Princeton University Press, 2003).

4 *Oxford English Dictionary Online*; http://www.oed.com, 2003.

5 The regime of living is, thus, a tool for investigating what Paul Rabinow has called a "problem-space." Paul Rabinow, "On Anthropological Work: Or an Untimely Adjacency," Department of Anthropology, University of California, Berkeley, unpublished MS, 2003.

6 Marilyn Strathern, "Robust Knowledge and Fragile Futures," Chapter 24, this volume, p. 470.

7 Idem.

8 Strathern does not specify these conflicts, but we might surmise that an example would be the sacrality of life at conception versus the health of the mother and the right of individuals to regulate their reproductive behavior.

9 For a discussion of the formation of assemblages that bring together ethics and technologies, see Paul Rabinow, *French DNA: Trouble in Purgatory* (Chicago: University of Chicago Press, 1999).

10 A number of medical anthropologists, for example, have critically analyzed the rise of bioethics in clinical and research contexts. See the contributions to *Daedalus* 128: 4, 1999, entitled "Bioethics and Beyond," coedited by Arthur Kleinman, Renee Fox, and Allan Brandt.

11 Alasdair MacIntyre, *After Virtue: A Study in Moral Theory* (Notre Dame, IN: University of Notre Dame Press, 1984), p. 110.

12 MacIntyre, *After Virtue*, pp. 110–111, p. 10.

13 Charles Taylor, "Justice after Virtue," in *After MacIntyre: A Critical Perspective on the Work of Alasdair MacIntyre*, John Horton and Susan Mendus, eds. (Cambridge: Polity Press, 1994). As Michel Foucault's work on the human sciences would seem to suggest, this use of "anthropology" is clearly anachronistic: see Michel Foucault, *The Order of Things: An Archaeology of the Human Sciences* (New York: Vintage, 1973).

14 MacIntyre, *After Virtue*, p. 148.

15 As John Horton and Susan Mendus summarize MacIntyre's position: "For Aristotle, the good life is the life lived in accordance with virtue (*arete*), where virtue is to be understood against the background of a teleological conception of man – a conception according to which human beings have a specific nature which determines their proper aims and goals. On his account, the virtues are excellences of character which enable people to move toward their goal (*telos*), and are an essential part of the attainment of that goal." See John Horton and Susan Mendus, "Alasdair MacIntyre: After Virtue and After," in *After MacIntyre*, p. 6.

16 MacIntyre, *After Virtue*, p. 150.

17 Taylor, "Justice after Virtue," p. 28.

18 MacIntyre, *After Virtue*, p. 162.

19 MacIntyre, *After Virtue*, p. 150. MacIntyre claims that the centrality of the *polis* as the proper milieu of ethics was common beyond the Aristotelian tradition. Of the four Athenian views of ethics he describes, "all do take it for granted that the milieu in which the virtues are to be exercised and in terms of which they are to be defined is the *polis*." (*After Virtue*, p. 135.)

20 Hannah Arendt, *The Human Condition* (Chicago: University of Chicago Press, 1958).

21 Arendt, *The Human Condition*, pp. 36–37.

22 Taylor, "Justice after Virtue," p. 31.

23 See Leo Strauss, *The City and Man* (Chicago: University of Chicago Press, 1964).

24 MacIntyre, *After Virtue*, p. 133.

25 MacIntyre's emphasis on the ability of Aristotelian ethics to accommodate itself to a more modern understanding of an ethics embedded in a cultural tradition is a distinctive feature of his reading of Aristotle. This emphasis is not to be found in other important readings of Aristotelian ethics.

26 CharlesTaylor, "Justice after Virtue," p. 19. For a similar argument, see Anthony Giddens' article in Ulrich Beck, Anthony Giddens, and Scott Lash, *Reflexive Modernization: Politics, Tradition and Aesthetics in the Modern Social Order* (Stanford: Stanford University Press, 1994).

27 That is, technological reason has a certain "global" character in the sense defined in Chapter 1 of this volume, "Global Assemblages, Anthropological Problems."

28 MacIntyre, *After Virtue*, p. 155.

29 MacIntyre, *After Virtue*, p. 155; Foucault, "On the Genealogy of Ethics.".

30 Max Weber, *Economy and Society* (Berkeley: University of California Press, 1978), p. 67.

31 As a large body of work in the social studies of science has shown, modern technical communities are also moral communities See, for example, Steven Shapin, *A Social History of Truth: Civility and Science in Seventeenth Century England* (Chicago: University of Chicago Press, 1994).

32 See also Taylor, "Justice after Virtue," p. 31.

33 Arendt, *The Human Condition*, p. 46. Peter Wagner dates the emergence of a discourse on "society" as a third term of political thought, in addition to *polis* and *oikos*, to the mid-18th century: "The new object society inherited the status of being neither state nor household. The new language thus affirmed that a moral–political entity consisted essentially of (a multitude of) households and a (single) state. It merely added a third category of phenomena; and in the way it did so, it also posited that this third category consisted of a single member rather than a multitude, though the oneness of society was of a different nature than that of the state." See Peter Wagner, " 'An Entirely New Object of Consciousness, of Volition, of Thought': The Coming into Being and (Almost) Passing Away of 'Society' as a Scientific Object," in *Biographies of Scientific Objects, Lorraine Daston,* ed. (Chicago: University of Chicago Press, 2000).

34 This situation, as Taylor notes, constitutes an effective reversal of the Aristotelian hierarchy in which ordinary life was only the unreflective basis for the ultimate aim of leading the good life. In modern culture, he writes, "the life of production and reproduction is the centre of human concern. The highest life does not reside in some supposedly higher activity, but rather in living ordinary life … rationally, that is, under rational control" (Taylor, "Justice after Virtue," p. 32). This is the theme of Michel Foucault's work on biopolitics and governmentality. Thus, Foucault defines biopolitics as "the endeavor, begun in the eighteenth century, to rationalize the problems presented to governmental practice by the phenomena characteristic of a group of living human beings constituted as a population" ["The Birth of Biopolitics," in *Ethics: Subjectivity and Truth* (New York: Free Press, 1997), p. 73]. See also Giorgio Agamben, *Homo Sacer: Sovereign Power and Bare Life* (Stanford, California: Stanford University Press, 1998).

35 For more detail on this argument in Arendt, see Hannah Pitkin, *Attack of the Blob: Hannah Arendt's Concept of the Social* (Chicago: University of Chicago Press, 1998).

36 Counter-politics is a Foucaultian term that Colin Gordon analyzes in "Governmental Rationality: An Introduction," in *The Foucault Effect: Studies in Governmentality,* Graham Burchell, Colin Gordon, and Peter Miller, eds. (Chicago: University of Chicago Press, 1991), p. 5.

37 Nikolas Rose and Carlos Novas, in "Biological Citizenship" (Chapter 13, this volume) offer a more general term for such situations.

38 Janet Roitman, "The Garrison–Entrepôt: A Mode of Governing in the Chad Basin," Chapter 22, this volume, p. 418.

39 Ibid., p. 432.

40 Ibid., p. 423.

41 Max Weber, *The Protestant Ethic and the Spirit of Capitalism* (London: Routledge, 1992), pp. 14–15; italics original.

42 Weber, *The Protestant Ethic*, p. 75.

43 Lawrence Cohen, "Operability, Bioavailability, and Exception," Chapter 5, this volume, p. 83.

44 Ibid., p. 87.

45 Taylor, "Justice after Virtue."

46 Max Weber, *The Methodology of the Social Sciences* (New York: Free Press, 1949).

47 For a description of the extension of audit regimes among different forms of social organization in Britain, see Michael Power, *The Audit Society: Rituals of Verification* (Oxford: Oxford University Press, 1997); and Marilyn Strathern, ed., *Audit Cultures: Anthropological Studies in Accountability, Ethics, and the Academy* (New York: Routledge, 2000).

48 Nancy Scheper-Hughes makes a similar point in "The Last Commodity: Post-Human Ethics and the Global Traffic in 'Fresh' Organs," Chapter 9, this volume.

49 Caroline Humphrey, "Russian Protection Rackets and the Appropriation of Law and Order," in *The Unmaking of Soviet Life* (Ithaca, NY: Cornell University Press, 2002).

50 Gordon, "Governmental Rationality."

3

MIDST ANTHROPOLOGY'S PROBLEMS

PAUL RABINOW

A term is an object so far as that object is undergoing shaping in a directed act of inquiry.

John Dewey[1]

In *The Order of Things*, Michel Foucault identified three arenas of discourse that in their (unstable and incomplete) coalescence at the end of the Classical Age constituted the *object* called "Man" – "*l'homme.*" This figure emerges at the intersection of three domains – Life, Labor and Language – unstably unified around (and constituting) a would-be sovereign *subject*. The doubling of a transcendental subject and an empirical object and their dynamic and unstable relations defined the form of this being. In 1966, Foucault held an epochal view of Man and of Modernity. In his conclusion, Foucault intimated the imminent coming of a new configuration of language about to sweep the figure of Man away like "a face drawn in the sand at the edge of the sea."[2] It now appears this presage was miscast: in the ensuing decades language (in its modality as *poiesis*) has not turned out to be the site of radical formal transformations through which this being, Man, would either disappear entirely (as Foucault intimated) or would transmute into a new type of being as predicted by Gilles Deleuze.[3]

Although Foucault did not directly return to his diagnosis of the "end of Man," he did modify his understanding of modernity as an epoch. In his essay "What is Enlightenment?" Foucault posed the challenge of inventing a new philosophic relationship to the present; one in which modernity was taken up not through the analytic frame of the epoch but instead through a practice of inquiry grounded in an ethos of present-orientation, of contingency, of form-giving. Perhaps today one (but only one) significant challenge of forging a modern ethos lies in thinking about how to relate to the issue of *anthropos*. Such a task presents different types of challenges to philosophical thinkers such as Foucault than to the anthropologist. Regardless of how one approaches those questions (an issue to which we return in the conclusion), what if we took up recent changes in the *logoi* of life, labor, and language not as indicating an epochal shift with a totalizing coherence (sovereignty, Man) but, rather, as fragmented and sectorial changes that pose problems, both in-and-of-themselves as well as for attempts to make sense of what form(s) *anthropos* is currently being given?

Labor, Life, Language

In 1966, capitalism was strong in its enclaves but not completely unchallenged: it had yet to face what now appears to have been a hopeless socialism and failed schemes of Third World development of whatever political and economic form. In 2001, no one can doubt that capitalism is more expansive, destructive, and productive than ever before. No one can doubt the growing scope and scale of market relations and the concomitant commodification of an ever-greater range of things previously held to be external to the realm of monetary value. However, today there exists neither a *logos* adequate to understanding this globalizing *oikeumene*, nor a means of regulating its volatility. In 1966, the mechanics of the genetic code and its extraordinary universality was just being discovered. The ensuing decades have seen the most dramatic and significant changes in the life sciences since Darwin. Yet no molecular Darwin has yet appeared to provide a unifying *logos*. Where and when and whether the technology-driven advances of genomics and biotechnology will transform into an understanding of living beings that is more adequate to their evident complexity remains to be seen. Although in 1966 semiotics, and/or cybernetics, and/or cognitive science, competed to unify all language, today – even though we are in the midst of a revolution in the invention and spread of technologies of communication and information – there exists no unifying *logos* of *discourse*.

At the very least, then, we can say that we are currently undergoing and participating in a distinctive set of inflections of labor, life, and language.[4] Perhaps, after all, the project of seeking Man – life, labor, language as the *logos* of modernity – has been dissolved. Or it may be that seeking such a *logos* actually was the wrong approach. Perhaps the multiplication and heterogeneity of recent *logoi* has put *anthropos* once again into question. We can see more clearly today that Foucault's Man was only one instantiation of the *figure* of *anthropos*. However, the one thing we should not be doing is attempting to find a new, hidden, deeper, unifying rationality or ontology. The alternative is not chaos. Rather, using the concept of problematization, and the topic of *anthropos*, we can direct our efforts toward inventing means of observing and analyzing how various *logoi* are currently being assembled into contingent forms.

Inquiry: From Reconstruction to Problematization

This surfeit of forms of knowledge is problematic. It is challenging to find ways to deal with such a situation. To do so, we pursue our convocation of Dewey and Foucault, two thinkers who made the issues of encumbrances, discordances, and problems into topics of inquiry.

In 1916, John Dewey re-published a group of his essays (originally published in 1903) under the title *Essays in Experimental Logic*. He opened his long "Introduction" by advising his readers that "the key" to his essays was to be found in his emphasis on "the temporal development of experience." Thinking was itself a temporal experience, or, to be more precise, thinking was a temporal experiment. Terms such as " 'thinking,' 'reflection,' 'judgment,' " Dewey asserted, are not faculties but, rather, "denote inquiries or the results of inquiries, and that inquiry occupies an intermediate and mediating place in the development of an experience."[5] Dewey's summation of the logic of experiment and experience places reason squarely in an intermediate position and assigns it a mediating function. Thinking takes place in a milieu; playing on the original sense of the term "mi-lieu" – between places – one can say that thinking takes place between places but not just anywhere, or anytime. Dewey explains: "From the standpoint of temporal order, we find reflection, or thought, occupying an intermediate and reconstructive position. It comes between a temporally prior situation (an organized interaction of factors) of active and appreciative experience, wherein some of the factors have become discordant and incompatible, and a later situation, which has been constituted out of the first situation by means of acting on the findings of reflective inquiry. The final solution thus has a richness of meaning, as well as a controlled character lacking in the original."[6] Dewey's claims are both persuasive and contestable.

For Dewey, then, thinking is not only a practice set in a dynamic milieu; it is an action called forth and set into motion by a discordancy. The function of thinking is to rectify – in the sense of "realign" – the factors that have produced, and/or have been altered by, a disruption. In order to fulfill its function, thinking (and hence, presumably the thinker) must take up an active relationship to the milieu in which she finds herself. Further, Dewey assigns thinking the task of providing a reconstructive "richness of meaning," although exactly what he means by "richness" remains vague. Thinking, then, is a situated practice of active inquiry whose role and goal is to initiate a motion that results in a movement from a discordant situation to a less discordant situation. Thinking is neither more nor less than this practice.

The value terms by which the norms of that motion (and the practice) are guided and judged are control and meaning. Control and meaning are not subjective terms. Neither the primary locus nor the yardstick of this practice is to be found in the subject. Dewey makes this point through a striking, if ambiguous, formulation: "it is the needs of a *situation* which are determinative."[7] We can gloss his claim by saying that thinking is a temporally unfolding, situated practice, the function of which is to clarify and to realign a problematic situation. The site of the trouble and the resolution is the problematic situation. Intervention is judged successful when it yields a reconstructive change through meeting the needs of a situation. Intervention and inquiry are essentially practical. Dewey, after all, was a pragmatist, an optimist, and an American. Thinking operated with no fixed universal principles, no pre-given and unalterable faculties. Whether there are situations that cannot be repaired is not a question that can be answered in the abstract. Nonetheless, one can raise the issue of whether Dewey allows sufficient space either for critical limits or a sense of pathos or tragedy, and if not, whether this lack is a major limitation of his work. The answer is complicated, as Dewey was made aware of these issues through repeated attacks by the Left and Right (theological and secular) in America over more than half a century.[8]

A core ambiguity of Dewey's position can be located in his noteworthy metaphoric frame. For a metaphoric frame it is: How, we wonder, do situations have *needs*? Without entering into the vast literature of debate about functionalism, organicism, and anthropocentrism that characterized so much of 20th-century social thought, not to mention the equally vast scholarly production around metaphor to which the cultural sciences for the past half century have devoted so much effort, let us simply suggest, following Georges Canguilhem, that it is epistemologically and historically preferable to say that modern situations are *normed*. Or that, to be more precise, norms function actively so as to ceaselessly spread a grid of normativity into an expanding range of situations. Taken up from this angle, we can move from Dewey's approach to situations in general to a historically more specific subset of discordant dynamism.

Problematization

One can find a partial but pronounced resonance, a purely arbitrary one in terms of direct influence, in Michel Foucault's concept of "problematization." A "problematization," Foucault writes, "does not mean the representation of a pre-existent object nor the creation through discourse of an object that did not exist. It is the ensemble of discursive and non-discursive practices that make something enter into the play of true and false and constitute it as an object of thought (whether in the form of moral reflection, scientific knowledge, political analysis, etc)."[9] The reason why problematizations are problematic, not surprisingly, is that something prior "must have happened to introduce uncertainty, a loss of familiarity; that loss, that uncertainty is the result of difficulties in our previous way of understanding, acting, relating."[10] For Foucault, there are always several possible ways of responding to "the same ensemble of difficulties." Consequently, the primary task of the analyst is not to proceed directly toward intervention and repair of the situation's discordancy but, rather, to understand and to put forth a diagnosis of "what makes these responses simultaneously possible." In contrast to Dewey, Foucault stops short, in a rigorously self-limiting manner, of proposing means of rectification. The extent to which Foucault's practice could be assimilated to a reconstruction (in Dewey's sense) is therefore complicated. He would seem to be constructing something like an ideal type, but since the sense of what Weber meant by ideal type has been massively misinterpreted, this comparison has limited utility.

For Foucault, the specific diacritic of thought is found not only in this act of diagnosis but additionally in the attempt to achieve a modal change from seeing a situation not only as "a given" but equally as "a question." Such a modal shift seeks to accomplish a number of things. First, it asserts that not only are there always multiple constraints at work in any historically troubled situation, but that multiple responses exist as well. Foucault underscores this condition of heterogeneous, if constrained, contingency – " this transformation of an ensemble of difficulties into problems to which diverse solutions are proposed" – in order to propose a particular style of inquiry. Foucault saw his calling as a contribution to the "freeing up" of possibilities. The act of thinking is an act of modal transformation from the constative to the subjunctive. From the singular to the multiple. From the necessary to the contingent.

A problematization, then, is both a kind of general historical and social situation – saturated with power relations, as are all situations, and imbued with the relational "play of truth and false," a diacritic marking a subclass of situations – as well as a nexus of responses to that situation. Those diverse but not entirely disparate responses, it follows, themselves form part of the problematization as it develops or unfolds (although both words are too Hegelian) over time. What Foucault is attempting to conceptualize is a situation that is neither simply the product of a process of social and historical construction nor the target of a deconstruction. Rather, he is indicating a historical space of conditioned contingency that emerges in relation to (and then forms a feedback situation with) a more general situation, one that is real enough in standard terms, but is not fixed or static. Thus the domain of problematization is constituted by and through economic conditions, scientific knowledges, political actors, and other related vectors. What is distinctive is Foucault's identification of the problematic situation (the situation of the process of a specific type of problem-making), as simultaneously the object, the site, and ultimately the substance, of thinking.

It is important to notice that Foucault differs from Dewey on this point: Dewey identified discordant forces and a breakdown of meaning as the locus of experience and the target of action. From the very start of his methodological work, Foucault sought to bracket meaning as well as the standard form of truth claims. What was substituted, if that is not too mechanical a word, was a series of forms of nominalist seriousness, of which problematization was the last. Foucault's concept of problematization is broad but not unlimited in scope. It is surely not as general as Dewey's "discordance." Rather, Foucault requires that the situation in question contain institutionally legitimated claims to truth, or one or another type of sanctioned seriousness (Bert Dreyfus and I called them "serious speech acts"). Without the presence of serious speech acts there is no problematization in the strict sense of the term (although obviously there could be problems).

In contrast to earlier positions that he held, Foucault's thinker is by definition neither entirely outside of the situation in question nor entirely enmeshed within it without recourse or options. The defining trait of problematization does not turn on the couplings of opposites (outside or inside, free or constrained), but rather on the type of relationship forged between observer and problematized situation. The specificity of that relationship entails taking up the situation simultaneously as problematic and as something about which one is required to think.[11]

The Market in Transnational Humanitarianism

The emergence of the complex of discourse, practices, and strategies lumped under the term "ethics," or "bioethics," or "medical ethics" indicates the presence of a problematized domain. One might well wonder: How did "ethical relations" become a zone of such charged importance? Upon reflection, however, we must pose some prior questions: When and under what circumstances did "ethical relations" become an object domain at all? How did they become a problem? And a solution? And thereby a new problem domain?

One can say that two of the most distinctive innovations of the 1990s inflection of *anthropos* were the visionary projects, technological developments, and institutional stabilizations of (1) genome mapping and (2) bioethics. Although bioethics is perhaps a decade older than genome mapping, their trajectories have been in part entwined in recent years. Both genomic mapping and bioethics are increasingly transnational, although both were powerfully spearheaded in the United States. Latterly, European Commissions and numerous authorized spokespeople have elaborated and disseminated the associated doctrines and practices around the world. Thus, for example, following in the wake of the venture capitalists, biotech startups, and multinational pharmaceutical companies, more and more people around the world are growing accustomed to thinking about themselves (and their pets and plants and food) as having genomes. These genomes, it is believed, contain precious information that tells the truth about who they (and their pets and plants and food) really are, as well as providing clues to what their future holds. Influenced by the aforementioned purveyors of biopolitical futures, more and more people are also coming to believe that their genomes contain information that is rightfully their property. Not only is their individual and collective identity being violated, it is being pirated. Both multinationals *and* NGOs frequently work – however unequal they may be in their political struggles – to reinforce this view of the body and the self, ownership and truth. Power and resistance, it has been claimed, can act mutually, if unwittingly, so as to re-enforce a type of rationality and the forms that it takes.

Human Rights: Human Good?

Historian and journalist Michael Ignatieff makes a claim that is striking and, upon reflection, perplexing. The striking claim: "There has been a revolution in the moral imagination in the last fifty years, and its most distinctive feature is the emergence and triumph of human rights discourse as the language of human good."[12] The perplexity: Is the claim true? A series of other perplexities spring to mind. What brought about this change? What was the dominant figure of moral imagination in Europe before World War II? Is there, in fact, a dominant figure of morality? Other related questions equally come to mind. For example: How does the human rights discourse relate to issues of health? How do both rights and health relate to biopolitics?

The contemporary self-evidence of the legitimacy of human rights discourse is even more striking when one realizes that before 1945 there existed no international legal framework for the protection of individual human rights. As Hannah Arendt made clear in her work on *The Origins of Totalitarianism*, those without passports ran the greatest risks, as only states (and their citizens) had rights.[13] The fact of having been stripped of an official attachment to a nation left one in the most precarious and vulnerable state. This fact underscores the historical originality but also the rather curious condition instantiated by the new formation of human rights to which Ignatieff refers. After all, rights discourses have been around for centuries without having been given an extra-discursive institutional location to defend those rights. If human rights are natural, or God-given, or merely self-evident, then: How is it that protection at the scale of "humanity" has not been previously invented? What has made this political and cultural shift toward such protection possible? Where has the urgency come from? To begin to make clear that these are questions, we must think more about the fact that the claim to self-evidence is itself problematic. It is both coherent and curious that the ethical domain that emerged was one that could, at least in principle, challenge and/or transform the sovereignty of the nation-state.

Although the Enlightenment idea of a common human history with cosmopolitan intent and reflections on what conditions would be required to produce "perpetual peace" had been a topic in a longstanding problematization (most famously in the writings of Immanuel Kant), it is only since the fall of the Soviet empire that the conditions have come about, Ignatieff argues, for the appearance of "an at least virtual global civil society." Ignatieff underscores that the Holocaust is not the main motive behind putting rights on the world agenda. The special consciousness of the Holocaust as an utterly singular event only became widespread in the 1960s and 1970s, when the generation after those who had lived through the war came to political consciousness. Peter Novick spells out a similar argument in detail for the United States in his book *The Holocaust in American Life*.[14]

Ignatieff specifies his claim when he asserts that with the fall of the Soviet empire there is now a "single human rights culture in the world." This claim is difficult to evaluate. After all, it is generally recognized within anthropology that the "culture" concept today raises more questions than it solves.[15] Whatever one wishes to make of, say, pre-contact "Hawaiian culture" after the lengthy, sophisticated, and acrimonious debate between Marshall Sahlins and Gananath Obeyesekere concerning its status and meaning, "rights culture" would certainly have to have a different status. Whatever kind of culture rights culture is, it certainly must exist and shape people's lives in a manner different manner from "Hawaiian culture."

Nor is it as self-evident, as Ignatieff claims, that rights discourses actually do dominate the moral landscape of the human good. Market cultures and religious cultures – to use a shorthand and to trouble the conceit of culture even more – remain potent contenders for the title of *who* speaks morally, *how* to speak morally, and *what* moral speaking is about. Secular rights cultures, cultures of consumption, and a wide range of religious and neo-traditionalist moral discourses, and the symbols deployed by all three, function at times and in specific settings as competitors (or rank enemies), at times and for certain issues as complexly complementary, and at times and for specific issues as simply co-present (or cordoned off one from the other). Claims to hegemony are typical of this moral landscape, but practices of coexistence are equally representative.

Ignatieff points in the direction of this elusiveness and substantive contradiction (or pragmatic flexibility) when he writes that "The legitimacy of human rights is not its authoritative universalism, so much as its capacity to become a moral vernacular for the demand for freedom within local cultures."[16] A moral vernacular? Perhaps, albeit one that derives in part from a highly articulated transnational form that is anything but vernacular. It is obvious that market cultures and religious cultures often are also the vehicle for such moral vernaculars, just as they are themselves transnationally located, a fact that cannot be readily accommodated into a narrative of hope and progress set within the essentially 19th-century grid of modernization and tradition.

Ignatieff remains, as he himself says, a Victorian (whatever such a claim could actually mean).[17] The 19th century, of course, was the time of a triumphant ascendancy of normalization – a time of World's Expositions and international competitions over capital, science, and sovereignty. As if surprised at himself, Ignatieff immediately draws back from his self-characterization as a Victorian when he writes: "Human rights is misconceived if it is understood as a breviary of values: rights talk can do no more than formalize the terms in which conflicts of values are made precise and therefore rendered amenable to compromise and solution. This is their dynamic: they do not, in themselves, resolve arguments; they create the steadily burgeoning case law, which in turn expands the ambit of human rights claims."[18] Rights language is dynamic, destabilizing; it is, in the sense in which Canguilhem and then Foucault used the term, normalizing: "Once rights language exists in public consciousness it sets up a dynamic directed at the inevitable gap between what a society practices and what it preaches." That gap is its engine, its steam, its normativity. Of course, just as "culture" is rather in disrepute as a concept today, so, too, is "society." Societies do not practice anything anymore than they preach. Spokesmen for regimes, ideologues, missionaries, and pastors preach, not society.

In any event, there is much about this talk of rights that is new; it is generally not autochthonous (at least not in the specific forms in which it is being disseminated around the world through a variety of practices – especially international bodies linked to the United Nations and a multitude of NGOs); it is not rooted in the longstanding beliefs, practices, and representations of a defined community. Rather, it would seem to be partly a doctrine and partly a module in what Robert Bellah has called a "life style enclave" (as a not entirely positive characterization of a trend to self-conscious and de-localized practices stitched together in a form of life that Bellah characterizes as "thin"). But new-ness and 'thin-ness' are derogatory only if one thinks that thick and old are better. If one sees the rise, spread, and triumph of "rights talk" as a good thing, then its new-ness, and perhaps the ready comprehensibility of its core message, would carry with them a positive valence. This positive valuation is one that Ignatieff shares.

Regardless of one's individual judgment of these matters, as human scientists we want to observe how this talk – in fact, a set of discursive and nondiscursive practices – is taking shape. Our imperative is to learn more about the variety and practices of human rights groups as well as the (now visible) preexisting moral landscapes to which the carriers of rights culture bring their message of change and improvement. Although there are governments that contest and combat 'rights talk' (and the groups that articulate it) on a variety of grounds, including national sovereignty and traditional culture, it is plausible to argue that currently no secular counter-discourse exists that has anything like the legitimacy, power, and potential for successful expansion that the human rights discourse currently possesses.

Transnational Virtue

A significant move in specifying how one might approach these developments sociologically is made by Yves Dezalay and Bryant Garth, in an article in Pierre Bourdieu's journal, *Actes de la recherche en sciences socials*, entitled "Droits de l'homme et philanthropie hégémonique." They provide a penetrating analysis of recent, seemingly contradictory, developments in the field of human rights: "The movement for human rights is often presented as an exemplary illustration of those new transnational practices that escape from state order. However, by a sort of paradox, it is the national state's recognition of this 'soft law' that represents the fulfillment of the militants' efforts, leading to a growing professionalization and competition within the market of political activism."[19] There are several claims embedded here. First, there is the perfectly straightforward and not especially paradoxical point that within a transnational field, national interests, institutions, and players remain significant actors; sovereignty in most domains remains national. Even when it is not absolute, national states and institutions remain funnels, as it were, through which things must pass on the way in or the way out. Although, as many authors have argued, we are witnessing new relationships between the national and the transnational, this transformation cannot be equated with the definitive eclipse of national sovereignty.

More original is a second claim that there is a *market for humanitarianism*. In their book, *Dealing in Virtue*, Garth and Dezalay provide a detailed account of one example of how a sector of this market – international legal arbitration – came into existence, changed, and how it currently operates. Strikingly, success within the humanitarian market depends on many of the same strategies employed in the venture capital world. These include capturing the attention of various traditional media as well as innovating in the use of new media (NGOs pioneered the use of the fax machine and then the Internet for political mobilization and the articulation of virtual communities), securing funding from "donor" institutions, translating into position for international conferences and agencies, high mobility of personnel, and so on. One sees a marketing of symbolic capital resources "whose investments and counseling strategy must prepare its clients to overcome the very intense competitions that reigns in the market of civic virtue."[20] Following Bourdieu, our authors do not assert that the market of humanitarianism and the capital markets are the same, only that there are parallel principles and forces at work. The analysts' task is to identify those principles and forces as well as to investigate how "capital" from one market is converted into "capital" (or advantage) in another. Garth and Dezalay analyze in some detail the changing players and goals involved in the "diffusion of this new symbolic imperialism." They speak of an "elitist democratic" project, conceived and carried by a small group of "learned men" (English in the text), "desirous of social, progress and civic morality, but very respectful of the interests of big capital whose inheritors, collaborators and beneficiaries they are."[21] The field of these civic engagements and disagreements is a microcosm of the fractures within the ruling class. To invest in civic virtue is also to construct the state and to assure oneself of a position of legitimacy on the international market of *savoirs d'état*, "state knowledges."[22]

In *Empire*, Tony Negri and Michael Hardt make a similar point. They argue that military intervention is only one form of imperial intervention (by imperial they do not mean "imperialist," but the regime of sovereignty that comes after imperialism).[23] Judicial and moral forms provide potent vectors as well. In fact, Negri and Hardt argue, the softer, "moral" forms are frequently deployed first. Following Weber, we might say that such moral intervention is less costly in both economic and political terms. The most potent new form of such intervention is the so-called nongovernmental organizations (NGOs) which, being nonstate based, are especially well suited to make moral claims. Such humanitarian NGOs as Amnesty International, Oxfam, and *Médecins sans frontières* (often despite the conscious intentions of their participants) are "some of the most powerful pacific weapons of the new world order. These NGOs conduct 'just wars' without arms, without violence, without borders. Like the Dominicans in the late medieval period and the Jesuits at the dawn of modernity, these groups strive to identify universal needs and defend human rights." Their modern universalism operates both at the level of rights and at the level of the most basic needs of life. It is the key symbol of a growing market of increasing sophistication for protectors of living beings and vital things. Its space is the space of the biopolitical.[24]

For those in the human sciences who would rather refer these grand themes back to historically specific cases and locations, David Rothman, in his book *Strangers at the Bedside*, provides helpful argument and chronology. Rothman shows that the rise of medical ethics boards was not the consequence of the Nuremberg trials. Rather, the lessons of Nuremberg in the United States (and in Europe) were held to be that there was a sharp line cordoning off the pathological from the normal. Nuremberg did not put into question the normal practices or the authority of paternalistic science and medicine. Bioethics in the United States arose from the scandals of Willow Brook, Tuskegee, and so on. The change in American medicine – the awareness that paternalistic authority needed regulation – took place during the period from 1966 to 1976. In 1966, Henry Beecher, a Harvard Medical school professor, exposed abuses in human experimentation. In 1973, the U.S. Congress established a national commission on medical ethics. A new formality was introduced that ushered in collective decision-making and what might be called a new publicity: "This formality transformed the medical chart from an essentially private means of communication among doctors to a public piece of evidence that documented what the doctor had told, and heard from the patient."[25] Tacit practices became objects of analysis, scrutiny, and regulation. As Rothman observes, wrongs abounded: "A series of exposures of practices in human experimentation revealed a stark conflict of interest between clinical investigations and human subjects, between researchers' ambitions and patients' well-being." These linkages were readily made in the light of the civil rights movements gaining strength in the 1960s, "largely because the great majority of research subjects were minorities, drawn from the ranks of the poor, the mentally disabled and the incarcerated." There was a move to juridical interventions, to bioethical treatises (a strange new word), to legislative resolutions. But there is more. Rothman observes that "some regulatory measures were bound to be imposed on medicine when the bill for national health care skyrocketed from $19 billion in 1960 to $275 billion by 1980 and $365 billion by 1985."[26] Indeed, new experiences, new experiments, new markets, new actors, and new rules mean a new game in which medical research, health care delivery, and capital (as well as the associated lawyers, advocates, ethicists, and others) were coupled in multiple positions in many sites beyond the bedside.

The developments that Rothman describes are part of a larger space of the articulation and problematization of an ethics of life and death, of the normal and the pathological, of well-being and deprivation, of degeneration and growth. This fluid space is one traversed by layered economies and multiple new *logoi*. Contrary to Negri, I do not think we should approach it as a space of epochal change driven and shaped by ghostly trans-historical forces – sovereignty – but rather as a space of concrete problems, dangers, and hopes that are actual, emergent, and virtual.

Restraint

Hans Blumenberg proposes an original solution to the question of why the practitioners of modern reason have proliferated totalizing systems, especially philosophies of history, and why these systems have all failed. In *The Legitimacy of the Modern Age*, Blumenberg provides a lengthy account of the background to these perpetually futile and ever-renewed efforts. In seeking to diagnose the root causes of the unceasing over-reaching that has characterized modern thought, Blumenberg locates the problem not in a supposed demonic essence of reason itself, or in a diabolically persistent "will to knowledge" – positions, he underscores, that are themselves symptomatic expressions of disappointment in failed hopes for reason – but in the historical fact that "Modern reason, in the form of philosophy, accepted the challenge of the questions, both the great and the all too great, that were bequeathed to it."[27] Bequeathed, that is, by the great systems of Christian theology. Although Blumenberg's book devotes hundreds of erudite pages to demonstrating that the great theological systems were themselves unstable, he nonetheless argues that there had been a proportionality of scale between the type of questions posed and the type of answers provided. That proportionality between problem and response broke down in the 17th century. Yet the former questions (about the nature of being, of logic, of general principles of the cosmos) continued to be posed, and more importantly, accepted as legitimate questions that required an answer. Blumenberg's diagnosis is that modern thinkers "found it impossible to decline to answer questions about the totality of history. To that extent the philosophy of history is an attempt to answer a medieval question with the means available to a post medieval age."[28] The wrong tools for the wrong job.

These broad historical problem-formations and the sequential answers provided constitute Blumenberg's subject matter: "The continuity of history lies not in the permanence of ideal substances but rather in the inheritance of problems." Blumenberg paints a massively detailed portrait of successive articulations of problems, philosophical/theological answers, their failure, displacement, and re-articulation or, in his vocabulary, a history of re-occupations. However, Blumenberg's thesis is not itself a philosophy of history, at least in the traditional sense. He does not see the developments that he chronicles as either unalterable or inevitable – that is, as fatal – for such an attitude would place him squarely in a reoccupation zone that Blumenberg steadfastly refuses to enter. Rather, it is only in later modernity that the long-term pattern of problem–failure–shift–problem has itself become the topic of theoretical curiosity. This new perspective has opened up because, as Blumenberg explains in his section on "The Trial of Theoretical Curiosity," theoretical curiosity, under constant attack from many quarters, has been obliged to question its own legitimacy. As Blumenberg's translator puts it in his introductory remarks, "By questioning the nature of our own questioning, we alter the dynamic of our curiosity not by fiat, by proscribing questions, but by extending it to and satisfying it on another level."[29] In sum, Blumenberg aims at a critical, curative, and affirmative diagnosis. His position is critical in that it seeks to establish through inquiry the contemporary limits of reason; it is curative because if his critical inquiry were to be sustained, a situation would arise in which certain of the current maladies afflicting the practice of reason would disappear; and it is affirmative in that it seeks not to denounce or proscribe reason but to articulate the condition of reason's current legitimacy.

Observing, naming, and analyzing the forms of *anthropos* is the *logos* of one type of anthropology. How best to think about the arbitrariness, contingency, and powerful effects of those forms constitutes the challenge of that type of anthropology (understood as *Wissenschaft* or *science*). To place oneself midst the relationships of the contending *logoi* (embedded as they are within problematizations, apparatuses, and assemblages) is to find oneself among anthropology's problems.

Notes

1   John Dewey, "Logic of Judgments of Practice," in *Essays in Experimental Logic* (New York: Dover, 1916), p. 435. In his "Introduction" (p. 51), Dewey says, "A term is not of course a mere word; a mere word is non-sense, for a sound by itself is not a word at all. Nor is it a mere meaning, which is not even natural non-sense, being (if it be at all) super-natural or transcendental nonsense. 'Terms' signify that certain absent existences are indicated by certain given existences, in the respect that they are abstracted and fixed for intellectual use by some physically convenient means, such as a sound or a muscular contraction of the vocal organs."

2   Michel Foucault, *Les mots et les choses* (Paris: Editions Gallimard, 1966), p. 398.

3   Gilles Deleuze, "Appendix: On the Death of Man and Superman," in *Foucault*, trans. Sean Hand (Minneapolis: University of Minnesota Press, 1988). Originally published as *Foucault* (Editions de Minuit, 1986).

4   Foucault identified "'l'homme moderne' as that being whose politics puts its existence in question." See Michel Foucault, "L'homme moderne est un animal dans la politique duquel sa vie d'être vivant est en question," in *La volonté de savoir* (Paris: Editions Gallimard, 1976), p. 188.

5   Dewey, *Essays in Experimental Logic*, p. 1.

6   Dewey, *Essays in Experimental Logic*, p. 19.

7   Dewey, *Essays in Experimental Logic*, p. 70.

8   This issue is explored at great length in the magisterial biography of Robert B. Westbrook, *John Dewey and American Democracy* (Ithaca: Cornell University Press, 1991). On the mis-reading of Dewey as "naïve," see Hans Joas, *The Genesis of Values* (Chicago: University of Chicago Press, 2000).

9   Michel Foucault, *Dits et ecrits: 1954–1988* (Paris: Editions Gallimard, 1994), p. 670.

10   Ibid., p. 598.

11   "A critique is not a matter of saying that things are not right as they are. It is a matter of pointing out on what kinds of assumptions, what kinds of familiar, unchallenged, unconsidered modes of thought the practices that we accept rest. We must free ourselves from the sacralization of the social as the only reality and stop regarding as superfluous something so essential in human life and human relations as thought. Thought exists independently of systems and structures of discourse. It is something that is hidden, but which always animates everyday behavior. There is always a little thought even in the most stupid institutions; there is always thought even in silent habits." Michel Foucault, "'Practicing Criticism,' or 'Is it really important to think?' May 30–31, 1981," interview with Didier Eribon, in *Foucault: Politics, Philosophy, Culture*, Lawrence Kritzman, ed. (New York and London: Routledge, 1988), p. 155.

12   Michael Ignatieff, "Human Rights," in *Human Rights in Political Transition: From Gettysburg to Bosnia*, Carla Hesse and Robert Post, eds. (New York: Zone Books, 1999), p. 313.

13   Hannah Arendt, *The Origins of Totalitarianism* (New York: Harcourt Brace, 1951).

14   Peter Novick, *The Holocaust in American Life* (New York: Houghton Mifflin, 1999).

15   James Clifford, *The Predicament of Culture* (Cambridge, MA: Harvard University Press, 1988).

16   Ignatieff, "Human Rights," p. 320.

17   The outline of a general anthropological critique of the universalism of bioethics is found in Arthur Kleinman, "Anthropology of Bioethics," in *Writing at the Margin, Discourse*

between Anthropology and Medicine (Berkeley: University of California Press, 1995). On the institutionalization of moral philosophy in England, see the various works of Stephen Toulmin and Albert Jonson.

18   Ignatieff, "Human Rights," p. 321.

19   Yves Dezalay and Bryant Garth, "Droits de l'homme et philanthropie hégémonique" in *Actes de la recherche en sciences sociales* 121–122, March 1998, pp. 23–41.

20   Dezalay and Garth, "Droits de l'homme," p. 23.

21   Ibid., p. 27.

22   Ibid., p. 40.

23   Tony Negri and Michael Hardt, *Empire* (Cambridge, MA: Harvard University Press, 2000), p. 36.

24   The general contempt for earlier generations of development theory and practice is widespread in the academic left in the United States. Perhaps for this reason few of these professors and their students seem to realize that they themselves are operating on the inside of an updated version of the enterprise that they are criticizing. In this light, the expansion during the 1990s of post-colonial, transnational, and human rights programs in elite American colleges is consistent. A whole new generation of (post-)modernization professionals is being trained with specialties in environmental, medical, and human rights issues. Dezalay and Garth's analytic apparatus (as well as the analysis of Negri) is especially helpful in making this shift visible. Human rights activism came of respectable academic age toward the end of the 1970s with the crowning success of Amnesty International. Human rights are a cosmopolitan, intellectual, political, and media object. Dezalay and Garth, diligent unmaskers of the dominant, express surprise that some multinational corporations are involved in articulating and funding these discursive networks, in addition to the governments, universities, and NGOs. Their surprise is surprising. It is based in the assumption that ethics or rights or truth is inherently external to forces of capitalism, or domination, of exploitation, of subjugation. Bourdieu knows better. What Dezalay and Garth are reluctant to acknowledge is that their own analysis functions within the market of civic virtue.

25   David J. Rothman, *Strangers at the Bedside, A History of How Law and Bioethics Transformed Medical Decision Making* (New York: Basic Books, 1991), p. 3.

26   Ibid., p. 12.

27   Hans Blumenberg, *The Legitimacy of the Modern Age*, trans. Robert Wallace (Cambridge, MA: The MIT Press, 1983), p. 48.

28   Ibid., p. 1.

29   Robert Wallace, "Introduction," in Blumenberg, *The Legitimacy of the Modern Age*, p. xxviii.

PART II

BIOSCIENCE AND BIOLOGICAL LIFE

ETHICS OF
TECHNOSCIENTIFIC OBJECTS

4

STEM CELLS R US:
Emergent Life Forms and the Global Biological

SARAH FRANKLIN

Introduction

Since the late 1990s, stem cell development has become one of the major growth sectors within the global biotechnology industry, and has attracted considerable attention as a site of bio-innovation. Like other "breakthrough" areas of bioscience, stem cell techniques have been accompanied by tremendous hype, emphasizing the speed of technological innovation and its "revolutionary" potential. A direct media feeder system links developments in stem cell research to the possibility of treatment for severe, disabling, and often fatal conditions – binding stem cell technology securely into a rhetorical fabric of hope, health, and an improved future through increasing biological control. Every country in the world that imagines itself a player in the future of genomics, biotechnology, or what is now being called "regenerative medicine" is today busy passing regulation that will facilitate public approval for rapid industrial development of stem cell technology.

The United Kingdom is currently the "world leader" in stem cell technologies. As *Business Week* reported in April of 2002, "In stem cell research, it's rule Britannia":[1]

> In Britain, home to the world's first test-tube baby and Dolly the cloned sheep, more than a decade of ongoing dialogue between scientists, government, and religious officials has resulted in the most conducive climate in the world for this important new area of scientific research.[2,3]

Both Germany and the United States, the U.K.'s major competitors, are hampered by strong public opposition to the use of human embryos for stem cell research – widely considered to be the most important resource for this area of scientific innovation. France, Spain, the Netherlands, and Sweden have plunged into the stem cell business enthusiastically, as have Australia and Canada. China and Singapore also have burgeoning stem cell industries, but since they are less defined by dominant Western systems of scientific publication, or intellectual property law, their competitiveness is harder to assess. Stem cell research combines human reproductive medicine (in particular, IVF programs) with agricultural applications (such as genetic modification of animals and plants) and traditional areas of biology; in particular, embryology, which, after a lengthy period of being sidelined by molecular biology, has burst back into the frame as a source of essential techniques, such as microinjection, and knowledge, such as expertise in cell cycles and embryonic metabolism. Stem cells offer the prospect of downloading genomics into a wealth of applications, making it the first major post-genomic bio-industry.

There are many emergent hybrid conjunctions that engender the stem cell field. The dominant post-genomic discourse of life's essentially shared molecular architecture (the we-are-50%-genetically-identical-to-cabbage trope of newfound affinities among everything from daffodils to fruit flies) is now increasingly fused with one of biology's oldest and most classical points of reference to describe life's commonalities – the cell. In the new flattened, respatialized, and recombinant genealogical topography of post-genomic designer organisms, life itself is repositioned outside the grid of neatly brachiated channels of ancestry that was formerly the master figure of life as a systematic unity. In place of the tree of life is the post-genomic, post-Darwinian, technique-led *genotopia* of the mix-'n'-match Petri dish, in which life components are assembled in ways that were, until quite recently, considered to be biologically impossible.

It is not so much that the pre-genomic beliefs that life has a structure, or some kind of internal design, have been displaced than that these long-held attitudes to "life itself" have been *repositioned alongside* a new enthusiasm for the potential of made-to-order recombinant outcomes. Ideas of naturalness, the inherent, the inherited, and the predetermined are still central vectors of assumed causality in contemporary biotechnological innovation. What has become more prominent is the idea, long established in the field of assisted human conception, and even longer in the field of animal breeding, that "nature can be given a helping hand." Darwin called this "the breeder's hand," and it was more important to the development of his ideas about natural selection than is commonly portrayed. IVF leaflets call it the hand of medicine, or the hand of science, and these "helping hands" provide a powerful image of regeneration under technological control, yet which is still being directed by nature's "own" dictates.[4]

This chapter explores stem cells as distinctive emergent life forms that refigure traditional understandings of economy, governance, and biology. Although I am focusing exclusively on the U.K., it is clear that the U.K. is responding to the stem cell issue within a global frame. In this, and other senses, stem cells are what might be called a *global biological*. Their production is a global biological enterprise, but it is also their "global," in the sense of totalizing, projected uses to which this term refers.[5] The idea of the global biological is already manifest in the human genome project, itself a description of a global totality (all of the human genes), the outcome of global cooperation, and a symbol of globalization – much as space exploration, and the image of the blue planet, inaugurated forms of global culture in the last century.[6] The conquest of inner space – the master narrative of genomics – is replete with the same imagery of technological potency, human frailty, and future salvation that framed an earlier century's lunar voyages. Stem cell technology is a prime example of the ways in which the global may come into being as a biocultural condition, as a form of identity, and as a realm of imaginary futures.

At the same time, stem cell technology is also, to mutate slightly Margaret Lock's phrase, a *local biological*. Describing the "local biologies" that emerge out of debates about menopause, brain death, and organ transplant, Margaret Lock has emphasized the ways in which the constitution of biological facts, the biological self-evident, or what are considered to be biological conditions, vary significantly according to their locations.[7] Stem cell technologies, as this brief portrait of the British situation attempts to suggest, demonstrate how biological properties are increasingly not only being "discovered," but are being created, in ways that reveal specific national and economic priorities, moral and civic values, and technoscientific institutional cultures.

Regeneration Narratives

A traditional anthropological entry point to begin to evaluate the cultural processes that are being made explicit in the stem cell field are the kinds of origin stories, conception models, or regeneration narratives through which stem cells are represented in both popular and scientific accounts. A typical example is the following opening paragraph from a description of stem cell technology in the European Commission's research and development newsletter, *RTD info*:

> At birth, human beings are made up of approximately 100,000 billion cells belonging to 200 different categories (nerve, muscle, secretory, sense cells, etc.). Each of these groups is able to effect a number of very specialised tasks. As the body develops, the cells multiply by a process of division: when tissues deteriorate or wear out, it is generally the cells in the vicinity of the damaged zone that proliferate and try to compensate for the losses. Over time, however, this regenerative ability is progressively lost and ultimately disappears in many vital organs. Also, when the cells divide they are only able to produce daughter cells that are similar to themselves.[8]

In this origin account, humans are described in terms of their cellular functions, over the course of an individual lifetime. The cells are classified in terms of both quantity (100,000 billion cells at birth) and type (200 different categories). Cellular function is described in terms of multiplication, division, replacement, specialization, proliferation, compensation, regeneration, development, deterioration, and disappearance. These are the key components of cellular effectivity, which are in turn organized economically, in terms of production and loss. Vitality is the outcome of successful replacement of cells, and age, or diminished vitality, results from the waning of this capacity. Significantly, regeneration alone is neither sufficient to produce beneficial outcomes, nor is it always a "good" in itself: successful regeneration requires the maintenance of appropriate specialization.[9]

The added-on concluding sentence, "Also, when cells divide they are only able to produce daughter cells which are similar to themselves," draws attention to this ambiguity of regeneration: more of the same is both good and bad, enough and not enough. The axes of regeneration and deterioration, and identity and difference, are both represented by the figure of the unilineal descent group, comprised of daughter cells. The next paragraph explains why the search for both dutiful and deviant daughters has proven to be so important:

> This is why the discovery of the role and properties of stem cells (known as *multipotent* when they can form several types of cells and *pluripotent* when they can form all of them) brings new and exciting prospects. Tissues formed from cells so specialised that they are virtually unable to be renewed could—if damaged—be "reconstructed" through the addition of a sufficient number of stem cells. In any event, that is the underlying idea of what is hoped is a new field of medicine in the making: regenerative medicine.[10]

Here, some of the functions of cells are spelt out in terms of the desirable and undesirable equations through which the viability, and profitability, of stem cell economics are being imaged and imagined: in a steady state, multiplication-plus-specialization, and division-minus-variation, equate to positive growth; however, this can transform into a state of deterioration, in which multiplication-plus-specialization (variation or no variation) equates to limited growth (or cessation). It is because specialization equals deterioration (over time) that a new source of renewable, specialized cells equates to *positive growth in perpetuity* – the ultimate bio-outcome.

Stem cells are important *because they are exceptional*. They are, according to the article cited above, "the exceptional exception" precisely because they offer unique regenerative capacities:

> Stem cells are a double exception to the rule of cell specialisation – hence their interest. Not only are they able to reproduce identically (and exceptionally quickly) throughout their lives but, more importantly, they are able to differentiate to form several (sometimes in very large numbers) distinct cell types.[11]

Stem cells, then, generate interest because they are multi-talented multipliers. "Not only do they reproduce identically," but they "are able to differentiate." In this account of stem cells, they are doubly valuable because they are a "double exception to the rule of cell specialisation." This makes them both doubly useful, and exceptionally interesting.[12]

What is evident in even the briefest descriptions of stem cells are emergent models of human life in which who we are, and what we are made up of, can be extracted and utilized in ways that are not only about the reuse of existing parts, *but their redefinition*. The redefinition of the human as a quantity of cells with different qualities is then further elaborated in terms of the ability to break down cellular capacities into specific functions, *and to redesign them*. The ways in which this emergent global cellular functionality is at once technologically assisted and "natural" repeats a common conflation, but in a new guise. At this early stage of stem cell research, a dominant language of cellular capacity is closely linked to the extraction of specific functions and effects. Extracted from the body, cellular functionality has become a field of property speculation, in the sense that cells are seen both to *have* new formal properties, and to *be* valuable as new property forms; that is, as various forms of biocapital. The language of engineering and design, applied to the fundamental units of the body – cells – offers the prospect of bespoke life forms which can be used to augment various kinds of life as we know it, including our own.[13]

In these ways, the RTD description of stem cells is typically global, referencing a global (all encompassing) set of future applications, and a global view of humanity (all of whom share a universal biological condition). Stem cells are also regionalized and localized in the description of several European projects at the close of the article, accompanied by a portrait of Eurocord, Europe's umbilical cord blood bank based in Paris: "Europe seems determined not to miss the stem cell train. The European Union already funds – to the sum of 27.4 million euro – 15 research projects involving 117 laboratories in countries from Finland to Portugal."[14] A description of the specific cell types under investigation, such as hematopoietic cells (the precursors of blood cells), completes the *compression of scale* from worldwide, panhuman applications of stem cell technologies, to major economic regions (the EU), to specific national projects, to distinct cell types, from which cell lines will be purified. The literacy that allows a movement, unfolding, or a "making sense," within and across all of these differently scaled contextual registers is also part of what is meant by the global biological.

Cellular Capacity

In classic biological terms, "differentiation" has always been associated with temporal progression and with the acquisition of form and shape. Together, these processes result in the development of both organisms and species, and it is to the mechanisms of generation, growth, and development that most of biological thought was directed until the advent of molecular genetics. "Differentiation" is a term derived from embryology and used to describe the way in which a body acquires specific parts out of a single undifferentiated whole. It describes the ways in which cells acquire specialized functions, and "to differentiate" is defined in the *American Heritage* dictionary as "to undergo a progressive developmental change to a more specialized form or function. Used especially of embryonic cells or tissues."[15]

At the close of the 19th century, in his now-famous treatise on "The Continuity of the Germplasm," August Weismann asserted that all the genetic material is contained in the cell nucleus and he forcefully rejected the idea of inheritance of acquired traits in any form.[16] Weissman had already explicitly stated that "heredity is brought about by transmission from one generation to another of a substance with a definite chemical and, above all, molecular constitution."[17] By the mid-20th century, following the discovery of the structure of the double helix by Watson and Crick, Weismann's continuity theory was recapitulated with even greater molecular authority in Crick's "central dogma" of molecular genetics, which stated that RNA makes DNA makes protein. This dogma expressed, in molecular terms, an affinity between differentiation and development that emphasized the one-way, irreversible, and progressive nature of both evolution and cellular specialization, which were united by the coding function of DNA.

According to the historian of biology Ernst Mayr, Weissman believed there were two possible relationships between genetic material and individual development.[18] Either all of the genes were divided up during embryogenesis, and then "turned on" to direct each specialist part of development, or all of the genetic material was contained in each cell, but was selectively activated to produce cellular specialization, or differentiation. Although evidence was established during Weismann's lifetime of continuity of the chromosomes, it was not until the 1930s that this idea came to be more widely accepted.[19] Shortly following the rediscovery of Gregor Mendel's experiments in 1900, according to Mayr, the embryologists Theodor Boveri and Walter Sutton began to combine genetic arguments about hereditary transmission with new kinds of cytological evidence, founding the subdiscipline of cytology. Bridging the gap between theories of hereditary transmission and the role of hereditary material in the process of individual development, Boveri and Sutton are historically credited with having offered the first substantial evidence of "the individuality and continuity of the chromosomes,"[20] which later became known as the *Sutton–Boveri chromosomal theory of inheritance*.[21]

Whiggish histories of biology such as Mayr's rely heavily on the assumption of a progressive reconciliation of elementary components of biological thought over time, leading to the eventual alignment of very broad approaches, such as evolution and embryology, so that an overall (Darwinian) complementarity is achieved. However, it is precisely the kinds of gaps described by Mayr that separated the researchers concerned with heredity-as-inheritance and those who investigated the relationship between inherited material and development in the early 20th century which have been redefined, and in many ways broadened, with the advent of molecular genetics. Today, fewer biologists have a general zoological approach to living systems, and many more have highly technical specialities that require very different kinds of interdisciplinarity; for example, between computation and biology. From this perspective, it is not so surprising that some of the fundamental laws and properties that shaped the emergence of modern biology, and indeed had become nearly sacrosanct, are undergoing substantial revision.

The increasing unity between ideas about development, differentiation, and cell division reached what may have been its culminating coherence in the late 20th century. In symphonic harmony, these processes were all seen to work together to a very considerable degree and, in a sense, reproduced each other in their movements. Despite obvious problems with Darwinian models, highlighted by provocateurs such as Steven Jay Gould, evolution, inheritance, and development worked within a system that favored recapitulation of certain key principles and forms. An economy of loss governed all of them. Evolution is, in Darwinian terms, dominated by extinction. Most species fail, and it is only the few successful adaptees who are favored by the hand of natural selection, all of whom are linked within a single system of descent that connects everyone to shared common ancestors, who survive. Similarly, differentiation is produced by the loss of cell functionality, specialization being conceived as an irreversible tapering off of genetic potential as an organism develops from simple to complex.

Stem cell technology offers not only to compensate for the losses inherent in cellular specialization, such as aging, disease, or organ failure, but to reverse them, and introduce an economy of growth in perpetuity. Stem cells are not only imagined as a supplementary source of tissue, but as a technology that can reprogram the cell in a way that transforms what were formerly thought of as its inherent one-way tendencies to decline into capacities for unlimited production. Stem cell technology, therefore, is not only offering new, lucrative, and "exciting" ways to harness the productive powers of the cell: what is most "interesting" about stem cell technology is that it is offering *a new means of creating them*.[22]

The Dolly Technique

In the experiments that led to the birth of Dolly the sheep, Ian Wilmut and his team at the Roslin Institute in Scotland made one of the major discoveries that has led to the development of the stem cell industry when they confirmed that the nuclear DNA of an adult cell could, in effect, be "reprogrammed" to go back in time and become totipotent, as if it were an embryonic cell, capable of forming all of the tissues in the body. Before the birth of Dolly the sheep, this was considered to be biologically impossible, because it contradicted one of the most fundamental laws of biology, namely the one-way process of specialization. Wilmut's team discovered that it is the very powerful cytoplasm, or cellular soup inside of the ovum, which, as he put it, "tells the DNA what to do." The egg cell used to make Dolly came from a Scottish Blackface sheep, and was, like all mammalian egg cells, 100 times larger than the mammary (adult) cell, from a white Finn Dorset sheep, with which it was fused.[23] The idea was to "trigger" the Finn Dorset DNA to make a sheep identical to its nuclear genetic mother (a "clone"). In sheer physical terms, the Blackface egg overwhelmingly dominated the cellular environment of the two cells once they were fused together with a jolt of electricity, which dissolved the cell wall of the microinjected Finn Dorset mammary cell. Wilmut describes the egg cytoplasm as a kind of super-computer that "reprogrammes" the DNA of the mammary cell to recommence development *as if it were an embryo* (see Figure 4.1).

Reversing the usual determinism attributed to DNA as the "blueprint" or master plan for cellular development, Wilmut's findings introduced an entirely new principle into reproductive biology, which is that DNA can, in a sense, be reactivated.

Wilmut was undoubtedly overstating the case when he concluded from the Dolly experiment that we have entered what he calls "the age of biological control" in which, in effect, nothing is "biologically impossible" anymore. However, as he states in the following passage, that term has certainly become a more unstable guarantee:

> As decades and centuries pass, the science of cloning and the technologies that flow from it will affect all aspects of human life—the things that people can do, the way we live, and even, if we choose, the kinds of people we are. Those future technologies will offer our successors a degree of control over life's processes that will come effectively to seem absolute. Until the birth of Dolly scientists were apt to declare that this or that procedure would be "biologically impossible"—but now that expression seems to have lost all meaning. In the 21st century and beyond, human ambition will be bound only by the laws of physics, the rules of logic, and our descendants' own sense of right and wrong. Truly, Dolly has taken us into the age of biological control.[24]

In overstating his case, Wilmut deliberately ups the ante of moral responsibility in the area of biological innovation. The implication of his statement is that the idea that something is biologically impossible is not going to be a very reliable guide in the future, and should not be cause for complacency. As a highly socially concerned and publicly active scientist, Wilmut is not being grandiose so much as urging caution, and expressing his eagerness to promote more substantial social,

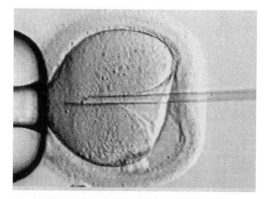

Figure 4.1 Microinjection of a human egg cell. In this image, which I argue elsewhere has become iconic of what I am calling in this chapter "the global biological," a new topography of "life itself" is characterized by the flattened focal frame of the cell's transluscent interior, out of which protrude the two "helping hands" of science: the suction, or "holding" pipette, and the microinjection needle, the source of new genealogical flows.
Source: Sue Pickering

ethical, and political discussion of how science should be regulated in the future, because, as he sees it, science is opening doors faster than anyone might have expected.

Wilmut's finding has led to considerable debate about the importance of the Dolly experiment within the scientific community itself. Wilmut and his own team would be the first to admit the term "clone" is very unhelpful, both because it is inflammatory and because it is scientifically inaccurate. Dolly would be a "proper" clone if she had been produced from *the adult cell alone* – a possibility the Dolly experiment may bring closer, but which it came nowhere near achieving. Since Dolly was created from a fusion of two cells, she is not accurately described as a clone – only the fact that her nuclear DNA came from one parent supports this view. More technically, the question of differentiation, and what happened to it, exactly, during the Dolly experiment, remains unclear. Initially, Wilmut and his team described the process by which the Finn Dorset mammary cell was "reprogrammed" as "dedifferentiation," because it was no longer functioning as a specialized mammary tissue cell, but as a germ cell. This was the "reversal" the Dolly experiment was seen to confirm. However, Wilmut has since suggested that "dedifferentiation" is the wrong term, since he suggests the Dolly experiment shows that adult cells do not "differentiate" irreversibly to begin with, and that specialization does not preclude recapacitation of "lost" functionality.[25]

While the importance of the Dolly technique remains in dispute, it has been widely interpreted as a formidable feat of biological experimentation that, at the very least, points toward dramatic new possibilities for harnessing cells as productive units. What has become the agreed position is that the technique used to make Dolly, somatic cell nuclear transfer, now shortened to cell nuclear transfer, or CNR, is extremely useful and promising. Already several versions of CNR have been developed, and a major battle over patenting its various components is under way. Attempts to replicate the Dolly experiment have been undertaken all over the world, on various species, many of which have been successfully "cloned."[26]

Economically, the success of the Dolly technique, and its implications for stem cell technologies, have been seen to offer the greatest commercial potential yet of any of the post-genomic bioindustries. The Human Genome project was never imagined to be very profitable itself, but was justified as a strategic investment in the development of biotechnology. Initially, diagnostic tests created from the ability to target specific genes were imagined to be a major consumer market, and to an extent this has been the case – for example, with Myriad Genetics' breast cancer test, on which it holds a patent. Gene therapy, another major application, has proved far more clinically challenging than initially imagined, and has led to several highly publicized and controversial deaths. Stem cell technology – with its enormous range of applications – has been seized upon by the biotechnology industry as a highly desirable R&D investment area. If we are not yet in the age of "biological control" envisaged by Wilmut, life is nonetheless substantially altered after Dolly.[27]

British Biology

Summarizing the scientific developments I have just described above, the British House of Lords Select Committee Report on stem cell research, published in February 2002, claims that:

> Until recently it has generally been considered that in mammalian cells the process of differentiation is irreversible. However, it has been demonstrated in animals that it is possible to reprogramme ("dedifferentiate") the genetic material of a differentiated adult cell by CNR. Following this seminal finding, many studies have also suggested that adult stem cells may have greater "plasticity" than previously suspected: they may be reprogrammed to give rise to cell types to which they normally do not give rise in the body. The potential of specialised cells to differentiate into cell types other than those to which they normally give rise in the body is little short of a revolutionary concept in cell biology. It has significantly increased the possibilities for developing effective stem-cell based therapies.[28]

In this description, the term "dedifferentiation" is retained, and equated with reprogramming, and the term "plasticity" is used to describe what is revolutionary about the CNR technique. Closely following scientific accounts of stem cell technology and nuclear transfer techniques, such as those provided by members of the Roslin Institute, the House of Lords' description of the basic biological "breakthrough" behind stem cell research endorses the view that it offers radical new possibilities, and emphasizes their therapeutic potential.

The House of Lords Report offers a thorough consideration of stem cell research and concludes that it should be "strongly encouraged by funding bodies and the Government" in the U.K.[29] Research on human embryos is described as "necessary, particularly to understand the processes of cell differentiation and dedifferentiation" and the report endorses the CNR technique, stating that "there is a powerful case for its use ... as a research tool to enable other cell-based therapies to be developed."[30] The report recommends the establishment of a British stem cell bank to be "responsible for the custody of stem cell lines, ensuring their purity and provenance"[31] and it concludes that existing mechanisms for regulation of research, and mechanisms for procuring informed consent from donors, are sufficiently robust to accommodate the new developments in the area of stem cell research.

The House of Lords would not have appointed a Select Committee to consider the issue of stem cells were it not a matter of significant national concern, while, in keeping with over 15 years of debate on related matters in Parliament, the outcome of the Committee's deliberations is extremely permissive – indeed almost radically liberal.[32] It is a more comprehensive and substantial endorsement of stem cell research than has been produced in any other country, including Sweden or the Netherlands, which also have very liberal legislation in this area.

Although the Committee acknowledges that it was only able to give limited attention to the role of commercial interests in stem cell research, it devotes an entire section of the report to this concern, and acknowledges that it has "been aware throughout that commercial interests could, and to some extent already do, play an important role in the development of such research."[33] It also acknowledges that "biotechnology is a growth industry," citing an Ernst & Young report that by the end of 2000 "the total value of Europe's publicly quoted biotechnology companies stood at 75 billion Euros, compared with 36 billion Euros a year earlier."[34] The Committee adds that

> According to a separate report, the United States, which has the largest number of companies in this field, market capitalisation of publicly quoted biotechnology companies fell over the same period (from $353.8 billion to $330.8 billion), but the number of public companies increased by 12.6%, and in the two years to June 2001 biotechnology stocks outperformed internet stocks on the Nasdaq index.[35]

These references, along with acknowledgment that the U.K. "has by far the most public biotechnology companies" in Europe, and that "investor interest is considerable and evidently based on the assumption that future profits may be significant" confirm the extent to which the British government recognizes the importance of economic growth in the biotechnology sector as a national priority. This is further underlined by reference in the House of Lords report to China and Singapore, which "provide examples that deserve special mention":

> In China the government has encouraged a number of universities to invest heavily in stem cell research. In doing so universities have attracted not only public funds but investment by private companies like the Beijing Stemcell Medengineering Company. Leading Chinese researchers are often U.S.-trained and have links with American laboratories. In Singapore, the Economic Development Board has provided initial finance for the Singapore Genetics Programme; it is said that by 2005 some $7 billion dollars will have been invested in relevant research. In both China and Singapore there is concern with ethical issues but also an interest to maintain the competitive advantage gained by light regulation.[36]

Between the lines of this description clearly lies a recognition of the intensely competitive economics of the global biotechnology sector, as well as a recognition of possible tension between "concern with ethical issues" and "the competitive advantage gained by light regulation."

To date, the U.K. has successfully promoted its highly regulated but unusually permissive biotech R&D environment by emphasizing its stability, in large part due to high levels of public confidence in the government's ability to regulate developments in the life sciences. This scene was largely set through the debates over IVF and embryo research that began in the mid-1980s, and resulted in the establishment of the Human Fertilisation and Embryology Authority (HFEA) in 1990. Public confidence in the HFEA remains high, and the combination of high public trust and robust regulatory guidelines is a competitively advantageous recipe for long-term R&D, which the British government is keen to protect and maintain. That a technique developed by an agricultural research facility largely concerned with livestock breeding has in such a short time become the lynchpin of an emergent global biotechnology industry, which, because it increasingly relies on human, not ovine, embryos, will soon come under the regulatory aegis of a Licensing Authority established to oversee reproductive medicine in the U.K., returns us to the theme of the complex hybridities, conjunctures, and mobilities that emerge in the stem cell field.

Stem Cell Futures

As part of an ESRC-funded ethnographic study of preimplantation genetic diagnosis in the U.K., conducted between 2001 and 2003, I interviewed Austin Smith, one of the U.K.'s leading stem cell scientists, in Edinburgh in March 2002.[37] An important finding of this study was the extent to which issues and concerns about stem cells had become intertwined with the cloning debate, genetic diagnosis, genetic screening, and the regulation of assisted reproductive technologies such as IVF during this period.[38]

The Centre for Genome Research, of which Smith is the Director, is based in an enormous science campus, on West Mains Road, a mile north of the city center. The historic campus is a hodge-podge of vast scientific facilities, varying in their architecture from 19th-century zoological collections housed in ornate stone edifices to logo-emblazoned ready-made warehouses large enough to house an Olympic-size swimming pool. Austin Smith's facility is vintage British public sector, with acres of linoleum, nondescript furnishings, and a plain, functional decor. He is a small, boyish figure with large blue eyes and an air of calm precision. He speaks so slowly and clearly, enunciating so precisely, it would be possible to transcribe his words as he spoke them.

I was unaware at the time of the interview, on March 7, that less than a week later, on March 13, Austin Smith would be the senior author of one of two articles published by the journal *Nature* casting doubt on many of the dramatic findings claimed for stem cell research.[39] If I had known this, I would have asked some additional questions. As it is, the *Nature* article sheds an interesting light, all the same, on his comments about stem cells.

Having previously interviewed Ian Wilmut, and conducted fieldwork at the Roslin Institute 15 miles south of Edinburgh (and also part of the university), I was particularly interested in the "dedifferentiation" question. Wilmut had suggested to me that he no longer considers the term appropriate, although, as the House of Lords Report demonstrates, it continues to be widely used, and has become a term that is in some ways defining of the CNR technique:

> SF: In terms of the language of what's happening to the cells, Ian Wilmut says that initially he used the term "dedifferentation" but then he came to feel it was an inappropriate term, because they didn't differentiate to begin with, and I wondered what you think about that term?

AS: Well, dedifferentiation means to me, its fairly precise meaning is just a loss of differentiated character of a cell, or of a group of cells, but it's of the same cell. So I don't think dedifferentiation actually has anything to do with cloning. It's totally inappropriate to use that word. But people did use it for a while, for a little bit, at the start, because they really didn't know how to describe the effects. But reprogramming is the correct terminology... Once you start doing a nuclear transfer experiment it's not the same cell, so I don't think you can talk about dedifferentiation... They didn't have cells, not in nuclear transfer. They're talking about this idea that there might be adult stem cells that could make other types of cells. So then it's a transdifferentiation, well, it is if it occurs.

The term "transdifferentiation" is the one preferred by the Royal Society, the U.K.'s leading scientific association, whose contribution to the stem cell debate in the form of their published literature uses that term throughout. For Smith, it is not possible to analyze any differentiation process "in itself" *once a cell has been combined with another cell*, which is what the Dolly technique involved. The fact that you have mixed a cell with another cell, to create a cell fusion, by definition, in his terms, means that you can no longer speak about cellular properties, since you are talking about a multicellular process.

As it turns out, this is exactly the message Austin was hammering home in the *Nature* article, which, by many, is considered a "blockbuster" for the industry.[40] Working with mouse cells, Smith and his colleagues mixed fluorescent embryonic (ES) cells with bone marrow and brain cells – that is, they mixed (totipotent) embryonic cells with adult stem cells (multipotent progenitor cells). This experiment precisely mimicked earlier research that had concluded that adult stem cells could be made to "go back in time," just as the Dolly mammary cell had apparently done. However, although the adult stem cells in Austin's experiment *appeared* to revert to the "blank slate state" of early embryos, it was revealed by further testing that they had simply *merged* with the ES cells, creating cells with two sets of chromosomes – one effectively "masking" the other. According to Robert Lanza, Medical Director of Advanced Cell Technologies in Worcester, Massachusetts (the main competitor to Geron-Bio-Med, the merged Geron/Roslin company that now holds the license to the Dolly technique), Smith's research "calls into question almost all of the data generated using stem cells."

Here again, the difference between how cells behave when they are merged and how they operate as single units, or as lineages of single cells, is the main target of Smith's concern. This raises a broader issue about which he spoke at some length during our interview, known as "characterization":

SF: In terms of getting a cell line that is *characterized*, that would be one that reliably produces a type of cell that will hold its identity and can be identified as having particular kinds of traits, is that what you would say?

AS: Yeh, I mean, well obviously there are many, there will be many levels to characterization. I mean it's up, it's different for different purposes for the scientist. You might want to set different thresholds, or criteria. I mean I think you'd really have to give me a specific example for me to be able to say, well, look.

SF: Yeh, OK, well, when we were at a medical conference in London on the day
the stem cell licensing announcement was made, there was a lot of discussion about
how many human embryonic cell lines there are, and people were saying there
are about 60 or 70 that are registered, and maybe now there are ten more from
Sweden, and one of the leading IVF practitioners stood up and said well there may
be that many cell lines but only a very few are *characterized* and *none* of these are in
the UK?

AS: Well, now, the answers are more [laughter], they're a little complicated. Firstly,
there are some cell lines in the UK, but they haven't been made here, the cell lines
have been brought in from the US. But there are not, er, there are not cell lines yet
that have been produced in the UK. So the issue of the 64 cell lines basically comes up
because what the NIH did, er, the 64 is basically a made-up number. It was a device to
get a green light for stem cell research. And so the NIH issued a call for people to
register. So people basically registered if they, er, had any ideas they thought they
might be making embryonic tissue: because then if they did get anything it would be
registered. That's why the "64 cell lines" has to be treated with a pinch of salt. Some
of these organizations may subsequently come up with cell lines, or they may yet do,
and they will be able to make out that they had them at the time of registration, so
that's one issue. Some of them just don't exist, and are just a prospective thing. The
other characterization issue is cell lines or cultures that were in the process at that
time, but which may not have gone onto lives as cell lines. And since a lot of it is not
published, there is really no way to know what the *status of those lines is*. Again, you
know, people will just inflate the numbers so a lot of these things will not transpire to
be cell lines. So this is where it gets even more complicated, because how do you
characterize the cell lines without any available data? All of the groups are assigning
slightly different properties to cells. Until you have a reasonable number of competent researchers who are not tied up with issues about companies, until you can do
some proper comparative evaluations, *you can't really say this is hard science*. You can't
say this is what the fundamental properties of these cells are as opposed to what you
would call their individual polymorphic properties.

According to Smith, in other words, it is very difficult even to say what cell line
characterization will be, because so many cell lines have such a speculative future.
Even if they are well established, they may not continue to reproduce reliably. At this
stage, he reported in our interview, "you can set criteria, but they would be
arbitrary." Since different researchers are using different culture methods, it is very
hard to standardize, on top of the fact there are so few human cell lines to compare.
Looking back at the history of murine cell lines, Smith pointed out that it took
ten years to learn best how to culture them, and another ten to decide how to
characterize them. "People just seem to have forgotten all of that," he noted.

The apparent stability of the "blank slate state" adult stem cells that Smith used for
the *Nature* article reproduces an *effect*, an experimental *artifact*, that led to what Smith
considers to be a possible source of major scientific error. Through a kind of experimental mimicry, Smith and his team sought to expose the kind of premature claims
that could impede progress in achieving either standardized culture methods or
anything like stable criteria for the standardization of human cell lines. In Smith's

view, the history of standardization of mouse cell lines sets a noteworthy precedent – it was not an achievement that occurred either quickly or very efficiently.

It is not surprising it is difficult to standardize cells that are being cultured into lines *precisely because* they are "exceptional," or even "doubly exceptional." While Austin Smith's concerns about the industry are substantial, and his *Nature* article is an elaborate staging of "what can go wrong," it is also clearly aimed at making the industry more robust and accountable, and thus building it on a stronger foundation. Significantly, the experiment also demonstrates the danger of assuming research can go forward using only adult stem cells – a major argument used by the anti-embryo research lobby to restrict stem cell research to adult cells alone, precisely on the basis of their newfound "plasticity." Hence, although it is highly critical of other studies, Smith's research is clearly protective toward the research field in general.

Cell Cultures

Among the multiplicities of stem cells are their identities as scientific, corporate, national, and public entities – in all of which capacities they are both unstable and contested. As individual lines, they have an ambiguous existence in relation to their collective future as either a research tool or as life forms. The cell lines that will eventually emerge into an orderly, characterized, typologized, patented, licensed, regulated, and marketable collection, such as the stem cell bank proposed in the U.K., will comprise a unique population of immortal, human life forms, whose existence, or origin, is technoscientific, organic, and historical.[41] Like genes, they currently elude stable characterization, in several senses of that term. At the same time, they have become a powerful global biocultural population, the imagined future of which already exercises a strong shaping force on scientific research, health priorities, commercial investment, and technological innovation. Learning how to "culture" stem cells has an additional meaning at the level of a report such as that prepared by the House of Lords, which, like the feeder cells necessary to grow cell lines, is creating fertile social and political soil for their successful cultivation. Cultivating public opinion in order to create a robust climate for bio-commerce turns out to be one of several generative activities out of which stem cells will be hot-housed into fruition.[42]

In striving to depict the "cultures of technoscience" out of which stem cells emerge as one of many multi-talented progeny, it is necessary to move beyond the "culture of no culture" that Sharon Traweek established as a kind of ground zero for the ethnography of laboratory life.[43] We have become increasingly familiar with the assemblages and artifacts with "lives of their own" that populate the process of technoscientific innovation. We have also come to take for granted the ease of pointing out the nature–culture hybrids that make a nature–culture distinction less and less meaningful. It may be that Paul Rabinow is right; it is no longer very meaningful to refer to culture at all, any more than it is to imagine we are now in "the age of biological control."[44]

However, if either biosociality or bioculture, or for that matter biocapital, are to become more robust analytic concepts, with which a certain amount of critical work can continue to be done in either a sociological or an anthropological vein, we might want to think about "culturing up the culture medium," as it were. Borrowing the trope of traffic in analogies from Strathern's work on new reproductive technologies, it may be worth thinking about how the culture concept "travels back" *out of* the Petri dish. It is, after all, culture in the sense of cultivation, or horticulture, from which anthropology borrowed the term to begin with.

In that case, cell cultures ask for both an ingredients list and a recipe for preparation. The stem cells "in culture" at the moment are being "fed" by the production of norms, principles, values, and laws, as they are also being "nurtured" by venture capital investments, media coverage, and public-sector funding. Certainly stem cells are being carefully tended by highly trained scientists, who are trying to teach them basic obedience lessons in state-of-the-art laboratories from Singapore to Silicon Valley. They are being watched over carefully by presidents, prime ministers, and innumerable professional organizations concerned with their welfare, their rate of population growth, and their international travel arrangements. Few offspring have their provenance, ancestry, reproductive behavior, or genetic composition more carefully scrutinized by highly trained custodians.

Like the enormous populations of frozen embryos that have become official legal entities, with protected status under the law of most countries, stem cells and their immortal progeny are increasingly becoming part of public, national, and civic culture. Like Dolly, they will eventually have names, and some will undoubtedly go on to enjoy worldwide celebrity and commercial success. In addition, they are destined to become parts of future people, carrying the genetic identities of their founder cells into new kinds of organic union with the as-yet unborn organ failure cases of the next generation.

The cellular trajectories marked by the passage of stem cells into the future forge a corporeal path out of scientific desire in ways that challenge existing current models of biological scale, temporality, and form. Moreover, human embryonic cell lines are "related" to us by genealogical and genetic links that challenge the meaning of relation, or relative, in the same way they establish excessive connections among themselves. Their lack of calibration awaits proper, and proprietary, denomination, according to criteria only their future systematic comparison will yield. For this reason, and all of the others, stem cell lineages are inevitably curious doppelgangers for their human cultivators, whose existences are being mutually transformed by new kinds of biocultural connections.

Appendix A

In one of the most concise accounts of embryology currently available, combining medical, historical, and evolutionary issues under one cover, the British embryologist Lewis Wolpert provides a definition of stem cells that clarifies the difference between stem cells and embryonic stem cells, as well as the two types of daughter cells:

> All the cells in the blood come, remarkably, from just one special progenitor cell – the multipotential stem cell. The essential nature of a stem cell is that it is self-renewing and, as its name implies, the source of other cells. When the stem cell divides, one of the two daughter cells may go on to give rise to other types of cell, whereas the other daughter cell remains a stem cell, capable of dividing again and always giving one daughter to diversification. Thus a characteristic feature of stem cells is this asymmetry; one daughter keeping the stem cell character, the other proceeding along a pathway of diversification. In principle, because stem cells are self-renewing, they are, unlike the cells they generate, immortal.[45]

Notes

1   Kerry Capel, "In Stem-Cell Research, It's Rule Britannia," *Business Week Online*, April 4, 2002, p. 1.

2   Ibid., p. 2.

3   The article goes on to claim that "Britain is the only country on the globe with a regulatory structure in place that provides a clear road map for both public- and private-sector research on embryonic stem cells" and points out that the U.K. will house the world's first stem cell bank – issues I will be discussing in more depth further on in this chapter.

4   Sarah Franklin, *Embodied Progress: A Cultural Account of Assisted Conception* (London: Routledge, 1997); Marilyn Strathern, *Reproducing the Future: Anthropology, Kinship, and the New Reproductive Technologies* (Manchester: Manchester University Press, 1992).

5   In describing the post-genomic shift from structural to functional genetics, Keller cites geneticists Hieter and Boguski's definition of functional genomics as: "the development and application of global (genome-wide or system-wide) experimental approaches to assess gene function by making use of the information and reagents provided by structural genomics." See Evelyn Fox Keller, *The Century of the Gene* (Cambridge, MA: Harvard University Press, 2000), p. 7. This is not strictly a definition of how stem cells are being used, but there are strong family resemblances, and this is one of the ways in which I am using the idea of the "global biological" in this chapter.

6   Sarah Franklin, Celia Lury, and Jackie Stacey, *Global Nature, Global Culture* (London: Sage, 2000).

7   Margaret Lock, "Deadly Disputes: the Calculation of Meaningful Life," in *Living and Working with the New Medical Technologies*, M. Lock, A. Young, and A. Cambrosio, eds. (Cambridge: Cambridge University Press, 2000); Margaret Lock, *Twice Dead: Organ Transplants and the Reinvention of Death* (Berkeley: University of California Press, 2002).

8   European Commission, "Stem Cells: Promises and Precautions," *RTD info* (Brussels) 32, 2001, p. 4.

9   Hannah Landecker, "On Beginning and Ending With Apoptosis: Cells and Biomedicine," in *Remaking Life and Death: Toward an Anthropology of the Biosciences*, Sarah Franklin and Margaret Lock, eds. (Oxford: James Currey, 2003), pp. 23–59.

10   European Commission, "Stem Cells," p. 4.

11   Idem.

12 "Stem cells" is a confusing term because it refers both to *embryonic cells* (ES cells, which are taken from early, undifferentiated embryonic tissue) and to *undifferentiated progenitor cells* derived from specific types of tissue (such as blood and bone marrow). ES cells are considered to be "totipotent" – i.e., capable of producing any tissue in the body – whereas stem cells taken from blood or marrow are "multipotent," meaning they can form most, but not all, tissue types. ES cells are the "ultimate" stem cells, but, in a sense, they are not really stem cells at all, since that term more accurately describes the undifferentiated progenitor cells that produce specific cell types. See further in Appendix A.

13 Linda F. Hogle, "Life/Time Warranty – Rechargeable Cells and Extendable Lives," in *Remaking Life and Death: Toward an Anthropology of the Biosciences*, Sarah Franklin and Margaret Lock, eds. (Oxford: James Currey, 2003), pp. 61–96. It is important to note that the productivity of stem cells is described in terms of mimicking, copying, or duplicating the *in vivo* functions of cells. In this way, cellular modelling, or simulation, forms part of a structural coupling: it is the *in vitro* version of an *in vivo* process. I have not developed in this chapter the question of what kind of productive economy results from this structural coupling, but I have explored elsewhere the "Warhol effect" of cloning on the traditional biological model of development as growth and differentiation, arguing that the mode of production cloning inaugurates is digital. See Sarah Franklin, *Dolly Mixtures: Cloning, Capital and Immortality* (forthcoming).

14 European Commission, "Stem Cells," p. 7.

15 *American Heritage Dictionary*, 3rd edition (1992), p. 521.

16 August Weisman, "The Continuity of the Germplasm," in *Das Keimplasma* (Jena: Gustav Fischer, 1892).

17 August Weisman, *Essays upon Heredity* (Oxford: Clarendon Press, 1889), p. 167.

18 Ernst Mayr, *The Growth of Biological Thought: Diversity, Evolution, and Inheritance* (Cambridge, MA: Harvard University Press, 1982).

19 Ibid., p. 749.

20 Ibid., p. 747.

21 A useful and comprehensive source of information on embryology can be found at the virtual embryo website (http://www.ucalgary.ca/UofC/eduweb/virtualembryo/index.htm).

22 The way stem cells are being redefined as productive mechanisms brings to mind comparisons to early industrialization in the north of England; for example, in the way rivers came to be seen as energy sources, and could be redesigned through sluices and weirs to drive waterwheels.

23 The mammary cell from the Finn Dorset sheep came from an animal that had died six years previously, and whose cells had been frozen in culture by PPL therapeutics, which both funded the Dolly experiment and contributed many of the materials for it, including cells. PPL is housed next to the Roslin Institute, just outside the village of Roslin, in what has become the Roslin Science Park. Roslin Biomed was founded as a public–private partnership to pursue commercially profitable research, and it is Roslin Biomed that later merged with the Geron Corporation in the United States, to which they have granted an exclusive license to the patented Dolly technique.

24 Ian Wilmut, Keith Campbell, and Colin Tudge, *The Second Creation: The Age of Biological Control by the Scientists who Created Dolly* (London: Headline, 2000), p. 17.

25 I first interviewed Ian Wilmut in 1999, which was the first time I had encountered this questioning of the dedifferentiation terminology. Since that time, Roslin has become

increasingly involved in stem cell research using human embryos, and they are likely to play a significant role in the application of their highly developed micromanipulation technology for sheep eggs to human embryos in the pursuit of basic understanding of cellular processes such as differentiation.

26 Royal Society, *Stem Cell Research and Therapeutic Cloning: An Update* (London: The Royal Society, 2000); Royal Society, *Stem Cell Research: Second Update* (London: The Royal Society, 2001).

27 Ironically, the ways in which experiments designed for sheep-breeding have led to the development of a huge industry for the replacement of human tissue fulfills one of Marx's many claims about the lessons to be learned from sheep-breeding in Scotland during the Highland Clearances, notably that "the British aristocracy, who have everywhere super-seded man by bullocks and sheep, will, in a future not very distant, be superseded, in turn, by these useful animals." See Karl Marx, "The Duchess of Sutherland and Slavery," *The People's Paper* no. 45, March 12, 1853.

28 House of Lords Select Committee on Stem Cells, *Stem Cell Research* (London: HMSO, 2002), p. 13.

29 Ibid., p. 48.

30 Ibid., pp. 48–49.

31 Ibid., p. 50.

32 The recent debates are very similar to those that took place in the late 1980s in their combination of elaborate discussion in great detail of embryology, and highly liberal, even radical, permissiveness. See Franklin, *Embodied Progress*; Sarah Franklin, "Making Representations: the Parliamentary Debate of the Human Fertilisation and Embryology Act," in *Technologies of Procreation: Kinship in the Age of Assisted Conception*, J. Edwards, S. Franklin, E. Hirsch, F. Price, and S. Strathern, eds. (London: Routledge, 1999), pp. 127–165.

33 House of Lords, *Stem Cell Research*, p. 32.

34 Idem.

35 Idem.

36 Idem.

37 The current project, which was undertaken in collaboration with Dr. Celia Roberts in the Department of Sociology at Lancaster (who also took part in this interview), is primarily aimed to produce an ethnographic portrait of the changing role of genetic selection within reproductive choice by studying the technique of PGD at two of the U.K.'s leading PGD centers.

38 See Sarah Franklin and Celia Roberts, *Born and Made: An Ethnography of Preimplantation Genetic Diagnosis* (Princeton, NJ: Princeton University Press, forthcoming, 2005).

39 Qui-Long Ying, Jennifer Nichols, Edward P. Evans, and Austin G. Smith, "Changing Potency by Spontaneous Fusion," *Nature* 416, 2002, pp. 545–548.

40 I would like to thank Linda Hogle for longstanding and ongoing assistance and very reliable information on the stem cell field during the writing of this chapter, and other papers, on this topic.

41 The ways in which the identities of stem cell lines vacillate between a discourse based on origins, or lineage, and ownership, or provenance, extends many of the arguments developed in *Global Nature* about what Donna Haraway calls a "shift from kind to brand." See Sarah Franklin, Celia Lury, and Jackie Stacey, *Global Nature, Global Culture* (London: Sage, 2000); and Donna Haraway, *Modest_Witness@Second_Millennium: FemaleMan meets*

OncoMouse (London: Routledge, 1997). It also raises important issues about property and creation, such as those that have been the subject of Marilyn Strathern's most recent work on "emergent forms." See Marilyn Strathern, "Emergent Relations," in *Scientific Authorship: Credit and Intellectual Property in Science*, M. Biagioli and P. Galison, eds. (New York: Routledge, 2003); also Marilyn Strathern, *Property, Substance and Effect: Anthropological Essays on Persons and Things* (London: Athlone Press, 1999).

42 I have written elsewhere about the ways in which the Geron Corporation has "built in" a cultural/ethical component to their cell lines, in a variation of this generative, or fertilizing, effect. See Sarah Franklin, "Culturing Biology: Cell Lines for the Second Millennium," *Health* 5(3), 2001, pp. 335–354.

43 Sharon Traweek, *Beamtimes and Lifetimes: the World of High Energy Physicists* (Cambridge, MA: Harvard University Press, 1988).

44 Paul Rabinow, *French DNA: Trouble in Purgatory* (Chicago: University of Chicago Press, 1999).

45 Lewis Wolpert, *The Triumph of the Embryo* (Oxford University Press, 1991), p. 94.

5

OPERABILITY, BIOAVAILABILITY, AND EXCEPTION

LAWRENCE COHEN

Empire and Exception

Formulations of old (sovereign, world system) and new (biopolitical, deterritorialized, neo-Hobbesian) imperial formations in the early 21st century may fail in their specific commitments to history to be attentive to forms recasting the reason of life, distribution, and control.[1] The regional and global circulation of organs taken from one broad set of bodies (whether alive, almost dead, or dead) and redistributed, and the lattice of scandal, piracy, rumor, denial, and fabrication that has enveloped it, have been productively read in the terms of persistent core–periphery dynamics[2] and new millennial capitalisms.[3] This chapter takes a different approach. Through ethnographic engagement with the social apparatus of kidney redistribution in South India, I frame the exception as a critical governmental form. I work toward an anthropology of the exception that does not presume that exceptional life is and is only bare life, the understandably bleak and quasi-apocalyptic post-humanism of Giorgio Agamben's influential rereading of Foucauldian biopower. To illustrate different approaches to what I am by way of contrast calling "exceptional life," I frame the distributive stakes in transplantation within two complementary but distinctive concepts, bioavailability and operability. I alternate concept development with ethnographic example.

Life at a Distance

Chennai, 2000. I am waiting outside a five-star hotel with the Medical Director of that city's Apollo Hospital. Apollo is arguably both the most prestigious and most successful of the thousands of private hospitals and hospital chains that appeared in India in the 1980s and 1990s and transformed inpatient care for a growing urban middle and working class. The Medical Director used to be Director of Madras Medical College, the most senior health bureaucrat below cabinet level in Tamil Nadu state and, in effect, the highest one can get in medicine outside active politics. Apollo is recasting the equation.

On this day a different sort of recasting looms. A Bangkok-based American reporter for the *Asian Wall Street Journal* is in town covering two stories, Ford's entry into Indian high-end automobile manufacturing and Apollo's newest program for the rural poor. We have just met: he is smart and informed and has already decided that nothing in India is going to disabuse him of his certainty that it can muster at best C-grade globalization, but a shadow of Southeast Asia.

The three of us are heading off to the ancestral village of Apollo's founder, Pratap Reddy, a place called Aragonda, by car some hours to the west, not too far from where Rajiv Gandhi got blown up a decade earlier. Reddy has built a clinic in Aragonda to showcase his introduction of "telemedicine" into rural India. A webcam links clinicians in the rural site with experts in Apollo's metropolitan hospitals in Hyderabad and Chennai. The idea is that from now on India's rural masses will have access to top-flight medical advice no matter how far they may be from tertiary care resources. The weblink was inaugurated by none less than Bill Clinton when he was visiting Hyderabad as President and paying a courtesy visit to Andhra Pradesh Chief Minister and high tech booster N. Chandrababu Naidu. The stakes in telemedicine, as government-integrated rural health development programs continue to wither, may or may not be worth engaging if Reddy is serious about targeting more than his old neighbors. The reporter is trying to figure out if Aragonda is a model for other corporate investment in rural health, but at this point seems doubtful of its sustainability. He has gone into his hotel and the Medical Director and I are standing by the hospital car talking.

All my conversations at this point tend to be about transplant organs. As ex-head of Madras Medical College, the Medical Director used to be in charge of something called the Tamil Nadu Authorization Committee that allowed for exceptions to the law forbidding organ sales. I've asked him about it and, like most medical bureaucrats in analogous positions, he is remarkably open about his discomfort with the ban. He is explaining to me why, despite the letter of the law, he felt it was more ethical to let such sales transpire, to push the exception to its extreme.

Loving Exception

In 1994 – in the face of widely publicized scandals in Bombay and Bangalore, in which physicians were accused of tricking a person into giving up a kidney – the Parliament of India passed the Transplantation of Human Organs Act (THOA). The Act ended a period of ambiguity: before it, forensic authorities responded variously to the question of whether donor nephrectomy as a nontherapeutic operation (for the body in question) constituted assault under the Indian Penal Code. Drawing on vigorous debate in the Indian press and NGO (nongovernmental organization) circles, as well as European and North American examples, the authors of THOA made the sale of a solid organ illegal. They mandated bureaucratic structures drawing on localized medical expertise to specify, recognize, diagnose, and certify brain death; these were termed Appropriate Authorities. They allowed for the transplantation of kidneys from living as opposed to brain-dead persons if donors were related to recipients in one of four permitted ways: as parents, children, siblings, or spouses. And they authorized exceptions to the latter rule delimiting these four classes, to be handled by a second set of medical–bureaucratic structures termed Authorization Committees.

THOA carried jurisdiction only in territories and institutions administered by the central government. Southern and western Indian states, where the primary scandals had broken, were quick to follow the central government and pass THOA or some variant of it. As more transplant clinics appeared in the then "less developed" north and east of the country, a similar pattern ensued in these states: clinic proliferation, increased competition, experimentation with procedures ensuring a steady supply of kidneys, the routinized recruitment of donors and sellers, the proliferation of broker-age forms, and the spiral of accusation, scandal, and audit, followed by the passage of some version of THOA.[4]

In most cases when a state initially set up a new Authorization Committee, a brief post-scandal period of "strict" observance in which exceptions were seldom granted was followed by the liberalization of the exception to cover most appeals. Authorization Committees required an application and formal interview with donor and recipient. As procedures for evaluating legitimate exception were standardized, physicians, brokers, and patients' associations found ways to coach sellers and other persons who might be considered vulnerable to coercion – servants and poor relations – with the necessary answers for the interview. Within a year of an Authorization Committee's establishment, it paradoxically became easier than it had been during the pre-THOA era for clinics and brokers to negotiate kidney sales and to avoid state audit and criminal accusation.

More precisely, it was easier than ever for clinics with Indian-looking patients and Indian-looking donors. Committees would approve, for example, a German recipient and Tamil donor, but elaborate fictions of patronage and affection had to be sustained, coaching was more difficult, and other payments were needed to grease the system. With the emergence of more accessible markets in China, Turkey, and other countries, buyers and other foreign recipients increasingly looked elsewhere. Transnational circulation was replaced by overlapping diasporic circulations: Malaysian Chinese to China; British Indians and Pakistanis to India and Pakistan; others. Bangladesh and Sri Lanka emerged as major markets for Indian kidneys. The "South Asianness" of bodies was normalized through such regional and diasporic distributive fields.

With these new practices of authorization, "caste" and "community" came to matter in how families chose a donor or seller in ways they hitherto had not. Patricia

Marshall has described the concern of recipient families that dissimilar donors would not get through the Authorization Committee.[5] Though few families I interviewed expressed or demonstrated much concern with the biomorality, to use McKim Marriott's apt concept of a transactional and "dividual" ethic,[6] of a lower-caste kidney being inserted into a higher-caste body, practical concerns over which caste bodies would be able to perform the state of exception necessary for committee approval were more common. Conversely, with brokers' growing experience in a given region and their ability to create sustainably exceptional narratives for clearly discordant donor bodies, caste and other performances could again diminish somewhat in relevance.

Committee members in several states agreed that the majority of appeals made to them once THOA precedents were established were transparently commercial, and yet they seldom turned donors down. They offered a series of explanations – interpellated by my presence as a presumed ethical auditor – for their practice. In effect, these constituted a set of exceptions to the formal logic of exception under the law of THOA: (1) One had to be ethical and not just let people die. (2) The formal questions you were allowed by law to ask made coaching and cheating likely and unenforceable. (3) Politicians pressured you to make additional exceptions. (4) The entire system was corrupt and the exception had become the norm to preserve reasonable standards.

THOA's formal logic of exception is organized as a mediation between sovereign protection and familial love. The sovereign state protects persons from practices deemed exploitative and uncivilized. Out of love, family members and friends may desire to give a kidney to one who needs it. To prevent the moral economy of the latter from degenerating into the uncivil economy of the former, only four permitted classes of kin are constituted as *normal* donors. To prevent state protection from shutting down other life-saving circuits of love and flesh, the formal logic of exception is set up.

The actual and doubled state of exception – exceptions to exception's formal logic – preserves the particulars of mediation but inverts love's relation to sacrifice. Out of love, family members and friends may still desire to give a kidney to one who needs it. But the by now routinized ethic of the prospective recipient – summed up in a phrase I often heard, to wit "why should I put someone I love at risk when I can just buy a kidney?" – is to act, *out of love*, to refuse another's sacrifice. What is of course erased in such equations is the question of the *seller's* sacrifice. As critically but less obviously, what is also erased is the question of the seller's *love*. The first erasure converges with Agamben's account of *Homo Sacer*: the seller is not only taken out of the relational frame of being a person, but he or she is denied the recognition of sacrifice.[7] But such an account is complicit with the second erasure. Sellers usually sell to support loved ones, particularly in conditions of everyday or extraordinary debt. The violence, if it is that, done to their bodies is the cost of love for the poor and marginal, and for them this violence and this love is indeed and obviously sacrificial. What is exceptional in these situations is less one's reduction to a zone of indistinction in which political life and bare life collapse together, but a more articulated zone in which one trades in one's bare life – kidneys, other biomatter – in order to remain a political subject of sacrifice and love.[8]

Though Indian transplant professionals often line up on one side or the other of legalizing organ sales, with proponents of a regulated market calling for a revocation of THOA, the logic of exception built into the Act supports the practice of both groups.

Bioavailability

The iterated opposition of sale and gift in such debates fails to engage their common bioavailability. I borrow the term from pharmacology; in brief, to be bioavailable in my terms is to be available for the selective disaggregation of one's cells or tissues and their reincorporation into another body (or machine). The language of disaggregation is not offered to convey moral concern. Like labor and marriage, bioavailability implies a wide range of potentially harmful bodily exchanges, and any comprehensive sociology of its reason or futures would have to think through its various links – metonymic, metaphoric, and otherwise – with these and perhaps others. Like them, bioavailability has a distinctly modern provenance overdetermined by the *longue durée* of its imaginary double – the vampiric and usurious extractions and transposed parts that have constituted and been constituted by the body of value and value of body. The story of bioavailability that I find most useful goes something like the following.

Over the 20th century, more and more live human tissues became available for extraction from one body followed by infusion or implantation into others, and both routine and end-stage medicine became increasingly reliant on tissue transfer to replenish blood and enable certain surgeries (through transfusion), and to replace failing organs (through transplantation). One can schematically represent this movement in terms of three technical shifts.

First: mechanical techniques for safely and effectively extracting, transporting, and grafting tissues were developed, in the case of renal transplantation early in the century. The work of surgical pioneers such as the Lyonnais researcher Alexis Carrel revealed a limit to mechanical innovation in the body's tendency to reject foreign tissue. Carrel was supported for a time by Auguste Lumière, the senior of the two cinematographer brothers. Carrel was a vitalist after Claude Bernard, with a deep commitment to the invention. His first major invention was a method solving the problem of arterial suture; that and subsequent work on renal autotransplants in dogs eventually gave Carrel the Nobel Prize. By that time he had left France without finishing his formal medical training, in disgust at the attacks he received for a pamphlet he wrote attesting to cures that he witnessed at Lourdes. He became a longtime collaborator of the former aviator Charles Lindbergh, in their efforts to create a tissue medium and pump to preserve living tissue indefinitely.

As a student, Carrel was successful in solving the technical problems allowing for a dog's kidney to be successfully moved to its neck; but transplanting the kidney to a different dog usually led to graft failure. The situation was the same for humans. Only very close relations were bioavailable, and even then there was great likelihood of graft rejection unless one had an identical twin willing and able to donate. Bioavailability, in other words, required complete identity, a situation complexly revisited as an element of a recognizable future by diverse actors at the end of the century, with the premature word out on human cloning efforts. Elsewhere I cite the self-described "father" of THOA, Dr. R. R. Kishore of Delhi, who came around to reversing his earlier conviction that organ sales from the poor must be stopped.[9] It's a win–win situation, he told my colleague Malkeet Gupta and myself, "life for life." And in a few years, the entire debate will be moot, for with cloning "I will be able to make babies like popcorn."

Second: through the development of transfusion medicine as defensive technology in World War II and the science it made possible, immunological techniques for recognizing degrees of tissue relatedness at the subcellular level were developed. Tissue rejection could be minimized through screening, and an effective transfusion medicine created large-scale possibilities for the management of human hematologic bioavailability. An effective organ transplant medicine, however, was not so readily achieved. In the case of most organs, live extraction was only possible by killing the donor, as now occurs in the current articulation by the newly entrepreneurial PRC military of organ demand among overseas Chinese and law and order campaigns shoring up the legitimacy of the postsocialist Chinese state through the expansion of capital punishment. Even in the case of kidneys, there were more tissue factors to consider than with transfusion, and correspondence between a biological match (blood and tissue typing) and a social match (someone close enough, charitable enough, dependent enough, or desperate enough) was not yet feasible.

Transplant bioavailability came to depend on the stabilization of large populations of potentially bioavailable recruits to ensure the likelihood of a match.[10] The only postwar population both large enough and *available* enough to enable a transplant medicine was that of the almost dead, bodies still and yet barely alive because of the development of the ventilator in the face of polio. For this population to be rendered bioavailable, as the work of Margaret Lock richly illustrates, several technical problems required solution.[11] New ways of conceiving of these bodies as more or less dead needed to be articulated and acceded to; thus the emergence of "brain death." New communications techniques to mobilize a large enough catchment of potentially almost dead bodies and rationalize their distribution were required. And new *forms of care*, new understandings of organ donation as "saving a life" despite the limited promise of risky, imperfect, and frequently experimental procedures, needed to be crafted and publicized. The result in effect was that accident victims and suicides became particularly bioavailable, but under the conditions of large national registries and audits of living and almost dead bodies at a continental scale. Western Europe and North America became the dominant bioavailable fields.

Though many transplant professionals have understandably taken the emergence of tissue typing with the research of Peter Medawar and others as the originary moment of the transplant era, the recognition apparatus they developed was not transposable to social worlds in which large-scale auditing of the almost dead and near-instantaneous redistribution of their tissues was unrealistic.[12] Brain death as the primary vector of bioavailability created the new moral economy of the waiting list.

Third: it was the most recent technical shift, the development and manufacture of effective immunosuppressant drugs, that made possible both the globalization of the transplant operation and the emergence of multiple bioavailable populations, not only the almost dead. With the invention by the Sandoz corporation, later Novartis, of cyclosporine and its use in tandem with other agents, close matching of transplant tissue was no longer essential. The game was suddenly not to improve the recognition apparatus but to suppress it altogether. Renal transplantation became almost as decentralizable as transfusion. In the 1980s, clinics around the world began to turn to multiple, usually smaller, and more easily mobilized populations. What characterized the mobilization and stabilization of bioavailable populations in this era was the flexibility of these processes. Transplant centers were more competitive the more they could ensure a constant supply of donors, and they experimented with methods of recruitment from transfusion medicine along with other techniques. As far more persons could serve as donors, bioavailability was no longer determined solely by consanguinity or brain death, but additionally by economic need, by political vulnerability, and by frequently gendered moral demands of prestation.[13] The mix of these multiple potential sites and sources of bioavailability was experimental. Common norms of regulated bioavailability became increasingly incoherent.

Thus I find myself, along with my colleague Nancy Scheper-Hughes, chronicling an extraordinary range of marked donor populations in and across different places and moments. In my own field and archival work I have begun to delineate as bioavailable groups ranging across space and scale: from poor relations to loving husbands to migrant labor, from indebted weavers after a cotton drought to small peasants struggling with diminished productivity after the adoption of cotton monoculture, from prisoners in China under an entrepreneurial military to evangelicals in America and their particular commitments to life after life, from men in rural villages to women in urban slums. These groupings share little except their *contingent* bioavailability, organized variously around the loving or charitable or anxious gift, the commoditized sale, or the authoritarian or covert seizure.

Studying transplantation as a critical engine and index of bioavailability foregrounds certain relations and not others. What matters in delineating structures and genealogies of bioavailability is an articulation of vital technique and forms of care with neoliberal entrepreneurship. Ethical conversation hovers around utility and the fragile claims of deontology, or it implodes under the swiftly shifting terrain of incommensurabilities that the intensified experimentation with flexible bioavailability generates. What are reduced to passive (or at most, weakly regulatory) players are the law and other instances and agencies of the state in its current conjuncture. The exception is but complicity: the stakes are pure *zoe*, bare life. To take the life of the exception more seriously, then, I need to reintroduce the state – and specifically, what I am calling the question of political form – as more than the site and instance of failed regulation. I do so here in two ways: through what I term operability and, related to it, what we might term the medicalization of politics.

Operability

For now, I will define operability as the degree to which one's belonging to and legitimate demands of the state are mediated through invasive medical commitment. In my current research and writing, I engage four classes of surgical operation that I argue have been of extraordinary importance in India in shaping a conversation we might wish to have about modernity, reason, and the will, utilizing in addition to the transplant the instances of sterilization, of trans- or ungendering – specifically, *hijra* (third gender or eunuch) castration – and of cataract surgery. To hint at the larger concept, and why I think it can be fruitful to juxtapose different kinds of operations (beyond their subdisciplinary relevance for an anthropology of surgery), I turn to a finding from my earlier work on organ transplantation in South India, and specifically to interviews with women in several slums of Chennai who had sold a kidney to the clinic run by famed transplant physician Dr. K. C. Reddy (unrelated to the head of Apollo Pratap Reddy) in the face of chronic indebtedness.

Organ transplantation expanded quickly in the south and west of India with the advent of cyclosporine. Local bioavailability was characterized by specific relational vectors (often but by no means exclusively or predictably parents to children, brothers to sisters and to brothers, wives to husbands, and asymmetric gifts from poor relations and family servants), by the expanding recruitment of urban and rural poor as sellers, and by very little use of the new brain death. Transplantation was profitable and advertised the hypermodernity of a clinic: numerous centers were set up in Chennai, Mumbai, and Bangalore, and these began to compete for stable bioavailable populations. In the southern state of Tamil Nadu, bioavailable populations were recruited in urban Chennai slums and rural towns near the city of Erode. Chennai sellers were predominantly women and the rural sellers, who were recruited for Bangalore clinics, were predominantly men. Though clinic directors I interviewed differed widely in their estimates of the relative number of family donors versus paid unrelated donors, most agreed that the majority of donations before 1994 were commercial and deferred the question of post-THOA.

What intrigued me in Chennai during my 1998 interviews was the ubiquitous presence for these women of a *prior* operation: specifically, every one of the almost thirty sellers with whom I spoke had had a tubal ligation, the "family planning operation." The matter of the first operation came up in interviews because the women were informed, early on in their enlisting, that for health reasons they would have to have had the family planning operation in order to be able to sell a kidney. But each in turn related that she had already had *that* operation.[14]

I was struck not only by the ubiquity of the prior operation but what I would call its intimacy, its identity with or proximity to the everyday. Work on poor women's often extensive use of available obstetric and prophylactic technology in Chennai by Cecilia Van Hollen has suggested that both the agency and governability of urban slum dwellers – their commitment, in other words, to state intervention in their lives – was in Tamil Nadu in the 1990s mediated through invasive medical technology.[15] Kalpana Ram has examined the forms of political subjectivity and citizenship that women's enlistment in health development articulates[16] and Darren Zook has contributed to a broader genealogy of development and docile bodies in Tamil Nadu.[17] My reading of accounts of the prior operation is in conversation with this literature.

Thus, at least as a thought-experiment if not the analysis of accepted social fact: I will venture that a person is hailed through the family planning operation as a pre-modern and pre-capitalist breeder for whom appeals to modern or bourgeois asceticism will be inadequate. In other words, the operation works within (among other things) a discursive field that presumes that the proper subjects of development are peasants or slum-dwellers marked by excessive passion and limited reason, prone to pathology rather than discipline of the will. From nationalist debates over mass will to the past five decades of Indian family planning, the operation as a proxy for a presumptively failed project of reason and will has continually been asserted. Thomas Hansen locates the genealogy of such pathology in what he terms 19th-century British colonialism's "double discourse" – the native subject split between reasoning elites and passionate masses – and its extension in the "antipolitical" governance of the Gandhian–Nehruvian state, and its separation of a sublime realm of culture and reason from the debased space of mass politics.[18] The operation is thus necessary to remake one's mindful body in accordance with the demands of developmental modernity, to remake one *as if* one were a modern.

If the operation becomes a form through which constitutively marginal, pre-modern subjects can secure some form of modern participation in the nation-state, it may become a critical desideratum. The trouble with viewing operability as fixed and tragic discipline, as opposed to a far more productive and complex governmentality, is more than a matter of either necessity or resentment. The logic of operability resists both the bleak accounting of the subaltern's meager agency and the win–win scenarios of THOA-apostate Dr. Kishore and many bioethicists. To be operable is to submit to one's differentiation, with all possible attendant violence; in so doing, one both participates in the impossibility of a universal subject and constitutes, perhaps, the ground for a political future.

The Medicalization of Politics

India has moved away from enforced quotas at the national level in its family planning, part of an international move recognizing the almost predictable violence that can and has resulted from sterilization targets. Andhra Pradesh, a state of contrasts, with its aggressive information economy championed by Chief Minister Chandrababu Naidu (who models himself as "national CEO" on Malaysia's

Mahathir) and growing wealth set against increasingly impoverished small peasants and *adivasis*, so-called tribals, has held fast to quotas with a vengeance. Naidu is frequently contrast with the populist erstwhile Chief Minister of the northern Indian state of Bihar, Laloo Prasad Yadav. Within the logic of neoliberal expectation, Bihar and Laloo are to backwardness and economic isolation what Andhra Pradesh and Chandrababu are to progress and global prominence. Chandrababu has publicly succeeded at claiming a status that former Prime Minister Rajiv Gandhi had sought but failed to secure: the status, that is, of being *the* sovereign body identified with the bringing of computers – and with these, global recognition and global wealth – to India. Laloo has publicly succeeded in preserving the classic political aesthetics of the post-Gandhian state: iterative commitments to a recognizably agrarian ethos in service of particular congeries of large and small peasant interests. Nepotism and fecundity are central to the maintenance of the Laloo image and the interests it both instantiates and serves: when the Bihar Chief Minister was imprisoned on corruption charges, his rustic wife was brought in to replace him; and largesse and benefits to his many children organize and locate the gift economy of a polity whose formal accounting is simulacrous. Chandrababu Naidu, in contrast, has become so associated with the promotion of vasectomy that on two or three occasions I was assured by people in Andhra Pradesh small towns that he himself must have had one.

The operability of leaders has been directly at stake in the recent and extensively publicized election of a number of *hijras* – transgendered, or more accurately ungendered, "eunuchs" – to municipal and state office. Like Naidu's imagined vasectomy, cutting out the parallel economy by removing the biological impediment to ascetic modernity, *hijra* political rhetoric has centered on the failure of their electoral opponents to be operated upon. Capitalizing on the frequent use of the epithet "eunuch" (or related terms *hijra*, *napunsak*, and *namard*) by famed orators of the Hindu communal right (Shiv Sena party leader Bal Thackeray, for example, repeatedly attacks his opponents as eunuchs for being too soft on Muslims), the *hijras* invert the political capital of castrating language. In speeches and media interviews, they challenge their uncastrated opponents as being the *real* eunuchs. At stake is the potential to have children, especially sons: *hijra* candidates point out again and again that these politician–eunuchs make promises to the electorate but pervert everything to settle their own children. What they evoke is a critical form, part social contract and part classical and agrarian imaginary of *dan* or *jajman*, the counter-gift from the sovereign: politicians promise the counter-gift to the citizen–subject but do not deliver. Their promises are false because they have sons. *Hijras* cannot have children, at least to the extent that they define and signify themselves operatively, and therefore their promises to the people will not be deferred. As the masses lack the will to be ascetic moderns, the leaders lack the will to be modern ascetics. India's would-be Mahathir may have a harder road than his Malaysian fellow traveler, at least if the truths of the *Asian Wall Street Journal* constitute expert knowledge. But his operable career locates itself against the failure of will of Laloo Yadav, and by extension those of his fellow Andhra citizens who resist the procedure.

Figures of the politician's body, its sickness, and the stakes in a cure proliferate, in India and elsewhere. Many of the Chennai women interviewed who had already had *that* operation knew of kidney failure as MGR's disease. M. G. Ramachandran was a wildly popular Chief Minister of Tamil Nadu, whose near death from renal failure (he received a transplant in New York, from his niece) created a moment of statewide crisis. But the medical identifications of and by the leader go far beyond the overdetermined terrain of sovereignty's bodily stakes, real and imaginary. From the late 1980s onward, increased and increasingly visible numbers of state and local politicians avoided arrest – usually on charges of corruption or the improper movement of undeclared funds – by checking into a hospital. The same was true for industrialists and others who negotiated the new possibilities and unanticipated limits of a complexly liberalizing economic field. Apollo and other high-end chains became known as five-star hospitals, less for the quality of their services than as they came to function as five-star hotels for surprisingly large numbers of politicians and business people. Political journalists in Delhi or the state capitals could tell you the names of the doctors of all major political figures and narrate the anatomy of a political crisis through the space of medical consultation. Medical scandals, including the kidney scandals that precipitated THOA, were often laid at the feet of the political investments and affiliations of rival medical–political assemblages. In such a context, THOA becomes as much an instrument of political discipline as ethical reaction, and the space of exception stands less on the margins of the ethical norm than the political cure.

Notes

1   I am grateful to Stephen Collier and Aihwa Ong for their generous invitation to present the original version of this chapter in Prague and their critical engagement throughout, along with that of conference participants. This research would not have been possible without the continued support and research collaboration of Nancy Scheper-Hughes; my understanding of what I here term "diasporic circulation" in the organs world is particularly indebted to Nancy's work across the globe. Funding for the research came from the Open Society Institute. Most thanks must be deferred until the publication of an eventual book, but the specific argument undertaken here also owes much to conversations with Warwick Anderson (on the operation), Amita Baviskar (on the Gandhian), Veena Das (on the everyday), Mariane Ferme (on the secret), Don Moore (on operative scale), Paul Rabinow and Tobias Rees (on the limits to bare life), Gayatri Reddy (on *hijras*), and Cecilia Van Hollen (on family planning), for all of which I am grateful.

2   Lawrence Cohen, "Where It Hurts: Indian Material for an Ethics of Organ Transplantation," *Daedalus* 128(4), Fall 1999, pp. 135–165; Nancy Scheper-Hughes, "The Global Traffic in Human Organs," *Current Anthropology* 41(2), 2000, pp. 191–224; Nancy Scheper-Hughes, "Commodity Fetishism in Organs Trafficking," *Body and Society* 7(2–3), 2001, pp. 31–62.

3   Jean Comaroff and John L. Comaroff, "Millennial Capitalism: First Thoughts on a Second Coming," *Public Culture* 12(2), 2000, pp. 291–343.

4   Cohen, "Where It Hurts."

5   Patricia Marshall, personal communication with author, 1998.

6   McKim Marriott, "Hindu Transactions: Diversity without Dualism," in *Transaction and Meaning: Directions in the Anthropology of Exchange and Symbolic Behavior*, Bruce Kapferer, ed. (Philadelphia: Institute for the Study of Human Issues, 1976).

7   Giorgio Agamben, *Homo Sacer: Sovereign Power and Bare Life*, trans. Daniel Heller-Roazen (Stanford: Stanford University Press, 1998).

8   Lawrence Cohen, "The Other Kidney: Biopolitics beyond Recognition," *Body and Society* 7(2–3), 2001, pp. 9–29.

9   Cohen, "Where It Hurts."

10 Cohen, "The Other Kidney."

11 Margaret Lock, *Twice Dead: Organ Transplants and the Reinvention of Death* (Berkeley: University of California Press, 2002).

12 Cohen, "The Other Kidney."

13 Idem.

14 Cohen, "Where It Hurts."

15 Cecilia Van Hollen, "Birthing on the Threshold: Childbirth and Modernity among Lower Class Women in Tamil Nadu, South India," Ph.D. dissertation, Department of Anthropology, University of California, Berkeley, 1998.

16 Kalpana Ram, "*Na Shariram Nadhi*, My Body Is Mine: The Urban Women's Health Movement in India and Its Negotiation of Modernity," *Women's Studies International Forum* 21(6), 1998, p. 617.

17 Darren Zook, "Developing India: The History of an Idea in the Southern Countryside 1860–1990," Ph.D. dissertation, Department of History, University of California, Berkeley, 1998.

18 Thomas Blom Hansen, *The Saffron Wave: Democracy and Hindu Nationalism in Modern India* (Princeton: Princeton University Press, 1999), pp. 32–35, 50–57.

6

THE ICELAND CONTROVERSY:

Reflections on the Transnational Market of Civic Virtue[1]

GÍSLI PÁLSSON AND PAUL RABINOW

A critique is not a matter of saying that things are not right as they are. It is a matter of pointing out on what kinds of assumptions, what kinds of familiar, unchallenged, unconsidered modes of thought the practices that we accept rest.

Michel Foucault[2]

At a time of spectacular announcements about the completion of a draft of the human genome – in the twin sense of impressive achievement and media spectacle – it is appropriate, indeed urgent for intellectual and civic reasons, to reflect on the social implications of the production of knowledge on biomedicine and the human genome, on social-scientific engagements with this production, and on its transnational institutional conditions of existence. This task is still in the early stages.[3]

An important dimension is the so-called "ethical issues" associated with central medical databases such as the Icelandic one. Recently, deCode Genetics was granted exclusive rights to develop a comprehensive Health Sector Database on Icelanders, following controversial laws passed by the Icelandic Parliament in December 1998. deCode Genetics burst on the local and global scenes with a larger biogenetic project, the aim of which is to combine, for the purpose of locating multifactorial diseases, clinical records dating back to 1915 (the Health Sector Database), genetic information, and a genealogical database that seeks to locate all living Icelanders, as well as a substantial proportion of those who have ever lived.[4] In this chapter, we propose to explicate (1) the transnational context of the deCode experiment, (2) the specificity as well as significance of the case of Iceland, and (3) the challenging and complex relations of knowledge production and circulation in genomics and bioethics, and their implications for the anthropology of human genomics and for ethnography more broadly.

Plans similar to the Icelandic one (with less comprehensive records but on a larger scale) are under way in several other nations and provinces, including Australia, Denmark, Estonia, Newfoundland, Norway, Quebec, Singapore, South Africa, Sweden, Tonga, and the United Kingdom. While these projects represent different scales, samples, and approaches, and moreover, different forms of collaboration between the state, the academy, and the private sector, they all pose, or seem to pose, we contend, fundamental questions of research ethics, biological and ethnographic. Gaining clarity on what those issues are is a logically prior step to taking sides, and turns out harder to do than first appears. The Icelandic plans, as we shall see, have been fiercely opposed both in Iceland and internationally, usually from a ''bioethical'' vantage point emphasizing patients' rights, informed consent, and the protection of privacy.

There is good reason to respect academics who speak out on public issues, taking responsibility as both scientists and citizens. However, following Yves Dezalay and Bryant Garth,[5] we suggest that it is equally important to critically examine the transnational development and practice of bioethics, to identify the principles it operates under and the forces and interests behind it as symbolic, academic ''capital'' is moved from one market sphere to another. In the social sciences and the humanities, as Arjun Appadurai has observed, there is a strong tendency to associate particular themes with particular places.[6] Just as India is the official site for caste, Iceland is emerging as *the* site of biotech and bioethics. There is a peculiar fascination with the Icelandic case, as we shall see, while the similar projects of the U.K., Estonia, and Sweden are almost completely ignored. It is important to try to understand why the social-scientific and ethical gaze is focused on some sites, themes, and issues and blind to others.

Humanitarian Markets

In the following, we explore the consequences of the failure of bioethicists and social scientists to take a comparative perspective, or to acknowledge the need to achieve some distance from their own opinions, or to clarify the bases for their own pronouncements. Such failures, we think, are symptomatic of the emerging global market for civic virtue at a time when the terms of trade are being radically redefined, following structural changes in biomedicine and biotechnology. We are not suggesting that ethical concerns with biogenetic projects – concerns over eugenics, patient rights, the impact of capitalism on the life sciences, transnational inequalities, and so on – are trivial issues in general or particularly in Iceland. Quite the contrary: it is precisely because we take them seriously that we insist on rigor, seriousness, and commitment on the part of those addressing these issues. We fully agree that there are potentially high stakes in the outcome of these events, financially, politically, and morally. The challenge is precisely not to pigeonhole things lest one misses what is actually taking shape, however dangerous, beneficial, or trivial it may turn out to be. We fully understand that our own work is subject to these same criteria and we welcome constructive criticism.

In an article in *Actes de la recherche en sciences sociales* on "The cunning of imperialist reason," provocatively entitled "Rights of man and philanthropic hegemony," Yves Dezalay and Bryant Garth provide a penetrating analysis of recent, seemingly contradictory, developments in the field of human rights: "The movement for human rights is often presented as an exemplary illustration of those new transnational practices that escape from state order. However, by a sort of paradox, it is the national state's recognition of this 'soft law' that represents the fulfillment of the militants' efforts, leading to a growing professionalization and competition within the market of political activism."[7] There are at least two claims embedded here, both of which bear upon our analysis of public debates on the ethics of biogenetic projects, including the Icelandic one.

First, there is the perfectly straightforward and not especially paradoxical point that within a transnational field, national interests, institutions, and players remain significant actors; sovereignty in most domains remains decidedly national. Even when it is not absolute, national states and institutions remain passage points, a funnel, as it were, through which the actors must travel on the way in or the way out to attain authority. Although we are witnessing new relationships between the national and the transnational, as many authors have argued,[8] this transformation cannot be equated with the definitive eclipse of national sovereignty.[9]

Second, and more original, is the claim that a transnational *market for humanitarianism* is in formation. In their book, *Dealing in Virtue*,[10] Dezalay and Garth provide a detailed account of one example of how a sector of this market – international legal arbitration – came into existence, changed, and how it operates at present. Strikingly, success within the humanitarian market depends on many of the same strategies employed in the venture capital world. These include capturing the attention of various traditional media as well as innovating in the use of new media (NGOs pioneered the use of the fax machine and then the Internet for political mobilization as well as the articulation of virtual communities), securing funding from "donor" institutions, translating these resources into position papers for international conferences and then agencies, ensuring a high mobility of personnel, and so on. One sees a marketing of symbolic capital resources "whose investments and counseling strategy must prepare its clients to overcome the very intense rivalries that reigns in the market of civic virtue."[11]

Dezalay and Garth do not assert that the market of humanitarianism and the capital markets are the same, only that there are parallel principles and forces at work in them. The analyst's task is to identify those principles and forces as well as to investigate how "capital" from one market is converted into "capital" (or advantage) in another. Dezalay and Garth show in some detail the changing players and goals involved in the "diffusion of this new symbolic imperialism." They speak of an "elitist democratic" project, conceived and carried by a small group of "*learned men*" (in English in the French text) "desirous of social progress and civic morality, but very respectful of the interests of big capital whose inheritors, collaborators and benefi- ciaries they are."[12] The field of these civic engagements and disagreements is a microcosm of the fractures within the ruling class. To invest in civic virtue is also to construct the state and to assure oneself of a position of legitimacy on the international market of *savoirs d'État*.[13,14]

Iceland provides an excellent case study to observe some of these players at work in the transnational market of virtue, just as it provides a fertile ground to scrutinize parallel agents and structures at work in the market in the economic sense, and a variety of scientific players either involved in deCode Genetics or competing with it (locally in Iceland or elsewhere). Here, a strong ethical and political body – the Association of Icelanders for Ethics in Science and Medicine (*Mannvernd*) – was formed in direct response to the medical database project. The Association, at present the main platform for bioethical criticism in Iceland, is also well connected to the international scene of bioethics, providing the base from which many observers position themselves. The responses to medical and genetic databases both among the public at large, the media, and within the scientific community raise interesting questions of social scientific practice, research ethics, and situated accounts.

The comparison of Iceland, the U.K., Estonia, and Sweden is particularly revealing in this respect, as it helps to pose the issue of how and where biomedical issues become bioethical problems. Said another way, it is not the issues alone that are at stake but a specific historical, political, and economic conjuncture in which an issue becomes a problem. Methodologically, those dealing in universals have major difficulties in addressing adequately the place of either particulars or singularities, and how each of these terms (universals, particulars, singularities) becomes a problem.

Contemporary Biopolitics in Estonia, Iceland, Sweden, and the U.K.

The founders of the company deCode Genetics were Icelandic physician Kári Stefánsson and U.S. biologist Jeff Gulcher, of Harvard University and the University of Chicago, respectively. Established in 1996, the company operates entirely in Iceland, although it was originally funded by venture capital funds coordinated in the United States.[15] deCode Genetics soon strengthened its financial position through a well-funded business arrangement with a pharmaceutical giant, Hoffmann La Roche, an agreement that focuses on research on the potential genetic bases of 12 common diseases. The company has grown phenomenally since its establishment. In a country of 280,000 people, with an economy previously largely based on fishing, in 2001 deCode employed about 700 people. Its significance for the national economy is sometimes compared to one of the major fisheries, the capelin fishery. When Hoffmann La Roche arrived on the scene, a contract was signed with Icelandic clinical collaborators, generally linked with patient groups. It is important to under- score that the company's research on common diseases operates on the principle of informed consent. This fact is often ignored within Iceland and almost entirely outside. What is most controversial on ethical grounds is the proposed Health Sector Database; its construction, its uses, and who has access to it, and the power thus acquired by the company within the Icelandic institutional landscape. Many of those working for deCode Genetics are university trained. This has meant many things, among them that the Icelandic scientific and medical diaspora has been able to return home.[16] It has also meant that the field of scientific and medical institutions has been profoundly altered. Not surprisingly, not everyone is happy about these changes.

About two years after the company began its operation, the Icelandic Ministry of Health dramatically and abruptly announced its plans for the construction of a Health Sector Database on the entire Icelandic population. These plans, initiated by deCode staff and emphasizing a research strategy outlined by Gulcher and Stefánsson,[17] specified how and under what conditions to assemble medical records – and, possibly, combine them with genetic data and genealogical records for the purposes of tracking the presumed genetic bases of diseases and economizing the National Health Service. The first bill for the Health Sector Database was drawn up in secret, presented as a *fait accompli*, and placed before the Parliament in March 1998 as an item demanding urgent action. Immediately, there was a strong public reaction. Critics argued that the measures introduced for the encryption of personal data were insufficient and, moreover, that clauses on patient consent and the monitoring of the database, as well as the rules of access, were poorly developed, at best. Given the "pioneering" nature of the enterprise, a legal model or framework for such a comprehensive project was nonexistent. deCode and the government were forced to retreat. The arrogant and clumsy handling of the bill yielded many enemies, and helped produce a climate of distrust concerning deCode and the current Icelandic government that continues to pervade significant sectors of Iceland's professional classes.

The bill was withdrawn and a second and extensively revised version was soon introduced. There was heated debate and criticism within and outside Parliament, especially over the protection of individual records. After nine months of national debate, the Icelandic Parliament passed the second bill, authorizing the construction of the Health Sector Database (see Figure 6.1). The license to construct the database would be open to competition, the licensee would finance it, and the resulting product would belong to the National Health Service, with the licensee retaining privileged rights to commercialize it for 12 years. Most controversially, the database was expected to operate on the principle of presumed consent, offering Icelanders the opportunity to opt out rather than explicitly requesting informed consent. Although information on DNA, medical data, and genealogical records will only be combined in the context of specific research projects, monitored by ethics committees and public officials, their synergistic coexistence is supposed to enhance each other's economic and medical value. As seems to have been the government's plan all the way through, deCode Genetics received the license to construct the database, in return for a fee paid to the medical service. A rival biotechnological company, Urður, Verðandi, Skuld (UVS) was established in the heat of the debate on the medical

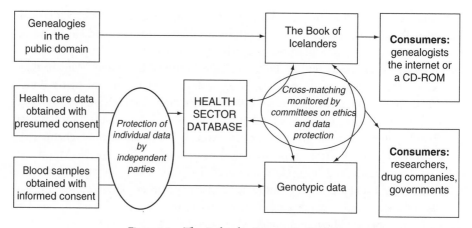

Figure 6.1   The Icelandic Biogenetic Project.

database, partly to challenge deCode's "monopoly" of biomedical research in Iceland. It is not a true rival, however, as it lacks the financial, political, and perhaps scientific resources to compete.

In Sweden, a medical database had already been constructed at the time of the Icelandic debate: Medicinska Biobanken of Västerbotten, a northern region of Sweden. It had been known for years that certain heart and cardiovascular diseases ran in families in Västerbotten.[18] In order to examine the distribution and causes of these diseases, blood samples from most adults in the region were collected over many years and compiled in a biobank. By the end of the 1980s, a sizeable information pool had been amassed, one of the largest ones in the world. Researchers and the state argued, however, that to systematically tap that resource a private genomics company had to become involved. In March 1999, the regional council of Västerbotten signed a contract with the University of Umeå and a newly established biotechnological firm called UmanGenomics for the use and further development of the biobank. According to the agreement, UmanGenomics owns the exclusive right to exploit for commercial purposes genetic information obtained from blood samples collected in Västerbotten over the years and in the near future. The agreement was prepared in the absence of debate from the public and the media, although the public would respond a few years later.

In the early years of the Swedish Biobank, blood donors were requested to sign a statement (a so-called "donation contract") testifying to their agreement to the use of their samples for research purposes. Samples were collected as contributions to the medical service and the Swedish welfare state, often known, significantly, by the term "*Folkhemmet*," literally meaning "the people's home." With the arrival of UmanGenomics, one form of informed consent entered the scene. From then on, blood donors were supposed to be informed about the specific use of their samples. However, it is apparently not the case that donors are consulted each time a new experiment is done or a new use of the material is proposed.[19] Such an approach is "pragmatic" and is widely employed in many countries, including Scandinavia, the

U.K., and the U.S.A. However, it does not fulfill the promise of fully informed consent that is being presented by some critics in the Icelandic case as the ethical standard.

In the U.K., there are plans for advancing genetic epidemiological research along those represented by the Icelandic and Swedish medical databases, namely the U.K. Population Biomedical Collection of the Medical Research Council and the Wellcome Trust. The Population Collection is expected to contain DNA samples from up to 500,000 adults aged between 45 and 60 years, which will be linked to personal medical records and family histories.[20] While this database is still in the planning stage, ongoing collection of data from research subjects is assumed, and genotyping of participants will be done in centralized facilities. The aim of the project is to explore interactions between genes, environment, and lifestyle, focusing on cancer and cardiovascular conditions. Companies are expected to have access to the data on a nonexclusive basis. However, important aspects of the design of the British Collection remain unsettled, including the selection of participants and forms of consent, monitoring and control, and the nature and degree of commercial involvement. In Estonia, the Human Research Act was passed in December 2000 to facilitate the establishment of a Gene Bank Database that will contain phenotype and genotype data of the entire adult Estonian population, around one million people. Again, the chief purpose is to explore the purported genetic causes of common diseases. The major anticipated clients of the bank are research institutions and companies in the fields of bioinformatics, biotechnology, and pharmaceutics.

In sum, the Icelandic, British, Estonian, and Swedish biogenetic projects are fairly similar – despite differences in terms of financing and ownership. As Jane Kaye and Paul Martin point out in their recent legal comparison of the U.K. Population Biomedical Collection and the Icelandic Health Sector Database, "the parallels are striking and the social and ethical issues raised are almost identical."[21] All four projects, moreover, were launched about the same time, at least publicly – in 1998–9. Iceland and Sweden have national health care systems that cover all citizens.[22] Hence the implications for the people in Iceland and Sweden of such projects are probably rather different than they would be in other places such as the U.K. and, especially, the U.S.A., where the health service is more market-driven, selective, and fragmentary. Given, however, the family resemblance of the British, Icelandic, and Swedish projects, one might expect similar debates in all three countries. As we will see, this has not been the case.

Divergent Problematizations

Anthropologist Klaus Høyer has explored the construction and the responses, domestic and international, to the Swedish Biobank.[23] In Västerbotten, he argues, among the subjects of research whose blood is being exploited for commercial purposes by UmanGenomics, there was little discussion of the Biobank – and practically none outside of the local university. There was no significant debate on the national Swedish scene either. While the media discussed the ethical implications of biomedical collections in general, reports on Medicinska Biobanken were fairly positive, praising the people responsible for setting a new standard, the so-called "ethical model of informed consent" developed by UmanGenomics. That model was also praised on similar grounds in international journals, including *Science* and *Nature*.[24]

In the U.K., too, neither the public nor the academic community have paid significant attention to the issue of the medical database. Kaye and Martin point out that the issue of the British Collection has hardly been raised domestically.[25,26] Nor has it been significantly publicized internationally. While the construction of centralized medical databases has gone largely unnoticed in Estonia, Sweden, and the U.K., in Iceland there has been extensive public discussion for over two years, leading to the publication of several hundred articles in national newspapers.

According to opinion polls, the majority of Icelanders support the Health Sector Database; in 1998 a Gallup survey showed that 59 percent were in favor of its development, and a similar poll 16 months later showed that an astonishing 81 percent of the population supported it. On the other hand, public discussion has been fairly critical.[27] Between April 1998 and July 2000, a total of 569 items (news reports and articles) appeared on the biogenetic project in the major Icelandic newspaper *Morgunblaðið* ("The Morning Paper") in connection with four major events: the initial introduction of the bill in the Icelandic Parliament in April 1998; the debate of a revised bill introduced in July 1998; passage of the final bill in December 1998; and the granting to deCode Genetics of the license to construct the database by the Ministry of Health in January 2000.[28] Figure 6.2 shows the distribution of articles over time and the relative proportion of articles "for" the database, "neutral," or "against" it. Out of 190 articles published during the period in question, 121 articles (64 percent) were against the medical database, 65 (34 percent) supported it, and four (2 percent) were neutral. Such coverage and polarization of

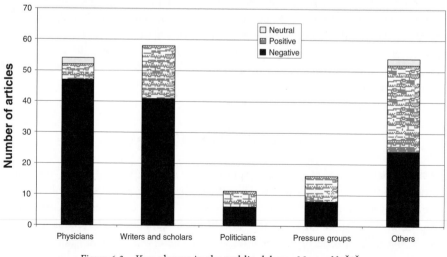

Figure 6.2   Key players in the public debate: *Morgunblaðið*.

biopolitical issues is exceptional in the Icelandic context; certainly no other "medical" issue has been debated to such an extent. The only equivalent, perhaps, in Iceland's recent history is the massive debate on privatization of fishing rights, following a decision by the Icelandic Parliament in 1983 to regulate access to the major Icelandic fisheries by a system of individual transferable quotas (ITQs).[29]

The authors of the articles in Morgunblaðið fall roughly into five main categories: (1) physicians; (2) professional writers (creative writers and journalists), scholars, and experts on biology and informatics; (3) politicians; (4) spokespersons for particular companies, institutions, associations, or pressure groups; and (5) the general public – that is, people who only identify themselves by personal names. Physicians wrote a full 28 percent of all of the articles and their contributions turn out to be overwhelmingly against the project. It should be noted, however, that a small subset of very active doctors wrote most of the negative items. One doctor was the author of 27.8 percent of the items, 15 out of 54 items in this category. Only in the sixth category, representing the "general public," do positive items outnumber negative ones. As to the main issues discussed, they turn on concerns about the protection of privacy, the potential misuse of personal information on health and genetic characteristics, the principle of "informed consent" vis-à-vis "presumed consent," property rights and returns to the community (the state) for the privileged use of the data involved, and rules of access for researchers.

Interestingly, the different components of the biogenetic project have not raised identical ethical questions of privacy and consent. One of its components is the Icelandic genealogical database, the so-called "Book of Icelanders" developed by Frisk Software, a computer company in Reykjavík, in collaboration with deCode Genetics. The Book of Icelanders collapses information from a variety of available sources, focusing on 12 censuses taken from 1703 to 1930. "Pretty much everybody is included," as Friðrik Skúlason, the Director of Frisk Software, put it in a recent talk.[30] It has taken about four years for a whole team of researchers and computer programmers to compile all of the information contained in the Book of Icelanders, and to design the necessary programs for displaying and analyzing it. The point, of course, is not simply to record information about individuals but, rather, to be able to connect them to each other. The "connectivity factor," the rate of documented connections between recorded parents and children, is close to 85 percent. Unlike the medical and genetic records, the Book of Icelanders has not raised major ethical concerns, despite the fact that it is in the public domain, with personal names included (www.islendingabok.is).[31] There are numerous publications of family records in Iceland, and some include photographs of family members. Icelanders have not been bothered by such an exposure of identities, images, and relationships. On the contrary, the public has welcomed the opportunity to explore genealogies electronically and on a grand scale. Significantly, the laws on the Recording and Treatment of Personal Information (§I. 2, 121) from 1989 deliberately "exempt recording [of personal information] for the benefit of genealogical research and the documenting of family histories." Restrictions on these, along the lines of those applied to medical and genetic information, would probably have caused a public outcry.[32] Yet, genealogical records and family trees are rarely innocent phenomena, in the sense that they have a social life of their own, informed by the contours of power and social discourse, by contesting claims about expertise, authority, and control.[33]

The Icelandic biogenetic project, then, has been the center of controversy and widespread discussion, while in Estonia, Sweden, and the U.K., by contrast, there has been virtually no public dialogue on similar projects. Moreover, the international press, the transnational scientific community, and the emerging informal international network of bioethicists have been heavily focused on the Icelandic Database, whereas the British Collection and the Swedish Biobank have only received scant attention, and, if anything, received praise rather than critique. Part of the reason why the Icelandic case has frequently been reported in most of the major international media, usually in a negative fashion, has something to do with the skilful, but somewhat risky, handling by deCode Genetics of public relations, including its frequent reference to genetic "roots" and the "Viking" past. There must be more to the story, however. While it is tempting to conclude that the architects of the British Collection, the Estonian Gene Bank Database, and the Swedish Biobank have somehow avoided the pitfalls of the Icelandic context, the available evidence does not seem to lend support to such a conclusion. The Swedish Biobank[34] and the Icelandic Database are similar in several respects; both projects emphasize the role of private, commercial initiative in human genome research, in collaboration with the public health service, assuming public access to the database for research purposes as long as the commercial interests of the licensee are not being violated. And both involve the use of public medical records collected for decades.

As to the comparison between the British and the Icelandic databases, Kaye and Martin argue that the "current situation in the U.K. is inadequate compared to the measures taken in Iceland and the Government should review where the law may need to be strengthened."[35] "In contrast to Iceland," they point out,

> the UK has historically left the regulation of medical research to the profession rather than to Parliament. An example of this contrast is that in Iceland the Patients Act 1997 controls medical research on humans, whereas there is no such specific legislation in Britain. However, it is notable that in the Britain there is long-established legislation controlling medical research on animals, which allows for an inspectorate to audit and enforce compliance with the statutory standards.[36]

In their study for the Wellcome Trust, Kaye and Martin go on to argue that the experience of Iceland "shows the need for fully independent regulatory bodies that have sufficient powers of investigation and enforcement. The current situation in the U.K. is contrary to this, as the funders of research, the managers of the database, and the regulators can be the same institutions."[37] This comparison is sound and convincing.

It seems, then, that the difference in responses to the British Collection, the Estonian Gene Bank Database, the Icelandic Health Sector Database, and the

Swedish Biobank in the international press and the transnational bioethical community has as much to do with partisan accounts, and pre-formed narratives, as it has to do with any differences between the projects in terms of design and implementation.

Notes

1   This chapter was originally written in the spring of 2001, during Pálsson's sabbatical leave at the University of California at Berkeley. The authors wish to thank Kristín E. Harðardóttir (University of Iceland), Halldór Stefánsson (European Molecular Biology Laboratory, Heidelberg), and Klaus Høyer (University of Copenhagen) for their comments upon earlier drafts. None of these people, of course, is responsible for our arguments or the errors we may make. The research on which this chapter is based has been supported by several funds, including the Nordic Committee for Social Science Research (NOS-S), the Icelandic Science Fund, the University of California at Berkeley, and the University of Iceland.

2   Michel Foucault, "'Practicing Criticism,' or 'Is it Really Important to Think?'" May 30–31, 1981," interview with Didier Eribon, in *Foucault: Politics, Philosophy, Culture*, Lawrence Kritzman, ed. (New York and London: Routledge, 1988), p. 155.

3   See Marilyn Strathern, *After Nature: English Kinship in the Late Twentieth Century* (Cambridge: Cambridge University Press, 1992); Paul Rabinow, *Making PCR: A Story of Biotechnology* (Chicago: University of Chicago Press, 1996); Paul Rabinow, *French DNA: Trouble in Purgatory* (Chicago: Chicago University Press, 1999); K. Finkler, *Experiencing the New Genetics: Family and Kinship on the New Medical Frontier* (Philadelphia: University of Pennsylvania Press, 2000); Lily E. Kay, *Who Wrote the Book of Life? A History of the Genetic Code* (Stanford: Stanford University Press, 2000); Hans-Jörg Rheinberger, "Gene Concepts," in *The Concept of the Gene in Development and Evolution*, R. Falk, P. Beurton, and H.-J. Rheinberger, eds. (Cambridge: Cambridge University Press, 2000); Gísli Pálsson and Kristín E. Harðardóttir, "For Whom the Cell Tolls: Debates about Biomedicine," *Current Anthropology* 43(2), 2002, pp. 271–301; Sarah Franklin and Susan McKinnon, eds., *Relative Values: Reconfiguring Kinship Studies* (Durham, NC: Duke University Press, 2001).

4   The public debate in Iceland often simply refers to "the database issue" (*gagnagrunnsmálid*), subsuming the three databases and their combination. For that reason, it makes sense to collectively label the three databases – medical, genetic, and genealogical – as the "Biogenetic Project." That larger, collective project, it needs to be emphasized, does not result in a permanent database; special permissions are requested from commissions on ethics and data protection to combine the information that the three databases contain for particular projects with detailed research protocols (see Pálsson and Harðardóttir, "For Whom the Cell Tolls").

5   Yves Dezalay and Bryant Garth, *Dealing in Virtue: International Commercial Arbitration and the Construction of a Transnational Legal Order* (Chicago: Chicago University Press, 1996); Yves Dezalay and Bryant Garth, "Droits de l'homme et philanthropie hégémonique," *Actes de la recherche en sciences sociales* 121–122, March 1998, pp. 23–41.

6   Arjun Appardurai, "Introduction: Place and Voice in Anthropological Theory," *Cultural Anthropology* 3(1), 1988, pp. 16–20.

7   Dezalay and Garth, "Droits de l'homme et philanthropie hégémonique."

8   See Arjun Apparadai, "Global Ethnoscapes: Notes and Queries for Transnational Anthropology," in *Recapturing Anthropology: Working in the Present*, Richard G. Fox, ed. (Sante Fe: NM: School of American Research Press, 1991), pp. 295–310; Ulf Hannerz, *Cultural Complexity* (New York: Columbia University Press, 1992); Akhil Gupta and James Ferguson, eds., *Anthropological Locations: Boundaries and Grounds of a Field Science* (Berkeley: University of California Press, 1997); Ulrich Beck, *What is Globalization?*, trans. Patrick Camiller (Cambridge: Polity Press, 2000).

9   For a recent discussion, from a variety of ethnographic perspectives, of Iceland's place in the global context, see Gísli Pálsson and E. Paul Durrenberger, eds., *Images of Contemporary Iceland: Everyday Lives and Global Contexts* (Iowa City: University of Iowa Press, 1995).

10   Dezalay and Garth, *Dealing in Virtue*.

11   Dezalay and Garth, "Droits de l'homme et philanthropie hégémonique," p. 23.

12   Ibid., p. 27.

13   Ibid., p. 40.

14   "Internationalization, however, does not refer only to activity that takes place at the transnational level. The transnational level, in fact, is best understood as a virtual space that provides strategic opportunities for competitive struggles engaged in by national actors..." (Dezalay and Garth, *Dealing in Virtue*, p. 3). Specific individuals are "purportedly selected for their 'virtue' – judgment, neutrality, expertise – yet rewarded as if they are participants in international deal-making. In more sociological terms, the symbolic capital acquired through a career of public service or scholarship is translated into a substantial cash value in international arbitration" (Dezalay and Garth, *Dealing in Virtue*, p. 8).

15   Gísli Pálsson and Paul Rabinow, "Islande: le cas decCode," *Biofutur: le mensuel Européen de biotechnologie* 206, December 2000, pp. 108–111.

16   In recent decades, a number of Icelandic students have carried out postgraduate work at foreign universities, particularly in the U.S.A. and Scandinavia. This is partly because the main university in the country, the University of Iceland in the capital city, offers limited postgraduate opportunities. Many young Icelandic researchers have later taken postdoctoral positions abroad, establishing a more or less permanent basis away from Iceland. This brain drain has been partly stopped or reversed by recent developments in Icelandic biotechnology, largely through the founding of deCode Genetics.

17   Jeff Gulcher and Kári Stefánsson, "Population Genomics: Laying the Groundwork for Genetic Disease Modeling and Targeting," *Clinical Chemistry and Laboratory Medicine* 36, 1998, pp. 532–537.

18   See Klaus Høyer, "Blod, aktier og 'etik'," master's thesis, Institute of Anthropology, University of Copenhagen, Denmark, 2001.

19   Idem.

20   Jane Kaye and Paul Martin, "Safeguards for Research Using Large-scale DNA Collections," *British Medical Journal* 321(4), 2000, pp. 1146–1149.

21   Ibid., p. 1146.

22   On the history and social implications of genetic research in Scandinavia, see T. H. Nielsen, A. Monsen, and T. Tennøe, *Livets tre og kodens kode: fra genetikk til bioteknologi, Norge 1900–2000* (Oslo: Gyldendal Akademisk, 2000); and Lynn Åkesson and Susanne Lundin, *Arvets kultur: Essäer om genetic och samhälle* (Lund: Nordic Academic Press, 2000).

23   Høyer, "Blod, aktier og 'etik'."

24   "Sweden Takes Steps to Protect Tissue Banks," *Science* 286, 1999, p. 894; "Sweden Sets Ethical Standards for Use of Benetic 'Biobanks'," *Nature* 400, 1999, p. 3.

25   Kaye and Martin, "Safeguards for Research."

26   The British scene may be changing, judging from a public statement (of May 9, 2001) by GeneWatch UK, suggesting that, because of lack of appropriate legislation to safeguard genetic privacy and human rights, "plans to develop a national gene-bank – or 'bio-collection' – should be shelved."

27   An extended discussion of the Icelandic debate is presented elsewhere; see Pálsson and Harðardóttir, "For Whom the Cell Tolls."

28   The reason for the focus on *Morgunblaðið* is that it is seen by almost every household in Iceland. Approximately 54,770 copies of *Morgunblaðið* are sold every day. About 64 percent of Icelanders read it every day, as do 71 percent of the inhabitants of the capital city, Reykjavík. For all age groups, *Morgunblaðið* is the most important newspaper. Moreover, it prints almost every article sent to it. As a result, *Morgunblaðið* gives a fairly good idea of public discourse in the country. There are other newspapers, but they are far less significant.

29   See Gísli Pálsson and Paul Rabinow, "The Icelandic Genome Debate," *Trends in Biotechnology* 19(5), 2001, pp. 166–171.

30   Gísli Pálsson, "The Life of Family Trees and the Book of Icelanders," *Medical Anthropology* 21(3/4), 2002, pp. 337–367.

31   The genealogical database takes two forms. One version is available on the Internet for genealogical enthusiasts and the general public. This version includes personal names. It allows users of the Book of Icelanders to trace family trees and to check in a split second their genealogical connection with any Icelander. Another version is being issued to deCode Genetics. In the latter case, no names are included, only numbers or IDs that allow for the combination of different data sets on a limited basis for particular purposes. Such a database, it is argued, combined with genetic and medical data, provides an important historical dimension to the search for mutant genes and the causes of common diseases. A complex process of encryption, surveillance, and monitoring is designed to prevent, if not exclude, any illegitimate use of the data.

32   The laws, however, have recently been changed, as of 2000, partly as a result of the debates on the biogenetic project. The recording of genealogical data no longer enjoys the privilege it had in earlier legal clauses. It remains unclear, on the other hand, how the new laws will be interpreted with respect to genealogical records and their publication.

33   Christiane Klapish-Zuber, "The Genesis of the Family Tree," *I Tatti Studies: Essays in the Renaissance* 4(1), 1991, pp. 105–129; Mary Bouquet, "Family Trees and their Affinity: the Visual Imperative of the Genealogical Diagram," *Journal of the Royal Anthropological Institute (Incorporating Man)* 2, 1996, pp. 43–66.

34   See Høyer, "Blod, aktier og 'etik'."

35   Kaye and Martin, "Safeguards for Research," p. 1148.

36   Ibid., p. 1147.

37   Ibid., p. 1148.

VALUE AND VALUES

7

TIME, MONEY, AND BIODIVERSITY

GEOFFREY C. BOWKER

Introduction

Biodiversity is the feel-bad word for the new millennium. We all know that we want it, and that there is a lot less of it around than there used to be. Indeed, as a species, we have irrupted into timelines stretching back some 700 million years as the cause of the sixth great extinction event in the history of the earth. Extending into the far reaches of Braudel's *longue durée*,[1] we are up there with the meteor that (possibly) killed the dinosaurs. We operate truly globally – affecting every nook and cranny on the planet – except, perhaps, the huge frozen Lake Vostok in the Antarctic, which:

> is absolutely devoid of interference. The youngest water in it is 400,000 years old. It doesn't know anything of human beings, fossil fuels, or plastics. It is a window into life forms and climates of primordial eras.

And even this we are working to explore – at first noninvasively, with "radar sounding, laser altimetry, magnetics, and gravity surveys," and at the end of the day we will probably send a putatively clean robot down there.[2] We commandeer an astonishing percentage of the sun's energy stored on earth and the fresh water that sculpts its features, and we are even digging into the earth's archives to release energy trapped in the form of petroleum.

There are two dramatically different modalities for dealing with the question of biodiversity. In the first, one tries to accord every category of living thing a single biodiversity value, so that the policy-makers can start the work of determining what should be protected and what should not – in much the same way as we now internationally barter pollution. Drawing on Donna Haraway's work,[3] I will call this a modality of implosion. In the second, one tries to list every last living thing – a frenzy of naming that is reaching its apogee with several multi-million dollar international efforts to record just what there is out there. I will call this a modality of particularity.

The two modalities immediately call to mind two great creations of bureaucracy – the coin of the realm (which Schmandt-Besserat[4] places at the origin of writing) and the list (which Jack Goody[5] places at the origin of writing). Each are learned responses developed over millennia to deal with complexity and scope – how to handle a large-scale enterprise through abstraction and classification. So it's unsurprising that these two behemoths are stalking biodiversity.

I show how these two modalities are constructed around a similar temporality: background stasis and foreground change (as in the production of animation pictures). My argument is that in order to write our "natural contract,"[6] we are producing a singular and rich temporality as complex in its own way as that read out of myths by, say, Lévi-Strauss. It is a temporality that as well as being powerful in the world (for who can doubt the power of bureaucracies and the efficacy of technoscience?) is integrally eschatological and mythic. I argue that paying due attention to the full richness of our current discourse about biodiversity entails reading our own emergent global society's discourse just as we would read any other discourse in societies which have never been modern.[7]

The argument comes in three parts. First, I give a brief account of some recent work in the history of money, as a way of opening up the issue of what we can look for in the modalities of accounting for biodiversity that will be the topic of my inquiry. Second, I look at one organization of the modality of implosion. Third, I look at one organization of the modality of particularity. My examples will be drawn from current efforts to database – figuratively, or as we shall see, literally – life on earth.

Money, Memory, and Discourse

The archetypal figure adjudicating between boundaries is that of the merchant, who is the trader between the inside (members of the *polis* in classical Greece) and the outside (neighboring communities that wish to operate some kind of trade). In his book *Le prix de la verité* (the price/prize of truth),[8] Marcel Hénaff traces the vicissitudes of this mediation over time, tying it initially to Plato's apothegms against the sophists selling that which is beyond price – philosophic truth. At this historic conjuncture when we are renegotiating the natural contract, the array of characters may be different, but the figure remains the same. We have something beyond price: the miraculous bounty of the earth – that gift we enjoy or invaluable creation we steward.[9] We are in the process of setting a price on it. The boundary between nature and culture we are creating is similarly textured to that of the definition of a community – it can be strictly geographic (natural wilderness on one side and urban mean streets on the other) but it is more generally the outcome of heterogeneous, partly conflicting, operational definitions. The merchant figures in this case are international organizations such as the Organization for Economic Cooperation and Development (OECD), which has in the past decade taken up the banner of brokering international deals on the environment:

> A healthy environment is a pre-requisite for a strong and healthy economy, and both are needed for sustainable development. The OECD provides a forum for countries to share their experiences and to develop concrete recommendations for the development and implementation of policies that can address environmental problems in an effective and economically efficient way. . . . Increasingly the problems they face are more complex, and will require co-operative action at the international level (e.g. climate change) or coordinated packages of policies across regions and/or sectors (e.g. biodiversity, agricultural pollution, and transport). . . . OECD supports its governments in addressing these problems primarily through the work of its Environment Policy Committee, through Joint Working Parties on Agriculture and Environment and on Trade and Environment and through Joint Meetings of Tax and Environment Experts. Overall, these activities contribute to the crosscutting work of the OECD on sustainable development.[10]

Sustainable development marches under the proud banner of OECD's programmatic definition, which has been endorsed by the World Bank, the International Monetary Fund, the World Wildlife Fund, and World Heritage among others, and was common to participants in the World Summit on Sustainable Development held in Johannesburg in 2002.[11] Contemporary discourse of biodiversity is structured within this policy framework.[12]

In order to render two things (species, wetlands, pollutants) comparable, one needs a token that can circulate in their stead – so that, for example, you can trade off a marine habitat with such and such a degree of richness with a wetland area with a comparable degree. Not even the spatio-temporal unit comes prepackaged. In order to preserve a wetland you have to preserve its adjacent water table, since otherwise draining an adjacent field can drain the wetland indirectly. Similarly for time – if you look at the decimation of caribou stock through current logging practices, you get a very different picture of sustainability if you take the base unit to be ten or 200 years.[13] Yet you do need a tradable unit that can circulate freely without containing too much historical baggage. In *Genèse* ("Genesis"),[14] Michel Serres writes that money is the "degree zero of information." He argues that in order to render a thing (a commodity) or an action (digging a field) into money, then all detail about the nature of the thing or action has to be blackboxed, so that what is left is the smooth surface of a coin or note, with a quantitative value attached to it. Money by this account constitutes the least possible information that can be shared about events and objects while still maintaining a viable discourse around them.

When he refers to money as a degree zero, Serres is not asserting that it is an empty set. Indeed not. As Keith Hart remarks:

> The word *money,* as I mentioned at the beginning, comes from Moneta, a name by which the Roman queen of the gods, Juno, was known. . . . Moneta was a translation of

the Greek Mnemosyne, the goddess of memory and mother of the Muses, each of whom presided over one of the nine arts and sciences. Moneta in turn was clearly derived from the Latin verb *moneo*, whose first meaning is 'to remind, put in mind of, bring to one's recollection' ... There seems little doubt that, for the Romans at least, money in the form of coinage was an instrument of collective memory that needed divine protection, like the arts.[15]

What is remembered in the coin is precisely that which is needed in order to carry on economic discourse. So doing, the coin continually evokes (recalls) the compact made with the state to honor information about value expressed in the form of an amount on a coin. Hénaff traces the etymology of *alatheia* (the female avatar of truth in attic Greece) to "memory" as well. The struggle between the "sophists" and the "philosophers" about selling truth mirrors that between the global policy-makers and deep environmentalists about dealing in biodiversity. The philosophers and environmentalists go for deep, "real" truth or wilderness (total memory of thought or world), the sophists and policy-makers for marketable truth (a minimal memory set).

The trouble is that while it is clear in a general sense that we as a globalized species and globalizing economy are currently deeply renegotiating the relationship between nature and culture, we really have no place to site a reflective discourse about the range of ecological and economic issues. We can take a lead from Lesley Kurke's brilliant *Coins, Bodies, Games, and Gold*.[16] Kurke explores the discursive dimension of money through analyzing texts in Herodotus. She starts from the curious fact that there is exceedingly little mention of coins in texts for the first 200 years after the first minting. Indeed, one must go as late as Aristotle to find a philosophic treatment of money. However, she notes, there is a rich thread tying together two alternative modes of discourse. The first is the discourse of the symposium. This is associated with leisure, aristocracy, the masculine ideal, and pure metals (gold and silver). Then there is the discourse of the agora, associated with bustling labor, merchants, effeminacy, and base metals (alloys standing as surrogates for the coin). In this chapter, I locate a similarly rich and heterogeneous list associated with the language of developing a single currency for biodiversity; figuring prominently in that list is a reading of social time and of memory – here, I concentrate on social time.

Modalities of Implosion: The Language of Money in Biodiversity Discourse

The word "biodiversity" is of relatively recent coinage – it is no more than 40 years old. It was developed within the emerging field of conservation biology – a science with a mission[17] to preserve our ecology. Nils Eldredge[18] argues that the ecological perspective (as opposed to the taxonomic perspective, which I look at in the next section) is an economic one – talking as it does about the way in which species interact in the economy of nature. It thus harks back to the common roots of ecology and economics in the Greek word for household, *oikos*.[19]

It has increasingly been seen as important within the biodiversity community to bring ecology and economy together, to find a way of expressing the value of "ecosystem goods and services" for humanity. The argument goes that biodiversity conservation can only take place if we have a powerful language shared between scientists (who often see themselves as philosophers who have been forced into sophism) and policy-makers. The former want to pack as much complexity as they can into the token that policy-makers can then exchange, without knowing anything of the science – just as the customers don't want to know details about the labor and art that went into forging a bust; they want to know just enough so that they can be assured that the outlay of money is reasonable. Thus the policy-makers can say: "We will take this bit of wilderness but we will give you another bit, which has, in the best of all possible worlds, an equal or greater biodiversity value. Or we can lose that species if we preserve another of similar value." Only if we can account for diversity will we be able to preserve it.

So how does one go about measuring biodiversity? The intuitive step of assigning a unit value to each species and then totaling species counts in a given area will not work for two reasons. First, if you want to save a useful minimum set for life on earth, you want maximum *spread* of biodiversity value:

> For example, a dandelion and a giant redwood can be seen to represent a richer collection of characters in total, and so greater diversity value, than another pair of more similar species, a dandelion and a daisy... This shows how the phenotypic characters (or the genes that code for them) could provide a 'currency' of value for biodiversity. Pursuing this idea, we will then need to maximize richness in the character currency within the conservationists' 'bank' of managed or protected areas.[20]

In other words, there's no point in preserving a large number of species within a small spread of genetic difference. Second, there's no way to preserve just one species – so it is not a useful unit of analysis:

> Often, higher-order species on the food chain have the most exacting environmental requirements and are thus valuable indicators of the health of the entire ecosystem; they or others may be critical 'keystone' species because they are located at the center of a network of interdependencies. Thus, as a practical matter, species values become proxies for ecosystem values: the Endangered Species Act in the United States is an embodiment of this principle in policy. And of course we regularly justify large expenditures to save some species (e.g., the African rhinoceros) but not others (there is no Save the Furbish Lousewort Society).[21]

Some species, then, are more important than others, since they stand as proxies for ecosystems. Species congregate in complex ecological groups.

The species, which is the proximate unit we most intuitively respond to,[22] holds then a tension between information (going down to the gene level) and community (going up to the ecosystem level). Further, the species concept is of itself highly controversial – there are a number of conflicting ways of severing the great chain of being.[23] Central here is that species are not stable, well-defined entities. The difficulty is in trying to snip up emergent processes into stable analytic coins. Much biodiversity discourse is centered on preserving that which is – a current set of species, our current climate conditions, and so forth. We talk about preservation and conservation, not potentiating dynamic change. On this logic, we should be preventing orogenesis, which has a huge impact on climate change – the thrust of the Indian subcontinent into Asia, which is throwing up the Himalayas, has been a significant cause of the lowering of temperature through trapping carbon dioxide; volcanic outgassing is seen as a major variable in lowering the temperature through causing higher reflection of the sun's energy.[24] Paradoxically, preventing global warming is extremely harmful for biodiversity – when there were temperate forests up in the Arctic, the biodiversity potential of the world was higher than it now is. A second paradox of the battle between saving stable sets and potentiating change is that it leads to preserving ecosystems which in the present might seem particularly uninteresting to those who care about the environment. Thus Terry Erwin and others talk of preserving evolutionary potential – "species-dynamo" areas:

> However, there are great difficulties in predicting future patterns of diversification . . . in patchy and changing environments, particularly as projected human-driven changes are unlikely to reflect simply those of the past. Following Erwin and Brooks et al.'s arguments, the perverse result of extrapolating future diversification 'potential' from recent history is that it leads to favoring conservation of species that are particularly similar to another (e.g. faunas with large numbers of rodents), in preference to biotas with more dissimilar and diverse species.[25]

The projects of preserving the possibility of change for a rich future or preserving the current set of species are at best kissing cousins.

Most units defined analytically in conservation biology run into this problem. If you go up a level to the ecosystem, you run into the problem of defining just what sort of a thing an ecosystem is. R. V. O'Neill, for example, argues that the ecosystem concept stabilizes the system "at a relatively constant equilibrium point";[26] indeed, he goes on to say that:

> Concepts like stability and ecosystem are ambiguous and defined in contradictory ways. In fact there is no such thing as an integrated, equilibrial, homeostatic ecosystem: It is a myth . . . !²⁷

The word "myth" is a useful one here, since it is surely what we are dealing with. Much biodiversity currency discourse is concerned with rendering the present eternal – moving ourselves and our planet out of the flow of history. We want this set of species to last, we want this climate to continue, and so forth. The background (our canvas) should stay stable while the foreground (human attainment of perfection) should be changing rapidly – even if we no longer use the term in vogue from the 1830s to the 1960s in the West: progress. The *nec plus altra* is the cloning movement.

Thus a company in San Diego offers gene banking by holding out the possibility of pet cloning (see Figure 7.1).

Indeed, one vision (popularized in the film *Jurassic Park*) is that we can preserve biodiversity by banking gene sequences and rolling out diversity when we need it . . .

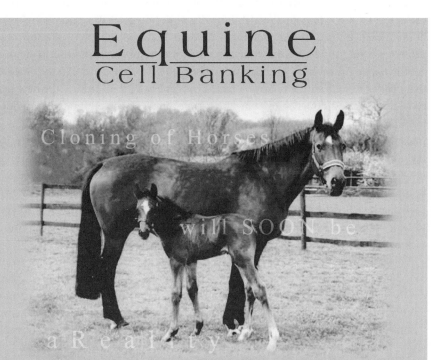

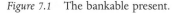
Figure 7.1   The bankable present.

Here is one of the central problems of trying to collapse multiple registers into a single currency that contains just the necessary information – the resulting units of analysis will be riven with contradictions:

> If there is no stable equilibrium, why bother to conserve?...How do you restore ecosystems when you don't know what to restore them to?[28]

Reid Helford[29] has written of this difficulty within the oak savannah restoration project in Illinois. He points to the difficulty of deciding what is natural and what is human (and, indeed, to engineering a division between the two). The restoration project is trying to restore the ecosystem as it was before European settlement. And yet the native Americans – through fire technology[30] – were central in the creation of that ecosystem. Given the relatively recent orogenesis of the Rockies, the new prairie ecosystem turned duocrop (except along train lines) of the American Midwest has been created out of a string of invasive plants, animals, and people. For the policy-makers in the project, white humans fall on the side of culture and so are external to the ecosystem, whereas native Americans fall on the side of nature and are internal to it. O'Neill points out that, in general, we constitute "the only important species that is considered external from its ecosystem, deriving goods and services rather than participating in ecosystem dynamics."[31] That old nature/culture divide – so central to Lévi-Strauss's mythologies – is alive and well and equally torqued within modern technoscientific mythology.

This brings us to the question of the work that is being done in order to effect that divide today. The mode that I will examine here is the move to value "ecosystem goods and services" – this move has structured the discourse of seeking to value biodiversity. Now if we are external to nature, we stand in the position of the Creator – outside of the flow of history, acting on, but not being of, the world. It is possible to argue that this move's current form is associated with the science of the Industrial Revolution, and in particular Lyell's geology (which discusses the question of man and nature at length). However, establishing the case is too long a project for this chapter.[32] For now, I treat solely the contemporary form of the divide.

So. Nature is external. We need to find a way of expressing nature in terms of our own value systems. If we start putting number values on aspects of our environment, we quickly run into the problem of infinity:

> As a whole, ecosystem service have infinite use value because human life could not be sustained without them. The evaluation of the tradeoffs currently facing society, however, requires estimating the *marginal* value of ecosystem services (the value yielded by an additional unit of the service, all else held constant) to determine the costs of losing – or the benefits of preserving – a given amount or quality of services.[33]

And there is a lot of infinity about. Take the soil, for example:

> Soil provides an array of ecosystem services that are so fundamental to life that their total value could only be expressed as infinite. . . . Human well-being can be maintained and fostered only if earth's soil resources are as well.[34]

Now infinite values are not of much use in economics, so in general the shift is toward dealing with units of analysis that produce finite numbers and delete inconvenient infinities (a ploy borrowed from the physics community, perhaps).

There has accordingly been an attempt to separate out the different kinds of value that nature provides. Use value is our current use of the ecosphere. This produces a very large, but vaguely quantifiable number:

> Despite recent estimates that the Earth's ecological systems are worth about $33 trillion annually, the comparatively low cost of maintaining the biological diversity that underpins these services is ignored.[35]

Not even Bill Gates can rival the ecosystem; however, he may well be worth Australia. This use value can be taken at any unit of analysis – the ecosystem, the species, or the germplasm:

> In common with all agricultural crops, the productivity of modern wheat and corn is sustained through constant infusions of fresh germplasm with its hereditary characteristics ... Thanks to this regular 'topping up' of the genetic or hereditary constitution of the United States' main crops, the Department of Agriculture estimates that germplasm contributions lead to increases in productivity that average around 1 percent annually, with a farm-gate value that now tops $1 billion ...[36]

This last is from a paper describing our genetic "library" – the modern form of the book of nature metaphor, which has a history stretching back many centuries. The figures given are frankly absurd – there is no way that such measures can be made of a system we are part of, and in a world in which we don't build statistics in such a way that they could possibly reflect use value – but at least they are finite. We are moving into the implosion of multiple registers into a single value.

But use value alone is not enough to describe the value of biodiversity – there is also option value. Option value is the interest that we have in keeping our current stock of biodiversity against possible future uses – thus a rare strain of corn in Mexico might help us if a new parasite emerges which attacks all other strains of corn apart from this one ... Infinity rears its ugly head again: option value with genetic features as the basic currency

> gives any included attributes equal value because of the inevitable ignorance or uncertainty of precise future needs. Biodiversity conservation would then focus on maximizing the amount of 'currency' (the number of valued biological attributes, features or characters) to be held within the protection system 'bank' (the set of protected species, ecosystems or areas). Thus the paradoxical consequence of equal value for attributes as units of currency is that their owners, the individuals, species or areas, may have different values because they contribute different numbers of complementary attributes for representation in the protection system.[37]

A third major category added to option value is existence value – the value that I derive from the existence of the Grand Canyon, say, even though I have no intention of ever going there.[38] I feel that way about Mount Uluru (the rock formerly known as Ayer's). This value is rarely quantified.

With use value and option value as the key components of a biodiversity currency – being those components that produce numbers – they are expected to do a lot of work. They should stand as proxies for other measures, which get a mention but are then to be ignored. For example, the World Conservation Union has stated that:

> the justification for preserving genetic diversity is that it is 'necessary to sustain and improve agricultural, forestry and fisheries production, to keep open future options, as a buffer against harmful environmental change, and as the raw material for much scientific and industrial innovation – and as a matter of moral principle.'[39]

The potentially infinite – the moral principle in this case – gets pushed into the sidelines, with the unstated assertion that moral principle will be served by maximizing use and option value. Gretchen Daily makes the same move – relegating the infinite to the sidelines; and structuring the economic argument in such a way that its value is incorporated:

> Our concentration is on use values; aesthetic and spiritual values associated with ecosystem services are only lightly touched upon in this book, having been eloquently described elsewhere.[40]

However, surely Derrida gets it right: that which is excluded is often that which structures the discourse.

The valuation is created as a way of collapsing multiple registers (aesthetic, religious, spiritual) onto an artificially created unit of currency that can then circulate within modes of discourse hostile to just these sets of registers. In a sense, it's surrogacy all the way down in biodiversity research: the only way you can measure all the life in a given area is to follow Terry Erwin's model, say, and fog the area to count dead beetles – an efficient mode of counting that has the down side of possibly destroying some highly specialized species (beetles can be specific to a given tree). All Taxa Biodiversity Inventories are slow, clumsy, and very expensive – all else is surrogacy, such as the aerial map of vegetation cover standing as a surrogate of animal life, with the assumption that we know which species tend to be associated with which cover. Williams and Gaston start their excellent paper on biodiversity by sidelining the difficult issue of surrogacy when trying to implode multiple values (here "the aims of conservationists"):

> We ask whether maximizing inter-specific genetic diversity necessarily fulfils the aims of conservationists most directly, or whether the consequences of this choice may actually be at odds with their objectives, and whether more appropriate currencies for conservation can be identified. We are not concerned here with the extent to which one currency can serve as a surrogate for another, which is regarded as a separate issue.[41]

They conclude by embracing it:

> In reality, currencies may yet prove to be highly correlated among species, so that any direct diversity measurement could present an approximate surrogate for any other, although this remains to be confirmed.[42]

The currency, then, holds out the promise of collapse of multiple social values onto a single measure. If engineered correctly, this currency will enter into policy discourse in just such a way as to promote a broadly common set of values held by conservation biologists. This is a dangerous move, akin to one (studied by Bowker and Star[43]) by nurses seeking recognition for their *process* work by cutting it up into regular temporal units (half-hour work units), which could then be recognized within hospital accounting systems. In the case of biodiversity, the currency move is collapsing emergence into units (the commodity form) that circulate in a very flat, linear time and space.[44]

The money tokens that are created must be kept in circulation, and in a space that has been evacuated of events. The eye should be on foreground change (human development, defining the boundary of culture) against a persistent canvas (background stasis, defining the boundary of nature).

Modalities of Particularity: The Tree of Life

A second modality for accounting for biodiversity is that of the tree of life. This is the art of the particular – any surrogate is a counterfeit, and to counterfeit (as the old paper money used to say) is death.

The tree of life is a venerable mode of representation of our knowledge about life, its origins and development. Life starts at the root, the single-celled protoplasm, and then claws its way up the tree until it pinnacles at Homer Simpson;[45] or devolves, *à la* McLuhan, into a biker.[46] This representation is an extremely powerful one – it stems from an unsystematic but very general move in the 19th century away from classifying objects by their innate qualities (the Aristotelian turn) to classifying them by their genesis (Tort 1989).[47] This new classification modality was associated in complex ways with the regime of governmentality (Foucault 1991).[48] The emergent technoscientific empires of the 19th century developed the discipline of statistics (which etymologically refers to the state) and new systems of classification to deal with the vast amounts of impersonal information that had to be collected in order for the Empire to function efficiently.[49]

Today, in both the social and the natural sciences, the tree is starting to look somewhat ragged. A more modern form of the tree is less attached to its roots.[50] This new tree has no clear roots in the ground – it's an exercise to work out where the origin is stashed away. Viruses don't have simple genetic histories in the way that larger organisms do:[51] they are sometimes seen as being devolved from higher life forms (a parasite – that prototypical troubler of inside and outside, both physiologically and socially[52] – that discovered a simpler way to get its genetic message across), or as evolving in pace with their host – not from any internal mechanism. This is the problem of Occam's razor. It is a computationally huge task to calculate all the possible phylogenies (branches of the tree of life) – there are many possible routes that lead to the present. Thus when producing computer models it is assumed that time is unidirectional – species cannot lose characteristics once acquired. And yet we know empirically that some species do just that. It is assumed that history is simple. One species can never branch off more than one species at a time. There's no particular reason for this assumption other than it makes the calculation possible with current technology (and this is perhaps reason enough...). It is assumed that this simple history only has one underlying cause. If genes can spread by contagion rather than be adopted from parents, then the problem of calculation becomes truly staggering. And yet we know that some genes spread by contagion.[53] For some trees, it is assumed that the clock of this unidirectional, simple, monocausal history is also as regular as clockwork. These trees were drawn by the molecular biologists of the 1980s and 1990s who sought for mitochondrial Eve – our shared progenitor – and who attacked phylogenies produced in other disciplines as being historically inaccurate. Their phylogenies were based on the assumption of a regular rate of mutation – so that the current percentage of difference from the root stock represented the amount of time since divergence. Given the overwhelming evidence for differential rates of mutation, the quest today is to find sites on genes that can serve as relatively reliable timekeepers. So trees as representations of life or knowledge are a problem for the white-coated molecular biologist as well as for the unwashed postmodern. There is nothing surprising in these convergent representational problems – Gerald Holton,[54] for example, produces a number of others from the fields of history, physics, and mathematics over the past century and a half.

The tree of life maps the diversity of life. To do so, it breaks the web of life into countable units. These units are assumed to be entities in the world – although there is fierce debate over their nature. These countable units are then aligned in a regular (in some cases, metronomic) historical time – in which there is no turning back and no speeding up. The unchanging species is mapped onto the flat time. Although temporality is thus doubly invoked, and is clearly central to the discourse, it is often invisible in discussions of the tree. And yet this folded temporality is precisely our effort to map the world, in all its complexity, onto a linear, featureless time.

A tree, then, is an expression of the modality of particularity. It is an attempt to represent all of life in its infinite diversity within a single representational structure – so that even the ephemeral mayfly can find its place. Such modalities are constitutive of much biodiversity discourse today. Stewart Brand's All Species Foundation,[55] as well as the All Taxa Biodiversity Inventories,[56] are recent multi-million dollar efforts to produce better lists of life on this planet. This is the other side of the coin from the modality of implosion described above. With the modality of particularity we find background stasis. Events – which would involve entities, a place, and a time – are systematically excluded from the representational framework, thus creating background stasis and an argument for taxonomists about whether cladistic trees have roots (represent change over what we have seen to be a deliberately smoothed, anisotropic time) or are formal devices for assigning names. The result is a packaging of species that guarantees humans some kind of immunity from the flow of natural time (we are a single, well-defined species) and so creates room for a foregrounding of the changes we induce on the external object "nature."

Conclusions

In a modality of implosion, representations are made of several registers within a single structure – the representations are imploded into a singular form rather than exploded into full detail. A rich example of this comes from the Lukasa memory board,[57] which contains topographical, historical, property, and political relations within a single handheld board (see Figure 7.2).

Within biodiversity discourse, the standard modality of implosion is scarcely so rich. This modality seeks to reduce plants, animals, viruses, bacteria, and so forth into a single "biodiversity value," which can used in making policy decisions about what to save and how to save it: for example, it might turn out more efficient in biodiversity terms to let a rare species die out if a sister species, with much the same genetic stock, is unthreatened.

Temporal orientation (how we conceive of the present, past, and future and the flow) is central to the operation of contemporary modalities of implosion and particularity; and this orientation simultaneously operates on the register of the nature of the world and the operation of our political economy. In the case of the coin, we saw the mapping of infinity onto an amount. In that process, which revolved around the construction of a nature/culture divide, we saw the cutting up of emergent forms into units that could circulate within Newtonian space and time. In the case of the tree, we saw the breaking down of complex historical time into regular, calculable units. Common to the enterprise of both modalities is the incorporation of natural objects into cultural discourse. Describing biodiversity and its value through these modalities involves creating databases out of which only certain sets of narrative form can emerge – the story of the house that Jack built, a simple story that proceeds in a regular rhythm.

Attention to these modalities draws us to a (global) anthropological reading of biodiversity discourse. This new discourse is confronting other ways of knowing (referred to as indigenous, local, and vernacular – all terms have their problems if you think about their other – knowledge), not as another myth system that revolves around the construction of the nature/culture divide, and yet which has some valuable nuggets of truth, but as a truth system that revolves around the way the world is. This seems unfair. Money is not the optimal symbolic form for bringing together the various actants in mutual accord. As currently being worked through, money discourse encourages the evacuation of event-based ontologies through the exclusion of just the sort of memory we should be exploring in order to deal with planetary management. In so doing, it settles the question of the mediation between

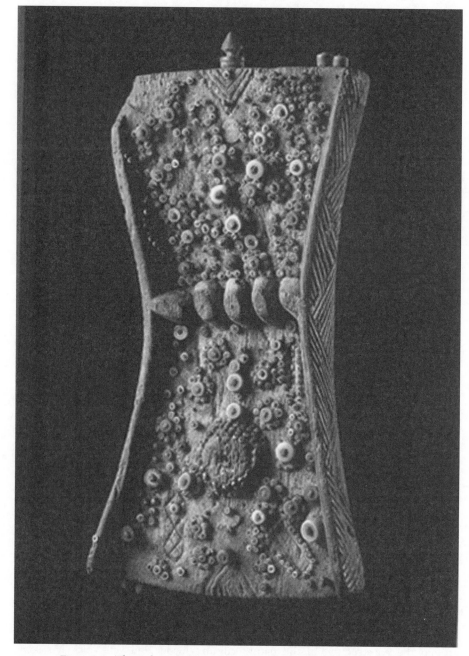

Figure 7.2   The Luba tribe's memory device, the Lukasa memory board.

inside and outside (nature and culture) in a way that is ineluctably ethnocentric. It is ethnocentric because the discourse is structured by the way "we" handle the nature/culture divide; it casts the world and time according to the very singular *oikos* of our emergent globalizing late-capitalist *ethnos*. Stable tokens beget tokenism.

Notes

1   Fernand Braudel, *Capitalism and Material Life, 1400–1800* (London: Weidenfeld and Nicolson, 1973).

2   Robin E. Bell, Michael Studinger, Anahita A. Tikku, Garry K. C. Clarke, Michael M. Gutner, and Chuck Meertens, "Origin and Fate of Lake Vostok Water Frozen to the Base of the East Antarctic Ice Sheet," *Nature* 416, March 21, 2002, 307–310.

3   Donna Haraway, *Modest-Witness@Second-Millennium. FemaleMan-Meets-OncoMouse: Feminism and Technoscience* (New York: Routledge, 1997).

4   Denise Schmandt-Besserat, *Before Writing* (Austin: University of Texas Press, 1992).

5   Jack Goody, *The Logic of Writing and the Organization of Society* (Cambridge: Cambridge University Press, 1986).

6   Michel Serres, *Le contrat naturel* (Paris: F. Bourin, 1990).

7   Bruno Latour, *We Have Never Been Modern* (Cambridge, MA: Harvard University Press, 1993).

8   Marcel Hénaff, *Le prix de la verité* (Paris: Seuil, 2002).

9   Donald Worster, *Nature's Economy: A History of Ecological Ideas* (Cambridge: Cambridge University Press, 1994).

10 See http://www.sourceoecd.com/content/templates/co/co_main.htm?comm=environm

11 Miriam Padolsky, "Environmental Justice at the Canadian Environment Ministry: Boundary Objects and Boundary Work in Sustainable Development Policy," unpublished MS.

12 David Takacs, *The Idea of Biodiversity: Philosophies of Paradise* (Baltimore: Johns Hopkins University Press, 1996).

13 Richard Jonasse, "Making Sense: Geographic Information Technologies and the Control of Heterogeneity," thesis, Department of Communication, University of California at San Diego, 2001.

14 Michel Serres, *Genèse* (Paris: B. Grasset, 1982).

15 Keith Hart, *The Memory Bank: Money in an Unequal World* (London: Profile Books, 1999), pp. 256–257.

16 Lesley Kurke, *Coins, Bodies, Games, and Gold: The Politics of Meaning in Archaic Greece* (Princeton, NJ: Princeton University Press, 1999).

17 Takacs, *The Idea of Biodiversity.*

18 Nils Eldredge, "Where the Twain Meet: Causal Intersections Between the Genealogical and Ecological Realms," in *Systematics, Ecology, and the Biodiversity Crisis* (New York: Columbia University Press, 1992), pp. 59–76.

19 Raymond Williams, *Keywords: A Vocabulary of Culture and Society* (London: Fontana Paperbacks, 1983).

20 The Natural History Museum, London, http://www.nhm.ac.uk/science/projects/worldmap/diversity/index.html; accessed 2002.

21 On the problems of "charismatic megafauna," see, for example, Thomas C. Edwards, Collin G. Homer, et al., *Utah GAP Analysis: An Environmental Information System* (Logan, UT, National Biological Service, Utah Cooperative Fish and Wildlife Research Unit, Utah State University), section 1, para. 1.

22 George Lakoff, *Women, Fire, and Dangerous Things: What Categories Reveal about the Mind* (Chicago: University of Chicago Press, 1987); Peter F. Stevens and S. P. Cullen, "Linnaeus, the Cortex-Medulla Theory, and the Key to his Understanding of Plant Form and Natural Relations," *Journal of the Arnold Arboretum* 71, April 1990, pp. 179–220.

23 Edward O. Wilson, *Species: New Interdisciplinary Essays* (Cambridge, MA: The MIT Press, 1999).

24 Richard J. Huggett, *Environmental Change: The Evolving Ecosphere* (London: Routledge, 1997).

25 Paul H. Williams, Kevin J. Gaston, and Chris J. Humphries, "Do Conservationists and Molecular Biologists Value Differences between Organisms in the Same Way?" *Biodiversity Letters* 2(3), 1994, pp. 67–78.

26 Robert V. O'Neill, "Is it Time to Bury the Ecosystem Concept? (With Full Military Honors, Of Course!)," *Ecology* 82(12), 2001, pp. 3275–3284; see p. 3275.

27 Ibid., p. 3276.

28 Idem.

29 Reid M. Helford, "Rediscovering the Presettlement Landscape: Making the Oak Savanna Ecosystem 'Real,'" *Science, Technology and Human Values* 24(1), 1999, pp. 55–79.

30 Stephen J. Pyne, *Fire in America: A Cultural History of Wildland and Rural Fire* (Seattle: University of Washington Press, 1997).

31 O'Neill, "Is it Time to Bury the Ecosystem Concept?" p. 3299; compare Nils Eldredge, *Dominion: Can Nature and Culture Co-Exist?* (New York: H. Holt, 1995).

32 See Geoffrey C. Bowker, *Memory Practices in the Sciences* (forthcoming).

33 Gretchen C. Daily, "Introduction: What are Ecosystem Services?" in *Nature's Services: Societal Dependence on Natural Ecosystems*, G. C. Daily, ed. (Washington, DC: Island Press, 1997), pp. 1–10.

34 Gretchen C. Daily, Pamela A. Mattson, and Peter M. Vitousek, "Ecosystem Services Supplied by Soil, " in Daily, ed., *Nature's Services*, pp. 113–132.

35 Williams et al., "Do Conservationists and Molecular Biologists Value Differences between Organisms in the Same Way?"

36 Norman Myers, "Biodiversity's Genetic Library," in Daily, ed., *Nature's Services*, pp. 255–273.

37 Williams et al., "Do Conservationists and Molecular Biologists Value Differences between Organisms in the Same Way?"

38 Lawrence H. Goulder and Donald Kennedy, "Valuing Ecosystem Services: Philosophical Bases and Empirical Methods," in Daily, ed., *Nature's Services*, pp. 23–47.

39 Williams et al., "Do Conservationists and Molecular Biologists Value Differences between Organisms in the Same Way?"

40 Daily, "Introduction: What are Ecosystem Services?"

41 Williams et al., "Do Conservationists and Molecular Biologists Value Differences between Organisms in the Same Way?"

42 Idem.

43 See Geoffrey C. Bowker and Susan Leigh Star, *Sorting Things Out: Classification and its Consequences* (Cambridge, MA: The MIT Press, 1999).

44 Alfred Sohn-Rethel, "Science as Alienated Consciousness," *Radical Science Journal* 5, 1975, pp. 65–101.

45 Matt Groening, *Bart Simpson's Guide to Life* (New York: HarperCollins, 1993), pp. 90–91.

46 Marshall McLuhan and Quentin Fiore (produced by Jerome Agel), *The Medium is the Massage: An Inventory of Effects* (San Francisco: HardWired, 1996).

47 Patrick Tort, *La raison classificatoire: les complexes discursifs – quinze études* (Paris, Aubier, 1989).

48 Michel Foucault, "Governmentality," in *The Foucault Effect: Studies in Governmentality,* Graham Burchill, Collin Gordon, and Peter Miller, eds. (Chicago: University of Chicago Press, 1991).

49 The "information revolution" is often misascribed to the invention of computing technology – the real revolution in information gathering accompanied the Industrial Revolution in Europe: information technology accompanied but did not occasion the changes.

50 See http://peptide.ncsa.uiuc.edu/tutorials_current/Tree_of_Life/

51 See http://tolweb.org/tree?group=life

52 Michel Serres, *The Parasite* (Baltimore: Johns Hopkins University Press, 1982).

53 For a full discussion of these issues, see Wayne P. Maddison and David R. Maddison, *MacClade: Analysis of Phylogeny and Character Evolution. Version 3.*

54 Gerald J. Holton, *Thematic Origins of Scientific Thought: Kepler to Einstein* (Cambridge, MA: Harvard University Press, 1988).

55 See http://www.all-species.org/

56 See, for example, http://iris.biosci.ohio-state.edu/projects/atbi_db.html

57 Mary Nooter Roberts and Allen F. Roberts, with contributions by S. Terry Childs et al., *Memory: Luba Art and the Making of History* (New York: Museum for African Art, 1996).

8

ANTIRETROVIRAL GLOBALISM, BIOPOLITICS, AND THERAPEUTIC CITIZENSHIP

VINH-KIM NGUYEN

Early in 1998, a small youth group in Ouagadougou, Jeunes sans frontières, which had become successful in carrying out model sexual health and AIDS awareness raising campaigns, embarked on a new project. In a small house with a courtyard in an outlying neighborhood of Burkina Faso's capital city, the group opened a "Friendship Centre" for people with HIV. An erratic flow of donated medicines from France provided a small stock for the dispensary – "nothing much," but certainly better than what was available at the nearby state-run dispensary, where years of World Bank mandated cost-recovery had long ago emptied the pharmacy.

The Friendship Centre was successful in attracting people with HIV in its first year – even though there were not enough medicines, there was always at least a warm welcome afforded by Madame Justine, the volunteer receptionist. Madame Justine had come to the group after her husband's death, which she believed had been caused by AIDS. Widowed, and with three small children to support, she had come to ask for support. The charismatic founder of Jeunes sans frontières, Abdoulaye Ouédraogo, couldn't offer her a job, but as she was an older woman he thought she would have the right social stature to be the Centre's receptionist. He suggested she volunteer, and he would do his best to make sure that enough would come her way that she could keep paying her children's school fees and put food on the table.

As the volume of patients grew, an informal camaraderie was struck up in the house's living room, which doubled as a waiting room. Its two wooden couches around a small table, a shelf-full of AIDS literature, and a large color television and VCR painstakingly obtained through a complicated World Bank program, gave it a homey feel. The patients often sat watching the television, unaware of its complex Bretton–Woods genealogy, exchanging long formulaic greetings as others arrived or left. The TV and VCR anchored the ill-defined sense of solidarity felt by strangers who await the same train. All of them had at some point learned they were HIV positive, and all of them knew that the others were HIV positive too, and some were visibly ill. Yet never, in those first months of operation, did they discuss this situation amongst themselves.

This wall of silence was a common reaction to these early attempts to foster a culture of self-help as a response to the AIDS epidemic in Africa. It did not long resist the onslaught of empowerment workshops, role-plays, self-esteem exercises, and the panoply of confessional technologies that trained people with HIV to "live positively" and "come out into the open," in order to "break the silence" and "overcome the stigma" surrounding life with HIV in Africa. By 2001, three years after the first attempts at initiating empowering dialogue had resulted in a laconic silence, African activists had begun to take center stage at international conferences and, even in remote villages, people with HIV were starting to talk openly about being HIV positive.

Within that same historical time-span, media coverage of the lifesaving potential of the new combination antiretroviral treatments for HIV furnished a faint glimmer of therapeutic hope, one nourished by contacts fostered by the intensifying institutional networks that linked Northern AIDS activists with individuals such as Abdoulaye and, through him, the people who attend the Friendship Centre. While the millennium marked a huge increase in the numbers of Africans living with HIV taking antiretroviral drugs, the total numbers are miniscule relative to the massive scale of the epidemic on that continent – of the over 30 million HIV positive Africans in 2002, fewer than 10,000 are estimated by UNAIDS to be on treatment.

These individuals, although few in number, have become the vanguard of a much broader phenomena emerging in the wake of the success of transnational campaigns to increase access to the lifesaving treatments in developing countries. This vanguard, I argue here, is much more than a new social movement pre-articulated around explicit objectives. Rather, it is a complex biopolitical assemblage, cobbled together from global flows of organisms, drugs, discourses, and technologies of all kinds. Institutionally, this assemblage roughly corresponds to what others have called an AIDS industry.[1] As AIDS emerges as the foremost issue threatening economic and political futures in many countries around the world, this AIDS industry has become ever-more entangled with the development industry, a salient example of how humanitarian issues are quietly reconfiguring the contours of Bretton–Woods modernity.

The increasing scope of humanitarian intervention in today's world has drawn attention to how the humanitarian industry constructs a logic of intervention that displaces local politics and contributes to the fashioning of new identities, a process that has been described as "mobile sovereignty."[2] The humanitarian "apparatus," blending military and biomedical intervention, is a specialized and highly structured crystallization of broader, more diffuse transnational processes wherein a diversity of groups, often referred to as nongovernmental organizations (NGOs), involved in a plethora of activities ranging from advocacy to service delivery, coalesce across different settings around specific issues. Humanitarian issues are most sharply expressed as health issues – threats to the lives and well-being of populations, as in the case of famines, war, and epidemics, are those that call forth the deployment of humanitarian apparatuses and the need for timely intervention.

In this chapter, I wish to capture how the humanitarian/development complex that has emerged around the HIV/AIDS issue has grown to encompass a heterogeneous and uneven congerie of practices and techniques, present and active in everyday life, to produce particular kinds of subjects and forms of life – AIDS activists, resistant viruses, and therapeutic citizens. Within science studies, the concept of "actor-networks" has been advanced to examine how practical and institutional arrangements tie together human and nonhuman agents (such as retroviruses) in order to stabilize scientific facts.[3] Certainly, this approach is useful in considering how HIV has been able to stitch together such apparently disparate phenomena as condom demonstrations, CD4 counts, sexual empowerment, retroviral genotyping, an ethic of sexual responsibility, and compliance with complex drug regimens, into a remarkably stable, worldwide formation. In this chapter, I am concerned with describing the forms of action that may result from such networks; specifically, I wish to draw attention to how these assemblages prefigure the emergence of new forms of therapeutic citizenship; that is, claims made on a global social order on the basis of a therapeutic predicament. As I will show here, therapeutic citizenship broadens "biological" notions of citizenship, whereby a biological construct – such as being HIV positive – is used to ascribe an essentialized identity, as in earlier forms of eugenics and racial ordering. Therapeutic citizenship is a biopolitical citizenship, a system of claims and ethical projects that arise out of the conjugation of techniques used to govern populations and manage individual bodies.

The notion of therapeutic citizenship points to the growing transnational influence of biomedical knowledge and practice in the government of human and nonhuman affairs. This discussion draws on the concept of therapeutic economy, which is used here to refer to the totality of therapeutic options in a given location, as well as the rationale underlying the patterns of resort by which these therapies are accessed. These therapeutic options comprise the practices, practitioners, and forms of knowledge that sufferers resort to in order to heal affliction. Therapy always involves a form of exchange and is embedded in "regimes of value."[4] Exchange may be monetary, as in the purchase of medicines, or it may constitute "moral economies" as individuals call on networks of obligation and reciprocity to negotiate access to therapeutic resources,[5] thus drawing attention to the constraints that shape therapeutic itineraries.[6] In this sense, the notion of a therapeutic economy builds on ethnographic studies that have taken medical pluralism as their object of scrutiny[7] to emphasize the link between therapies and wider economic and social relations.

As the full social and demographic consequences of the relentless global AIDS epidemic become clearer, calls for increased access to treatment for this disease in poor countries have been made by a coalition of AIDS activist groups, humanitarian organizations, and health advocacy networks. By engaging governments, international aid donors, biomedical researchers, and the pharmaceuticals industry with these therapeutic claims, this coalition has configured a therapeutic economy that conjugates confessional technologies, self-help strategies, and access to drugs in novel ways. This represents an increasingly biomedicalized form of governmentality, and my argument here is that the ways in which these coalitions produce subjects and citizens cannot be limited to the discursive and the material, but increasingly encompass the biological itself.

The Global Biopolitics of HIV: From Prevention to Treatment

Efforts to address the HIV epidemic in developing countries had, until very recently, almost exclusively focused on preventing HIV infection. A first generation of programs was focused on raising awareness through large-scale "information, education and communication" (IEC) programs, assuming that this would lead to an increase in safer sex. This was followed by the adoption of "social marketing" campaigns that sought to generate demand for, as well as supply, what was deemed to be the key preventive intervention: condoms. Condom social marketing represented a significant shift from IEC programs in that it extended beyond awareness-raising to measuring efficacy in terms of condom distribution and sales. These approaches were developed by Northern development agencies that relied on consortia of large international NGOs as implementing agencies. It was in many respects a "top-down" approach, with international agencies targeting the populations of developing countries, and with little local involvement in the process.

A second generation of programs stressed the direct involvement of affected communities in the response to the epidemic, largely through the idioms of "self-help" and "empowerment." These strategies were a hybrid of approaches pioneered by communities affected by the epidemic in Northern countries, which drew on local forms of solidarity to organize "buddy" systems and support groups, and forms of community organizing indigenous to African, Asian, and South American contexts. A handful of pioneering AIDS groups from Brazil, Thailand, and Uganda were founded by charismatic leaders who were able to obtain funding from progressive foundations and other funders outside of the mainstream development organizations and consortia that implemented the first wave of AIDS programs. Their funding success resulted from their ability to successfully translate Western notions of solidarity into locally meaningful action; most notably, by rephrasing the "buddy" system of therapeutic companionship – pioneered by the North American gay community in the early years of the epidemic – in the post-colonial idiom of evangelical organizing. These local NGO responses became the reference for subsequent attempts to replicate "indigenous" responses around the globe.

These programs encouraged the creation of groups of people living with HIV/ AIDS (PWA) and the promotion of people with HIV to visible leadership roles within organizations active in the response to the epidemic. Achieving "greater involvement of people with HIV," or GIPA, as this approach came to be called after the 1994 Paris summit on AIDS, translated into resources as funding agencies rushed to fund new PWA groups and organizations that undertook to visibly promote persons with HIV in their ranks. Understandably, this stimulated the creation of groups and a plethora of "self-help" and "empowerment" activities, although in the early years many of these seemed to exist more out of mimicry of their Western inspiration than out of any heartfelt desire to participate in self-help groups – a process referred to by development workers as "resource-capture driven."

Abdoulaye Ouédraogo is the founder of Jeunes sans frontières, the youth group in Ouagadougou that opened the Friendship Centre in 1998. Shortly before, in late 1997, Abdoulaye had gone to Europe for the first time – he had been invited by a French NGO to come and attend a workshop. Traveling to France, former colonial metro-pole for Francophone West Africa and the primary reference for all that is Western and "modern," was enormously exciting – an opportunity that few Burkinabè would ever have. At the time, Abdoulaye was spending most of his time putting together HIV projects for Jeunes sans frontières, and once in Paris trips to the Eiffel Tower, the Louvre, and the Champs-Élysées were complemented by visits to the French AIDS organizations whose material Abdoulaye had been reading and whose names were by now important references for him. Abdoulaye took the "exchange and sharing of experiences" purpose of the trip seriously, and as he had been writing about HIV testing centers and counseling groups he decided to visit a number of testing sites and activist groups in the French metropolis. He also had an HIV test, which turned out to be positive. Parisian friends found a doctor who was able to supply him with triple therapy for himself.

After he returned from Europe, inspired by the self-help groups he had seen there, Abdoulaye opened the Friendship Centre and convened – but did not participate in – a discussion group of people who had come to him because they were HIV positive and had heard that Jeunes sans frontières was involved in the "fight against AIDS." However, none spoke about being HIV positive. Discussion was centered around the details of everyday life and the difficulties of getting by. By 1999, Abdoulaye was faced with a new problem. Some of the people he had invited to the group, he realized, were better off than others – some of them were even able to pay for some form of medical treatment. This would surely "inhibit" any of the kind of fluid discussion that was important to mutual support. "It will only create jealousies and frustrations," he told me.

During the time he was trying to set up the "talking group," one of Abdoulaye's aunts in the family compound fell ill. She had been ill for some time, and unbe-knownst to her she had tested positive for HIV at the local hospital. As is customary, the diagnosis was confided to her father, the head of her household, and he had summoned his knowledgeable Abidjan-educated nephew to discuss the matter. Abdoulaye arranged for medical care, and made sure that she was properly looked after and that basic medications were paid for. Her diagnosis was never discussed. At the time, lifesaving antiretroviral drugs were unaffordable to all but the very wealthy. She died six months later, not having been told she had AIDS.

In the eyes of Western donors, NGOs and other "community-based organizations" (CBOs) were representative, and even expressive, of preexisting communities. Thus NGOs and CBOs could be used to target interventions at these communities and mobilize a response to the epidemic. They became the lynchpin of efforts to get at the roots of the epidemic. However, such organizations can be "artificial," in the sense that they are not expressions of endogenously occurring collectivities, such as those organized through kinship relations. Programs such as GIPA promote particular kinds of people, in effect conjuring them into existence through testing programs and a wide range of narrative technologies that empower them to represent themselves to others and shape their own experiences.

In harnessing NGOs and CBOs as mechanisms to implement programs, donors actually create new forms of social relations and, over time, new communities. However, these communities do not spring up de novo; rather, they are bricolages of preexisting social relations (such as kinship relations), global therapeutic strategies, and local tactics. In this sense, they recapitulate earlier attempts to translate kinship into strategies for accessing and redistributing resources during colonial modernity. In colonial Africa, what are today called CBOs or NGOs were referred to as voluntary associations. These are described in the classical ethnographic literature on urbanizing Africa as "acculturating" and "modernizing" influences, destined to whither away once cultural modernization was complete. More recent historiographic work on Africa suggests that voluntary associations were rather more like social laboratories, sites of heightened reflexivity where the terms of engagement with the new colonial – and global – modernity were negotiated and enacted. Significantly, these social laboratories produced historically robust phenomena, whether large historical formations such as nationalism or the persistence of a myriad of micropolitical forms that continue unabated in contemporary everyday life.

From Diagnosis to Therapy; From Biosociality to Biopolitics

Between 1994 and 1999, it seemed as though the disconnection between "coming out," or talking about one's experience of being HIV positive, and "solidarity" or self-help would remain refractory to the best efforts of westerners to bring them together. For the development workers with whom I spoke, it seemed obvious that self-disclosure was cathartic and a first step to the organization of therapeutic social relations. Although Abdoulaye said he believed this too, this was belied by the differential manner in which disclosure occurred around him.

Abdoulaye told me that, after his initial depression upon discovering he was HIV positive in Paris, he did not speak to anyone about it. After all, whom could he trust in Ouagadougou? As the leader of Jeunes sans frontières, he told me he was afraid that "it would discourage everyone in the group, if they find out that even I am positive too."

The Friendship Centre's World Bank television set was a welcome source of diversion, but ultimately *poulet télévisé* (the local term for the chickens grilled on a spit, referring to their presentation behind a window) would have been more welcome. Talking about being HIV positive was of little relevance when the pressing concerns were about getting food and medicines.

Things began to change, however, in early 2000. By then, Abdoulaye had been on his antiretroviral treatment for three years, managing with donations from his Parisian doctor. Together with him, Abdoulaye had devised a treatment plan to deal with erratic supplies; he would just switch medicines according to what he had on hand, making sure that he was taking at least three different and complementary drugs. He had bought a small fridge to store those medicines that had to be refrigerated. As a result, by late 1999 his T4 cells had shot up, from 14 to over 400; the virus had been undetectable in his blood for almost three years.[8]

He put on weight, regaining the stocky build of his early twenties. His wife also thrived with a supply of medicines from Marseille, but his daughter Salimata was often ill with fevers. While this is not unusual for a child in West Africa, Abdoulaye was distraught every time she took ill. For the first year of life, HIV tests are unreliable, as infants have their mother's antibodies and, Fatou being positive, Sali would have been positive too. By the time she was two, Sali still had not had a test, even though it could have been reliably ascertained whether or not she had contracted HIV from her mother at that point. By that time, Abdoulaye had resigned himself to preferring uncertainty – punctuated by attacks of anxiety every time Sali had a fever – to risking the certainty of knowing his daughter had HIV.

Meanwhile, Abdoulaye's visible recovery was not without an impact on his surroundings. Rumors circulated that he had supernatural healing powers, and this brought a new influx of the ill to the Friendship Centre. Those who knew about his consumption of medicines did not suspect HIV, he told me, because he had always been "easy to take medicines," a modernist quirk that his Ouagadougou friends assumed had been acquired in Abidjan, where, like many Burkinabè, Abdoulaye had been born and raised. His stock of antiretrovirals did seem ostentatiously modern, laid out in their brightly colored boxes by the foam mattress he slept on in the adobe room in the family courtyard where he lived.

The doctor in Paris was also impressed, having "never imagined" that such a striking clinical response could have been obtained with rotating medicines and a long-distance therapeutic relationship. As a result, from early 1999 Abdoulaye left his doctor's office with armfuls of medicines that had been collected for other patients in Ouagadougou. By 2000, Abdoulaye was telling some people he was HIV positive, but "only my friends who are taking the test or have taken it," he told me, "because only they can understand." That year, he moved out of the family compound. His daughter's frequent illnesses had led to his aunt being accused of witchcraft by the other women in the family compound. As I helped him pack up his antiretrovirals in their pristine packages, Abdoulaye told me he was "tired" of these "African stories" and wanted a holiday.

Faced with the influx of newcomers at the Friendship Centre, Abdoulaye tried again to start a "talking group." Initially, the patients maintained an awkward silence. Discussion invariably turned to the problems of material subsistence. In the words of a European psychologist who tried to work with the group, "these people are completely overwhelmed by their material needs and difficulties – how can you expect to do any psychological work until these more basic issues get resolved?" The laconic nature of these exchanges, whether in Abdoulaye's discussion group or in his own family, would seem to point to the difficulties of fostering an ethic of self-help oriented around a biomedical diagnosis and a culture of talking. At first glance, it could be surmised that ease of self-disclosure, and the ability to generate therapeutic communities on that basis, is a cultural particularity of westerners in general and Americans in particular. However, these have proven to be robust even in the alien soil of an impoverished Africa. Abdoulaye's persistence paid off, and gradually over the next two years, the "talking groups" flourished as more members joined and awkward silence gave way to at times animated discussion. The subject of discussion, however, was not the kind of self-disclosure familiar to North American readers steeped in a culture of talk shows and confessional media, but a more pragmatic to-and-fro about the vicissitudes of everyday life.

Abdoulaye's, and Jeunes sans frontières' story is not unique, and parallels the evolution of community groups that inevitably moved to being confronted with the problems of persons ill with HIV after having started out in prevention work, extolling the benefits of condoms, safer sex, and HIV testing. Community groups involved with AIDS inevitably have many HIV positive people who know their diagnosis amongst their members – either because they join these groups in the hope of getting access to treatment or they take the test themselves (as Abdoulaye did) in order to "practice what they preach." Encouraging testing is one of the pillars of development agencies' prevention strategies, the argument being that testing is a powerful tool for raising awareness and changing behavior. In countries with a high prevalence of HIV, the odds are good that some of those tested will turn out to be HIV positive.

Training Africans with HIV to "come out" with their stories of being diagnosed, and living, with HIV were the cornerstone of development organizations' attempts to foster self-help. It would be a mistake to take these early silences, as we have seen, as evidence that these techniques were culturally inert and pragmatic failures. These confessional technologies, deployed by the AIDS industry, were taken up by individuals to fashion themselves. The evangelical idiom within which "living positively," "taking responsibility," and "caring for others" was phrased was not merely a form of religious mimicry, but an ethical project, a way of integrating being HIV positive in a moral order. The direction this ethical project took was determined by the inequalities inherent in the global therapeutic economy.

The evolution of contemporary PWA groups and other community organizations initially "recruited" into the battle against a terrible epidemic shows how they, like their historical predecessors, do act as social laboratories where globalized discursive forms – from discourses such as GIPA to discursive practices organized around "self-help" – are negotiated and indeed fashioned. The story of Abdoulaye and the patrons of the Friendship Centre indicates how testimonials and other confessional technologies, used by the AIDS industry to foster self-help and empowerment, fashioned local subjectivities and social relations, something I will return to later. HIV/AIDS led to the organization of social relations according to a shared biological affliction, inadvertently in the case of many community groups drawn into awareness-raising campaigns by the availability of donor funding, and explicitly in the case of the PWA groups that were funded by GIPA programming.

What was at stake in these social relations, mediated through various NGOs, was dramatically raised by news of the lifesaving potential of antiretroviral treatments. What may have been regarded as just theatre, mimicry-for-money, became a matter of life and death. In retrospect, it seems that the arrival of the antiretrovirals subtly shifted what was at stake in the discussion groups. With circumspection, Abdoulaye and an inner circle of Friendship Centre staff began to carefully – "little by little" – distribute the medicines. He explained to me that they used the talking group to identify candidates for the medicines – those who came regularly were more likely to observe the rigorous treatment schedules, and those who "contributed" most to the group were favored. These "dynamic" members should have access to treatment, they reasoned, because they would be able to help others more than those who remained passive. The "talking group" began to fulfill a function unintended by those who championed it as a model of self-help: it served as a kind of laboratory for determining how to identify those who should have access to treatment. Thus, the self-help group functioned as a triage system, a method for determining who would benefit most from medicines – just as in wartime, when military physicians must decide who of the wounded can be saved and who cannot.

Biopolitical Production and Antiretrovirals

These micro-ramifications of GIPA show how policies developed in geopolitical centers take on a life of their own in the peripheries where they are enacted; however, they also indicate how techniques for managing populations and bodies produce particular kinds of subjectivities. Foucault used the term "biopower" to group these forms of the government of life together and map the transformations in the nature of power and sovereignty in the modern age. While the globalization of HIV/AIDS prevention set the stage for the emergence of a globalized politics of access to treatment, it also shows how a biosocial formation – self-help organized according to a biomedical diagnosis – can articulate with biopolitical processes. But here, in the globalized therapeutic economy of the current age, the biopolitical production of subjects becomes is ever more intimately tied to the biomedical.

Organizations such as Jeunes sans frontières inevitably find themselves confronted with the issue of treatment for their own members as well as those who come to them for help. Ultimately, access to treatment is contingent on social relations and the ability to capitalize on social networks. Jeunes sans frontières made treatment decisions based on a social calculus: Who would translate improved health into the greatest good for others? This explicit form of local triage is, however, the exception. The lucky few who obtain antiretrovirals do so through contacts with northerners. For these individuals, the key to survival is to be able to "tell a good story." Stories may mediate access to medicines by being told to the right person or, more significantly, can get the teller to a European haven. French authorities, like those in other European countries, quietly renew foreigners' residency permits when they are HIV positive, subsequent to domestic political pressure denouncing early deportations of HIV-positive Africans. Many of the founders of the first PWA groups now live in Europe, having stayed behind after obtaining a visa for a conference or having gotten sponsored by fellow activists. The lucky ones found work with European AIDS groups; others scrape by, at least assured of free treatment. These early activists were the vanguard of a small movement of Africans who migrate to the North to obtain treatment, a fact that has come to the attention of HIV clinicians in Europe and Canada. To those who are left behind, these therapeutic migrants are the truly lucky ones, whose stories got them to Europe.

The UNAIDS Initiative and the Local Biopolitics of Treatment

As we have seen, confessional technologies were initially used to attempt to elicit narratives of distress as a means of fostering mutual support. In a context of material want and of growing awareness of the benefits of treatment, these narratives were used tactically – either to improve one's own chances of obtaining treatment or to select those who could best benefit from obtaining medications. As Jeunes sans frontières' pragmatic decision-making around using antiretrovirals makes clear, once biosocial relations were in place, the biological potency of drugs articulated these social forms to predicaments where what was at stake was eminently biopolitical: a question of the government of life.

This biopolitical dimension emerges clearly when examining the strategic positioning that narratives must take when used to negotiate access to resources mediated through large, stable institutions. In the early years of the therapeutic revolution ushered in by the new "cocktails" of antiretroviral drugs, few options existed outside of the informal networks scaled by those with the social and symbolic capital necessary for reaching sites where resources could be accessed more easily.

The inability of public health care institutions in Africa to offer much in the way of accessible services to the general population is well known, the result of decades of structural-adjustment mediated underfunding and ill-conceived schemes to "recover costs" from users who cannot possibly pay. The HIV epidemic only exacerbated the situation, by increasing demand for services at the same time as the burden of illness meant that those who needed it were in even less measure to pay, a marked example of the illness/poverty trap. Private for-profit institutions treat those with HIV only as long as they can pay, at times with treatments of doubtful efficacy. The AIDS industry's efforts had neglected medical treatment for people with HIV, preferring to concentrate on prevention and, in a minority of cases, "cost-effective" interventions aimed at offering people with HIV "care and support": largely supportive listening and home-based palliative care. In those early years, the only exception to this was a UNAIDS initiative that attempted to make antiretrovirals available to the general population.

The UNAIDS initiative was a pilot program coordinated by the agency to improve access to antiretrovirals – programs were launched in Chile, Vietnam, and Côte-d'Ivoire. The agency hired a consulting firm to negotiate reduced prices for antiretrovirals with pharmaceuticals firms and implement a local distribution system. In Côte-d'Ivoire, the government pledged one million dollars to a drugs purchasing fund that would be used to subsidize the purchase of antiretroviral medicines. Interestingly, UNAIDS did not itself make any financial contribution to drug purchases, as this was "beyond their mandate" as a "co-ordinating and technical support agency." For UNAIDS, this was to be a pilot project to demonstrate the feasibility of using "private–public partnerships" (public funding to purchase drugs produced by the private sector, which would guarantee reasonable prices).

The program got under way in late 1998, recruiting patients at the Infectious Diseases Service of the Treichville University Hospital, one of the city's TB control clinics, and at a handful of NGO outreach sites. The program quickly became embroiled in controversy. Several hundred people were treated through the program, although the subsidies were insufficient to allow them to keep paying for the drugs for more than a few months. Almost all of those who continued could only afford inadequate two-drug cocktails. As a result, the majority became resistant to these drugs, as demonstrated by their CD4 counts, viral load measurements, and resistance testing done by the CDC's retrovirology lab in Abidjan, Projet RétroCI. The laboratory data collected by CDC was compromised by the irregularity of follow-ups, which meant that blood specimens were collected at more or less random intervals, rendering any kind of meaningful epidemiological analysis difficult. Prescribing physicians, who had been selected from a variety of public health institutions across the city, had minimal training in using the drugs, limited to a three-day seminar conducted by a French AIDS NGO.

The selection criteria for subsidies were never made clear. One group of activists, which had been quite vocal at the Geneva AIDS Conference in 1998, received an unprecedented 95 percent discount and were able to afford the triple therapy cocktail with this subsidy. Curiously, the group ceased to be visible on the local AIDS scene at about that time. The coordinator of the program explained to me that the generous subsidy had been an administrative error. It was never clear what role the distribution system was to play, and the whole program became quickly mired in an ongoing corruption scandal that resulted in the suspension of European Union aid to the country. It subsequently emerged that the prices that had been negotiated by the consulting firm were in fact going market rates, and that as prices for antiretrovirals dropped through 2000 and 2001, the program was briefly locked into a higher price.

The 1999 coup complicated things even further. According to the incoming military government, outgoing officials had looted the Treasury and the state was near bankruptcy. The military government's evaluation was credible, given the financial track record of the previous government. Arrears to the Public Health Pharmacy, which purchased the antiretrovirals, mounted to the point of compromising its ability to purchase other essential generic medicines. Discontinuations in ARV purchases ensued that, combined with poor inventory management, led to sustained interruptions of deliveries of antiretrovirals. Thus, throughout 2001, the supply was patchy at best, meaning that almost all those on the UNAIDS program had intermittent, partial therapy – a situation certain to generate drug resistance in all involved patients. While the situation was denounced, and some patients even went on a hunger strike, little could be done.

In retrospect, it seems that it was unreasonable to expect that Abidjan's crumbling public health facilities should have been to shoulder the burden of such an ambitious program. Staff in hospitals and clinics complained that they were not compensated for the extra work that the program entailed. Furthermore, it seems that, after launching the process, UNAIDS did not follow through as enthusiastically as it might have with technical support to monitor drug procurement and distribution, and training of physicians. Subsequent evaluations of the program were conducted, and indexed "dysfunctional institutional relationships" and "fuzzy decision-making," as well as lack of technical support and resources, as contributing to the program's mitigated success.[9]

While the program was intended as a demonstration, a pilot project, it needs to be also understood as obeying a specific biopolitical imperative. The French had for some time been arguing that treatment needed to be part of the fight against AIDS in developing countries, and Côte-d'Ivoire, the jewel in the post-colonial French crown, was to be a showcase; similarly, UNAIDS was being held accountable to an AIDS activist constituency that was increasingly vocal about the issue of access to antiretroviral drugs in developing countries. At one level, then, the UNAIDS Ivoirian initiative was more about showing that something was being done for political ends domestically and internationally than about achieving meaningful public health results. It should be underlined that, precisely because of the high political stakes of the program, its evaluation had benefited from an unprecedented degree of transparency from Ivoirian officials, who were held accountable both to a local HIV-positive public and a wide international audience. The preferential involvement of groups of people with HIV should also be seen in this light.

Little commented upon was the observation that a large number of the initial group of patients were found to harbor drug-resistant virus – sure evidence that they had had already had partial access to ARVs.[10] The decision to start off with biotherapy, taken under material duress, was in retrospect a perilous one, for it could only lead to short-term therapeutic efficacy that wore off as patients quickly developed resistance to the two drugs they were treated with. The situation is analogous to that described by Farmer and colleagues, who showed that multidrug-resistant tuberculosis epidemics in Peru and then Russia were directly attributable to inadequacies in government TB control programs, and evidence of the perils of scaling back of global health capacity in an era of globalized health expectations and therapeutic resort.

The outcome of the program – expanded access to antiretrovirals and clear short-term therapeutic benefit, but also partial treatments and drug-resistant viruses – reflected the welter of conflicting organizational and individual priorities. International consultants set up an unwieldy drug procurement and distribution mechanism that neither patients nor physicians knew how to negotiate; local priorities did not necessarily correspond to the concerns of international organizations. The gap between local patterns of resort, the therapeutic economy within which that occurred, and international humanitarian imperatives, was one that only a few could bridge – as in the case of the one group that was able to get a 95 percent discount on drug prices from the program.

How patients got access to drugs through UNAIDS' initiative in Côte-d'Ivoire contrasts with Jeunes sans frontières' tactical form of social triage. In Abidjan, at least, allocation of treatments obeyed programmatic imperatives about treating the greatest number of patients while balancing conflicting agendas, resulting in a worst-case scenario in which many got partial treatment and, therefore, resistance to the drugs. For the majority of patients, the institutional landmarks within which strategies could be oriented were absent; indeed, the only individuals who were able to successfully leverage full treatment were the members of that small group who correctly "read" the political dimension of accessing treatment.

From Local to Global Biopolitics

Confessional technologies, therapeutic tactics, and biopolitical strategies are, as we have seen, most legible in the local frame of everyday life. However, consideration of the global therapeutic economy requires they must be read in the context within which the creation and dissemination of biomedical knowledges and practices occurs globally. The UNAIDS program showed how global biopolitical goals may not be effectively translated into locally available strategies. In contrast, a local initiative in the same city was able to expand its social relations internationally to access resources: the Abidjan Institute for Biomedical Research. It was founded in 1995 with the intention of treating people with HIV without outside help, and attracting clinical research to expand access to treatment to those who could not afford even the cost of ARVs. Like Jeunes sans frontières, the Institute's drive stems from the charisma of one individual, and its therapeutic mission from that individual's experience with illness. However, in the case of the Institute, the ability to translate that experience into concrete resources for people with HIV in Africa derived from its founder's position in a well-placed social network that spanned Abidjan and Paris.

The Institute was the first institution in West Africa to concentrate on the issue of treating people with HIV openly, long before it became fashionable amongst international agencies, and even before local groups realized that this was an issue at the very heart of their own survival. Bertrand Dupont, a surgeon, is the Institute's founder, driving force, and current director. Dupont banked that there would be a market of paying patients who could keep the Institute running, and wagered that if he could attract the research infrastructure he would then be able to use clinical trials to treat patients for free. As the son of prominent settlers, he was able to access and mobilize networks of support in the metropole, contacts that led him to meet and finally persuade Professor Luc Montagnier, hailed as one of the discoverers of HIV, to raise funds to fully equip a laboratory in Abidjan. Dupont's "village" was the cosmopolitan sphere that linked Abidjan and Paris. Dupont's maverick style allowed him to scale networks and "go to the top" to mobilize resources.

But Dupont's trump card in the battle for research resources is not the Institute's laboratory facilities, as impressive as they are. It is its loyal cohort of patients. Being able to put together, and retain, a cohort of patients is a greater challenge than setting up a laboratory, and patients are the key ingredients to conducting clinical research. Being able to conduct clinical research in Africa will become increasingly important as the pool of patients who have not been yet treated with antiretrovirals dries up in Northern countries, and with the advent of vaccines that will need to be tested against the strains of HIV circulating in Africa. Yet it is only now that the idea of using research to drive resources into African clinical settings is starting to gain currency.

This is because it has been widely believed that conducting clinical research in African settings is fraught with "cultural," as well as economic, barriers. African patients, it is often said, and not only by Western physicians and bureaucrats but by African physicians as well, are notoriously "noncompliant." Why? The common reasons given are because "they go to the witch doctor," "they do not return for appointments," and "they stop their treatments when they feel better." This way in which efforts to improve patients' access to treatment is dismissed contrasts with the colonial period. Then, patients were more actively sought after – so much so that they were forcibly injected or were even interned for treatment. The colonial medical authorities' frustration with this kind of behavior in the face of their well-meaning efforts led them, at times, to blame the natives' evasiveness on ignorance, irrational fears, or even moral ineptness. Nowadays, frustrated physicians and public health officials – most of them African – resort to culturalist explanations, blaming patients' noncompliance on the ease with which they either resort to what is offered in "the village" or just stop coming back once they feel better.

The Institute's patients, however tell a different story. In the first year of the Institute's operation, over 900 patients consulted there, and half of them came back, a retention rate considered to be excellent by clinical epidemiologists. Many do not return because the $7 consultation is expensive and, if they are poor, they are told to save the consultation fees by coming back only if they are ill. Those for whom the registration fee was not an obstacle kept coming back regularly because they felt well treated – "the receptionist is always friendly," or "the doctor explained things to me." Patients were appreciative that an effort was made to give them appointments rather than it just being expected that they would turn up and wait, as is the case in the public sector. Rudeness, long waits, and "not being told anything" were patients' most common complaints about the welcome they received in public institutions. In these institutions, staff cited lack of time for not explaining things to patients, frequently adding that patients would not understand anyway. While this is often the case, I found that a fear also exists that by explaining and demystifying medical knowledge, practitioners will lose some of their status and prestige.

Considering it normal for staff to barely speak to patients ("treating them like animals" commented one physician, who had left the public service) makes it easier to blame patients for not complying with medical treatment. Dupont, while at times perfunctory in his explanations to his patients, instilled a culture of explanation at the Institute that had served him well in building up his private practice. His almost abrupt familiarity reassured patients, as did his popular ways of "acting like everyone's brother," as some put it. He succeeded in dissolving the hierarchy that normally separates patients from physicians.

Dupont was, I was told by expatriate French I interviewed, the first Frenchman to be infected with HIV in Abidjan. This happened between 1980 and 1983, when he cut himself while operating at the Treichville University Hospital. Dupont's patients returned to him even after news of his diagnosis wound its way through the grapevine, as they were already a loyal clientèle. There is no doubt that this also encouraged HIV-positive patients to come to him. After his diagnosis, he took particular interest in treating people with HIV, and was certainly the first physician in the country to openly counsel and test his patients. Being himself HIV positive, he was also keenly aware of treatment issues and up to date on the indications and use of antiretrovirals before they became available in Côte-d'Ivoire. Sure enough, word got around, and the sheer volume of Dupont's AIDS practice weighed in heavily in the decision to set up the Institute which, Dupont thought, could function as the "research arm" of his private practice. Indeed, many of Dupont's patients left the homey feel of the family practice in the leafy colonial district of the Plateau for the gleaming sterile quarters of the Institute. They did this first out of loyalty to Dupont and then because of the service they received there.

The first clinical trial was conducted at the Institute in 2000. Twenty patients were enrolled into a study where they all received triple therapy for HIV. These patients were representative of the Institute's patients – a few had good jobs, but most were poor. The study showed rates of adherence to follow-up that were superior to rates observed in Western settings, and that the most important determinants of adherence were economic. Patients were not paid to be in the study, and some had difficulty finding the money to travel to the Institute. The study also showed that the combination was biologically as effective as in Western patients. Yet the Institute has been unable to attract any further trials sponsored by drug companies, largely because of concerns that results will not be considered generalizable to the Northern markets where they earn their profits. (However, with an emerging market in antiretrovirals for HIV, companies have become interested in using African sites to generate clinical data that can be used to market the drugs for the African setting – see below.)

Despite the Institute's relative isolation from the Western research world, and the difficulties of developing a culture of research that this isolation entails, its loyal cohort of patients and laboratory infrastructure make it well positioned to take advantage of a growing market for clinical data. Essential to this has been Dupont's ability to a foster an institutional culture that enables, in Foucaultian terms, disciplined patients. The laboratory allows patient loyalty – adherence to follow-ups and medication schedules – to be translated into universally recognized measurements of biological efficacy. Its ability to produce biomedical knowledge – knowledge that, because of its universal aspiration, is able to circulate globally – where others have not, illustrates how globalized forms of biopolitical production (that is, the production of particular kinds of subjects) may allow global capital to articulate with local biologies and politics that would otherwise remain refractory to abstraction and circulation.

This raises an important question. Transnational socioeconomic inequalities, and the gradients of disease and inequity in access to health care that are associated with them, may unwittingly produce ideal conditions for the conduct of clinical research that furthers the marketing concerts of the pharmaceutical industry. Does the Institute's drive to provide treatment through research not risk enhancing the market power of the pharmaceuticals firm that commission research? Does the increasing market power of pharmaceuticals firms increase the barriers to making treatment accessible? Or might increasing return on pharmaceutical capital in Northern markets make the industry more susceptible to public pressure there, and more likely to tolerate generics competitions and two-tiered pricing for the South? While there is no clear answer to this difficult question, it underlines the importance of understanding the increasing blurring of the boundaries between science and marketing within the global therapeutic economy.

Clinical Research and Bio-Capital

If biopolitics allows science and the global organization of "bio-capital" (in this case, the pharmaceuticals industry) to articulate local and global therapeutic economies, what is the driving force? In this case, it is the market for clinical data, as this is the cornerstone of the market power of the pharmaceuticals industry. Data from clinical research carried out in developing countries will be of increasing strategic important to the pharmaceuticals industry, particularly for infectious diseases, as research costs escalate in developed countries relative to the number of research subjects available.

When the Institute first opened in 1998, the pharmaceuticals industry was skittish about doing clinical research in developing countries. Merck's "028" study, conducted in Brazil, compared triple therapy using AZT, 3TC and its drug Indinavir (Crixivan™) with treatment with only one of these drugs ("monotherapy"). The study generated some controversy because some patients were kept on the single therapy arm of the study long after it had become accepted that triple therapy was superior to mono-therapy, and had therefore become the standard treatment. Although controversial, the trial never became a major media issue, but the potential for "ethical trouble," along with clinicians' suspicion of trials conducted in developed country settings, made companies skittish about pursuing such trials throughout the past decade.

The situation began to change in 2001. In the late 1990s, the epidemic had slowed in the North, and patients who were not already on antiretrovirals were hard to find. But these "naïve" patients (so-called because they had never been treated with antiretrovirals) were extremely valuable for companies' marketing needs. In order to create a market share for a new drug, a company must show that the drug is superior to standard treatment in clinical trials. By 1998, AZT-3TC-Indinavir was considered the standard combination against which all new drugs were to be judged. But, for virologic and pharmacologic reasons, most new drugs in the pipeline are unlikely to be significantly superior to this standard – they are "me-too" drugs, whose mechanism of action is no different from existing treatments.

As a result, new drug combinations require large numbers of patients to be recruited into clinical trials, in order that any small improvements in patients' clinical outcomes can be attributed to the drug's effect rather than to random variation in these outcomes. Since previous treatment with antiretrovirals attenuates the impact of subsequent treatments, the therapeutic impact of new drugs is much more likely to be seen in ARV-naïve patients. However, recruitment of large numbers of previously untreated patients is difficult in the North – as a result, companies must conduct expensive multi-center international trials that can take years to recruit patients, delaying a drug's arrival on the market and increasing its research and development costs substantially.

With more and more new drugs coming out of their development "pipelines," competition for suitable patients is fierce. This requires companies to recruit patients across a greater number of clinical research sites and to offer more generous inducements to these sites for recruiting such patients. The enormous expense implied by these clinical trials encourages companies to conduct trials with combinations of exclusively "in-house" drugs. If an "all-in-house" combination can be proven to be as effective as the best available treatment, all three drugs will generate profits for the company for the cost of a single trial. For instance, GlaxoWellcome (now GlaxoSmithKline) strategically conducted a large international trial comparing three of its drugs (zidovudine, lamivudine, and abacavir) with two of its drugs plus Merck's indinavir, the "gold standard" of treatment. At the time the trial was designed and implemented (1997–8), it was widely thought that HAART required a protease inhibitor (PI) to be effective, and GlaxoWellcome's abacavir was a nucleoside reverse transcriptase inhibitor (NRTI), just like zidovudine and lamivudine. GlaxoWellcome "gambled," scientifically speaking, that three-drug NRTIs might be as good as two NRTIs and a PI. The trial was a success, demonstrating that either combination was equivalent, and setting the stage for GlaxoSmithKline to dominate the market with a twice-a-day HAART cocktail, formulated in a single capsule and aptly named Trizivir,™ which was marketed in late 2001 and then went on to be the leading HIV drug – and one of the company's most profitable products – until a subsequent trial in 2003 showed it to be less effective than another triple-drug combination.

Trizivir's development points to how marketing concerns are built in up-front into the design of the clinical trials that are conducted to bring drugs to market. GlaxoSmithKline's marketing acumen, however, has gained it little advantage in the African market, where the drug is still largely unavailable and has been upstaged by a copycat triple-therapy in one pill. In 2001, Indian generic pharmaceutical manufacturer Cipla began selling Triomune, a single-pill combination of zidovudine, lamivudine, and nevirapine (an NNRTI), for a dollar a day.

Although pharmaceutical capital and production is concentrated in Europe and North America, and despite an unprecedented wave of mergers and corporate concentration, the industry is organized transnationally across regionally segmented markets; and still remains fragmented, with firms tending to specialize in a handful of therapeutic drug classes. Companies' market power is the result of the highly technical nature of pharmaceutical production and the industry's ability to exert control over raw materials and technological know-how, largely through intellectual property laws (see below). To this must be added the power of brand names and a subtle, but vast, array of marketing strategies. As shown above, the design of pharmaceutical industry clinical research is one of those strategies.

Although their success was mitigated, public health campaigns served to create a biological "vanguard" of individuals who had been tested for HIV and had discovered they were positive. Of those who were not already active NGO members, many joined and have joined others in become increasingly vocal in demanding access to treatment for their condition, setting a global stage for what I have called a therapeutic citizenship. In this new age of biomedical globalization, the humanitarian logic of health has inadvertently spawned a political movement. This is a biopolitical movement because what is eminently at stake is life itself, both in access to lifesaving and -shaping drugs and the new forms of life – from therapeutic relations to drug-resistant organisms – that it spawns.

Conclusions

As a result of the access-to-treatment campaign and the media attention it has drawn, there have been a series of declarations announcing dramatic price reductions in the cost of these drugs. However, these only began once Cipla offered to make the nine antiretrovirals it produces in India available at cost to African countries. Subsequent offers of price cuts by – in order – Merck, Bristol-Myers Squibb, and GlaxoSmithKline can be read as an attempt to protect their market share in the face of competition from generics. In fact, generic antiretrovirals are now being manufactured in Thailand and Brazil as well as in India. As a result, Brazil has been able to achieve public health benefits from combination therapy that are similar to those of Western countries, but at a fraction of the cost. More worrisome for these companies, however, is the threat posed to their patents, which they have been enforcing vigorously through international intellectual property conventions such as TRIPS, and lobbying of the U.S. government to keep other nations in line.

The access-to-treatment campaign has brought to the fore the role of international conventions and agreements governing intellectual property, and the institutional mechanisms by which these are enforced, in ensuring the profitability of the pharmaceutical industry. Recent attention has also focused on patenting of the human genome and indigenous knowledge. While not strictly part of the process of drug production, this transnational institutional sphere nonetheless is an important part of bio-capitalist accumulation. In this case, changes in drug pricing and in the capitalist regulation of intellectual property cannot be viewed separately from the conjugation of biosocial forms (HIV-positive groups) and technologies of the self that leveraged the broad transnational advocacy coalition that has contributed to bringing down drug prices. Increasing drug availability will have a multiplier effect, as the voices of people with HIV are no longer extinguished by illness but grow louder as their bodies respond to the treatments. It is this dialectic between a global therapeutic economy, local tactics for mobilizing resources, and the biopolitical processes through which humanitarian interventions produce particular subjectivities that gives birth to what I have called a therapeutic citizenship – a form of stateless citizenship whereby claims are made on a global order on the basis of one's biomedical condition, and responsibilities worked out in the context of local moral economies.

In many Northern countries, national health insurance has meant that citizenship automatically confers access to treatment. This is obviously not the case in developing countries. There, individuals must draw on their financial capital or, as is the case for the vast majority who cannot afford medicines, on their social capital to pay for drugs. Social capital, in this case, designates the proximal network of social relations through which resources may be mobilized. Material resources may be used directly to pay for drugs, or they may be used to invest in businesses that will generate revenues to cover the cost of procuring drugs. In the latter case, one's social network can be used to obtain introductions to individuals – such as physicians or politically powerful figures – who may be able to help access drugs.

Individuals make use of social networks to mobilize the resources they need to purchase medicines or gain access to sites where these are available – public health facilities, research institutes, or NGOs, where drugs may be available at lower cost than in the private sector, or may be completely free, as in the case of research protocols. Social networks may also channel treatments directly to affected individuals, as when relatives, friends, colleagues, or fellow activists in Northern countries with access to drugs send medicines to individuals or institutions in countries with limited access, a process referred to as "drug recycling."

The ability of individuals to leverage social relations to obtain treatments, however, is constrained by the political economy of the transnational pharmaceuticals industry and, behind it, the global organization of capitalist production. Transnational advocacy groups appear to have achieved some success in pointing out, and reducing, these structural barriers to treatments, but it remains to be seen how sustained these will be.

Treatments influence biology, and through these embodied effects representations of the disease, and in turn the subjectivity of those who are able to access them. One result has been the advent of a therapeutic activism spearheaded by those who have had access to treatment on behalf of those who do not. This concatenation of biology (epidemics and the therapeutic effect of drugs) and social relations (those that condition the spread of epidemics and those that condition access to treatments) is an example of biosocial change. The biosocial changes brought by the epidemic have begun to crystallize in a notion of "therapeutic citizenship."

Therapeutic citizenship is emerging as a salient force in the local African settings that have been explored here, where widespread poverty means that neither kinship nor a hollowed-out state can offer guarantees against the vicissitudes of life. It has also emerged as a rallying point for transnational activism in a neoliberal world in which illness claims carry more weight than those based on poverty, injustice, or structural violence.

Notes

1   C. Patton, *Globalizing AIDS* (Minneapolis: University of Minnesota Press, 2002).
2   M. Pandolfi, "L'industrie humanitaire: une souveraineté mouvante et supracoloniale: réflexion sur l'expérience des Balkans," *Multitudes* 3, 2001, pp. 97–105.
3   S. Pigg, "Introduction," in *The Moral Object of Sex: Science, Development and Sexuality in Global Perspective*, Vincanne Adams and Stacy Leigh Pigg, eds. (Durham, NC: Duke University Press, forthcoming).
4   Arjun Appadurai, "Introduction: commodities and the politics of value," in *The Social Life of Things*, Arjun Appadurai, ed. (Cambridge: Cambridge University Press, 1986), 3–63.
5   The notion of a "moral economy" draws on E. P. Thompson, "The moral economy of the English crowd in the eighteenth century," *Past and Present* 50, 1971, pp. 76–134. Thompson shows how capitalist markets brought into conflict different régimes of value. I use it here in a somewhat broader sense, to draw attention to how different social relations produce value.
6   The manner in which individuals access therapy has also been a staple of medical anthropological studies of patterns of resort, also called "therapeutic itineraries." Multiple medical traditions can be accessed either serially or simultaneously. These have drawn attention to "therapy managing groups" that debate options and make decisions on both economic and cultural grounds about which practitioners should be consulted and when. See John M. Janzen, *The Quest for Therapy* (Berkeley: University of California Press, 1978); Marc Augé and Claudine Herzlich, *Le sens du mal: anthropologie, histoire, sociologie de la maladie* (Paris: Editions des archives contemporaines, 1984).
7   See M. Lock, *East Asian Medicine in Urban Japan* (Berkeley: University of California Press, 1980); Paul Brodwin, *Medicine and Morality in Haiti: The Contest for Healing Power* (Cambridge: Cambridge University Press, 1996).
8   A normal T4 cell count is over 600; with less than 50 cells, patients are at high risk of serious opportunistic infections and death within the year.
9   Vidal Msellati and J.-P. Moatti, eds., *L'accès aux traitements du VIH/sida en Côte-d'Ivoire: Évaluation de l'Initiative Onusida/ministère ivoirien de la santé publique, aspects économiques,*

sociaux et compartementaux (Paris: Éditions de l'Agence nationale de recherché sur le sida, Collection sciences sociales et sida, 2001).

10 C. Adjé et al., "High Prevalence of Genotypic and Phenotypic HIV-1 Drug-Resistant Strains among Patients Receiving Antiretroviral Therapy in Abidjan, Cote d'Ivoire," *Journal of Acquired Immune Deficiency Syndromes* 26(5), April 15, 2001, pp. 501-6.

9

THE LAST COMMODITY:
Post-Human Ethics and the Global Traffic in "Fresh" Organs

NANCY SCHEPER-HUGHES

The neoliberal readjustments of societies worldwide to meet the demands of economic globalization have been accompanied by a depletion of traditional modernist, humanist, and pastoral ideologies, values, and practices. New relations between capital and labor, bodies and the state, inclusion and exclusion, belonging and extraterritoriality have taken shape. Some of these realignments have resulted in surprising new outcomes (for example, the emergence and applications of democratic ideas and ideals of "medical" and "sexual" citizenship[1] in countries such as Brazil and India, which have challenged international patent laws and trade restrictions to expand the production and distribution of generic, lifesaving drugs), while others (for example, the spread of paid surrogacy in assisted reproduction[2]) have reproduced all too familiar inequalities.

Nowhere are these trends more stark than in the global markets in bodies, organs, and tissues to supply the needs of transplant patients who are now willing to travel great distances to procure them. But rather than a conventional story of the lamentable decline of humanistic social values and social relations, our discussion is tethered to a frank recognition that the material grounds on which those once cherished modernist values and practices were based have shifted today almost beyond recognition.

The entry of free markets (black and gray) and market incentives[3] into organs procurement has thrown into question the transplant rhetoric on "organs scarcity." There is obviously no shortage of desperate individuals willing to sell a kidney, a portion of their liver, a lung, an eye, or even a testicle for a pittance. But while *types of scarcity)*

erasing one vexing scarcity, the organs traffic has produced a new one – a scarcity of transplant patients of sufficient means and independence and who are willing to break, bend, or bypass laws and longstanding codes of medical ethical conduct.

Transplant Ethics

From its inception, transplant medicine put severe demands on modernist conceptions of the body, the person, and the meanings of life and death. For one, transplantation demanded a radical redefinition of death, to allow the immediate harvesting of organs from bodies neither completely dead nor yet still living, which to this day still troubles many of the world's religious leaders and a surprising number of medical specialists[4] – not to mention the relatives of the nearly dead, who so often refuse to allow the term to be applied to their loved ones and prevent harvesting from taking place.

Diametrically opposed to the "softer" medical ethic of the clinic and the emergency room, based on a commitment to save the sickest, transplant ethics operates on the less civil and more brutal ethic of the lifeboat and of the battlefield, based on a commitment to save the salvageable and to allow the sickest to die. In the United States, one needs to be relatively healthy and financially solvent (or at least well insured) to be recommended for a transplant. How can a surgeon recommend transplant to a patient without dependable access to expensive anti-rejection drugs? But as transplant capabilities have developed and the desires for transplant have "democratized," medical consumers have begun to challenge the old battlefield triage and are demanding an end to "wartime" rationing based on scarcities that could be addressed by "simply" tapping into and plundering the bodies of the *living*.

This move has required a radical breach with, or highly selective use of, classical medical ethics, based worldwide on a blend of Aristotelian theories of virtue (wisdom, courage, temperance, and justice), and the Hippocratic ethic of purity, loyalty, compassion, and respect for the dignity of the individual. In recent years, modern theories of right action, especially John Rawls' theory of distributive justice to redress inequities by redistributing scarce goods to the most disadvantaged social groups,[5] has had made some inroads on medical ethics – but not in the field of transplant medicine, where these ideas are simply anathema.

Historically, transplant physicians have been trained in the Hippocratic tradition of medical ethics, with its markedly individualist conception of physician responsibility and virtue. In this tradition, the physician owes his loyalties to the patient alone, as if society – let alone the rest of the world – did not exist. In recent years, and in response to the privatization and commercialization of medicine (transplant in particular), many surgeons now espouse a frankly post-humanist utilitarian ethic based on the moral philosophy of John Stuart Mill[6] and Jeremy Bentham,[7] but stripped of their original social content and concerns. In a recent essay in *The Lancet*,[8] Dr. Michael Friedlaender, of Hadassah Hospital in Jerusalem, explains his about-face with respect to accepting the "greater good" that can result from adopting a utilitarian ethic with respect to the individual's right to buy (or sell) a kidney. He opens his essay pointedly: "Recently I was told that I am a utilitarian. I had always considered myself a humanitarian, but recently I developed some doubts about my beliefs." He follows this with a discussion of his many kidney patients, both Jews and Arabs, who have returned from abroad (Jews from eastern Europe and Arabs from Iran and Iraq) after purchasing a kidney.

The advent of the kidney trade evokes a timeless moral and ethical "gray zone"[9] – the lengths to which it is permissible to go in the interests of saving or prolonging one's own life at the expense of diminishing another person's life or sacrificing cherished cultural and political values (such as social solidarity, justice, or equity).

The Research Problem: A Note on Method

At the heart of this exploratory, multi-sited, ethnographic research project are a few basic first questions: How does the human organs market function? Who are the key players? How are the relations between organized crime and illicit transplant medicine structured? Whose needs are privileged? What invisible sacrifices are demanded? What "noble lies" are concealed in the tired transplant rhetoric of gifting, scarcities, and human needs?

In the course of this research I have interviewed kidney patients in their homes, clinics, and their hospital beds to try to understand the specific conditions of their suffering.

I have followed a much smaller number of them from their dialysis clinics to meetings with brokers and intermediaries in suburban shopping malls and hotel lobbies, and from there to illicit surgeries in rented operating rooms of public and private hospitals, some resembling the clandestine back-alley abortion clinics of the 1940s and 1950s. I have tracked down some notorious organs brokers, only to discover that many began as desperate kidney sellers themselves, who were later hired by their surgeons as local kidney hunters. My research associates and I have met with local kidney sellers in township *shabeens* in Soweto, in squatter camps in Manila, in shantytowns in Brazil, in jails in Israel, in smoke-filled bars in Chisenau, and in the wine cellars of Mingir in Moldova.[10]

In short, we have gone to many of the places where the economically and politically dispossessed – including refugees, the homeless, street children, undocumented workers, prisoners, AWOL soldiers, aging prostitutes, cigarette smugglers, petty thieves, and other marginalized people – are lured into selling their organs. At the same time I have followed, observed, and interviewed over one hundred international surgeons and transplant specialists who are knowledgeable about or implicated in illicit surgeries, their lawyers, and their often far-flung medical and financial connections which make these surgeries possible.

In its odd juxtapositions of ethnography, documentation, surveillance, and human rights work, this project blends genres and transgresses longstanding distinctions between anthropology, political journalism, scientific report, moral philosophy, and human rights advocacy.[11] These new ethnographic engagements require the fieldworker to enter spaces and into conversations where nothing can be taken for granted, and where a hermeneutics of suspicion replaces earlier fieldwork modes of bracketing and suspension of disbelief.

Because of the covert nature of these illicit transplant transactions, I have had to operate under cover at times, realizing that this represents a serious deviation from classical anthropological and fieldwork ethics. In Turkey in February 2002, I posed as a potential buyer desperately seeking a kidney in order to meet with kidney sellers at a "Russian suitcase market" in a run-down, immigrant section of Istanbul. In Buenos Aires, I posed as the American niece of a missing woman who had disappeared at the end of the Argentine "Dirty War" in order to access the grounds of a large, closed state asylum for the profoundly mentally retarded, a site long suspected of being involved in illegal blood, organs, and tissues harvesting. While these obvious deviations from standard fieldwork practice and ethics certainly gave me pause, I could not think of another way to learn of the hidden suffering of an invisible and silenced population. This project required a certain militancy, as well as a continual and relentless form of self-criticism and a constant rethinking of *anthropological* as well as medical ethics and practice. In short, I claim no innocence for myself.[12]

Here, I will contrast the *variable* meanings of selling (or buying) a body part (in Israel, Moldova, and the Philippines) with a growing consensus in the transplant community that supports a patient-centered ethic that includes the right to purchase advanced, expensive, and experimental biomedical/surgical procedures, as well as to buy and sell body parts from the living and the dead. Both are compatible with neoliberal economics.

Indeed, commercialized transplant exemplifies better than any other biomedical technology the reach of economic liberalism. Transplant technology trades comfortably in the domain of postmodern biopolitics, with its values of disposability and free and transparent circulation. The uninhibited circulation of bought and sold kidneys exemplifies a neoliberal political discourse based on juridical concepts of the autonomous individual subject, equality (at least, equality of opportunity), radical freedom, accumulation, and universalism, expressed in the expansion of medical rights and medical citizenship.

Under the rubric of "circulation," I will focus on the networks of organized crime ("body mafia") that are responsible for putting into circulation and bringing together ambulatory organs buyers, outlaw surgeons, illicit and sometimes makeshift transplant units, and clandestine laboratories in an example of what economist Jagdish Bhagwati[13] refers to as " rotten trade." Rotten trade refers to any trade in "bads" – arms, drugs, stolen goods, and hazardous and toxic products, as well as traffic in humans, babies, bodies, and slave labor. The organs trade is fueled by a dual "waiting list," one formed by sickness, the other by misery.

I will explore some of the implications of this shift in medical practice and ethics, and the social, political, and economic quandaries resulting from it. And I will conclude with an *anthropos*-centric critique of the stripped-down conceptions of human life (what Giorgio Agamben called naked or brute life[14]) that this brutal form of medical intervention requires.

In all, I shall make three points. The first is about invented scarcities and artificial needs, within a new context of highly fetishized "fresh" organs. The chronic scarcity of cadaver organs has evolved into a trade in "surplus" body parts from living "suppliers," which has sustained the growth of "medical tourism" as well as new forms of "biopiracy." The second point concerns altruism versus invisible sacrifice. The third point concerns surplus empathy and the relative visibility of two distinct populations – excluded and invisible organ givers and included and highly visible organ receivers. We have found almost everywhere a new form of globalized "apartheid medicine" that privileges one class of patients, organ recipients, over another class of invisible and unrecognized "nonpatients," about whom almost nothing is known – an excellent place for a critical medical anthropologist to begin.

Transplant Tourism

What Jean and John Comaroff refer to as millennial or "second coming" capitalism[15] has facilitated the spread of advanced medical procedures and biotechnologies to all corners of the world, producing strange markets and "occult economies." Together, these have incited new tastes and desires for the skin, bone, blood, organs, tissue, and reproductive and genetic material of others. Nowhere are these processes more transparent than in the field of organ transplants that now takes place in a transnational space, with both donors and recipients following new paths of capital and technology in the global economy.

The spread of transplant technologies initially created a global scarcity of transplantable organs at the same time that economic globalization released an exodus of displaced and "surplus" persons to do the shadow work of production and, *alter*, to provide bodies for sexual and medical consumption. The "open" global market economy provided the ideal conditions for an unprecedented movement of people, including mortally sick bodies traveling in one direction and "healthy" organs (encased in their human packages) in another direction, creating a bizarre "kula ring" of international body trade. Like any other business, the organs trade is driven by a simple market calculus of supply and demand. Its brokers organize and bring together affluent kidney buyers from Japan, Italy, Israel, and Saudi Arabia with the stranded Moldovan and Romanian peasants, Turkish junk dealers, Palestinian refugees, AWOL soldiers from Iraq and Afghanistan, and the unemployed stevedores of Manila's slums from whom they will buy a lifesaving commodity.

Transplant tourism is vital to the medical economies of rapidly privatizing clinical and hospital services in poorer countries that are struggling to stay afloat. The "global cities"[16] in this nether economy are not London, New York, Tokyo, and Frankfurt, but Istanbul, Lima, Lvov, Tel Aviv, Chisenau, Bombay, Johannesburg, and Manila. However, the United States has not been isolated from this global market that pits desperate transplant patients against equally desperate poor people, each trying to find a solution to basic problems of human survival. Transplant tourism packages, arranged in the Middle East, have brought hundreds of affluent kidney patients to U.S. transplant centers for surgeries conducted with paid donors or with cadaver organs that are otherwise described as painfully scarce.[17] The University of Maryland Medical Center, for example, advertises its kidney transplant program in Arabic, Chinese, Hebrew, and Japanese on its website.[18] Mt. Sinai Hospital in New York City has published promotional advertisements on its transplant capabilities in the *Wall Street Journal* and in the *International Herald Tribune*. The U.S.A. is very democratic in at least one sense – anyone with enough cash, regardless of where they come from, can become a "medical citizen" of the U.S. and receive a *bona fide* "made in the U.S.A." transplant organ.

To give them their due, however, these new transplant transactions are a blend of altruism and commerce; consent and coercion; gifts and theft; science and sorcery; care and human sacrifice. On the one hand, the spread of transplant technologies, even in the murky context of illicit surgeries, has given the possibility of new, extended, or greatly improved life to a select population of mobile kidney patients from the deserts of Oman to the rain forests of Central Brazil.[19] On the other hand, the spread of "transplant tourism" has exacerbated older divisions between North and South, core and periphery haves and have-nots, spawning a new form of commodity fetishism in demands by medical consumers for a quality product – "fresh" and "healthy" kidneys purchased from living bodies. In general, the circulation of kidneys follows the established routes of capital from South to North, from poorer to more affluent bodies, from black and brown bodies to white ones, and from females to males, or from poor males to more affluent males. Women are rarely the recipients of purchased or purloined organs anywhere in the world. We can even speak of organ donor versus organ recipient nations.

In these radical exchanges of body parts and somatic information, lifesaving measures for the one demand a bodily sacrifice of self-mutilation by the other. And one man's biosociality[20] is another woman's biopiracy, depending on whether one is speaking from a Silicon Valley biotech laboratory or from a sewage-infested *barangay* in Manila. The commodified kidney is, to date, the primary currency, in transplant tourism; it represents the gold standard of organ sales worldwide. In recent months, however, markets in part-livers from living vendors are beginning to emerge in Southeast Asia.

New forms of "social kinship" (and a promise of biosociality) must be invented to link strangers, even at times political "enemies" (see below), from distant locations who are described by the operating surgeons as "a perfect match – like brothers," while they are prevented from seeing, let alone speaking to, each other. If and when these "kidney kin" meet at all, it will be by accident and like ships passing in the night, as they are wheeled, heavily sedated, on hospital gurneys into their respective operating rooms, where one surgeon *removes* the seller's kidney of last resort and the other *inserts* the buyer's kidney of opportunity.

In all, the strange markets, excess capital, occult medical economies, renegade surgeons,[21] and local rings of "kidney hunters" with links to an international Mafia [22] exist side by side with a parallel traffic in slave workers, adoptive babies, drugs, and small arms. This confluence in the flows of immigrant workers and itinerant kidney sellers is a troubling subtext in the story of late 20th and early 21st century globalization, one that juxtaposes aspects of pre- and postmodernity. The only voice of protest comes, however, in the form of inarticulate and unpalatable rumors of body-, baby-, and organ-stealing – rumors that were quickly squelched as an urban legend.

Scenes from the Field

Avraham R., a retired lawyer of 70, stepped gingerly out of his sedan at the curb of the Beit Belgia Faculty Club at the University of Jerusalem in July 2000. The dapper gent, a grandfather of five, had been playing a game of "chicken" with me over the past two weeks, ducking my persistent phone calls. Each time I asked the genial grandfather for a face-to-face interview, he demurred: "It's not to protect me," he said, "but my family." Then, one afternoon, Avraham surprised me, not only agreeing to meet me but insisting that he come over to my comfortable quarters where, over a few bottles of mineral water, he explained why and how he had come to the decision to risk traveling to an undisclosed location in eastern Europe to purchase a kidney from an anonymous "peasant," and to face transplant in a spartan operating room ("I have more medicines in my own medicine chest than they had in that hospital," he said) rather than remain on dialysis at Hadassah Hospital, as his nephrologist had suggested.

Avraham was still eligible for a transplant, but at his at his age, his doctors warned, such a long operation was risky. Dialysis, they told him, was really his best option. But Avraham protested that he was not yet ready for the "medical trash-heap," which is the way he and many other Israeli kidney patients now view hemodialysis. And, like a growing number of kidney patients, he rejected the idea of a cadaver organ (the "dead man's organ") as "disgusting" and unacceptable:

> Why should I have to wait years for a kidney from somebody who was in a traffic accident, pinned under a car for many hours, then in miserable condition in the I.C.U. [intensive care unit] for days and only then, after all that trauma, have that same organ put inside me? That organ isn't going to be any good! Or worse, I could get the organ of an old person, or an alcoholic, or someone who died of a stroke. That kidney has already done its work! No, obviously, it's much better to get a kidney from a healthy person who can also benefit from the money I can afford to pay. Believe me, where I went the people were so poor they didn't even have bread to eat. Do you have any idea of what one, let alone five thousand dollars, means to a peasant? The money I paid him was 'a gift of life' equal to what I received.

Then, in December 2001, during an early snowstorm, I ducked into a small, dark, subterranean wine cave in the rustic little village of Mingir, Moldova. There, once out of earshot of his elderly father and beyond the prying eyes of disapproving neighbors, 22-year-old Vladimir, a skinny lad with a rakish metal stud in his lip, explained how he had been approached a few years earlier by Nina, a local kidney hunter, who arranged his passport, visa, and bus ticket to Istanbul, a bumpy 18-hour overnight ride. With the demise of the Soviet Union, the agricultural economy of rural Moldova collapsed in the mid-1990s. Here, in the heart of central Europe, economic globalization has meant one thing only for agricultural villagers – that 40 percent of the adult population has had to leave home to find work abroad. Today, Moldova is the poorest country in Europe: an indigenous "third world" within European borders.

Once in Istanbul, Vladimir was housed in the basement of a run-down hotel facing a notorious Russian "suitcase market" in the tough immigrant neighborhood of Askary. He shared the space with several other Moldovan villagers, including a few frightened village girls barely out of high school. First, Nina arrived to break the news to one of the girls that her "waitressing" job would be in a bar where "exotic" dancing was required. Then Vladimir was told that he was wanted for more than pressing pants. He would start by selling a few pints of his blood and once a "match" was found, he would be taken to a private hospital where he would give up his "best" kidney for $3,000, less the cost of his travel, room, and board and the fees for his "handlers." And a few days later Vlad was told that an elderly transplant patient from Israel, who had traveled to Istanbul with his private surgeon, was matched and ready to go. When Vlad demurred, Nina arrived with her pockmarked, pistol-carrying Turkish boyfriend, who told Vladimir that he was quickly losing patience. "Actually," Vlad says ruefully, "If I had refused to go along with them, my body minus *both* kidneys, and who knows what else, could be floating somewhere in the Bosporous Strait."

But once safely home, hapless kidney sellers such as Vladimir face ridicule and ostracism. Both kidney sellers and female sex workers are held in contempt in rural Moldova as shameless prostitutes. Months and even years later, these young men suffer from feelings of shame and regret – like Nicolae, a 26-year-old former welder from Mingir, who broke down during an interview in December 2000, calling himself "a disgrace to my family, my Church, and my country."

While kidney selling is a deeply stigmatized act in Moldova, it has become a routine event in slums and shantytowns half a world a way in the Filipino capital of Manila. This is despite the fact that the operation has put a great many young men permanently out of work. Kidney sellers say they are no longer able to lift heavy cargoes: "No one wants a kidney seller on his work team," an unemployed father of three told us, while his wife fumed at him from a distance.

Bangon Lupa is a garbage-strewn slum built on stilt shacks over a polluted and feces-infested stretch of the Pasig River that runs through the shantytown on its way to Manila Bay. In Bangon Lupa, "coming of age" now means that one is legally old enough to sell a kidney. But, as with other coming of age rituals, many young men lie about their age and boast of having sold a kidney when they were as young as 16 years old: "No one at the hospital asks us for any documents" they assured me. The kidney donors lied about other things as well – their names, addresses, and medical histories, including their daily exposure to the general plagues of the third world – TB, AIDS, dengue, and hepatitis, not to mention chronic skin infections and malnutrition.

In this *barangay* of largely unemployed stevedores, I encountered an unanticipated "waiting list," comprised of angry and "disrespected" kidney sellers who had been "neglected" and "overlooked" by the medical doctors at Manila's most prestigious private hospital, St. Luke's Episcopal Medical Center. When word spread that I was looking to speak to kidney sellers, several scowling and angry young men approached me to complain: "We are strong and virile men, and yet none of us has been called up to sell." Perhaps they had been rejected, the men surmised, because of their age (too young or too old), their blood (difficult to match), or their general medical condition. *rejected* But whatever the reason, they had been judged as less valuable kidney vendors than some of their lucky neighbors, who now owned new VCRs, karaoke machines, and expensive tricycles. "What's wrong with me?," a 42-year-old man asked, thinking I must be an American kidney hunter. "I registered six months ago, and no one from St. Luke's has called me . . . But I am healthy. I can lift heavy weights. And my urine is clean." Moreover, he was willing, he said, to sell below the going rate of $1,300 for a fresh kidney.

When one donor is rejected, another, younger and more healthy looking, family member is often substituted. And kidney selling becomes an economic niche in some families that specialize in it. Indeed, one large extended family Bangong Lupa supplied St. Luke's Hospital with a reliable source of kidneys, borrowing strength from across the generations as first father, then son, and then daughter-in-law each stepped forward to contribute to the family income.

The Consumers – The Expansion of Medical Citizenship and Commodity Fetishism

Finding an available supply of organ vendors was only a partial solution to the new scarcities produced by transplant technologies. Even Jesus knew that "the poor ye shall always have with you," and the all too tempting "bio-availability" of poor bodies has been a primary stimulus to the "fresh" organ trade. Today, a great many eager and willing kidney sellers wait outside transplant units; others check themselves into special wards of surgical units that resemble "kidney motels," where they lie on mats or in hospital beds for days, even weeks, watching color television, eating chips, and waiting for the "lucky number" that will turn them into the day's winner of the kidney transplant lottery. Entire neighborhoods, cities, and regions are known in transplant circles as "kidney belts" because so many people there have entered the kidney trade.

More difficult is locating patients of sufficient economic means to pay for these expensive operations, as well as sufficiently courageous to travel to the largely third world locations where people are willing to self-mutilate in the interests of short-term survival. Here is a classic problem in microeconomics – one of supply and demand side sources separated by vast geographies, different cultures, and even by fierce religious and political hostilities.

Who, for example, would imagine that, in the midst of the longstanding religious and ethnic hostilities and an almost genocidal war in the Middle East, one of the first "sources" of living donors for Israeli kidney transplant patients would be Palestinian guest workers; or that, as recently as March 2002, Israeli patients would be willing to travel to Istanbul to be transplanted in a private clinic by a Moslem surgeon who decorates his waiting room with photos of Ataturk and a plastic glass eye to ward off evil? Or that the transplanted kidneys would be taken from impoverished Eastern Orthodox peasants from Moldova and Romania, who came to Turkey to sell smuggled cigarettes until they ran into the famous kidney brokers of Askary flea market?

A new source of organs scarcity is, however, being socially produced by the artificial expansion of organs waiting lists in North America and Europe to include patients from the medical margins – those over 70 years, infants, those with hepatitis C and HIV seropositivity, and those proven to be immunologically prone to organ rejection. There is little recognition that these experiments are inflating the demand for organs and promoting desperate means to obtain them. Rather, these experiments are defended by officials from UNOS and by EUROTRANS[23] as a democratic gesture and a service to those potential transplant consumers who are demanding the right to any and all advanced medical procedures now available.

New transplant patient advocacy groups have sprung up in many parts of the world, from Brazil to Israel to Iran to the U.S.A., demanding unobstructed access to transplant and to the lifesaving "spare" organs of " the other," for which they are willing to pay a negotiable, market-determined price. They justify the means by recourse to the mantra that it will "save a life." However, most kidney patients around the world have the option of long-term hemodialysis, weakening the "life-saving" argument. The problem is that dialysis, even as a bridge while waiting for transplant, is increasingly viewed by sophisticated kidney activists today as unacceptable suffering. In September 2000, a 23-year-old university student from Jerusalem flew to New York City for a kidney transplant with an organ purchased from a local "donor," arranged through a broker in Brooklyn. The cost of the surgery ($200,000) was paid for by his Israeli "sick funds" (medical insurance that is guaranteed to all Israeli citizens). Noteworthy in his narrative is an almost seamless "naturalization" of living donation accompanied by a rejection of the artificiality of the dialysis machine:

> Kidney transplant from a living person is the most natural solution because you are free of the [dialysis] machine. With transplant you don't have to go to the hospital three times a week to waste your time, for three or four hours. And after each dialysis you

don't feel very well, and you sleep a lot, and on weekends you feel too tired to go out with your friends. There are still a lot of poisons in the body and when you can't remove them, you feel tired. Look, it isn't a normal life. And also you are limited to certain foods. You are not allowed to eat a lot of meat, salt, fruits, vegetables. Every month you do tests to see that the calcium level is OK, and even so your skin becomes yellow. Esthetically, it isn't very nice. So, a kidney transplant from a living donor is the best, and the most *natural* solution.

Similarly, many kidney activists reject conventional "waiting lists" for organs as archaic vestiges of wartime triage and rationing, or reminiscent of hated socialist bread lines and petrol "queues." In the present climate of biotechnological optimism and biomedical triumphalism, any shortage, even of body parts, is viewed as a basic management, marketing, or policy failure. The ideology of the global economy is one of unlimited and freely circulating goods. And these new commodities are evaluated, like any other, in terms of their quality, durability, and market value. In today's organs market, a kidney purchased from a Filipino costs as little as $1,200, one from a Moldovan peasant $2,700, and one from a Turkish worker up to $8,000, while a kidney purchased from a housewife in Lima, Peru, can command up to $15,000 in a private clinic.

Internet brokers prey on consumer prejudices and on the anxieties of transplant candidates. "Livers-4-You" (http://www.kidneysurgery@s-s-net.com) advertises the following: "Want a living donor next week, or a morgue organ in five years? We are a new organization with a New York City phone number and unique experience in locating the overseas pathway for those waiting too long for a transplant." This website states that it has "joined with medical professionals in the Philippines (and nearby countries) to help 'fill the gap' between the supply and demand for organs." For those who are nervous about traveling to a "developing" country for transplant surgery, the site notes that "medical schools in the Philippines are carbon copies of U.S. schools and that Philippine surgeons are all trained in the United States." The organization's head surgeon is himself a U.S.-trained and -licensed doctor, who has "done many operations in the United States."

Bioethics – The Handmaiden of Free Market Medicine

What goes by the wayside in these new medical transactions are the modernist conceptions of bodily holism, integrity, and human dignity, not to mention traditional Islamic and Judeo-Christian beliefs in the "sacredness" of the body. Free market medicine requires a divisible body with detachable and demystified organs seen as ordinary and "plain things," simple material for medical consumption. But these same "plain" objects have a way of reappearing and returning like the repressed, when least expected, almost like medieval messengers and gargoyles from the past, in the form of highly spiritualized and fetishized objects of desire. As Veena Das once wryly observed, "An organ is *never* just an organ."

Indeed, the highly fetishized kidney is invested with all the magical energy and potency that the transplant patient is looking for in the name of "new" life. As Avraham, the Israeli kidney buyer, put it: "I was able to see my donor [from a village of eastern Europe]. He was young, strong, healthy, and virile – *everything* I was hoping for."

In the context of this volume on "*anthropos*," it might be fair to ask if the life that is teased out of the body of the living donor bears any resemblance to the ethical life of the free citizen (*bios*) or whether it is closer to what Giorgio Agamben,[24] drawing on Aristotle's *Politics*, referred to as *zoe* – brute, bestial, or bare life, the unconscious, unreflective mere life of the species? Thomas Aquinas would later translate these ancient Greek concepts into medieval Christian terms that distinguished the natural life from the good life.[25]

But neither Aristotle nor Aquinas is with us. Instead, medical practitioners consult and take counsel from the new specialists in bioethics, a field finely calibrated to meet the needs of advanced biomedical biotechnologies. Even as conservative a scholar as Francis Fukuyama refers to the "community of bio-ethicists" as having "grown up in tandem with the biotech industry" and being, at times, "nothing more than a "sophisticated (and sophistic) justifiers of whatever it is the scientific community wants to do.""[26]

The field of bioethics has to date offered little resistance to the growth of markets in humans and body parts, and many now argue that the real problem lies with outdated laws, increasingly irrelevant national regulatory agencies (such as UNOS), and archaic medical norms that are out of touch with economic realities today – and with the "quiet revolution" of those who have refused to face a premature death with equanimity and "dignity" while waiting patiently on an official waiting list for a cadaver organ.[27] Some argue for a free trade in human organs; others argue for a regulated market. In the meantime, the rupture between practice and the law can be summarized as follows: while commerce in human organs is illegal according to the official legal codes of virtually all nations where transplant is practiced, nowhere are the renegade surgeons (who are well known to their professional colleagues), organs brokers, and kidney buyers (or sellers) pursued by the law, let alone prosecuted. It is easy to understand why kidney buyers and sellers would not be the focus of prosecution under the law. Compassion rather than outrage is the more appropriate response to their acts. But the failure on the part of governments, ministries of health, and law enforcement agencies to interrupt the activities of international transplant outlaws, their holding companies, money laundering operations, and Mafia connections, can only be explained as an *intentional* oversight.

Indeed, some of the most notorious outlaw transplant surgeons are the medical directors of major transplant units, who serve on prestigious international medical committees and on ethics panels. None have been censured by their own profession, though a few have been investigated, briefly arrested, arraigned, and are awaiting trials in Israel and South Africa. But all practice their illicit surgeries freely, though some move their bases of international operations frequently so as to avoid medical or police surveillance. One of transplant medicine's most notorious outlaws, Dr. Zaki Shapira, of Bellinson Medical near Tel Aviv, served on the prestigious international "Bellagio Task Force" investigating the global traffic in organs, of which I was also a member.[28] In one of his subsequent trips to Italy, he was the recipient of a prestigious human service award. Meanwhile, one of Dr. Shapira's patients in Jerusalem provided me with copies of his medical documents that led to a fraudulent medical society in Bergamo, Italy, to whom the patient had sent the $180,000 that his illicit transplant (in Turkey) had cost. When I called the "medical society" in Bergamo, I was told that they were only a "clearinghouse" for medical encyclopedias.

The impunity of these transplant outlaws concerns more than government lassitude and obvious professional corruption. Outlaw surgeons are also protected by the charisma that accompanies their seemingly miraculous powers over life, death, and adverse circumstances. As much as his younger colleagues worry about Dr. Shapira's questionable ethics, they praise his surgical technique and his "golden hands." The head of the Turkish medical ethics committee lamented that Dr. Yusef Somnez, the "Doctor Vulture" of Istanbul fame, was one of Turkey's most celebrated transplant surgeons. "Somnez is the man who put transplant on the map in Turkey," he said.

Some transplant surgeons themselves see themselves as "above the law," a tradition they inherited from the early days of transplant, when the "founding fathers," such as Christian Barnard in South Africa and Thomas Starzel in the U.S.A., battled against prevailing social norms and those who resisted transplant's redefinition of death to allow the removal of organs from those still at that time designated as living, though most certainly dying, patients. That same sense of embattlement continues today among transplant surgeons who may publicly support international regulations against buying and selling organs, but who privately say that this is the *only solution* to organs scarcities. In the face of illicit transplants with paid donors, many surgeons simply look the other away. Others actively facilitate sales, while others counsel kidney patients for transplant trips overseas and care for them on their return from a trip to South America, South Africa, or China, where organs are purchased from the living or (as in the case of China) taken from an executed prisoner.

In the rational choice language of contemporary medical ethics, the conflict between nonmalfeasance ("do no harm") and beneficence (the moral duty to perform good acts) is increasingly resolved in favor of the libertarian and consumer-oriented principle that those able to broker or buy a human organ should not be prevented from doing so. Paying for a kidney "donation" is viewed as a potential "win–win" situation that can benefit both parties.[29] Individual decision-making and patient autonomy have become the final arbiters of medical and bioethical values. Social justice and notions of the "good society" hardly figure at all their discussions.

In the post-human, consumer-oriented context, the ancient perceptions of virtue in suffering and grace in the art of dying can only appear patently absurd. But the transformation of a person into a "life" that must be prolonged or saved at any cost has made life into the ultimate commodity fetish. The belief in the absolute value of a single human life saved or prolonged at any cost ends all ethical inquiry and erases any possibility of a global social ethic. And the traffic in kidneys reduces the human content of all the lives it touches.

Medicine and the Mafia

Illicit transplant transactions are obviously complex and require expert teamwork among technicians in blood and tissue laboratories, dual surgical teams working in tandem, nephrologists, and post-operative nurses. Travel, passports, and visas must be arranged. These awesome organizational requirements are arranged in many parts of the world by a new class of organs brokers, ranging from sophisticated business-men, medical insurance agents, and travel agents to criminal networks of armed and dangerous Mafia to the local "kidney hunters" of Istanbul, Bangong Lupa, and Mingir. In Israel and the U.S.A. religious organizations, charitable trusts, and patient advocacy organizations sometimes harbor organs brokers. I have identified a large network operating between Israel and several cities in the U.S.A. on both coasts. Some have recruited organ donors locally, while others have recruited Russian and Moldovan immigrants, ex-prisoners, and other marginalized people who have been smuggled into the U.S.A. as tourists.

The outlaw surgeons who practice their illicit operations in rented, makeshift clinics or, just as often, in operating rooms of some of the best public or private medical centers in the city, do so under the frank gaze of local and national governments, ministries of health, regulatory agencies, and professional medical associations. In short, the illegal practice of transplant tourism, which relies on an extensive network of body brokers and human traffickers, is a public secret, one that involves some of the world's most prestigious hospitals and medical centers. Transplant crimes – even when they explode into gunfire and leave a trail of blood – go officially undetected and unpunished. Even the most aggressive surgeons can find themselves trapped and more deeply involved in "the business" than they had ever anticipated.

But in addition to organized crime, the organs business is also not infrequently protected by military and state interests, particularly during periods of political conflict and war. A footnote to the story of military terrorism during (and following) the "Dirty War" in Argentina and the dictatorship years in Brazil is that doctors there provided – in the case of Argentina – not only children for military families but also blood, bones, heart valves, organs, and tissues for transplant taken from the bodies of the politically "disappeared" and from the socially disappeared, including the captive populations such as the mentally retarded in state institutions, such as the infamous Montes de Oca and Open Door asylums in Lujan, Bsás province. There are indications that the organs trafficking business in eastern Europe began amidst the chaos and dehumanization of the death camps during the genocides in the former Yugoslavia.

Israel, for complicated reasons having to do with moral, political, and institutional obstacles to the procurement and distribution of cadaver organs, is a major player in the global market for "fresh" (living donor) organs. The search by Israeli surgeons and patients for living donor organs began in the West Bank and Gaza, and then moved to Turkey, India, and Iraq, and, later to Moldova, Romania, and Russia. When these options closed down, the Israeli market for kidneys moved to Brazil[30] and South Africa. Thus, today, one half of all Israelis who have a transplanted kidney purchased that kidney abroad. Caught between a highly educated and medically conscious public and a very low rate of organ donation, the Israeli Ministry of Health has expedited the expansion of transplant tourism by allowing Israeli patients to use their national insurance to pay for transplants conducted elsewhere, even if illegally. The cost of the transplant "package" increased from $120,000 in 1998 to $200,000 in 2001. The cost includes the air travel, bribes to airport and customs officials, "double operation" (kidney extraction and kidney transplant), the rental of operating and recovery rooms, and hotel accommodation for accompanying family members. The donor fee of between $3,000 and $20,000 (depending on the status of the donor) is also included.

Well known Israeli businessmen and their associates have formed "corporations" (including the firms of Kobi (Jacob) Dyan and Ilan Perry) with ties to illicit medical centers and rogue transplant units (public and private) in Turkey, Russia, Moldova, Estonia, Georgia, Romania, South Africa and the U.S.A. The specific sites of the illicit surgeries are normally kept secret from transplant patients until the day of travel, and the locations are continually rotated to maintain a low profile. The surgeries are performed at the dead of night in rented operating rooms. In one scenario, Israeli patients and doctors (a surgeon and a nephrologist) fly to a small town in Turkey, where the kidney sellers sometimes include young Iraqi soldiers or guest workers. In another scenario, the Israeli and Turkish doctors travel in tandem to a third site in eastern Europe, where the organ sellers are unemployed locals or guest workers from elsewhere. In a third scenario, living kidney donors are recruited from the slums and favelas of Recife, Northeast Brazil (by brokers who include a military police officer) and sent by plane to Durban and Johannesburg in South Africa, where they are met by South African brokers, who will match these unfortunates up with Israeli patients arriving from Tel Aviv. In this instance, South African surgeons operate alone, without the presence of Israeli surgeon accomplices.

The collaboration of the Israeli government and Ministry of Health in this multi-million dollar business, which is making Israel something of a pariah in the international transplant world, requires some explanation. Between 2001 and 2003, medical insurance programs under Israel's national health care system (*Kupot Holim*) funded 319 foreign kidney transplants with living unrelated donors who were paid. According to government tax investigators looking into the illegal trade, each Israeli transplant tourist was paid prior to, or reimbursed following, kidney transplant abroad $120,000 plus an additional $25,000 for pre- and post-op testing, treatment and care of the living donor and the patient. In the absence of a strong culture of organ donation and under the pressure of angry transplant candidates, each person transplanted abroad is one less demanding and angry client with which to contend. More troubling, however, is the support and involvement of the Ministry of Defense in the illicit transplant tourism. Israeli patients who traveled on the transplant junkets to Turkey and eastern Europe recorded the presence of military officers accompanying their flights.

Similarly, medical human rights workers in the West Bank complained of gross violations of Palestinian bodies by Israeli pathologists at the National Legal Medical Institute in Tel Aviv. An official investigation committee appointed by the Minister of Health confirmed the suspicions of Palestinian health workers. The harvested organs and tissues were sold by the Institute to hospitals and medical centers for surgical procedures, research, and medical teaching. A special "squad" of surgeons on military reserve duty performs the harvesting. This practice was established by the head of the national skin bank, who was formerly also Chief Medical Officer of the Israeli Defense Forces. Relying on "presumed consent," the staff of the Forensic Institute and the surgeons who illegally harvested skin and organs said that they believed they were helping to save lives, and that this was more important than trying to procure the consent of ill-informed and grieving family members. As elsewhere, tissues and organs were regarded as mere detachable objects that could be transformed into something valuable. Some bodies were, however, exempt from this practice, specifically the bodies of Israeli soldiers, which are always returned intact to their families for burial.

Beyond Bioethics – Regulating the Black Market in Organs

If a living donor can do without an organ, why shouldn't the donor profit and medical science benefit?

Janet Ratcliffe-Richards[31]

From the exclusively market-oriented "supply and demand" perspective that is gaining ground among transplant specialists and bioethicists today, the buying and selling of kidneys is viewed as a potential solution to the global scarcity in organs and as a "win–win" situation that benefits both parties. In so doing, however, the human and ethical dilemmas are reduced to a simple problem in management. The problems with this rational solution are many. The arguments for "regulation" are out of touch with the social and medical realities operating in many parts of the world, but especially in second and third world nations. The medical institutions created to "monitor" organs harvesting and distribution are often dysfunctional, corrupt, or compromised by the power of organs markets and the impunity of the organs brokers, and of outlaw surgeons willing to violate the first premise of classical medical bioethics: above all, do no harm.

The Secretary of Health of the Philippines, Dr. Manuel Dayrit, had two proposals on his desk at the time of my interview with him in February 2002. The first would create a government-regulated kidney bank (to be called KIDNET) that would allow poor people to sell and deposit a kidney into a virtual "organs bank" that would presumably make these available to all Philippine citizens who needed them. Dr. Dayrit was, however, reluctant to discuss just how the Ministry of Health might set a "fair price" for a poor person's kidney, preferring to leave this task to the free market. Dr. Clemente, the director of Capitol Hospital in Manila, agreed:

"Some of our 'donors' are so poor that a sack of rice is sufficient. Others want medical care for their children, and we are quite prepared to provide that for them." The second proposal is a government-sponsored program to grant death row prisoners (most of them killers) a reprieve in exchange for donating a kidney. Their death sentence would then be replaced by life imprisonment. Supporters of this program believe that the donor incentives program could end up convincing society that the death penalty is a terrible waste of a healthy body. "Organ donation is a medical equivalent of Catholic Lenten rites of self-flagellation," Professor Leonardo Castro, of the University of the Philippines said in defense of the prisoner organ donation incentives program.

For most bioethicists, the "slippery slope" in transplant medicine begins with the emergence of an unregulated market in organs and tissue sales. But for the critical medical anthropologist, the ethical slippery slope occurs the first time one ailing human looks at another living human and realizes that inside that other body is something capable of prolonging or enhancing his or her life. Dialysis and transplant patients are highly visible and their stories are frequently reported by the media. Their pain and suffering are palpable. But while there is empathy – even a kind of surplus empathy – for transplant patients, there is little empathy for the donors, living and brain dead. Their suffering is hidden from the general public. Few organ recipients know anything about the impact of the transplant procedure on the donor's body. If the medical and psychological risks, pressures, and constraints on organ donors and their families were more generally known, transplant patients might want to consider opting out of procedures that demand so much of the other.

In the absence of any national or international registries of living donors or mandatory reporting laws concerning complications following living donation for the donor/seller, there is really no reliable data on the medical/psychological risks and complications suffered by living organ donors anywhere in the world. In the U.S.A., two kidney donors have died during the past 18 months and another is in a persistent vegetative state as a result of donation.[32] The fact that many living donors have either died immediately following the surgical procedure, or are themselves in dire need of a kidney transplant at a later date, sounds a cautionary note about living donation and serves as a reminder that nephrectomy (kidney removal) is not a risk-free procedure.[33]

Bioethical arguments about the right to sell an organ or other body part are based on Euro-American notions of contract and individual "choice." But the social and economic contexts make the "choice" to sell a kidney in an urban slum of Calcutta, or in a Brazilian favela or Philippine shantytown, anything but a "free" and "autonomous" one. Consent is problematic with "the executioner" – whether on death row or at the door of the slum resident – looking over one's shoulder. Putting a market price on body parts – even a fair one – exploits the desperation of the poor, turning suffering into an opportunity. Asking the law to negotiate a fair price for a live human kidney goes against everything that contract theory stands for. When concepts such as individual agency and autonomy are invoked in defending the "right" to sell an organ, anthropologists might suggest that certain "living" things are not alienable or proper candidates for commodification. And the surgical removal of nonrenewable organs is an act in which medical practitioners, given their ethical standards, should not be asked to participate.

The problems multiply when the buyers and sellers are unrelated, because the sellers are likely to be extremely poor and trapped in life-threatening environments where the everyday risks to their survival are legion, including exposure to urban violence, transportation- and work-related accidents, and infectious disease that can compromise their kidney of last resort. And when that spare part fails, kidney sellers often have no access to dialysis, let alone to organ transplant. While poor people in particular cannot "do without" their "extra" organs, even affluent people need that "extra" organ as they age, and when one healthier kidney can compensate for a failing or weaker kidney.

Transplant surgeons have disseminated an untested hypothesis of "risk-free" live donation in the absence of *any* published, longitudinal studies of the effects of nephrectomy among the urban poor living anywhere in the world. The few available studies of the effects of neprectomy on kidney sellers in India[34] and Iran[35] are unambiguous. Even under attempts (as in Iran) to regulate and control systems of "compensated gifting" by the Ministry of Health, the outcomes are devastating. Kidney sellers suffer from chronic pain, unemployment, social isolation and stigma, and severe psychological problems. The evidence of strongly negative sentiments – disappointment, anger, resentment, and even seething hatreds for the doctors and the recipients of their organs – reported by 100 paid kidney donors in Iran strongly suggests that kidney selling there represents a serious social pathology.

Our research with 22 kidney sellers in Moldova and 20 sellers in the Philippines, which in several cases included diagnostic exams and sonograms, found that kidney sellers face many post-operative complications and medical problems, including hypertension and even subsequent kidney insufficiency, without access to medical care or necessary medications. On returning to their rural villages or urban shanty-towns, kidney sellers often find themselves weakened, sick, and often unemployable, because they are unable to sustain the demands of heavy agricultural or construction work, the only labor available to men of their skills and backgrounds. Kidney sellers are most often alienated from their families and coworkers, excommunicated from their churches, and, if single, they are even excluded from marriage. The children of kidney sellers are ridiculed as "one-kidneys."

In my sample of 22 kidney sellers in Moldova, my assistants and I found that not one had seen a doctor or been treated at a medical clinic following their illicit operations in Istanbul and Georgia (Russia). I had to coax the young men to agree to a basic clinical examination and sonogram at the expense of Organs Watch. Some said they were ashamed to appear in a public clinic, as they had tried to keep the sale a secret; others said they were fearful of learning negative results from the tests. All said that if serious medical problems were discovered, they were unable to pay for follow-up treatments or necessary medications. Above all, they said, they feared being labeled as "weak" or "disabled" by employers and coworkers, as well as (for single men) by potential girlfriends and brides. "No young woman in the village will marry a man with the tell-tale scar of a kidney seller," the father of a village kidney seller said sadly. "They believe that he will be unable to support a family." Sergei, a married man from Chisenau, revealed that his mother was the only person who knew the reason for the large, saber-like scar on his abdomen. Sergei's young wife believed that he had been injured in a construction accident while he was away in Turkey.

How can a national government set a price on a healthy human being's body part without compromising essential democratic and ethical principles that guarantee the equal value of all human lives? Any national regulatory system would have to compete with global black markets that establish the value of human organs based on consumer-oriented prejudices, such that in today's kidney market Asian kidneys are worth less than Middle Eastern kidneys and American kidneys worth more than European ones. The circulation of kidneys transcends national borders, and international markets will coexist and compete aggressively with any national, regulated systems. Putting a market price on body parts – even a fair one – exploits the desperation of the poor, turning suffering into an opportunity. And the surgical removal of nonrenewable organs is an act in which medical practitioners, given their ethical standards, should not be asked to participate. Surgeons whose primary responsibility is to provide care should not be advocates of paid self-mutilation, even in the interest of saving lives.

Market-oriented medical ethics creates the semblance of ethical choice (for example, the right to buy a kidney) in an intrinsically unethical context. Bioethical arguments about the right to sell an organ or other body part are based on cherished notions of contract and individual "choice." But consent is problematic when a desperate seller has no other option left but to sell an organ.

The demand side of the organs scarcity problem also needs to be confronted, especially the expansions of waiting lists to include patients who would previously have been rejected. Liver and kidney failure often originate in public health problems that could be treated more aggressively preventively. Ethical solutions to the chronic scarcity of human organs are not always palatable to the public, but also need to be considered. Foremost among these are systems of educated, informed "presumed consent," in which *all* citizens are assumed to be organs donors at brain death unless they have officially stipulated their refusal beforehand. This practice, which is widespread in parts of Europe, preserves the value of organ transplant as a social good in which no one is included or excluded on the basis of their ability to pay.

Conclusion – A Return to the Gift

The material needs of my neighbor are my spiritual needs.
Emmanuel Levinas, *Nine Talmudic Readings*

I end this chapter with a return to the radical premise entailed in organs sharing which envisions the body as a gift, meaning also a gift to oneself. The body and its parts remain inalienable from the self because, in the most simple Kantian or

Wittgensteinian formulation, the body provides the grounds of certainty for saying that one has a self and an existence at all. Humans both *are* and *have* a body. For those who view the body in more collectivist terms as a gift (whether following Judeo-Christian, Buddhist, or animistic beliefs and values), the body cannot be sold, while it can be re-gifted and re-circulated in humanitarian acts of caritas.

From its origins, transplant surgery presented itself as a complicated problem in gift relations and gift theory, a domain to which sociologists and anthropologists from Marcel Mauss to Levi-Strauss to Pierre Bourdieu have contributed mightily. The spread of new medical technologies and the artificial needs, scarcities, and the new commodities that they demand have produced new forms of social exchange that breach the conventional dichotomy between gifts and commodities and between kin and strangers. While many individuals have benefited enormously from the ability to get the organs they need, the violence associated with many of these new transactions gives reason to pause. Are we witnessing the development of biosociality or the growth of a widespread bio-sociopathy?

In his 1970 classic, *The Gift Relationship*, Richard Titmuss anticipates many of the dilemmas now raised by the global human organs market. His assessment of the negative social effects of commercialized blood markets in the U.S.A. could also be applied to the global markets in human organs and tissues:

> The commercialism of blood and donor relationships represses the expression of altruism, erodes the sense of community, lowers scientific standards, limits both personal and professional freedoms, sanctions the making of profits in hospitals and clinical laboratories, legalizes hostility between doctor and patient, subjects critical areas of medicine to the laws of the marketplace, places immense social costs on those least able to bear them—the poor, the sick, and the inept—increases the danger of unethical behavior in various sectors of medical science and practice, and results in situations in which proportionately more and more blood is supplied by the poor, the unskilled and the unemployed, Blacks and other low income groups.[36]

The goal of this project is frankly adversarial in its attempt to bring *social justice* concerns to bear on global practices of organs procurement and transplant. This chapter has been an attempt to delineate some of the contradictions inherent in a market-driven solution to the problem of "scarcity" of human organs; as well as an attempt to recapture the original biosociality inherent in the once daring proposal to circulate human organs as a radical act of fraternity; and, finally, to bring a critical medical anthropological sensibility into the current debates on the commodification of the body.

Amidst the tension between organ givers and organ recipients, between patients and nonpatients, between North and South, between the illegal and the unethical, clarity is needed about just whose values and whose notions of the body and embodiment are being represented.[37] Are the frank concerns, expressed here, for bodily integrity and human dignity a residue of the Western Enlightenment? In fact, these modernist values, so embattled and under assault in the late modern world, are intensely defended in pockets of the third and fourth worlds. Beliefs in bodily integrity and human dignity lie behind "First Peoples" demands for the repatriation and reburial of human remains now warehoused in university museum archives.[38] They lie behind the demands of the wretchedly poor for dignified death and burial.[39] And they certainly lie behind the fears of organ theft, the deep anger expressed in eastern European villages today toward the medical "vultures" and "mafia dogs" who have turned them into "communities of half-men and women." Indeed, the division of the world into organ buyers and organ sellers is a medical, social, and moral tragedy of immense and not yet fully recognized proportions. We hope that this project will help to establish an ethical blueprint for medical anthropology and for medicine in the 21st century.

Notes

1   On biological citizenship, see Adriana Petryna, *Life Exposed: Biological Citizens after Chernobyl* (Princeton University Press, 2002); on sexual citizenship, see Nancy Scheper-Hughes, "AIDS and the Social Body," *Social Science & Medicine* 39(7), 1994, pp. 991–1003.

2   See Elizabeth Roberts, "Examining Surrogacy Discourses: Between Feminine Power and Exploitation," in Nancy Scheper-Hughes and Caroline Sargent, eds., *Small Wars: The Cultural Politics of Childhood* (Berkeley: University of California Press, 1998), pp. 93–110.

3   See Francis Delmonico, Robert Arnold, Nancy Scheper-Hughes, et al., "Ethical Incentives – Not Payment – For Organ Donation," *New England Journal of Medicine* 346(25), 2002, pp. 2002–2005.

4   For example, Alan Shewmon, a respected pediatric nephrologist at UCLA, has argued persuasively that on neurological grounds alone, while the brain dead are incontestably and probably irreversibly dying, they are quite simply not yet dead. Margaret Lock, who has exhaustively explored the topic of brain death, refers to the brain dead as *"as good as dead."* Alternatively, I call them the "good enough" dead. But the point is that the brain dead are not dead in the more usual "deader than a door nail" sense of the term.

5   See John Rawls, *A Theory of Justice* (Cambridge, MA: Harvard University Press, 1971).

6   See John Stuart Mill, "Utilitarianism," in *Ethical Theories: A Book of Readings*, A. I. Melden, ed. (Englewood Cliffs, NJ: Prentice-Hall, 1967), pp. 391–434.

7   Jeremy Bentham, "An Introduction to the Principles of Morals and Legislation," in *Ethical Theories: A Book of Readings*, A. I. Melden, ed. (Englewood Cliffs, NJ: Prentice-Hall, 1967), pp. 367–390.

8   Michael Friedlaender, "The Right to Sell or Buy a Kidney: Are we Failing our Patients?" *The Lancet* 359, March 16, 2002.

9   This is a reference to Primo Levi's description, in his book *The Drowned and the Saved*, of the extent to which inmates of the concentration camps would collaborate with the enemy in order to survive.

10   This project has been a thoroughly collaborative one. Lawrence Cohen and I co-founded Organs Watch in November 1999 as a research, documentation, and medical human rights project. In each of the nine countries in which I have worked, I have collaborated with younger anthropologists, medical students, and law students, as well as with human rights workers, political journalists, and documentary filmmakers.

11 See Nancy Scheper-Hughes, "Parts Unknown: Undercover Ethnography on the Organs-Trafficking Underworld," *Ethnography* 5(1), 2004, pp. 29–72.

12 In one of his last public lectures, delivered in Athens in the summer of 2000, Pierre Bourdieu embraced the life of the "engaged and militant intellectual," by which he meant direct political engagement in new social movements as well as with labor movements in a united struggle against the forces of globalization. See also Nancy Scheper-Hughes, "The Primacy of the Ethical: Towards a Militant Anthropology," *Current Anthropology* 36(3), 1995, pp. 409–420.

13 Jagdish Bhagwati, "Deconstructing Rotten Trade," *SAIS Review* 22(1), 2002, pp. 39–44.

14 Giorgio Agamben, *Homo Sacer: Sovereign Power and Bare Life* (Stanford: Stanford University Press, 1998).

15 Jean Comaroff and John Comaroff, eds., *Millennial Capitalism and the Culture of Neoliberalism* (Durham, NC: Duke University Press, 2001).

16 See Saskia Sassen, *The Global City: New York, London, Tokyo* (Princeton: Princeton University Press, 1991).

17 The United Network for Organ Sharing (UNOS) allows 5 percent of organ transplants in U.S. transplant centers to be allotted to foreign patients. However, only those centers reporting more than 15 percent foreign transplant surgery patients are audited.

18 See, for example, the Arabic (as well as Hebrew and Japanese) version of the university's advertisement; http://www.umm.edu/transplant/arabic.html

19 In São Paulo Hospital, Mariana Ferreira and I encountered Dombe, a Suyá Indian from the forest of Mato Grosso who, to our amazement, faced kidney transplant (including two rejection crises) with remarkable equanimity and calm. See Nancy Scheper-Hughes and Mariana Leal Ferreira, "Domba's Spirit Kidney – Transplant Medicine and Suyá Indian Cosmology," in *Disability in Local and Global Worlds*, eds. B. Ingstad and S. Reynolds (Berkeley: University of California Press, in press).

20 See Paul Rabinow, "Artificiality and Enlightenment: from Sociobiology to Biosociality," in *Essays on the Anthropology of Reason* (Princeton: Princeton University Press, 1999), 91–111.

21 See Marina Jimenez and Nancy Scheper-Hughes, "Doctor Vulture – The Unholy Business of Kidney Commerce," part one of a three-part series in *The National Post* (Toronto), March 30, 2002, B1, B4–B5.

22 See Flavio Lobo and Walter Fangaaniello Maierovitch, "O Mercado dos Desperados," *CartaCapital*, January 16, 2002, 30–34.

23 UNOS, the United Network for Organs Sharing, and EUROTRANS, are organizations that manage the capture and distribution of organs in the U.S.A. and Europe. UNOS is an official government-regulated program in the U.S.A., while EUROTRANS is a voluntary association among several European countries.

24 See note 10.

25 Both Agamben, *Homo Sacer*, pp. 2–3, and Hannah Arendt, *The Human Condition* (Chicago: University of Chicago, 1958), pp. 12–49, treat the translation from ancient Greek to Church Latin in slightly different ways.

26 Francis Fukuyama, *Our Postmodern Future* (New York: Farrar, Straus and Giroux, 2002), p. 204.

27 "Offering Money for Organ Donation Ethical, HHS Committee Says," December 3, 2001.

28 See David Rothman et al., "The Bellagio Task Force Report on Global Traffic in Human Organs," *Transplantation Proceedings* 29, 1997, pp. 2739–2745.

29   See Janet Radcliffe-Richards et al., "The Case for Allowing Kidney Sales," *The Lancet* 352, 1998, p. 1951.

30   Nancy Scheper-Hughes, "The Cutting Edge: Trans-Atlantic Transplants," *The Center for Latin American Studies Newsletter*, Berkeley, California, May 14, 2002, pp. 14–17.

31   Radcliffe-Richards et al., "The Case for Allowing Kidney Sales," p. 1951.

32   "Man Keeps Vigil for Comatose Wife who Gave him Kidney, Life," *The Holland Sentinel*, February 15, 2001.

33   "The Live Donor Consensus Conference," *Journal of the American Medical Association* 284, 2001, pp. 2919–2926.

34   See Madhav Goyal, R. Mehta, L. Schneiderman, and A. Sehgal, "The Economic Consequences of Selling a Kidney in India," *Journal of the American Medical Association* 288(13), 2002, pp. 1589–1593.

35   Javaad Zargooshi, "Iranian Kidney Donors: Motivations and Relations with Recipients," *Journal of Urology* 165, 2001, pp. 386–392.

36   Richard Titmuss, *The Gift Relationship: From Human Blood to Social Policy* (New York: Pantheon, 1970), p. 314.

37   See Ong's commentary in *Current Anthropology* on Scheper-Hughes, "The Primacy of the Ethical."

38   See Nancy Scheper-Hughes, "Ishi's Brain, Ishi's Ashes," *Anthropology Today* 17(1), February 2000, pp. 12–18.

39   Ruth Richardson, *Death, Dissection and the Destitute* (Chicago: University of Chicago Press, 2000); also Nancy Scheper-Hughes, "Two Feet Under and a Cardboard Coffin," *Death Without Weeping: The Violence of Everyday Life in Brazil* (Berkeley: University of California Press, 1992), pp. 249–264.

PART III

SOCIAL TECHNOLOGIES AND DISCIPLINES

STANDARDS

10

STANDARDS AND PERSON-MAKING IN EAST CENTRAL EUROPE[1]

ELIZABETH C. DUNN

A Tale of Two Sausages

The Mięso meat factory sits high on a hill outside the town of Rzeszów, in the southeastern corner of Poland. The building is new, and the grounds are spotless. In the back, trucks full of hogs pull up to unload animals into the slaughterhouse. Inside the plant, pigs proceed along a (dis)assembly line, where they are efficiently carved into cuts of meat. Workers in white coats load hams into the smokehouse, test the internal temperature of cooking sausages, check the tracking numbers that indicate the date and the batch number of the meats, and record data about the production process into logbooks. Inspectors from the sanitary-epidemiological service (SANEPID) and the Veterinary Inspection Service patrol the facility and monitor the logs, ensuring that the complex Polish standards for food production are being met.

Not far away, in the town of Przemyśl, working-class Poles and scruffy Ukrainian traders stand in line outside a wooden booth in the town's bazaar. They buy mostly parówki (hot dogs), and other low-quality ground meats made by small, often unregistered, meatpacking plants that operate without state inspections and without paying taxes. The meats come wrapped in twists of paper or packed into cardboard boxes. There are no tracking numbers on these meats that might indicate when or where they were made. No SANEPID inspectors are in evidence, as they are at Mięso's retail outlets. Some of the meat will be packed up and shipped eastward into the Ukraine. The rest will show up on Polish tables, stirred into a juicy pot of bigos (sauerkraut stew), made into kanapki (sandwiches), or served as kiełbasa.

The Przemyśl marketplace is almost a throwback to communist times, when suitcase traders transshipped product around the Eastern Bloc, working to circumvent shortages in the planned economy by buying and selling in illegal, but tolerated, black markets. In the postsocialist era, the scene is particularly ironic, because the "transition" from socialism was supposed to eradicate informal markets. During the 1980s, theorists of state-socialist economies divided the economies of the Eastern Bloc into two sectors: the formal centrally planned "first economy" and the informal market-based "second economy."[2] Service activities, informal manufacturing, and trading in everything from razor blades to machine parts took place in the second economy, but one of its largest sectors was agricultural goods. Produced by peasants working outside the formal quotas of the plan, meat, fruits, vegetables, and other farm produce showed up in unofficial markets throughout the socialist period.

Working from the conceptual model outlined by János Kornai,[3] analysts assumed that the second economy existed as a stopgap measure, which was necessary to compensate for the shortages produced by the problems of redistribution caused by central planning.[4] Because the second economies of eastern Europe worked on market principles, they were often portrayed as "islands of capitalism," where people could express entrepreneurial talents.[5] It was no surprise, then, that when the first economy collapsed along with the rest of the socialist system in 1989–90, many onlookers assumed that the second economy would simply expand to take the place of the first. There would be no black markets in legal goods, the argument ran, because without the shortages caused by the socialist first economy, there would be no need for them. Eastern European black marketers would be transformed into entrepreneurs, operating in the new above-board capitalist markets.

Firms such as Mięso seemed to shore up the hypothesis that formerly illicit traders would become licit entrepreneurs. Like literally thousands of other small slaughterhouses, Mięso was founded by a man who had run a small village abattoir, and who had operated semi-legally during the socialist period to supply villagers and informal markets with smoked meats and sausages. After 1989, as the market demand for meat began to rise, Mięso's founder gathered together enough capital to build a new, higher-volume slaughterhouse. The new plant incorporates western European slaughter and processing methods, and complies with Poland's stringent food safety requirements. It is, in many ways, a poster-child for postsocialist entrepreneurship: not only is it privately owned and market-oriented, but it is amenable to oversight by government authorities who ensure that Mieso's products meet applicable standards and regulations.

However, at the same time that firms such as Mięso operate, illicit markets in unregulated agricultural produce are flourishing. Vegetables, milk, eggs, and meat are also informally traded, either in bazaars or through chains of personal connections.[6] Yet, both local "mom-and-pop" stores and large western European chain supermarkets exist in most markets, and sell the same commodities that are traded informally. Why don't the orderly rule-governed entrepreneurial businesses and legitimate markets that were supposed to be the outcome of transition obviate the need for informal markets? Why do black markets persist?

The answers to these questions have bigger stakes than merely unearthing subterranean economic practices. Understanding why black markets endure is an important means of understanding how new modes of governmentality operate in postsocialist eastern Europe. The reestablishment of black markets, I argue, is a backlash of the normative form of governmentality characteristic of the European Union. Normative (or "neoliberal") governmentality attempts to integrate new geographic spaces and populations not by overt coercion, but by instituting a host of "harmonized" regulations, codes, and standards. It facilitates the flow of capital and goods by demanding specific forms of record keeping and audit that claim to make the production process "more transparent" to regulators, investors, and consumers. The EU's standards for food processing make a particularly good case for investigating this form of governmentality, because the food industry is one of the most highly regulated sectors in Europe. To ensure food safety, the EU's sanitary and phytosanitary standards specify not only the qualities of the product, but particular production processes and the creation of auditable records. Food processing standards thus illustrate the ways in which normative governmentality claims to reveal truth, to transform economic structures, and to be applicable across geographies with diverse histories and institutions.[7]

Examining normative governmentality in the context of eastern Europe opens up a window to critique claims that the EU and its standardizers make about harmonization and inclusivity in an expanded EU. In Poland, because of the institutional legacy of socialism, standardization may regulate some producers but it provides strong incentives for others to leave formal markets. It does so by creating a kind of personhood that evokes responses developed under socialism and impelling people to seek out ways to circumvent discipline. Looking at Poland's black markets, then, is a way not only to understand this new form of power, but also to understand the ways in which people resist, avoid, or modify it.

Transition as the Transfer of Standards

When the Berlin Wall fell in 1989, the first order of business for many reformers in eastern Europe was *destatization*, or the dismantling of the Party-State. Neoliberal principles such as the formation of nonregulated (or loosely regulated) markets and the privatization of state assets were essential part of destatization.[8] By putting property in the hands of private owners and then subjecting those owners to the pressures of the newly liberalized market, reformers hoped to create a more efficient organization of industry and hence economic growth. Neoliberal reformers such as Leszek Balcerowicz, the architect of Poland's "Shock Therapy" plan, assumed that managers in newly privatized enterprises would behave like their capitalist counterparts in the West, and restructure production, increase product quality, and tighten managerial control of the work process.[9]

Market discipline, however, turned out to involve more than the creation of private property. Facing uncertainty about the permanency and direction of change, many mangers of state-owned enterprises opted to continue with their previous managerial routines, changing almost nothing about their firm's performance. In some cases, instead of trying to turn the state-owned firm around, they focused their attention on transferring as many of the enterprise's assets to their own private companies as they could.[10] This unruly "political capitalism" led to an anarchic privatization process and to corporate management often based on the owners' social connections rather than ideal-typical market rationality.

The failure of neoliberal destatization as a development strategy led to a different approach to governing eastern European economies and societies, which began by changing corporate governance. Rather than focusing exclusively on market pressures, many corporate managers began to focus on meeting norms and standards set by global institutions such as the European Union or the International Organization for Standards (ISO). Because standards such as the ISO's 9000 series dictate not only the qualities of the finished product but also the manufacturing process itself, they offered the possibility of disciplining firms from the inside out. Standards soon came to shape the organization of production by outlining how a firm should measure quality at various points in the production process and how it should correct the process when target measures fall outside particular ranges.

As Marilyn Strathern points out,[11] standardization and its associated disciplinary tool, audit, have become globally dispersed because they promise to act as internal mechanisms for self-improvement. In eastern Europe, standards were held up as a way of correcting some of the fatal flaws of state socialism. The first was the erratic – and usually low – product quality that was the result of the socialist economy of shortage.[12] Process-based standards, with their emphasis on controlling variability in manufacturing, promised to make products consistent across batches (although they could not promise to ensure that the products were tasty, nutritious, or of particularly high quality).

But standards were not just aimed at making products alike: they also aimed at making *firms* alike, by making standards into targets as well as measures, and by using audit technologies to make the activities of the firm visible.[13] As a form of internalized discipline, standardization offered to make eastern European enterprises converge on the forms and practices of western European companies. Bafoil makes this point explicit when he argues that state-socialist enterprises were disorderly and asserts that standards could be the "mainspring of order, whether of discipline or of hierarchical structure."[14] He and his informants make the direction of change very clear: while the standards are meant to be "effective" in changing the Polish firm, the direction of change is to be purely unilateral. Poles are not to argue, and the rules are not to be modified in any way to suit the particular constraints of the postsocialist enterprise.[15]

The object of introducing standards in postsocialist enterprises was thus not just to increase product quality, but to reshape firms in order to make them more closely resemble the organizational forms of their Western counterparts. In this sense, standards in eastern Europe are expected to function as what Bowker and Star call "boundary objects"[16] or what Latour calls "immutable mobiles": objects transferred from one community of practice to another, which have profoundly transformative effects without being transformed themselves.[17] As Brunsson and Jacobsen point out, this project is not unique to eastern Europe, but is part of the process of restructuring global capital:

> We argue that standards generate a strong element of global order in the modern world such as would be impossible without them. People and organizations all over the world follow the same standards. Standards . . . create similarity and homogeneity even among people and organizations far apart from one another.[18]

As in many other developing countries, standardization in Poland became an intrinsic part of bringing in much-needed capital. By demanding auditable records of production and finance, standards supposedly increased "transparency" and made it possible for Western managers and investors to judge whether a Polish firm was potentially profitable.[19] In doing so, it also promised to make Polish firms look like the organizations that Western investors were familiar with, thereby boosting their confidence and willingness to invest. The implementation of standards became what Michael Power calls a "ritual of verification," or a social practice aimed at persuading onlookers that accountability, in its larger sense, had been rendered.[20] Importing a specific administrative technology – standards – into Poland thus became the quiet backbone of the transition project. It started as a means of connecting Poland to the world economy and ensuring foreign investment. But it soon became part of a much more tightly focused plan: the Polish drive to join the European Union. As a prerequisite for joining, Poland had to agree to adopt the *acquis communautaire,* or the body of EU common law. Adopting the *acquis,* the EU promised, would integrate Poland into what Barry has called the European "technozone": a technologically homogeneous space which cuts across geographic and social divisions, thereby insuring a greater flow of capital, people, and goods.[21]

Within the European Union, the capacities of eastern European states thus soon became defined not as the ability to deregulate, or even simply to regulate, but to adopt specific regulations coming from Brussels. As the case of the Polish meatpacking industry shows, however, being accountable to Brussels can sharply constrain the postsocialist state's ability to address the needs of many of its own citizens.[22]

Meatpacking as a Site of Normative Governance

The "technozone" that the *acquis communautaire* seeks to create in the agricultural sector rests on very detailed standards for food processing, including meatpacking. The regulations are designed to protect animal health by reducing the risk of foodborne illnesses such as trichinosis and Creuzfeld–Jakobs ("mad cow") disease, as well as to protect the economic health of farmers by reducing the spread of livestock epidemics such as foot-and-mouth disease (FMD). There are regulations on how live pigs and cows must be fed and housed, and rules about how they must be inspected, transported, and held prior to slaughter. The regulations set out detailed specifications for the physical plant of abattoirs and meat processing plants: the surface and the color of the walls are specified by law, as are the flooring, doors, employee locker rooms, number of wash basins, and type of wash basin taps. The layout of the plant is strongly determined by the regulations: there must be walls separating raw and finished materials, locker rooms may not open onto work rooms, and there must be a separate room for storing detergents. Finally, regulations also contain specifications on documentation and tracking. Under the newly required Integrated Administration and Control System (IACS), each animal, farm, abattoir, processing plant, and individual piece of meat must have a number, and those numbers must be recorded so that the path of each piece of meat from farm to table can be traced. The length of documentation on each piece of meat that must be archived is also specified by law. The regulations, which came into effect for every meatpacker in Poland in late 2003, are enforced via regular inspections both by the Polish Head Veterinarian's Office and EU inspectors.[23]

Introducing new, more rigorous standards had the desired effect in the Polish meatpacking industry: it elicited trust on the part of foreign investors and opened the flow of capital into Poland. In 1999, Smithfield Meats, an American corporation, bought up Animex, Poland's largest socialist-era meatpacker. Smithfield, the largest producer of pork in the world,[24] grew to prominence by developing a highly industrialized strategy for pork production in North Carolina and Iowa. It contracts with local farmers for specially bred fast-growing piglets, and then raises the hogs in vertically integrated mega-factories, where thousands of hogs per year are raised in specially designed intensive growing facilities, slaughtered, and then processed on site.[25] The advent of EU pork processing regulations created a significant opportunity for Smithfield: by replicating contract farming and vertically integrated processing in Poland, Smithfield stood a chance of not only capturing the large Polish market, but of exporting into the lucrative markets of western Europe.[26] With the amount of capital that giant Smithfield could invest in upgrading Animex, and the familiarity with EU regulations it gained by operating plants in France, Smithfield had a significant advantage over domestic Polish producers. Smithfield moved quickly to buy Animex and to assist contract farmers in creating factory hog farms on former socialist collective farms.[27] Smithfield's CEO, Joseph Luter, was explicit about his aims: "We want to create the same model in Poland that has worked so well for us in the U.S.," he said. "In the next five or six or seven years, I could see as much profitability from Europe as we have in this country."[28]

For most Polish farmers and small agricultural processors, the imposition of EU standards and the arrival of Smithfield and other multinational packers promises disaster. Of Poland's roughly 2,800 slaughterhouses and processing facilities, only 19 abattoirs and 23 processing plants – most of which were already owned by foreign firms – met EU requirements in 2001.[29] For the other plants, meeting EU regulations will require that many plants rebuild almost from scratch, and install expensive computers to implement farm-to-table tracking and other forms of audit. Because these renovations are so expensive, current estimates suggest that only 833 slaughterhouses and 944 processing firms have any possibility of meeting requirements and staying in business.[30] This means that enforcement of EU regulations will force two out of three firms to go out of business. Most of the firms likely to close are the small and medium meatpackers in the countryside. This creates a significant opportunity for multinational meatpackers, who will see their largest aggregate source of competition fall by the wayside once standards are implemented.

For Poland's smallholder farmers, standardization and industry consolidation also spell disaster, because the closure of village abattoirs and processors poses a significant threat to their livelihoods. The average farm in Poland is only about 5 hectares, in comparison to the European Union average of 17 hectares.[31, 32] Small farms do not produce very many pigs per year. In fact, over 56 percent of Polish farmers have fewer than nine hogs, which means they usually have only a sow or two and piglets.[33] Village abattoirs were willing to buy pigs in small lots, which was an important source of cash for resource-poor farmers. Large industrial processors, who make their profits by buying large lots of virtually identical very lean hogs, are much less willing to buy the small lots of genetically irregular, often fatty, hogs that smallholder farmers have to offer.[34] The new regulations will affect Polish retailers, most of whom operate small, nonchain shops, as well. The large-volume processors have focused on selling their wares at low cost to large retail chains such as Tesco, a British supermarket chain, and LeClerc, a French retailer. Small shops, that will be forced to pay the markups charged by wholesalers, will find it increasingly difficult to turn a profit and stay in business.

The adoption of EU norms and standards thus exerts strong pressure to make the Polish meat-processing sector similar in structure to the agribusiness and food retailing commodity chains found in the United States and western Europe – that is, to ensure that "integration" means not just technical harmonization, but also the harmonization of infrastructures. Although the standards may not have been written with this intent, the EU is aware of this effect and endorses it, as the EU's Special Adjustment Programme for Agriculture and Rural Development (SAPARD) shows:

> The meat processing sector is characterized by a big number of enterprises with low capacities. As there is also over-capacity in slaughtering and the sector has low productivity, investments aimed at increasing processing efficiency will be supported. Special attention must be given to attaining compliance with EU requirements... This specific measure (Measure 2) is meant to restructure the food processing industry...(while) avoiding increase of capacities available.[35]

Normative governance and the introduction of standards thus create significant barriers to market participation by smallholder farmers. They threaten to push small processors out of formal markets, where government inspectors will demand they comply with EU regulations, and to create such strong incentives for economies of scale that they collapse formal markets for smallholder farmers. The Polish state, eager to join the European Union, is thus becoming the transmitter and the enforcer of rules that benefit multinational corporations at the expense of its own citizenry. By demanding the right to inspect premises and audit production records, the Polish government is actively excluding its own citizens from market participation. Rather than building up connections between Polish farmers and larger economies, the Polish state is actively disarticulating local people from regional and global market structures.[36] And, at the same time that village farmers are being barred from wider economic participation, they are also being barred from democratic political participation in the structures of power that so deeply affect them. The European Union's food safety regulations are written in Brussels, by transnational teams of experts. Even though the Polish government can send a representative to these teams, it is unlikely that Polish smallholder farmers will have access to that representative or any voice in the standards-setting process. The Polish state, acting as a normative agent, thus has a significant potential to assign some groups of people not only to the economic periphery, but to the political periphery as well.

Hierarchies of Value, Topographies of Taste

The normative state (in this case, the EU, via offices of the Polish government) makes certain kinds of claims when it advances new standards. In the first place, by transferring standards from one geography to another, the normative state makes the implicit claim that each place in a given technozone shares the same set of problems – the problems that the standards were developed to address. But why is it that the standards developed for one set of circumstances appear to be applicable or attractive in a completely different context?[37] As recent work in science studies suggests, the rise of new ideas and the ways particular depictions of the world are stabilized as "facts" through scientific practice is a social problem.[38] The rhetoric of standards – including the ways standards depict the world, highlight particular problems as deserving of regulation and scientific solutions, and make assumptions about practices and institutional infrastructures – is one place to look at how specific places come to be known and made. The EU's meatpacking standards make these assumptions and portray Poland as a particular kind of place by defining the problem of food safety as one of *risk*, redefining farmers and processors as risk-bearing subjects, and positing standardization as the antidote to risk. Yet these standards ignore the fact that Poland, because of state socialism, has a very different institutional and social configuration. This different configuration makes traditional indices for assessing risk misleading.

The EU argues that its standards are designed to reduce the risk of both animal-borne and food-borne diseases, including viral infections, neurological diseases, parasites, and bacteriological contamination. For example, rules written for beef production aim at stopping the spread of "mad cow" disease, which can be transmitted to humans and cause a fatal neurological disorder called Creuzfeld–Jakobs disease. Throughout 2001 and 2002, countries that did not quickly adopt the EU's food safety standards were portrayed as potential carriers of disease that endangered the European food consumer and the food system. In 2001, Poland was assigned a "Group 3" rating by the EU, indicating the "probability" of widespread "mad cow" in Poland. Yet Poland did not report its first case of "mad cow" until 2002! Poland was deemed risky because the Polish state was judged incapable of effectively transmitting norms and standards, and because Poland's informational infrastructure (which might be used to track zooepidemics) was deemed low capacity.

However, although EU standards portray Poland as a *high-risk* country because Poland's infrastructure is different from that of western European countries, Poland in fact poses a low risk of widespread "mad cow" precisely *because* its economic infrastructure is different. "Mad cow" is a disease of industrial agriculture. It originates from the practice of feeding the remnants of dead cattle (including bone meal) back to live cattle, which enables the transfer of the prion that causes "mad cow." It therefore affects highly concentrated, highly industrialized farms – such as the large-scale operations found in the United Kingdom – disproportionately. But in Poland, where farms are small and farmers poor, smallholder farmers face such severe shortages of cash that they prefer to feed cattle homegrown hay rather than the commercially prepared feeds that were responsible for the "mad cow" outbreak in the U.K. The result is a strategy of "involution" – or a turning away from the market for industrial feeds – which dramatically reduces the risk of a "mad cow" epidemic in Poland.

Likewise, trichinosis, a disease sometimes transmitted via undercooked pork, has also been used as justification for introducing EU food safety standards in the meatpacking industry. Yet, in 2000, for example, there were only 176 cases of trichinosis in Poland, almost all of which were linked to wild boar rather than to commercially produced pork.[39] The risk of widespread trichinosis is quite low, and the costs of preventing the disease disproportionately high. Similarly, the EU justifies the need for Poland to adopt its hog-processing regulations on the need to avoid the spread of foot-and-mouth disease. Both the EU and the U.S. Department of Agriculture have classified Polish farms and processing facilities as posing a "high risk" of FMD. Yet Poland has no reported cases to date and has been classified as FMD-free by the U.S. Department of Agriculture. The "high-risk" classification is because Poland has not yet implemented the EU's tracking system – its regulatory architecture – for managing animal disease.

The EU's rating systems thus classify Poland as "risky" not because Poland's own standards are less stringent (they are not), but because Poland's informational and physical infrastructure for agricultural production is not the same as the one developed to address problems of western European agricultural production – problems that Poland, with its fragmented structure, does not share. The hierarchy of value that standards lay out quickly transmutes *difference* into *impurity*. Standards thus act as more than technologies for organizing and regulating markets, and express fundamental social relations between groups.[40] They set up a distinct power differential between the rule-making western European members of the EU, and Poland, which is construed as an infested, disease-bearing, less technologically sophisticated candidate for membership. By making Poland's infrastructure more like that of western Europe and purging it of small-scale producers and processors, the standards equate the reduction of difference with an increase in product quality. An administrative technology makes the reduction of difference into a process of purification.[41]

Normative governmentality not only defines particular states and their products as risky, but creates power relationships among particular social groups by (re-)defining the specific products they make and ordering them in a hierarchy of purity, quality, and value. The EU's EUROP meat grading scale is an example. The EU requires that the amount of fat on each pig carcass be measured with an electrical current so that the pork can be graded. Less fatty meat is labeled "E" and deemed to be of higher quality, while "P" meat is highly fatty and therefore less desirable. The intent of the EUROP grading program is to encourage the production of leaner meat overall, but particularly to encourage the production of meat suitable for export to western Europe, where it will earn a price premium.

The effect, however, is to grade producers and consumers as well as meat. The EUROP standards place pigs such as the ones from western European hog lines at the top of the scale. These pigs most often come from industrial piglet producers such as the Pig Improvement Corporation (PIC), which breeds pigs that grow fast and lean, and which have the highly standardized body size and type that facilitates mechanization on large-scale slaughter lines. These are the same kinds of pigs that multinational packers such as Smithfield use in their operations, since they keep both line speeds and profit margins high. Polish pigs, however, are different. In the past, Poles have generally had a preference for fattier meat, so Polish pigs have been bred to produce fat. On the EUROP scale, Polish pigs do not score well. They rarely produce "E" grade meat, and their body sizes vary substantially from pig to pig. These differences might – in a different context – be prized as markers of genetic biodiversity or cherished as "heirloom species." However, the EUROP scale ensures that Poland's installed infrastructure – here the genetic lines of the country's livestock – is placed on an evaluative grid that deems it inferior because it is unstandardized.[42]

More than just pork is measured on this scale. The EUROP system also grades consumers. "E" grade pigs are bought by EU-compliant processors, slaughtered, and then shipped to the EU, where they garner a high price. "U" and "R" grade pigs generally go to larger or medium-sized processors and stay on the Polish domestic market, while "O" or "P" grade animals are slaughtered by small noncompliant processors who make them (along with the unwanted parts of higher-grade animals) into hot dogs, sausages, and ground meat. This is the meat that appears in the Przemyśl marketplace, where it is bought by small traders, and shipped east to the Ukraine or Russia. Polish meatpackers map this hierarchy of meat onto hierarchies of geography and people when they envision their clients. They say that "Europeans" (meaning EU citizens) like high quality and will pay for it. Poles, they say, would like to eat good meat but cannot afford it, and prefer slightly fattier meat anyway. They portray Russians as people who do not care what they put in their mouths as long as it is cheap. Such gradations are not just differences in wealth, but in worth. As meatpackers envision their clients according to the framework that standards lay out, they create topographies of taste in which the further east one travels, the less discerning the residents are about quality and perhaps the less deserving they are of high-quality products. As Julie Goldman points out, this kind of sorting creates "an aesthetic of cognitive mapping," or a hierarchy of national selves that embeds farmers, processors, and distributors in a global hierarchy of value.[43] When Polish meat fails to meet EU standards (which soon will become domestic standards as well) and has to be shipped to the Ukraine or Russia, the workers become second-class producers of second-class products. As they classify meat into superior meat that is exportable to the West and inferior meat that is good only for the East, workers themselves are constructed as inferior people who only deserve to consume inferior, impure, unstandardized product.[44]

Standards are thus not only about forcing parts of the industry to take on the forms and practices of western European firms, but about categorizing all producers, assigning them value, and marginalizing those who will not or cannot comply.[45] By making the adoption of standards such as EUROP a condition of EU accession, the EU holds out the promise that "harmonizing" rules will allow countries like Poland to join the club and hence, eventually, to "harmonize" economies, incomes, and lifestyles with western Europe as well. Quietly, however, standards such as EUROP open up another possibility: that Poland will become the Arkansas of Europe, a place with a stable and structured but economically peripheral role within a hierarchically ordered division of labor.[46]

Of Pigs and Personhood

EU standards, and the normative power they contain, have become key tools of the "transition" in eastern Europe because they claim to have a kind of disciplinary power that makes economies and producers commensurable. By using a single metric (here, the ability to transmit regulation from international bodies to the level of the firm) to compare and rank states, firms, and goods, standards make unlike things into comparable units. A Polish pig becomes comparable to an industrially bred Smithfield pig, small-scale slaughterhouses become comparable to vertically integrated hog farms, and the Polish government, once part of a species completely "other" to market democracies, becomes like, but inferior to, the governments of western European states.

Standardization thus implies *legibility, commensuration*, and *hierarchy*. That combination is part of what makes standards efficacious, and an important part of why they became crucial parts of the transition process. However, the brunt of standards' disciplinary force is not felt at the national, sectoral, or even firm levels. Standards work to shape economies because they are able to drive new norms down to the level of the individual. As Andrew Barry writes of the EU's harmonized standards:

> Harmonization depends not just on written statements and procedures, but also on the transfer and monitoring of practical skills. Harmonization is apparently a rationalistic and legalistic enterprise; but to be successful it demands the presence of persons.[47]

Barry's statement might be rephrased as "the presence of *particular kinds of* persons." Food safety standards make strong claims to efficacy because they wield a kind of disciplinary power that promises to reshape both people and the practical skills they deploy on the job. They promise to turn postsocialist farmers, workers, and managers into people like (but not necessarily equal to) their western European counterparts.[48] Using audit to enforce the targets that standards lay out, the EU hopes to turn Poland's food processing sector into a visible, calculable, and governable space by making the people in it in to governable, calculating, self-regulating selves.[49]

Audit works to shape personhood by making the internal workings of firms – and hence, the individuals in those firms – perfectly visible. Like other firms seeking to comply with EU regulations, Mięso's job is not only to produce healthy, clean meats, but also to produce a set of records that will convince auditors from the EU and the Polish government that it is being compliant. To do so, Mięso has come up with a HACCP (Hazards Analysis of Critical Control Points) plan that demands monitoring throughout the production chain and produces a set of auditable documents. As animals are taken in to the abattoir, slaughterhouse workers read the IACS tracking numbers from the *kolchiki* or "earrings" hung from the animals' ears, and record them in a logbook. As the animal is slaughtered and the meat passes down the production line, processing line workers assign the animals' numbers to individually numbered batches of processed meat. Workers pull samples from each batch off the line every few minutes and test them for visual appearance, fat content, and levels of microbiological or chemical contamination. They record the temperature of the refrigerated warehouse where meat from the batch is stored and the temperatures of any cooking or smoking processes. If, at any moment, one of the samples exceeds the targets for the "critical control point" being measured, the record for the entire batch is shifted to a "corrective action log" which specifies the nature of the problem, its potential for causing food-borne illness, and the remedies taken to ensure that the batch is safe. The account of itself that the firm gives through this documentation can be hundreds of pages thick.

Standards function here as "fact factories." Not only do they import knowledge about how things should be made, but also, by specifying particular forms of data collection, recording, and analysis, they act as engines for generating knowledge about products, processes, and people. For the EU veterinary inspectors or the Polish Sanitary and Epidemiological Service inspectors, the batch logs at Mięso create a narrative that tell more than the microbiological status of the meat. The logs also reveal important things about what kinds of persons are in the plant. First of all, they demonstrate how compliant senior management is, and show how strong is the firm's desire to produce for highly regulated markets such as the EU or Poland. Looking at the corrective action logs shows how attentive plant managers are to the nuances of the production process, and how quickly they respond when data from one of the critical control points exceeds acceptable tolerance levels. A moment's inattention shows up on the log, ready for an alert inspector to catch and possibly penalize.

As theorists such as Michael Power have shown, the indirect spot-checking of records lends more disciplinary force, not less, to the audit process.[50] In this case, it makes production logs into paper panopticons that view and discipline individuals. Just as the prisoners on the hexagonal prison described by Michel Foucault never knew if the guard in the tower in the center was watching them, but always knew that he could be,[51] Mięso managers know that external auditors can use the logs of meat temperatures to judge their performance and their willingness to comply. This transforms audited managers as acting subjects: they now have strong incentives to constantly monitor and discipline themselves in order to ensure that the EU's production objectives are met. Now microcosms of the Polish state, managers are judged by their abilities to *internalize* the EU's norms and values and make them the basis for self-regulation, while at the same time *transmitting* those norms and values down the hierarchy of production to the shop floor.

The normative discipline that managers transmit to workers when they transfer standards and audit to the shop floor is a different kind of discipline from the kind deployed under socialism. Because of endemic shortage, socialist factories were often characterized by highly erratic production rhythms: hours or days when work ground to a halt because critical inputs were missing, followed by furious "storming" in an attempt to meet the quotas of the planned economy. These fits and starts in production made it possible for workers to dodge off the shop floor to go to the bathroom or sneak a smoke, or even to dash out to do some shopping or run to the doctor's surgery. Now, because they must render accounts of themselves as they create accounts of the products they make, workers must discipline themselves to stay at their machines and fill out the logs.[52] Also, the discipline of audit is different from the direct surveillance and often brutal physical control deployed in Fordist-era capitalist factories.[53] At Mięso, managers do not need to constantly watch the workers to ensure the speed and quality of their work, or to use piece rates as a disciplinary tool.[54] The production logs take care of that: just by looking at the logs, managers can tell if workers are taking samples every five minutes, if they are attending the vats or smokers properly to prevent large variations in cooking temperatures, and if the work team is keeping the production line moving at a steady pace. Managers' disciplinary gaze thus becomes more powerful, not less, as it is mediated through paper logs.

The combination of standardization and audit is not effective merely because workers can be "viewed" and disciplined through the production logs, however. By demanding that workers and managers constantly render accounts of themselves as they render accounts of the products they make, audit requires employees to constantly monitor themselves. While standards inculcate new norms and values in workers, the addition of audit asks them to use the constant stream of data about the qualities of the product to actively bring their own performance into accordance with the targets specified by the state.[55]

In short, external subjection and internal subjectification are combined so that individuals conduct themselves in terms of the norms through which they are governed. Audit thus becomes a political technology of the self: a means through which individuals actively and freely regulate their own conduct and thereby contribute to the government's model of social order.[56]

By providing a new framework within which employees strategize about their own behavior and shape the firm's strategy in a state-regulated marketplace, standardization and audit align persons, organizations, and objectives by acting "at a distance."[57] They govern individuals without violating their formal rights to autonomy, and control enterprises without impeding their abilities to act in an open market.

Shore and Wright argue that "challenging the terms of reference" that standards provide "is not an option."[58] These terms of reference are based on a western European norm. They not only valorize Western institutional structures, such as factory farming and industrialized agriculture, but also attempt to create it when they encounter new landscapes with different institutional legacies. Likewise, they valorize western European forms of personhood. They demand that people become calculative actors, willing to orient their activities to produce the desired figures on a record sheet. Just as they present standardization and audit as a form of "empowerment" to western European workers, they ask eastern European workers to see limited choices in a highly constrained field of action as a kind of "empowerment" or freedom, and to willingly become self-activated, yet self-disciplined, microcosms of the regulatory state. This assumption is fundamental to the project of reshaping the structures and rationalities of firms in the mold of western European businesses, and of transforming the eastern European economies, since both these endeavors work by changing the micropractices of the enterprise. Standardization thus operates not only by crossing the boundaries of nation-states, but also by crossing scales from the supranational to the individual.

However, just as the standards developed for western Europe fit uneasily with Poland's rather different agricultural infrastructure, they also fit uncomfortably with Polish views of personhood and social relations. In this new geography, a place with remarkably different mores and ideas about sociality as well as different farms and processing techniques, standards cannot discipline as effectively. Instead of encompassing more and more people in the "iron cage" of reflexive rationality, standards' evaluative grids work to exclude many people from audit's discipline. Producers who are already in compliance with EU regulations – such as Animex – or those who produce "E" grade meat for the European Union may be forced to strategize within the frame of rationality set by standards.[59] However, those small producers who cannot afford to comply with EU regulations, or who cannot produce meat of high enough quality or profit margins to make compliance worthwhile, are pushed beyond the borders of standards' discipline. Seen as the bearers of too much risk to be absorbed into the system, they are forced out of the frame of governance that standards create and pushed outside formal markets. Instead, as they are forced into the gray market, they must depend instead on a very different form of personhood altogether: the networked and relational form of personhood created under the property regime of state socialism.

Creatures of Disease and Deceit

Polish peasants have survived for decades in legal frameworks that disadvantage them. During the socialist period, they deflected central planners using a combination of overt political opposition and covert semi-legal "gray market" economic action. Now, just as state socialism's planned economy produced its own "second economy," the European Union's regulated *capitalist* economy may produce its own second economy. The emergence of a semi-hidden, "corrupted," or informal market in agricultural products may emerge as a direct result of increased standardization and the persons it creates.

During the Communist period in eastern Europe, the socialist state sought to regulate its economy not only through central planning but also by seeking to atomize individuals by severing all social connections except those linking individual and state. Ironically, however, the centrally planned economy ended up creating just the opposite kind of social relations: instead of social isolates whose economic activities were completely controlled by the Party-State, the acute shortages of socialism created people who had to make extensive networks of personal connections in order to siphon materials from the state, to make products, and to trade them. Within these networks of carefully cultivated personal ties, peasants hid land and animals from planners, cultivated crops that were never reported to the state, and sold city-dwellers produce that the state never got the opportunity to redistribute. Their eggs found their way to the bureaucrats who made the decisions about which children would be admitted to more prestigious schools, their cucumbers to the shop attendants who decided which customer would get the hard-to-find coat, and their homemade liquor to the office workers who approved passports for potential emigrants.[60] Rev saw these practices as sources of power for farmers in their struggles against the socialist state:

> Peasants make nonobjects: food that cannot be found, grain that has never been harvested, land that is nonexistent, people who are phantomized. The technique of the resistance is the nonevent, the means is the nonobject, the actors are anonymous.[61]

Rev calls the power created by these shadowy nonobjects "the advantage of being atomized." Even though atomization was a source of oppression for peasants, it also led to informal economic action, which could be used to weaken socialist power. Informal economic activity prevented the state from controlling the economy, exacerbated shortage, undermined the Party-State's legitimacy, and eventually became one of the most important factors in undermining state socialism.

The kinds of persons created in these webs of exchange were strikingly different than the kinds of selves that standards create. Standards and audit constitute the "self-activating selves" of workers or managers as bounded and disciplined individuals. Spurring themselves to action by constantly monitoring their *individual* performance and reflecting back on their *individual* personality characteristics rather than on the quality of the relation among workers or firms, audit's self-regulating selves meet the norms that standards set by managing their *own* capacities. The persons characteristic of state socialism, however, were in many ways the direct opposite of the standard-ized self. They were relational and evasive rather than bounded and disciplined. Instead of being bundles of measurable qualities, they were deeply embedded in networks of reciprocal exchange. Dependent upon one another, they emphasized their abilities to mobilize others to give or to act rather than their own abilities for autonomous action.[62] Rather than holders of autonomous rights, socialist-era persons were junctions for the transfer of goods and favors within loosely bounded networks. Most importantly, rather than "shoppers," choosing among easily available goods, socialism's persons were "hunters" who used their networks to evade the blockages created by the planned economy. The ability to dodge regulations, to get goods that the state denied, and to covertly sell the fruits of one's private labors became highly valorized as *spryta,* or "cleverness." People spoke admiringly of exploits in evasion, making a snaking gesture with their hands to demonstrate the agility with which rules were circumvented.

With the advent of standards, the price premiums put on "E" grade or EU-compliant goods, and the almost omnipresent talk of entrepreneurship in the post-socialist period, Polish producers were primed to become self-activating. As entrepre-neurship and the virtues of the free market were lauded in the press and by the EU, Poles were quickly sold on the idea of becoming self-starters who were personally responsible for their own economic well-being inside the integrated European market. But those same people, once they had invested the capital and energy in founding their own abattoirs and meatpacking firms, were soon told that they and their products were impure and inferior, too risky to be admitted to licit markets. Instead of becoming the self-contained, self-monitoring disciplined rational *individ-uals* that critics of accounting might predict they would become, they have responded to their exclusion and the possibility of being permanently assigned to Europe's economic periphery by reactivating their *relational* selves and continuing the flow of gifts and favors that undermined the socialist economic system. Rather than seeking to fit themselves to standards' disciplinary grids, they seek the holes in those grids through which the crafty and clever may slip.

Mobilizing socialist-era personhood and recreating systems of personal relations opens up multiple possibilities for economic action in what Poles call "the gray zone." Some smallholder farmers build relationships with abattoirs that are willing to accept small lots of pigs that come without tracking numbers. They give "gifts" to the abattoir employees in charge of grading meat, hoping that their fattier pigs will receive "R" or "O" grades (and higher prices) instead of the lowest "P" grade. Managers of some small abattoirs or processing firms seek to evade regulation by bribing veterinary inspectors or by convincing SANEPID inspectors to turn a blind eye to irregularities in the processing logbooks. They try to create commodity chains other than the industrialized ones controlled by the multinationals. They buy cheap, undocumented, untracked pigs and sell them to the owners of small shops, or to traders who export the meat from Poland to the former Soviet Union. They build up all these relationships not by analyzing themselves or giving accounts of themselves, but by exchanging gifts and favors, and creating webs of reciprocal obligations.

Standardization thus does not homogenize persons, as it claims to. Instead, it creates significant inequalities between them, some of which are brute-economic and others of which are metaphorical and related to identity. It also gives people strong incentives to find ways *around* the standards, because they can gain new markets, reduce costs, and raise profits by doing so. They once again become "hunters," seeking to find paths around the economic blockages thrown up by standards. Relying on alternate forms of personhood, such as the network-embedded personhood characteristic of socialism, becomes one way to circumvent the standards and to reap the economic and social rewards of doing so. Overcoming new forms of atomization, networks of underground producers may be able to reserve certain market segments to themselves and, by creating alternate commodity chains, create some barriers to the penetration of Polish agriculture by foreign capital.

Conclusion: Black Markets and Technozones

Both the EU and the Polish government present standards as tools with which to create a homogenized technological zone. Promising to "harmonize" Polish regulation and the Polish economy, they hold out a vision of Polish producers and consumers integrated in a flow of capital and goods. Standards work to create these "technozones" not only by regulating products and manufacturing processes, but also by standardizing people and making them into self-monitoring, self-motivating persons who use audit to align themselves with EU regulations. Yet, because there is an uneasy fit with Polish agricultural infrastructure, standards fail in their stated aims. They cannot make all firms and all farmers across Europe commensurable. The evaluative grids that standards present cannot encompass the millions of smallholder farmers and small-scale processors that Poland presents. Instead, obscuring their very existence, the EU speaks dispassionately about "restructuring the food processing industry," "reducing overcapacity," and "increasing processing efficiency."[63] The small processing firms and small farmers caught in this web of efficiency will not be subject to standards' discipline or made to become auditable persons, but instead will be pushed off the EU's evaluative grids and forced out of the sector. Millions of Poles who depend on agricultural livelihoods have few alternatives but to fall back on a kind of personhood developed under a very different regulatory order: the lived experience of state socialism. They rely on the mores, techniques, and relationships developed under socialism to form illicit markets and to avoid standardization and audit.

The reemergence of midnight meat companies and postsocialist black markets in eastern Europe highlights critiques of – and alternatives to – standardization, audit, and new modes of normative governance. Although normative governmentality claims to be totalizing and to be able to encompass whatever it touches inside its own system,[64] it is often unable to digest social forms, cultural values, and infrastructures that are truly foreign to it. This is particularly true at the level of the person: standardization cannot always make people commensurable, as it claims to. Instead, it can often make them incomparable, both in economic and cultural-symbolic terms. In pushing some kinds of people outside the frame of standards, normative governmentality gives them strong incentives to find new paths around regulatory obstacles.

In Europe, the process of installing normative governmentality is referred to as "harmonization" and "integration." But rather than accepting these words with their positive overtones, it is important to also see the ways that the power of standards excludes certain groups, disarticulates them from the European order, and leads to patterned and structured inequalities. Standards can create barriers to both market and political participation, and catalyze new forms of conflict, both open and covert. Ironically, in its drive to govern the ungovernable spaces of postsocialism, the European Union may find that the products and people it wants to regulate become less regulated than ever before.

Notes

1 This chapter was vastly improved by a series of conversations with David Stark, Aihwa Ong, Paul Rabinow, Katherine Verdery, Elizabeth Ferry, and Stephen Collier – my thanks to all of them.

2 József Böröcz, "Informality Rules," *East European Politics and Societies* 14(2), 2000, p. 355.

3 János Kornai, *The Socialist System: The Political Economy of Communism* (Princeton: Princeton University Press, 1992).

4 Steven Sampson, "The Second Economy of the Soviet Union and Eastern Europe," *AAPSS Annals,* 493, 1987, p. 122.

5 For example, Hedrick Smith, *The Russians* (New York: Quadrangle, 1983), p. 86.

6 According to *Gazeta Wyborcza,* a Polish daily newspaper, if one compares the number of loaves of bread that bakers report selling (and paying tax on) with the number of loaves of bread that Poles report consuming, Poland appears to eat about three times as much bread as it produces – and this in a country which by and large does not import bread.

7 See Martha Lampland, "Rationalizing Methods: Studying Measures of Modernization," unpublished manuscript, n.d.

8 For example, Jeffrey Sachs, *Poland's Jump to the Market Economy* (Cambridge, MA: The MIT Press, 1993).

9 Ian Taplin and Carola M. Frege, "Managing Transitions: The Reorganization of Two Clothing Manufacturing Firms in Hungary," *Organizational Studies* 20(5), 1999, pp. 721–722; Elizabeth C. Dunn, *Privatizing Poland: Baby Food, Big Business and the Remaking of Labor* (Ithaca, NY: Cornell University Press, 2004).

10 Taplin and Frege, "Managing Transitions," p. 722; Jadwiga Staniszkis, "Political Capitalism in Poland," *Eastern European Politics and Societies* 5(1), 1991, pp. 127–141; David Stark, "Recombinant Property in East European Capitalism," NCSEER Working Paper, 1993.

11 Marilyn Strathern, "Robust Knowledge and Fragile Futures," Chapter 24, this volume.

12 Kornai, *The Socialist System,* p. 310.

13 Kenichi Ohmae goes so far as to argue that the combined pressure of accounting standards and manufacturing standards is leading to a standardized corporate form.

That is to say, he argues that corporations around the world are becoming structurally more and more like one another due to firms' needs to comply with process-based standards. See Kenichi Ohmae, *The Borderless World: Power and Strategy in the Interlinked Economy* (New York: The Free Press, 1990).

14   François Bafoil, "The Formation of Rules in Post-Communist Firms in Poland," in *Poland Beyond Communism: Transition in Critical Perspective*, Michal Buchowski, Edouard Conte, and Carole Nagengast, eds. (Fribourg: University of Fribourg Press, 2001), pp. 323–340.

15   In interviews that I conducted in both Poland and the Czech Republic, managers of food-processing firms expressed much the same sentiments: While the introduction of Western standards by a western European or American partner was supposed to effect a dramatic change in the former state-owned enterprise, neither eastern European nor foreign managers had any expectations that the experience of working with or even owning a formerly socialist enterprise would change the character of the foreign company.

16   Geoffrey Bowker and Susan Leigh Star, *Sorting Things Out: Classification and Its Consequences* (Cambridge, MA: The MIT Press, 1999).

17   Bruno Latour, *Science in Action* (Cambridge, MA: Harvard University Press, 1987).

18   Nils Brunsson and Bengt Jacobsson, *A World of Standards* (Oxford: Oxford University Press, 2000), 1.

19   While these kinds of record-keeping practices revealed some of the internal workings of eastern European firms to Western investors and managers, the omnipresence of informal production and accounting practices made it quite difficult in practice for outsiders to understand the activities of eastern European firms or to judge their potential profitability. See Dunn, *Privatizing Poland*.

20   Michael Power, *The Audit Society: Rituals of Verification* (Oxford: Oxford University Press, 1997).

21   Andrew Barry, *Political Machines: Governing a Technological Society* (London: Athlone Press, 2001), p. 58.

22   Laszlo Bruszt and David Stark, "Who Counts? Supranational Norms and Societal Needs," *Eastern European Politics and Societies* 17(1), 2003, p. 2.

23   European Commission, "Opinion of the Scientific Committee on Veterinary Measures Related to Public Health," http://europa.eu.int/comm/food/fs/sc/scv/out47_en.pdf; accessed 2001.

24   At least by its own reckoning; see http://www.smithfieldfoods.com

25   Robert Morgan, "Legal and Political Injustices of Industrial Swine Production in North Carolina," in *Pigs, Profits, and Rural Communities*, E. Paul Durrenberger and Kendall Thu, eds. (Albany, NY: State University of New York Press, 1998), p. 140.

26   Michael Davis, "Smithfield Expects to See International Growth," *Virginian-Pilot*, December 7, 2002; http://www.pilotonline.com/business/bz1207smi.html

27   Elizabeth C. Dunn, "Trojan Pig: Paradoxes of Food Safety Regulation," *Environment and Planning A* 35, 2003, pp. 1493–1511.

28   Cited in Davis, "Smithfield Expects."

29   Robert Gmyrek, "Polityka Panstwa w dziedzinie dostosowania polskiego przemysłu miesnego do standardów europejskich" (Public Policy Relating to the Polish Meat Industry's Adaptation to European Standards), *Gospodarka Miesna*, May 2001, pp. 24–25.

30   Idem.

31   "Europe: Poland's Pig-headed Farmers," *The Economist*, February 20, 1999, p. 47.

32 Among current EU countries, only Greece (where farms average 4 ha) has smaller farms than Poland. In France, which is largely viewed to have fragmented holdings, the average farm size is 42 ha, while in England the average farm size is 69 ha, or over ten times as large as the average Polish farm. See Assemblée Permanente de Chambres d'Agriculture, "Agriculture in France," http://paris.apca.chambagri.fr/apca/data/aagrifr.pdf; accessed 2000.

33 Główny Urzad Statystyczny (GUS), *Budzety Gospodarstw Domowych w 1999 r* (Household Budgets in 1999) (Warsaw: GUS, 2000), p. 12.

34 The purchasing manager for Animex told me that until more factory farms are set up on the former collective farms, even Animex is being forced to buy small lots at village purchasing stations. However, this irregular supply of irregular-quality hogs is a serious impediment to Animex's profitability, and so the company is seeking to set up stable large-scale supply chains near its processing plants.

35 SAPARD, "Rural Development Measures" (2000); electronic document available at http://www.agri.ee/SAPARD/En/RDP_measures.htm (February 20, 2003).

36 Bruszt and Stark, "Who Counts?", pp. 4–5.

37 Lampland, "Rationalizing Methods," p. 5.

38 Bruno Latour, *The Pasteurization of France* (Cambridge: Harvard University Press, 1988); Michael Callon, "Some Elements of a Sociology of Translation: Domestication of the Scallops and the Fishermen of St. Brieuc Bay," in *The Science Studies Reader*, Marco Biagoli, ed. (New York: Routledge, 1999), pp. 67–83.

39 European Commission, "Opinion of the Scientific Committee."

40 Lawrence Busch, "The Moral Economy of Grades and Standards." *Journal of Rural Studies* 16, 2000, p. 273.

41 See Barry, *Political Machines*, p. 43.

42 A similar statement might be made about the USDA's beef grading standards in the United States. USDA "prime" and "choice" grades are awarded for highly marbled beef, which is best achieved by pulling cattle off the range and putting them into large-scale feedlots where they eat corn.

43 Julie Goldman found a similar hierarchy of national selves when she worked as a sorter in a Chilean fruit-packing factory. Her work on the Chilean fruit industry remained unpublished at the time of her death. I am grateful to her colleague Lida Junghans for granting me access to her manuscripts. See Julia Goldman, "The World According to Fruit," unpublished MS, n.d.

44 Cf., Goldman, "The World According to Fruit," p. 2.

45 Bowker and Star, *Sorting Things Out*.

46 Bruszt and Stark, "Who Counts?," p. 8. Bruzst and Stark argue that countries which enter the EU as marginal players may be able to "upgrade" their positions in the industrial hierarchy much as Taiwan or Japan did. I am more skeptical, given that the eastern European countries face much higher barriers to entry in industries such as high tech than Taiwan or Japan did, precisely because Taiwan and Japan – and increasingly, Korea, China, and India – are already in markets for cheap, highly skilled labor.

47 Barry, *Political Machines*, p. 78.

48 Or at least the people Eurocrats would like western Europeans to be. See Maryon McDonald, "Accountability, Anthropology and the European Commission," in *Audit Cultures: Anthropological Studies in Accountability, Ethics and the Academy*, ed. Marilyn Strathern (London: Routledge, 2000), pp. 106–132.

49   See McDonald, "Accountability," p. 109.

50   Power, *The Audit Society.*

51   Michel Foucault, *Discipline and Punish* (New York: Vintage, 1979).

52   See Dunn, *Privatizing Poland.*

53   See Aihwa Ong, *Spirits of Resistance and Capitalist Discipline: Factory Women in Malaysia* (Albany: State University of New York Press, 1987).

54   Cf., Maria-Patricia Fernandez-Kelly, *For We Are Sold, I and My People: Women and Industry in Mexico's Frontier* (Albany: State University of New York Press, 1983).

55   William Maurer, "Forget Locke? From Proprietor to Risk-Bearer in New Logics of Finance," *Public Culture* 11(2), 1999, pp. 47–67; Marilyn Strathern, "Bullet Proofing," paper presented at the Seminar in Political Thought and Intellectual History, Faculty of Philosophy, Cambridge, May 1999; John Law, "Organizing Accountabilities: Ontology and the Mode of Accounting," in *Accountability: Power, Ethos and the Technologies of Managing,* Rolland Munro and Jan Mouritsen, eds. (London: Thomson, 1996), pp. 283–306.

56   Cris Shore and Susan Wright, "Coercive Accountability: the Rise of Audit Culture in Higher Education," in *Audit Cultures: Anthropological Studies in Accountability, Ethics and the Academy,* Marilyn Strathern, ed. (London: Routledge, 2000), 62.

57   Peter Miller and Nikolas Rose, "Governing Economic Life," *Economy and Society* 19, 1990, pp. 1–31; Marilyn Strathern, "Critique of Good Practice," paper presented at the Annual Meeting of the American Anthropological Association, Philadelphia, November 1998; Keith Hoskin, "The 'Awful Idea of Accountability': Inscribing People Into the Measurement of Objects," in *Accountability: Power, Ethos and the Technologies of Managing,* Rolland Munro and Jan Mouritsen, eds. (London: Thomson, 1996), pp. 265–282.

58   Shore and Wright, "Coercive Accountability," p. 62.

59   Large multinational corporations, who produce "E" grade meat for export to the West, can also afford to engage in the very costly forms of self-evaluation and self-monitoring that the application of process-based standards to employees requires. Smithfield, for example, strongly prefers to hire managers for its Polish Animex subsidiary who have worked in the United States and who have been exposed to American human resource management practices as well as American factory farming techniques. Smithfield, which uses process-based standards for employee evaluation in the United States, then also applies those techniques to its top Animex employees in Poland. Slowly, Smithfield is letting these techniques filter down Animex's hierarchy into the meatpacking plants themselves. Creating these privatized, auditable, *legible* selves in its Polish workforce is an integral part of Smithfield's plan for speeding the flow of investment into Poland and the flow of profits out exactly because it provides control at a distance. Managers who understand Smithfield's imperatives and are willing to constantly transform themselves to meet Smithfield's expectations are not only easier to control from far-away Virginia, but also more likely to try and transform the employees and plants they control to meet Smithfield's models.

60   Katherine Verdery, *What Was Socialism and What Comes Next* (Princeton: Princeton University Press, 1996).

61   Istvan Rev, "The Advantages of Being Atomized," *Dissent* 34, 1987, p. 349.

62   Cf., Strathern, "Critique of Good Practice"; Dunn, *Privatizing Poland.*

63   SAPARD, "Rural Development Measures."

64   Strathern, "Critique of Good Practice."

11

THE PRIVATE LIFE OF NUMBERS:
Pharmaceutical Marketing in Post-Welfare Argentina

ANDREW LAKOFF

In this chapter, I analyze pharmaceutical marketing practices as techniques for managing contemporary biomedical expertise on a global scale. The chapter is based on research conducted among drug representatives (hereinafter, "reps"), sales managers, health bureaucrats, and psychiatrists in Buenos Aires. Specifically, I focus on the uses of data generated by pharmaceutical audit firms, both domestic and multinational. The numbers that such firms generate are elements of technologies that work to modulate the behavior of the key actors involved in the pharmaceutical market. In looking at how pharmaceutical sales strategists use these numbers, it is possible to see how a specific market is both constituted and transformed. The market is both that which directs strategy and that which strategists try to reshape. Firms that audit pharmaceutical sales and prescriptions, which produce the numbers that make the market and its transformations visible, are crucial to this reflexive loop. Their numbers operate to make the pharmaceutical market palpable as a kind of living entity that can be both a target of strategists' intervention and a source of rectifying "feedback." As a form of knowledge about health practices that is used in guiding expertise, pharmaceutical audit data emerges as a kind of neoliberal epidemiology, whose trajectory I term "the private life of numbers."

The chapter has two sections. The first section examines the use of audit data by pharmaceutical firms in Argentina as a means of regulating expertise and as a way of constituting the market as a domain of practice. Such techniques of government are particularly salient in places such as Argentina, where the role of the state has receded in the wake of neoliberal reforms. The second section investigates recent shifts in the Argentinean psychopharmaceutical market. Specifically, I ask whether steeply rising antidepressant sales in recent years should be attributed to the country's severe economic and social crisis or to the practices of regulation described in the first section.

Neoliberal Contraband

"The history of Argentina is the history of contraband," said Daniela, a pharmaco-epidemiologist employed at a pharmacy benefits management firm in Buenos Aires, by way of explanation of the country's pharmaceutical industry. While the statement implied a more general analysis of the trajectory of capitalism in the Rio de la Plata, her specific reference was to the sanctioned prevalence of unlicensed copies in the domestic pharmaceutical market.

To understand the central role of copies in the Argentinean pharmaceutical industry, it is useful to begin with some background on changing forms of political rationality in Argentina and their relationship to innovation and industrial policy. The domestic pharmaceutical industry was founded according to a logic of import-substitution, producing copies for the internal market in a climate in which patent rights for pharmaceuticals were not recognized. This was part of the broader strategy of the postwar Argentinean welfare or "planning" state, which constituted its citizens as subjects of need and the state's task as one of gathering knowledge about such needs and providing services to satisfy them. The developmentalist program was oriented toward state-led industrialization that would, it was hoped, not only lead to independence from external powers but also provide work and affordable goods for the population.[1] But mounting debt crises and hyperinflation eventually led to the abandonment of this model and to the embracing of IMF-designed structural adjustment policies that demanded a reduction in the role of the state.[2] In the late 1980s and early 1990s, after more than a decade of fitful attempts to shift away from the planning state, the Peronist government of Carlos Menem began a radical experiment in market liberalism, through rapid privatization of state-owned entities such as electric utilities, railroads, and the oil company, and the deregulation of protected markets.

The goal of these neoliberal reforms was to limit the role of the state in overseeing human welfare, and to extend market rationality to areas that had not previously been seen as economic – such as education, health, and security.[3] The premise was that market competition rather than state planning was the most efficient and effective way to provide such goods: given a space of ideal competition, entrepreneurs would quickly step in to offer the best service at the best price, whereas states were hampered by bureaucratic inertia, corruption, and inflexibility – the inability to deal with rapid change.[4]

The pharmaceutical industry is a good place for looking at the uneven and contingent effects of such "liberalization." Under neoliberal reform in the early 1990s, price controls were dropped, the protection of local markets was eliminated, and the process of registration and authorization of medications was eased by giving automatic approval to a new drug if it had been approved by regulators in a "leading country" – that is, in western Europe or North America. The idea was to regulate prices not by state-imposed controls but through competition structured by the free choices of consumers.

Argentina agreed to comply with the multilateral TRIPs accord on intellectual property that emerged from the 1986 Uruguay Round of GATT. Multinational pharmaceutical companies were encouraged to expand their efforts in the market through their local subsidiaries. This was obviously bad news for the domestic industry, which controlled most of the market but was dependent on the absence of an effective patent regime. To continue their operations the domestic industry depended on the ability to freely expropriate intellectual property, and during the 1990s it was able to repeatedly delay implementation of the patent regime. Under these circumstances, many domestic firms thrived in the neoliberal transition by turning exact copies of multinational drugs into local brands. This strategy should be distinguished from generic production: these products were marketed brand names, sold at comparable prices to those of the multinationals. In other words, domestic firms took advantage of the value structure of the transnational pharmaceutical industry, which is based on patent protection, while at the same time defying such protection.[5] As in many other areas of late capitalism, key developments were taking place in terms of crafting brand–consumer relationships rather than at the level of the production of new things.

The Argentinean pharmaceutical market was thus a peculiar one: it is in an unlikely grouping with the United States, Germany, Switzerland, and Japan as the only countries whose domestic producers have a greater market share than foreign ones. But it was unique in that this thriving domestic production was founded on high-priced brand-name copies. Therefore, of 54 marketed brands of antidepressants, as of the summer of 2001, there were 14 kinds of fluoxetine (Prozac) and six brands of paroxetine (Paxil).

Under these circumstances, the Menem government's deregulation policies in the early 1990s produced a striking change in the Argentinean pharmaceutical market. Drug prices rose sharply despite the lack of enforcement of patent protection, and while overall pharmaceutical consumption declined by 13 percent in the first five years after reforms, revenues increased by 70 percent.[6] This was in part the result of informal collusion between drug firms and insurance providers, and the systematic blockage of the emergence of a generic industry. But it also had to do with the role of doctors as gatekeepers to consumption. In this sense, the model of consumer choice is clearly an inappropriate one for the pharmaceutical market, which is inherently "imperfect," in economic terms: the one who chooses the drug is not the one who consumes it, and the one who consumes it is not (or often is not) the one who pays for it.[7] Doctors' decisions about medication are not typically shaped by price competition.

Pharmaceutical relations

Observers of the recent shifts in the global economy have noted an increasing emphasis on consumption rather than production. In turn, social analysts have turned to strategies for shaping consumer demand as a source of insight into contemporary forces of social regulation and identity-formation.[8] But in the case of "ethical" pharmaceuticals (those drugs whose consumption is restricted to physician prescription), identifying the actual consumer is a complex problem. Professional and state regulation of the pharmaceutical market means that consumption is based not directly on need or desire, but is mediated by expertise. The problem for pharmaceutical marketers, then, is to link doctors' selection of their products to the practice of authorized knowledge. The boundaries between capitalism and science seem to blur: the generation of demand must be at the same time an appeal to professional authority. This merging of domains can inspire either denunciations on the grounds of impurity or celebrations of the benefits of entrepreneurialism to health.[9] On the basis of research into the psychopharmaceutical market in Argentina, I would suggest, however, that the mutual imbrication of science, state regulation, and private industry in the circulation of pharmaceuticals is best seen not as a contamination of pure science but, rather, as part of a distinctive and emergent regime for authorizing knowledge claims and expert action.

The pharmaceutical gift relation is an apt site for investigating the operations of this regime. Given the presence of so many copies (and the continued prohibition on direct-to-consumer advertising) in Argentina, there is intense competition among both domestic and multinational firms for the loyalties of doctors. Meanwhile, there is an oversupply of professionals, who have difficulty finding enough private patients and receive abysmally low salaries in public hospitals or social insurance based clinics. With no research costs, domestic firms can reinvest their earnings directly into marketing – and the key strategy is to build relationships of reciprocity with doctors through gifts of access. In this environment major gifts are common: at the 2001 American Psychiatric Association (APA) meetings in New Orleans, the largest foreign contingent was from Argentina, with 500 psychiatrists attending, the vast majority of whom had received sponsored trips from pharmaceutical firms.

In the United States, the ubiquity of such gifts from pharmaceutical firms to doctors has drawn increased scrutiny in professional and ethical discourse. The anxiety provoked is of a "conflict of interest" between the doctors' duty to the patient and a reciprocal obligation to the pharmaceutical company that might compromise doctors' professional integrity.[10] This framing in terms of conflict of interest assumes that a clear distinction can be made between "rational pharmacology" and marketing. However, as David Healy and others have shown, marketing and expertise cannot be so easily disentangled: pharmaceutical companies are producers not only of pills but of knowledge about their safety and efficacy, and their gifts to doctors provide access to the latest expertise.[11] The fortress that is supposed to guard against the crude logic of profit – biomedical expertise – is itself ensconced in the market.

Moreover, pharmaceutical gift relations should be seen not in terms of a transfer of goods (your conference for my prescription) but as the forging of a relationship, which involves something like (*reciprocal access to guarded resources.*[12]) This will become clearer below, as I describe the structure of relations between doctors and pharmaceutical companies in the Argentinean context. From the vantage point of firms, these relations obviously enable access to patients – either as drug consumers or as subjects of clinical trials. From the perspective of Argentinean psychiatrists, the kinds of gifts that are offered – e-mail accounts, computer equipment, travel to international congresses – represent the possibility of engagement with centers of knowledge production and professional authority. Given a lack of other means of accessing cosmopolitan systems of expertise, pharmaceutical relations become portals to the global biomedical infrastructure. In their relations with pharmaceutical companies, it is not so much that doctors are faced with a conflict of interest between science and the market, then, as that they are embedded in a structure of *interested knowledge.*

This does not in itself de-legitimate knowledge produced and disseminated about pharmaceutical safety and efficacy. Rather, it directs us to consider how doctors come to invest authority in the information that comes to them via pharmaceutically mediated circuits.[13] This requires the investigation of the structure of the relationships between pharmaceutical companies and doctors. While such relations are strengthened through exchange, the form of trust involved is deliberative: there are sources of accountability on each side.[14] Let me begin by looking at how firms monitor the effectiveness of promotional strategies focused on shaping the behavior of doctors.

Post-'social' regulation

The goal of the sponsored conference trip and other major gifts is to forge a relationship of loyalty between the doctor and the firm. There are two kinds of doctors who are particularly sought after for such relationships: prescription leaders and opinion leaders. The basic strategy of building brand loyalty among doctors takes a different form depending on whether the doctor is an opinion or prescription leader. The delicate work of forging ties with opinion leaders is the job of the sales director or product manager. The key figure in relation to prescription leaders, on the other hand, is the rep – to which the Argentinean pharmaceutical industry devotes 15 percent of its total revenue ($3.6 billion in 2000). There are 90,000 physicians and 8,000 reps in the country.[15] The rep's task is to work within an assigned territory to increase the market share of his company's products. Strategies for gaining loyalty also differ somewhat between domestic and multinational firms. Multinationals rely on their links to prestigious knowledge centers, and regulate themselves (at least in appearance) according to transnational norms; domestic firms, unable to capitalize on such links, tend to focus on more direct rewards, and at the level of marketing invent tactics based on knowledge of the local terrain.

The pharmaceutical audit industry provides data that enables pharmaceutical companies to gauge the results of their marketing campaigns, as well as to monitor their relations with individual doctors. I first became interested in the uses of pharmaceutical sales data through a psychiatrist who edits a leading Argentinean journal of psychiatry. He had complained at one of the journal's editorial meetings about sales reps from Lilly who had rebuffed his request for sponsorship of his journal, saying "Why are you asking us for help, when you only prescribe Foxetin?" Gador's Foxetin, a copy of Prozac, was at the time the leading antidepressant on the Argentinean market, while Lilly's patented original languished in sixth place.[16] The psychiatrist, who was known for having been a militant activist in the Left during the early 1970s, was outraged: first at the extortionary tactics of the reps, and secondly at their in-depth knowledge of his prescription practices. How did they know what he prescribed? It turned out that there were database firms that microfilmed individual prescriptions in pharmacies, collated the data, and then sold it to pharmaceutical companies. I was impressed at the detail of this private-sphere knowledge – especially in a place where, in the public sector, it is nearly impossible to find any epidemiological data on the prevalence of mental illness in the population or information on rates of pharmaceutical use.[17]

The gathering of detailed knowledge about prescriptions that the psychiatrist had stumbled upon is a window into a more general set of practices that have to do with the regulation of contemporary expertise, and which are particularly salient in sites – such as Argentina – where other forms of knowledge and regulation typically associated with the state or with professional organizations have fallen away. The "avalanche of numbers" about the population's health status and practices produced by audit firms, and its stark contrast with the lack of data available elsewhere, shifts attention to the role these numbers play in governing expertise.[18]

In his genealogy of governmental rationality, Michel Foucault showed that sciences concerned with gathering knowledge about public health first appeared as part of an art of government whose aim was to improve the health and welfare of populations, in the service of increasing the strength of the state.[19] Understanding and fostering the well-being of subjects understood as living beings gradually became a central task of state administration. Forms of knowledge about the health of populations – from statistics (which first referred to "the science of the state") to demography to epidemiology – have since been linked to a variety of modern state-building projects, as well as efforts to modernize colonial and post-colonial territories.[20] The gathering of detailed data about the condition of the population is thus crucial to modern forms of government, in that these numbers constitute the domains that become sites of its intervention – economy, society, and population.[21]

If sciences such as epidemiology emerged in the context of regulating the health of collectivities within a territory, how can we understand new forms of knowledge such as audited sales data with respect to the problem of government? It might be said that the role of the social scientist in the welfare or planning state – to constitute and intervene in the collectivity understood as a national population – finds an analog, in a post-"social" order, in the contemporary market strategist.[22] Gilles

Deleuze hinted at this shift in his 1990 "Post-Script on Control Societies," describing the importance of marketing to the new form of capitalism oriented toward "meta-production."[23] Deleuze thought that predominant forms of power relations had shifted: disciplinary power had given way to control, and the problem of confinement to the problem of *access*. This new form of power operated through constant modulation and transmutation rather than surveillance or confession, he argued. But where and on whom does such power operate? In the case of pharmaceutical marketing, the figure who is being modulated through the question of access is not the patient but the doctor. This complex, interactive control is made possible by audit data, the information collected on pharmaceutical sales and doctors' prescription behavior.

Audit firms' numbers operate to make the pharmaceutical market palpable as an entity that can be both a target of strategists' intervention and a source of rectifying "feedback." A field of possible action such as the pharmaceutical market has to initially be made present in order to be operated on and transformed. As a form of knowledge about health practices that is used in guiding expertise, pharmaceutical audit data emerges as a kind of "neoliberal epidemiology." These numbers provide a vision of the territory as containing a market rather than a population. While the notion of a sales territory is not new, information technology now makes possible an immediacy and detail of knowledge that changes the character of territory management.[24] A veteran psychopharmaceutical marketer told me how he used such data to find prescription leaders, referring to an upper middle class neighborhood of Buenos Aires: "You know that Palermo's postal code is 1425 and so you say, 'I want anti-psychotic prescriptions from Palermo.' You find the five best prescribers, and how much they prescribe of what. These are often doctors who are affiliated with high volume insurance plans." The strategist can then do targeted marketing. Older places devoted to the clinical encounter can be used as sites of encounter and transaction: thus, in Buenos Aires, public hospitals provide important opportunities for access to prestigious doctors who commute to private practices in places such as Palermo in the afternoons, and to patient populations for use in clinical trials.[25]

Bringing the market to life

As I explored this milieu, my specific interest was in recent changes in psychopharmaceutical sales, but it was quite difficult to get hold of the actual numbers and trends. In visits to pharmaceutical companies' sales divisions in Buenos Aires, I was sometimes allowed to surreptitiously glance at the huge IMS binder listing monthly sales figures, but not to make copies. One sales director I met with in a café had written them down on a piece of paper before coming, let me look at them before we talked, then tore up the piece of paper. Sales data were private numbers. They were quite valuable: it cost pharmaceutical firms up to $150,000 per year to subscribe to the IMS service, which was only one kind of audit. The other service, Close Up, which collected prescriptions from pharmacies, provided a different and complementary set of data, which was equally difficult to access. Both came with software that allowed one to move through their databases, and that broke down the information into significant components: For what pathology did doctors generally prescribe a given drug? Who were the leaders in a given therapeutic class over the past 12 months, and what was the pattern of change? And, more impressively, how did sales of specific medications break down by region – by city, neighborhood, or even postal code?

IMS Health is a multinational firm headquartered in the United Kingdom, with a subsidiary in Buenos Aires. It is the leading collector and distributor of pharmaceutical sales data in the world. The firm's "primary material" is standardized information on overall sales and specific therapeutic classes in terms of units and value at the level of regional and global markets. IMS information can also be specified down to the level of the postal code of the pharmacies where drugs are sold. In Argentina, IMS buys this information from wholesale drug distributors. As an executive at IMS Argentina told me, they provide only the "pure information" and it is up to the companies themselves to figure out what the data means.

In looking at the practices of market strategists, one can see how a specific market is reflexively constituted and transformed through the use of audit data. Information from IMS makes it possible to grasp the market as a kind of living entity, evolving in unpredictable but measurable ways. With it, the market's evolution becomes visible. Gabriela, product manager for a new antidepressant that had 33 percent sales growth last year, showed me how strategists distinguish between markets according to therapeutic class:

> Studying the market in the past, we deal with the sales statistics to see what specialties use our products, and seeing, for example, the *evolution of the numbers* I was just talking about. *Which are the markets that evolve most rapidly or which are the markets that are growing*. I have a general market that is shrinking and this market is growing [pointing to the antidepressant sales column], this one is attractive.

The IMS executive explained how to use its database of qualitative information gathered from interviews with panels of experts to plan a campaign: "So—I'm thinking of launching a tranquilizer. The first thing I'm going to do is enter [the database] by pathology, and what am I going to see? From my information, which products do doctors use, which brands, what do they associate it with, in what cases do they use them?" The market is both that which directs strategy as well as that which strategists try to reshape. It can also be seen as a foe, an antagonist. Martin, CNS sales director at a multinational firm whose antidepressant is struggling in the overcrowded field, talks about how he uses audit information to design a market strategy:

> First you analyze the market . . . What volume it has, how it is evolving, who are the companies that participate, what percentage that company has in sales of its products in

the market ... this means: *whether I'm going to attack it, whether it's going to react or isn't going to react, how it's going to react,* what is the age of the products, what is the index of penetration of the new products that were launched onto the market, what differentiation do you have with what already is there, who are the doctors that prescribe the products in this market, how many there are ...

Integrated control

An executive at Close Up, the Argentinean firm that audits prescriptions, told me why IMS' data on territorial sales alone is not enough – one must also have individual doctors' prescription numbers at hand: "It's sort of an integrated control. We don't claim that the pharmaceutical companies don't have to see the territorial sales, but they also have to see the prescriptions. They ... have to be analyzed at the same time, to be able to have more coherent and more precise explanations of what is going on in the field." With a subscription to Close Up's databases, you can look up which doctors prescribed your products, which prescribed competitors, and how much each doctor prescribed. To get this information, Close Up buys or barters microfilmed copies of actual doctors' prescriptions from pharmacy chains. They claim to cover 18 million (out of an estimated 300 million yearly) prescriptions, and to have profiles on the behavior of over 90,000 physicians in Argentina, including nearly 2,000 psychiatrists in the city of Buenos Aires. Their data, in the hands of Lilly reps, had been the source of the journal editor's ire.

Close Up's promotional material advises that "Success, for a pharmaceutical company, depends on a primary factor: The physician's prescriptive behavior." How do these numbers work to know and shape such behavior? Their literature provides a rather sinister vision of government by surveillance, targeted specifically at doctors. It seems to confirm recent analyses of audit cultures in terms of the prevalence of "technologies of mistrust" – means of monitoring and shaping behavior that otherwise cannot be checked.[26] If you use Close Up, they tell prospective clients, you will know "what the doctor does, not what he says he does." Their "Audit Pharma" database can be loaded onto handheld computers that reps consult while in the field. As one psychiatrist told me, "You feel like you're being watched by the CIA."

But why would doctors lie to the medical reps? The sales audit is a way of checking whether the firm's gifts are actually paying off. As Gabriela told me, "If [the doctor] says, 'why don't you pay for my trip to the APA because I'm prescribing a lot of this product,'" she needs to know whether or not this is true; "Because the doctor can tell all the laboratories that he's prescribing a lot of every product"—and thereby get a lot of trips. Sometimes this negotiation between the firm and the doctor is quite direct: "Doctor, if you get me 20 more prescriptions a month, I'll send you wherever you want to go." But usually it is more subtle – "How can I help you?" the rep asks.

Territory management

But doctors are not the only parties subject to audit surveillance. While detail men (reps) track doctors' behavior armed with knowledge of their actual prescription practices, sales managers monitor how their reps are doing. Gabriela pointed out a number in her IMS binder and explained:

> This statistic shows the "market-share" of each visitor in each zone. So you know that you have a visitor in Santa Fe and you see the market-share of each product in this zone, so you see how this visitor is doing in the zone. And you are doing what is called "Territory Management," you are seeing the profitability of each zone or how each visitor is doing.

The fact that sales performance is constantly monitored colors the interactions of doctors and reps. Reps, who try to form relationships of "friendship," or at least mutual obligation, with doctors, plead for help from doctors in raising their territorial sales figures. With this information on their own salespeople, the audit becomes a reflexive technique for the firm, a way of directing intervention but also of self-modulation, given the precarious uncertainty of the market. Close Up claims that its service for measuring reps' productivity, called "Feedback," allows the sales manager to know exactly what is happening in the territories:

> Measure the prescriptive productivity of each one of the representatives and their supervisors, through prescriptions captured from the visited doctors. Eliminate the deviations of productivity measurement according to territory [*this is a dig at IMS*]. An objective and valid measure of the results from promotion with visited doctors. Feedback is the only technical report that makes it possible to make precise decisions to identify market opportunities.

How well is a given campaign – of samples, information-diffusion, symposia – going? The reflexive loop provided by the audit database allows for self-evaluation and transformation. As Martin, CNS sales director at the Argentinean subsidiary of a U.S.-based multinational, said upon getting the disappointing results of his new campaign: "We thought we would grow 15 percent this year, and we're getting there, we're doing pretty well. But *one has to be permanently monitoring what's happening*." The "market" – here, the accumulated prescribing decisions of the country's 90,000 physicians – is a semi-controllable entity that on the one hand is what one wants to act upon but which also reacts – reinforcing successful decisions and throwing unsuccessful ones into question. The modulation is interactive: pharmaceutical marketers regulate doctors, but doctors – as a collectivity represented in the market's monthly evolution and the inevitable bell curve of any specific product's "life cycle" – shape the behavior of marketers as well.

Opinion leaders

While directly surveying prescriptions helps to manage relations with prescription leaders with whom one can make certain arrangements of exchange, a more subtle set of dynamics occurs with opinion leaders. Explicit negotiation and direct exchange is not the typical quality of the relationship between the opinion leader and the firm. In fact, it can be counterproductive to bring sales numbers into these interactions. Here the main technique is to develop long-term, trusting relationships. This task is not left to the reps in the field, but is the responsibility of the sales director or product manager. Audit numbers play a role in the process, but in a more complex way. The young CNS product manager at an upstart European firm told me how they decide with whom to develop contacts:

> We work with doctors with high prescriptive power, very prestigious doctors, who can establish some trend in the use of psychopharmaceuticals, either because they have a lot of patients or because they are well known, for example, they are "Speakers." Or because they decide on purchases, for example in hospitals, or they participate in some important institution or in the psychiatric associations, so these doctors are those that enable us – through a good, fluid contact and relation with this doctor – to get the message we need out to the doctors who follow his trends.

In the case of opinion leaders, it is not a question of monitoring prescriptions, but of developing alliances – of having these respected figures available for seminars, symposia, the authorship of "scientific literature" to be disseminated. The role of the opinion leader is something like a brand spokesman – although you will see opinion leaders allied with multiple firms. There is a hierarchy of opinion leaders, and of firms. Market strategists know as well as anyone who the key players in the field are – and in fact can play a major role in making them opinion leaders. Through these relationships, companies are able to ally themselves with experts who command respect and have the trust of other doctors. Conversely, these experts are able to reaffirm their authority and to disseminate their knowledge through their relationship with pharmaceutical firms – such as one well-respected leader whose book on "practical psychopharmacology" was sponsored by the Dutch firm Organon and introduced by the head of Pharmacology at the University of Buenos Aires. Another technique for forging links with opinion leaders is to offer them a marketing-oriented "Phase IV" clinical trial. This is a trial of an already approved medication, whose results are more or less known beforehand. The ostensible study results in a "poster" that is presented at an international scientific congress, with travel expenses paid for by the company. For young doctors, this is one way to begin to appear in circuits of expertise as an emerging opinion leader.

Firms must tread lightly with opinion leaders. A veteran strategist told me that if he is putting on an event, he makes sure to invite all the most important opinion leaders: if you leave someone out, they will be upset and they won't prescribe your product. The opinion leaders are very sensitive, he said: "they want to feel important." In this respect multinational firms have an advantage, given their ability to link local opinion leaders to their networks of prestigious transnational experts. Companies strive to develop a reputation for taking good care of their opinion leaders. Gabriela, the product manager, said of her company's efforts at conferences, "If there is something that distinguishes us it's that we don't make huge investments of money but we do make high quality investments, we are with them all the time, it's not that we invite them and then they go alone. *We are very careful with the relationship of the doctor with the laboratory,* because we don't have such a big [sales] force." And the psychiatrists cared about how they were taken care of as well. At an editorial meeting of the leading Argentinean psychiatry journal, two members of the board talked about their upcoming trip to the APA meetings in Washington, D.C.: the younger of the two was going early to attend a Lilly course on anti-psychotics and depression. "Oh, it's marvelous," enthused the more experienced one, "you're going to love it, and they look after you so well."[27]

Opinion leaders insist that they never endorse a specific product, and only accept offers from reputable companies whose products they believe in. The reputation of the firm then becomes a means of ethical regulation. In other words, firms that wish to ally with prestigious opinion leaders must maintain a reputation for propriety: they do not give out samples ("like the others do"); they provide access to information, sponsor studies, help patients. A former Janssen marketing director described a campaign he ran for Risperdal that won a prize from an international patient organization. Its theme was "reinsertion" – an attempt to go further than just medication, to resocialization. Ten patients from a schizophrenic patient support group were hired at Janssen for short periods, to do simple tasks such as photocopying, were paid small salaries, and then received scholarships for training and certificates of having worked. The program showed that these patients needed less medication and had fewer relapses – that they could be successfully "reinserted." More than being directly about sales, he said, the campaign was about shaping the image of the company as one that was interested in the "quality of life" of patients.

Local knowledge

The Risperdal campaign was ingenious in its awareness of the importance of questions such as social reintegration to the epistemic milieu that it targeted, Argentinean psychiatry. Psychiatry is distinctive from other fields in biomedicine in the multiple forms of expertise that coexist within it, each of which has a distinct model of the cause, site, and optimal modes of treatment of mental disorder. While in the United States psychiatry has recently shifted toward a "neuroscientific" approach that locates illness in the brain of the patient, in Argentina social and psychoanalytic explanations remain predominant.[28] This poses a challenge for pharmaceutical marketers accustomed to campaigning in terms of serotonin levels and synaptic receptors. How, for example, might one appeal to former activists such as the journal editor, a staunch critic of globalization who associates neuroscientific psychiatry and the extension of DSM-IV with American imperialism, and who says of neoliberal policies more generally, "in the same way that they open the market to foreign products and liquidate the state, they liquidate the forms of hospital care, the training criteria, training institutions, and the public university as the center of knowledge-production"?

Here we can distinguish between the kinds of knowledge about the market that strategists gather. One is quantitative, grid-like, evolving over time, displaying trends, providing a picture of the market – this is what IMS and Close Up provide. The other form of knowledge is local, qualitative, picked up gradually through interactions with doctors. It shows an awareness of the ethos of the market. This distinction might help answer the question of why Gador's generic fluoxetine was the leading antidepressant in 1998, while Lilly's Prozac remained far behind. A long-time veteran of marketing psychiatric medications, the CNS product manager for Gador is something of a legend in the field. He claimed that audit data was only necessary if one did not already know the market – "they are orienters, but they are not [so] important . . . We don't apply some of the tools that other companies do, because our strength, in the case of the sales force, is very different, this is a totally atypical company." In what sense? "In the average seniority of our men . . . in each of their zones . . . our man has a lot of stability and is someone who inspires trust."

Given his knowledge of the terrain, he intuited that, unlike in the United States, lock-and-key illustrations of neurotransmitter re-uptake inhibition might not be the most effective technique for pitching psychopharmaceuticals to Argentinean psychiatrists. In the late 1990s, a critical social psychiatry actually became the basis for Gador's marketing campaign, using globalization and the anxieties it provoked to promote its large anxiolytic and antidepressant line. One advertisement featured a series of grim figures traversing a map of the world, suffering from symptoms of globalization: "Deterioration of interpersonal relations," "Deterioration in daily performance," "Unpredictable demands and threats," "personal and familial suffering," "loss of social role," "loss of productivity." Gador's claim that pharmaceuticals were a means to alleviate social suffering indicates how medication can operate in distinctive ways according to its milieu of use.[29]

I asked the product manager how he came up with the "Globalization" campaign: "For as long as Gador has been putting together molecules, the work has been, in some way, to establish clearly the niches to which each one of these molecules is directed and, in this sense, globalization as a cultural concept – it is too strong not to use it." He told me about the next phase of the campaign: "Right now we are in a later stage; we realized that the medical audience and even the users are absolutely conscious that globalization brings all these problems and we are in a campaign that is in the next stage, and this is that of *vulnerability*." Another product manager noted the cleverness of this word choice, pointing out its resonance with a popular television series, called *"Los Vulnerables,"* about an eclectic group of patients involved in group therapy. The Vulnerability campaign was kicked off by a symposium in October 2000 called "Stress, Anxiety and Depression: A Progressive Clinical Sequence," at which a number of important local opinion leaders spoke. Among the organizers of the symposium was the journal editor who had objected to Lilly's tactics: Gador had succeeded where Lilly had failed – by approaching the opinion leader on his own terrain. Even if the editor could not fully embrace the role of opinion leader, at least this campaign resonated with his own political and epistemological inclinations as a socially oriented psychiatrist.

High Contact

How do these relations function to shift doctors' prescribing behavior? The recent relationship between anxiolytic (or tranquilizer) sales and antidepressant sales in Argentina provides a glimpse into the work of transforming a market. But it is a complex story, intersecting with very recent events in Argentinean political and economic life. I began my research into the pharmaceutical market in the summer of 2001, with the question of how to explain a dramatic rise in antidepressant sales revenue over the previous few years. While the pharmaceutical market as a whole had shrunk over the years of hyper-recession between 1998 and 2001, income from antidepressant sales jumped – by 16.5 percent from June 2000 to June 2001 alone.[30]

I asked market strategists and database managers why antidepressant sales were rising so much while the rest of the industry was in recession. The Close Up executive suggested a couple of reasons: on the one hand, older anxiolytics were losing market share to antidepressants; but also, a tremendous increase in panic attacks, especially in Buenos Aires, was driving up antidepressant sales. "Why were there more panic attacks?" I asked:

> Because there is a totally confusing situation in this country... a very stressful situation; there's a huge amount of unemployment, there's under-employment, and on the other hand we Argentineans are in a dead end. It seems like we don't have or *we can't find the way out... You're an anthropologist, you understand well.* Problems of social relations are being added to personal problems.

The overwhelming sense of insecurity linked to the ongoing economic crisis was generally the first answer pharmaceutical industry executives gave to the question of why antidepressant sales were increasing. When I asked the IMS executive in his Puerto Madero office, he said:

> You've been here for a month. You must know by now... the socio-economic situation and the politics of the country make it so that people are consuming more anxiolytics all the time and are going to the psychiatrist more all the time... Imagine a man who works, who has... who had a decent quality of life and has an income around a thousand or twelve hundred dollars a month. A few years ago he could live on this, now it's not enough to live on, so he becomes anxious. Don't forget that everyone in Argentina, everyone, has a tremendous fear, which is to be left without work.

In August 2001, announcements of "Anxiety Disorders Week," an information campaign designed to bring patients to hospitals where they could consult with experts, appeared in a number of Buenos Aires newspapers. "One of every four Argentineans suffers from them," one article proclaimed: "panic attacks, phobias. Specialists say that they are increasing; factors such as insecurity or incertitude with respect to the future can influence them."[31] The reference to uncertainty and insecurity was apt: the country was entering its fourth year of recession, the unemployment rate had reached 20 percent, and the widely tracked index of *riesgo-pais* or "country-risk" was spiking to record levels each day. And the campaign was successful beyond the expectations of its sponsors: the city's hospitals were inundated with patients complaining of symptoms of stress. The articles did not mention that the campaign had been co-sponsored by the domestic pharmaceutical firm Bago, makers of Tranquinil-brand alprazolam. Since in Argentina it is still prohibited to market a drug directly to the general public, an alternative is to "grow the market" by making general practitioners and patients more aware of the illness. In an article that appeared two months later in the daily *Clarín*, on the role of the growing economic crisis in increasing tranquilizer sales, a Bago sales manager reported that August had been a month of record sales for Tranquinil. The piece was subtitled, "Illnesses brought on by the crisis are increasing medical visits and anxiololytic use."[32] What might have been seen as evidence of the success of the Bago information campaign was instead cited as a sign of the nation's social and psychic crisis.

In the months that followed, as the crisis in Argentina reached its zenith with the fall of two presidents and the record default on its $132 billion national debt, the apparent increase in psychopharmaceutical sales became a subject of increasing interest to the press. A Spanish-language *BBC Online* article from late January 2002 cited reports from the pharmaceutical industry that while overall sales had decreased by 10 percent in the last year, antidepressant sales had increased by 13 percent and tranquilizer sales by 4 percent.[33] *The Observer* cited similar statistics in a piece called "Argentina Hits Rock Bottom," again linking the crisis to increased symptoms of anxiety and increased suicide rates.[34] Audit numbers extended their use here. Not only did they provide a map for strategists in their efforts to regulate expertise, they could also serve as evidence of effects of the crisis on the mental health conditions of the population. After mentioning an increase in stress-related medical visits in the wake of the crisis, the BBC article quoted an Argentinean psychiatrist: "Argentineans feel devalued. People feel lost. The rules of the game have changed. Working hard for many hours doesn't mean economic security any more."[35]

It was not clear, however, whether it was the effects of the crisis or the promotional strategies that harnessed them that were the primary cause of changes in the psychopharmaceutical market. These articles at first seem to provide evidence of the growing medicalization of social disorder, but it is important to try to sort out the relation between data on the transformations of the market and the stories that were being told about this data.

While mass media attention to psychopharmaceutical consumption seemed to increase toward the end of 2001, it was not a wholly new phenomenon. In 1996 – a moment that now looks like the height of the 1990s economic boom in Argentina – a piece called "The Ranking of Remedies" appeared in *La Nacion*.[36] In it, the President of the Argentinean Federation of Pharmacies said of the consumption of pharmaceuticals, "Perhaps what is most notable is the boom of the antidepressants, whose massive consumption took off in our society at the beginning of the seventies. And not by chance, as will be understood." The author of the article commented, "Of the five products most sold annually in our country, one is an antibiotic and the

rest are a faithful reflection of the two great maladies of our time: stress and *nervios*."
More pharmaceutical industry representatives added their interpretations: "Who isn't
nervioso in Argentina today?" asked the Executive Director of the CAEME, the
council of multinational laboratories. The President of the College of Pharmacists
gave a sociological reading of the sales data: "Life conditions are getting worse . . . and
we live in a permanent state of alteration. In 1994 alone more than 16 million boxes
of psychotropics were sold."

Such social analyses of psychopharmaceutical sales patterns were common among
market strategists. A veteran of the industry told me his theory of the relation of
social change to drug consumption: "In the seventies you had the cold war, and a
heightened sense of tension and nervousness – so valium sold well. Then in the
eighties with the phenomenon of the yuppies and their emphasis on career success,
the drugs of choice were anxiolytics. In the nineties anti-depressants became popular,
for two reasons: first there were those who had failed to meet their expectations in
the eighties and so they were depressed. But pharmaceutical marketing strategies
also had to do with it."

To analyze increased psychopharmaceutical sales as an instance of the medicalization of suffering seemed somehow redundant in this context. It was a part of assumed
knowledge that increased symptoms of anxiety and depression were linked to social
and political phenomena – so much so that the very salience of social accounts of
suffering served not as a *critique* of the role of pharmaceutical marketing but as its
basis, as we saw in the case of the Gador globalization and vulnerability campaigns.
The Gador campaign had captured a more generally prevalent explanatory model
of mental illness as grounded in the social.[37] Even CNS product managers did
not have a neural model of disorder. Thus Martin, discussing the question of the
sources of depression, protested the predominance of psychoanalytic explanations in
Argentina – in favor of a social one. He could have been describing one of the figures
on Gador's "*globalizacion*" map:

> It's not necessarily the case that the current modification, which is the cause of the
> depression, has its origin in what happened to me during my infancy. It's very likely that
> this marks us, but also the context and this sense of feeling ever-more vulnerable before
> change . . . The world is changing very fast, too fast for all of us. Today I was talking
> with someone about this issue and how we're *stuck* now – the deficit, the default or not,
> devaluation or not, it's such an uncertain horizon.

Media pundits, sales directors, and database firm executives agreed: insecurity linked
to the economic crisis was driving up psychopharmaceutical sales. But in fact it was
not clear that actual consumption had changed significantly. Martin told me, "the
quantity of patients treated with antidepressants hasn't increased that much; what has
changed is the average price of antidepressants." This would make sense given the
pattern in the early 1990s in the rest of the market – an increase in revenue generated
not by an increase in consumption but by the use of newer, more expensive drugs. In
this case, the explanation for increasing antidepressant sales could be a gradual

switch, among nonspecialists, from anxiolytics – still used far more than antidepressants – to the new SSRIs.

In fact, he thought that the market was still relatively untapped. "I think it's the tip of the iceberg, what we have today. Today the antidepressant market, even though as you said it's growing, I think that the potential is, easily ten times more than what it is now." How did he know the potential since there was no data available on the prevalence of depression in Argentina? He used transnational epidemiology, combining it with audit data: "If you take the index of the prevalence of depression in any country in the world, which is around – let's take a conservative number, 3% – you would be talking about a million or so people … in reality that would be pure depression, but if you begin to take the different types of depression, dysthemia, we're talking about three million people, more or less. And *today you have, treated patients, 350,000, more or less.*" I was impressed by the latter number – not because it was low, or because it was right, but because I hadn't been able to get even an estimate from anyone before – not from the health ministry (they didn't have them), nor the database firms (they wouldn't give them away), nor health insurance managers.

His argument that it was higher prices more than the actual number of patients treated that was driving up sales revenue was substantiated by a study that I initiated – given the paucity of other available data – with a group of pharmaco-epidemiologists affiliated with the University of Belgrano. The study compared the pattern of anxiolytic and antidepressant use over the period from 1997 to 2000 among members of four separate health plans, comprising a population of about 600,000 people.[38] It turned out that over this period there was a sharp *decline* in anxiolytic exposure, from 21 percent to 14 percent, and a slight increase in antidepressant exposure, from 3.6 percent to 4.5 percent of affiliates. These results are striking in comparison with the steep rise in psychopharmaceutical sales figures cited by the media as evidence of the effect of the economic crisis on the population's mental well-being. They are substantiated by data obtained from the IMS on changes in psychopharmaceutical unit sales volume in Argentina over the past five years, which indicate that overall anxiolytic unit sales declined by 5 percent between 1997 and 2001, and antidepressant unit sales increased by 9 percent over the same period.[39] While the gap was narrowing, anxiolytics were still sold at nearly six times the rate of antidepressants.

If we add to the results of this study another piece of information, we can be more precise about what was happening in the market: it turned out that the impressive growth in antidepressant revenue between December 1998 and June 2001 – from $45 million per year to $54 million per year (20 percent) could be mostly accounted for by sales of Paxil and Zoloft alone, which leapfrogged Gador's Foxetin to become the market leaders.[40] This was due to "high contact" between reps and doctors, and to the enviable position of these drugs within the product life cycle. Thus GlaxoSmithKline and Pfizer had apparently been successful in getting generalists to switch from anxiolytics to their new antidepressants – which were now indicated for anxiety disorders as well as for depression.

Rather than a precipitous increase in overall psychopharmaceutical consumption due to the economic crisis, the increase in antidepressant revenue could best be explained in terms of a specific tactic: the work by sales reps and opinion leaders to convince doctors to prescribe the newer antidepressants instead of tranquilizers for symptoms of stress, anxiety and depression. It is worth noting that such a shift is in accord with the recommendations of leading health authorities, who have expressed alarm at high rates of anxiolytic use (often tied to addiction and self-medication) in countries such as France and Argentina. In other words, "high contact" – the intensification of relations between pharmaceutical companies and doctors – worked in this case to shape prescription habits more or less along the lines that officially sanctioned expertise would authorize. This technique of regulating doctors' behavior depended on knowledge about prescription practices and disease prevalence that was not available in the public domain; that is, it relied on intensive efforts to acquire, compile, and disseminate – at a steep price – a set of private numbers with a life of their own.

Notes

1   Kathryn Sikkink, *Ideas and Institutions: Developmentalism in Brazil and Argentina* (Ithaca, NY: Cornell University Press, 1991); Carlos Waisman, *Reversal of Development in Argentina: Postwar Counterrevolutionary Policies and Their Structural Consequences* (Princeton: Princeton University Press, 1987).

2   Martin Hopenhayn provides a lucid account of this process from the perspective of Latin American intellectuals and policy-makers. See M. Hopenhayn, *No Apocalypse, No Integration: Modernism and Postmodernism in Latin America* (Durham, NC: Duke University Press, 2001).

3   Andrew Barry, Thomas Osborne and Nikolas Rose, eds., *Foucault and Political Reason: Liberalism, Neo-Liberalism and the Rationalities of Government* (Chicago: University of Chicago Press, 1996).

4   Despite the extremity of its reform measures, the Argentinean state was by no means completely stripped away. In fact, per capita spending on health (40 percent of which is public) increased by 50 percent from 1990 to 1999, and in 2000 was approximately 10 percent of the $285 billion GDP. Per capita health spending increased from $827 to $1291 over this period, according to the World Bank's standardized units of calculation. See World Bank, "Health, Nutrition and Population." World Health Organization, *Atlas: Country Profiles on Mental Health Resources in the World* (2001). About one quarter of the health budget was spent on pharmaceuticals – $6 billion in 1999.

5   The brief submitted by the lobbying group PhRMA claimed, as part of the U.S. case against Argentina before the WTO, that "Argentina is widely recognized as the worst expropriator of U.S. pharmaceutical inventions in the Western Hemisphere, as local firms dominate over 50% of the pharmaceutical market currently estimated at almost U.S. $4.1 billion. Substantial and continuing loss of market share, in the range of hundreds of millions of dollars, is directly attributable to Argentina's defective intellectual property regime."

6   ISALUD, "El Mercado de Medicamentos en la Argentina," *Estudios de la Economia Real*, no. 13 (Buenos Aires: Fundacion ISALUD, 1999).

7   Idem.

8   Gilles Deleuze, "Post-Script on Control Societies," in *Negotiations* (New York: Columbia University Press, 1995); for a wide-ranging description of the experiential implications of new forms of global capital, see Jean and John L. Comaroff, "Millennial Capitalism: First Thoughts on a Second Coming," *Public Culture* 12(2), 2000, pp. 291–343.

9   For the description of the practice of denunciation as the uncovering of impurity within regimes of action, see Luc Boltanski and Laurent Thevenot, *De la Justification: les economies de la grandeur*(Paris: Gallimard, 1991). Paul Rabinow shows that as early as Pascal's plan to sell transportation infrastructure to the Parisian bourgeoisie, truth-seeking has coexisted with enterprise. See P. Rabinow, *Anthropos Today: Reflections on Modern Equipment* (Princeton: Princeton University Press, 2003). On the "impurities" that patient activism introduced to clinical research into HIV/AIDS, see Steven Epstein, *Impure Science: AIDS, Activism, and the Politics of Knowledge* (Berkeley: University of California Press, 1996).

10 See, for example, Marcia Angell, "Is Academic Medicine For Sale?" *New England Journal of Medicine* 342(20), 2000, pp. 1516–1518.

11 David Healy, "The dilemmas posed by new and fashionable treatments," *Advances in Psychiatric Treatment* 7, 2001, pp. 322–327.

12 See Arjun Appadurai, ed., *The Social Life of Things: Commodities in Cultural Perspective* (New York: Cambridge University Press, 1986).

13 As Steven Shapin has shown, relations of trust and socially sanctioned authority have underpinned scientific knowledge production from the earliest moments of what came to be known as the Scientific Revolution. See S. Shapin, *A Social History of Truth* (Chicago: University of Chicago Press, 1996).

14 Charles Sabel, "Constitutional Orders: Trust Building and Response to Change," in *Contemporary Capitalism: The Embeddedness of Institutions*, J. Rogers Hollingsworth and Robert Boyer, eds. (Cambridge: Cambridge University Press, 1997).

15 ISALUD, "El Mercado de Medicamentos en la Argentina." Data on the number of reps in 2002 comes from the union of *agentes de propaganda medica* (APMs). Their website, which features an animated suitcase-bearing rep, can be found at http://www.apm.org.ar

16 IMS Health website; http://www.imshealth.com (accessed December 1998).

17 As the Pan American Health Organization reports of Argentina, "information on the prevalence of mental illness is very scant."See *Health in the Americas* (Washington, DC: Pan American Health Organization, Pan American Sanitary Bureau, Regional Office of the World Health Organization, 2002). As for spending, in its *Atlas* of global mental health, the World Health Organization notes of Argentina: "Details about expenditure on mental health are not available." See World Health Organization, *Atlas: Country Profiles on Mental Health Resources in the World* (2001), p. 148.

18 Ian Hacking describes the "avalanche of printed numbers" produced by nation-states, beginning in the Napoleonic era, in *The Taming of Chance* (Cambridge: Cambridge University Press, 1990).

19 Michel Foucault, "'Omnes et Singulatim': Toward a Critique of Political Reason," in Foucault, *Power*, James Faubion, ed. (New York: New Press, 2000).

20 See Paul Rabinow, *French Modern: Norms and Forms of the Social Environment* (Cambridge, MA: The MIT Press, 1989).

21 Nikolas Rose, "Numbers," in *Powers of Freedom* (Cambridge: Cambridge University Press, 1999).

22 See Nikolas Rose, "The Death of the Social? Refiguring the Territory of Government," *Economy and Society* 25(3), 1996, pp. 327–356.

23 Deleuze, "Post-Script on Control Societies."

24 For the history of the use of "territory" measures in sales management, see Timothy Spears, *100 Years on the Road: Traveling Salesmen in American Culture* (New Haven: Yale University Press, 1995).

25 I describe this dynamic in more detail in Andrew Lakoff, *Pharmaceutical Reason: Technology and the Human at the Modern Periphery* (Cambridge: Cambridge University Press, forthcoming).

26 Michael Power, *The Audit Society: Rituals of Verification* (New York: Oxford University Press, 1999); Marilyn Strathern, ed., *Audit Cultures: Anthropological Studies in Accountability, Ethics and the Academy* (New York: Routledge, 2000).

27 The course was part of Lilly's efforts to promote new uses of its anti-psychotic medication Zyprexa as Prozac went off patent.

28 Two important recent histories of the Argentinean *mundo-psi* (psy-world) are Hugo Vezzetti, *Las Aventuras de Freud en el País de los Argentinos: de José Ingenieros a Enrique Pichon-Rivière* (Buenos Aires: Paidos, 1996); and Mariano Plotkin, *Freud in the Pampas: The Emergence and Development of a Psychoanalytic Culture in Argentina* (Palo Alto: Stanford University Press, 2001).

29 Van der Geest et al. make this point in their important survey of the anthropology of pharmaceuticals: "Pharmaceuticals are often recast in another knowledge system and used very differently from the way they were intended in the 'regime of value' where they were produced." See Sjaak van der Geest, Susan Reynolds Whyte, and Anita Hardon, "The Anthropology of Pharmaceuticals: A Biographic Approach," *Annual Review of Anthropology* 25, 1996, p. 166.

30 IMS Health sales reports. Data obtained through anonymous sources.

31 Horacio Cecchi, "Una noticia para comerse las uñas," *Página 12*, August 16, 2001.

32 "El Consumo de Tranquilizantes creció entre un 8 y un 9 por ciento." *Clarín*, October 3, 2001. The article also cites IMS figures: "the total sales of prescription medications declined in the last year by 5.63%. But this number isn't the same for all remedies. The sales of anxiolytics grew 3.86% and that for heart ailments grew 1.31%. The data does not seem coincidental."

33 "Los Argentinos se sienten devaluados," *BBC Online*, January 24, 2002.

34 Sophie Arie, "Argentina Hits Rock Bottom," *The Observer*, December 9, 2001.

35 "Devaluation" here referred to the uncoupling of the dollar–peso peg, which for ten years had provided Argentineans with a tenuous sense of economic security, while at the same time hampering the government's capacity for macroeconomic intervention to promote growth.

36 Jorge Palomar, "El Ranking de los Remedios," *La Nación* On Line, 1996.

37 For the concept of explanatory models in psychiatry, see Arthur Kleinman, *Rethinking Psychiatry: From Cultural Category to Personal Experience* (New York: Free Press, 1988).

38 Miriam Gattari, Susana Scarpatti, Inés Bignone, Ricardo Bolaños, and Ulises Romeo, "Estudio de utilización de ansiolíticos y antidepresivos en cuatro entidades de la seguridad social de la Argentina, periodo 1997–2000," unpublished MS, 2001.

39 I am very grateful to Nikolas Rose for obtaining and sharing this most valuable data.

40 Unofficial data: over the two and a half year period, Paxil sales had gone from an annual $6.2 million to $11.5 million. Unit sales of paroxetine and sertraline also increased markedly.

12

IMPLEMENTING EMPIRICAL KNOWLEDGE IN ANTHROPOLOGY AND ISLAMIC ACCOUNTANCY

BILL MAURER

In 1999, the Supreme Court of Pakistan ordered the government to "Islamize" the country's economy by the summer of 2002. In June 2002, just a few days before the deadline, the court suspended that judgment.[1] The earlier decision had sought the elimination of all forms of interest charges, or *riba*, which the court had ruled was forbidden by Islamic law. While apparently reversing that earlier judgment, the court's decision in 2002 did leave open the possibility of Islamic economic reforms sometime in the future. The manner in which it did so speaks directly to a crisis in Islamic banking, one that strongly resonates with an analogous crisis in contemporary anthropology. Those crises motivate this chapter.

For Islamic banking, the impracticality of creating a financial system that does not rely on interest-bearing debt produces a crisis in knowledge, for the Qur'an is unequivocal in its outlawing of *riba*, and Islam is unequivocal in its acceptance of the Qur'an as the word of God. To accept that interest has practical necessity is thus to deny the Qur'an its status as universal knowledge. For anthropology, the act of creating new knowledge from others' practices, when those practices are themselves knowledge-producing, points up the "surfeit of forms of knowledge"[2] that throws open the pretension of anthropology to be the universal science of "man." The problem is particularly acute, and absorbing, when others' knowledge practices share with anthropology's a specific moral and epistemological form. In the end, the Pakistan Supreme Court decided that no "Islamic" reform of the country's economy would be possible until after "thorough and elaborate research and comparative study of the financial systems which are prevalent in the contemporary Muslim countries of the world."[3] In short, the court called for rigorous, empirically based comparison and synthesis, a knowledge practice of the sort an ethnographer, not a theologian, might conduct – although the contrast may turn out to be more apparent than real. Indeed, as this chapter argues, the moral form of empirical facts made by knowledge techniques such as anthropology and Islamic banking testifies to an uneasy unity that obviates any clean distinction between fact and value. I am interested in Islamic banking, and, in this chapter, Islamic accountancy, because its participants at times make that unity an explicit element of reflection on the status of the empirical and, in the same instant, the divine.

While Pakistan's effort to create an interest-free economy may have been put in abeyance, various movements to craft Islamic financial alternatives continue apace, and even in the sites of production of hegemonic financial knowledge (what Islamic bankers call "conventional finance"), and even after the events of September 11, 2001. The United States' Department of Treasury, for example, hosted a seminar titled "Islamic Finance 101" in Washington, D.C., in the spring of 2002.[4] And throughout 2002, the U.S. Federal Home Loan Mortgage Corporation ("Freddie Mac") expanded its underwriting of interest-free mortgage alternatives devised by a number of Islamic financial institutions in the country.[5]

The question of practicality and implementation continue to vex Islamic financial experiments, however, as it did the Pakistan Supreme Court. The taint of illicitness, too, before and after September 11, 2001, has also hindered the development of Islamic finance. Islamic banking professionals (and the regulators who look over their shoulders) have settled upon one knowledge-generating tool to address both problems: accounting standards-setting. Islamic banking professionals have been calling for clear Islamic accounting standards ever since the Bank of Credit and Commerce International scandal of the 1980s, linked in the business press to Islamic banking in Caribbean tax havens. Founded in 1990 as the Financial Accounting Organization for Islamic Banks and Financial Institutions (FAOIBFI) and renamed in 1991, the Accounting and Auditing Organization for Islamic Financial Institutions (AAOIFI) disseminated Islamic accounting procedures in 1996–7 as part of this effort, and continues to revise and update them.

At its inception, the AAOIFI entered a field previously dominated by Shari'a Supervisory Boards (SSBs). Most Islamic businesses of any appreciable size rely on the seal of approval granted by an independent SSB made up of clerics and scholars. The AAOIFI has been careful not to tread on the toes of independent SSBs, and relies on their standards-setting to guide its own. The AAOIFI itself boasts an SSB made up of internationally prominent individuals. While the AAOIFI has drafted standards that are readily grasped by its counterpart non-Islamic organizations and agreements such as the International Accounting Standards Committee or the Generally Accepted Accounting Principles, it is not engaged in a struggle for authority with local, national, or regional SSBs. Indeed, the AAOIFI needs SSBs, and vice versa, for the AAOIFI relies on SSBs to provide the "data" from which it crafts universally applicable Islamic accounting standards. The AAOIFI collects information on already existing Islamic accounting practices and distills from the available empirical data the "best practices" that will have the most universal transferability and, ultimately, transparency to both Islamic and non-Islamic businesspeople and regulators. It is a process analogous to the establishment of the Uniform Commercial Code (UCC) in the United States during the early 20th century,[6] and the empiricist orientation of much anthropology. The name Karl Llewellyn, of course, underscores their shared institutional and personal histories.

Indeed, the way accounting in Islamic banking and finance creates particular kinds of facts and engages a specific rhetoric of rationality bears a family resemblance to the knowledge projects of the social sciences, including anthropology. Garfinkel early on asked scholars to appreciate the multiple ambiguities of the word "accounting," stressing the unity of the numerical and narrative forms of accounts-keeping that render organizational forms "tell-able." As he put it, "Any setting organizes its activities to make its properties as an organized environment of practical activities detectable, countable, recordable, reportable, tell-a-story-about-able, analyzable – in short *accountable*."[7] Although religion was not specifically within his purview, Garfinkel's comments illuminate the moral valence of accounting in its multiple senses, a valence that is integral to its form and forms of knowledge allied to it.

Accounting standards-setting and scholarship that seeks to understand it, such as the so-called critical accounting literature,[8] both rely on the same perspective-shifting analytics as anthropology and its underlying empiricism. Both create knowledge by abstracting general principles from discrete data that is understood to preexist the act of abstraction and the shift in perspective (that is, to "another level") that abstraction entails. For standards-setting, the principles are quite simply the standards that end up getting written down and disseminated. For critical accounting scholarship, which seeks to understand the accounting profession in terms other than the profession's own, the principles have to do with something else – politics, values, meanings – lying before or behind accounting practice. Critical accounting scholarship thus replicates the analytics of standards-setting at a different level of abstraction. It often does so by using anthropological tools such as ethnography. Many critical accounting scholars also want to reshape that content and create a new accounting, and from a new accounting, a new world.

Regardless of its transformative aspirations, critical accounting's recursivity should be familiar to anthropologists used to finding "culture" in winks. Drawing on the work of Mary Douglas, the influential accounting theorist Trevor Gambling argued that "accounting theory and culture are not readily separable"[9] and that " 'accounting theory *is* the culture' at least in the anthropological sense. Perhaps one could go further and define a society as a 'group of people who subscribe to a common accounting theory.' "[10] The idea that everything is accounting and accounting is everything plays on the ambiguity of the term in English (accounting as audit, accounting as narration, and accounting as religious or cosmopolitical judgment), an ambiguity made material in the transformations of scale that accounting in all of its senses permits. If accounting is everything, can analysis, itself a form of accounts-keeping, get a critical perspective on it?

This problem takes on a particular significance in Islamic accountancy. In Islamic finance, some very anthropological ideas – such as debate over the social construction of reality and the role of values and beliefs in bureaucratic practice – have become a terrain of struggle. As anthropologists have turned to bureaucratic forms such as accounting, the discipline has confronted the separation of text from context, form from content, and theory from data that stabilized its technique in the late 20th century. Those oppositions now seem to characterize the knowledge practices of those we study, and turn up in precisely those bureaucratic quarters to which we now direct our attention.[11] This places anthropology in an uncomfortable position, different from the reflexivity of an earlier era, because it is concerned less with the partiality of a particular observer's perspective than with the metapragmatics of analytics of parts and wholes that make perspectival knowledge possible, yet guaranteed very quickly to reach its own limits.[12] This chapter is thus concerned as much with the implementation of anthropology's empirical claims as it is Islamic accountancy.

Making Reasonable Accounts

The facts of accounting are special facts: they are supposed to help people make good decisions about the management of their assets. It is a textbook truism that the principal objective of accounting practice is to guarantee the "decision-usefulness" of the information that accountants collect, analyze, and present to auditors, shareholders, managers, and others. The underlying assumption of the decision-usefulness framework is that rational economic actors need information in order to make effective economic decisions that will serve their self-interest. Since, in this framework, the aggregate activities of self-interested maximizers create the most efficient allocation of resources, decision-usefulness is the cornerstone of the efficient functioning of markets.

Regulators and other observers not directly involved in Islamic banking cite a lack of accounting standards as one of their main concerns about the movement. *Euromoney* reports that Islamic banking's "long-term ambition" of "taking on world markets" may be hindered by a lack of "uniform and consistent accounting and auditing standards and . . . proper regulation," and that "standardization is desperately needed."[13] A vice-president of the Federal Reserve Bank of New York attached the success of Islamic banking to decision-useful accounting standards. While stating before an audience of Islamic bankers that "issues of religion are not supervisory matters of concern,"[14] this official argued that "qualitative" considerations must be taken into account by supervisory agencies. He continued:

> it involves an assessment by bank examiners of the financial strength and managerial controls of the bank. This is done in a 'hands on' way by examiners looking at the bank's systems, books, and records on site and assessing the quality of its management. In addition, we rely on reports of the bank which are issued quarterly and made public

to allow the public – investors, depositors and counterparties – to assess the credit-worthiness and risk profile of the bank.[15]

Concerns about standardization, decision-usefulness, and possible regulatory inter-ference led to the establishment of the FAOIBFI/AAOIFI.[16] Here, certain "ceremo-nial" or "window-dressing" functions of accounting seem evident.[17] It is evidentiary, however, in the same way that the facts of accounting are: based on induction from the observation of a moment of social life, a process that delimits the accountant's, regulator's, and, just as importantly, social analyst's field of practice. It is evidentiary, too, only within the terms of an implicitly functionalist theory of culture (window-dressing, after all, functions to make something prettier, or to hide something else). This is a point to which I will return later.

Decision-usefulness criteria are supposed to mitigate information asymmetry and provide a means of bracketing the conflict of interests between the manager of a financial institution and the shareholders. In the accounting literature, this potential conflict is called the agency problem. The decision-usefulness framework only makes sense in a world in which a person can be called forth into social interaction as a maximizing individual; only in such a world would the agency problem manifest, and the decision-usefulness framework actually be useful. One would need to be possessed of (by?) the spirits of capitalist utilitarianism for conventional accounting to lessen information asymmetry and foster efficient markets.

The argument could be made that different spirits do or ought to possess Islamic economics, rendering conventional accounting irrelevant. A recent Western com-mentator on Islamic accountancy explicitly rejects the AAOIFI's approach to stand-ards-setting – beginning with data from actual practices and "objectives established in contemporary accounting thought" tested against Islamic religious norms – in favor of proceeding from "objectives based on the spirit of Islam."[18] Others agree,[19] arguing that Islamic economics in general needs to be exorcised of its Western underpinnings so that its true spirit will come forth. In an e-mail post to the Islamic banking Internet listserv that generated heated, highly theoretical debate, a promin-ent Islamic economist argued:

> Islamic economics and finance being entrenched body and soul in mainstream economic doctrines has remained without a distinctive birth-pang of its own. Its epistemology...remained in foreign moorings just as the early rationalist Muslim scholars distorted the Qur'anic worldview with Greek thought. [It remains] subservi-en[t] to modernity rather than upholding [the] purity of human faculty to the Qur'anic worldview and its deep analytical vision...

In a later posting, the same scholar invoked *tawhid*, or "unity," a core element of neo-Sufi and neo-Platonist Islamic theology. He also directly addressed the accounting criterion of decision-usefulness as a core element of Western economics:

> What I am taking out of the Qur'an is the epistemology of *Tawhid* in which Allah is manifested as the Complete and Absolute in Knowledge Stock, from which premise

emerges the immaculate premise of Unity as the Fundamental Unity. Yet this is a topological reality from which is derived the organization of flows of incomplete knowledge in the world-system, but that ever grows and unifies as it does so with the elements of the world-system . . . [The] essence of pairedness is the resemblance of universal complementarity within the acts of systemic realization. Hence, the essence of Qur'anic pairedness is combined with the incompleteness of knowledge to know, creatively evolve and organize in the framework of the self-same unification of relations. Such a Process negates all claims on the agent to have full-information. Terminality and scarcity, marginalism and optimality of neoclassicism are totally replaced by the process-oriented, creatively learning and evolving universally complementary process in this Qur'anic framework of *Tawhidi* [*sic*] epistemology.

Such an analytic move attempts to redraw the process of knowledge and the objects of the known. The *tawhid* approach demands a fundamental reconfiguration of epistemology – indeed, a dissolution of epistemology itself into the incompleteness of approaching but never reaching the overarching unity of divine thought, as if a mathematical limit-function.

Both within and outside Islamic banking circles, however, this sort of argument is often cast as mystical, irrational, and otherizing. More damning, it is considered impractical – it does not generate the kind of facts that economic practice needs in order to "work," much less to work "efficiently." And, as the Pakistan Supreme Court case that introduced this chapter made explicit, the criterion of practical workability is of signal importance in implementing economic rationality. As another prominent Islamic economics expert wrote, in countering the *tawhid* approach, "there is no point in trying to re-invent the wheel (especially if you don't end-up with a round one). The machinery of neo-Classical economics, and many of its assumptions, is mostly in harmony with the canonical Islamic texts . . . , as well as the opinions of Muslim jurists over the centuries."

Why, for Islamic banking adherents who reject *tawhid*, is their understanding of a convergence between neoclassical economic theory and Islamic jurisprudence not unnerving?[20] Do the facts of Islamic accounting invoke in outside observers, as well as devotees, trust and confidence in the stable entities and clear agents of Islamic banking? If so, they are less constitutive of an essential Muslim subject of economics than they are persuasive that the business practices from which they are distilled are sound, reputable, and consistent with a range of business practices that are not specifically Islamic. In that, they take on the same performative window-dressing functions as the facts of conventional accounting that Carruthers has discussed.[21]

Yet Islamic accountants must abstract the facts of Islamic accounting out of a field of practice. As is the case with conventional accounting that abstraction, like induction generally, is never straightforward.[22] A closer look at technical problems in Islamic accounting created by Islamic banking practices shows that the question of Islamic accounting being merely window-dressing, or the more classically anthropological question of Islamic accounting's difference from conventional accounting, is perhaps slightly beside the point.

Mudarabah Accounting in Theory

A *mudarabah* or profit-and-risk sharing contract is a ubiquitous financing mechanism in Islamic banking. In a classic (that is, medieval, not modern) *mudarabah*, the *rabb-al-mal* (henceforth, depositor–investor) provides money to an *mudarib* (henceforth, manager) who uses it to conduct an agreed-upon business, and then returns to the depositor–investor the principal and a preset proportion of the profits. Once she or he has turned over the money as an initial investment, the depositor–investor has the right to verify that the manager is complying with the terms of the contract. The manager is not liable for any loss that occurs in the course of the business except when such loss occurs because of a breach of trust. There is an understanding that the manager will act according to the customary practice of any businessperson. Further, the depositor–investor has a right to share the profits as agreed upon at the contract's commencement. Finally, the depositor–investor's liability is limited to the capital that he or she initially invested. The manager is not permitted to commit any sum of money greater than the capital in hand to the partnership without the depositor–investor's authorization. Similarly, once the depositor–investor has handed over the initial investment as specified in the contract, the manager has no right to demand any further financial liability or contribution from him or her.[23]

Modern Islamic banks can use *mudarabah* contracts to generate liquidity and turn a profit, acting as go-betweens between the depositor–investors and the managers of business ventures. In effect, modern Islamic banking takes the classic *mudarabah* contract and scales it up: the depositor–investor becomes the *rabb-al-mal* in relation to the bank, as *mudarib*, which manages the depositor–investor's money. At the same time, the bank assumes the position of the *rabb-al-mal* in relation to the business enterprise the bank invests in, which is the *mudarib* in relation to the bank. Under this scaling principle, the bank can accept money from many depositor–investors via the *mudarabah* contractual form and, in turn, invest it in several different enterprises through the same *mudarabah* contractual form. Should the enterprises turn a profit, the enterprises, the bank and the depositor–investors are entitled to a predetermined percentage of the profit. Should they turn a loss, the depositor–investors (and possibly the bank, depending on its operating principles) share in a predetermined percentage of the loss. The enterprises themselves (and also the bank) can pass off the loss onto their depositor–investors, since the enterprises are considered to have "lost" the expertise and labor invested in prosecuting the contracts.

Mudarabah provides a means for enterprise financing and a sort of consumer banking that are Islamically acceptable. Instead of financing its activities with interest-bearing loans, a business could accept funds from an Islamic bank and give up a predetermined percentage of its profits (and losses, effectively spreading some the risk of doing business). Rather than a depositor earning interest on a savings account, the depositor–investor would earn a predetermined percentage of the profits (or losses, effectively bearing the risk of market activities) of all the enterprises in which the bank had invested the pooled resources of its depositor–investors.

Mudarabah presents a number of problems for conventional accounting. First, consider conventional accounting's "entity theory," according to which accounting draws meaningful boundaries around business entities for the purpose of audit. Entity theory poses problems for Islamic banks using *mudarabah* accounts, especially when it comes time to account for *mudarabah* holdings on a balance sheet. *Mudarabah* contracts confound the clear boundaries between the entity taken into consideration for the purposes of accounting and its owners. In a *mudarabah* contract, the depositor–investor who contributes capital in return for a share of the profit or loss "owns" that capital. The bank is "managing" it and investing it in productive enterprises. The bank sees the depositor–investors on its own balance sheets, but the enterprises that receive the depositor–investors' capital from the bank do not. Yet the depositor–investors are the "owners" of the ventures the bank has invested in. And they are not merely financially responsible for them, but morally as well: should an enterprise engage in un-Islamic activities, then ethically the depositor–investors are just as at fault as the bank.

In conventional accounting, the entity concept effects a separation between owners and corporate entities, morally insulating the former from the decisions of the latter; if owners disagree with a particular decision, they can vote at shareholders' meetings to change policies, or, more simply, disinvest. Accounting and audits are supposed to help them make exactly these sorts of decisions. But *mudarabah* contracts are a moral/ethical form that demands a close relationship, indeed, an identity, between the morality of the business ventures and that of the depositor–investors. Depositor–investors are in a sense insulated from the business ventures they are invested in by the intermediation of bank, but they have no say in the activities of those ventures and have to rely on the bank's judgment to make wise investments. The bank's own venture, its own corporate status, meanwhile, is not a separate entity from the depositor–investors' capital, but rather an extension of the depositor–investors.[24] Given this, how should an accountant "entextualize," as it were, the entity for the purposes of an audit?[25] How should the accountant draw meaningful boundaries around and abstract from the business practices of the depositor–investors, the bank, and the enterprises in which the bank has invested depositor–investors' money?

The second problem that *mudarabah* poses for conventional accounting concerns the separation of ownership from management in the corporate form.[26] When corporations are managed by one set of individuals (managers) and owned by another (shareholders), the managers are obliged to act in the interests of shareholders. In other words, managers are the agents of the shareholders, who are the "principals" of the corporation. Yet (as was made abundantly clear by the Enron, WorldCom, and Arthur Anderson accounting scandals of 2001–2) the separation of ownership from management means that shareholders do not have access to the same information about the day-to-day operations of the corporation as the managers. Shareholders must take on faith that the information managers divulge to them is an accurate reflection of an underlying reality. The postulate of self-interested maximization would suggest that managers would attempt to act in their own interests, not those of the shareholders. The condition of "information asymmetry" that obtains between agents and principals opens a space of possibility for the free reign of managers' self-interest. Just as significantly, it also opens a space for the insertion of faith into finance: the faith that representations do suggest an underlying reality, and that that reality precedes the representation of it.[27]

An Islamic bank relying on *mudarabah*, however, has an agency relationship with potentially two kinds of investors – those who invest in the financial company itself as shareholders and have voting privileges on its board, and those who simply deposit their money into *mudarabah* investment accounts. Unlike an interest-bearing savings account, a *mudarabah* account carries no guarantee of return. The bank calculates the amount of profits (or losses) disbursed to investment account holders. At the same time, the bank calculates the amount of the profits (or losses) disbursed in the form of dividends to shareholders. In effect, the bank must take into consideration two sets of interests – those of the shareholders, and those of the depositor–investors – that are at odds with one another, since a loss to one is a gain to the other. For whom, then, is the bank the "agent?" For whose decisions should any information produced by an audit of the bank be "useful?" For some in the Islamic banking community, it makes sense to think of the bank as multiply agentive. This does not necessarily solve the agency problem, however, because it leaves open the question of how an accountant ought to delimit decision-useful information. In other words, as with entity theory, *mudarabah* creates an entextualization problem from the point of view of the accountant: how to delimit and bound and abstract from the field of practice the specifically relevant aspects of a bank's activity for depositor–investors and shareholders.

The third problem that *mudarabah* poses for conventional accounting has to do with income. To calculate income, one must first determine the value of an entity's assets. And there are different methods for doing so. For example, how should one determine the value of real property held by the bank? Should one enter a value based on what one originally paid for it, based on what one paid for it adjusted for inflation, or based on projections of its value at some future liquidation date? From the point of view of Islamic banking, most calculations of value of this sort introduce the possibility of *riba*. This is because each of these calculations adds a value to the real property that is not specifically tied to any of the risks involved in holding the property. They constitute paper-based augmentations of value. Conventional accounting theory does offer an alternative to these methods of valuation; namely, current cash equivalent valuation (CCE). CCE essentially demands that all assets be marked to market – based on the assumption that markets efficiently set prices and that the value of any item at any given moment in time is equal to the price of that item in an open and unrestricted market. Islamic accounting scholars recommend that CCE be used to value assets in any determinations of income.[28] Again, however, this is a particular kind of entextualization problem: How should the accountant literally record the value of real property in this case?

Consider the effect of *mudarabah* on the three legs of conventional accounting. Entity dissolves, or, rather, multiplies, into proprietors. Agency disperses into multiple agents. And income gets disaggregated and temporally fixed into contemporary assessments of cash equivalencies, in a continuous and real-time marking to market. Each leg undergoes a sort of fractal transformation: each component part of the account is a smaller version of the whole, in a potentially infinite reiteration at all levels of scale. Imagine a ledger for an Islamic bank. Contained within it would be ledgers for each *mudarabah* account and, within those, ledgers for each proprietor. Imagine the budget line for income: within each would be a constantly changing figure based on continuous and indefinite valuation through the marking of assets to the market. This marking to market is a recursive process that guarantees the perpetuation of the fractal pattern of the imaginary *mudarabah* account. The multiple agents constituted by multiple proprietors lend a scaling shape to the imaginary account. At whatever level the accountant looks, she or he will see "similar patterns at different scales"; "enlarging a tiny section will produce a pattern that looks similar to the whole picture, and shrinking down the whole will give us something that looks like a tiny part."[29] Our imaginary fractal account begins to resemble nothing so much as the knowledge-flows of *tawhid*, where epistemology dissolves into the unity of divine thought.

Mudarabah Accounting in Practice

I ask my reader to imagine a fractal ledger because there are no real ones to show. The fractal form was only revealed to me when, out of utter desperation and confusion over the multiple levels of ownership possible with nested contracts, I asked people to draw me the mechanisms of *mudarabah*. I discuss one such example below. But the accounting books of Islamic banks and the accounting standards put forward by the AAOIFI are hardly fractal or neo-Platonist. Indeed, what is so striking about the standards is that they are virtually silent on the practical and epistemological problems that *mudarabah* might pose for conventional accounting. In effect, they erase the oneness of *tawhid* in the *mudarabah* form. Like other documents of bureaucratic rationality, the AAOIFI standards provide clear rules, straightforward justifications for those rules, and guidelines for following the rules. The standards explicitly invoke the need for impartiality, consistency, universal applicability, and procedural precision. The very form in which they are presented embodies these principles: the standards are labeled with a letter or number and divided into sections, subsections, and paragraphs. In such form, they embody order and logic and hierarchy, appealing to bureaucratic reason and logic recast as fundamental human nature. AAOIFI Standard A section 4 subsection 1, headed "The importance of establishing objectives," begins as follows:

> Human experience proves that any work which does not have clear objectives encounters limitations, conflicts, and blurred vision in its implementation. Financial accounting and financial reporting are no exception to this precept. Accounting scholars and practitioners alike have found that the process of developing financial accounting standards without establishing objectives leads to inconsistent standards which may not be suitable for the environment in which they are expected to be applied.[30]

That said, the objectives of the AAOIFI standards are the same as for any set of accounting standards: the provision of decision-useful facts for large investors, not for small depositors or *mudarabah* account holders. *Mudarabah* accounts are treated exactly like any other liability, and *exactly* like deposit accounts in a conventional bank. The problems that *mudarabah* poses for conventional accounting are transformed into nonproblems, the practices of Islamic accounting are identical to conventional accounting, and the distinction between the two seems to disappear.

Two brief examples will suffice to illustrate the nonproblem of *mudarabah* accounting. The first is the 1999 Annual Report of Bank Muamalat Indonesia (BMI), the largest Islamic bank in that country (BMI 1999). Unlike most other financial institutions, BMI weathered Indonesia's recent financial crisis (1998–2000) rather well, and has entered the post-Suharto *era reformasi* in a better position than almost all other banks. Its success during the crisis was due in no small measure to fact that its consumer-based liabilities are in the form of *mudarabah* accounts rather than conventional savings accounts. When the Indonesian currency, the rupiah, lost 600 percent of its value against the U.S. dollar between August 1997 and February 1998, most banks could not meet their obligations to their depositors, and folded. BMI's investments in "real" assets, however much affected by inflation and the crisis, proved more stable than the debt-based investments of conventional banks. Profit-and-loss sharing investments in the export commodity sector, for example, brought *increased* profits as the rupiah's value fell. As a direct result of the crisis, cities in provinces that were heavily reliant on export commodity production became boom towns, and many rural producers suddenly found themselves rich. As one banker in Makassar (formerly Ujung Pandang), South Sulawesi, told me, "The monetary crisis was the best thing that ever happened to South Sulawesi."

BMI's ledger, however, hides the role of *mudarabah* accounts in its success by recording them as simple liabilities, exactly the way AAOIFI standards suggest it be done. They are treated under the category *Kewajiban*, "Obligations" or "Liabilities," and placed under the heading *Simpanan*, or "Deposits," as *Tabungan Mudharabah* or "*Mudarabah* Savings Accounts." *Tabungan* is derived from the word *tabung*, a "bamboo tube used for storage,"[31] evoking an image of money hidden in a sack in the rafters of a house rather than invested in productive enterprise. AAOIFI procedures thus convert living agreements into dead savings, skirting the problems of accounting for all the nested and hierarchical contractual agreements of *mudarabah*.

The second example is from a small Islamic cooperative credit association (ICCA) in Makassar, organized for the benefit of teachers and students at a local Muslim university. ICCA, in the words of its manager, "operationalizes the university's credit" as part of the university's government-mandated role to support local businesses. With seed money from a faith-based private foundation, ICCA provides two types of credit to members of the university community and small business owners in town. Small business owners – mainly street vendors – enter into *mudarabah* agreements with ICCA, while ICCA enters into *mudarabah* agreements with the university and the foundation, in a nested hierarchy. All the contracts stipulate a preset profit-and-loss sharing ratio of 60 percent to 40 percent. In a contract with a street vendor, the profits are divided on a 60:40 ratio in favor of ICCA. Of ICCA's 60 percent of the profits, 60 percent is returned to the university, while 40 percent is retained by ICCA itself. Of that 40 percent, 60 percent is returned to the foundation that originally granted the university funds to set up ICCA, and the remaining 40 percent is for the "prosperity and welfare of the staff" of ICCA.

In addition to this form of "productive credit," members of the university community can borrow from ICCA for consumption. Consumption loans are interest-bearing, in spite of ICCA's Islamic credentials. The interest rate is *back-calculated* from the effective rate of return of ICCA's productive *mudarabah* accounts with street vendors. In other words, in the example above, ICCA earns an effective rate of return of 9.6 percent. In a consumptive loan, then, ICCA would charge 9.6 percent interest. This is a calculation made possible by ICCA's ledger-books, which, like BMI's, enter *mudarabah* accounts as deposit-type liabilities. It is only by aggregating *mudarabah* accounts with street vendors into one balance-sheet item that they can be offset by consumption loans to university professors and students. Not only are the fractal accounting problems of *mudarabah* skirted here; so, too, is the prohibition of interest – a side-stepping made possible by AAOIFI standards that allow *mudarabah* accounts to enter the liabilities side of the double-entry account without acknowledging their different conceptual and Shari'atic status from that of regular deposits.

The accounting trick is made more dramatic by the fact that in 2000 ICCA had extended consumption loans totaling 700 million Rp, and shared productive *mudarabah* accounts with vendors totaling 100 million Rp. It had 700 clients with outstanding consumption loans, and only about 70 with *mudarabah* accounts. The AAOIFI standards have allowed ICCA to base a rate of interest for the 90 percent of its clients who borrow for consumptive purposes on the rate of return generated by only 10 percent of its clients and extrapolated into a general principle, into a literal "rate of return" without regard for the actual value of that return at any given point in time. In theory, and in the books, consumption loans are backed by productive *mudarabah*. This both helps ICCA extend credit and achieve Shari'a compliance. In practice, however, productive *mudarabah* could only cover about one-seventh of the outstanding loans.

Notice how closely the nested *mudarabah* accounts resemble the fractal transformation of accounting discussed earlier. There are similar patterns at every scale, both within the ICCA's structure of *mudarabah* accounts and between ICCA's structure and the pattern suggested by *mudarabah's* in-folding and multiplication of the three legs of conventional accounting theory: entity, agency, and income. *Mudarabah* accounting in practice has the structure of the knowledge-flows of *tawhid*. It permits a detour to consumption-oriented, interest-bearing credit on the way to divine oneness. But then again, that detour is already built into the design.

Accounts of Islamic Accounting

For some, the procedures through which the AAOIFI extrapolates best practices out of existing practices and translates those into standards are highly suspect.

Complaining in an online forum about the changes in direction he saw Islamic finance taking to satisfy the demands of standardization, one Islamic accounting specialist argued, "If Islamic economics must make U turns to remain in business, I suggest that we cut the whole crap and join mainstream *riba* economics under the *fiqh* [legal] category of *dharurah* [necessity] and the modern criteria of efficiency." Another, however, responding to the demand that an Islamic accounting must somehow be "Islamic," replied,

> Accounting in whatever sense or use whether it be for Islamic purposes or otherwise is only meant to be used as a science to enable an organization to identify, assemble, analyse, calculate, classify, record, summarize and report transactions and other events ... Accounting is only a method of presentation of facts and figure [*sic*] about an organization in such a manner that the user can use that info according to his own needs whether the need is the promotion of welfare or something else.

A third replied, to this second interlocutor:

> I had the same thoughts as you a few years ago, insisting that Accounting is a technical subject and therefore there is no question of an Islamic or Christian or Buddhist Accounting ... Unfortunately, modern corporate accounting is not a matter of just numbers but a whole philosophy. Accounting can lead to perceptions of reality ... Ultimately, what accounting tells us [is that] what makes more money is the best thing. Over time, people will become mesmerised with this infactuation [*sic*] and act accordingly.

That the debate gets framed in the same terms as contemporary academic theorizations of the social construction of reality reveals a convergence between internal debates about Islamic accounting and modalities of academic knowledge production such as critical accounting scholarship. As one Islamic accounting scholar writes, citing a classic article in that scholarship, "Islam accepts the fact that accounting is a social construction[32] and itself constructs social reality but this social reality which the accounting constructs must conform to the dictates of Islamic belief."[33] Rifaat Ahmed Abdel Karim, one of the figures responsible for the creation of the AAOIFI, was a former student of the accounting theorist Trevor Gambling. The two coauthored the book *Business and Accounting Ethics in Islam*, a work deeply influenced by social accounting theories.[34]

What interests me is the convergence between the creation of AAOIFI international accountancy standards, the internal debate on Islamic accountancy, and ethnography. Like ethnographers (and like the early 20th century compilers of the U.S. Uniform Commercial Code, one of whom was an ethnographer), the members of the AAOIFI have observed, recorded, and compiled the "best practices" of Islamic accounting worldwide and abstracted from them a written set of proscriptive rules for Shari'a-compliant accountancy. Like ethnography, this process includes the debates about the process itself, embodied in the comments of Islamic accountants who echo critical accountants – or, rather, share the same field of discourse and citational authorities, and the same techniques for generating knowledge. Knowledge is produced through shifts in scale, levels of abstraction from a reality. In internal debates over Islamic accounting, as in critical accounting, there is a further instrumentalization of the knowledge thereby produced. As a construction, social reality is cast as a particular kind of resource, something that can be used for specific purposes, or struggled over like a terrain. At the same time it is something that can create or instantiate other things in people and social spaces: it is a construction that can make more constructions. It creates "values" and "behaviors," as well as, recursively, itself, a part of "social reality," even as it is the product, constructed out of, values, behaviors, and social realities. It has parts, which are related to other parts – either explicitly, by the actors in social worlds themselves, or implicitly, only to be drawn out by social analysts determining the distinctions between domains, between form and content, text and context, subjective from objective.

That the techniques of knowledge in Islamic accounting, critical accounting, and anthropology are homologous to one another should lead us to explore their metapragmatics in the debates and practices that call accounting forth as a topic of concern for differently positioned social persons. This means engaging in a sort of "triangulation" and studying the simultaneous entextualization and contextualization processes that produce social realities (and produce them as something both constructed and productive): here, Islamic accounting practice, Islamic accounting standards, critical accounting scholarship, and debates over the status of constructivism in Islamic accounting and social science.[35] These techniques of knowledge involve transformations in the scale of phenomena. They involve nested hierarchies of practice, as in the credit cooperative example, and both the erasure of those hierarchies, as in international Islamic accountancy standards and Bank Muamalat Indonesia practice, and the making explicit of those hierarchies, as in the internal debate over Islamic accounting. In that debate, recall, knowledge techniques make up the flows of divine knowledge into an always-already present unity that, paradoxically, is founded in its own unfolding incompleteness.

Toward Anthropological *Tawhid*

The fact that AAOIFI standards ended up mirroring conventional international accountancy standards does not mean that Shari'a compliance is simply standard practice with Islamic window-dressing. AAOIFI standards do not produce information that serves the rhetorical function of marking organizational practice as Islamic. Rather, AAIOFI standards and organizational practice exist in a coordinated relationship, and that relationship produces a nervous grammar that makes the distinction between rhetorical and technical, and Shari'a-compliant and conventional or non-Islamic, intelligible and real, albeit unstable. Is there a difference between Islamic accounting and conventional accounting? The answer depends on the analytic status of the unmarked (and implicit) terms in each: the (nonreligious) modern bureaucratic practices of standardization, and the (nonreligious) status of conventional accounting.

The Shari'a, after all, is not a book of rules but a system of rule-making, a meta-grammar for securing the conditions for the practice of Islamic virtues in a morally organized universe. Following those rules calls forth Shari'a compliance, even if the product looks exactly like conventional international accountancy standards, because the performative event here is the coordination of the AAOIFI standards with the accounting practices.

The AAOIFI standards do not so much replace religious authority as reveal the rhetoricality of conventional accounting practice. They do so through their own failure, a failure noticed by *tawhid*-oriented participants in the debate over Islamic accounting, just as critical accounting scholars note the failures of conventional accounting. The failure of the former, to the extent that it is a failure of Islam, is of cosmological significance. That failure does not derive from the act of trying to create standards, or from the bureaucratic standardization of Islamic principles. From the Islamic accounting standpoint – as for the critical accountants – bureaucratic standardization is a social and cultural process, embedded with and productive of social and cultural values. The task, as the Islamic accountant quoted earlier put it, is to construct an accounting knowledge that will create *different* values. So, the failure can be reversed, or changed, and the culture thus constructed anew.

At the same time, however, Islamic accounting makes explicit that which is only implicit in conventional accounting. The fractal form of *mudarabah* accounts and the fractal form of *tawhid* are of a unity with the techniques of knowledge of anthropology, conventional accounting, and critical accounting. Recently, scholars concerned with the status of accounting as a form of knowledge production have moved away from the critical accounting position that accounting possesses rhetorical functions. They instead put forward the idea that accounting is itself a form of rhetoric for making empirical facts, and the reality-effect that such facts precede their representation.[36] As a form of rhetoric, accounting renders itself a transparent practice of recording the empirical as already-there in the world. In the process, it denies own its status as a modality of argumentation constituted by various levels of scale: a set of techniques for making things; a set of rules for making things tell-able (in Garfinkel's sense); a toolkit for constructing those rules; and the metapragmatic *ad hoc* and *post hoc* relating of those rules to each other and to actual practices. Poovey is on the mark when she argues that the very separation of (mathematical) technique from (linguistic) rhetoric was itself an effect of the invention of double-entry accounting. And those who hold out *tawhid* as the unity of flows of incomplete knowledge are on the mark, too, in revealing the oneness of apparent levels of the cosmos, or, here, levels of analysis that make up a modality of social and moral argument.

Marilyn Strathern has observed that ethnographic research and anthropological comparison have traditionally proceeded through transformations of scale: the singular fieldworker apprehended "culture" by talking to multiple informants and abstracting general principles.[37] What emerged for the singular fieldworker was not just the particularity of each individual encounter or informant, but "more"; this more was generalized as the culture of a people.[38] The problem of perspective arose when the field of the ethnographer's vision came into question: it was necessarily limited, only one perspective on the flow of social life. With certain ethnographic subjects, Hagen flutes as well as accountancy, the problem gets compounded, as the anthropologist's "contexts and levels of analysis are themselves often at once both part and yet not part of the phenomena s/he hopes to organize with them. Because of the cross-cutting nature of the perspectives they set, one can always be swallowed by another."[39] In such cases the ethnographic object and ethnographic practice seem out of scale, and the logic of proportionality undergirding anthropological analytics seems to fall off-kilter,[40] or at least to be made explicit as an "organizational facility of Western pluralist cultural life."[41] Once it is made explicit, however, it can be put to use. Strathern argued that the fractal form could provide a way out of the sameness/difference and singular/plural frameworks of anthropology and create "maps without centers and genealogies without generations."[42] The distinction between data and theory collapses, or resolves itself into a self-same pattern at another level of abstraction.

The significance of Islamic accounting, then, is not its religious basis or veneer, the culture behind it, or the values it generates in turn. Instead, its significance is that in striving for Shari'a compliance, Islamic accounting throws itself into the open-ended metapragmatics that demonstrate the fractal form of accounting and its allied modes of social inquiry such as anthropology. Islamic accounting demonstrates that empirical facts are moral acts. The challenge for accounting, as for its anthropological accounts, is to be as open-ended and incomplete-yet-whole as *tawhid*, to dissolve its self-understanding as a reflection of reality, but not its appreciation as a very special kind of moral tool: to focus more on the implementation, perhaps, than the empirical.[43]

Notes

1 Pakistan Supreme Court, Civil Shariat Review Petition No. 1 of 2001; hereafter, C.SH.R.P. 1/2001.

2 Paul Rabinow, "Midst Anthropology's Problems," *Cultural Anthropology* 17(2), 2002, pp. 135–149, esp. p. 136; see also Paul Rabinow, "Midst Anthropology's Problems," Chapter 3, this volume.

3 C.SH.R.P. 1/2001, para 18.

4 "U.S. Treasury Hosts Islamic Finance Seminar," *Islamic Horizons* July/August 2002, p. 18.

5 "Islamic home financing starting in the nation's capital," *The Minaret* July/August 2002, pp. 19–20.

6 Karl N. Llewellyn, *The Bramble Bush: On Law and its Study* (New York: Oceana Press, 1951).

7 H. Garfinkel, *Studies in Ethnomethodology* (Englewood Cliffs, NJ: Prentice Hall, 1967), p. 33; original emphasis.

8 For example, A. Hopwood and P. Miller, eds., *Accounting as Social and Institutional Practice* (Cambridge: Cambridge University Press, 1994).

9 Trevor Gambling, *Societal Accounting* (London: George Allen and Unwin, 1974), p. 107.

10 Trevor Gambling, *Beyond the Conventions of Accounting* (London: Macmillan, 1978), pp. 2–3; original emphasis.

11 A. Riles, *The Network Inside-Out* (Ann Arbor: University of Michigan Press, 2000).

12 Marilyn Strathern, *Partial Connections*, ASAO Special Publications No. 3 (Lanham, MD: Rowman and Littlefield, 1991).

13 N. Dudley, "Islamic banks aim for the mainstream," *Euromoney* 349, May 1998, pp. 113–116.

14 Ernest Patrikis, "Islamic Finance in the United States: The Regulatory Framework," remarks by Patrikis, First Vice-President, Federal Reserve Bank of New York given to the Islamic Finance and Investment Conference, New York, May 23, 1996, p. 1.

15 Patrikis, "Islamic Finance," p. 4.

16 T. Gambling, R. Jones, and R. A. A. Karim, "Credible Organizations: Self-regulation v. External Standard-setting in Islamic Banks and British Charities," *Financial Accountability and Management* 9, 1993, pp. 195–207; F. Pomeranz, "The Accounting and Auditing Organization for Islamic Financial Institutions: An Important Regulatory Debut," *Journal of International Accounting, Auditing and Taxation* 6, 1997, pp. 123–130.

17 See B. Carruthers, "Accounting, Ambiguity, and the New Institutionalism," *Accounting, Organisations and Society* 20, 1995, pp. 313–328.

18 M. K. Lewis, "Islam and Accounting," *Accounting Forum* 25, 2001, p. 112.

19 For example, M. U. Chapra, *Towards a Just Monetary System* (Leicester: The Islamic Foundation, 1992); M. A. Choudhury, *Money in Islam: A Study in Islamic Political Economy* (London: Routledge, 1997).

20 After J. Pemberton, *On the Subject of "Java"* (Ithaca, NY: Cornell University Press, 1994), p. 9.

21 Carruthers, "Accounting."

22 M. Poovey, *A History of the Modern Fact* (Chicago: University of Chicago Press, 1998).

23 See F. Vogel and S.L. Hayes, *Islamic Law and Finance: Religion, Risk, and Return* (The Hague: Kluwer Law International, 1998).

24 T. Gambling and R. A. A. Karim, *Business and Accounting Ethics in Islam* (London: Mansell, 1991), p. 103.

25 M. Silverstein and G. Urban, "The Natural History of Discourse," in *Natural Histories of Discourse*, M. Silverstein and G. Urban, eds. (Chicago: University of Chicago Press, 1996), pp. 1–17.

26 A. Berle and G. Means, *The Modern Corporation and Private Property* (New York: Macmillan, 1932); B. Maurer, "Forget Locke? From Proprietor to Risk-bearer in New Logics of Finance," *Public Culture* 11, 1999, pp. 365–385.

27 See T. Mitchell, "Fixing the Economy," *Cultural Studies* 12, 1998, pp. 82–101.

28 Gambling and Karim, *Business and Accounting*; S. Ibrahim, *Review of Income and Value Measurement Concepts in Conventional Accounting Theory and their Relevance to Islamic Accounting*, Department of Accounting and Business Finance, University of Dundee, 1999; also at http://www.islamic-finance.net/islamic-accounting/acctg3.html (September 29, 2000).

29 R. Eglash, *African Fractals* (New Brunswick: Rutgers University Press, 1999), p. 18.

30 *Accounting and Auditing Standards for Islamic Banks* (Manama, Bahrain: AAOIFI, 2000), p. A4/1; also at http://www.islamic-finance.net/accounting (September 29, 2000).

31 J. M. Echols and H. Shadily, *Kamus Indonesia Inggris*, 3rd edition (Jakarta: Penerbit PT Gramedia, 1997), p. 540.

32 R. Hines, "Financial Accounting: In Communicating Reality, We Construct Reality," *Accounting, Organisations and Society* 13, 1988, pp. 251–261.

33 Ibrahim, *Review of Income*, p. 17.

34 Gambling and Karim, *Business and Accounting*.

35 See Silverstein and Urban, "The Natural History of Discourse," pp. 4–5.

36 Poovey, *A History of the Modern Fact*.

37 Strathern, *Partial Connections*.

38 Ibid., p. 9.

39 Ibid., p. 75.

40 Idem.

41 Ibid., p. xx.

42 Idem.

43 For further reading on the issues addressed in this chapter, see B. Carruthers and W. Espeland, "Accounting for Rationality: Double-entry Bookkeeping and the Rhetoric of Economic Rationality," *American Journal of Sociology* 97, 1991, pp. 31–69; T. Kuran, "The Genesis of Islamic Economics: a Chapter in the Politics of Muslim Identity," *Social Research* 64, 1997, pp. 301–337; M. Maududi, *The Economic Problem of Man and its Islamic Solution* (Lahore: Islamic Publications, 1975); B. Maurer, "Engineering an Islamic Future: Speculations on Islamic Financial Alternatives," *Anthropology Today* 17, 2001, pp. 8–11; R. Munro and J. Mouritsen, eds., *Accountability: Power, Ethos and the Technologies of Managing* (London: International Thomson Business Press, 1996); A. I. Qureshi, *Islam and the Theory of Interest* (Lahore: Shaikh Muhammad Ashraf, 1946); M. D. Rahardjo, "The Question of Islamic Banking in Indonesia," in *Islamic Banking in Southeast Asia*, M. Ariff, ed. (Singapore: Institute of Southeast Asian Studies, 1988), pp. 137–163; M. Strathern, ed., *Audit Cultures: Anthropological Studies in Accountability, Ethics and the Academy* (London: Routledge, 2000); and A. M. Tinker, *Paper Prophets: A Social Critique of Accounting* (New York: Praeger, 1985).

PRACTICES OF
CALCULATING SELVES

13

CULTURES OF EXPERTISE AND THE MANAGEMENT OF GLOBALIZATION:
Toward the Re-Functioning of Ethnography

DOUGLAS R. HOLMES AND GEORGE E. MARCUS

It is very striking that the classic technique devised in response to the impossibility of understanding contemporary society from experience, the statistical mode of analysis, had its precise origins within the period of which you are speaking. For without the combination of statistical theory . . . and arrangements for the collection of statistical data . . . the society that was emerging out of the industrial revolution was literally unknowable. I tried to develop this contrast in The Country and the City between the knowable community, a term used with irony because what is known is shown to be incomplete, and the new sense of the darkly unknowable . . . New forms had to be devised to penetrate what was rightly perceived to be to a large extent obscure . . . From the industrial revolution onwards, qualitatively altering a permanent problem, there has developed a type of society which is less interpretable from experience—meaning by experience a lived contact with the available articulations, including their comparison. The result is that we have become increasingly conscious of the positive power of techniques of analysis, which at their maximum are capable of interpreting, let us say, the movements of an integrated world economy, and of the negative qualities of a naïve observation which can never gain knowledge of realities like these . . . Experience becomes a forbidden word, whereas what we ought to say about it is that it is a limited word, for there are many kinds of knowledge it will never give us, in any of its ordinary senses.

Raymond Williams[1]

In this quotation from a classic book of interviews with Raymond Williams lies the reason why it might be difficult for cultural and social anthropologists to extend their mode of basic research to the worlds of financial experts, bankers, and bureaucrats, Yet, if they are to engage in an anthropology of the contemporary, and now of a globalizing world, they must do so, as they have already been doing impressively in science and technology studies, by making other kinds of experts their subjects rather than being able to largely exclude them from the domain of their own research practices by classifying them as colleagues, or "like colleagues." In our experience, ethnographers trained in the tradition of anthropology do not approach the study of formal institutions such as banks, bureaucracies, corporations, and state agencies with much confidence. These are realms in which the traditional informants of ethnography must be rethought as counterparts rather than "others" – as both subjects and intellectual partners in inquiry. These are technocratic milieus in which, as suggested by Williams, that which is valued most by ethnographers – "understanding contemporary society from experience" – is most devalued within them.

Would one have gone into anthropology if one wanted to study such people or places? The anthropologist does not study the lives of central bankers, for instance, because they have the same kind of interest that the everyday lives of the Tikopia, the Tongans, or the Nuer have had for anthropologists. Indeed, rarely do ethnographers have access to the details of the everyday lives of expert subjects. Working through the complex techniques of experts in various ways tied to the flow of money – "the statistical mode of analysis in context" – is of course one potentially valuable option in undertaking an ethnography of such experts. But we seek to connect this sort of inquiry to more conventionally social and cultural factors that underpinned traditional ethnography. In short, what is the anthropological interest in studies of domains of expertise dominated by particular forms of the statistical mode of knowledge production? And how do we reclaim "experience" as an analytic bridge to these distinctive domains?

In the following schematic consideration of central bankers, we want to take on some of these questions, especially the latter ones. We believe that certain ingrained assumptions in constituting the field of ethnographic research, especially when it comes to experts, have to be rethought. Is the point of doing fieldwork among experts to do a conventional ethnography of them? We believe it is highly unlikely that a robust ethnography of "everyday life" can be done within these cultures of expertise, where the public and private spheres are strictly demarked. If we study not only the practice of statistical modes of knowledge-making, then what other kinds of "native points of view" remain to study in the domain of experts? Here we suggest a particular strategy for *re-functioning ethnography* around a research relation in which the ethnographer identifies a para-ethnographic dimension in such domains of expertise – the *de facto* and self-conscious critical faculty that operates in any expert domain as a way of dealing with contradiction, exception, facts that are fugitive, and that suggest a social realm not in alignment with the representations generated by the application of the reigning statistical mode of analysis. Making ethnography from the found para-ethnographic redefines the status of the subject or informant, asks what different accounts one wants from such key figures in the fieldwork process, and indeed questions what the ethnography of experts means within a broad, multi-sited design of research. Crucial to this re-functioning is the status of the construct of the para-ethnographic as a kind of illicit, marginal social thought – in genres such as "the anecdotal," "hype," and "intuition" – within practices dominated by the technocratic ethos, which in the era of integrated global markets simply does not serve to discipline this thought of experts perhaps as efficiently as it once did.

Central Banks

From preliminary investigation, we have chosen to pursue an illustration of the form that the para-ethnographic takes in the work of the personnel of central banks. The para-ethnographic here provides, as we will argue below, a somewhat subversive, yet controlled, access to fugitive social facts in a key contemporary system of techno-cratic expertise, which conceives and produces the idea of the global as daily practice. Central banks operate not merely under the sway of fast-capitalism; they have played a direct role in creating and mediating it. The lever that a central bank wields, as an agency regulating financial markets, is both strategic and simple: by determining interest rates by which money can be borrowed, it can influence decisively the tempo of activity in an entire economy. But to wield this lever requires the constant monitoring of massively complex representations of the entire economy and its articulations within a world system of markets. It is of course elaborate technologies of quantification that ensure that dominant theories and perceptions of this constantly monitored representation of the economy are perpetuated.

To the extent that central banks lose a complacent and bland confidence in their technocratic performance, although that is still very much the face and professional ideology that they continue to present, they begin to share governing functions that can only be understood as "political." Once there are sustained puzzles or displace-ments in the models that track and represent the behavior of an entire economy, the opportunity emerges for the influence of ways of knowing that are normally re-pressed, subordinated, and considered slightly illicit – the ways of knowing relegated in such technocratic organizations to the realm of the anecdotal, of hype, of intuition, of experience. Just as the decision-makers in central banks become more powerful in the public sphere as symbolic and political actors – as broader governing agents – so do para-ethnographic insights on the margins compete with what "the numbers" indicate.

In the recent (now past) period of unexpectedly sustained prosperity in the United States, the central bank became very visibly recognized in an unprecedented manner as the governor of the nation's welfare, especially in the awareness of the power of global financial flows. While, in retrospect, this recasting of the central bank's role might be seen as an anomaly of an aberrant period of "irrational exuberance," it still accented deeply embedded balances in modalities of knowledge and power practice of such banks that are bound to be further affected by the course of growing understandings of the globalizing contexts in which national economies operate.

Pivotal to the monumental changes that have attended contemporary agendas of neoliberalism has been the relinquishing of the control exercised by parliaments and legislatures over broad domains of society and economy, and the transfer of that authority ostensibly to "the market." These strategic powers, seemingly relinquished by politicians and government regulators and conferred on "the market" are, in fact, recaptured in part by a small coterie of officials working within central banks. Moreover, the instruments used conventionally by central banks to regulate monetary policy by influencing money market conditions and growth of money and credit have assumed far wider influence and authority over broad domains of a globalized economy in which "money" serves as the basis for austere forms of "social" integration.[2]

Elsewhere, we have referred to the cultural formation created by this wide-ranging program of neoliberal reform as fast-capitalism. We have argued that the most distinctive feature of fast-capitalism is its propensity to subvert the science, political economy, and metaphysics of solidarity upon which modernist conceptions of society rest. Indeed, the abiding irony is that the personnel working within central banks must overcome precisely the subversions of the social that they have had a direct hand in creating through their promotion of neoliberal reform. In other words, they must reconstruct a meaningful engagement with society in order to pursue their own knowledge work and expert practice. Para-ethnography is the means by which they recast a semiotics of the social in the face of the corrosive influence of fast-capitalism.

In "The Beige Book" section below, we will be looking at personnel in the research divisions of the Federal Reserve (the "Fed,") whose expertise is centered on continuous representations of the intricate dynamics of a technologically advanced and fully globalized world economy. Through the analysis of vast amounts of quantitative data drawn from governmental and nongovernmental agencies, these expert subjects generate narratives of the changing nature of key aspect of the economic life within and beyond the borders of the U.S.A. The role of the research division is not merely to glean and summarize these data, but to actively engage and refine these measures and critically scrutinize their relevance for policy formulation. By any measure, so to speak, the Fed is one of the most formidable cultures of expertise organized for the production and analysis of quantitative economic data. Yet, when the Fed seeks to enter the contemporary, to assess economic activity in something that approximates real time, its personnel employ a strikingly different set of practices. These practices are illustrative of key aspects of what we mean by para-ethnography.

The Anecdotal amid other Genres of the Para-Ethnographic: A Glimpse at Alan Greenspan's Practice of the Para-Ethnographic

Anecdote: "Secret, private, or hitherto unpublished narratives or details of history." "The narrative of a detached incident, or of a single event, told as being in itself interesting or striking."

Oxford English Dictionary[3]

In an earlier paper, we argued that Alan Greenspan was a para-ethnographer extra-ordinaire, who established his particular persona and reputation at the Fed by frequently countering the methods and modalities of econometrics in relying on the kind of information that those who represent the movements of the economic leviathan through measurement would dismissively characterize as "anecdotal."[4] The following collection of fragments from Bob Woodward's book on Greenspan supply interesting details for our argument, revealing how the para-ethnographic engages the "darkly unknowable":

Over the next months, when Greenspan analyzed data, he saw that the future orders were down in a wide range of businesses. That meant demand for goods was falling and economic growth was slowing. Greenspan tapped into his network of business contacts in New York. One was E. F. "Andy" Andrews, who has written the monthly National Association of Purchasing Management Business survey for 19 years. Greenspan knew Andrews from back in the 1970s, when Andrews had made the survey available to Greenspan, who was then a private citizen, a day in advance . . . Another of his regular contacts was Robert P. Parker, 49, the associate director for national income, expend-iture and wealth accounts at the Bureau of Economic Analysis in the Department of Commerce. He had known Parker for 18 years . . . Greenspan also phoned Jack Welch, the CEO of General Electric. GE had its tentacles just about everywhere, Greenspan found . . . Sounding out his long list of contacts took a great deal of time, and Greenspan eventually set up a system in which Fed staff members would formally call a long list of companies each week to get their real-time numbers. Only a small fraction of Green-span's information came to him orally, though he listened to the BBC. Reading was more efficient, and he kept up with the newspapers and specialty magazines such as *Aviation Week*. He tried not to over-schedule himself, making only three or four appointments or meetings a day. The rest was for study and reading.[5]

Greenspan went to lunches at the Business Council, an organization of business leaders, and listened to the CEOs of America's largest corporations. As soon as they saw he wasn't going to disclose much or press his own conclusions on them but instead wanted to listen, they poured out their anxieties or latest good news. Greenspan insisted that he nearly always learned more from the people who came to hear him speak than they learned from him.[6]

This pain in the stomach was a physical awareness Greenspan had experienced many times. He felt he had a deeper understanding of the issue—a whole body of knowledge in his head and a whole value system—than he was capable of stating at that moment. If he was about to say something that wasn't right, he would feel it before he was intellectually aware of the problem. It was this physical feeling, this sense in the stomach, that he believed kept him from making dangerous or absurd statements that might appear on the front page of the newspapers.[7]

Greenspan realized that his arguments amounted to little more than back-of-the-envelope calculations to the PhD's on the FOMC [Federal Open Market Committee] and the staff. Only vast models and years of statistics would convince them—a kind of care he appreciated, on the one hand. On the other hand, he was pretty certain he was right... Why was there no burst of inflation? The old belief held that with such a low unemployment rate, workers would have the upper hand and demand higher wages. Yet the data showed that wages weren't rising that much. It was one of the central economic mysteries of our time. Greenspan hypothesized at one point about the "traumatized worker"—someone who felt job insecurity in the changing economy and so was accepting smaller wage increases. He had talked with business leaders who said their workers were not agitating and were fearful that their skills might not be marketable if they were forced to change jobs. Janet Yellen was sympathetic to Greenspan's hypothesis and she was deeply bothered that the Fed staff seemed too set in their ways to engage alternative views of how the economy was functioning. Each staff forecast before the FOMC meetings insisted that inflation was about to take off unless interest rates increased substantially. Greenspan appeared to be going it alone... Yellen thought Greenspan spoke a language different from what was taught in graduate school. Outsiders and noneconomists thought his Fedspeak was the language of economics, but the chairman's language was highly idiosyncratic, often not fully grounded in the data. He was prone to take leaps. At the FOMC, Yellen noticed that the PhD's on the committee, or some of the members of the staff, would be nearly rolling their eyes as the chairman voiced his views about how the economy might be changing. Nobody challenged him or dared say anything, but it weakened his hold on the committee. Yellen told Greenspan that she might be able to find a theoretical underpinning for his job insecurity thesis... Working with data, graphs and some 14 complex equations, she drafted a 13-page memo that she sent Greenspan on June 10, 1996. It concluded that since workers had been paid more in the earlier years of the 1990s, the higher pay had induced them to feel greater attachment to their jobs and to be more productive... The memo was an economically conventional way of saying what he wanted to say. He had it circulated to the FOMC.[8]

It is the so-called fugitive social facts in the continuously changing contemporary that give rise to the sorts of knowledge-making among experts that can be identified as para-ethnographic by the ethnographer. Woodward, among others, doesn't quite know what to make of Greenspan's counterdiscourse which defines so much his special qualities as a leader – as someone shaped in sensibility and habitus by the routines of economic discipline, partial to its formalities, yet distinctively in rebellion to its conventional wisdom and guidance.

Para-Ethnography as Method

The generative potential for anthropology of the idea of the para-ethnographic is what concerns us in this initial formulation of the concept. We frame the para-ethnographic from the standpoint of the way it produces a series of distinctive substantive, methodological, and theoretical questions as a means to enter fields of expertise.

How do we make ethnography of the para-ethnographic found in the marginal ways of knowing – centrally the anecdotal – within technocratic regimes? When deployed counterculturally and critically, by the most privileged within these regimes such as chairman Greenspan, these genres suggest where ethnography might literally go in fieldwork. How to move within the space or vision of the referents of the para-ethnographic? And what is the implication for these regimes of the return of this ethnography derived from the subversive para-ethnographic by some strategy of overture, writing, and presentation back to the project's orienting milieus. These are the issues that would make multi-sited projects of varying thickness and thinness out of the orienting ethnography of the balance of modes of representation that chairman Greenspan and his administration of the Fed have put in place.

It is regrettable that, in the absence of bridges or alliances between his interest and other kinds of scholarship, Greenspan was left to "go it alone" in his development of an anecdotal critique of the dominant econometric mode of representing the economy. In the above example of Greenspan's positing "the traumatized worker," he only had his colleague Yellen, on one side, to make his concept acceptable to the paradigms of economic thought. On the other side – the side that would have supported the sociology or ethnography in Greenspan's para-ethnographic insight – there is already a large amount of research – much of it ethnographic and qualitative – about the current state of workers in their own domestic and everyday contexts. It could greatly enhance the intuition or insight of Greenspan based on anecdotal evidence in his own milieu. Yet, this knowledge simply does not count in Greenspan's world, and there is no bridging contact to make it count; it is as if this relevant research exists in another world. It is certainly an urgent task, then, of ethnographies that enter into cultures of expertise through the finding of para-ethnographic linkages that create intellectual bridges with such *de facto* critical genres "inside." This would not be the unmodified presentation or importation of supporting genres from anthropology, sociology, or cultural studies into the spontaneous para-ethnographic genres within the realm of expertise – this simply would not work – but some sort of mutual modification of the formal character of ethnography to meet the passionate nature of countercultural experience. In essence, how to relate what the ethnographer knows to the visceral mediation of the para-ethnographic by Greenspan – in short, how to relate relevant ethnography from something he experiences as much as a "pain in the stomach" to formally thought out concepts? This requires a very different presentation of ethnography than one makes to professional peers.

Of course, the engagement of ethnography with the para-ethnographic in central banking is not likely to be with the chairman himself, but collectively with the sorts of projects he puts in play to prove his insights. Here, the above example is illustrative of Greenspan's attempt to prove the structural changes in the levels of productivity in the economy that the standard models were missing. The research that Greenspan orders is an interesting roundabout means from within the world of economics to find more systematic evidence for what arises at first anecdotally. It is trying to do the sociology or the anthropology without the aid of either one. Efforts to explore these issues through techniques at hand are precisely what the ethnographer looks for in order to grasp the fugitive social.

Finally, there is the question of to what degree Greenspan operates within a global or globalizing vision of his work as chairman of the Fed.[9] Is he still very much an operative of the nation-state, or has he become one of the "symbolic analysts" that Robert Reich described in *The Work of Nations* more than a decade ago, when he argued that there had emerged a class of elite technocrats and politicians who, while appointed or elected within nation-states, now had an international if not global outlook in a qualitatively different way than before. These actors stand in contrast to much of their publics, who still vestigially – as false consciousness, so to speak – see their affairs in terms of states and nations to which they belong. While Robert Rubin and Larry Summers might be candidates for Reich's conception of the symbolic analyst, it is clear that Greenspan is firmly still oriented to thinking of his functions in terms of the U.S. economy and society. His countercultural, critical production of the para-ethnographic is conceived in the frame of U.S. culture, society, and conditions. The ethnography that would support Greenspan's development of the anecdotal in his own sphere would be that devoted to American culture and society. Yet, Greenspan clearly understands globalizing forces as accounting for the changes that are not registered in the reigning econometric models of the Fed, thus creating the opportunity for countercritique through para-ethnographic conjecture. But this understanding exists through indirection or as a trace in his thought.

So how would we design a study located among U.S. central bankers that would bring out and highlight the repressed, traced nature of globalization in their found para-ethnographic musings? This would involve a different strategy for multi-sited research. Rather than supplement the insights of a Greenspan with basic ethnographic findings in U.S. society, the challenge would be to juxtapose these fully exposed treatments against what such insights repress or only refer to indirectly. Thus, the relations that define the "traumatized worker" – or, even more importantly, the different ways increased productivity is registered in the U.S. economy – are globalizing factors involving new technologies and the markets that define them. For the purposes of his own discourse and politics, this kind of juxtaposition is not something that Greenspan would do himself, but it might be an interest of a complementary critical ethnographic project that is multi-sited in its purview. To make visible or elaborate on certain relations that are ignored or not seen among central bank actors themselves – either inadvertently or quite intentionally – is the provocation that might offer the orienting framework through which to enter these globalizing domains. Postulating and finding the situated equivalent of ethnography in the para-ethnographic can provide access to an emergent social that gains articulation first as a moral framework, and then as an analytic construct, and empirical fact.

In the following section, we turn to an illustrative example of how the para-ethnographic operates as an overt form of knowledge production within the research division of a district branch of the Fed.

The Beige Book

Its formal title is *Summary of Commentary on Current Economic Conditions by Federal Reserve District*, and it is a spiral-bound report that runs to about 40 double-spaced pages, with a beige cover (hence the name). The report is published eight times a year, about a week prior to the regularly scheduled FOMC meetings. The FOMC is composed of the seven members of the Board of Governors of the Federal Reserve System and five of the twelve presidents of the Federal Reserve district banks. The president of the New York Reserve Bank is a permanent member and the other reserve bank presidents serve one-year terms on a rotating basis. The Committee is charged under law "to oversee open market operations, the principal tool of national monetary policy."[10]

This legal authority over the management of monetary policy, exercised primarily through the setting of interest rates, makes the Committee one of the most – if not the most – powerful single institutions governing financial markets. The Beige Book is the Committee's briefing document and a means by which its members assess the current state of the economy. Thus, this innocuous-looking document, which could easily pass for an undergraduate term paper, is one of the most influential and carefully scrutinized reports on the overall U.S. economy and its implications for global markets. We turn now to the distinctive knowledge practices of those expert subjects who draft this document.

The material that follows is drawn from a conversation (by Holmes) with Richard Peach, Vice-President of Research at the New York Fed, and Jason Bram, the analyst who does the research and has written the Beige Book entry for the New York District of the Federal Reserve for the past five years or so. The discussion took place in December 2001 at the branch headquarters located in lower Manhattan, about two blocks from the site of the World Trade Center.

Mr. Bram solicits accounts from a network of strategically positioned informants. He seeks an acute anecdotal portrayal of the economy under the administrative purview of the New York District. Significantly, there is no formal protocol specified by the Fed for how this analysis should be undertaken. Rather, the research divisions of each of the 12 district banks pursue this work independently – and, in fact, competitively – to provide a descriptive tableau of the U.S. economy. Mr. Bram, working with a small staff, begins calling his contacts about a week before the report is due and drafts the actual document at the last possible moment to make it as contemporaneous as possible.

What are these "anecdotal reports"? Rather than informal observations and casual asides, as the term "anecdotal" might suggest, these reports constitute a sophisticated means of tracking and interpreting the economy. Mr. Bram cultivates highly developed "contacts" with human interlocutors who oversee daily transactions within strategic spheres of the economy. These interlocutors are not employees of the Fed, but informants – bankers, manufacturers, real estate brokers, and retailers – who transact loans, book orders (and cancellations), and track store sales minute-to-minute, hour-to-hour. These interlocutors operate in real time, providing the closest approximation to a contemporaneous engagement with the economy.

These men and women, typically senior and mid-level managers, have access not merely to an extraordinary range of quantitative data, but they are constantly in conversations with clients, customers, and colleagues: this can include auto executives walking showroom floors talking to potential car purchasers; bank executives conversing with prospective borrowers about the state of their businesses and their outlooks for the future; and manufacturers discussing with their customers their future needs in order to plan capital expenditures. By gleaning knowledge from these interlocutors, Mr. Bram gains access to those profound and elusive cultural forces guiding the economy: expectations and sentiments.

This para-ethnographic labor reveals an unusual problem whereby "expressed preferences" – in other words, the actual buying or lending or borrowing decisions that have already taken place – do not capture expectations and sentiments in the near future, and that the thing to be understood, therefore, is not just "what is going on" but some phenomenon at the very core of the capitalist system that can only be expressed as a recent past, but not as a likely near future. This space of the para-ethnographic, in this sense, is not simply an exception but seems to be a structural feature of economies of the market type, that can be gleaned as a structure of feeling expressed anecdotally.

It is not merely that these reports amassed by Mr. Bram provide a means to overcome the inevitable "lag" attendant with quantitative data; rather, it is their inherently social nature that provides these "anecdotal reports" with an agile purchase on the contemporary. And these reports would have little force if it were not for the fact that these informants speak from an intimate, subjective sense of the situated business practices and predicaments that they track anecdotally from day to day. These anecdotes are not just a different kind of supplementary data; rather, they have a distinctive cogency in their own right, legitimized through a socially mediated "native point of view." Thus, what makes these reports persuasive is the experience of the interlocutors, their judgment, their feel. These intricate exchanges that report on the economy in something that approximates "real time" constitute an acute illustration of para-ethnography and its analytic purchase.

Mr. Bram's para-ethnography yields the following kind of textual account of the state of the New York economy in the aftermath of September 11. This short excerpt is from the October 24, 2001, Beige Book and is in many respects unusual. The prior Beige Book entry for the New York District had been completed on September 10. For the two weeks after the attack, the offices were closed and the research staff almost immediately began working from their homes, calling their networks of contacts to assess the impact on the economy. An internal document – compiled using essentially the same method as the Beige Book though with a larger staff – was generated that served as a starting point for assessing the disaster. In redrafted form, it became the basis of the October 24 Beige Book entries.

In Mr. Bram's restrained prose, elements of the disaster are tightly summarized. Unfortunately, what gives this account its power and its legitimacy – its rich engagement with remarkably situated human interlocutors – is edited out from the report, as the following short excerpt shows:

> Home sales in and around New York City have slowed drastically since the last report, and both apartment prices and rents have fallen by an estimated 10 percent. In general, contacts note that the high end of the market has been the most affected. Contrary to initial post-attack expectations, Manhattan's office market has not tightened—availability rates at the end of September were slightly higher than a month earlier. Hotels, taxi drivers, and Broadway theaters experienced a steep falloff in business in mid-September, but activity has reportedly recovered somewhat in the weeks since. Finally, bankers again report weaker loan demand, tighter credit standards, and moderately higher delinquency rates in the latest survey, taken in early October.[11]

Mr. Bram described his autodidactic method in terms that are familiar to an anthropologist. "It's sort of an art, you have to know the people you are talking to." "I can't put it into a formula, it is very opportunistic." "It is very wide open." "As you do it, I have been doing it for four or five years, you learn. When you start out you ask [a retailer] about sales and inventories. But then [I learned] you have to know how retailers think [to interpret these numbers] . . . It's a very subjective kind of thing, you have to learn what kinds of questions to ask." "You try to find common threads." Though Mr. Bram's method lacks a formal disciplinary identity, it yields a refined analytic engagement with staggeringly complex economic activity and human behavior.

What is compelling about this approach to cultures of expertise is that it immediately provides a basis of exchange with expert subjects. By marking out the para-ethnographic character of their expert practices, an intricate basis of discussion is opened between the anthropologist and subject. The anthropologist's presence in these domains is thereby legitimized and the basis of meaningful exchange is created. A critical seam is opened up – through a shared ethnographic enterprise – that allows the anthropologist entry into these intriguing cultural domains.

Mr. Bram's research expertise converges with our conceptualization of para-ethnography. His knowledge practices, however, also expose a deeper dimension of the workings of the native point of view and its engagement with the contemporary. His informants, his interlocutors, and his contacts are themselves engaged in a direct para-ethnography that is so deeply embedded in their consciousness and aligned to their practices as to be virtually invisible. Once these knowledge practices are opened to scrutiny, they reveal how the contemporary is socially reproduced through the cumulative action of multiple and manifold para-ethnographies. Acutely drawn anecdotal material is the fabric of this dynamic contemporary. Mr. Bram's contacts summon para-ethnographies as they act within and upon the contemporary and by so doing give it – the contemporary – social form and cultural content.

This harks back to our earliest collaborative insight that under the sway of fast-capitalism, discourses of the social are rendered not just "darkly unknowable," but illicit. This illicitness of the anecdotal in many discourses of expertise summons up again the quotation that opened this chapter. From extensive interviews that

Raymond Williams gave in 1980, he described the decline in the prestige of *experience-based* knowing with the rise of industrial societies. Yet these knowledge practices have retained a power and élan when practiced as "craft" or "intuitive skill" by bureaucratically powerful officials such as Greenspan. As suggested above, from their privileged networks of relationships these subjects can construct representations of the economy, drawn from experiential material that is fundamentally different from those representations that arise through the application of the statistical modes of analysis. Again, what makes these anecdotal accounts something more than merely another form of "information" or "data" is their social character – mediated through networks of interlocutors – conferring on these accounts distinctive authority that can inform policy formulation and action. Jason Bram – as a mid-level technocrat within the research division of the New York Branch of the Fed – can, by drawing on the prestige of the U.S. Central Bank, create a similarly privileged network of contacts.[12] Refracted through his para-ethnography is not just a contemporaneous take on the economic situation, but inklings of deeper transformation in the alignments of society and economy. It is this latter possibility that reveals how the para-ethnographic can be employed to further the production of fundamental *anthropological* knowledge.

As the political economy of the nation-state is effaced by transnational forces, conventional accounts of society as a discrete construct are increasingly superceded. Class, status, and power no longer cleave merely to the instrumentalities of the state; they are unbound. The overarching interpretive challenge for the ethnographer is to gain access – through para-ethnographic practices of expert subjects – to these emergent formations of political economy. We believe that what is revealed in the cumulative para-ethnographies of experts such as Mr. Bram are crucial ways in which social and economic phenomenon are being reconfigured as global process. More fundamentally, it is through the knowledge work of these experts that society and economy are re-created as analytic constructs and empirical facts.

The Materialization of the Global Subject In the Design for Multi-Sited Ethnography

This chapter has been a study within a larger ongoing project in which we are systematically reimagining the norms and design of ethnography, especially as it has developed in the discipline of anthropology, under the changed contemporary circumstances in which it is practiced. We are very much guided by the strategy and tropes of the influential 1980s so-called Writing Culture critique of ethnography,[13] but now fully extended to the conditions of fieldwork as well and in terms of a different *mise-en-scène*, so to speak, for the practice of ethnography in which objects of study are often diffuse, fragmented, and multi-sited. We also come out of the recently strong, and also strongly critiqued, interpretative tradition in cultural anthropology, in which the core of ethnography is apprehending, by any of a number of theoretical and methodological tendencies, a so-called "native point of view."

Other traditions of anthropology, notably that of British social anthropology, would undoubtedly generate different styles of the reenvisioning of ethnography. In any case, for us, the postulation of para-ethnography as a variety of traditional interpretive concerns with "native points of view" is the crucial methodological issue that this chapter has taken up.

We have been imagining a particular strategy for the conduct of ethnography, specific to our collaboration. It is not yet fully worked out through application to a particular subject of study. Rather, specific elements or facets have emerged from different research interests that we each and together have had over the last few years – in European Rightist politics, in dynastic fortunes, in financial systems, in art worlds, in foundations, in aristocracies, in corporations, in social movements, and, in the case of this study, in central banking. We envision a coherent set of positions on the conduct of ethnography that is alternative to the still reliable traditional localized model of a place/people-bounded research project, contextualized by stipulated macro-historical and social systemic forces. We believe that these positions – only one part of which, the postulation of para-ethnography and its implications, has been examined in detail here – articulate a viable and coherent conception of practices that are circumstantially emerging in the projects of all those researchers who find themselves outside the norms and forms of the standard model, and have to improvise or even reinvent ethnography itself.[14] In sum, it might be said that our priority interest is methodological, but not in the sense of the markedly formal methodological discourse that was current in the high positivist days of post-World War II social science. After years of theory, and the use of theory in texts as an "alibi" for what should be changes in ethnographic design, we believe that articulating explicitly the ongoing changes in the practices of knowledge production should be the priority focus of current meta-discussion and awareness in anthropology.

The goad for this, that virtually everyone would recognize today, is globalization discourse. Undoubtedly, globalization and the category of the global gesture toward real historic conditions of change – most commonly referring to the spread of less fettered market operations throughout the world, speeded up and modified by technological change in communication, transportation, and manufacture – that social inquiry in its many disciplinary forms wants to explain or in terms of which it is contextualized. Yet, like similar terms such as modernization and postmodernity before it, globalization is less an object for comprehensive theorizing or empirical investigation than the referent or symptom that conditions diversely posed challenges to disciplines, knowledge practices, and forms of expertise. The organization of knowledge about society and culture is not dissolving into new interdisciplinary spaces – at least not yet – but the reinvention, recalibration, defense, and debate about long-established doctrines of method are occurring on a widespread basis in disciplinary and expert communities whose mainstreams seemed to have survived the interdisciplinary rumbles of the *fin de siècle* just past. Globalization is not the common object or theoretical frame to which what are indeed diversely experienced problems in method orient themselves, but it does signify a commonly expressed symptom of these problems for still quite disciplinary apprehensions of the contemporary world.

The use of globalization is perhaps different compared to that of earlier similar terms of symptomology in its intensity and comprehensiveness, as the favored term of common focus among specializations, experts, and scholars in academia and elsewhere. This in itself establishes an important suggestion or clue in the re-envisioning of ethnography about the contemporary affinities between anthropologists and expert subjects; the sharing of globalization discourse suggests the latter as counterpart rather than traditional "other" to the former. If the opening gambit of the ethnography challenged by the symptom of the global is an orienting foray into some strategically selected culture of expertise, then that milieu of fieldwork cannot be treated conventionally or traditionally. Such experts are to be treated neither as collateral colleagues helping to inform the framing for fieldwork to occur elsewhere, nor as conventional "natives," as tokens of their cultures to be systematically understood. Instead, they must be treated as subjects fully within the "multi-sited field" itself. What's left is for them to be treated "like" collaborators or partners in research, a fiction to be sustained more or less strongly around the key issue of the postulation of para-ethnography as the object of research.

Whereas once the ethnographer in contemplating a culture could erase the writings and perspectives of the missionary or colonial official from the scene of fieldwork, today the corporate executive, the banker, the diplomat, the lawyer, or the bureaucrat cannot be so erased; even if one retains interests beyond their purview. The question is how to work within and through these domains of representation and practice (by including "insider" fieldwork) in order to define with ethnographic integrity of the "global" subject of one's interest. This ultimately is what is at stake in trying to come to terms, in the exercise that this chapter offers, with the para-ethnographic dimensions of central bankers' practices. It is important to understand this effort not as a contribution to the long-deferred and awaited anthropological study of elites (as another item of categorical coverage after anthropology has studied peasants, workers, tribals, and so on), which by this time is belated. Indeed, the object of study is not the interior lives of experts as an elite as such, but rather to understand their frame, which we assimilate by collaboration and complicity, for a project of tracking the global, being engaged with its dynamics from their orienting point of view.

This sort of ethnographic interest and staging of research on the global field requires a rethinking of the basic assumptions and regulative ideals of the anthropological research process. For us, this is the most urgent task; the pursuit of a global anthropology with far-reaching implications for how the sort of knowledge form that such ethnography produces takes shape.

The Warrant for the Postulation of the Para-Ethnographic in Cultures of Expertise

We want merely to stipulate here the interesting debate that might ensue from our postulation of the "para-ethnographic" as a key construct in the design of multi-sited ethnography. This debate might focus on the phenomenological bases of the recognition and accessing of such a dimension of subjects' discourse and actions as the "para-ethnographic"; it would focus on the nature and capacity of the faculty of practical consciousness and whether anything about it could ever be equated with "the scholastic point of view,"[15] the domain of distanced reflective reason which we reserve for ourselves as academics. And if one were able to establish such collaborative relations with subjects on this level, what implications would this have for the whole project of ethnography, where certain defining distances are closed between ethnographer and subject, at least in certain reaches of the domain of multi-sited fieldwork? Not only is our proposal here based on these debates, but so is a whole school of interpretative theory within the American tradition of cultural anthropology, in which the so-called native point of view has been valorized over the architecture of social relations as the emphasized object of study. In multi-sited research, the social is not ignored, but it emerges in fieldwork from a priority concern with subject models through a more active and explicit practice of collaboration in ethnography.

Recall here the strong images of these 1980s critiques – the central trope being fieldwork strongly enacted by dialogue – where the anthropologist's informing ideas and theories are challenged by informants – the relativization of the scholastic point of view *à la* Pierre Bourdieu by upgrading the intellectual capacity of subjects, in the terms in which the anthropologist is interested. This is to reassert that one of the strongest images of the 1980s discussions was the idea of multiple authorship in any ethnography. The informant became more active than he or she was ever thought to be, involving an enhanced standing of native knowledge in its own forms, of the dialogue settings from which it is accessed, of relationships that can generate ethnography with equal intellectual capacity on both sides. There have been exemplary texts in subsequent years that have enacted just this kind of relationship. But beyond these instances, the point, while provocative, remained ambiguous, unfinished, the implications for practice undefined.

Another issue raised in postulating the para-ethnographic would be its implication for prominent styles of critical argument that ethnography now typically makes by the closing of the distance between ethnographer and expert subject. Most often, critical ethnography has served to undo and demystify the common sense of established institutions, centers, dominant discourses, and elite practices, but such critiques are delivered from the distance of the "scholastic point of view," and often in sympathy with some subordinated, often silenced, subject which gives shape to the moral economy of the ethnography. It is precisely this distance that is closed and this pure sympathy that is made ambiguous in developing the orienting design of multi-sited ethnography by some complicit engagement with the found critical dimension or potential already in play within expert practices. Thus, this standard strategy of critique is not an option. The danger, then, is that the ethnographer will actually be seduced by, or join, the intellectual game of the sphere of expertise with which she or he is engaged, thus eviscerating the project of critique altogether (by indulging the "going native" option). Anyone who studies corporate managers, scientists, policy-makers, and so on by finding collaborative alliances within the field of study can easily slip into being a sort of adviser or taking up the role improvised for the ethnographer. We have seen this threat of seduction materialize in a number of projects, where the researcher nearly joins the community of subjects as ethical adviser or house anthropologist. This is an increasingly tempting role within such research, and it appeals both to a sense of new personal opportunity as well as to widespread desire for some sort of activist dimension to ethnographic work, along with the dissatisfaction with the anticipated indifferent or merely positive, but not sustained, reception to one's work by professional peers. The desire to shape work for those who really understand it and care about it not only leads to a possible shift in the nature of ethnography that maintains its professional boundaries by folding dimensions of reception among subjects into its results, but threatens to motivate the ethnographer to work primarily with and for his expert subjects in developing a new technique for them, or a better analysis. So there is a potentially serious problem in how critical perspective is redeemed once one develops a complex relation with expert or elite subjects, signaled by the postulation of the para-ethnographic as the object of ethnography.

The other option is to explore the social fields that expert imaginaries in the course of practice evoke, in what we referred to as para-ethnography. There are many possible stories or outcomes of ethnography from this premise, but none that can return to the strategy of demystifying critique, although the danger of slipping into pure participation remains. It is the worldview, so to speak, of experts that is most wanted, their attempt to define a rapidly changing or evaporating social field that is intimately tied to and defined by their purposes. This is most often what the ethnographer wants too, but not only this. An evolution of fieldwork from orienting engagements with expertise also guarantees them independence from expert complicities. It is the literal and figurative movements away from the orienting focus on expertise that make the ethics of multi-sited research really complicated, but it is also through the ethical questions themselves posed by working through cross-cutting commitments that the reflexive and recursive shape of such fieldwork projects emerges. The knowledge product of ethnographic research must thus arise from contending with the complicities that materializing the multi-sited design of ethnography entails, and any focused object of critique secured by the distance of the constructed professional role of fieldwork can no longer be relied upon.

In sum, within traditional ethnography one never would have asked for the para-ethnography of the Trobriand islander or the Nuer. The need for radical translation was assumed. The ethnographer wanted modes of thought, systems of belief, ritual performances, and myths as the means to "the native point of view." What does it mean to substitute the "para-ethnographic" for this traditional apparatus of ethnographic knowing? As we have suggested, it means that when we deal with contemporary institutions under the sign of the global symptom, as we have termed it, we presume that we are dealing with counterparts rather than "others" – who differ from us in many ways but who also share broadly the same world of representation with us, and the same curiosity and predicament about constituting the social in our affinities. This condition of orienting ethnography in a multi-sited project changes fundamentally many of the norms and forms of the established model of fieldwork and ethnographic writing.

At base, then, the postulation of the para-ethnographic is a somewhat veiled, maybe even hesitant, overture to partnership or collaboration with our counterparts found in the field. There is quite a bit of ambivalence in making this overture. It may or may not work out. It is perhaps disturbing to think that we are more like some managers of capitalism or some politicians than we would like to admit. The overture may even be the path toward eventual betrayal, as the project eventually establishes independence from the orienting, collaborative ethnography with counterparts. All of this complexity in the reshaping of fieldwork relations in order to establish the multi-sited field under the sign of the global symptom is conveyed, we believe, by evoking the para-ethnographic as the appropriate version of the interpretative tradition of seeking to understand "native points of view." This postulation of the para-ethnographic seems perhaps anemically to arise as an extension from the interpretative tradition, but it carries with it rather profound re-identifications of the fieldwork relationships that define and complicate ethnography.

Notes

1 Raymond Williams, *Politics and Letters: Interviews with New Left Review* (London: Verso, 1981), 164–165.

2 Georg Simmel, *The Philosophy of Money*, trans. David Frisby and Tom Bottomore (London: Routledge, 1990).

3 *Oxford English Dictionary* (1971), p. 319.

4 Douglas R. Holmes and George E. Marcus, "The New Economy in Real-time: Para-Ethnography and the Production of Anthropological Knowledge," unpublished MS, 2000.

5 Bob Woodward, *Maestro: Greenspan's Fed and the American Boom* (New York: Simon & Schuster, 2000), pp. 60–61.

6 Ibid., p. 67.

7 Ibid., p. 120.

8 Ibid., pp. 168–169.

9 The Chairman of the Board of Governors has significant responsibilities within global financial institutions representing, for example, the U.S. central bank on the Board of Directors of the Bank for International Settlement (BSI) in Basle. Representatives of the Federal Reserve also participate in the work of the International Monetary Fund (IMF), the Organization for Economic Co-operation and Development (OECD), and with the Governors of Central Banks of the American Continent. See Board of Governors of the Federal Reserve System, *The Federal Reserve System: Purposes and Functions* (Washington, DC: Board of Governors of the Federal Reserve System, 1994), pp. 61–69.

10 See Board of Governors of the Federal Reserve System, *The Federal Reserve System*, pp. 12–13.

11 Federal Reserve Second District, New York, October 24, 2001.

12 Para-ethnographic practices are by no means limited solely to elits, but can emerge as robust accounts of strategically positioned subalterns. See Douglas R. Holmes, *Integral*

Europe: Fast-Capitalism, Multiculturalism, Neofascism (Princeton, NJ: Princeton University Press, 2000), pp. 105–161.

13 James Clifford and George E. Marcus, eds., *Writing Culture* (Berkeley: University of California Press, 1986).

14 George E. Marcus, *Critical Anthropology Now* (Santa Fe: School of American Research Press, 1999).

15 Pierre Bourdieu, *Practical Reason. On the Theory of Action* (Stanford: Stanford University Press, 1988).

THE DISCIPLINE OF SPECULATORS

CAITLIN ZALOOM

Financial speculators do business with individual traders from London to Singapore, yet they enter into global capital flows that they understand as a single aggregate entity called the market. For futures traders who make their living interacting with this financial power, the market is an object with an existence separate from and larger than the sum of its individual participants. It is "an object of attachment" that is both their source of profits and a judge of their personal worth.[1] Traders consistently describe the market as the highest authority. For traders, these speculators told me, "The market is always right."

Joshua Geller, a manager at the London dealing firm (LDF), where I worked in 2000 as both a trader and an anthropologist, stated his view that the market acts as an instrument of the divine.[2] "We don't know value. Only God knows value." Geller points to worth as something obscured and absolute that partakes in sacred authority. Yet every day Geller and his trainees work to find the value of financial commodities by identifying their price. In the language of economics, futures markets perform "price discovery," assigning a monetary value to a financial product.[3] In Geller's formulation, this is an act of engaging God.

Geller provides a potent description of traders' relationship to the financial domain. The market holds absolute truths. It determines traders' financial fates, and it acts as the arbiter of the speculators' moral worth. Geller told me that in the market, "You test yourself every single day. You either made money or you lost money. I'm a good person or I'm a bad person." This widely held understanding directs traders to adhere closely to the norms of speculation that mediate the individual trader's relationship to the market. To enter into exchange with the market, traders submit to a set of strictures they call "discipline."

The religious language that traders use expresses the urgency they bring to their financial conduct. Yet their ways of working within futures markets are consummately secular. Traders make themselves worthy of their profits by practicing a regimented form of action before the market. The faith and humility traders display expose an economic ethic forged within the circuits of global markets. This chapter examines futures traders' sense of vocation by examining discipline as an ethical practice. Weber's classic questions guide this inquiry into contemporary global finance: at the heart of the financial system today, how do traders' ascetic practices and capitalism interact? What modes of self-conduct does this relation produce?[4]

In traders' discourse, discipline is both an idealized state and a concrete set of internal strategies. Traders use discipline as a tool to shape themselves into actors who can produce appropriate and successful interactions with the market. These techniques work to separate each individual's concerns and desires from his economic judgments. Discipline demands that, while engaging with the market, traders purge themselves of affect and individuality. According to the logic of this technique, they must manage their personal investments and reactions to make possible unobstructed perception. The central virtue of the responsible trader is precise reading of financial information. Speculators train themselves to become embodied instruments for sensing the market and reacting to its every twitch. According to traders' professional norms, discipline enables them to coast with the uncertainties of the market and to judge effectively when to enter and exit the game.

Managing a trading self requires the artful application of disciplinary methods.[5] There are four core elements of discipline: first, traders separate their actions on the trading floor from their lives outside; second, they control the impact of loss; third, traders learn to break down the continuities between past, present, and future trades, by dismantling narratives of success or failure; and fourth, they create a stance of acute alertness in the present moment. Techniques of discipline are at the center of becoming a proficient speculator, of inhabiting the identity and body of the trader. But the work of discipline does not end there. Discipline creates the conditions to become one with the market. "You can experience the market and become a part of this living thing, intimately connected to it," one trader told me.

Speculators labor to strip themselves of their individual stories and circumstances. According to the LDF managers, the market cares nothing for individuals and their obligations. The LDF trainers warned, "The market doesn't care what you think or who you are." Discipline helps traders to fashion a market actor in harmony with the impersonal and anonymous nature of the market. Philip, one of the LDF directors, told me that he has spent years trying to figure out a profile that assures that someone will be a good trader. However, according to him there is only one common denominator among excellent speculators. A good trader must "get rid of [his] ego." The quality of a trader, according to this logic, is located not in the personal characteristics of any individual but, rather, in the talent to undo those marks of individuality with discipline.

I learned about the significance of discipline first-hand during my fieldwork in financial futures markets. In 1998, I trained in market techniques on the trading floor of the Chicago Board of Trade (CBOT), where I was employed as a clerk. With hand signals, shouts, and slips of paper, I relayed orders for financial contracts from outside clients on the phone to traders in the pit. During slow times and after hours, the traders whom I assisted tutored me by explaining their strategies for working in and profiting from the market. In 2000, I extended my research to London. There I worked as a trader in the electronic dealing room of LDF. Along with ten other new recruits and scores of more experienced traders, I made deals on the electronic exchange Eurex, working to apply discipline to my own trading practice eith discipline.

I did not expect to find subtleties of self-control in either site. A hypermasculine, crass persona dominated both the trading floor and the dealing room. Traders were often proud of their own grotesque showmanship. Swearing, shoving, and indulging in language of sexual violence were common. Traders' performance of self is marked by excess and recklessness. Yet the answer to one of my standard questions, "What makes a good trader?", yielded a consistent response: discipline. At first, I found this reply surprising. It seemed to contradict what I had observed. Discipline did not appear to have a place in their trading strategies. However, as I came to learn, the self-regulation of these market actors is governed by strict control.

Discipline breaks traders from the social principles that guide the outside world and places them inside the market sphere. With discipline, a specific market being can emerge. Although each trader must regulate himself, the market also acts as an enforcer. If the trader breaks from his internal codes, the market "punishes" him. This discipline from above imposes norms of behavior on those who lack the resolve to do it themselves. Traders labor to internalize this mode of control and avoid the consequences of a lapse.[6]

Scalpers

CBOT and LDF speculators fill or empty their accounts with skimmings from the vast flow of financial capital that circulates through futures markets. Although all the traders I worked with operated under the demands of discipline, its workings are most visible in a particularly risky trading style called "scalping." Scalping is a technique for buying and selling futures contracts "outright," or without hedging the position. Scalpers work second-by-second, buying in anticipation of a quick rise in price or selling in expectation of a rapid fall. In the language of finance, they do not "offset" any risk by buying or selling products that will limit their losses. Instead, the financial consequences of scalping are immediate and stark, win or lose. With this technique, a trader frees himself to take advantage of every price movement. In an ideal trade, the scalper observes the market's motions, makes a judgment, and executes a sale or purchase. He monitors each price change and its effect on his stake, looking for the best moment to complete the trade and reap his profit or take his loss.[7] If he gauges that the market is going to turn against his position, he may "scratch" the trade, getting in and out of the market at the same price only to reenter seconds later.[8] This simple technique allows the trader the flexibility to move in and out of the market in an instant, taking advantage of every rise and fall of the commodity's price. According to the ideals of discipline the speculator should never look back, whatever the outcome. To be an effective scalper, the trader must maintain sharp attention and responsiveness every moment that he has money on the line. He must move on to the next trade with a clear mind, looking to evaluate the market conditions as they present themselves.

Scalpers learn discipline in both formal and informal ways. On the floor of the CBOT, new traders often work as apprentices, absorbing trading norms from the experienced members who sponsor them. In electronic dealing rooms such as the one at LDF, these opportunities are limited. The LDF trainers knew that their neophyte traders would not have learned trading's central tenets. They created a training program to drive home the lessons of discipline and create a cohort of reliable risk-takers. The managers claimed that they didn't care if money was made or lost as long as each trader practiced obedience to discipline. For them, the responsibility of the trader was to his techniques of self-regulation, not to the profit and loss figure at the end of the day. With adherence to discipline, the managers believed that traders proved themselves worthy. Profits would follow.

The two-week training at LDF devoted part of each session to drilling the new traders in the principles of self-regulation. Yet, this is a difficult task. The LDF trainers, Andrew and Joshua, monitored their traders to ensure that they were developing and using their discipline. To promote trader's internalization of their techniques, the managers required the traders to turn in weekly journals. These documents supplied a written analysis of each deal, forcing traders to objectify their own reasoning processes. The managers expected a logic for each trade and its timing, as well as confessions of lapses in maintaining a regulated trading practice. The online risk management system provided manager Andrew Blair with an electronic view of every computer on the trading floor, in both London and Chicago. In the patterns of profit and loss that registered on Blair's screen, the managers discerned marks of discipline. The weakening of self-control is easy to detect, they claimed. When traders are unable to maintain the divisions between the market and their outside lives, the trainers believe their trading suffers. Adam Berger, a third LDF manager, told me, "I can tell by watching trades come across my screen when someone has had a fight with their wife." According to the strictures of discipline, dissolving those ties while inside the market is essential to making oneself into an instrument that can receive market signals, act on them spontaneously, and take advantage of every opportunity.

LDF traders dreaded early-afternoon phone calls from Adam. Having arrived at his Chicago office at 7 a.m. (1 p.m. London time), Adam would look over the trading records for the day, see who was racking up the marks of unruly trading, and dial the offender's extension to snarl in his ear.

Market Space

For a trader to achieve the total focus required to merge with the market, he must first erect a division between the trading floor and life outside it, isolating the market from the arena of family and friendship obligations. Creating a boundary around the space of the market allows speculators to hone and execute purified economic logics when they are dealing.

Traders make a similarly rigid distinction between market currency and money that is exchangeable for other goods and services. This practice divides action in the market from consequence in their lives outside of it. Market money is specific to the time and space of trade. It is divided from its exchangeability for food, mortgages, tuition, cars, and vacations, all of which draw the trader into a web of relationships outside the market arena.

Discipline redefines the trading object. Traders transform the dollar-denominated cash balances in their accounts into the abstract measurement of "ticks." A "tick" is the generic term for a price interval. The market moves up and down by "ticks." For instance, in the futures market on the Dow Jones Industrial Average (DJIA), ticks are measured in 1/100 increments in the price. If the price of one contract moves from 110.80 to 110.81, the 0.01 increase in the price is a tick. In the DJIA each tick on one contract equals $10 but, according to the logic of the discipline, traders should not calculate the sums of money at stake. Traders count their gains and losses in ticks; these measurements further separate market dealing from the exchanges required for necessities of everyday life.

An underlying tenet of discipline is a conviction that market and emotional matters are irreconcilable. When traders bring family financial concerns to the domain of trading, it impairs their ability to act and react in the temporal and physical space of the market. Discipline allows traders to separate market and family frames. Making this separation takes concentrated labor. Dividing ticks and dollars segments space. The space of money and the space of ticks are physically and socially separated by their assigned currencies. Maintaining different names and accounting strategies for each currency divides the space of the market from the world outside the trading floor. Separating market and social space allows traders to eliminate outside consider-ations and purify market calculations.

Classically, from Simmel and Weber forward, money has been thought of as the ultimate tool of exchangeability. In contrast, Viviana Zelizer has written about the ways in which people assign specific functions and significance to certain pots of money.[9] Yet Zelizer uses examples from actors who are outside a formal market context. Traders' use of ticks sheds new lighton Zelizer's insight. These financial professionals whose task is to create a market, de-commensurate the money *in the market in order to work in the market*.

Traders must labor to strip money of its nonmarket connotations. In the market, where money should appear in its most abstract and depersonalized form, it fails to live up to a pure quantitative logic. Zelizer's claim that money is used to foster and sustain social relationships underestimates the strength of her argument. Money's imbrication with social obligations should be the starting point for analysis. Rather than asserting that money can sustain social connections, we can see a more powerful fact in traders' invention of a currency of ticks. Money must be transformed – purified of its basic social reality – to operate according to economic logic.

Losses

Discipline manages the emotional effects of financial risk-taking while maintaining an intense concentration and focus on the present moment; this is an especially difficult task when they are taking losses. One of traders' greatest vocational challenges is to suppress their individual reactions, desires, and concerns.

Even the best traders take losses over and over again during a day. As Joshua Geller explained, "We are wrong all the time." Losing ticks is an inevitable and unavoidable part of speculation, but the emotional impact of losses can be devastating. Joe Rose told me, "If you are losing money on a regular basis it hurts. You feel like you can't trade. I feel like I never even knew what I was doing. When I lost money a couple of days in a row, I felt like I was just a fake." The repercussions of losses can invade the trader's confidence and self-assurance. Both of these qualities are crucial in traders' rapid-fire work.

Ideally, traders are able to forget about the consequences of each trade. Adam Berger instructed the LDF trainees that "you can't ever make your money back. If you've lost money have a funeral for it. You have to have closure. It is gone . . . you have to look at the next trade." But in a one-on-one interview he admitted the difficulties of containing the effects of financial loss: "You can't make that money back. It's gone . . . And believe me, it is a lot like having a death. You go through that." Yet scalpers may take a hundred losses in a day.

Although discipline as a principle covers all speculators, each trader must come to understand his own personal limits. This requires a special kind of self-knowledge. The trader must assess how many ticks he can lose before he loses his composure. The disciplined trader binds himself to take his loss after the market has gone a certain number of ticks against his position. After, say, three ticks, he will complete the trade and take the loss.

Traders use discipline to manage the act of taking losses and to control the emotional impact of losing ticks. Everett Klipp, an old-timer at the CBOT, was famous for his techniques for training young traders. He was utterly devoted to trading. Even after he retired, he would walk the halls wearing his signature bow tie and a trading jacket that draped from his aging frame. One friend of his told me, "He'd say, 'You'll never become a millionaire if you don't learn how to take small losses.' . . . He didn't teach [new traders] how to win. He taught them how to lose." Klipp's belief in the salutary effects of discipline was unshakable. He would stand behind the neophyte trader under his care and force him to take small losses, which is a crucial part of discipline. Discipline directs a trader to exit the trade before the position moves against him more gravely. Klipp's theory, as several of his admirers described to me, was that taking small losses teaches traders to become familiar with losing, to gain control over the impact of a loss. In May 1999, *Futures* magazine quoted him saying, "You have to love to lose money... to be successful."[10]

Taking losses is so significant for traders' discipline that traders often claim that their best trades were the ones where they cut their losses. When I asked the question "What was the best trade that you ever made?" I naïvely assumed that the one with the largest financial yield would be the most prized. Yet traders insisted on the distinction between the "best" trade and the trade in which they had made the most money. The responses below show the premium placed on applying discipline and taking the loss that the market has doled out:[11]

> The most important thing... is you have to be able to take your loss... If you don't take your losses then you're just going to get killed. You have to take your losses. It's just so important. And oftentimes at the end of the day you'll remember the best trade you had was a loser and you took your loss right away and if you hadn't you'd have gotten killed. As far as great trades, the best trades that I can recall were scratching [getting out of a trade with no gain or loss] and then seeing [the market] go just totally against [the position I just left]. And had I stayed in it [I would have lost a lot of money], like wow, that was great. So I used the discipline, I stuck to my guns and it just totally worked out... So I was trying to become really aware of just doing the right thing, making the *right* trade, doing the *right* thing, following the rules. And that's very tough. [my italics]

The quality of a trade is measured by the exercise of principled dealing. Taking small losses is the mark of a virtuous trader. Both the act and the loss prove the trader's worthiness to search for profits in the market. The loss is not simply a financial debt; it is a tangible mark of adhering to discipline's limits and guidelines.

The Danger of Narratives

Breaking down continuities between past and present helps traders to form and sustain economic judgments in the maelstrom of the market. This temporal separation reinforces the boundaries between market and outside space.[12] To observe the quick movements of the market in accordance with discipline, the trader must immerse himself in the market and block out external influences, including the memory of success or failure.

Traders segment time into small, disconnected increments to stop narratives of success or failure from building. They try to treat each trade as if it has no effect on the next. A disciplined trader leaves every trade in the past. He is reactive to the market, leaving his own judgments quickly behind when the market proves him wrong. He does not build stories about his successes or failures that would provide a sense of weakness or invincibility that could effect his decisions and timing in the market.

Discipline demands that traders leave the consequences of each trade behind – whether it made a profit or a loss. One good trade never guarantees the next. Developing a sense that there is a continuity of success or failure is the trader's Achilles heel. In the practice of speculation, traders divide time in the market to accentuate the constant regression to the mean that is a necessary part of discipline.[12] Traders work to isolate one decision from the next, dividing now from then. In the trade, there is no past and no projection ahead. The present moment takes precedence. Ideally, scalpers carry nothing forward into the next trade. One veteran trader lectured me, "Once the trade is done it is history." Part of discipline is learning how to divide the consequences of the last trade from the work of the next to limit the psychological effects of success or failure.

The dissociation from each individual decision is accompanied by dissociation from the circumstances of the individual decision-maker – whether profits are up or down on the day, week, or year. Traders work hard to maintain the kind of division that breaks down any narrative that might arise from a series of successive losses and gains. It takes active efforts to break down the sense of continuity that comes with repeated success or failure.

Wishing, Hoping, and Praying

When traders are unable to divide the consequences inside the market from the potentials of wealth and devastation outside the market, they run the risk of bringing their personal desires into their economic actions. Traders whose discipline has lapsed may also invest themselves in a given position, personalizing the success or failure of a single decision. Joshua Geller warned against what he considers to be the greatest danger of trading: "wishing, hoping, and praying." On the days when Geller wandered the LDF trading floor, he would stand at a trader's shoulder watching the rhythms of his trades. As the trader increased a position that was already posting losses, or hung on minute after minute in a trade that was running against him, Geller would hiss, "Wishing, hoping, and praying," into the trader's ear.

Both wishing and praying break discipline's cardinal rule. They bring personal desires and convictions into market judgments. Without discipline, traders' own assessments cloud their view of the objective movements of the market. These desires then mediate between the trader's actions and his reactions to the constantly changing information before him. To structure the self as an instrument of perception and reaction, traders must give up their desires.

The scalpers' ability to skim a profit from market fluctuations relies on a constant clarity of vision. Traders must maintain an acute reactive stance to work in their second-by-second time frame. With every extra moment spent on the losing trade, a profitable position passes. Taking the loss removes the constraints that block a quick move into the next prospect. Geller warned us, "If you are hoping for something to change or come back you are missing opportunities. You are not taking advantage of opportunities." Successful discipline allows traders to take action instantaneously.

Wishing, hoping, and praying undermine the trader's ability to react. They alter the time frame of a trader's decision-making capacity. These expressions of individual desire extend the present moment forward in time. When a trader attaches hope to an individual trade, he is no longer responding to the information available at the moment. When a trader breaks his discipline, the consequences of an individual trade begin to matter. Wishing, hoping, and praying can easily slide into an attachment to an individual decision.

If the keen trader spends a few minutes in the same position, watching the gains or losses tick up and down with the market, his neighbors may begin to heckle him : "Are you married to it [the position] yet? Hey, I think Charles has gotten married." The unlucky groom may elicit a spontaneous performance of the wedding march from the other traders. "Marriage" betrays a trader's weakness. It means that he has formed a connection with his position that goes beyond the moment and the explicit purpose of making money. He has invested his self in the object. When the individual trade has gained some value in its own right, it loses the status of pure instrument. "Getting married" to a trade is a way of saying that a trader has abandoned his senses. An inability to separate market reason from personal attachments has undermined his trader's craft.

Entering the Zone

The immediacy of the market

From the point of view of the scalper, the market resides in the present. In an online exchange, the market is located between the buyer and seller that are in the process of closing. On the floor of the CBOT, the agreement that is being made between traders in the pit at this very moment is the market. As the CBOT traders explained to me, once the clerks record a trade and the prices are printed on the electronic screens above the trading floor, the market that they represent is history. Traders try to apprehend the ungraspable, the elusive presence of the market. Because it is always moving forward in time, it always remains uncertain. Scalpers' work exists in a just emerging future, one step ahead of the market.

On the CBOT trading floor, the pit is the space of the market. Anything outside the pit is beyond the market. Although "outside events" (as traders refer to them) affect the flow of orders into the pit and the price of the contracts, scalpers' attention remains focused on the action in the pit. The pit links the time and space of the market into a discrete present.

This bias for the present lends itself to Zen-like aphorisms. Joshua Geller advised, "Accept the market as it is and try to be with it." A popular book that outlines the path to success counsels traders to follow the *Tao of Trading*.[14] And, indeed, traders speak of their best trading moments in ways that sound like mystical engagements.

For traders, it is necessary to abandon self-consciousness to gain full access to the market's interior. Traders use discipline to excise outside contexts from their conscious thoughts and to enhance their abilities to read, interpret, and ultimately merge with the market. Traders often talk of their best moments in terms of being "in the zone," or being immersed in a flow, in terms that parallel Csikszentmihalyi's description of peak experiences.[15] In the zone, economic judgments and actions seem to roll without effort from the trader's instincts. The market and the trader seem to merge, giving him special access to the natural rhythms of financial patterns.

The moments traders value most come with a sense of total absorption in the market, of entering "the zone." For traders, the zone is where conscious thought disappears and an ultimate sense of presence takes over. Their senses are heightened to the sounds and cadence of the market. In the zone they are able to act without explicit thought. Achieving oneness with the market can wipe away concerns beyond the moment. As Joe Rose, a successful senior trader in equity index futures, told me, "The only time in my life when I am not anxious is when I'm trading. I am just out there making money, losing money. And it absolutely wipes out all anxiety. I live in the moment when I trade."

This absorption in the present echoes descriptions of the athlete's and musician's craft. Joshua Geller attributed the success of one of his traders to his musician's access to the rhythmic flow of the market. The man had been a drummer in a jazz band. "He sways with the market," Geller said. This trader followed the market pulse, switching his positions with the changing tempo of trading in a kind of improvisational technique.

A disciplined scalper always remains in the moment. He is flexible and reactive to the market situation immediately at hand. He cannot put too much confidence in his own judgment, or carry a sense of weakness. This paring down of the self leaves only the part that can become absorbed in the market, with no outside commitments. The technique enables a feral sense for market action that little resembles a strictly calculating subject. He reacts to each move of price regardless of his own judgment and desire about what the market "should" do according to his individual estimate.

Pit traders speak of living within the heart of the market. Traders must have the physical discipline to remain in the pit through the adrenalin spurts brought on by volatile markets and the boredom associated with the deadened tempo of trading lulls. In the pit, this means standing shoulder to shoulder with hundreds of other men, hour upon hour, without sitting. The physical aches and pains of a trader cannot distract him from soldering his attention to the market and its movements. Bodily immersion in the market is both a challenge to traders' focus and a powerful force for drawing them in. On the CBOT floor during fast-moving markets the collective excitement of the trading pits, the rousing noise, and the jostling bodies draws traders into the market. They are surrounded and soaked in the sweat of exchange.

The need for discipline, both of body and spirit, is heightened in online exchange. Where the CBOT traders have the advantage of physical immersion in the market, the LDF traders are distanced from their dealing partners by electronic networks and trading screens. In the electronic dealing room, the market does not surround the trader. Instead, he trains his attention on the numbers that represent the market on his screen.[16]

Nonetheless, Joshua Geller stressed the importance of constant physical readiness in our training. He demonstrated the disciplined crouch that brought his eyes inches from the screen. His index and middle fingers rested lightly on the right and left click buttons on his mouse. From this alert stance he could spontaneously sell or join the offer. "Have your cursor over the relevant hot button so that when the opportunities happen you are there to act on it immediately," he told us. Mustapha, the most profitable scalper at LDF, visited the hospital because the tendons in his hands were throbbing and stiff. The physical therapist there told him that clicking the mouse was not to blame for his injury. The pain was not caused by overly frequent trading. Rather, the damage came from holding his index finger slightly above the mouse, poised to click at any moment. Hours of hovering in readiness each day had injured his hand.

These periods of anticipation are vital challenges for traders. "Flat" markets, when very little is happening, can be deadly. Each day, a flurry of activity surrounds the market opening. But that burst soon wanes, rolling slowly into the afternoon. Depending on external events, or other market news, there may be surges of activity or simply a steady drone of trades that carries into the concentrated action around the closing bell. These temporal rhythms of the market try the speculators' patience.

A trader must be unreactive to monotony as well as excitement. Boredom tempts speculators to "over trade," to take a position for the sheer stimulation of being in the game. Tedium is dangerous because it dulls the senses and tempts the trader into chatting, taking long lunches, and making telephone calls. Discipline is as important for deciding to stay *out* of the market as it is in making decisions to enter. Discipline supports the trader as he stands in the pit, or keeps his eyes glued to his screen, resisting the quicksand of boredom.

Geller held up a coworker in the pit as the greatest example of this aspect of discipline:

> The guy was a trading machine. He would make one, maybe two trades a day. He would just stand there waiting to pick off a perfect trade. Put the entire stake on one moment where he was sure. He never left the pit. He didn't eat. He didn't go to the bathroom. I don't think he even blinked. He was an awful human being but he was a great trader.

Despite his own inaction, this trader was able to stay totally focused on the market. The claim that he was a trading machine points to the speculators' ideal. In Geller's portrait, his successful neighbor was able to excise the human urges that lead others into the trading traps of boredom. The neighbor's machine-like quality reverses the usual notion of mechanical movement. Instead of associating the machine with repetitive action, in this case, he describes how the dictates of discipline raise his neighbor to inhuman extremes of *inaction*. The trader, in Geller's estimation, successfully transformed himself into a machine for reading the market. In his role as an LDF trainer, Geller's goal was to produce these kinds of human machines.

Don't think

The immediacy of the market as it is localized in a particular time and space forces traders to focus on each price movement. Traders act as if they are tracking an animal. Calculations or elaborate strategies that take them out of the immediacy of market time are seen as an impediment. Traders ultimately value reactive speed and perceptive clarity rather than complex calculative skill.

Sean Curley, who was trained as a lawyer, explained how his legal training sometimes impedes his trading abilities:

> Sometimes I think [my legal education] hurts me because I'm more prone to get set in my ways. I'll reason to a particular conclusion based on assumptions that I've got built into the market whether it's based on fundamentals or it's based on some technical thing. You know, just like I'd craft an argument... There are a lot of guys who may never look at a chart, they never read a newsletter, they don't care. They just want to know what's bid and what's offered. And they just trade... A lot of those characters aren't the kind of guys who went to dental school or have a law degree. Maybe they didn't get out of high school but they're damn good traders because they trade the market. They know the market. The market has been their education.

Tom Walsh, who holds an MBA from MIT in finance, agrees. He believes that his university education leads him to consider situations *too closely.* Early on in his career, Neil Marks, now a veteran trader, acquired the nickname "Don't tell me anything" Marks, because of his belief that knowledge of events or analyses outside the immediate market are a distraction. When he began trading at the CBOT he canceled his subscription to the *Wall Street Journal.* He said that the minute he began incorporating the newspaper's information into his trades, he started losing money. Marks commented that the traders' advantage lies in their presence in the heart of the market. He says that "Traders have the pulse of the market. They are on top of it every second." For him, the adrenaline rush of trading and the feeling of being in the zone come with the gut-level immediacy of being directly inside and surrounded by the market.

Discipline checks the instinct to *out-think* the market, a practice that draws traders out of the market and into their heads. Strong convictions are dangerous for traders. The LDF trainers instructed us with the phrase "Don't think." Traders must remain flexible – ready to react immediately to changes in the market. As one trader told me, "It doesn't pay to have too much of a view." A trader with too much confidence in his judgment can become wedded to a strategy. Instead of getting out of a losing position and reassessing his judgment, he may hold on as the position loses more and more money. Assurance in his original judgment can convince him that the market will soon turn around and go in his favor. Discipline places a limit on the role of explicit calculation. If a trader persuades himself that he has "figured out" the market rather than sticking to his discipline, he risks becoming tied to his decision, and exposing himself to further losses. Setting limits for losses helps the trader to reject calculations that place his intellect above the objective movements of the market.

Conclusion: The Ethical Practice of Discipline

Discipline is an ethical system and profit-making strategy. It is a method both for engaging the market and being accountable to it. Maintaining discipline allows traders to allay the ethical dangers of acting in the market. Overconfidence brings punishment:

> You [can] become very opinionated on the market, instead of just trading it and scalping in and out. I go in with a set feeling that I'm right. Sometimes I just don't want to give up. And that is when it [the punishment] happens, after I'm doing really well and I'm feeling omnipotent. You think you're bigger than the market and then you just ask for it.
>
> As soon as you think you're bigger than the market, and [you say to yourself] "I'm a great trader...I can sell at the top and buy at the bottom," you get killed.

Most importantly, discipline demands that the trader acknowledge that the market itself is the only authority. The movements of the market represent financial truth. It is not surprising that traders' attitude to the market takes on a quasi-religious aura. Discipline is, therefore, both a technique of the self and a technique of the sacred.[18]

Practicing discipline allows traders to attain a proper state to engage the overwhelming force of the market. Traders speak about the market in religious ways that make this analogy appropriate. The adage "The market is always right" locates the market as possessing ultimate truth. Men must fit themselves to its requirements.

The market is the moral authority; it monitors traders' discipline and judges their worthiness for profit. It is both the single truth and the arbiter of a trader's work. In many of my discussions with traders, they returned often to the idea that the market required obedience. When traders gain too much confidence over recent successes, they say that the market "knocks me down." The traders' code of action is based on a belief that "You can never be smarter than the market," a conviction that demonstrates that the market is a mysterious and powerful force that can be apprehended only if approached with the correct humility.

Humility in relation to the market demands the recognition that success can be perilous. A trader's claim to special knowledge or access to the mysteries of the market invites retribution. A successful trader must maintain a fine balance between a basic confidence in his ability to interact with the market and an arrogance that will draw its wrath. A disciplined trader knows that such arrogance results in having to "give back" profits. The market takes away the earnings of the arrogant trader. Loss is the moral penalty for the breakdown of discipline. The trading journal of one LDF trader stated bluntly, "Just when you think you're starting to figure these markets out, they come back and squash your ego like a peanut." The market seems to insist on the complete remaking of the trader in line with its requirements. It does not give out subtle hints: "Any crack or psychological weakness the market will find it . . . and will put a chisel in there and bang, bang rip it apart," Adam Berger warned.

When discipline breaks down and the trader's self-mastery is called into question, he begins to use the language of dire consequences. Common descriptions of losing money include "getting killed" and "getting burned." These physical metaphors of loss draw attention to the dangers of close contact with the market. The break from discipline lends these losses moral meaning. One trader, David, described to me the unraveling of his proper trading technique:

> There have been [trades] when I just got killed. Everything goes against you. You sell it when you shouldn't. You buy it when you shouldn't. All day long and it's a busy market, you're trading numbers you shouldn't. The value's down. [You're] trying to get it back so you're trading bigger. When you have a profit normally you'd get out. But because you're down money you're trying to squeeze it, get more out of it. [You] turn it into a loser. Hate yourself. Hate yourself. Consumed with self-hatred.

When he cannot manage his profit-making strategies and emotions with discipline, David's downward spiral of loss and self-inflicted violence gathers force. The more losses he incurs, the greater his self-loathing and the more losses he takes on. He is consumed by emotion and unable to divest himself.

Discipline is a both an ideal and a technique that traders work to enact. Traders use the methods of discipline to enter into the financial domain and manage their engagements with the market. Traders apply this practice in their daily work with greater or lesser competence. Yet, even for those who can successfully lose themselves in the market, there are significant obstacles to maintaining discipline over time. The greatest challenges to the competent execution of a disciplined trading practice are the pressures that impose themselves on traders from beyond the market frame. The strains of wealth and dependents tempt traders to allow their thoughts to wander beyond the market present and, therefore, to break the ethical imperative to separate economic and social spheres. Shaping the self into an instrument that can read and exchange with the market is not a one-way process. Traders' practices of discipline require daily acts of separation. Adherence to discipline waxes and wanes. It is a challenge for traders to maintain their techniques of separation and humility. Traders operate under the constant threat of losing their discipline, and with it their focus and trading skills.

The ascetic practices of discipline that shape men into market actors are difficult and painful to maintain. These techniques of self-conduct extract a price from the traders, who must subject themselves to the market. Discipline can create a self that can read, interact, and draw profit from the market. However, submitting to the authority of the market, stripping oneself of thoughts, analyses, and desires, requires several acts of separation. This stripping places the trader in a complex relationship to his sense of success, his reflection on past actions or hopes for the future, and his responsibilities to others outside the market. In other words, it brings him into direct conflict with other ethical domains. Traders believe that indulging any of these competing ethical imperatives will lead to punishment by the market. The language of death that traders use to describe their failures shows that they stand on the edge of an ethical precipice. Their balance depends on their skillful performance of discipline.

Notes

1 Karin Knorr Cetina and Urs Breugger, "The Market as an Object of Attachment: Exploring Post-Social Relations in Financial Markets," *Canadian Journal of Sociology* 25(2), 2000, pp. 141–168.

2 All names, including the name of the firm, are pseudonyms, except for the Chicago Board of Trade and Everett Klipp, who is deceased.

3 Futures are traded in auctions markets. According to Charles Smith's argument, auctions thrive where the value of objects is ambiguous or uncertain: see Charles Smith, *Auctions: The Social Construction of Value* (New York: Free Press, 1989). Futures contracts are just such objects. They represent an obligation to buy or sell a financial commodity weeks or months in the future. Traders constantly process events that affect national economies and new information about the future health or weakness of stock markets, and adjust their assessment of a financial commodity's value. This evaluation is reflected in the changing price of the commodity.

4 Max Weber, *The Protestant Ethic and the Spirit of Capitalism*, trans. T. Parsons (New York: Routledge, 1992 [1930]).

5 For Foucault, the arts of self-governance are the uses of techniques for "training of oneself by oneself": see Herbert Dreyfus and Paul Rabinow, *Michel Foucault: Beyond Structuralism and Hermeneutics* (Chicago: University of Chicago Press, 1983), p. 246. Techniques of the self treat the self as an object to be formed in harmony with a specific end. For traders, exercising this "exact mastery" eliminates nonmarket influences to create a person who can be absorbed completely in the rhythms of the market.

6 Foucault has most famously employed the concept of discipline in *Discipline and Punish* (New York: Vintage, 1995 [1979]). Discipline, in this sense, produces individuals. However, despite the similarity of language with his earlier project, Foucault's work on ethics has more salience for the analysis of traders' practices of discipline. Discipline fits closely with Foucault's concept of ethical work. Paul Rabinow explains that "[t]he task of ethical work for Foucault is to establish the right relationship between intellect and character in the context of practical affairs": see his introduction to *Michel Foucault: Ethics* (New York: The New Press, 1994), p. xxxiii. Traders forge this relationship of the self to the self in and for the practice of speculation. The process of Foucault's discipline is inverted. Trading as a performance of discipline sublimates the individual and his particular interiority to the larger market.

7 I use the masculine pronoun for gender realism. The vast majority of traders are men. During my time at LDF, there were three women in a room of 65 traders. At the CBOT, the largest pit holds 600 traders. While I worked there, two were women.

8   Traders may also try to reap a profit from the difference between the price bid and the price offered, called the "bid/ask spread." They buy at the lower price and sell at the higher price (or vice versa), taking advantage of the insider's "edge." The spread is the market maker's premium, but it is not always easy or available to take.

9   Viviana Zelizer, in *The Social Meaning of Money* (Princeton, NJ: Princeton University Press, 1997), has shown that people create specific uses and meanings around money as they "cope with their multiple social relations." Working against the classical theories of Weber and Simmel, Zelizer shows how people use money to maintain social ties and how these ties mark money. In Zelizer's analysis, money cannot simply create "sensualists without spirit," as Weber worried. Rather, money is subservient to logics of the family, charity, and the gift. Yet the ability of money to distance social ties must also be taken as an anthropological object. If we begin with Zelizer's observation that social connections personalize money, the trader's techniques of separation are all the more surprising. On the trading floor, money must be crafted into a technology of social distance. It is not a property that inheres in money *per se*. The forging of dollars into ticks shows just how difficult it is to strip money of its power as a social connector.

10 Andrew Schroedter, "Everett Klipp: 'Babe Ruth of the CBO,'" *Futures*, Chicago 28(5), 1999, p. 102.

11 A paper funded by the Commodity Futures Trading Commission (CFTC) documents that the most profitable traders are the most willing to take losses quickly: see Peter R. Locke and Steven C. Mann, "Do Professional Traders Exhibit Loss Realization Aversion?" (Washington, DC: Commodity Futures Trading Commission, 1999). In the language of behavioral finance, they do not exhibit "loss realization aversion." The CFTC paper claims that critics of behavioral finance will find satisfaction in the fact that the more successful traders demonstrate less loss aversion than those who draw fewer profits, proving that they behave "rationally" according to profit motive. In other words, they apply discipline to their trading practices. The source of traders' success does not lie in their ability to be impervious to "behavioral" traits. Traders who work to implement the separation of a market self from their social selves strictly adhere to discipline's demands. They take small losses rather than letting their losing positions run.

12 The bias for the present and the short frame of market action are very different from other financial actors. Financial strategists for investment banks, or even mortgage brokers who are looking to hedge simple interest rate risk, work with time frames that can look months into the future. Scalping, and its techniques, is a form of speculation particular to the market makers who provide consistent liquidity for futures markets.

13 Richard Sennett has pointed out that "Risk-taking . . . lacks the quality of a narrative, in which one event leads to the next": see Richard Sennett, *Corrosion of Character: The Personal Consequences of Work in the New Capitalism* (New York: W. W. Norton, 1998), p. 83. In futures markets, we can see how traders actively produce this quality. Narrative is an active obstacle to risk-taking practice. Lack of narrative is not an inherent quality of risk, but one structured by the techniques of discipline.

14 Robert Koppel, *The Tao of Trading: Discovering a Simpler Path to Success* (Chicago: Dearborn Trade, 1998).

15 Mihaly Csikszentmihalyi, *Flow: The Psychology of Optimal Experience* (New York: Harper & Row, 1990).

16   For more on the role of screens in calculation, see Caitlin Zaloom, "Ambiguous Numbers: Trading Technologies and Interpretation in Financial Markets," *American Ethnologist* 30(2), 2003, pp. 258–272.

17   This flat effect and absence of desire seems especially strange. Geller's neighbor cuts a figure at odds with the willful entrepreneur usually associated with risky capitalist pursuits.

18   Henri Hubert and Marcel Mauss' essay on sacrifice helps to illuminate the problem of actors engaging a divine presence: "Sacrifice is a religious act that can only be carried out in a religious atmosphere and by means of essentially religious agents. But, in general, before the ceremony neither sacrifier nor sacrificer, nor place, instruments or victim possess this to a suitable degree. The first phase of the sacrifice is intended to impart it to them. They are profane; and their condition must be changed . . . All that touches upon the gods must be divine; the sacrifier is obliged to become a god himself in order to be capable of acting upon them." See Henri Hubert and Marcel Mauss, *Sacrifice: Its Nature and Function* (Chicago: University of Chicago Press, 1922), pp. 19–20.

15

CULTURES ON THE BRINK:
Reengineering the Soul of Capitalism – On a Global Scale[1]

KRIS OLDS AND NIGEL THRIFT

Where do you produce your entrepreneurs from? Out of a top hat?
There is a dearth of entrepreneurial talent.
We have to start experimenting. The easy things—just getting a blank mind to take in knowledge and become trainable—we have done. Now comes the difficult part. To get literate and numerate minds to be more innovative, to be more productive, that's not easy. It requires a mind-set change, a different set of values.

Senior Minister Lee Kuan Yew[2]

Q.   How do you size up made-in-Singapore graduates?
A.   What strikes me about those I meet is that many are very good at solving a problem but very bad at defining a problem. I've noticed if I say 'This is the problem solve it', they are very dedicated, intelligent and come back faster than I expected. But if I say 'I'm not sure what I would do here, how do you define the problem?' then they have problems.

Arnoud De Meyer, Dean, INSEAD Singapore[3]

Introduction

It is a near constant in the history of capitalism that what there is to know about the conduct of business is surrounded by a garland of institutions that not only impart that knowledge but attempt to codify and improve upon it, so producing new forms of conduct. But since the 1960s this roundelay has accelerated as the institutions of business knowledge have joined up to form a fully functioning "cultural circuit of capital."[4] This cultural circuit of capital is able to produce constant discursive-cum-practical change, with considerable power to mold the content of people's work lives and, it might be added, to produce more general cultural models that affect the rest of people's lives as well. Indeed, it would not be too much of an exaggeration to say that the omniscience once claimed by Marxism-Leninism in large parts of the world as a means of rehabilitating the economic, social, and cultural spheres has now passed to the fleeting ideological products of the cultural circuit. These are the equivalent of capitalism's commissars.

But we cannot stop there. For the discursive and practical tenets of this world have increasingly become entangled with state action, producing new practices of government that are also redefining who counts as a worthy citizen. In other words, the kind of subject positions that are deemed worthy managers and workers are increasingly similar to the kinds of subject positions that define the worth of the citizenry (and, it might be added, other actors such as migrant workers). This is particularly true of that network of global cities where these tenets are most likely to be put into action.[5]

In turn, we can also begin to see how global corporate power is deployed nowadays. More often than not translated by the cultural circuit of capital, the discursive style of state policy has become ever more closely aligned with the discursive style of corporations. They both share a common background of expectations of how, and on (and in) what terms, the world will disclose itself. But we should be careful here. The products of the cultural circuit of capital tend to see the world as fast moving, ambivalent, difficult to predict, and "on the brink," and this frame of mind (which can equally be found now in much state policy) does not make for an easy imperium.

The different centers of "calculation" (if calculation is quite the right word) that make up the cultural circuit of capitalism can perhaps best be thought of as shifting assemblages of governmental power, made more powerful by their strictly temporary descriptions and attributions. It is a set of assemblages which – fuelled by the raw material of events as sieved through the discursive-cum-practical sequences of the cultural circuit – are in constant motion, constantly inventing new moves.

We want to use the world "assemblage" here in a Deleuzian way, to signal that we do not want to think of these centers of calculation as homogenous and tightly knit structures or even as a loosely linked constitution, but rather as "functions" that bring into play particular populations, territories, affects, events – "withs." They are not therefore to be thought of as subjects but as "something which happens."[6] Assemblages differ from structures in that they consist of cofunctioning "symbiotic elements," which may be quite unalike (but have "agreements of convenience") and coevolve with other assemblages, mutating into something else, which both parties have built. They do not, therefore, function according to a strict cause-and-effect model.

In turn, the denatured notion of assemblage makes much more room for space. Assemblages will function quite differently, according to local circumstance, not because they are an overarching structure adapting its rules to the particular situation, but because these manifestations are what the assemblage consists of. Indeed, the cultural circuit of capital allows the knowledges of very different situations to circulate much more freely (and rapidly), and to have a much greater say than previously within a space which is precisely tailored to that circulation, consisting of numerous sites and specialized route ways.

In this chapter, we want to look at one of these spaces, a space that is attempting to recast itself as a "global schoolhouse" for business knowledge. Singapore, a Pacific Asian city-state with a population of 3.9 million (of whom about 600,000 are foreigners) is a rapidly evolving laboratory for the corporate interests of both the cultural circuit of capital and the state. But while Singapore is a very intense example, we would argue that the trajectory it has set out to follow – toward a kind of kinetic utopia – is one that many Western and some Asian states (for example, India or Malaysia) would like to emulate to a significant degree. This is a space in which accumulation becomes the very stuff of life, through persuading the population to become its own prime asset – a kind of people mine (in a mineral sense) of reflexive knowledgeability.

This chapter consists of five sections, including these introductory comments. In the second section, we go on to consider the cultural circuit of capital, concentrating especially on the role of business schools as the key nodes in this circuit. In the third section, we will consider the Singaporean state as both test bed for, and to some extent progenitor of, a number of the ideas that have been circulating in the cultural circuit. The fourth section of the chapter is then concerned with a study of the actual process of negotiation between state and the cultural circuit of capital in which a number of elite "world-class" business schools established formal presences in Singapore between 1998 and 2000. Finally, we offer a few speculative comments and about the future direction of the Singaporean management experiment, for the phase that we focus on in this chapter was designed to lay the groundwork for a much more ambitious goal of transforming Singapore into an "enterprise ecosystem," not just for Singaporeans but for the entire Pacific Asian region.[7]

The Cultural Circuit of Capital

The world may consist of a constantly moving horizon of situated actions, learning experiments, and makeshift institutional responses, but that does not mean that it cannot be held together. Since the 1960s, one of the more impressive of these holdings together has been the link-up of a series of institutions to produce and disseminate business knowledge. In particular, this circuit arises from the concentration of three different institutions – management consultants, management gurus, and especially business schools – all surrounded by the constant swash of the media, which in itself constitutes a purposeful part of the circuit.

Management consultancies date from the late 19th and early 20th centuries. But their heyday has been since the 1960s, when companies such as Bain and Co. and McKinsey began to gel into vast consulting combines. Consultancies subsequently became the important producers and disseminators of business knowledge through their ability to take up ideas and translate them into practice – and to feed practice back into ideas.

Management consultancies were helped in these ambitions by the oracles of business knowledge, management gurus, nearly all of whom were (or are) consultants. Gurus packaged business ideas as aspects of themselves. Although they existed before the 1980s, gurus have become particularly prevalent since the phenomenal success of Peters and Waterman's *In Search of Excellence*,[8] "a Zen gun that was fired 20 years ago."[9] Gurus tend to embody particular approaches to business knowledge through performances that are meant to both impart new knowledge while also confirming what their audiences may already know (but need bringing out or confirming). Increasingly, gurus come replete with moral codings: "they do not only tell managers how to manage their organisations, they also tell them what kind of people they should become in order to be happy and morally conscious citizens with fulfilling lives."[10]

But the primer for the system of producing and disseminating management knowledge is now the business school. Though a small elite of business schools was formed in the late 19th and early 20th centuries in the United States, the main phase of expansion took place much later – from the late 1940s on – on the back of the Master of Business Administration (MBA) degree. In the rest of the world, business schools only slowly came into existence until, in the 1950s and 1960s, they began to open and expand in Europe and then in Asia. They now form the most visible tips of a vast global business education iceberg, one that turns over billions of dollars per year.

Producers of business knowledge necessarily have to have a voracious appetite for new knowledge, since it is the continuous conveyor belt of new knowledge that keeps the system going. In particular, this means a central bank of knowledge that can be stripped of many of its local contingencies and can therefore be made mobile across the globe. So, for example, ideas such as "complexity theory"[11] or "community of practice"[12] can be made into ready-made resources that give up a hold on certain aspects of the world for the sake of portability. But while the universalizing nature of much business knowledge is evident, business schools also produce rich case studies of actual corporate strategy that more often than not recognize the sociospatial embeddedness of firms and market processes. The case study method is a prominent one in many business schools, with upper tier schools such as Harvard Business School, the Richard Ivey School, Darden, and INSEAD producing the bulk of the 15,000-plus cases that now circulate through business school classrooms and corporate education centers. Given the interdependencies between business schools and corporations, business school academics have relatively deeper access to the primary "movers and shapers" of the global economy than the vast majority of social scientists.[13]

The kinds of knowledge that are pursued in business schools necessarily range widely, of course. So there is functional knowledge of all kinds – from principles of accounting and finance to logistics. Then, there is knowledge that is organizational and strategic. And, finally, there is knowledge that is especially concerned with subjectification; how to be a "global leader," for example.[14] But, whatever the case, what is effectively being pursued is a constant process of adaptation through continuous critique of the status quo.[15] The critical feedback loop produced by the cultural circuit of capital is meant to produce a kind of dynamic equilibrium in which the brink (the "edge of chaos") is the place to be.

Weaving in and out of this set of actions and ideas are the media, key means of transport, amplifiers, and generators of business knowledge in their own right. Through the vast range of different general and special media outlets that now exist, and through the vast range of general and special media intermediaries that vie to get their ideas circulated in these outlets, the media acts to force the production of ideas. Newspapers such as the *Financial Times* also shape institutional conduct at a wide variety of levels via their regular surveys and ranking exercises. In addition, business knowledge is also circulated via the continual production of conferences, seminars, workshops, and the like, as the meeting has increasingly been turned into a means of dissemination, which is itself sold as a product.

Through these different sets of institutions that make up the cultural circuit of capital, dispersed knowledges can be gathered up and centered, practical knowledges and skills (including soft skills such as leadership) can be codified, the miasma of "too much information" can be cut down and simplified, and large numbers can be made into small and handleable numbers. But three points need to be made here. First, we are not claiming that the knowledge being produced is somehow false; for example, because it is caught up in "fashion." The hard and fast lines between the kind of studied objectivity which, in its various forms, academic knowledge still strives for and the mutable contingencies of management knowledge were long ago broken down by surficial models of relativist or quasi-relativist approaches to knowledge, and the continuous process of osmosis between academic and management knowledge. But, second, that does not mean that we consider management knowledge to be neutral. The process of instrumentalized commodification that calls it into being brings with it a set of highly politicized values that cannot be denied;[16] values that underlie the influential spread of neoliberal policies through much of the world. Still, and third, both academic and management knowledges increasingly share certain values: a commitment to conceiving the world as continuously rolling over, continually on the brink; a commitment to fantasy as a vital element of how knowledge is constructed; and a commitment to tapping the fruitfulness of the contingency of the event.

One element of management knowledge that we want to foreground here is the constant attempt to produce new, more appropriate kinds of *subjects*, what we might call "souls" that fit contemporary, and especially future, systems of accumulation. In pursuit of high performance, both workers and managers must be refigured. Of course, this kind of explicit engineering is hardly new. F. W. Taylor and others plotted bodily configurations that they believed would produce better workers at the end of the 19th century. Similarly, by the middle of the 20th century, managers were beginning to be expected to embody themselves in ways that would make them better leaders. But the emergence of the subject as a quite explicit focus of management knowledge has taken on a new urgency of late, boosted by the growing power of human resources departments and the growing body of knowledge and practice devoted to such practices. In particular, we can see much greater attention being paid to attempts to produce "knowledgeable" subjects – by harnessing tacit knowledge, by producing communities of practice within which learning is a continuous activity, by working with and making more of affect, by understanding the minutiae of embodied time and space, and so on. In other words, a partially coherent set of practices of "government of the soul"[17] is starting to be produced by the cultural circuit of capital, a kind of instrumental phenomenology that can produce subjects that disclose the world as one that is uncertain and risky, but that can also be stabilized (in profitable ways) by the application of particular kinds of intense agency that are creative, entrepreneurial, and businesslike.

The State and the Global Schoolhouse

Of course, other organizations have interests in producing pliant but enterprising subjects, not least the state. And, as has been shown many times now, a considerable part of this interest has come about as states have become more and more aligned with global corporate interests, redescribing themselves as guarantors of economic growth through their ability to produce subjects attuned to this objective. *Enterprise* becomes both a characteristic and a goal of the new supply-side state. Nearly all Western states nowadays subscribe to a rhetoric and metric of modernization based upon fashioning citizens who can become an actively seeking factor of production, rather like a mineral resource with attitude. And that rhetoric, in turn, has been based upon a few key management tropes – globalization, knowledge, learning, network, flexibility, information technology, urgency – which are meant to come together in a new kind of self-willed subject whose industry will boost the powers of the state to compete economically, and will also produce a more dynamic citizenry.

Many of the states of Asia have bought into this rhetoric of a knowledge economy, often with good reason. Thus, beyond the purely economic advantage that is seen to arise from it, there is also its ability to both respect and minimize ethnic difference and to provide an unthreatening (or difficult to critique) national narrative.[18] Of these states, perhaps the most enthusiastic participant has been the paternalist but ultimately pragmatic Singapore,[19] which has been an independent city-state since 1965. Indeed, it would not be entirely unfair to say that Singapore has become a kind of management primer come true, with the fantasies of the serried rows of management texts in its main bookshops embodied in the person of its citizens and its "professional" migrant workers. In Singapore, accumulation often seems to have become the work of life, a passion of production (and consumption – Singaporeans are expected to be "prosumers") in its own right.

Periodically, prompted by circumstance, Singapore refocuses its economy. In the process, this "modern day garrison state" reworks a post-independence discourse of *survivalism*. Frequent tropes include both real and manufactured concerns about the country's small size and its resultant openness to competition from Malaysia, Hong Kong, and most recently China; the gradual run-down of its traditional long-term geographic advantages (such as the port); and its lack of natural resources and consequent dependence upon its people. This concern seemed to be confirmed by the Asian economic crisis of 1997–8, which meant that Singapore, though on the edge of events, saw its growth rate fall from 8 percent in 1997 to 1.5 percent in 1998. Singapore reacted predictably, with a 15 percent wage cut, a 30 percent reduction in rentals on industrial properties, and the liberalization of its financial sector (allowing for more foreign bank presence in the domestic banking sector). But the crisis also hastened a longer-term strategic shift, fuelled especially by the later downturn in information technology industries, as well as more general concerns about a sluggish world economy.

The government of Singapore, a technocratic "soft-authoritarian" adminstration that has been controlled by the People's Action Party (PAP) since 1959, is responsible for reshaping the economy. The Ministry of Trade and Industry (MTI) is the most important formal institutional mechanism for economic governance. While the MTI has only one functional department – the Singapore Department of Statistics – nine statutory boards (semi-independent and well resourced agencies) under the MTI jurisdiction carry out policy and program work. The most significant MTI statutory boards are the following:

- the Economic Development Board (EDB)
- the Singapore Productivity and Standards Board (PSB)
- the Singapore Trade Development Board (TDB)

The Singapore EDB[20] was founded in 1961 to formulate and implement economic development strategy for Singapore.[21] While relatively well resourced and staffed by Singaporeans, the EDB is open to the cultural circuit of capital through regular visits by management gurus and consultants – figures such as Tom Peters, Gary Hamel, and Michael Porter (the latter having worked with the EDB since 1986, and having been anointed as a "Business Friend of Singapore" in 2001).

While the EDB is the shaper and mediator of most economic change within Singaporean territory, a powerful guidance role is played by select committees that report on a one-off or *ad hoc* basis. An example of the former is the Committee on Singapore's Economic Competitiveness, which reported in 1998 on matters related to the Asian crisis. An example of the latter is the Economic Review Committee (ERC),[22] a Singapore-based network of state- and private-sector representatives responsible for making recommendations to generate structural shifts in the economy and society. The most recent ERC was set up by Prime Minister Goh Chok Tong in October 2001, with a mandate "to fundamentally review our development strategy and formulate a blueprint to restructure the economy, even as we work to ride out the current recession." The Committee's composition is revealing: nine members of the government or government functionaries (including the President of the National

University of Singapore), two trade union representatives, and nine private-sector representatives (including Arnoud De Meyer, the Dean of INSEAD's Singapore campus). Arnoud De Meyer also serves on the Sub-Committee on Service Industries in the ERC.

While the current ERC was given a relatively new mandate in 2001, it is building upon initiatives first established in the mid-1980s to promote the *services* sector as actively as manufacturing, thereby firing up "twin engines" in a city-state drive for more diversified economic growth.[23] This service-oriented agenda subsequently merged with the trope of the "knowledge-based economy" (KBE) that began circulating at a global scale in the 1990s. As Coe and Kelly demonstrate in the Singaporean case, this phrase first surfaced in a speech by the Prime Minister in 1994.[24] By 1998, the phrase was gaining some currency. By 1999 it was in wholesale circulation, having "seemingly entered the common vocabulary of all Ministers, bureaucrats and media commentators in Singapore."[25]

In line with the goal of transforming Singapore into "a vibrant and robust global hub for knowledge-driven industries," the EDB accordingly announced its detailed *Industry 21* strategy, a strategy whose product would be a Singapore capable of developing

> manufacturing and service industries with a strong emphasis on technology, innovation and capabilities. We also want to leverage on other hubs for ideas, talents, resources, capital and markets. To be a global hub and to compete globally, we require world-class capabilities and global reach. The goal is for Singapore to be a leading center of competence in knowledge-driven activities and a choice location for company headquarters, with responsibilities for product and capability charters.
>
> The knowledge-based economy will rely more on technology, innovation and capabilities to create wealth and raise the standard of living. For our knowledge-based economy to flourish, we will need a culture which encourages creativity and entrepreneurship, as well as an appetite for change and risk-taking.[26]

As this quote, and Lee Kuan Yew's statement at the start of this chapter, make clear, this strategy involves constructing an assemblage made up of a different set of "withs," and not least a major cultural change that consists of an upgrading of Singapore's labor force so as to make it more knowledgeable and entrepreneurial through a continuous process of learning.[27]

An important part of the *Industry 21* strategy is the creation of a "world-class" education sector that would import "foreign talent," both to expose Singaporean educational institutions to competition (thereby forcing them to upgrade), and to produce a diverse global education hub that is attractive to students from throughout the Pacific Asian region. In theory, this cluster of educational institutions would produce and disseminate knowledge at a range of scales, supporting local and foreign firms in Singapore, state institutions in Singapore, and firms and states in the Southeast, East, and South Asian regions.

Significantly, much of this educational strategy was concerned with those key institutions of the cultural circuit of capital, business schools. In turn, this hub would hypothetically act as the core of a series of industrial clusters, through spin-offs and the like in industries such as medicine, engineering, and the applied sciences. This education upgrade strategy hinged on attracting ten world-class educational institutions to set up independently or in collaboration with Singaporean partners by the year 2008, plus a series of large corporate training concerns. In fact, by late-2002 that target had been nearly been reached, with eight major educational institutions having signed agreements (see Table 15.1), three of them elite Western business schools.

Foreign education institutions are still arriving, with other universities from the United States and Australia apparently on the cards. This is without taking note

Table 15.1   Substantial Singapore–foreign university initiatives (as at November 2002)

	Initiatives (by date of establishment)
Johns Hopkins University (JHU)	Three medical divisions of JHU were established in January 1998: Johns Hopkins Singapore Biomedical Center, Johns Hopkins Singapore Affiliated Programs, and Johns Hopkins – National University Hospital International Medical Centre. These institutions facilitate collaborative research and education with Singapore's academic and medical communities. Web link: *http://www.jhs. com.sg/*. JHU's Peabody Institute is also collaborating with the National University of Singapore (NUS) to create the Singapore Conservatory of Music. An agreement was established in November 2001. Web link: *http://www.scm.nus.edu.sg/*
Massachusetts Institute of Technology (MIT)	The Singapore–MIT Alliance (SMA) was established in November 1998. Local alliance partners include the National University of Singapore (NUS) and Nanyang Technological University (NTU). The focus is on advanced engineering and applied computing. Web link: *http://web.mit.edu/sma/*
Georgia Institute of Technology (GIT)	The Logistics Institute – Asia Pacific (TLI–AP) was established in February 1999. TLI–AP is a collaboration between NUS and the Georgia Institute of Technology. TLI–AP trains engineers in specialized areas of global logistics, with emphasis on information and decision technologies. Web link: *http://www.tliap.nus.edu.sg/*
University of Pennsylvania (Penn)	Singapore Management University (SMU) was officially incorporated in January 2000. Wharton School faculty from the University of Pennsylvania (Penn) provided intellectual leadership in the formation of SMU's organizational structure and curriculum. The Wharton–SMU Research Center was also established at SMU: 306 students were enrolled in 2000, and 800 in 2001, with eventual enrollment levels expected to top out at 9,000 (6,000 undergraduates and 3,000 graduate students). A US$ 650 million campus is currently being built in Singapore's downtown. Web link: *http://www.smu. edu.sg/*

Continued

Table 15.1 *(continues)*

	Initiatives (by date of establishment)
INSEAD	INSEAD established its second campus in Singapore in January 2000. A US$ 40 million building was built to enable Singapore-based faculty, and European campus visiting faculty, to offer full- and part-time courses, as well as executive seminars. Web link: *http://www.insead.edu/*
University of Chicago	The University of Chicago Graduate School of Business (GSB) established a designated Singapore campus in July 2000, to offer the Executive MBA Program Asia to a maximum of 84 students per program. The curriculum is identical to the Chicago-based Executive MBA Program, and faculty are flown in from Chicago to teach on it. Web link: *http://gsb.uchicago.edu/*
Technische Universiteit Eindhoven (TU/e)	The Design Technology Institute (DTI), jointly administered by National University of Singapore (NUS) and Technische Universiteit Eindhoven (TU/e), was established in May 2001. The courses and projects offered by DTI are aimed at providing a balance between basic engineering concepts and product design and development. TU/e has strong links to Philips, both in the Netherlands and in Singapore. Web link: *http://www.dti.nus.edu.sg/*
Technische Universität München (TUM)	The National University of Singapore (NUS) and the Technische Universität München (TUM) established a joint Master's degree in Industrial Chemistry program in January 2002. The German Institute of Science and Technology (GIST) in Singapore coordinates this program, which is a joint entity established by TUM and the NUS Department of Chemistry. A significant proportion of specialists from industry will also be involved. Web link: *http://www.gist-singapore.com/*

of the numerous corporate organizations that have set up training facilities in Singapore, including the New York Institute of Finance (set up in 1997), which trains senior financial executives and professionals, Motorola University South East Asia, Cable and Wireless, Citibank, ABN Amro, St Microelectronics, Lucent Technologies, and so on.

In summary, elite institutions of higher education are recognized by the Singaporean state as playing a fundamental role in restructuring the economy via the refashioning of the local citizenry, while simultaneously providing retooling opportunities for the 75,000–100,000 professional migrants who use Singapore as a temporary base. The key idea is the creation of a virtuous circle: draw in the "best universities" with global talent; this talent then creates knowledge and knowledgeable subjects; these knowledgeable subjects, through their actions and networks, then create the professional jobs that drive a vibrant KBE. As Tharman Shanmugaratnam (Senior Minister of State for Trade and Industry) puts it, the government seeks to create "a new breed of Singaporean":

We have strong institutions and a highly credible government. We start from a position of strength, both financially and socially. All we want to have now is a stronger individual, more adaptable to the business world with a global mindset and concrete experience.[28]

And, again, elite business schools are perceived by the state to support (and attract to Singapore) the highly prized "global talent" associated with transnational corporations.

Negotiating the Global Schoolhouse

But these bare facts hide much of the process by which international educational interests were initially brought into alignment with the Singaporean state. Therefore, in this section we look at the way in which that alignment took place, by concentrating on the counterposed strategies of the Chicago GSB, INSEAD, and Wharton with the Singaporean state. Much of this section is based upon dialogue with people associated with new business schools in Singapore and with the National University of Singapore, as well as life experience and fieldwork in Singapore between 1997 and 2003.[29]

The Singaporean state had to make some significant changes of emphasis in order to accommodate these educational institutions with the aim of fashioning new subjects, while simultaneously branding Singapore as a global business education site.

The *first* change of emphasis relates to enhancing the *depth* of linkages between foreign universities and Singapore. Given that education can be viewed as a "service," it is helpful to delineate four modes or channels for the provision of educational services to "foreign" consumers:[30] (1) cross-border supply (for example, distance education); (2) consumption abroad (for example, foreign students studying in the United States); (3) commercial presence (for example, supplier of education via a newly established campus, or via the formation of a joint venture); and (4) the presence of natural persons (for example, academics travelling to a foreign country to run courses). Until the mid-1990s, Singapore was strongly incorporated into the first two modes of educational service provision. But a shift began to occur in the mid-to-late 1990s, when Singapore formally permitted and indeed encouraged foreign universities to establish relatively *deeper* commercial presences (3) in the city-state. However, this change of emphasis was selectively applied to Western universities deemed to be of "world-class" stature.[31]

The *second* change of emphasis related to the educational model that Singapore followed at the tertiary level. A geo-institutional realignment took place that demoted the long hegemonic British-based educational model, replacing it with the *American* model:

KO: I'm not assuming here, but is there a preference for universities from a particular geographic region?

LK/NUS: I think again this is interesting, because when we were talking about benchmarking issues, up to about three or four years ago, we were still talking about looking towards Britain and an RAE [Research Assessment Exercise] kind of model of evaluation and benchmarking. And it was quite clearly and quite starkly [altered] with this particular DPM's [Deputy Prime Minister] entry into the educational arena. I think it was around 1997, 1998 maybe. And there was a very clear, I think, and marked shift towards a North American, and in particular, a United States kind of a model and at that point in time, there also was this talk about being the Harvard of the East. It wasn't just North America, or just USA, but Harvard specifically. The institutions that we now look towards are of course more varied, more realistic perhaps, but certainly it is very much a United States sort of thing.

The reframing of the geo-institutional reference point for Singapore's higher education system took place quickly, and was driven by the Deputy Prime Minister and Minister of Defense (Tony Tan).[32]

LK/NUS: The common belief is that DPM Tony Tan came to know the North American system quite well, in part through his son who studied there [in Boston]. That may have influenced the way he thought about the higher education system.

Janice Bellace of Wharton echoed Lily Kong's comments as well. Tony Tan, though, was in no way the only Singaporean politician to look favorably upon the American system. Senior Minister Lee Kuan Yew has also pushed the American model *vis-à-vis* the development of more "entrepreneurial culture":

The difference between British and American values cannot be more profound. The US is a frontier society. By and large there were and are no class barriers. Everybody celebrated getting rich. Everybody wanted to be rich and tried to be. There is a great urge to start new enterprises and create wealth. The US has been the most dynamic society in innovating, in starting-up companies to commercialise new discoveries or inventions, thus creating new wealth. American society is always on the move and changing. They have led the world in patents, striving to produce something new or do something better, faster and cheaper, increasing productivity. Having created a product that sold well in America, they would then market it world-wide.

When I saw America's amazing recovery in the last ten years after it had lost so much ground to industries in Japan and Germany in the 1980s, I appreciated in full the meaning of Americans being "entrepreneurial." But for every successful entrepreneur in America, many have tried and failed. Quite a few tried repeatedly until they succeeded. Quite a few who succeeded continued to create and start up new companies as serial entrepreneurs. This was the way America's great companies were built. This is the spirit that generates a dynamic economy.[33]

This said, it is important to place our comments about these two admittedly powerful individuals (Lee and Tan) in context: the late 20th and early 21st centuries are an era in which American universities have generated increasingly positive (for the most part) attention in many parts of the world.

In turn, it is also clear that this move toward the United States was in part an attempt to increase Singapore's economic visibility across the Pacific, with select Americans associated with producing this prized "entrepreneurial culture." For many Americans, especially elite business school faculty, Singapore did not exist in their geographic imagination, or else it was viewed casually as an authoritarian hothouse, Asian style.

> JB/SMU&WHARTON: I want to stress that few people have visited Singapore. A significant number of Wharton faculty have been to Hong Kong, and some have been to China. And since the 1980s, everybody has managed to get to Japan. But Singapore is a place that people just have never visited. So for most of the Wharton faculty, it was unknown. The question I heard repeatedly was "What's Singapore like?" In the first two years here, the big challenge has been to get Wharton people out here, just to come out to visit. As you would expect, nearly everyone who has come out has been pleasantly surprised. The first surprise is that it is not like Hong Kong. Many people didn't realize that everything is in English here, and how modern and prosperous it is. The second surprise, and you can quote me on this, is that Singapore is not some sort of a police state. For many Wharton faculty, their vague impressions of Singapore are based on articles like those in *The Economist*. I tell my colleagues that they don't understand what *The Economist* means when they call Singapore "the nanny state," and that some mistakenly assume it is like a former Communist eastern European state. I tell them to think about how a British nanny interacts with the children. She exhorts them to behave themselves and to improve themselves. It might seem strange in the U.S. if the head of the government in a major speech were to tell the people to speak better English, but to Singaporeans it seems natural for the Prime Minister to say that, and they simply view it as something the government should say if it is important for the economic vitality of Singapore. Once Wharton faculty visit and experience how Singaporeans act in everyday life, they better understand exactly what is meant by "the nanny state."

The *third* change of emphasis was concerned with freedom of speech for foreign academics. Some of the principles that the Singaporean government held dear had to be shifted a little – but only a little – in order to accommodate academic concerns:

> ADM/INSEAD: I don't want to put words in their mouths but they really don't care about publishing research results in journals that nobody reads. What they are concerned about is publishing in nonacademic journals with wide circulations in Singapore. More specifically, there are three specific areas that we have to be careful about. First, we cannot get involved in any activity that stimulates racial or religious tensions. If we do so, we are going to get immediately cracked up. Second, and they didn't phrase it this way but this is my reading of it: Singapore has two big Muslim countries as neighbors and we have to be careful, we cannot start insulting Muslims, etc. And third, they basically said that if we get ourselves involved in local politics, we better get our bags packed . . . We as faculty said that we have no problems with the first two areas because we are not in the business of creating racial or religious tensions, and we are not in the business of insulting countries. Local politics, we are

not interested in it, because Singapore is far too small for our interests. So it was like yes, we can live with it.

KO: Was this a written agreement or was it just a verbal understanding?

ADM/INSEAD: This was a verbal understanding; we don't have that on paper, but it was very consistent throughout our conversations.

The comments of Arnoud De Meyer were matched in tone by Janice Bellace and by Gary Hamada, Dean of the University of Chicago GSB.[34] In other words, the Singaporean state made it relatively clear (in comparison to its policies toward indigenous universities and academics) that greater academic freedom was being permitted, subject to some locally – and regionally – oriented "out-of bounds" topics. This policy generated some realignment within the three Western business schools (for they are used to complete academic freedom), but it left them satisfied that they could conduct their type of work in what is a relatively more authoritarian political context.

These three changes of emphasis – a deeper foreign university presence within Singaporean space, a different kind of educational model, and relatively more academic freedom – laid the foundations for the stretching of the institutional architecture of elite Western universities across global space. The realignment of Singaporean priorities was clearly not enough, however, to draw in elite universities that had already embarked upon globalization drives. What also mattered was government support via the powers and capacities of the developmental state (for example, targeted financial subsidies), along with doses of bureaucratic persistence and persuasion. For example, the EDB played an important role in courting select universities in R&D-rich contexts (for example, Boston). However, universities are less hierarchical than the transnational corporations that Singapore is used to dealing with. As Tan Chek Ming, Director of EDB Services Development, put it, "Every faculty member has to agree. All you need is one person to disagree and the whole deal will be thrown out of alignment." In this context, EDB

team members act as tour guides, flying in faculty staff for a look-see trip to Singapore. The usual highlight is a meeting between the dons and senior Cabinet Ministers, namely Deputy Prime Minister Tony Tan, who oversees university education, Education Minister Teo Chee Hean, and Trade and Industry Minister George Yeo.

These meetings are important, stresses Mr Tan, as they send a strong signal to the visitors of the political will and commitment in drawing reputable universities to Singapore. Team members also double up as property agents, scouting around for suitable premises in Singapore to locate the foreign university. They also help look into the legal and financial aspects of setting up shop in Singapore.[35]

In order to tempt business schools, the EDB played up Singapore's cosmopolitan nature, and then used tangible material resources in the form of financial and other incentives. For example, INSEAD received $10 million in research funding over four years, plus soft loans, reduced land values (about one-third of the commercial price), easier-to-get work permits, housing access, and so on. The University of Chicago GSB received several million dollars worth of subsidy via the renovation of the historic House of Tan Yeok Nee building that they now use as their "campus." Finally, the government of Singapore effectively funds the Wharton–SMU Research Center at SMU,[36] providing monetary and in-kind support for research projects, seminars, scholarships, and the like.

These forms of material support are clearly important, and short- and long-term financial opportunities needed to be viewed favorably by the three business schools before they would commit the necessary intellectual and material resources required to stretch complicated institutional fabric across space. But there were some additional factors that led the cultural circuit of capital into Singapore space: the city-state's strategic geographic position within Asia (boosted by Changi Airport, an efficient award-winning airport 20–30 minutes' taxi ride from all three campuses), "quality of life" for expatriates, the fact that many alumni were Singaporean, and the large number of transnational corporations with presences in Singapore. All of these factors were often put together as "international feel" or a genuinely "cosmopolitan nature;" characteristics associated with global cities.[37] As Arnoud De Meyer of INSEAD put it:

> ADM/INSEAD: We developed a business plan and finally chose Singapore because it stood out in terms of government support for business, and for us the "international feel." I often say, and you would be able to relate to this, that Singapore is more international than Hong Kong. Hong Kong is a Chinese city. I remember when I took two groups of faculty and major administrators for a tour of Hong Kong, Kuala Lumpur and Singapore. When visiting each city I brought them outside the central business district. I brought them to Woodlands, in the case of Singapore, to show them an HDB [public housing] environment. Some of our faculty and administrators might live in such areas, or else in expatriate enclaves, yet often be forced to interact with such areas. I still remember when one of my colleagues made an interesting remark: she said that when she went to Hong Kong and she got out of the city [i.e., the city center], she really felt that she was in a "Chinese" city. When she went to KL [Kuala Lumpur] she saw Indians, Malays, Chinese, and Caucasians on the streets but she never saw them together. But when she went to Woodlands [in Singapore] she saw these people together. Or the fact that all taxi drivers understand English. That was part of why we felt comfortable here. It's little things like that.

The selection process in all cases was relatively systematic:

> ADM/INSEAD: I initiated INSEAD's Asia campus feasibility study in June 1995. In 1996, I visited 11 cities in Asia amidst my other work. At this time there was a lot of pressure from the [INSEAD] Board to move fast. We had six criteria to judge the potential of each of the locations. We wanted, from the very beginning, to have faculty stationed in Asia because the Euro-Asia Centre was already flying faculty in and out. The additional objective of establishing an Asia campus for INSEAD was to develop our faculty. This idea of linking the establishment of an Asia campus to the development of our faculty makes us very different from Chicago or Wharton.

The first criterion we considered was quality of life for professionals.

The second criterion related to good communications infrastructure. There also had to be a bit of time-zone overlap between our French campus and the prospective Asian campus. The time-zone differential effectively excluded Japan because of the eight-hour time difference during the European winter. In other words, time-zone overlap with respect to telephone usage becomes much more complicated in Japan.

Thirdly, we wanted to have a place that had "international" appeal.

Fourthly, we wanted a place that had other good universities. We were aware that even with 50 faculty in Singapore, we would be a very small group and we wanted interaction with other scholars, a place with a lot of flow of people so that we would have visitors.

The fifth point is that we looked for a place where there was government and business support for the concept.

There was probably a sixth element, that of the perceived "neutrality" of the place, although it was really an afterthought. For example, KL [Kuala Lumpur] is less neutral than Singapore. Similarly, Shanghai is less neutral than Singapore.

Cost was actually not part of our decision criteria. It would be foolish to say that it was irrelevant but it was not a major issue. When we developed that grid of five to six criteria and related it to the 11 cities that I looked at, about eight disappeared very quickly. Shanghai was impossible in terms of its politics. Perth was too far away in terms of communications. Tokyo and Osaka fell through very quickly as well. In short, applying this grid to the potential cities led to a number of them falling out very quickly. We were left with KL, Hong Kong, and Singapore. But in each place we were considering three different development models. Here, in Singapore, we have a free-standing campus. In KL we were looking at a joint venture with a number of large companies. In Hong Kong, we were looking at either a free-standing campus, a small subsidiary, or a takeover/joint venture with an existing business school.

As Arnoud De Meyer's last comment points out, there are a variety of modes of entry to Singapore space, and the government of Singapore allowed the business schools to identify their own mode of entry (versus forcing them to engage in joint ventures, as is required in Malaysia). Though each of the three schools (Wharton, INSEAD, and Chicago) were simultaneously globalizing their business education and research programs, INSEAD chose a relatively high-risk new-product strategy, building a completely new offshoot of INSEAD, with some of its own priorities and research agendas (in comparison to the larger Fontainebleau campus). At the other end of the spectrum of risk was the Wharton approach via intellectual influence on a local provider. Through collaboration with the Singapore government in the establishment of Singapore Management University, most risk for Wharton was dispersed to the state. Finally, the Chicago GSB was somewhere in between, seeking to export its fixed products more efficiently. It had already established a new subsidiary campus in Europe (Barcelona) in 1994, and it wanted to reproduce a similar model in Pacific Asia.

These three divergent models were, in part, prompted by willingness to take financial risk, but also by the forms of business knowledge that were being developed and diffused. INSEAD has a more heterogeneous and institutionalist view of business knowledge. This form of knowledge requires the formation of relatively deep regional (that is, Asian) knowledge and networks. In contrast, Chicago has a very explicit, fixed, and universal model, based on economics, statistics, and the behavioral sciences:

> BB/CHICAGO: When we planned to establish our two international campuses in Barcelona and Singapore, we wanted to offer an educational product identical to what we offer in Chicago. Since the quality of our faculty members is so integral to the quality of our MBA programs, we felt that the only way to assure that the programs offered in Barcelona, Singapore and Chicago were identical was for the same faculty to teach in all three programs. So our regular Chicago-based faculty members "commute" to Barcelona and Singapore for one week at a time to teach in these programs. Each faculty member makes two trips to deliver his or her course in two one-week modules, rather than two 90-minute sessions per week over ten weeks, for example, as in our full-time program in Chicago.
>
> Now clearly, the limitation of this model is that we cannot expand very much. We admit 84 students per year to each of the three branches of the Executive MBA program. Because of the limitation on faculty resources, we do not have any plans to add to the size of our existing programs or to establish additional campuses.

As Beth Bader's comments imply, the Chicago School trains up students via a universal program that need not account for significant difference across space. Gary Eppen, the GSB's associate dean, put it even more bluntly: "Demand curves don't slope up in Taiwan. Demand curves slope down everywhere in the world." The GSB teaches "fundamental concepts that you should be able to apply wherever you are."[38]

Conclusions

This chapter has sought to describe the way in which the cultural circuit of capital has become aligned with the state and has thereby increasingly become involved in global geo-political interventions. These interventions are producing new forms of governmentality that privilege the mass production of knowledgeable and enterprising subjects, subjects who can simultaneously optimize their relationship to themselves and to work. We paid particular attention to the case of Singapore as a story of how what are still relatively loose functions that bring into play populations, territories, affects, and events can find *common cause* in particular places, at particular times, and can coevolve new strategies of government that are intended to recode Singapore's citizens. The injection of new knowledges into Singapore space is designed to create "a new breed of Singaporean," one that will be more entrepreneurial, connected to the world, yet (so the state hopes) still committed to "our best home." Moreover, these new strategies of government are designed to enable the local and regionally based professional migrants (expatriates) to discipline themselves through a continual "upgrading" process, spur on restructuring in indigenous universities, and simultaneously "brand" Singapore as a suitable hub for "global talent."

So far as Singapore is concerned, the strategy of bringing the cultural circuit of capital and the state together as a relatively loose and opportunistic assemblage is clearly intended to be a critical element of "Remaking Singapore," one that – if successful – may lift Singapore further out of the Southeast Asian region, flinging it into an orbit where its region can be the globe itself:

> ADM/INSEAD: The locational advantages of Singapore, and the nearby region (including Johor Bahru in Malaysia and Batam in Indonesia) are eroding. Singapore is being challenged by China, Vietnam, and some parts of India. In other words geographical proximity is not as valuable as it once was. How do you replace that? At the level of the Singapore government, an idea is developing that Singapore should "move out of the neighborhood." So I see the development model being focused on remaking Singapore into a center of excellence that is linked to Tokyo and San Francisco and Munich, rather than being a service center for the region. Is this a good idea? I'm not sure. That's very difficult for me to judge, but I do see a policy that is moving in this direction. It is clearly a big bet; one that is being pursued at the top level of government.

Of course, as Arnoud De Meyer implies, no strategy is without risk. One risk is that the strategy of attracting the cultural circuit of capital will be too successful, and that the pile-up of new educational institutions of one sort or another will grow beyond what the student market in Singapore and the region can deliver. Indeed, in September 2002 the ERC recommended that Singapore become a "Global Schoolhouse" for an "additional 100,000 international fee-paying students and 100,000 international corporate executives for training,"[39] a challenging policy goal for both the state and the cultural circuit of capital, to put it but mildly. Another risk is that the informal agreement on academic freedom for these foreign universities will be tested, just as foreign media freedoms in Singapore are tested from time to time. One more risk is that contradictions may emerge between economic sectors in this small island nation: a services sector, and services employees, that demand high quality of life, versus a fast-growing chemicals sector, one that is injecting increasing volumes of noxious emissions into the atmosphere of the coastal zones. In any of these cases, the elite brand-name business schools may move on to pastures new, in which case an Asian tiger may find itself having caught a rather larger tiger by the tail; a tiger that can consign it to the place where all the old management ideas go. What is clear, then, is that the future shape and effectiveness of the set of assemblages that are associated with making "literate and numerate minds to be more innovative, to be more productive" has yet to be fully worked through.

Notes

1   We would both like to thank the National University of Singapore (especially the Department of Geography) for its generous support. Aihwa Ong and Stephen Collier were most

gracious hosts for the workshop at which the original version of this chapter was first presented. Kris Olds would also like to acknowledge the assistance of all interviewees, some anonymous Singapore-based professionals, and important financial support from the U.S. Department of Education via the University of Wisconsin-Madison Center for International Business Education and Research (CIBER).

2 K. Hamlin, "Remaking Singapore," *Institutional Investor*, May 2002.

3 *Straits Times*, February 9, 2001.

4 N. J. Thrift, "The Rise of Soft Capitalism," *Cultural Values* 1, 1997, pp. 29–57; N. J. Thrift, "Virtual Capitalism: Some Proposals," in *Virtualism: The New Political Economy*, J. Carrier and D. Miller, eds. (Oxford: Berg, 1998); N. J. Thrift, "The Place of Complexity," *Theory, Culture and Society* 12(3), 1999, pp. 31–70; N. J. Thrift, "Think and Act Like Revolutionaries: Episodes from the Global Triumph of Management Discourse," *Critical Quarterly* 44, 2002, pp. 19–26.

5 K. Olds, *Globalization and Urban Change. Capital, Culture and Pacific Rim Mega-Projects* (Oxford: Oxford University Press, 2001).

6 G. Deleuze and C. Parnet, *Dialogues*, trans. H. Tomlinson and B. Habberjam (New York: Columbia University Press, 1987), pp. 51–52.

7 ERC, *Developing Singapore's Education Industry* (Singapore: ERC, 2002); available at http://www.erc.gov.sg/frm_ERC_ErcReports.htm

8 T. Peters and R. Waterman, *In Search of Excellence* (New York: Warner Books, 1982).

9 T. Peters, "True Confessions," *Fast Company* 53, 2001, p. 78.

10 R. ten Bos, *Fashion and Utopia in Management Thinking* (Amsterdam and Philadelphia: John Benjamins Publishers, 2002), p. 22.

11 Thrift, "The Place of Complexity."

12 K. Vann and G. Bowker, "Instrumentalizing the Truth of Practice," *Social Epistemology* 15(3), 2001, pp. 247–262.

13 P. Dicken, *Global Shift: Transforming the World Economy*, 3rd edition (London: Paul Chapman, 1998).

14 S. Roberts, "Global Strategic Vision: Managing the World," in *Globalization and Governmentalities*, R. Perry and B. Maurer, eds. (Minneapolis: University of Minnesota Press, 2002).

15 L. Boltanski and E. Chiapello, *Le nouvel esprit du capitalisme* (Paris: Gallimard, 1999).

16 Vann and Bowker, *Instrumentalizing the Truth*; Y. Dezalay and B. Garth, *The Internationalization of Palace Wars: Lawyers, Economists, and the Contest to Transform Latin American States* (Chicago: University of Chicago Press, 2002).

17 N. Rose, *Powers of Freedom: Reframing Political Thought* (Cambridge: Cambridge University Press, 1999).

18 Cf., T. Bunnell, "(Re)positioning Malaysia: High-Tech Networks and the Multicultural Rescripting of National Identity," *Political Geography* 21, 2002, pp. 105–124.

19 L. Low, ed., *Singapore: Towards a Developed Status* (Singapore: Oxford University Press, 1999).

20 See http://www.sedb.com/

21 E. Schein, *Strategic Pragmatism: The Culture of Singapore's Economic Development Board* (Cambridge, MA: The MIT Press, 1996); Low, *Singapore: Towards a Developed Status*; C. B. Chan, ed., *Heart Work: Stories of How EDB Steered the Singapore Economy from 1961 into the 21st Century* (Singapore: EDB, 2002).

22 See http://www.erc.gov.sg/

23   ERC, *Report of the ERC Subcommittee on Services Industries: Part 1* (Singapore: ERC, 2002); available at http://www.erc.gov.sg/frm_ERC_ErcReports.htm

24   N. Coe and P. Kelly, "Distance and Discourse in the Local Labour Market: the Case of Singapore," *Area* 32(4), 2000, pp. 413–422.

25   Coe and Kelly, "Distance and Discourse," p. 418; also see N. Coe and P. Kelly, "Languages of Labour: Representational Strategies in Singapore's Labour Control Regime," *Political Geography* 21, 2002, pp. 341–371.

26   See http://www.sedb.com, May 20, 2001.

27   While beyond the scope of this chapter, it is important to note that a series of interrelated reform initiatives took place in Singapore in the latter half of the 1990s via the Ministry of Education (especially the "Thinking Schools, Learning Nation" initiative that was launched in 1997), and the Ministry of Manpower's M21 initiative. These reforms continue to be developed, implemented, and debated, and are now becoming more tightly integrated with higher education reforms as guided by Dr. Ng Eng Hen, Singapore's Minister of State (Education and Manpower) (Ministry of Education, 2003).

28   *Straits Times*, March 17, 2002, p. 18.

29   Formal interviews and correspondence with key actors took place in June 2001 and October 2002. JB/SMU&WHARTON refers to Janice Bellace, President, Singapore Management University. Professor Bellace was the first President of SMU, and she stepped down in September 2001, becoming Vice-Chairman (Academic Affairs) of SMU's Board of Trustees. Professor Bellace is Samuel Blank Professor of Legal Studies, The Wharton School, University of Pennsylvania. LK/NUS refers to Lily Kong, Dean, Faculty of Arts and Social Sciences, National University of Singapore. ADM/INSEAD refers to Arnoud De Meyer, Dean, INSEAD Singapore Campus. BB/CHICAGO refers to Beth Bader, Managing Director, Executive MBA Program Asia, University of Chicago Graduate School of Business. KO is Kris Olds. Kris Olds worked in Singapore from 1997 to June 2001 at the Department of Geography, National University of Singapore, and conducted field research in Singapore in November 2001 and January 2003. It is also important to note that Nigel Thrift acted as an external examiner for Nanyang Technological University, and was a Distinguished Visiting Professor at NUS from January to April 2002.

30   S. Kemp, "Trade in education services and the impacts of barriers to trade," in *Impediments to Trade in Services: Measurement and Policy Implications*, C. Findlay and T. Warren, eds. (London: Routledge, 2000), pp. 231–244.

31   Some visiting academics to NUS from universities not included in the "world class" line-up have spoken of Singapore's "Gucci complex."

32   Tony Tan's current positions as Deputy Prime Minister, Minister of Defense, and Minister of Higher Education began in 1995 and continue to the present date. This is the same period in which the U.S. higher education model gained much more influence in Singapore. Tony Tan is relatively unusual in that whereas the majority of similarly aged Singaporean politicians studied in England, he has a master's degree from MIT.

33   Lee Kuan Yew, "An Entrepreneurial Culture for Singapore," address by Senior Minister Lee Kuan Yew at the Ho Rih Hwa Leadership in Asia Public Lecture Series, Singapore Management University, Singapore, February 5, 2002.

34   X. Boruk, "Chicago Business School picks Singapore – university to open permanent campus for Executive MBA students," *Asian Wall Street Journal*, January 25, 1999, p. 6.

35   M. Nirmala, "Campus Courtships," *Straits Times*, June 24, 2001, p. R1.

36 See http://www.smu.edu.sg/research/

37 K. Olds, *Globalization and Urban Change*; S. Sassen, *The Global City: New York, London, Tokyo*, 2nd edition (Princeton, NJ: Princeton University Press, 2001).

38 B. Dolven, "Business Class," *Far Eastern Economic Review*, February 10, 2000, pp. 48–49.

39 ERC, *Developing Singapore's Education Industry*.

MANAGING UNCERTAINTY

16

HETERARCHIES OF VALUE:
Distributing Intelligence and Organizing Diversity in a New Media Startup

MONIQUE GIRARD AND DAVID STARK

Introduction

What's valuable? Economic sociologists, like their discipline in general, have given considerable attention to the problem of *values*.[1] But in doing so they have conceded the problem of *value* to economists. In its modern form, economic sociology arguably began with Talcott Parsons' pact with economics: You, the economists, study value; we, the sociologists, will study values. You study the economy; we will study the social relations in which economies are embedded. But economic sociology can be recast with a different agenda – as the *sociology of worth*.

In this move, the polysemic character of the term – worth – signals a concern with core problems of value while recognizing that the task of valuation can work with multiple evaluative frameworks. We see this in everyday life. "What are you worth?" is a question that can be unambiguous when constrained by context (as, for example, when applying for a mortgage). But the question "Yes, but what is it worth?" already suggests that value might be different from price. And the question, "Girl, do you really think he's worth it?" is one that brings several evaluative criteria into play. Social life is a place of perplexity and sometimes wonder precisely because of these problems of incommensurability. Political life, similarly, is rich not simply in competition over worthiness but in contention over the very criteria to assess it.

The life of business organizations is no less an arena of puzzlement and contention over issues of worth. To take even one step from the simplest textbook is to move into a world of competing metrics rather than easy consensus about the proper yardsticks. By which metric should I measure the value of a property, a stock, a company? What are the relevant criteria for assessing the value of an employee's contribution? These questions are particularly acute in times of rapid economic, technological, and social change when contention about how to measure "performance" is less a by-product of change than an engine of dynamism. Such was the time of the "New Economy" and such is our object of investigation. Our task is not to assess whether that phenomenon was "new" but to examine the challenges facing the companies and the people that participated in it. We seek to document the process whereby firms navigated in uncertain territory. We examine in detail the process of collaborative organization and demonstrate how the multiple registers for assessing performance were a source of innovation. We do so by studying construction sites.

These construction sites had subcontractors but no cement; they had architects, but no steel; they had engineers and designers and builders who built for retail firms, financial services, museums, government, and cultural institutions, but no one ever set foot into their constructions. These architects were information architects, the engineers were software and systems engineers, the designers were interactive designers, and the builders were site builders – all working in the Internet consulting firms that were the construction companies for the digital real estate boom that marks the turn of the millennium.

From the spring of 1999 through the spring of 2001, we were fortunate to be able to observe one of these startup firms and watch its website construction projects, not through a Plexiglas peephole, but close-up as ethnographic researchers. What we found, in almost every aspect, was a project perpetually "under construction." At the same time that the software engineers and interactive designers were constructing websites, they were also constructing the firm and the project form. And this relentless redesign of the organization was occurring simultaneously with the construction, emergence, consolidation, dissipation, and reconfiguration of the industry itself. "What is New Media?" This was the question we encountered numerous times scribbled on whiteboards in brainstorming sessions during or just prior to our meetings in various interactive companies. Or, as one of our informants posed the question, "People are always trying to come up with a metaphor for a website. Is it a magazine, a newspaper, a TV commercial, a community? Is it a store? You know, it's none of these . . . and it's all of these and others, in many variations and combinations. So, there's endless debate." Of one thing you could be certain: if you were sure you knew the answer, the pace of organizational innovation to make new business models, the pace of technological innovation to make new affordances, and the pace of genre innovation to make new conceptualizations had likely combined to make your answer already obsolete.

What is a new media firm? In answering the question, the startups did not start from scratch. The form of the firm and the shape of projects were borrowed from prior existing models. Many were shaped around the consulting firm model; others adopted the model of an architectural firm, an advertising agency, a film or television studio, a software engineering or systems integration company, a design studio, a venture capital firm, or the editorial model of a magazine.[2] Forming the basic template, these models were repurposed for new functionalities as well as recombined for new purposes (e.g., consulting model + systems integrator, media production studio + venture capital model, etc.).

But whatever the choice of model (and note that, with few exceptions, most firms studiously avoided the "construction company" moniker), every new media firm that was in the business of constructing websites had to cope not only with the problem that the field was in flux but also that every successful innovation in carving a niche, creating a new product, defining a new business model, or introducing a new technology could be replicated by competitors. Unlike other high tech firms in fields such as biotechnology where patents could protect intellectual property, in the new media field innovations were not likely to yield a stream of rents. Under circumstances of low barriers to entry (because innovations—in genre, technology, and organization—could be easily assimilated), firms were forced to be relentlessly innovative.

Thus, firms could not prosper simply by learning from their construction projects. It was not enough to master the project form, to codify, routinize, or even perfect what they had been doing. If you locked-in to what you had done previously, regardless of how much you improved performance by your existing criterion, you would be locked out of markets that were changing rapidly. On the other side, if you spent all your organizational resources searching for new products and processes, always and everywhere exploring for new opportunities, you would never be able to exploit your existing knowledge. For the new media companies, March's problem of "exploration versus exploitation" could be rephrased as the problem of staying ahead of the curve without getting behind on your deadlines.[3]

When coping with complex foresight horizons,[4] where dislocations can be anticipated in general but are unpredictable in their specific contours, firms must be perpetually poised to pursue innovation. They must build organizations that are not only capable of learning but also capable of suspending accepted knowledge and established procedures to redraw cognitive categories and reconfigure relational boundaries – both at the level of the products and services produced by the firm and at the level of the working practices and production processes within the firm. Organizations must innovate in ways that allow them to re-cognize, redefine, recombine, and redeploy resources for further innovation. In other words, organizations must "invest in forms"[5] that allow for easy reconfiguration and hence minimize the costs of "divestment" or reorganization. Such capacities for organizational innovation must go beyond the discovery of new means to carry out existing functions more effectively and efficiently. Under conditions of radical uncertainty, organizations that simply improve their *adaptive fit* to the current environment risk sacrificing *adaptability* in subsequent dislocations.[6]

Organizational ecologists have long held that adaptability is promoted by the diversity of organizations within a population. The perspective adopted here, by contrast, is that adaptability is promoted by the *organization of diversity* within an enterprise. The adaptive potential of organizational diversity may be most fully realized when different organizational principles coexist in an active rivalry *within the firm*. By rivalry, we do not refer to competing camps and factions, but to coexisting logics and frames of action. The organization of diversity is an active and sustained engagement in which there is more than one way to organize, label, interpret, and evaluate the same or similar activity. Rivalry fosters cross-fertilization. It increases the possibilities of long-term adaptability by better search – "better" because the complexity that it promotes and the lack of simple coherence that it tolerates increase the diversity of options.

We explore these themes by examining the collaborative interactions among the multi-disciplinary project teams working in a Silicon Alley new media firm. First, we establish the highly uncertain environment within which new media firms operate, with the paramount uncertainty being the shifting content, parameters, and value of the new media industry itself. What is the meaning and where is the value of new media? We then sketch the organizational features required of new media firms to deftly reassess the shifting terrain and adjust their positioning and strategy. Most salient among these features is the organization of diversity and lateral accountability, properties constitutive of a new mode of organizing that we characterize as *heterarchy.* We then explore the dynamics of heterarchical organization by examining the process of collaborative engineering involved in the construction of websites. In this process prominence given to the competing evaluative and performance criteria specific to the multiple disciplines is matched by a scaling back of administrative hierarchy. In place of directives, the multiple disciplines engage in a discursive pragmatics in which the disciplined judgment needed to do a good job is balanced with compromise needed to get the job done. Sharing the responsibility for getting the work done, one fights to promote the values of one's discipline, but one yields out of allegiance to the project and the firm. By distributing authority, the firm yields control of disciplined argument but wins the competitive edge that results by cultivating a diversity of options in face of uncertainty.

An Ecology of Value

Silicon Alley: new firms in an uncertain environment

Silicon Alley is a (post)industrial district that can be thought of first as *a place*, running south of 41st Street along Broadway through the Flatiron District and Soho into Chelsea and down to Wall Street. But it is also, and just as importantly, *a social space* between Wall Street and Midtown, linking the financial district to the traditional big advertising firms and the traditional big media companies in broadcast and publishing. In this case, the physical place and the social space are, not coincidentally, isomorphic. By 1999, new media was one of New York's fastest growing sectors with almost 100,000 full-time equivalent employees in Manhattan alone (that is, more than the city's traditional publishing and traditional advertising industries combined) and with an estimated 8,500 new media companies in the larger New York City area.[7] In that same year, the New York new media industry produced revenues of $16.8 billion and generated $1.5 billion in venture capital funding and $3.5 billion in IPO funding.

Bolstered by industry associations, promoted by government officials, and exuberantly championed by its trade publications, the public face of these new media companies showed a brash self-confidence. But they were acutely aware that they were operating in a highly uncertain environment. Their statements to the Securities and Exchange Commission (SEC) upon filing for an Initial Public Offering (IPO) provide a chorus of this uncertainty. (All statements in bold or italics are quotations from SEC filings by Silicon Alley new media firms.)

Among the risk factors reported by these new media firms are some standard items commonly found in almost all SEC filings. More interesting are those factors common to early stage companies in which the elapsed time from startup to IPO is brief:

(1) **We have an extremely limited operating history and may face difficulties encountered by early stage companies in new and rapidly evolving markets.**
(2) **Our recent growth has strained our managerial and operational resources.**
Our recent acquisitions have created financial and other challenges, which, if not addressed or resolved, could have an adverse effect on our business. We acquired five businesses during 1998 and completed our merger with [another new media firm] in January 1999. We are experiencing certain financial, operational and managerial challenges in integrating these acquired companies. This process of integration . . . will require the dedication of management and other resources, which may distract management's attention from our other operations.

For some new media firms, the liabilities of newness were extreme, as in this case where almost all the senior personnel were newcomers to the company:

(3) **Several members of senior management have only recently joined the company.**
Several members of our senior management joined us in 1998 and 1999, [this from a March 1999 filing] including our Chief Financial Officer, Chief Operating Officer, Senior Vice President for Sponsorship, General Counsel, Vice President for Finance, Controller and Chief Accounting Officer, Senior Vice President for Human Resources, and the Chief Technology Officer. These individuals have not previously worked together and are becoming integrated as a management team.

In a tight labor market, loss of "old hands" is a real threat and, in this knowledge-based industry, would spell a loss of the company's primary assets, especially where contacts to clients are contacts through personnel:

(4) **The loss of our professionals would make it difficult to complete existing projects and bid for new projects, which could adversely affect our business and results of operations.**

Moreover, assets are not contained within the boundaries of the firm but are distributed across a network of interdependent firms. In choosing partners, alliances, and technologies, winners cannot be known in advance:

> **(5) We may not be able to deliver various services if third parties fail to provide reliable software, systems, and related services to us**.
> *We are dependent on various third parties for software, systems and related services. For example, we rely on [another Internet company's] software for the placement of advertisements and [another Internet company] for personal home pages and e-mail. Several of the third parties that provide software and services to us have a limited operating history, have relatively immature technology and are themselves dependent on reliable delivery of services from others.*
> **(6) Our market is characterized by rapidly changing technologies, frequent new product and service introductions, evolving industry standards, and changing customer demands. The recent growth of the Internet and intense competition in our industry exacerbate these market characteristics.**

In a newly emerging field, measuring assets is also complicated by the absence of industry standards and by uncertain government regulations:

> **(7) The market for Internet advertising is uncertain.**
> *There are currently no standards for the measurement of the effectiveness of Internet advertising, and the industry may need to develop standard measurements to support and promote Internet advertising as a significant advertising medium.*
> **(8) Government regulation and legal uncertainties could add additional costs to doing business on the Internet**.

Being a frontrunner in an emerging field is only a temporary advantage where there are few barriers to entry, no patentable rents, and larger and more established firms ready to exploit the profitable activities revealed by the trials and errors of the pioneering startups:

> **(9) We compete in a new and highly competitive market that has low barriers to entry.**
> **(10) We do not own any patented technology that precludes or inhibits competitors from entering the information technology services market.**
> **(11) We expect competition to intensify as the market evolves. We compete with: Internet service firms; technology consulting firms; technology integrators; strategic consulting firms; and in-house information technology, marketing and design departments of our potential clients.**
> **(12) Many of our competitors have longer operating histories, larger client bases, longer relationships with clients, greater brand or name recognition and significantly greater financial, technical, marketing and public relations resources than we have.**

Above all, will e-commerce prove viable? Will the Internet as we know it be sustainable? Will it continue to grow? And might it mutate into unpredictable forms?

(13) **Our business may be indirectly impacted if the number of users on the Internet does not increase or if commerce over the Internet does not become more accepted and widespread.**

(14) **If the Internet is rendered obsolete or less important by faster, more efficient technologies, we must be prepared to offer non-Internet-based solutions or risk losing current and potential clients. In addition, to the extent that mobile phones, pagers, personal digital assistants or other devices become important aspects of digital communications solutions, we need to have the technological expertise to incorporate them into our solutions.**

Hence, at the height of exuberance of the Internet bubble, the following sober assessment:

(15) **We anticipate continued losses and we may never be profitable.**

Searching for value in an evolving ecology

Our litany of risk factors in the Silicon Alley IPO filing statements points to the difficulties of evaluating Internet stocks. But over and above the problem of the market figuring out what these firms are worth is an even more interesting uncertainty: How do the firms themselves figure out what is *the basis of their worth*? To be clear, the problem is not in establishing the level of their market capitalization, which in any case is set by the market, but of surveying their actual and potential activities to discover what they are doing (or could be doing) that is of value.

Many of the Silicon Alley new media firms that were formed during the initial expansion of the web around 1995 began their operations designing websites. Suddenly, every corporation, it seemed, needed a website. This surge in demand for the skills of designers and programmers created a sizeable niche, with relatively few players, and a yawning knowledge gap between producers and clients. The folk history of the industry is strown with stories by the startup entrepreneurs who tell of their early experiences with mid-level corporate managers who had never surfed the web but who had been instructed by senior executives of major corporations to "get us a website!"

Many of the twenty-something new media pioneers were rebounding from a string of marginal jobs, having graduated from college after the 1987 stock market crash and the following recession that devastated the New York City economy. With the sudden expansion of the web, their generational position, which had seemed such a liability, now became an asset: having grown up in the computer age, they were quick to grasp the implications of the web. Equipped with a couple of PCs, an Internet connection, and the rudiments of HTML they could make some kind of living, doing something they enjoyed, while making up the rules as they went along.[8] Here was an opportunity to prove their worth – in circumstances where their marginality to the corporate world could be recast into a source of authority as legitimate interpreters of an alternative medium. With nothing to lose and with little or no experience in the corporate world, they met corporate executives who had little or no experience in the emerging field of new media. Frequently negotiating in their apartments-*qua*-offices, the six-figure contracts they landed for building websites were instant proof (sometimes surprising in magnitude) of their value.

If the corporate world was not only paying attention but also willing to pay, what was it paying for? In these early days, their corporate clients were anxious to establish a presence on the web, imagining websites as little more than billboards alongside the information superhighway. But, as the new media entrepreneurs were introduced to the business operations of the firms, their interactions with various units yielded new insights about the capabilities of interactive websites as innovative corporate tools. Looking inside marketing departments, they realized that the web could provide new kinds of information about customers; in interactions with production departments, they learned that the web could establish new kinds of relationships to suppliers; and probing technology departments they recognized how the web could exponentially extend the network of information transfer well beyond the task of integrating proprietary data.

Although they were being paid for design work, the new entrepreneurs concluded that the real value they brought to the deal and to the client was as consultants. And so they adjusted their positioning. As "web shops" they were like construction companies, building in a digital medium to be sure, but nonetheless basically working to the specifications of the client. Reconfigured as "web developers," they were in the business of advising clients about how to develop an overall strategy on and for the web. The new mottos and redesigned logos on their own websites told the story: "Interactive Strategy," for example, and "digital.change.management."

The new management consulting/web design hybrid took the web developers more deeply and more intensively inside the organizations of their corporate clients (as the price of a well-designed corporate website rose into seven figures). And this increased interaction brought them into new fields with yet different identities. Their increased interaction with marketing departments, for example, resulted in "interactive advertising" and brought them onto the domain of the Midtown advertising agencies. As they began to design intranets and virtual offices for flexible communication within the corporation, the web developers learned that their programming skills in graphic design had to be augmented with programming skills for the "information architecture" of knowledge management. And with the development of e-commerce, the front end of the website (the interface with the customer) quickly became more integrated with the entire organization and its "legacy systems" working on older operating platforms in production, purchasing, billing, and data archiving. To deliver a comprehensive product that linked the user interface to the "back end," the graphic designers, thus, also found themselves moving onto the terrain of the system integrators.

And so from graphic designers the web developers had evolved into interactive designers – management consultants – advertising agencies – information architects – system integrators. Some of them were now being approached by a new kind of client – not simply major corporations who needed a website to augment their bricks and mortar facilities but also startup entrepreneurs with no physical plant and equipment but ideas to build click-and-order operations. Whereas the mid-level executives of the earlier period had come with a corporate charge to "build me a website," the exclusively e-commerce entrepreneurs now came with venture capital backing to "build me a company." The entrepreneurs for galoshes.com, soapsudsonline, YouNameIt.com brought financing, contacts to suppliers, and usually some modicum of marketing experience in a specific line of goods; but everything else from server farms to user interfaces, from e-carts to returns policies, from supplier interfaces to knowledge of online consumer buying practices rested in the knowledge base of the web developer.

After creating one or two such virtual companies for fees, the web developers were confronted yet again with the problem of value: Why simply charge a fee for a professional service when so much of the value of the virtual company resulted from their efforts? The answer: in addition to fee for service, acquire partial equity in the new online companies. But things were usually not so additive, and the resulting deals often involved trading off some part of fees for equity. So, to protect their "investments" in deferred fees, some web developers began incubating their client companies, working closely with the managers of the startup ventures to guide them to the market. In doing so, the web developers entered yet a new field of skills. In taking on a new project it was no longer enough to assess whether a new client could pay its bill. As equity holders, their value as a firm now rested in part on their ability to evaluate the potential of new ventures, their profitability, and/or their marketability. The more they began to think of their product as building a company, the more they had to consider the built company as a product; that is, the likelihood that it could be sold whether through an IPO or to another round of investors. As such, in addition to all their other new identities, these web developers were taking on some of the roles of venture capitalists. Whereas the Silicon Alley new media firms were once digital construction companies, now they joined the venerable New York City tradition of real estate developers – developing properties on the digital landscape.

But as the web developers evolved in a zigzag course of learning where the value is, other actors, of course, were doing the same. The major Midtown advertising agencies, for example, established interactive units or spun off their own dedicated interactive agencies; the big consulting firms did not leave the field of interactive management to the new media startups but moved aggressively into the field; and the big systems integrators developed their own e-commerce units and launched new initiatives in the lucrative business-to-business (B2B) web development field. From a scarcely populated niche, the field of new media services was now filled with more established competitors, coming to it from multiple starting points.

Meanwhile, the nascent industry was faced with new waves of technological innovation disrupting its emerging digital ecologies. On one side, players in the field were anticipating major breakthroughs in the development of broadband technologies which promised the convergence in one device of the various functionalities now parceled across your television, computer monitor, stereo, VCR, and telephone. But just when one might think that this hails a new "single appliance" era, we saw, on the other side, the proliferation of myriad electronic devices (e.g., wireless palm pilots, and the like) through which you can receive and transmit digital information in a mobile environment.

These simultaneous processes of convergence and divergence would have two consequences. First, the joint appearance of broadband technologies, on one side, and multi-appliance mobile interactivity, on the other, would have important consequences for the website genre form. That is, just at the point that the website genre seemed to be stabilizing, that moment of stabilization was revealed as a tiny moment in the history of the medium. Second, as bandwidth was expanding to broadband proportions, another set of actors entered the field – cable companies, network broadcasters, recording companies, and telecommunications firms. Sony, NBC, AT&T, and Telefonica (the Spanish telecommunications firm), for example, were among the major corporations who moved most aggressively. They were joined, with the arrival of mobile interactivity (from *Wired* to the "wireless revolution"), by new hardware manufacturers such as Nokia, Ericsson, and Palm, Inc. (as well as rapidly growing companies such as Symbol Technologies, makers of hand-held, bar-code devices).

This crowding of the field happened at the same time as its economic contraction. As the IPO market for dot.coms slowed and then stopped altogether, firms that had put too many resources into developing companies instead of developing competencies found themselves with worthless holdings. Those who had scored early successes by tapping into the Internet Gold Rush with a timely IPO and who had pegged their worth according to their soaring stock values (from $12 to $120 in months or even weeks), now found (with their shares trading in pennies) that allowing the market to be the measure of their worth could just as easily undervalue as overvalue a company's actual performance. Those who had turned away clients in 1998 and 1999 because "our cultures just don't fit," now found themselves making pitches in the most improbable places. And those who hoped that their reputations – as capable professionals who delivered value on deadline – would help them weather the storm now found themselves competing for clients that were not only fewer in number but also much more cautious about allocating resources for Internet services.

Heterarchy

Companies striving to make headway amidst such dizzying impermanence were in constant search of that "sweet spot" which consisted of finding the right temporary permanence to commit to – the winning clients, technology, marketing strategy – that would position them favorably for the next imminent shift of course. The challenge for these companies was not only to have the operational flexibility needed to change direction quickly; they needed to maximize their capacity to recognize opportunities and realize their promise, not only by exploiting their immediate benefits but by exploring them as openings to new opportunities. To enhance their innovative capacity, new media firms experimented with new organizational forms that we characterize as heterarchy.

Heterarchy represents a new mode of organizing that is neither market nor hierarchy: whereas hierarchies involve relations of *dependence* and markets involve relations of *independence*, heterarchies involve relations of *interdependence*. As the term suggests, heterarchies are characterized by minimal hierarchy and by organizational heterogeneity.

Heterarchy's twinned features are a response to the increasing complexity of the firm's foresight horizons[9] or of its "fitness landscape."[10] In relentlessly changing organizations where, at the extreme, there is uncertainty even about what product the firm will be producing in the near future, the strategy horizon of the firm is unpredictable and its fitness landscape is rugged. To cope with these uncertainties, instead of concentrating its resources for strategic planning among a narrow set of senior executives or delegating that function to a specialized department, firms may undergo a radical decentralization in which virtually every unit becomes engaged in innovation. That is, in place of specialized search routines in which some departments are dedicated to exploration, while others are confined to exploiting existing knowledge, the functions of exploration are generalized throughout the organization. The search for new markets, for example, is no longer the sole province of the marketing department if units responsible for purchase and supply are also scouting the possibilities for qualitatively new inputs that can open up new product lines.

These developments increase interdependencies between divisions, departments, and work teams within the firm. But because of the greater complexity of these feedback loops, coordination cannot be engineered, controlled, or managed hierarchically. The results of interdependence are to increase the autonomy of work units from central management. Yet at the same time, more complex interdependencies heighten the need for fine-grained coordination across the increasingly autonomous units.

These pressures are magnified by dramatic changes in the sequencing of activities within production relations. As product cycles shorten from years to months, the race to new markets calls into question the strict sequencing of design and execution. Because of strong first-mover advantages, in which the first actor to introduce a new product (especially one that establishes a new industry standard), captures inordinate market share by reaping increasing returns, firms that wait to begin production until design is completed will be penalized in competition. Like the production of "B movies" in which filming begins before the script is completed, successful strategies integrate conception and execution, with significant aspects of the production process beginning even before design is finalized.

Production relations are even more radically altered in processes analyzed by Sabel and Dorf as *simultaneous engineering*.[11] Conventional design is sequential, with subsystems that are presumed to be central designed in detail first, setting the boundary conditions for the design of lower-ranking components. In simultaneous engineering, by contrast, separate project teams develop all the subsystems concurrently. In such concurrent design, the various project teams engage in an ongoing mutual monitoring, as innovations produce multiple, sometimes competing, proposals for improving the overall design.

Thus, increasingly rugged fitness landscapes yield increasingly complex interdependencies that in turn yield increasingly complex coordination challenges. Where search is no longer departmentalized but is instead generalized and distributed throughout the organization, and where design is no longer compartmentalized but deliberated and distributed throughout the production process, the solution is *distributed authority*.[12]

Under circumstances of simultaneous engineering where the very parameters of a project are subject to deliberation and change across units, authority is no longer delegated vertically but rather emerges laterally. As one symptom of these changes, managers socialized in an earlier regime frequently express their puzzlement to researchers: "There's one thing I can't figure out. Who's my boss?" Under conditions of distributed authority, managers might still "report to" their superiors; but increasingly, they are accountable to other work teams. Success at simultaneous engineering thus depends on learning by mutual monitoring within relations of lateral accountability.

As it shifts from search routines to a situation in which search is generalized, the heterarchical firm is redrawing internal boundaries, regrouping assets, and perpetually reinventing itself. Under circumstances of rapid technological change and volatility of products and markets, it seems there is no one best solution. If one could be rationally chosen and resources devoted to it alone, the benefits of its fleeting superiority would not compensate for the costs of subsequent missed opportunities. Because managers hedge against these uncertainties, the outcomes are hybrid forms.[13] Good managers do not simply commit themselves to the array that keeps the most options open; instead, they create an organizational space open to the perpetual redefinition of what might constitute an option. Rather than a rational choice among a set of known options, we find practical action fluidly redefining what the options might be. Management becomes the art of facilitating organizations that can reorganize themselves.

This capacity for self-redefinition is grounded in the organizational heterogeneity that characterizes heterarchies. Heterarchies are *complex* adaptive systems because they interweave a multiplicity of organizing principles. The new organizational forms are heterarchical not only because they have flattened hierarchy, but also because they are the sites of competing and coexisting value systems. The greater interdependence of increasingly autonomous work teams results in a proliferation of performance criteria. Distributed authority not only implies that units will be accountable to each other, but also that each will be held to accountings in multiple registers. The challenge of a new media firm, for example, is to create a sufficiently common culture to facilitate communication among the designers, business strategists, and technologists that make up interdisciplinary teams – without suppressing the distinctive identities of each.[14] A robust, lateral collaboration flattens hierarchy without flattening diversity. Heterarchies create wealth by inviting more than one way of evaluating worth.

This aspect of heterarcy builds on Frank Knight's distinction between *risk*, where the distribution of outcomes can be expressed in probabilistic terms, and *uncertainty*, where outcomes are incalculable.[15] Whereas neoclassical economics reduces all cases to risk, Knight argued that a world of generalized probabilistic knowledge of the future leaves no place for profit (as a particular residual revenue that is not contractualizable because it is not susceptible to measure *ex ante*) and hence no place for the entrepreneur. Properly speaking, the entrepreneur is not rewarded for risk-taking but, instead, is rewarded for an ability to exploit uncertainty. The French school of the "economics of conventions"[16] demonstrates that institutions are social technologies for transforming uncertainty into calculable problems, but they leave unexamined the possibility of uncertainty about which institution ("regime of worth") is operative in a given situation.[17] Knight's conception of entrepreneurship as the exploitation of uncertainty posed within the heterarchy framework is thus rendered: entrepreneurship is the ability to keep multiple regimes of worth in play and to exploit the resulting ambiguity.

The Ethnographic Setting: NetKnowHow

Over a two-year period, we observed the organizational features of heterarchy in practice at NetKnowHow, a pseudonymous new media startup firm in Silicon Alley navigating the uncharted Internet territory. NetKnowHow is a full service Internet consulting firm. It was founded in 1995 by two young entrepreneurs, each with experience in the large corporate sector (traditional consulting and traditional media). In its formative years it was a software development company, but it quickly moved into the new media field producing intranets and websites for corporate and university clients. NetKnowHow acquired a reputation for excellence in retail e-commerce after its website for a famous department store won a prize for an outstanding e-commerce site. In 1999, while continuing to build retail e-commerce sites for nationally recognized corporate clients, it also built sites for startup dot.coms (striking partnerships with several of these) and merged with another smaller startup in the field of digital kiosks. In 2000, it stopped taking on dot.com clients, focusing instead on consulting for "click and mortar" operations that combined physical and digital retailing while experimenting on the side in developing applications for the wireless interface. Like the overwhelming majority of new media startups in Silicon Alley, it had no venture capital funding; and, also like the majority of new media firms during the period prior to the industry's downward spiral beginning in April 2000,[18] it was a profitable company. Also, like almost all firms in this sector, it is struggling in the wake of the dot.com meltdown. When we began our ethnographic research in the spring of 1999, NetKnowHow had about 15 employees. Within 18 months it had grown to over a hundred employees but has subsequently declined, in three rounds of layoffs, to about 40. Very painful, this survival is itself an accomplishment in circumstances where much larger and much better financed companies have bit the dust.

The physical setting of our research was in the Flatiron District, at the core of Silicon Alley. At the point of its maximum growth, NetKnowHow occupied four workplaces each several blocks apart—lofts converted from displaced printing operations with as many as 30 computer workstations in an open room where no walls, dividers, or cubicles separated the programmers, designers, information architects, and business strategists. It was not just open, but so closely packed that almost anyone could reach out and literally touch someone. And, like a construction site, it was a place in movement. Although there were periods, typically mid-morning and mid-afternoon, where it seemed that everyone was still, each concentrating on his or her own monitor, for much of the time the rooms seemed in motion with dozens of micro-meetings in twos or threes, some sitting, others standing, leaning over shoulders to point at lines of code or graphics on their monitors, some lasting 30 minutes, many only 30 seconds. Some formal project meetings took place around large tables in the conference rooms; but just as often, a project team would claim a part of the open room by wheeling chairs and sitting on tables around several workstations. For the most intense discussions, you could go to one of the "private conference rooms" in the stairways and on the fire escape where smokers congregated.

The social setting of our ethnography, like the *de rigueur* hardwood floors, was Silicon Alley standard: the workforce of NetKnowHow was tightly grouped around its median age of 27. But its demographics departed from the typical new media startup with a higher proportion of women and a broader ethnic and racial mix. The following job listing indicates the qualities that NetKnowHow was seeking in its employees. For this programmer position, beyond the obvious technical qualifications, it seeks "team players" who "take pride in their work" and who can thrive in its "flat organizational structure":

> NetKnowHow, Inc. seeks Cold Fusion/ASP/MS SiteBuilder (or CGI/Perl) programmers with proven experience developing a wide range of leading-edge Internet systems. The ideal candidate will have experience in database design and development (Oracle/SQLServer) and strong HTML and JavaScript skills. *Team players must be able to juggle multiple projects, prioritize to meet client needs and established deadlines.* Requirements include one year solid experience programming in Cold Fusion or equivalent language, as well as familiarity with database systems (MS Access, MS SQL Server, Informix and Oracle). *We are looking for quality people who take pride in their work and enjoy working in an eclectic, hard-working and creative environment.* If you're interested in beginning a career with a cutting edge new media company, drop us a line. NetKnowHow's *flat organizational structure permits self-starters to thrive.* Benefits include medical, dental, 401-k and gym membership. If you have something special to contribute, submit your résumé and a cover letter describing your work experience and *what you think you could bring to NetKnowHow's table,* to recruiting@NetKnowHow.com. [emphasis added]

Reflecting the casual work environment, NetKnowHow's refrigerators were well-stocked with soda, juice, and beer. And like a construction site, the place was frequently noisy, not from crane engines and jackhammers, but from the music that provided a nonstop umbrella of sound over the low hum of many conversations. In this setting, the counterpart of a hard hat was a headset wired to one's own music as some protection against the din and as a signal "not to be interrupted." If the work atmosphere was casual, the actual work was intense and the hours long. Both hours and intensity increased with the approach of a project deadline and reached manic levels each autumn when the hardwood floors were littered with futons and mattresses as NetKnowHow's employees worked literally day and night to build e-commerce sites that could be launched for the holiday buying season. Like pre-industrial work rhythms[19] with bouts of work followed by relative idleness, rush work to meet deadlines could be followed by less intense periods "between projects," but these were typically short. Opportunities for "learning by watching"[20] were limited where the general rule was "learning by doing": there was nothing pre-industrial about the overall experience of temporality. In the new media field, there was no sense of a "passage of time." Instead, time was compressed; like a time warp it was something that you were being shot through.

Distributing Intelligence: Collaborative Engineering as Emergent Design

The process of designing and building a website at NewKnowHow, as in new media firms generally, takes the organizational form of a project. A project is not a permanent construct but a temporary ensemble whose players had been working on other projects before and will move to other projects after its conclusion. Together with every new media firm we encountered in Silicon Alley, NetKnowHow devotes considerable energy not simply to monitoring projects ("building account-ability of the project and in the project") but also to monitoring the project process ("codifying our practice," "institutionalizing our process," etc.), in part as marketing strategy ("The Razorfish 5 Step Process"), in part because the project form is a critical component of the core competence of these firms.

Some projects last no more than a month. Some, whether because of their innate complexity or because of indecision or insolvency on the client side, can last five or six months. The typically sophisticated project runs 60–90 days, and this extraordin-arily compressed time to market is an important factor in project dynamics. Projects can bring earnings to the firm ranging from several hundred thousand to nearly a million dollars. Project fee structures can vary: NetKnowHow has sometimes contracted fixed fees, sometimes adopted a retainer model, and sometimes taken equity in lieu of partially defrayed or deferred fees. More typically, it negotiates overall price estimates based on material expenses plus billable hours.

On the firm's side, the participants in a project include business strategists, interactive designers, programmers and other technologists, information architects (IA), and merchandising specialists. Each project has a project manager; most projects will include a designated design lead and technology lead, and larger projects will designate a lead information architect as well as a lead business strategist. While they are temporarily the "members" of a project, personnel remain part of an ongoing functional unit (e.g., design, programming, IA, strategy, etc.) variously referred to as "communities," "disciplines," or "guilds," but most frequently called "teams" or "groups" (e.g., "the design team," "the technology group," etc.).

The life cycle of a web project typically has a preformative, "preproject," stage of matching firm and client followed by stages of identifying the project personnel, a formal "kickoff," planning and site design, production, testing, soft launch, and a celebration at hard launch. Figure 16.1 presents a diagram of a typical project life cycle at NetKnowHow.

From the idealized representation in Figure 16.1, it might seem that building a website is a matter of sequential engineering: in principle, all design and engineering should be completed before production begins. Within an overall sequence the diagram shows distinct moments of parallel engineering, for example, during weeks 3–5 when the information architects, technical architects, and graphic designers work in parallel to draw up their plans for the site, which are then "handed off" to the site builders. In the actual process, however, engineering is more simultaneous than sequential. At NetKnowHow, website construction is a process of collaborative engineering.

In an industry in which there can be extraordinary first mover advantages, strong pressures exist to be quick-to-market. The results are excruciatingly tight project deadlines that force production to begin before design is completed. Typically, the database managers and other programmers begin construction just as soon as they hear initial ideas about the project. Of course, they are not literally writing each of the many thousands of lines of code from scratch, but are looking to previous work to find promising templates for the various functionalities that are likely to be adopted for the project. At the same time that they are searching through

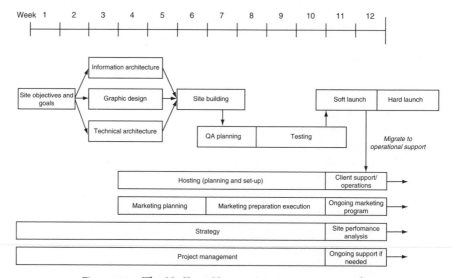

Figure 16.1   The NetKnowHow project management guide.

their existing stock of code, they are also searching for solutions to the new functionalities that were discussed in the kickoff meeting (as well as those that were not even mentioned there but that are literally overheard in the close quarters of the open workplace). If they started programming only after the information architect presented them with the finished "wire frame"[21] (a kind of blueprint specifying each part of the website and their inter-relations), the project could never be completed on deadline. Similarly, the information architect is consulting with the programmers about the code that they are already preparing, hearing their proposals about new solutions to old problems, and picking up new ideas that could be adopted in the site in progress. Without such iteration, she might draw up an exquisite wire frame – but one that could not be completed on time and on budget. In short, production workers participate in design as a process that involves bricolage.[22]

If production begins before design is completed, it is also the case that design is ongoing, continuing almost to the point that production is completed. First, even with the best efforts to manage the client's expectations and even within a project cycle as short as 90 days, it is nearly impossible to prevent "project creep" – the racheting up of project specifications. Because clients learn during the process of building the site, they will demand new functionalities. Some can be resisted ("that's not in the project specifications"). But they cannot all be deflected, especially when the firm has promised a "cutting edge" website and the client now sees a competitor's site with new features that "have to be adopted." From a narrow business logic, new functionalities can be incorporated with a corresponding increase in price ("yes, but it will increase the programming costs dramatically"). But from a design perspective, introducing new features can have enormous implications that ramify throughout the site. Seemingly simple changes in the order of steps within "check-out," for example, might require major restructuring of the database.

But there is a second, more important, reason why design – as the work of figuring out the whole – can continue well through the production process, even when no additional functionalities are introduced after the initial stages. Because of the rapid pace of organizational, technological, and genre innovation, website construction at NetKnowHow was almost always a process of engineering something they had not built before. Even when the project could benefit from utilizing existing templates, the particular combinations were likely to be novel, and likely to incorporate novel elements as well. Moreover, at NetKnowHow, learning was by doing. That is, instead of understanding a technology and then adopting it, one came to understand a technology by using it. As a result, the process of figuring out how all the pieces fit together did not take place in the initial "design" phase but, instead, occurred during and through the process of constructing the site. "It's like a puzzle," explained Aaron, age 27, one of the firm's two most senior project leads, "but it's peculiar because the picture on the cover keeps changing as you put it together." The passage from our conversation deserves quoting verbatim:

Early on in the project you have a kick off meeting and you do have an understanding of the project up front. You have a sense of what the project is, the size of it, the scope of it, and everything else. But as soon as that kick-off meeting is over, that whole concept just... [throws up his hands]. It's like a puzzle—you see the cover of the box, you know what the puzzle is supposed to look like, you have a really good idea of what you need to do, but then you open the box, you just see all those pieces, and then you have to start putting all those pieces together.

In trying to figure out how the puzzle pieces might fit together, the wireframes are not much help because the projects are always so fluid and there are always so many changes you have to go through, regardless. Every client wants changes; every project leader encounters some complexity that requires a change; so the deeper you go into changes, the farther you get from the realization. You'll have the puzzle pieces, and then someone will dump a whole other 50 or 100 pieces into your lap. And when they dump the additional pieces in your lap, you also don't know how those fifty pieces relate to the cover on the box, you don't know if it's the bottom, on the side, on the top, or the left. But you do know that what you're going to end up with is not like the initial picture you started with at the kick-off meeting, because you change so much.

No matter how many new changes come across, for every new change you can tie up and get your arms around, get a resolution to, and get it implemented, then that actually serves to be a greater step towards the realization than just figuring out how the two pieces you had in the beginning fit together the way that you thought they would, because it's now more like you're getting these undefined pieces and you're able to define them and that sort of leap frogs you toward that realization. At some point when you get all of those changes done and a good portion of the rest of it done and at that point, that's usually when I have that realization that YES! I see what it is that we're doing now. I have a good understanding of the whole thing and what it's going to end up looking like. For me it usually happens towards the end.

In these observations, Aaron is expressing a view that design is an emergent process, distributed across many actors in a highly interactive way. And, like design, innovation is not a moment that occurs at a particular stage in the web development process. At NetKnowHow, innovation is not an activity confined to an R&D department. Every unit, indeed everyone, is involved in the process of innovation as an immensely pragmatic activity of collaborating to "figure out how it fits together." In short, instead of the conventional view of innovation by design, in these website construction projects we find design by innovation. As a self-organized, emergent process, it is not engineered from above.

To understand the complexities of "figuring out how it fits together" we need to go beyond the simple "front end/back end" dichotomy that figures so prominently in discussions of websites. The distinction exists in the folk categories of the web: the "front end" is what you, the end user, experience when you go to a website, but it is like the tip of the iceberg; the "back end" is everything you do not see below the water line, but which makes it work. The distinction is meaningful, but misleading –

especially if it connotes website construction as parallel processes that have to be made to converge or leads to metaphors in which the "front end" people (designers and such) are building a bridge from one side, the back end people (programmers) are building from another side, and they have to meet in the middle. Their interdependencies are, of course, much greater.

In the simple version of the front/back end model, there are two computers and one interface: the server where the code of the website is resident, your PC, and the graphical user interface (GUI) through which you experience the site. But sophisticated e-commerce sites involve many computers and multiple interfaces – yours, the servers leased by the client of the web developer, the mainframes on which the client's multiple data bases are operating, as well as the computers of the client's suppliers and vendors, the computers of the order fulfillment service, credit card companies, and so on. Your click as end user can initiate a purchase, create a delivery form, enter a credit card payment, provide feedback to marketing, and route an order directly to a supplier. Some sophisticated e-commerce sites reach deeply into the production and inventory systems of multiple suppliers and use algorithms (with weights for the suppliers' price, location, level of inventory, opening or closing phases of production runs, and even the quality of the suppliers' data) to determine which supplier will fill a particular customer's online purchase.

The challenge for the website developers is to build a site in which the activities of the end user are seamlessly linked to the various other computers to which the site is interfaced. The performance of the website critically depends on the performance of an actor – the user – whose actions might be anticipated but cannot be controlled. It is this interdependence that most dramatically increases the interdependencies among the website construction crew. A programmer can design a beautiful interface between the website and the suppliers, but she needs to make sure that it does not interfere with how the information architect is thinking about navigational issues for the interface to the user. The more the site is truly interactive, the more the various parts of the team must interact. A change in the categories of the database, for example, can change parameters for the graphic designers and vice versa. The more the intelligence of the site is distributed – including, most critically, the user's intelligence – the more the construction site must use a distributed intelligence among the team in collective problem solving. When graphic designers and database programmers speak, the phrase "being on the same page" can refer to an injunction to focus on the same problem, a request to consider how an action will have consequences in another sphere, an opportunity to bring each other up-to-date on new methods, applications, functions, and reporting systems as well as quite literally being on the same page of code. The more they must take into account how their actions will shape the parameters of others, the more they must increase the lines of lateral accountability. As a young programmer explained to us in an apt epigram for collaborative engineering: "In this company, I'm accountable to everybody who counts on me."

Organizing Diversity

Multiple performance criteria

The directionality of accountabilities in heterarchical organizations such as NetKno-wHow is lateral. But these accountabilities are not of a singular logic. These are sites where evaluative principles operate in multiple registers.

Questions of value – the value of work and the value of the product of work – are central to a web project. At NetKnowHow, some criteria of worth are shared across all communities. Formal credentials are unimportant; actual skills are critical. Not surprisingly, in this project-based organization, an ability to work well with others is highly valued. This trait has several components. First, an ability to get along with others in an extraordinarily stressful and fast-pace environment.[23] Knowing the subtle cues for when and how you can interrupt is one of the skills relevant in this area. Second, an ability to convey knowledge (whether explicit or tacit) to others. Finally, and most ubiquitous, an ability to figure things out quickly. As important as (and for some even more important than) one's absolute or relative knowledge is the rate of acquiring new skills and knowledge as well as being talented in being able to re-think a problem so that it can be solved. "Picking things up quickly" is highly valued whether within a community of practice or across them.[24]

However, not all criteria of worth are shared. The different communities of practice at NewKnowHow differ in their conceptions of value and in their measures of performance:

> For **programmers**, a good programmer is above all *logical*, and a good site must be judged by the same criterion. When she performs well, she does so with *speed, efficiency,* and *accuracy*; and a good website must do the same. A good programmer can *translate*— express a functionality in the language of a computer code that is *categorical* and *hierarchical*. A good programmer understands the deep structure as well as the quirks and idiosyncracies of the program. When she speaks it is not simply on behalf of other programmers but on behalf of the program. The legitimate tests and proofs of worth are Quality Assurance tests and other instruments that measure the speed, efficiency, security, and reliability of the site.
>
> For **designers**, a valuable designer must be knowledgeable about processes of *perception*, and a good website must use graphic cues that conform to these processes. When he performs well, he does so with *creativity,* and the results will be *exciting* and *stimulating*. A good designer is also a *translator*—into a language that is *visual, intuitive,* and *interactive*. At work he engages in a visual dialogue with other designers, the client, and users. When this work of translation is successful it makes links to the *imagination* because both the client and the user live not only in a real world and a virtual world but also in *imaginary* worlds. The designer's translation creates multiple links among all these – in the process, making connections between the self-image of the client and that of the user. Exploiting interactive as well as visual features, he creates the overall "look and feel" through which the site achieves the desired *effects/affects* and conveys a branding *experience*. If necessary, he has authority to argue with the client provided he

speaks as an advocate of the brand. Winning clients, winning audiences, and winning competitions are legitimate proofs of worth.

For **information architects**, a good information architect must be knowledgeable about principles of *cognition*. A site that successfully applies these principles will be characterized by *clarity, ease*, and above all *usability*. A good website conveys information by creating navigable pathways that conform to cognitive pathways. An information architect's activities are valuable because they are based on *studies* that use *statistics* to understand user *behavior*. In discussions with other members of the project, including the client, the information architect is an advocate of the *user*. The user lives in a world of *information* that is accessed through *tools* some of which are more and some of which are less *appropriate* for the *tasks* that the user attempts to perform. "Conversion rates" and other statistical metrics of user activities are legitimate tests of a website's performance.

For **merchandising specialists**, a good website is one that moves product. To do so, a good online merchandiser exploits powers of *suggestion*. Because the *shopper* lives in a world of *desire*, she is open to suggestion. *Playfulness* takes precedence over information, surprise takes precedence over search, product *placement* takes precedence over navigation, and *pleasurability* takes precedence over usability. Proofs of value are metrics that measure how product is moving in relation to inventories.

OK, it works, but how does it perform?

In the section on collaborative engineering we focused on the pragmatic activity of figuring out how everything fits together. But collaborative engineering also involves the discursive activity of evaluating how it performs.

You build a website that works. But, as more websites get built, you cannot make a distinction between yours and others' simply on the grounds that yours works. You say that yours performs better. But then immediately you must begin to articulate your performance criteria.[25] You cannot silence the talk about evaluative principles and point to a purely pragmatic frame since your claim that you are making a valuable product raises the question not only of what is its value but why.

The various communities of practice at NetKnowHow were articulate and adamant about their respective performance criteria. "We yell and scream" was a repeated refrain in conversations when we talked about this friendly rivalry. Discussions could be heated, especially when proofs of worth[26] were not immediately recognized outside of the frames that made them seem so obvious to their proponents. The statistical studies on user behavior produced by the leading information architect, for example, were characterized by a leading designer as "arbitrary," provoking the counter-charge that this was yet another instance in which he, the designer, was being "irrational."

Despite occasional flare-ups, the temperature stayed cool since the dominant mode was persuasion rather than denunciation. Because every community of practice was a minority view, each attempted to enlist or enroll others in recognizing the legitimacy of their performance criteria. In this process of ongoing realignment,[27] people spoke openly about seeking allies.

We saw this process at work, for example, in a dispute over competing claims about who could speak on behalf of "the user" that raged for many months at NetKnowHow and was still ongoing when we concluded our fieldwork. This development was triggered by the information architects, who thought that they had a special claim on knowledge about the user. Their hope was that every group would start focusing on the user's performance and that, by maintaining their special definition, they could raise their own performance criteria to a special status to which all groups gave credence. The information architects' strategy was initially successful: as references to "the user" indeed circulated through the company, we could hear this theme more and more frequently in discussions, formal and informal.

But the strategy also had consequences unintended by the information architects: instead of deferring to the information architects, each of the disciplines began to articulate their own definitions of the user consistent with their value systems and metrics of performance. That is, each community developed its own distinctive claims to represent the user. The merchandizing specialists, who had previously seemed to be speaking on behalf of the merchandiser, offered seminars in which they presented their view of the user as "shopper" and mobilized an alternative set of findings. Similarly, the firm's leading designer, who was genuinely most attentive to the studies of the information architects, came to the defense of the designer who had derided them as "arbitrary," pointing out that these statistical studies were conducted at a particular stage of the development of the web. In a variety of settings, he suggested new directions in the evolution of the web that could make these findings obsolete. And, more quietly but quite forcefully in their individual interactions with the other communities, even the programmers began to articulate their own representation of the user.

Disputes such as these were vital for firms like NetKnowHow. If the firm locked-in to a single performance criteria, it could not be positioned to move with flexibility as the industry changed and the web evolved. Thus, even the principle we have not yet mentioned – profitability – was not itself an evaluative principle that trumped all others since continuing profitability was itself based on the ability to anticipate new developments and re-cognize new performance criteria for evaluating well-designed and well-functioning websites. Tolerating, even encouraging, such friendly rivalry was a source of innovation to navigate the search for value within the young industry.

To build a site, make settlements

Collaborative engineering is a discursive pragmatics. It is, at once, an ongoing conversation and an intensely practical activity. I present to you accounts of my work so that you can take my problems and goals into account in yours. We do what works to make it work. We need to talk to get the job done, but to get the job done we need to stop talking and get to work. We give reasons, we explain the rationale, but we use different rationalities. We do not end disputation so much as suspend it. To build sites, we make settlements.

Settlement of the web and settlement in web projects share some common features, not least because the two dynamics are recursive. As a frontier, the web is going through a process of settlement.[28] It is not simply that sites are built, but that they are built in settlements. Landscapes are reshaped and structures are recognizable by their contours. We can distinguish an e-commerce site from a portal site from an informational site. Things get settled.

For the members of web projects, the process of building websites has the result that things also get settled. From a very low division of labor, some professional boundaries develop. It is possible to recognize a graphic designer from a business strategist from an information architect. Things settle down, people settle in. They work out ways of dividing tasks and managing the relationships across their professional boundaries. On many issues they reach agreement.

But you cannot settle back in your ergonomic chair too long – because, unlike settlements on physical landscapes – things do not stay settled on the web. (Or at least they have not during the period we are experiencing.) The built structures on the digital landscape lack the permanence of physical structures. An abandoned warehouse is a boarded-up blight on the landscape until it is destroyed or gentrified into luxury apartments. An abandoned website is a Code 404, File "Not Found." Websites can be destroyed with ease and new ones created. Repurposing takes more work,[29] but in general the process of recombining forms takes place with marked rapidity when working in the digital medium.[30] Thus, just when we thought we could easily recognize the difference between e-commerce sites, portal sites, and information sites, fusions began that confused the distinctions. AOL's mall of affiliated storefronts began to double as a portal, the Yahoo portal adopted e-commerce features, and we can go to the dominant e-commerce site, Amazon, for information and for its affiliated shops. Things might be settling down, but they are not settled.

Life in web projects is much the same. Sometimes the parties actually come to agree. But frequently, instead of reaching an agreement, they reach a settlement. Like the term itself with its connotations of law and locality, our informants at NetKno-wHow reach settlements (1) by judicious appeals to other actors who are outside the dispute, and (2) through their highly localized practices. When the incommensurable systems of value come into conflict in a project they are sometimes settled by contingent compromises (often through appeals to the project lead) and by "relativization" (through appeals to the client). In relativization,[31] the parties to the disagreement can maintain their principled position; they merely agree to accede to whatever outcome is chosen by the "outsider." "So, it's settled, right?" The highly localized practices of the project, so confined in space and time, further contribute to temporary settlements. Working in such tight quarters creates a forced intimacy and a heightened tolerance. Where everything is overheard and everyone is monitoring not only what is said but also the tone of voice, project team members are on the alert for a pitch of voice that signals an unproductive impasse. "OK, let's settle this and get back to work." Deadlines have a way of settling disagreements. Not surprisingly, like those on the landscape of the web, these settlements are more provisional than permanent. Limited in time, localized in space, a project is a provisional settlement.

The provisional character of project settlements is an expression of discursive pragmatism. Pragmatic, because provisional settlements make it possible to get the job done. Discursive, because provisional settlements are open to reinterpretation when the project is concluded and the next begun.

Our understanding of collaboration in heterarchical organizations is thus more complex than coordination within a project. A frictionless coordination, in which everyone shared the same performance criteria, might make life smooth for project managers; but it would lose the creative abrasions[32] that are the source of ongoing vitality. Settlements facilitate coordination *within projects*; the unsettling activity of ongoing disputation makes it possible to adapt to the changing topography of the web *across projects* in time. Friction promotes reflection, exposing variation from multiple perspectives. Friction can be bountiful because complex coordination is a function not only of the values we share or of the language we have in common but also of our creative misunderstandings.

Conclusion

One of the more interesting aspects of the death of the New Economy was the rapidity with which both right and left rushed in to celebrate its demise. Always suspicious of the free-wheeling culture of New Economy firms such as the new media startups, op-eds in newspapers like the *Wall Street Journal* almost chuckled that "real value" and more sober business practices had triumphed. The startups had had their day, but now the grown ups were back in charge. (The scandals of the big boys' corporate board rooms, of course, were to follow.) But the left had also been suspicious, perhaps even a bit worried, that talk like "all the rules are changed, you either get it or you don't" was encroaching on its discursive domain. And so the left's periodicals almost crackled that the new media faux revolutionaries had got their comeuppance. It was capitalism after all, and the only thing that counts in capitalism is the bottom line.

Where left and right agree, and even for the same reason, seems to us to be an interesting place to be looking. We neither mourn nor celebrate because, regardless of whether the New Economy is alive or dead, the analytic problems survive. Valuation of knowledge-based activities where the effective unit of organization is a network of entities and not isolated firms will continue to be a challenge when available metrics all revolve around corporately bounded balance sheets. The heterarchical structures of lateral coordination will continue to operate in an uneasy coexistence with corporate hierarchies. The goal of workplace democracy will continue to be troubled by the realization that being accountable to one's peers might produce newly invidious forms of monitoring and that workers' self-management might involve management of the self. The emergence of new forms of communication will continue to destabilize established routines. Collaborative organization will continue to co-evolve with interactive technologies. And competing and coexisting evaluative principles will continue to make their productively noisy clash.

Notes

1   An earlier version of this chapter appeared in *Environment and Planning A* 34(11), November 2002, pp. 1927–1949. Our thanks to Daniel Beunza, Pablo Boczkowski, Beverly Burris, Gernot Grabher, Scott Lash, Gina Neff, Wanda Orlikowski, and Andy Pratt for their comments and suggestions on an earlier draft.

   Monique Girard and David Stark, "Heterarchies of Value: Distributing Intelligence and Organizing Diversity in a New Media Startup," *Theory, Culture & Society* 20(3), 2003, pp. 77–105. © 2003 Theory, Culture & Society Ltd. Reprinted by permission of Sage Publications.

2   These models are frequently made explicit in the names of firms and echoed in their décor; e.g., Plumb Design (architecture), Agency.com (ad agency), RG/A Studios, (design studio), Concrete Media (magazine + construction company), and so on. The décor of the offices of Pseudo in New York and Razorfish in NYC and San Francisco might seem to break out of any model – except that resembling a trendy nightclub is part of a branding strategy that shocking the corporate client can be a source of reassurance that the product will be unquestionably hip.

3   James G. March, "Exploration and Exploitation in Organizational Learning," *Organization Science* 2(1), 1991, pp. 71–87.

4   David Lane and Robert Maxfield, "Strategy under Complexity: Fostering Generative Relationships," *Long Range Planning* 29(2), 1996, pp. 215–231.

5   Laurent Thevenot, "Rules and Implements: Investment in Forms," *Social Science Information* 23(1), 1984, pp. 1–45.

6   Gernot Grabher, "Adaptation at the Cost of Adaptability? Restructuring the Eastern German Regional Economy," in *Restructuring Networks: Legacies, Linkages, and Localities in Postsocialism*, Gernot Grabher and David Stark, eds. (London and New York: Oxford University Press, 1997), pp. 107–134; Gernot Grabher and David Stark, "Organizing Diversity: Evolutionary Theory, Network Analysis, and Postsocialist Transformations," in Grabher and Stark, *Restructuring Networks*, pp. 1–32.

7   All figures in this paragraph are from the *3rd New York New Media Industry Survey*, sponsored by the New York New Media Association and conducted by PriceWaterhouseCoopers. Numbers of jobs listed are full-time jobs plus the full-time equivalent of part-time jobs and freelancers.

8   Casey Kait and Stephen Weiss, *Digital Hustlers: Living Large and Falling Hard in Silicon Alley* (New York: HarperCollins, 2001).

9   Lane and Maxfield, "Strategy under Complexity."

10 Stuart Kauffman, *The Origin of Order: Self-Organization and Selection in Evolution* (London: Oxford University Press, 1993).

11 Charles F. Sabel and Michael C. Dorf, "A Constitution of Democratic Experimentalism," *Columbia Law Review* 98(2), 1998, pp. 267–529.

12 Walter W. Powell, "Inter-Organizational Collaboration in the Biotechnology Industry," *Journal of Institutional and Theoretical Economics* 152, 1996, pp. 197–215.

13 Charles Sabel, "Moebius-Strip Organizations and Open Labor Markets: Some Conse-quences of the Reintegration of Conception and Execution in a Volatile Economy," in *Social Theory for a Changing Society,* Pierre Bourdieu and James Coleman, eds. (Boulder, CO, and New York: Westview Press and the Russell Sage Foundation, 1990), pp. 23–54.

14 A young business strategist in a leading new media consulting firm in Silicon Alley grasped the problem intuitively. When I asked whether he could speak the language of the designers and technologists on his project teams, he responded that he frequently does. But then he paused for a moment and added, "But I don't always do so. If I always talked to the technologist on his own terms, then he would never understand *me.*"

15 Frank H. Knight, *Risk, Uncertainty, and Profit* (Boston: Houghton Mifflin, 1921).

16 Luc Boltanski and Laurent Thevenot, *De la justification: les economies de la grandeur* (Paris: Gallimard, 1991); Luc Boltanski, "The Sociology of Critical Capacity," *European Journal of Social Theory* 2, 1999, pp. 359–377.

17 David Stark, "For a Sociology of Worth," paper presented at the Annual Conference of the European Association of Evolutionary Political Economy, keynote address, Berlin, November 3, 2000; also as David Stark, "For a Sociology of Worth," unpublished MS, Center on Organizational Innovation, Columbia University, http://www.coi.colum-bia.edu/workingpapers.html#fsw

18 New York New Media Association (NYNMA) 1999 Survey. April 14, 2000 marked the first dramatic drop in Internet stocks.

19 See E. P. Thompson, "Time, Work, and Industrial Capitalism," in *Classes, Power, and Conflict*, Anthony Giddens and David Held, eds. (Berkeley: University of California Press, 1982), pp. 299–309.

20 Gernot Grabher, "Ecologies of Creativity: the Village, the Group, and the Heterarchic Organisation of the British Advertising Industry," *Environment & Planning A* 33, 2001, pp. 351–374.

21 The wire frame is an example of a "boundary object" – stable enough to circulate, ambiguous enough to be an object of multiple meanings. See Susan Leigh Star and James Griesemer, "Institutional Ecology, Translations, and Boundary Objects: Amateurs and Professionals in Berkeley's Museum of Vertebrate Zoology, 1907–1939," *Social Studies of Science* 19, 1989, pp. 387–420.

22 Raghu Garud and Peter Karnoe, "Distributed and Embedded Agency in Technology Entrepreneurship: Bricolage vs. Breakthrough," unpublished MS, Stern School of Busi-ness, New York University, n.d.

23 As academics we might think about this as a collegial respect, but that would miss the physical dimension of working in such close proximity. Imagine five people all working together in a space the size of your office, if you have a big office imagine ten, and then you will get the idea.

24 In 2000 NetKnowHow initiated a formal evaluation process for all employees. Each employee was able to choose five coworkers to write evaluations. "Picking things up quickly" was one of the most frequently mentioned positive traits. The summary statements below draw from these evaluations, as well as from our field interviews and observations.

25 See Antoine Hennion for a fascinating analysis of performance criteria in the field of popular music. Antoine Hennion, "Baroque and Rock: Music, Mediators and Musical Taste," *Poetics* 24, 1997, pp. 415–435.

26 Boltanski and Thevenot, *De la justification.*

27   Bruno Latour, "Powers of Association," in *Power, Action, and Belief: A New Sociology of Knowledge*, John Law, ed. (London: Routledge, 1986), pp. 264–280; Bruno Latour, "Technology is Society Made Durable," in *A Sociology of Monsters: Essays on Power, Technology, and Domination*, John Law, ed. (London: Routledge, 1991), pp. 103–131.

28   On settlement, see the extraordinarily rich and insightful analysis of online newspapers by Pablo Boczkowski, "Affording Flexibility: Transforming Information Practices in Online Newspapers," Ph.D. dissertation, Department of Science and Technology Studies, Cornell University, 2001.

29   The analogy to physical buildings and landscapes has merit when we move from destruction (almost without cost in the digital case) to repurposing. Sites like Amazon, Yahoo, and AOL can be rebuilt only with considerable investment. Like newsmagazines, they can be cosmetically redesigned with some frequency; but changing their *form* and functionality is a major operation that is fraught with difficulties. Witness the calamity at Deja.com.

30   Even in the digital environment, relative stabilizations occur because of investment in forms. See Laurent Thevenot, "Rules and Implements." Genre forms are malleable but not infinitely so.

31   Boltanski and Thevenot, *De la justification*.

32   John Seely Brown and Paul Duguid, "Organizing Knowledge," *California Management Review* 401(3), 1998, pp. 90–111.

17

FAILURE AS AN ENDPOINT

HIROKAZU MIYAZAKI AND
ANNELISE RILES

An anthropologist working in the Japanese financial markets cannot help but confront widespread skepticism about the efficacy of knowledge.[1] In the aftermath of the collapse of certain Asian economies in which the state has played the major role, the subsequent failure of the IMF and World Bank to bring these economies to recovery, and the parallel collapse of many socialist regimes, the failure of economic knowledge to predict, plan, and regulate the market seems self-evident to market participants. On the other hand, the triumph of American-style thinking about markets also has turned out to be brief. A series of high-profile financial failures in the U.S. markets, such as the collapse of Long Term Capital Management, have led Japanese traders to question the superiority of American traders' "market genius," while accounting scandals such as the Enron Corporation case have led many to query the American free-market ideology. The dominant mode of apprehension of the market, at the moment, then, is one of failure.[2]

The failure of economic knowledge is hardly a new theme in social and economic theory. The free-market advocate F. A. Hayek argued that economic planning was destined to fail because the kind of knowledge required for successful planning – "knowledge of the particular circumstances of time and place" – was unattainable in statistical form.[3] Hence, only the market could coordinate collective action. In a different way, economic anthropology and economic sociology, likewise, were built on the assumption that economics fails to represent economic realities. In their early renditions, both aimed to demonstrate empirically the limits of the explanatory power of economic theories such as economic rationality.[4]

Recent work in the "social studies of finance" shares with earlier economic anthropology and sociology an assumption that economic theory has its limits both as a model of and model for economic action. Rather than seek to demonstrate the ways in which economic theory fails, this work has drawn attention to other mundane practices and technologies working in the interstices of economic knowledge that make the market work. Practitioners are aware of the limits of economic theory, these scholars assert, and they respond to these limits in unexpected, creative, and sociotechnically determined ways. Daniel Beunza and David Stark, for example, have argued that what is missing from economic theories of arbitrage is an understanding of the sociotechnical and sociospatial environment in which arbitrage takes place.[5] The gaps in the economic theory, for them, are literally constituted by sociotechnical relations.[6]

A measure of how commonplace and accepted this move to show the work of sociotechnical relations in the market has become is that most recently economic knowledge itself has been reintroduced, as an actant in the network of humans and nonhumans that is understood to constitute the market. Michel Callon recently has pointed to "the capacity of economics in the performing . . . of the economy."[7] Callon's point is that even if, as generations of economic sociologists and anthropologists have suggested, economic knowledge fails in its predictive and explanatory capacities, it has other sociotechnical effects, and hence serves as a kind of genitor of the very sociotechnical practices that make the market work.[8] Donald MacKenzie's attention to the performative quality of finance theory, while differently motivated, also seeks to demonstrate the work of economic knowledge in constituting the sociotechnical conditions of the market that sociologists have long emphasized.[9]

What these diverse approaches share is an ambition to construct an alternative theory of how the market works that might in one way or another supplement traditional economic knowledge. Beunza and Stark go so far as to suggest that sociotechnical analysis completes one's understanding of finance and hence has practical utility for market participants themselves.[10] In this endeavor, the social studies of finance does not challenge economic theory but, rather, fills in certain gaps – it provides what Harold Garfinkel long ago termed "that missing what."[11] In the social studies of finance, in other words, data and theory form a kind of pair, in which data is what is found in the world and theory is what is added to that data, once it is removed to the anthropologist's or sociologist's office, in order to make social scientific knowledge. The data has gaps to be filled in by analysis. And at the same time, the theories have gaps, to be filled in with ethnographic data. Either way – and, indeed, in both ways at once – it is the gaps that draw the social scientist in.[12]

In this chapter, we challenge this project for a number of reasons. First, the sociotechnical focus on how the market works celebrates more than we would like the mystique of finance.[13] Whether the marvels of the market are the marvels of sociotechnological innovations or of the invisible hand, we believe that the fascination is critically unwarranted and devalues actors' own orientations toward technologies, theories, and institutional arrangements. That is, the fascination fails to give ethnographic attention to the mundane quality of the mundane. Second, and more importantly, we argue that this focus on what makes the market work drowns out the currently dominant mode of apprehension of the market among the participants we knew in Japan. Drawing upon ethnographic research among derivatives traders conducted by Miyazaki in the context of our joint research project on the Japanese financial markets and their regulation, we argue that what is salient, rather, is a shared perception of failure. An ethnographic inquiry into market participants' apprehensions of the failure of economic knowledge suggests that failure is apprehended not as a series of limits or gaps in economic theory to be filled in, as is assumed in the social studies of finance, but as an endpoint.

Of course, sociologists of finance will respond that their ambition is not to give voice to practitioners' own understandings of the market or its failures but, rather, to explain the workings of the market from a wider, nonsubjective, and analytical point of view. In other words, what is at stake in the question of how anthropologists and sociologists of finance apprehend the failure of economic knowledge is a larger question about the nature and uses of ethnographic knowledge. This in turn raises questions about the parallels between apprehensions of failure in the market and apprehensions of failure in anthropological and sociological work. What makes financial markets particularly interesting for social theorists at this moment, we contend, is this shared sense of the failure of knowledge. In other words, part of what is new about subjects such as finance is precisely the way in which they eclipse our sociological pairing of theory and data.[14]

Retreat from Knowledge

Beginning in the late 1980s, new financial products known as derivatives, understood to demand high-level computer and mathematics expertise, were introduced to Japan. In response, Japanese securities firms hired scientists and engineers as traders. Since 1997, Miyazaki has conducted fieldwork among members of the proprietary trading team of one of Japan's largest securities firms, which we will call Sekai Securities.[15] At the time of Miyazaki's fieldwork, the unit managed approximately $150 million of the firm's assets through active participation in domestic and overseas derivatives markets. Many of the members of the team were mid-career engineers or recent graduates of graduate programs in engineering, applied physics, and applied mathematics.

At the outset, these scientists knew nothing about trading, and since the Japanese market was still in an embryonic stage, they meticulously devoted themselves to learning from American futures and options specialists. This learning took a variety of forms. First, the scientists carefully studied a number of American books on options pricing models and trading strategies, such as John Cox and Mark Rubinstein's *Options Markets*[16] and John Murphy's *Technical Analysis of the Futures Markets*.[17] Some of these traders also collaborated with American business school professors through Sekai's research arm in San Francisco.[18] The traders also devoured collections of interviews with famous American traders in search of tips and "trading philosophies" that they believed would not appear in mathematical and technical analyses.

At the same time as they pursued this knowledge of derivatives trading, they also sought to acquire what anthropologists and sociologists have termed "tacit knowledge" of the market. From 1993 to 1995, Sekai collaborated with a group of traders from a well-known options trading firm in Chicago, which at the time was the global center of options trading. The Chicago firm sent two traders to Sekai's trading room in Osaka to trade options on Nikkei 225 futures at the Osaka Stock Exchange, under the watchful eye of the Sekai traders. The goal of the project was straightforward, from the Sekai traders' point of view – through what Jean Lave and Etienne Wenger have called "legitimate peripheral participation,"[19] the Sekai traders sought to learn how to trade by example.

By the time of Miyazaki's fieldwork, however, the traders had grown skeptical about all this learning. Takahashi, a Sekai trader, observed that he did not learn any hidden secrets from observing the Chicago traders, although he told Miyazaki that he was impressed by their "stoic" attitude and disciplined approach to the market. The traders ultimately came to conclude that learning, as a mode of engagement with the market, was the wrong approach altogether. On the one hand, there were no secrets to learn. On the other hand, all the studying and refining of academic theories and trading models had not made them any more successful in actual terms.

The Sekai traders' awareness of the limits of knowledge reflected their shared sense of defeat in the market. In the summer of 1998, Sekai announced that it would become part of an American financial conglomerate, and that its "wholesale" wing (including the proprietary trading unit) would merge with an American investment bank within the group. At the end of 1998, as a result of this merger, the trading team would be disbanded. By 2002, some of the former members of the team had found jobs as fund managers at Sekai's asset management subsidiary firm, while others had joined securities firms newly established by major Japanese banking groups, such as the Industrial Bank of Japan (IBJ) and Tokyo-Mitsubishi Bank, or had joined foreign securities and management consulting firms.

Indeed, "defeat" (*haisen*) was a dominant metaphor within the Japanese markets in 1998. Many popular commentators described Japan's financial situation at the time as a second "occupation" (*senryo*).[20] History seemed to be repeating itself, they said. The Japanese *goso sendan* – the "fleet" or "convoy" of mutually supporting manufacturing companies, banks, and securities firms that had been triumphant overseas during the 1980s – was falling apart. Since the collapse of the so-called bubble economy in 1991, Japan's banks and securities firms had been plagued by bad debt and severe losses on their investments. The industry had also been tainted by a series of scandals.[21] Just as the Americans brought democracy to Japan following defeat in World War II, some market commentators and politicians said, American firms were bringing to the Japanese financial markets the moral principles of what the government, in its blueprint for a British-inspired "Big Bang" enthusiastically termed "free, fair and global" trading. The presence of American securities firms and investment banks in Japan visibly increased in 1998 as a result of several major mergers and acquisitions.[22] Sekai's merger with an American investment bank was an example of this trend.

Hayashi, a Sekai trader who held a master's degree in applied mathematics from the University of Tokyo, had been at the center of the team's learning projects. Upon joining Sekai Securities after working for a chemical company as a computer scientist, Hayashi had devoted himself to developing highly complex trading models, using his expertise in neural network, fuzzy logic, and chaos theories. During this period, in part because of his English-language skills but also because of his prestigious academic training, Hayashi also worked on joint research projects with the American academics hired by the firm, and he supervised the collaboration between Sekai and the Chicago-based options firm. In the team, he was counted on to know the very frontier of finance theory.

One of Hayashi's pet projects during this period was a model based on neural network theory. Collaborating with an American trader, Hayashi developed a system aimed at predicting the movement of the TOPIX index futures market at the Tokyo Stock Exchange. What made the system different from other models was that it had a built-in learning mechanism. It processed six different kinds of input data, such as volume, interest rates, the yen/dollar exchange rate, and the percentage of total market share made up of the ten most heavily traded stocks, into its own formula, in a way that simulated what a human trader was expected to do. Mirroring the practice of human traders, the system would learn for a certain period of time and then, on the basis of this learning, predict market movement in the following time period. One could say that Hayashi and his colleagues' pursuit of learning American knowledge about the market had resulted in a kind of learning that aimed to learn the very same material itself. What Hayashi and his colleagues aimed to create through the model was a perfect version of themselves – an entity so knowledgeable, indeed so indistinguishable from that knowledge, that it could be truly interactive with – that is, at one with – the global market.

By 1998, however, Hayashi had given up on constructing complex trading systems. Thinking back, in the fall of 1998, to his work in the early 1990s, he recollected that he had taken it as self-evident that the more complex a system, the better it would predict market movement. He also recognized, in retrospect, the allure that the project of developing such a model had had for him. Because his specialty in graduate school was very close to neural network theory, he "was naturally attracted to these complex models," he said. It is important to note that Hayashi was not led to rethink his intellectual commitments as a result of actual market losses sustained by the model. In fact, Hayashi never used his complex models in actual trading, although he performed a number of simulations using these models.

Hayashi's coming to terms with the failure of cutting edge mathematical approaches took a particular form. In 1993, he came to know about a very simple trading strategy known as the "Turtle strategy," because of its alleged use by a Chicago-based group of traders known in the market as the "Turtles." The strategy – long a secret in the financial markets – derives from an even simpler trading strategy dating to the 1960s, known as Donchian's four-week rule.[23] In Hayashi's understanding, the Turtle strategy, itself only a very slight innovation on Donchian's rule, holds that if one holds a long position in a particular future, one should simply close that position when the price falls below the daily low for the last ten days. Likewise, if one holds a short position, one should close that position when the price exceeds the highest of the daily high for the last ten days.

Hayashi first learned about the Turtles through a reference in a book the team had translated. Curious, he responded to an advertisement placed in the back of *Futures Magazine*, an industry publication, by a former member of the Turtles team. To his team members' dismay, he spent $2,000 acquiring a "Turtle Seminar Workbook" entitled *Turtle Trading Concepts* and an accompanying videotape aimed largely at an amateur trading audience. Hayashi told Miyazaki that his team had already reached much the same conclusions as those of the Turtle trading strategy by the time he purchased the materials.

It was the endpoint of Hayashi's expert knowledge about the market, both technical and tacit. Since 1996, Hayashi and his team have traded entirely on the basis of their own version of the Turtle strategy. As he told me, "no other model, however complex, can out-perform this strategy." However, Hayashi noted that even this simplest and yet most accurate of strategies correctly predicted market movement only six out of ten times.

In the spring of 1999, Hayashi quit Sekai and abandoned trading altogether to become a consultant for a foreign risk management system company. His new role was to support the company's sales team by explaining the company's risk management system to their trader-clients. When Miyazaki saw him in January of 2000, Hayashi justified his retreat from trading saying that he only lives once, and so should not "hold a sword over his head" (*daijodan ni kamaeru*, meaning "take a high-handed attitude"). Making money actually was quite easy, he said – there was no need to expend so much intellectual energy to develop new trading strategies that did not work anyway.

Hayashi's discovery resonates with many other traders' experience. From many former Sekai traders' viewpoint, their past efforts to learn and acquire what they took to be superior knowledge of the market were misplaced. In early 2000, the former head of the team sarcastically told Miyazaki that Sekai was just a "good school" (*ii gakko*). One former Sekai trader who moved to a French securities firm said that he had discovered that his new colleagues did not pay any attention to the latest financial theories at all. Having accepted that knowledge mattered little, he claimed that he was successful for the first time in his trading career.[24]

We want to suggest that Sekai traders' apprehension of the limits of knowledge about the market took the form of an endpoint, a moment at which a project is apprehended retrospectively as complete, closed,[25] and in the past. This apprehension, in our view, is part of a widely shared discovery of the limits of knowledge in the market in Japan and elsewhere. Riles finds a similar apprehension of failure as endpoint among regulators of the Japanese financial markets.[26] The central bankers she has studied believe that their ambition to know the market's needs prospectively and to plan for them belongs to an era that has passed. They now seek to develop devices such as real-time clearing and settlement that, in their conception, will take the planner out of the loop of knowledge and response. For these regulators, the appeal of these devices inheres in the way they mark an end to market knowledge.

Of course, this apprehension of failure as an endpoint and the retreat from knowledge is not permanent.[27] By the summer of 2000, for example, Hayashi was seeking out a new kind of market knowledge – in particular, he had turned to new books about "human relations" (*ningen kankei*) for tips about how to read other people's minds. Whereas initially, for him and other traders, the turn to the relational side of business – networking and favor-swapping – exemplified their retreat from knowledge, soon they came to see social relations as its own object of knowledge.[28] Likewise, for central bankers, the needs of real-time machines fostered new demands for knowledge, albeit of different kinds. Yet although a sociological observer might emphasize the way one form of knowledge was emergent from another, our point is that this does not diminish the effect of retrospective closure at the moment of failure as an endpoint, from actors' own points of view.

Knowing the Endpoint

This brings us back to the social studies of finance. As we noted at the outset, Hayashi's approach to the market is paradigmatic of a pervasive awareness of and response to the failure of economic knowledge. It will be apparent how different this conception of failure as an endpoint is, in aesthetic and temporal terms, from the working view of the limits of economic knowledge in the social studies of finance, in which economic knowledge is imagined as incomplete – as leaving gaps to be filled in with sociotechnical truths. For us, this ethnographic fact has important implications for what the project of the social studies of finance should be. From the point of view of market participants such as Hayashi, the gap-filling approach is simply misdirected. There are no gaps to be filled in with detailed local knowledge or sociotechnical facts. If the social studies of finance is to take seriously the value of ethnographic research, its project must lie elsewhere.

The "anthropology of the contemporary" exemplified by this volume suggests a different way of engaging ethnographically with the failure of economic knowledge we have described. This project foregrounds the "instability" and "indeterminacy" of "emergent" articulations of rationality. Michael Fischer describes this position, which he terms, "emergent forms of life," as follows:

> "Emergent forms of life" acknowledges an ethnographic datum, a social theoretical heuristic, and a philosophical stance regarding ethics. The ethnographic datum is the pervasive claim (or native models) by practitioners in many contemporary arenas of life (law, the sciences, political economy, computer technologies, etc.) that traditional concepts and ways of doing things no longer work, that life is outrunning the pedagogies in which we have been trained. The social theoretic heuristic is that complex societies, including the globalized regimes under which late and post modernities operate, are always compromise formations among, in Raymond Williams's salutary formulation, emergent, dominant, and fading historical horizons.[29]

In this approach, it is not so much the failure of knowledge *per se* that is interesting, but rather the way this failure precipitates the "assemblage" of old and new knowledge practices in expected and unexpected manners.[30] As Paul Rabinow writes, "one seeks 'as yet unspecified singularities,' assembled in action."[31]

Another approach to the current ethnographic moment focuses on parallels between the representational practices of anthropologists and their subjects. In their chapter for this volume, for example, Holmes and Marcus have proposed "para-ethnography" – a focus on the quasi-ethnographic analytic practices of expert subjects.[32] To put the point in our own terms, what defines the "new ethnographic subjects" such as finance is a condition in which the subjects of ethnography – the data – are producing "theories" and indeed (as in the case of financiers) may even share an aesthetic of theory and data pairs.[33] This parallel obviates the ground of conventional genres of anthropological engagement such as sociological analysis or critique, since these genres are already incorporated into the "para-ethnographic" knowledge practices of experts.[34] But like the tradition of anthropological theory that has found in the effectiveness of indigenous analytical practices analogs for anthropological knowledge,[35] this focus on parallels between "what they do" and "what we do" reestablishes a kind of distance, a descriptive vantage point for ethnography.

From this point of view, what is interesting to us are the parallels between the way anthropologists of the contemporary and the traders we have described each respond to the failures of their own knowledge practices. For the anthropologist of the contemporary, the failure at issue is a failure in the ability to "know" the ethnographic subject. In response to such failures of knowing, the focus on "emergence," "complexity," and "assemblage" implicitly resigns itself to the fact that little can be known about the world except for the fact of complexity, indeterminacy, and open-endedness, since reality, in this view, is always emergent, indeterminate, and complex. Many of the analytical strategies that populate the anthropology of the contemporary – including those strategies that Miyazaki has elsewhere identified as the aesthetics of emergence[36] and those strategies that Riles has elsewhere identified as the aesthetics of instrumentality[37] – are analogous to Hayashi's Turtle strategy in our view: in response to the apprehension of the endpoint of their own knowledge, they retreat from knowing. And they also retreat from the recognition of the failure of their own knowledge by locating indeterminacy and complexity "out there," as if to be discovered, documented in real time. For Rabinow, for example, anthropology becomes "a chronicle of emergent assemblages."[38]

We do not want to be misunderstood as advocating a return to meta-theory here.[39] Rather, we want to suggest that the example of traders' apprehension of the failure of their knowledge of the market goes beyond mere parallelism between their knowledge practices and our own: it allows us to reflect ethnographically in turn on our own moment, and theirs, as a kind of endpoint. Under these conditions, which we term "epistemological sameness," it may seem that social scientific knowledge "fails" in aesthetic terms; that is, that the forms that define it as knowledge cease to produce the effects they once did.[40] The condition of "epistemological sameness" we wish to foreground is also by definition a condition of explicit acknowledgment of the failure of anthropological knowledge. It is quite literally failure as an endpoint.

What is necessary at this endpoint is not a description of points of parallelism between expert and anthropological knowledge but, rather, a response to expert knowledge. In the archetypal disciplinary understanding, the moment of ethnographic research is a moment of submission and response: the ethnographer abandons analytical control and submits to the agency of others. This submission occurs with another moment in mind, however: the ethnographer is looking forward to a future moment at which he or she will reassert analytical control over "the material" (the ethnographic moment, formulated retrospectively as material).[41]

This radical disjuncture between the moment of ethnography and the moment of writing is made untenable, however, by the new ethnographic subjects. Conversely, from the point of view of epistemological sameness, the knowledge practices and their failures that constitute finance are worthy of engagement because of the responses they invite in ethnographic knowledge. Following the collapse of distance between "data" and "theory" in the new ethnographic subjects, an ethnographic response in turn collapses the distance between the moment of the ethnographic encounter and the moment of description and analysis. We think that bringing the abeyance of agency that is at the heart of ethnography into the analytical and descriptive project, by understanding anthropological analysis as an act of response, is a means of resetting and reorienting the terms of anthropological knowledge at its endpoint.

What specific anthropological response would Hayashi's abandonment of economic knowledge seem to demand? Current projects that retreat from the limits of anthropological knowledge in a self-consciously limited way by pointing to assemblages and indeterminacies, or to parallels between other experts' knowledge and our own, projects that immediately turn endpoints into new beginning points, do not respond in kind to Hayashi's own stark encounter with the endpoint of his knowledge. Rather than simply passing through the endpoint on the way to new (but self-consciously limited) beginnings, therefore, we prefer to know the endpoint in a sustained way. This involves more than simply demonstrating that failure can be "productive" or "generative" of further knowledge, or further emergent complexities.

Notes

1   This essay draws on fieldwork that Miyazaki conducted among members of a trading team at a major Japanese securities firm in Tokyo, from August to September 1997, from September to November 1998, from August 1999 to July 2000, and from August to September 2001. Miyazaki spent every day at the team's trading room during his 1998 fieldwork. The trading team was disbanded in March 1999 due to the internal reorganization of the firm following its merger with a major American financial conglomerate.

During the 1999–2000 research, most of the members of the team left the firm, and Miyazaki met former members of the team on a regular basis outside their workplace. Unless otherwise noted, all quotations are taken from Miyazaki's field notes and all translations are Miyazaki's.

Joint research in 1997 and 1998 was conducted under the auspices of the American Bar Foundation. Miyazaki's 1999–2000 research was supported by the Abe Fellowship Program of the Social Science Research Council and the American Council of Learned Societies, with funds provided by the Japan Foundation Center for Global Partnership; Riles' research was funded by the Howard Foundation, the Japan Foundation, the National Endowment for the Humanities, and the American Council of Learned Societies. We thank audiences at the University of Lancaster and the University of St. Andrews, where earlier versions of this essay were presented. For comments, criticism, and help of many kinds, we thank Stephen Collier, Tony Crook, Sarah Franklin, Iris Jean-Klein, Aihwa Ong, Nigel Rapport, and Adam Reed.

2   Nigel Thrift has recently pointed out a shared sense of the limits of knowing in both academic and practical writings about the market: "until recently we were in love with expectations about what we could know and how we can know it which have only now, and rather painfully, been dismantled." See Nigel Thrift, "Shut Up and Dance, Or, Is the World Economy Knowable?" in *The Global Economy in Transition*, P. W. Daniels and W. F. Lever, eds. (Harlow: Longman, 1996), p. 12.

3   F. A. Hayek, *Individualism and Economic Order* (Chicago: University of Chicago Press, 1980 [1948]), p. 80.

4   See, e.g., Mark S. Granovetter, "Economic Action and Social Structure: The Problem of Embeddedness," *American Journal of Sociology* 19(3), 1985, pp. 481–510.

5   Daniel Beunza and David Stark, "Tools of the Trade: The Socio-Technology of Arbitrage in a Wall Street Trading Room," working paper available at http://www.coi.columbia.edu/pdf/beunza_stark_tott.pdf, 2002.

6   Ibid.

7   Michael Callon, "Introduction: The Embeddedness of Economic Markets in Economics," in *The Laws of the Market*, Michel Callon, ed. (Oxford: Blackwell, 1998), p. 23.

8   Cf., Fabian Muniesa, "Performing Prices: The Case of Price Discovery Automation in the Financial Markets," in *Facts and Figures: Economic Representations and Practices*, H. Kalthoff, R. Rottenburg, and H. Wagener, eds., *Ökonomie und Gesellschaft, Jahrbuch* 16, 2000, pp. 289–312.

9   Donald MacKenzie, "Physics and Finance: S-Terms and Modern Finance as a Topic for Science Studies," *Science, Technology and Human Values* 26(2), 2001, pp. 115–144.

10 Daniel Beunza and David Stark, "Trading Sites – Destroyed, Revealed, Restored," working paper available at http://www.coi.columbia.edu/pdf/beunza_stark_ts.pdf, 2002.

11 Michael Lynch, *Scientific Practice and Ordinary Action: Ethnomethodology and Social Studies of Science* (Cambridge: Cambridge University Press, 1993), p. 271.

12 Cf., Annelise Riles, *The Network Inside Out* (Ann Arbor: University of Michigan Press, 2000), pp. 143–170; Marilyn Strathern, *Partial Connections*, ASAO Special Publications 3 (Savage, MD: Rowman and Littlefield, 1991).

13 Cf., Karin Knorr Cetina and Urs Bruegger, "The Market as an Object of Attachment: Exploring Postsocial Relations in Financial Markets," *Canadian Journal of Sociology* 25(2), 2000, pp. 141–168; see also Bill Maurer, "Finance," in *The Handbook of Economic Anthropology*, James Carrier, ed. (London: Edward Elgar, 2004).

14 Riles, *The Network Inside Out*.

15 A propriety trading team is a team that invests the firm's own capital, rather than the capital of its clients.

16 John Cox and Mark Rubinstein, *Options Markets* (Englewood Cliffs, NJ: Prentice-Hall, 1985).

17 John Murphy, *Technical Analysis of the Futures Markets: A Comprehensive Guide to Trading Methods and Applications* (New York: New York Institute of Finance, 1986).

18 Hirokazu Miyazaki, "The Materiality of Finance Theory," in *Materiality*, Daniel Miller, ed. (Durham: Duke University Press, forthcoming, 2005).

19 Jean Lave and Etienne Wenger, *Situated Learning: Legitimate Peripheral Participation* (Cambridge: Cambridge University Press, 1991).

20 Tsuneo Iida and Takanori Mizuno, *Kinyu haisen wo koete* [Overcoming defeat in the financial war] (Tokyo: Toyo Keizai Shinpo-sha, 1998); Takanori Mizuno, *Beikoku kinyu meja no Nihon senryo* [The occupation of Japan by the U.S. financial industry] (Tokyo: Jitsugyo no Nihon-sha, 1998); Eiji Ohshita, *Shosetsu Nihon baishu* [Buying out Japan: a novel] (Tokyo: Shodensha, 1998).

21 Top executives of the Big Four firms had been prosecuted for directing their firms to compensate preferred clients for their losses. These clients included institutional investors, politicians, and *yakuza* (Japanese gangsters).

22 The presence of American securities firms and investment banks was not new in Japan, although up until then, the range of their business activities had been considerably limited. Merrill Lynch opened its Tokyo branch office in 1972, following the passage of a law that allowed foreign securities firms to operate in Japan. Several other American securities firms opened branch offices in the first half of the 1980s. None of these was allowed to obtain a membership at the Tokyo Stock Exchange. In 1986, however, Merrill Lynch, Goldman Sachs, and Morgan Stanley acquired memberships at the Tokyo Stock Exchange, following negotiations between the Japanese and American governments concerning American firms' access to the Japanese market. See Maximilian J. B. Hall, *Financial Reform in Japan: Causes and Consequences* (Cheltenham, U.K.: Edward Elgar, 1998), pp. 114–117; Shigeo Uchida, *Nihon shoken shi* [History of the Japanese securities markets], Vol. 3 (Tokyo: Nihon Keizai Shinbun-sha, 1995), pp. 106–108.

23 According to Donchian's rule, one takes a long position (buys) when the price of a bond future exceeds the highest of the daily highest prices of the last four weeks, and one takes a short position (sells) when the price falls below the lowest of the daily lowest prices for the last four weeks.

24 Hirokazu Miyazaki, "The Temporalities of the Market," *American Anthropologist* 105(2), 2003, pp. 259–260.

25 Hirokazu Miyazaki, *The Method of Hope: Anthropology, Philosophy, and Fijian Knowledge* (Stanford: Stanford University Press, 2004).

26 Annelise Riles, "Real Time: Unwinding Technocratic and Anthropological Knowledge," *American Ethnologist* (forthcoming, 2004).

27 Cf., Miyazaki, *The Method of Hope*.

28 Hirokazu Miyazaki, "Economy of Dreams: The Production of Hope in Anthropology and Finance," unpublished MS, n.d.

29 Michael J. Fischer, *Emergent Forms of Life and the Anthropological Voice* (Durham: Duke University Press, 2003), p. 37.

30 Stephen J. Collier and Aihwa Ong, "Global Assemblages," Chapter 1, this volume.

31 Paul Rabinow, *French DNA: Trouble in Purgatory* (Chicago: University of Chicago Press, 1999), p. 174.

32 Douglas R. Holmes and George E. Marcus, "Cultures of Expertise and the Managements of Globalization: Toward the Re-functioning of Ethnography," Chapter 13, this volume.

33 Bill Maurer, "Implementing Empirical Knowledge in Anthropology and Islamic Accountancy," Chapter 12, this volume; Annelise Riles, "Making White Things White: Legal Theory as Ethnographic Subject," unpublished MS, n.d.

34 Kim Fortun, *Advocacy after Bhopal: Environmentalism, Disaster, New Global Orders* (Chicago: University of Chicago Press, 2001).

35 Roy Wagner, *The Invention of Culture* (Chicago: University of Chicago Press, 1981 [1975]); Roy Wagner, *Symbols that Stand for Themselves* (Chicago: University of Chicago Press, 1986); Marilyn Strathern, *The Gender of the Gift: Problems with Women and Problems with Society in Melanesia* (Berkeley: University of California Press, 1988); Strathern, *Partial Connections*; Riles, *The Network Inside Out*.

36 Miyazaki, *The Method of Hope*.

37 Riles, "Real Time"; Riles, "Making White Things White"; Annelise Riles, "Law as Object," in *Law and Empire in the Pacific: Fiji and Hawaii*, Sally Merry and Donald Brenneis, eds. (Santa Fe, NM: School of American Research Press, 2004); Annelise Riles, "Property as Legal Knowledge: Means and Ends," *Journal of the Royal Anthropological Institute* (forthcoming, 2004).

38 Paul Rabinow, *Anthropos Today: Reflections on Modern Equipment* (Princeton: Princeton University Press, 2003), p. 86.

39 Cf., Benjamin Lee and Edward LiPuma, "Cultures of Circulation: The Imaginations of Modernity," *Public Culture* 14(1), 2002, pp. 191–213.

40 Marilyn Strathern, *After Nature: English Kinship in the Late Twentieth Century* (Cambridge: Cambridge University Press, 1992).

41 Miyazaki, *The Method of Hope*.

PART IV

GOVERNMENTALITY AND POLITICS

GOVERNING POPULATIONS

18

ECOLOGIES OF EXPERTISE:
Assembling Flows, Managing Citizenship[1]

AIHWA ONG

'Today, wealth is generated by new ideas, more than by improving the ideas of others . . .

The US economy has done immensely well because it enjoys a "brain gain" year after year.

For example, one quarter of the companies in Silicon Valley are created by or led by Indian and Chinese immigrants . . . That is why we have to bring in multi-national talent, like the way we brought in MNCs [multinational corporations]. Like MNCs, multi-national talent, or MNTs, will bring in new expertise, fresh ideas and global connections and perspectives. I believe that they will produce lasting benefits for Singapore.

Goh Chok Tong, Prime Minister of Singapore[2]

We shall all become citizens of the K-economy . . . Survival in a borderless global economy based on knowledge requires everyone to be equipped with new skills and assimilate the culture of high technology and dynamic entrepreneurship. This is not wishful thinking. In fact, the Government has painstakingly endeavoured to build a strong foundation, in particular through education and human resource development. I am confident that there is someone in every village who has acquired skills and knowledge in the field of technology from an institution of higher learning. I believe this was not possible five or ten years ago . . . To ensure success from the new economy, we need a pool of the best talent from at home and abroad. Efforts need to be taken to hire

*the best brains regardless of race or nationality, from Bangalore to California. This is a
step towards creating a world-class workforce.*

The Malaysian Minister of Finance[3]

Reassemblage

The above discourses about technology and the nurturing of an enterprising culture
encode rather specific kinds of hope, orientation, and scope for Southeast Asian
nations. They also suggest that networks of mobile technology, government practice,
and political values can be brought into a new kind of engagement for the production
of a knowledge society. Such emerging configurations of technology, biopolitics, and
ethics, however, fly in the face of existing theories about information society. Manuel
Castells provides a view of how "global networks" are organized by elite managers
operating at a global scale.[4] In the Asian region, Castells argues that developmental
states mainly depend on links with indigenous business firms and actors to form
distinct regional networks that are separable from networks of greater extension.[5]
Castells' model thus claims that the information technologies produce networks at
global and regional scales, suggesting that these systems are aligned in terms of
hierarchical levels based on geo-economic positioning.

But the proliferation of technologies across the world produces systems that mix
technology, politics, and actors in diverse configurations that do not follow given
scales or political mappings.[6] Gilles Deleuze and Felix Guatarri use the term "assemblage" to denote a contingent ensemble of diverse practices and things that is divided
along the axes of territoriality and deterritorialization. Furthermore, particular alignments of technical and administrative practices extract and give intelligibility to new
spaces by decoding and encoding milieus.[7] In short, particular assemblages of
technology and politics not only create their own spaces, but also give diverse values
to the practices and actors thus connected to each other. Deleuze and Guattari call
any multiplicity of interconnected techniques and actors "a continuous self-vibrat-
ing" plateau.[8]

★ ★ ★

The recent experiences of state-planners in Southeast Asia provide an opportunity
to explore the new kinds of engagement between administrative rationality and
developmental projects, with direct consequences for the management of
citizens and foreigners alike. In the late 1990s, a financial upheaval challenged the
continuing feasibility of the dominant "Asian tiger" model of export-led manufacturing based on partnerships between state authorities and foreign factories.[9] In the
aftermath of the crisis, technocrats sought to reassemble new elements – research
institutions, expatriates, and administrative calculation – that constitute their own
environment.

It is perhaps not surprising that ecology has entered the lexicon of technocrats who use terms such as web, cluster, and ecosystem to suggest new forms of linkages, exchanges, and feedback loops that are being forged between the distribution of knowledge flows and the technical resources, and techniques of management. The deliberate orchestration of technical flows and interactions between global and local institutions, actors, and values engenders its own dynamism and intensity. Ecologists, for instance, have pointed to the jungle canopy as an ecosystem that allows diverse life forms to dwell in or move through it, a process of complex interaction that contributes to a high species density.[10] Perhaps inspired by such complexity theory, Asian technocrats are creating ecological conditions of intense mobility and inter-activity in order to generate nonlinear dynamics for the rise of new collective properties. Thus I call this new techno-administrative zone that depends on novel combinations of mobile knowledge and actors connected to diverse sites and labors an "ecology of expertise."

Particular alignments of knowledge, politics, and ethics also constitute an ecology of positions, whereby diverse subjects are administered in relation to each other. The government of diverse populations increasingly depends on neoliberal calcula-tion of worth, as individuals and populations become operable through specific knowledges, techniques, and expertise.[11] Nikolas Rose has argued that in Thatcherite Britain, a neoliberalist style of government reconceptualized citizenship as a mode of self-enterprise, an obligation to be an entrepreneur of oneself, to become knowledge-able citizen-subjects.[12] More recently, the Blair government has promoted a kind of technological citizenship that encourages citizens to be technologically informed as a way of engaging in public life.[13] But how is neoliberal calculation taken up in Southeast Asian contexts, where the value of knowledgeable, risk-taking, and entrepreneurial subjects is to be found mainly in circulating foreign professionals? In Singapore and Malaysia, the application of neoliberal rationality to the adminis-tration of subjects has political implications for the meaning of citizenship. Malaysia, and to some extent, Singapore practice a process of graduated sovereignty[14] whereby differentiated forms of social privileges and economic regulation are articulated over the population. Dominant ethnic groups – ethnic Chinese in Singapore, Malay *bumiputera* in Malaysia – have had their special status and privileges enhanced because of their capacity to engage global market interests. But in the quest for a knowledge society, expertise and entrepreneurial values are replacing ethnicity and political loyalty; and expatriates, including foreign Asians, are increasingly coded as exemplars of intellectual capital *and* risk-taking behavior. The two countries differ in the way in which they each assemble institutions, actors, and values in techno-poles of different orders that are linked to transnational networks of different technoscientific orders. Each is a distinctive constellation of specific presences and absences, of social privileges, values, and regulation that destabilize ethnic governmentality and promote new ethics of intellectual capital and market agility. But as we shall see, the new ecology of belonging produces a set of new problems, as citizens come to question the new regime of moral worthiness based on foreign expertise.

Singapore: A Biotech Tiger?

Recruiting foreign talent

Singapore prides itself on being a "green" nation-state, a pleasant, efficient tropical paradise that is the favorite site of multinational corporations. An island nation with practically no natural resources but a well-educated population of about four million, Singapore has built a manufacturing base in electronics, engineering, and chemicals. The political norm has been to maintain a tight control over the population while dispersing infrastructure systems in order in bring in food, water, and immigrant talent. The ecological language comes easily, then, in the campaign to get locals to accept a new kind of open society. In 1997, the Prime Minister Goh Chong Tock remarked that "gathering human talent is not like collecting different species of trees... to green up Singapore ... In the information age, human talent, not physical resources or financial capital is the key factor for economic competitiveness and success. We must therefore welcome the infusion of knowledge which foreign talent will bring. Singapore must become a cosmopolitan, global city, an open society..."[15] The "enterprise economy" represents the creation of a virtual ecological environment that is intended to attract global flows of intellectual capital and expatriates, while superseding the older ideas and stalwart workers associated with the Asian tiger model.

Wealth, a Singapore official declares, is now "generated by new ideas, more than by improving the ideas of others."[16] Marketable ideas depend on exploiting specific qualities of the population. However, the government faces the problem of a small but steady outflow of its own talented elite, while trying to maintain a critical mass of well-educated people who can be the basis of new knowledge industries. To attract international expertise, clustering infrastructure is built to localize world-class institutions and experts in technological zones. The "cluster-development" strategy connects the state, as venture capitalist, with foreign research institutes and global companies, creating a network that fosters interactions, risk-taking, and innovations among expatriate and local knowledge workers. An official told me that the state sees itself as a gardener providing fertilizer, thus acting as a catalyst to allow different organisms to thrive in the corporatized ecosystem. For instance, cluster projects include state–university–firm partnerships in the domains of business management,[17] engineering, and biomedical sciences. By incubating strategic knowledge domains, cluster projects hope to attract intellectual capital from overseas and investments by global companies, and to build a creative environment for further knowledge growth. By tapping into the huge population of smart students, professionals, and scientists from Asia (and beyond), Singapore hopes to become the hub of cutting-edge intellectual capital in the region.

Immigration, academic, and taxation policies have converged to make the island very attractive to foreign knowledge institutions and foreign experts. There are already a variety of expatriate populations in Singapore – Malaysians in all walks of life, European and American businessmen, bankers, industrialists, and professors, as well as old-time colonial British subjects. Nevertheless, the thrust toward a rapidly growing knowledge economy requires headhunting programs to recruit promising foreigners from China, India, Southeast Asia, and Australia to come train and work in the new industries in Singapore. Promising students from leading universities in China and India are given scholarships and places in the National University of Singapore (NUS), where they can enroll in programs and incubator projects overseen by professors and scientists from world-class institutions and companies. Special tax regimes favor expatriates over local citizens, and spouses of expatriates can find work easily. World-class research universities and companies are given tax breaks for locating in Singapore, and entering into partnerships with the National University of Singapore.

Biotech research as a Wild West frontier

This assemblage of science, administration, and foreign experts is focused on transforming Singapore into "Asia's biotech tiger."[18] Central to the attraction of foreign companies and scientists are a number of schemes that facilitate transnational training and research. First, there is a coordination of training programs between the National University of Singapore and American and European universities. The Singapore–Massachusetts Institute of Technology Alliance, founded in 1998, provides advanced distance learning facilities to Asian students gathered in Singapore. Such linkages – through the Internet and live technologies – provide MIT with a new model "to promote global science and engineering education and research."[19] Scholarships to students from China, India, Vietnam, and Malaysia cover all expenses at a higher level than normal expenses incurred by students in Singapore. Services for international students are expanded. The faculty (of approximately one hundred) is comprised of equal numbers of Singaporean and MIT professors, distributed across fields such as computer science, manufacturing technology, and molecular engineering. The university curriculum has been changed to accommodate the American semester cycle and the schedules of expatriate professors. Students have the option to spend one semester at MIT in Cambridge, Massachusetts. It is hoped that young engineers and scientists (with M.A. and Ph.D. qualifications) will develop spin-off companies that are based in Singapore. To nudge students toward that goal, foreign students enjoy guaranteed employment and high salaries upon graduation, as well as invitations to become residents and citizens. The expectation is that the national university will soon have a student body that is one-fifth foreign. The Singapore–MIT Alliance is therefore about more than training a new generation of Asian scientists. It is also about using engineering as a technology to forge an information society, thus transfiguring the meaning of citizenship and state in the process.

Scientists and observers are astonished at the huge sums of state money (close to 3 billion dollars) that bankroll all aspects of biomedical research. Nikolas Rose and Carlos Novas[20] use the term "biovalue" to denote the transformation by recent advances in the biomedical sciences of "the potentialities embodied in life itself into a source of value creation."[21] In Singapore, biovalue is accumulated by concentration on specific fields – molecular biology, bioengineering, and bioinformatics – that offer long-term profitability. Singapore is already the base for manufacturing for seven of the world's leading drug companies that enjoy ten-year tax breaks. The state offers venture capital and sets up institutes to both attract and train scientists, who will be employed by global companies and will transform intellectual property into market products. A major player is Johns Hopkins Singapore, which is extending new franchises in Asia. Johns Hopkins University has a historical connection with Asia – it set up the first American hospital in China in the 1910s – and it now views Southeast Asia as a site for applying its discoveries and techniques to diseases that are prevalent in the region. Johns Hopkins Singapore has established a doctoral program in immunology and a master's degree in clinical research. In short, new opportunities to undertake research on Asian genomics, and to conduct research on mechanisms of diseases endemic to the Asian region, have lured leading foreign professors and scientists to Singapore. Also a major draw are the new facilities – including a huge science park centered on a Biopolis – fluid funding programs, and an environment that encourages excellence in science. A Wild West frontier atmosphere is created that treats scientists as demigods in a place where education is already highly regarded. For an American university, Singapore becomes a step toward globalization.

But perhaps an even greater attraction for foreign scientists is an ethical regime that has a hands-off policy toward limits on research methods and access to data. In the initial euphoria, the stress was on essentially unregulated research unfettered by the debates and ethical concerns that limits research elsewhere. The head of a bioethics advisory committee describes the untrammeled research environment in this way: "When there are no traffic rules, people will park everywhere."[22] This is ironic in a country in which traffic rules are rigorously enforced through an arsenal of electronic monitors. But when it came to the harvesting of human embryonic cells for research, it seemed prudent to consult religious groups. Research on 14-day-old embryos was presented as being of benefit to mankind, but Buddhist leaders voiced objections against human cloning "just for fame and money," and Catholic doctors who opposed taking human life warned of a downward "spiral of moral deconscientisation."[23] But by defining life in strictly scientific terms, and getting endorsements from scientists around the world, therapeutic cloning received the green light in 2002. It was assumed that the informed consent of all parties concerned was required, thus conforming to global or American standards. Currently, research is based on six cell-lines developed in Singapore, which also supplies federally funded research in the United States. The Genome Institute has stressed that it engages only in therapeutic cloning (from unused embryos, left over from fertility treatment) and that it will not be producing human clones.

In addition to following international guidelines for stem cell research, a Singapore Tissue Network provides cell material for cancer and related disease research: "Genetic research today is global . . . In Singapore the relevant resources for human genomics research are the ethnic diversity and high quality clinical databases."[24] The country has computerized medical records, the ethnic groups are fairly discrete (because of limited inter-ethnic marriage), and personal identity cards make it easy to track patients. By drawing medical profiles along with identifiable racial or ethnic markers, the goal is to "understand the genetic architecture of Pan-Asian populations" as the basis for developing functional genomics for treating cancer and diseases that are endemic among Asian populations. The genomic data will be made available to public and private researchers alike, and thus will be a lure for foreign laboratories. In short, Singapore is capitalizing not only on the availability of Asian brains; it is also selling multiracial Asian gene lines to bring in biotech investments. A bioethical regime, driven more by the imperative to develop a life-science economy than by the ethical concerns of varied ethnic groups, woos foreign biologists who believe that in Singapore, there are fewer constraints on research and the best opportunities for career development anywhere.[25]

The state has orchestrated a sense of excitement over the life sciences, and the collective good that is assumed to contribute to public health and prosperity, as well as to benefit mankind. The successful recruitment of a number of high-profile scientists – including those who cloned "Dolly" – has stirred national pride that little Singapore can compete with the world's best biotechnology hubs. By forming an ecology of research and idea creation – Singapore wants to recast itself as "the Boston of the East" – a whole new space has also been created in the biopolitical regulation of citizens in relation to expatriates.

Technopreneurial citizenship

The quest for a knowledge society is the latest experiment in a Singaporean modernity driven by the relentless pursuit of new ideas, the manipulation of human resources, and recoding of the purpose of the city-state. Since independence from the United Kingdom in 1965, administrators have sought to steadily improve the human capital, through immigration of professionals and promising students (mainly ethnic Chinese from Malaysia), and by regulating the ethnic composition of its Chinese-dominated population. In the 1980s and 1990s, worries about declining birth rates shifted the government toward a eugenics program that favored marriage and childbirth among university "female graduates," a term coding elite women mainly from the Chinese population. This technology of "state fathering" is based on the assumption that children of the more fertile minority Malays are intellectually inferior, and the perceived need to secure the human capital of the future.[26] Despite various state interventions, including the arrangement of dating services and courtship venues, many professional women have remained single (men tend to marry much younger, less educated women). At the same time, tens of thousands of Singaporeans study or live abroad, adding to the shortfall in local talent. But the policy of building up a critical mass of well-educated people in the form of "graduate babies" has not been able to supply the kind of subjects who embody the new technological and entrepreneurial skills associated with the information economy.[27]

Seemingly overnight, a new official discourse stresses the defunct value of local Chinese economic networks and competitiveness. A manpower official reminded me: "Competition is a fact of life. This is an open economy in which global links predominate." The Chinese merchant who mobilizes kinship- or ethnic-based personal relationships (*guanxi*) is not an appropriate actor for forging transnational relations based on cutting-edge research and knowledge creation. What is needed, he stressed, is "the international risk-taking entrepreneurial figure who is beyond the Chinese merchant model. In the post-industrial society, there is the need for a Western attitude of risk-taking, a need to mix *guanxi* with Western global practices." Technopreneurial values, that stress a mix of technical and entrepreneurial excellence in citizen-subjects, are now detached from culture and ethnicity, putting a premium on agile knowledge subjects who can help build a globally connected knowledge society.

This recoding of citizenship ideals entails transforming all Singaporeans into technologically informed individuals. Besides universal access to computer training in schools, a variety of in-house retraining programs continually adjust workers to reskilling and lifelong learning.[28] In addition, retirees and housewives have access to neighborhood classes on using the Internet. Singapore is, proportionately speaking in terms of its population, the most wired country in Asia. The normative goal is that citizens must become competitive with global, or stereotypically Californian, entrepreneurs. But clearly, the attitudes and practices of the old Singaporean corporate culture look positively antiquated in relation to the fluid strategies of the new economy.

Heretofore, a scholarly-official class has operated government-linked corporations, controlling control large amounts of national savings and enjoying an oligopoly market position sponsored by the government. An economist from Morgan Stanley observes that the "civil servants turned corporate managers" do not have the appropriate skills, creative values, and innovations of American enterprising technological culture. The old planners should be replaced by "tomorrow's risk-taking New Economy entrepreneurs," who can convert these corporations into "genuine enterprises."[29] Even employment with multinational firms is no longer the sensible thing to do, since corporations teach technical skills but not entrepreneurial risk-taking and the capacity to hive off home-grown companies. Furthermore, the public, attuned to years of official messages about how it should be managed, has been socially conditioned to "instinctively go along with accepted wisdom," an official confided. In the post-1997 recession, the "shared values" talk has been abandoned. This would require a shift from the educational policy of rote-learning to one that is more "American," stressing independent thinking, initiative, and risk-taking at all levels of the education system. At a meeting on the Singapore–MIT Alliance, a business leader notes that the region "has strong advantages over the West" when it comes to diligence, loyalty, and teamwork, but that Asian graduates lack curiosity, innovation, and independent thinking, which are perhaps more crucial in the knowledge-based economy. There is the fear that such views would be considered to be "anti-traditional" Asian values, but he recommends that a calculative and creative approach in the workplace need not spread to the family and society, where Confucian respect for individuals and collectivities should remain the norm.[30]

To engender appropriate new-economy attitudes, the national university has forged links with overseas colleges, through which Singaporeans can acquire the kind of practices that mix scientific excellence with creative risk-taking. The University of Pennsylvania is one milieu in which students will also have the chance to work with biomedical and biotechnology companies located in the Philadelphia area. Another internship program, at Stanford University, allows Singaporean students to work briefly in Silicon Valley companies in order to pick up "technopreneurial" practices in the high-tech field. In a glowing write-up, a third-year material science student heading for Silicon Valley enthused that "we are young and not risk-averse." Through the internship program, "we hope to experience first-hand how a startup works. The practical experience will be invaluable."[31] Such overseas programs are intended to shake Singaporean university graduates out of their complacency, and suggest alternative entrepreneurial careers to their usual ambition of working for foreign business. Instead, it is hoped that through exposure to a variety of knowledge and business domains, Singaporeans and foreign Asians benefiting from these programs will form the core of new entrepreneurial subjects. Eventually, it is hoped that some of them will found startup companies in Singapore that attract global investments.

But as citizenship becomes invested with technological and risk-taking values, foreigners, it appears, have been the ones to benefit most handsomely from government largess. The moral demands of a technopreneurial citizenship have risen higher as citizens are expected to compete with Asian foreigners on home ground. The continual influx of expatriates, and their coding as the scientific experts or entrepreneurial subjects, have coincided with the retrenchment of less competitive workers in a variety of fields. Growing public anxiety has surfaced in the state-controlled newspaper. Some letters to the editors request that first job preference be given to locals, and that only unfilled positions be occupied by foreigners.[32] There is also suspicion that locals may be overlooked in favor of foreign but mediocre talent. Officials have responded through a double message of reassurance and the necessity of relentless competition. Singaporeans are told that there was no simple process of one-on-one substitution in different categories of expertise, that competitive Singaporeans will get the jobs for which they qualify. There is a growing sense of a moral regime of differential worth based on foreign talent. Expatriates seem to enjoy citizenship status, to be cajoled into becoming citizens when reluctant to do so.

The ecology of expertise is thus a "high-tension zone"[33] of constant cross-referral between the recent past and the projected future, between rigidity and flexibility, between insiders and outsiders. Singaporean citizens are used to considering themselves among the most Westernized Asian subjects, and yet they must now compete with educated expatriates from post-socialist China and impoverished India. There is mounting intra-ethnic Chinese strain as mainland Chinese students and professionals seem to enjoy greater benefits, scholarships, and jobs than local ethnic Chinese. Students are concerned about career chances, and they believe that they have become less eligible for university scholarships. State promotion advertisements feature

Japanese cancer researchers and musicians from the People's Republic of China singing effusive praises such as "Singapore gives life to new ideas" and "Life in Singapore is like an allegro. Fast, furious, and fun."[34] In this envisaged "top talent capital," people who do not aspire to be elite professionals or managers are beginning to feel a sense of reverse nativism or *bumiputera*-ism. As mentioned earlier, *bumiputera* ("sons of the soil") is a term for the native-born Malay majority in neighboring Malaysia. Most Singaporeans have long felt superior to Malays in Malaysia and in Singapore itself, considering them as less competitive and knowledgeable natives. But a new regime of graduated citizenship is giving foreigners first rank, seeming to demote Singaporean ethnic Chinese to the second level, to a scale of lower technical excellence formerly occupied by Singaporean Malays. Meanwhile, discourses of technopreneurial citizenship have remained silent about the heavy responsibility of Singaporean citizens, that all men must spend at least two years in military service during the critical years when they are ready to launch themselves into careers. Expatriates are not burdened by this requirement. There is a sense of being re-nativized, a reduction to the debased subaltern position of colonial times, except that this time the natives will be actual citizens, while expatriates – especially foreign Chinese – are the virtual citizens of an extended space of expertise.

Malaysia: A Knowledge Stepping Stone

Singapore has clearly positioned itself as a first-tier techno-hub in Asia, while the Malaysian knowledge project has come across mainly as a public relations campaign. Some American scholars have dismissed the project – "there's no multimedia super corridor!" – noting that the fancy infrastructure cannot conceal the limited supply of skilled workers. Others have treated the project as a discursive device to "reposition" Malaysia in the networked information economy, especially through a strategic invoking of Malaysia's multiculturalism. A closer investigation shows a rather more complicated picture: the forging of "smart partnerships" between the government and foreign business in order to reposition Malaysia as the site of high-technology sweatshops. The multimedia corridor links Cyberjaya, Putrajaya (a showpiece new capital), Kuala Lumpur, and the international airport, covering a former plantation area larger than the entire island of Singapore. Billions of dollars from oil wealth have been poured into the building of business centers, highways, academic institutions, and shopping malls. Unlike Singapore, where the localization of experts and intellectual property is under way, the Malaysian hub has attracted mainly assembly, manufacturing, and call centers. A new Multimedia University (compared to Stanford University) and surrounding colleges are supposed to graduate local talent, but what seems most compelling to foreign companies is the digital corridor as a stepping-stone to Asian markets.[35]

The cyber-hub is primarily a switching station between the global scale of high-technology applications and adaptations at the regional scale. It is a portal between global and regional scales of technological innovations whereby local actors are enrolled to make useable in local markets. Bruno Latour uses the term "translation" to denote the interpretations by actors of their own interests and that of the people they enroll.[36] By providing a series of translations, the cyber corridor hopes to become an important detour for global companies. First, the combination of impressive infrastructure and low costs makes the corridor comparatively attractive to software companies from India, but also from Australia and the West, that seek to test and develop their products for small and emerging markets. For Indian software servicing, the corridor is also an ideal site for expanding offshore business in Southeast Asia. Indian companies or their subsidiaries provide software packages – in the areas of banking, insurance, telecommunications, and manufacturing – that are "localized," or adapted for applications in a variety of venues in other developing countries. Second, being linked to high tech operations at the global scale, Malaysia can undertake the widespread computerization of the basic operations of government, the commercial, health, and educational sectors. Third, the multilingual skills of Malaysian workers – in English, Hindi, Malay-Indonesian, Chinese, and Thai – allow global companies to launch their products in other markets. Malaysian workers in effect help to identify and shape the interests of diverse groups in new technological products. For instance, firms customize multimedia technologies such as smart cards for use in Malaysia and in smaller markets such as Thailand, Burma, Saudi Arabia, and parts of Africa. Finally, firms such as Microsoft use the local center not only to stake out growing Asian markets for its software products, but also to introduce the notion of software piracy as something of economic interest to Asian consumers as well.[37] Through this series of translations – by linking the interests of its own and that of enrolled others – the digital hub transforms the detour into a corridor (if not a highway).

While they are not Silicon Valley firms, Indian companies have become key players in connecting the super-corridor to a second tier of the information economy, and in training Malaysian knowledge workers. HCL Infosystems, for instance, is the largest Indian software company, with 14,000 workers in software factories in India and at sites around the world. The company also operates as a body shop – that is, as a recruiter of knowledge workers who are sent to high tech centers worldwide. Indian software expatriates in Malaysia are mainly recruited from Chennai, and are recruited to work for periods from six months up to ten years. Most if not all view their sojourn in the corridor as strictly short term, though they enjoy the facilities and living conditions, which are superior to those in India. Because they have tested out of rigorous technology institutes in India, the engineers often feel disdain for the fruits of Malaysian technical education. They consider Malaysian workers as mediocre, narrowly specialized, "not well equipped for multi-platform work," and generally hampered by poor English. This means that Indian expatriates have to repeatedly intervene to correct their mistakes. Some have been quick to dismiss Malaysia's ambitions since they consider Malaysian knowledge workers half as effective as Indian counterparts, while others have been more optimistic, saying that it is a matter of years before the Malaysian corridor will become a big technology center.

The Indian expatriates consider the corridor as a "stepping stone" to America and other final Western destinations. While they enjoy living in Kuala Lumpur, in a familiar Indian neighborhood, few expect to settle down as permanent residents or citizens. Some feel exploited by the body shop system that pays them a set rate, by tricky apartment brokers, and by companies that do not pay them as well as expatriates from Western countries. A few are angry that Malaysia makes it almost impossible for their spouses to join them. Many if not all are biding their time in Malaysia, waiting for their friends in American cities to sponsor them for jobs in America. For instance, just before September 11, 2001, a female Indian engineer who had spent three years in Kuala Lumpur obtained an American work visa. As soon as the American economic climate improves, she expects to be reunited with her family in Chennai and to relocate to a New Jersey suburb: "We ask each other, 'Are you still here in Kuala Lumpur? After 2–5 years?' Sooner or later, all Indian expats will go to the U.S." In this connection, the Malaysian digital hub also functions as a site for translating Asian computer workers into experts suitable for higher-level techno-poles.

The digital corridor emerges as a space in which a certain kind of governmentality seeks to break the association between race privilege and citizenship, and instead produce ethical reflection on the moral figure of the native-born technocrat. For the past three decades, a pro-Malay affirmative action program had sought to benefit Malays or *bumiputera* who have, since colonial times, lagged behind ethnic Chinese in education and in the economy more generally. Among other things, *bumiputera* receive guaranteed quotas for university education and jobs in the government and private sector. While these rules are relaxed in the multimedia corridor, *bumiputera* students and employees are still the dominant work force. A new ethical regime is being enforced: it is not merely enough to be born *bumiputera*; one must also acquire intellectual capital in order to be citizens of the knowledge economy. An array of education practices targeting Malays have been introduced. They include English instruction in science and mathematics in primary and secondary education, and the opening of exclusive Malay science colleges to other ethnic students, in order to foster academic competition. An official discourse about the moral dilemma of Malays chides them for relying on affirmative action rights as the mark of a higher racial standing over non-Malays, and for neglecting to equip themselves with the necessary education and skills. *Bumiputera* are urged to discard this kind of "prosthesis" and the sense of a hollow security that rests on the knowledge of others.[38] Global competition that depends on new skills and knowledge will sweep away such racial benefits, threatening to reduce society to the status of some developing African countries. In short, the discourse warns that failure to adjust to the new technology will result in a form of moral crippling or suicide for the Malay nation.

In the fragmented Malay public, voices charge that the new values promoting technical expertise and brain gain are a reflection of the greed and corruption of the state, part of an attempt by politicians to stay in power through cultivating global corporations. I spoke to an English-speaking middle-aged Malay man who rejects the call for Muslims to equip themselves with scientific knowledge as a tool of political empowerment. Despite having received an M.A. degree from the National University, he has chosen to make money operating a taxi license rather than be a college professor. This is an example of a widespread practice whereby it may be more profitable for *bumiputera* to receive state subsidies for business ventures that may actually fail than to become professionals. But his rejection of the need to acquire intellectual capital is based on ethical grounds. As an adherent of a form of radical Islam, he feels that "Western" knowledge may be sinful and lacking in merit for the afterlife. After all, the natural wealth of the country – oil, gas, timber, rubber – will keep the Malay nation comfortable. Other positions are staked out by elite Malay professionals who support the state goal of knowledge development, but the taxi driver is part of a growing category of educated Malays (and the rural masses) who reject the need for scientific knowledge, even when they draw material benefits from a digital economy. Being plugged into the global knowledge networks inspires not the fear of being left behind, as is the case among Singaporeans, but the fear of being cybercolonized and set back by a developmental project that gives priority to science over race- and religion-based views of citizenship. There is an ethical skepticism about linking the fate of the Muslim society to a wider ecology of Western expertise and enterprise.

Ruptures in the Ecosystem

Government is a problematizing activity in relation to the population, and yet it cannot anticipate the problems that will ensue as a result. Increasingly, in neoliberal times, countries (like corporations) that lack enough human capital will import people with know-how and skills. Such calculations set into play various assemblages of biopolitics and technology that connect transnational relations, actors, and values. Singapore and Malaysia represent rather distinct orders of expert ecologies: one a clustering of world-class institutions and actors to develop a global center of intellectual capital, the other a second-level node for regional technology networks. Expatriates bearing intellectual capital – entrepreneurs, scientists, computer programmers – come to be inscribed with new values of citizenship, while citizens are found ethically (and ethnically?) deficient for their relative lack of market and technical skills. Despite their multiple allegiances and national origins, foreign managers, professionals, and knowledge workers are defined as insiders to research ecologies. They are in effect "virtual global citizens," who belong not to a single nation or region but are free to become citizens of knowledge hubs and techno-parks across the world. This capitalization of citizenship is linked to new regimes that are evaluating and disciplining ordinary citizens and low-skill migrants.[39]

But ecological networks are riven by ruptures, and various ethical concerns about links between public funds and private interests, foreign brains and local labors, competition and collaboration are raised by diverse subjects situated in relation to each other. For instance, the legitimacy of expatriates brought in under the legend

"Singapore Vision 21" has been challenged by a "Singapore First" vision proposed by the political opposition and labor groups. Instead of the current mass recruitment of foreigners, dissenters suggest a system similar to that in the U.K., where the first preference in employment goes to British citizens, and foreigners will only get jobs that are unfilled. There is also fear that the preference given to expatriates will replace qualified locals. It is suggested that a more stringent regulation of employment-pass holders will limit the influx of foreign workers to the upper reaches of the professional and managerial category. Expatriates are referred to as "citizens without local roots," a protest about citizens feeling uprooted in their own country.

That call for a stricter regulation of foreign expertise has acquired new ethical resonance has gained new resonance in recent events. In April 2003, a British neurologist in Singapore was charged with making unofficial blood tests and taking tissue samples of over one hundred Asian patients. This was a major scandal, since the scientist in question was recruited, with great fanfare, from a London university to head a new Singaporean institute, the core of a neuroscience cluster to fight diseases such as epilepsy, Parkinson's, and dementia. A government's inquiry revealed that the doctor had undertaken research on patients without seeking their informed consent. He resigned and returned to England, while his Ph.D. student fled back to India. The incident created much embarrassment for the government, and stirred the beginnings of a more serious debate on bioethics. Doctors acknowledge having little training in bioethics, and having depended on a system of mutual trust in their research. Singapore "must avoid becoming a cowboy town for scientists," and there is clearly a need for a human research protection agency.[40] The public raised anew questions about throwing money at foreign experts and investing so much of the nation's future in the human capital of outsiders. There is also a sense that Singapore is becoming a prosthetically enhanced nation. The bifurcation between an enterprising ecosystem on the one hand, and a national *oikos* being divested of its immediate past on the other, has induced feelings of inauthenticity.[41] The ethical regime of knowledgeable and risk-taking subjects, and its vision of the good life in the ecosystem, comes into conflict with a reduced sense of cultural moorings. What is the meaning of citizenship when those with technoprenerual skills can jump to the front of the line? Expatriates are courted into becoming citizens, with offers of sped-up process, jobs, and perks. Furthermore, the expatriate permanent residents do not have to perform national service. In addition, there seems to be something sinister in the implication that being native today may involve being biologically available as a resource to global actors.

Around the same time of the expulsion of the brain neurologist from Singapore, Malaysia also undertook its own eviction of Indian computer professionals suspected of visa violations. Hundreds were arrested for engaging in unauthorized economic activities and sent back to India. Especially since September 11, there have been growing fears that foreign experts in the technological hub will take away local jobs. Furthermore, there is insecurity that Indian tourists exploit the "Indian expert image" by applying for work in the digital corridor. A number of Indian body shops or labor brokers are also suspected of selling work permits to unskilled Indians who enter Malaysia illegally. Thus, the technological network is increasingly viewed as a space through which other Asians with counterfeit credentials can enter the country, intensifying the insecurity among a population that is already worried about keeping up with more technologically adept foreigners.

Whether in the creation of a biotech center or a digital corridor, the two cases are concrete examples of the assemblages of neoliberal reasoning, authoritarian rule, and governmentality that have created distinct regimes of human worth. In the new ecology of belonging, schemes that coordinate market or scientific skills with social citizenship have privileged foreign experts over most citizens. New ethical dilemmas are generated as local people feel themselves perilously close to becoming second-class citizens or biological resources made available to global drug companies. At the same time, the recent expulsions of foreign workers indicate the complex and contingent outcomes of such assemblages of power, and the ethical claims of ethnic majorities and religious groups that have to be negotiated in ecologies of expertise.

Notes

1 I am grateful to Stephen J. Collier, Jerome Whitington, and Shannon May for their helpful comments on earlier drafts of this chapter.
2 Prime Minister Goh Chok Tong, "New Singapore," National Day Rally 2001 Speech at the National University of Singapore, August 19, 2001 (Ministry of Information and the Arts, Singapore).
3 "The Budget Speech: Strategies and Thrusts," *New Straits Times Press*, Malaysia; http://www.nstpi.com.my/z/Focus/copy_of_Budget/Two/20001028010916/wartre-vamp (accessed March 22, 2002).
4 Manuel Castells, *The Rise of Network Society* (Oxford: Blackwell, 1996), pp. 473–474.
5 Ibid., pp. 173–179.
6 Bruno Latour, *We Have Never Been Modern*, trans. Catherine Porter (Cambridge, MA: Harvard University Press, 1993).
7 Gilles Deleuze and Felix Guattari, *A Thousand Plateaus: Capitalism and Schizophrenia*, trans. Brian Maasumi (Minneapolis: University of Minnesota Press, 1987), pp. 504–505.
8 Ibid., p. 22.
9 See Aihwa Ong, *Flexible Citizenship* (Durham: Duke University Press, 1999), chs. 8 and 9.
10 Ricard Sole and Brian Goodwin, *Signs of Life: How Complexity Pervades Biology* (New York: Basic Books, 2000), pp. 179–180.
11 Colin Gordon, "The Soul of the Citizen: Max Weber and Michel Foucault on Rationality and the Government," in *Max Weber, Rationality and Modernity*, Scott Lash and Sam Whimster, eds. (London: George Allen & Unwin, 1987), p. 298.
12 Nikolas Rose, "Governing 'Advanced' Liberal Democracies," in *Foucault and Political Reason*, A. Barry, T. Osborne, and Nikolas Rose, eds. (Chicago: The University of Chicago Press, 1996), pp. 37–64.
13 Andrew Barry, *Political Machines* (London: The Athlone Press, 2001), p. 129.
14 Aihwa Ong, "Graduated Sovereignty in Southeast Asia," *Theory, Culture, and Society* 17(4), August 2000, pp. 55–75.

15 Quoted in Brenda S. A. Yeoh and T. C. Chang, "Globalising Singapore: Debating Transnational Flows in the City," *Urban Studies* 38, June 2001, p. 1032.

16 Prime Minister Goh, "The New Singapore..."

17 See Kris Olds and Nigel Thrift, "Cultures on the Brink: Reengineering the Soul of Capitalism – On a Global Scale," Chapter 15, this volume.

18 "Asia's Biotech Tiger," *New Scientist* 175, I2360, September 14, 2002, pp. 54–58.

19 See http://web.mit.edu/sma/index.html

20 Nikolas Rose and Carlos Novas, "Biological Citizenship," Chapter 23, this volume.

21 Ibid., p. 455.

22 Chang Ai Lien, "Maintaining S'pore's lead in stem-cell race," *The Straits Times*, September 5, 2001.

23 Cybernews, "The Bioethics Advisory Committee took pains – and 10 months – to consult various professional and religious groups," *The Straits Times*, June 22, 2002.

24 Edison Liu, Genome Institute of Singapore brochure, 2002.

25 "Asia's Biotech Tiger," *New Scientist*, p. 3.

26 See Geraldine Heng and Janadas Devan, "State fatherhood: the politics of nationalism, sexuality and race in Singapore," in *Bewitching Women, Pious Men*, Aihwa Ong and Michael G. Peletz, eds. (Berkeley: University of California Press, 1995), pp. 195–215.

27 Three-quarters of Singapore's population are ethnic Chinese. A steady stream of ethnic Chinese professionals from Malaysia augments the pool of skilled workers. Singapore students perform at the highest global level in mathematics and the sciences, but even with the current intake of educated Asians from China and India, there is an ongoing policy to convert almost all of the island's population into people with high-technology knowledge and skills.

28 N. Coe and P. F. Kelly, "Languages of Labour: Representational Strategies in Singapore's Labour Control Regime," *Political Geography* 21, 2002, 341–371.

29 Daniel Lian, "Singapore: New Economy Proletariat or Bourgeoisie?" Morgan Stanley Global Economic Forum, January 16, 2001.

30 Morris Chang, "Human Resources for Technology and Innovation in Southeast Asia," presented at the Singapore–MIT Alliance Symposium, January 2002.

31 "The NUS Enterprise: A Hotbed for Entrepreneurship," *The Alumnus*, no. 48, January 2002, pp. 12–16 (The National University of Singapore).

32 For a sense of the complaints, see articles in *The Straits Times*: "Downturn, foreign talent – main issues," October 23, 2001; "Looming clash over foreign talent," October 24, 2001; "Foreign talent pet issue of engineer," October 25, 2001; and "Foreign talent boosted GDP by 20% in last decade: SM Lee," October 31, 2001

33 Martin Wood, "Cyborg: a Design for Life in the Borderlands," *Emergence* 1(3), 1999, pp. 92–104.

34 These statements, by an Asian expatriate scientist and a musical conductor, respectively, are featured in advertisements by Contact Singapore, a recruiting program of the state, which has offices in Boston, Chicago, San Francisco, London, Sydney, Chennai, Hong Kong, and Shanghai.

35 Malaysia is a country of about 14 million people, of whom approximately 60 percent are ethnic Malays, including aboriginal peoples, labeled as *bumiputera* ("sons of the soil"). Ethnic Chinese comprise some 30 percent and ethnic Indians some 10 percent of the total population.

36 Bruno Latour, *Science in Action* (Cambridge, MA: Harvard University Press, 1987), p. 108.

37 Malaysia is regarded as the country with the highest rate of software piracy in Asia. According to a Microsoft handout, it is estimated that almost 70 percent of business software applications in Malaysia are illegal, costing the software industry around $96 million a year.

38 Summary of comments by Mahathir Mohamed, "The New Malay Dilemma," speech by the Prime Minister Datuk Seri Dr. Mahathir Mohamed at the Harvard Club of Malaysia, July 29, 2002; see *The Straits Times Interactive*, July 30, 2002.

39 For a discussion of low-skill and extra-legal migrants in Southeast Asia, see Aihwa Ong, "An Exception to the Good Life: Foreign Maids, Feminist NGOs, and Bio-Legitimacy" in *Citizenship, Borders, and Gender*, Seyla Benhabib, ed. (forthcoming).

40 "S'pore must avoid becoming a cowboy town for scientists," *The Straits Times*, April 12, 2003; Andy Ho, "Medical Research: Who watches ethics panels?" *The Straits Times*, April 16, 2003.

41 For views on the profound cultural dislocations experienced by Singaporeans, see chapters in *Beyond Description: Time, Space. Historicity, Singapore*, Ryan Bishop, John Philips, and Yeo Wei-Wei, eds. (New York: Routledge, 2004).

19

GLOBALIZATION AND POPULATION GOVERNANCE IN CHINA

SUSAN GREENHALGH

China's 1983 sterilization campaign, launched four years after the historic Third Plenum set the nation on the path to modernization through globalization, stands as one of the most ethically troubling and intellectually challenging episodes in world population control history.[1] In the name of reaching urgent population control targets, the peasant masses were treated like mere objects of numerical control. The result was a harvest of numericized achievements – including an astonishing 58 million birth control surgeries – and a harvest of personal and communal sorrow, as baby girls' lives were snuffed out, women's bodies were damaged, and local party–peasant relations were frayed. China's leaders backed down from the campaign's control-the-numbers-regardless-of-the-cost approach, but the significance of that campaign, to this day a highly sensitive subject in China, goes far beyond that nation's borders, to touch on large – and largely unaddressed – questions about the invention and governance of populations in a globalizing world.

How did the 1983 campaign and the one-child policy it sought forcefully to impose on the Chinese masses originate? What larger dreams for a socialist nation newly entering the global capitalist economy brought it to life? What political rationalities made it not just thinkable, but even reasonable and desirable to its creators? What practices gave rise to the use of physical force – in Chinese, "coercion and commandism," practices specifically forbidden by the codes of the good communist cadre – against fertile bodies? For a number of complicated reasons, both specialists on China and students of population have shunned these questions. In the United States, and elsewhere, thoughtful scholarly accounts of this and other coercive moments in China's now decades-old population project are largely absent. In their absence, public understandings of China's population control work have come to be dominated by a powerful narrative of coercion created by a group of conservative politicians and like-minded intellectuals located outside the academy. Elaborated by grisly media images of family planning jails, forced abortions, and much more, this narrative views China's population project as the product of a cruel communist state willing to use force against what it deemed overly reproductive bodies to achieve its macroeconomic goals, regardless of the costs to individuals, families, and communities. In this story the high tide of 1983 is rooted firmly in communist coercion, a remnant of the not so distant past of Maoist "totalitarianism."

Coercion: this little word has done a lot of work. It has divided the political world into systems of coercion/freedom, socialism/capitalism, communism/democracy, and East/West, placing what not long ago was called "Red China" on the "bad" side of each of these and obscuring the blurrings, borrowings, and border crossings that mark the politics of an increasingly interconnected, post-cold war world. These oppositions miss important pieces of the ethical, economic, technocratic, and demographic assemblage that has come together around population policy in China over the past 25 years. With its orientalizing, Otherizing thrusts, the coercion narrative also keeps us from seeing the place of Western ideas and technologies, and of Chinese dreams of catching up with the West to become a global power, in that complex, continuously evolving assemblage around population. To understand the roots of the forceful logics and practices embedded in the Chinese program, we need to set aside these binaries and go to China to see what hopes, logics, and techniques animate actually existing population practice there.

To the makers of China's population policy, population control has not been about coercion; it has been about the nation's dreams of achieving wealth, power, and global position through selective absorption of Western science and technology. Could it be that the selective borrowing of Western science and technology played a role in the creation of the troubling 1983 campaign? I will argue just that. Indeed, I will show that sinified adaptations of particular Western sciences and technologies provided both the rationale for and the technical means behind the unusual ferociousness of the 1983 campaign. I will argue that the roots of the campaign's harmful practices lie in a yoking together of three fields of thought and practice – a particular version of Western population science, which created a "crisis" problematization; socialist state planning, which outlined the solution as a series of ever tougher targets; and party-led mobilization, which provided a set of tried-and-true techniques for fulfilling the planned targets on the ground. These three quite different fields of ideas and practices were tied together by numbers, a language each in its own way spoke. Radically simplifying and apparently precise, numbers enabled the three fields to link up and jointly construct a population control project so powerful that it aspired to – and for a while appeared to succeed in – planning the births of one billion Chinese. More than "communist coercion," it was these numbers and, even more so, the numerical logics that came with them, that led to the violences of 1983. Those numerical population control targets were so seductive and powerful because they were attached to deeply felt and widely shared yearnings, borne of 150 years of national humiliation, that China's historical greatness might be restored. The hope was that, by combining economic growth with the accelerated modernization of a "backward" population, China might finally escape its wretched poverty and become a prosperous, modern, globally prominent nation.

As Foucault[2] suggested, the management of population size and growth – the proliferation of life itself – is a powerful domain of governance in the modern world. In the past few years, students of modernity's making have begun to trace the emergence of the sciences and particular discourses of population.[3] Yet governmental projects to limit life have received less attention.[4] I begin by proposing some working concepts and methods that help render these sprawling enterprises accessible to research. I then turn to China to explore the transformations in population governance that attended that nation's entry into global circuits. With its enormous size, its controversial approach to population control, and its rapid post-1978 insertion into the global economy, China provides one of the world's most important and illuminating cases of population governance in a globalizing world. The next three sections examine the roles of population science, state planning, and party mobilization in the making and executing of the 1983 sterilization drive. A conclusion suggests what is at stake in unraveling the logics, aims, and practices that gave birth to this fearsome episode in the history of population governance. This chapter is based on nearly 20 years of research on Chinese population affairs, including rural fieldwork, documentary research on the history of Chinese population science and policy, and extensive interviews with Chinese scholars and policy-makers.

Follow the Numbers: Studying Population Governance

How might we study the governance of population size and growth? Conceptually, governmental projects of population control can be understood as one class of governmental project.[5] Such projects involve constituting the object of governance (in this case, "the population"), establishing the problematization (including the problem, such as "overpopulation," together with its solution, often the family planning program), and then implementing that solution among selected target population(s). These phases – object constitution, problem and solution delineation, and implementation – can be thought of as making up the "life cycle" of the governmental population project.[6] But with what methods might we study these phases? Rather than trying to study the full range of actors involved – a gigantic terrain that ranges from UN agencies to NGOs to state bureaucracies to individual health care providers – it might be more feasible and productive to find a strategy that hones in on the core intellectual and political techniques involved in regulating population growth. One such method is to follow the numbers.

Why numbers? As Nikolas Rose and others have argued, numbers have inordinate power within modern technologies of government.[7] Numbers are so powerful because they are the language of science and science is the source of *truth* in modern society. Numbers have particular force in the science and governance of populations.

Because population is seen as a biological object, an aggregation of bodies that exists unproblematically in nature, counting or estimating the "vital" attributes of populations such as fertility and mortality, and then manipulating the numbers so as to chart their variations and distributions, are seen as the fundamental activities of the science of population. It is for good reason that demography is defined as the statistical study of population.

Numbers also form the crucial building blocks of governmental projects for population control. Figures not only constitute the domain of interest, population; they also define the problematizations adopted. Numbers also play important roles in implementation, serving as key measures of program success. In China, figures have gained many other powers as well, as we shall see shortly. Tracing the social and political lives of these numbers provides keen insight into the making and workings of population science and governance.

Lest I be misunderstood, the task of the student of population governance is not to *do* demography – to count births, bodies, and other phenomena. It is, rather, to study how others – in particular, population scientists, state planners, and government bureaucrats – do so. It is to follow the numbers wherever they take us, asking how they have been deployed, in what contexts, following what rationales, in pursuit of what strategic aims, by what techniques, and with what practical effects. We must pay particular attention to numerical inscriptions – those mundane tables, figures, charts, and equations – for it is here, in the making of these little pictures, that population scientists, planners, and governors do some of their most important yet least studied work.[8] Far from being "dusty [and] replete with dried up old books," as Ian Hacking once described them,[9] the numbers of population turn out to be a fascinating ethnographic domain.

Population Science: Defining the Problem – A Crisis of Human Numbers Keeping China "Backward"

At the historic Third Plenum of the Eleventh Central Committee that met in December 1978, China's new leaders rewrote the script for the country's future, changing the nation's goals from socialist revolution and class struggle, Mao's failed program, to socialist modernization and personal enrichment, Deng's appealing dream for the future.[10] China's new program of "reform and opening up" (*gaige kaifang*) was to be based on the selective absorption of Western science and technology. Indeed, science and technology was designated the first of China's four modernizations, the key to achieving the other three. Like most of the social sciences, population studies had been abolished in the 1950s. In 1979 a new field of population science was assembled from fields as diverse as the natural sciences, the social sciences, and the humanities, with quantitative fields such as economics and statistics predominating. Drawing on two very different types of Western population sciences – demography on the one hand, and cybernetics and control theory on the other – the new experts used an array of numbers to define and vigorously expose the urgency of "the population problem".[11] In delineating the population problem, they also constituted population as a bounded, numerically describable field: a space of investigation and administration, in short, a space of governance.[12] At the same time, they placed *the numerical logic of population science* – that is, a sinified version of a certain cluster of transnational population sciences – at the heart of China's population problem.

In the late 1970s and early 1980s, China's newly minted population specialists mobilized a wide array of numbers, some from large-scale surveys, others pulled together from typical local studies, to delineate the population problem. The specialists defined two sets of problems, one surrounding the "abnormality" and thus "backwardness" of the population itself, the other concerning the effects of those irregularities on the nation's economy and thus the speed of its socialist modernization. Taken together, these two sets of quantitatively defined problems would establish China's backwardness in the global order and the immense difficulty the nation now faced in catching up with the advanced industrialized countries, a group to which it aspired to belong.

With their simplicity and apparent facticity (that is, their status as reflections of reality), the numbers provided a powerful means to communicate what specialists saw as the urgency of the population problem, and to tie the solution to the population question to the nation's deep desires to escape poverty and backwardness at long last. When China's numbers were compared with the numbers of more powerful nations, the numbers seemed to summarize all that was wrong with China, and all that needed to be done to make it right. The numbers thus expressed powerful yearnings that were widely shared. The numbers were particularly powerful because of the unquestioned assumption that any publicly presented numbers were by definition reliable and, perhaps more important, "scientific." In the reform era, science was seen as the antidote to the horrors of the Cultural Revolution and the sure route to a prosperous new future.[13] It is difficult to overstate the importance of "science" – not only as a field of practices, but also as the idea, known as "scientism," that science is the prime source of truth and an all-powerful solution to China's problems – in the new national order.[14] Anything represented as scientific was seen as powerful, modern, and progressive. These meanings and desires attached to science gave the numbers of the population scientists all the more power.

An "abnormal" population

Comparing China with the industrialized nations of the world, China's population specialists found their own population to be abnormal in four important ways.[15] First, it was inordinately large. China's demographic excess was not only a terrible burden; it was also a sign of the nation's backwardness in a world in which the small, controlled, "quality" population was the very sign of the modern.[16] With peasants making up 80 percent, the population was also too rural, a great burden on an aspiring industrial power. China's population was also excessively young, the product of the disastrous campaigns of the past. The huge demographic wave of young people would soon marry and produce more babies, compounding the problem of excess numbers. Finally, the population was growing too rapidly, indeed, three times more rapidly than the populations of the standard or "normal" countries, such as France, West Germany, the United Kingdom, and the United States. These "special characteristics" (*tedian*) marked features that separated China from its aspired peers. They would have to be altered for China to become modern. Following the logic of population science, normalization of the population would be a key aim of population governance.

A demographic–economic "crisis"

The abnormally rapid growth of China's already outsized population was a serious problem because it was eating up China's economic gains, ensuring China's continued backwardness in the global scheme of modernization. In the earliest formulations, China's problem was framed as one of imbalance in the planned socioeconomy, in which overly rapid population growth was delaying the four modernizations by impeding the development of capital accumulation, employment, and education. This problem was advanced by social scientists and it was rooted in Marxian theory. This more moderate construction of the problem was soon over-taken by another, more gripping framing, introduced by a handful of natural scientists and engineers. The natural scientists portrayed China's population problem as a veritable crisis, an explosion of numbers that would prevent China from catching up and becoming a modern, global power. Ordinary though the idea of a population crisis may seem to Western readers, in China of the late 1970s the image of China's population growth as a crisis was fresh and riveting. That construction of the problem was borrowed from Western science, in particular, from the Club of Rome, world-in-crisis cybernetic models popular in some quarters in the 1970s.[17] Chinese scholars learned of these models from discussions with European scientists whom they met on delegation visits to the West in the late 1970s. Tables and graphs created by Chinese specialists compared China to Western powers, showing how China's overly rapid population growth had eroded the growth of the nation's per capita income and productivity, keeping China poor and backward, even as the West grew rich and advanced.[18] The reader was invited to imagine China among the global powers and then to envision how drastically population growth would have to be curtailed for the crisis to be alleviated.

A global good citizen

So far, I have been elaborating a largely economic connection between China's globalization and the emergence of the problem of population. But there was another type of connection as well, one that had to do with China's desire for global respect, for membership in the global community of nations. In the late 1970s, China's population specialists began to portray China's population crisis as a major compon-ent of the "global population crisis." By controlling its own numbers, China would contribute mightily to resolving the world's population crisis, earning China the status of a responsible member of the world community. In speeches in international meetings, top population officials announced that China would strive hard to control its own population growth in order to avoid adding pressure to world population problems.[19] In these and other international forums, China's population leaders constructed China as a global good citizen that was doing its part to solve the world's population and thus development problems.

Reproduced endlessly and energetically, and in multiple contexts, the crisis problematization was to stick and become the official construction of the population problem for years to come. While it served the population experts well in conveying the urgency of their political project, the crisis representation treated large segments of the people who had been aggregated into a population as saboteurs of modernization and hence threats to the well-being of the nation. These representations would have dire effects when the crisis problem became joined to a strong solution.

State Planning: Mapping the Route to Demographic Modernity and Global Position

If the problem of population was an economically menacing explosion of human numbers, the solution was to drastically restrict those numbers to put the nation on the road to prosperity and global position. Clearly, the crisis problematization dictated an extreme solution. But how would such a solution be designed and carried out?

The solution adopted drew heavily on China's own post-1949 traditions of socialist state planning and party-led mobilization. These modes of governmental planning and practice had been used in previous population projects, especially in the highly successful later–longer–fewer project of the 1970s (promoting later marriage, longer child spacing, and fewer births). They were fully institutionalized. They worked remarkably well. They were the logical choice. Population thus became a hybrid domain of governance that wedded a rationality rooted in part in Western science to techniques of control that followed the logics of a socialist state and a long-Maoist Communist party. The three set of logics and practices – Western science, state planning, party mobilization – would combine to form a powerful nexus of reproductive control.

What tied them together, what enabled the makers of China's project of population governance to move with ease from problem to planned solution to implementation was the language of numbers. For despite their very different roots and aims, each of these fields of governmental practice spoke the language of numbers. Numbers enabled communication between the fields because they were radically simplifying, reducing complex phenomena to figures that seemed to map onto reality and nature in an unproblematic way. As the language of numbers facilitated the construction of a powerful project of population governance and reproductive control – one that combined the authority of science with the coercive power of the party-state – the numbers themselves gained new and formidable powers over people's minds and women's bodies.

State birth planning

Since Mao enunciated the concept of "birth planning" (*jihua shengyu*) in 1956–7,[20] population control in the People's Republic of China has meant not the planning of family size and composition by individual couples, but the planning of births countrywide by the socialist state. The commitment to state birth planning was formalized in the early 1960s, but it was not until the early 1970s, after the chaos of the Cultural Revolution had subsided, that population planning was integrated into the larger, target-driven process of economic and social planning. Between 1972 and 1975, a population control target was introduced into the Fourth Five-Year Plan (1971–5), and in 1975 targets set at the political center were divided up and handed down to localities all over the country.[21] From that point on, population control would be target-driven – in the plan and on the ground.

China's post-Mao drive to achieve modernization and global status was to lead not to the demise of state birth planning, but to its embrace with renewed vigor, at least for a time. Indeed, it was precisely the practice of socialist planning that was to give China the competitive edge in the world economy, enabling it to catch up with the West in an exceptionally short period of time.[22] The continued creation and aggressive pursuit of population control targets served not only the practical end of enabling China to catch up, but it had strategic political aims as well. For the successful use of state planning would demonstrate the superiority of socialism, ensuring the survival of Chinese socialism in an increasingly capitalist world. Equally important, it would secure the legitimacy of the ruling Communist party by enabling it to make good on its promises to improve the material well-being of the Chinese people. Nothing short of China's national identity, its global survival, and the survival of its ruling party were at stake in the creation and later fulfillment of population targets. It is not surprising that those targets would take on such urgent importance.

The creation of the one big figure

Because population planning was to serve economic (and ultimately political) ends, population targets were constructed on the basis of economic targets. In the late 1970s, the top leadership set the year 2000 as the date for the achievement of a "comfortable standard of living" (*xiaokang shuiping*), defined quantitatively as U.S. $800–1,000 per capita GNP. Since population was the crucial denominator in such per capita measures of economic modernization, population planning would take on immense importance. In a remarkably short time, this tiny little fraction – income over population – would acquire enormous political significance.

The task for population planners was to set interim population control targets that would allow the state to achieve the century-end's comfortable standard of living on which the people's welfare and the party's legitimacy now rested. The most important figure was the total population size by which aggregate economic measures would be divided. Through a process that remains opaque, in early 1980 that crucial number, that millennial measure of demographic modernity, was set at 1.2 billion. Although that number apparently had no sound empirical basis and it was wildly unrealistic – that is, it was demographically unrealizable without the use of extreme methods – in September 1980 it became enshrined as the official population control target.[23] Bearing the imprimatur of the party's Central Committee, it was effectively set in political stone. Students of Western politics have written of "the power of the single figure" in political life.[24] In China in the early 1980s, that turn-of-the-century target played the same role. As the aspirations of the party and nation got expressed in – and reduced to – that figure, that single figure became the *raison d'être* of all political efforts to avert the population crisis, the number in whose name everything was done.

Scientific planning at the State Birth Planning Commission

With an arduous task ahead, in 1981 the state established the interministerial State Birth Planning Commission to lead and coordinate the work of birth planning committees all the way down the administrative hierarchy. The Commission's primary charge was to fulfill the population control targets established by the political center, in that way keeping the nation on the road to demographic modernity and global position. As indicated by its name, the Commission's major bureaucratic assignment was to plan the nation's births. This gigantically complex task involved two major subtasks: managing population planning and target setting, and overseeing enforcement and hence fulfillment of the targets.

To keep population, then estimated at 1 billion, within 1.2 billion by 2000, the planners' major job was to calculate the interim targets for the intervening five-year and one-year plans. These interim targets would serve as a map to demographic modernity, a plot of the route that must be followed for the nation to achieve its demographic and, in turn, economic goals. In the early 1980s, the most pressing task was to figure out the goals for the Sixth Five-Year Plan (1981–5), which was just then unfolding. One of the first activities of the new Commission was to conduct a nationwide One-per-Thousand Fertility Survey to coincide with the 1982 Census, the first modern census ever conducted in China – complete with U.N. support, computers, and much more. (Other censuses had been conducted in 1953 and 1964, but they were relatively simple and technically unsophisticated.) The Fertility Survey was launched as part of a larger effort to "strengthen scientific management" of birth planning work.[25] Although China's newly emerging population scientists and state statisticians could not question the party's goal of 1.2 billion, they could, and were expected to, use their skills to specify the best way to achieve it. That was what was known as scientific management. What the work involved was manipulating more, and more reliable, numbers than had been available earlier, using newly available computers to process and store data, employing more sophisticated data-analytic techniques as the basis for formulating population plans and making population projections, and so on. (Many of these computers and techniques were introduced with the assistance of foreign organizations, themselves with investments in the process. I explore those international linkages elsewhere.) Calling these new practices scientific management connected them to a much broader national effort to use modern science to modernize the country. One can imagine the hopes invested in the work.

The magnitude of the problem that population planners faced became clear in the fall of 1982, when the initial results of the census and survey became available. Analyzed by statisticians at the Commission, the survey showed that between 1983 and 2000, 200 million women would reach the age of marriage and thus childbearing. (Planners assumed, reasonably, that most couples would have their first child immediately after marriage.) "Even if women's fertility is kept at 2 births each," the analysts wrote, "the net population at the end of the century will reach 1.290 billion," 90 million more than the target.[26] The Census itself apparently implied even grimmer prospects. Commenting on its results, Qian Xinzhong, the new Minister-in-Charge of the Commission, warned that if each rural couple had two children, the total population would reach 1.317 billion by the end of the century.[27] How, then, could the target be reached?

To answer that question, the statisticians performed some projections that allowed them to plot the downward path that the nation's fertility rate must follow over the next 18 years in order to keep the population within its assigned target. The results of their work are shown in Table 19.1. The very mundanity, the ordinariness, of this table belies its significance. For the little numbers in this table would have formidable material effects.

The results suggested that, in order to attain the crucial 1.2 billion target, the total fertility rate (TFR) – the average number of children per woman – would have to drop from 2.6 in 1981–2 to 1.7 in 1985 to 1.5 in 1990, and then remain at that level until 2000. Such extraordinary fertility declines have rarely been achieved anywhere. They were especially unrealistic for China, where children had enormous cultural, social, and economic value. That such fertility reduction targets were even imagined suggests the power of the numericizing and crisis logics at work, for their imagining required the construction of the objects of control as little more than numbers. These imaginings required the subordination of concerns for a host of complicating factors – from problems of enforcement, to cultural desires for children, to the health and safety of the bodies that would be operated on – to reach the planned target.

The analysts concluded that "The crucial factor lies in the period of the Sixth Five-Year Plan, for unless early achievements are made, fertility will have to be pushed below 1.5, which is very difficult".[28] The task the birth planners faced, then, was to lower the TFR from 2.6 to 1.7 in the three years 1983–5. Despite the Herculean nature of the task, the Commission's analysts suggested that it could be done "with some effort" by lowering the TFR by 0.3 births each year. (Of course, in this political system, the planners did not have the option of saying that the target could not be reached.) Scientific management had combined with socialist target setting to create a task of enormous difficulty.

Table 19.1 Population projections from 1983 to 2000

Year	Total population	Total fertility rate	Natural growth rate (per 1,000)
1983	1,027,690,000	2.30	13.00
1984	1,040,840,000	2.00	11.54
1985	1,050,710,000	1.70	10.25
1986	1,061,400,000	1.67	10.79
1987	1,072,020,000	1.65	9.63
1988	1,083,510,000	1.60	10.37
1989	1,095,490,000	1.55	11.02
1990	1,107,520,000	1.50	11.02
1991	1,119,080,000	1.50	11.00
1992	1,130,030,000	1.50	9.48
1993	1,140,320,000	1.50	9.41
1994	1,150,380,000	1.50	9.11
1995	1,159,880,000	1.50	8.70
1996	1,169,090,000	1.50	8.20
1997	1,177,180,000	1.50	7.38
1998	1,184,310,000	1.50	6.49
1999	1,190,520,000	1.50	5.65
2000	1,195,920,000	1.50	4.87

Source: Xiao Zhenyu and Chen Shengli, "Current Birth Planning Work Viewed from the Results of the National Fertility Sample Survey" (in Chinese), *Renkou Yanjiu* 2, 1983, pp. 20–23.

Party Mobilization: Fulfilling the Target – A Frenzy of Numbers

To reach the ambitious century-end targets, the Commission was instructed to enforce a policy encouraging one child per couple. While implementing such drastic restrictions was possible, if difficult, in the cities, it would be almost impossible in the countryside, where children played a multiplicity of crucial social and economic roles. Yet the countryside was the crux of the problem, the source of China's many demographic woes. The countryside was deemed the most "backward" area, with the most backward fertility culture and the highest fertility rates. Enforcement problems in the countryside were further compounded in 1982, when decollectivization was completed countrywide. The introduction of rural responsibility systems led to an increase in the desire for children, especially sons, and an increase in peasants' ability to resist cadre efforts to restrict births.

Despite repeated warnings and urgings, births rose throughout 1982. Top party leaders responded by increasing the pressure on the birth planning bureaucracy to stanch the rising tide of humanity. In September 1982 the 12th Party Congress designated birth planning and, by implication, the one-child policy, a "basic state policy" (*jiben guoce*) – that is, a top-priority policy that concerned the fundamental interests of the state – and reemphasized the century-end goal of 1.2 billion.[29]

To achieve these difficult goals, the two highest authorities in the land, the party's Central Committee and the governmental State Council, made the decision to launch a nationwide mobilizational campaign. Although the use of campaigns had been repudiated in the early reform years – campaigns, which involved intense mobilization of the masses to achieve specific party targets, were based on Maoist mobilizational logics, the antithesis of the scientific strategies that the Dengist party sought to promote – the campaign was the only technique in the party's toolkit capable of achieving such difficult targets in so short a time.[30] Moreover, since the introduction of "patriotic health campaigns" in the early 1950s, campaigns had been the primary means of enforcing public health policies in general and birth planning policies in particular. Both local cadres and the rural masses had grown accustomed to them. Especially when the political center threw its weight behind them, campaigns could work, at least in the short run, to achieve targets.

In December 1982, the Central Committee's Propaganda Department, along with eight other units, jointly issued a circular on carrying out national birth planning "propaganda month" activities from New Year's Day to Spring Festival (the Chinese New Year) of 1983.[31] Although publicly described as a propaganda month, the campaign's goal was to ensure the achievement of the year 2000 population control target by controlling the momentum of next year's population growth and, more generally, making numerical breakthroughs in reaching targets. Those targets would be fulfilled by focusing on the rural areas and strictly enforcing the one-child policy – in Qian Xinzhong's instructions, "forcefully raising the one-child rate" while "controlling second births as strictly as possible".[32] Based on the Maoist logic of voluntarism – the notion that people would "self-consciously" and "voluntarily" accept party policy once sufficiently educated about its advantages or, barring that, were "mobilized" (on which, more below) to accept it – the campaign sought to utilize all sorts of party forces to intensely propagandize the birth policy and then, once people were persuaded or mobilized, carry out "technical measures" so that the numerical targets could be achieved.

What distinguished this birth control campaign from previous ones, what made it more new and modern and promising, was the application of modern science and technology in the two major domains of practice, propaganda and education and the technical measures designed to ensure fulfillment of the targets – that is, birth control devices and surgeries. The hope was that modern science would combine with the party's longstanding and excellent tradition of voluntarism to ensure successful fulfillment of the targets.

Scientific propaganda and education: a pedagogy of numbers

As in all campaigns, in the 1983 drive, cadres' major means of enforcement was to conduct "deep and meticulous education and propaganda" to change fertility culture and persuade people of the correctness of party policy. The 1983 drive was seen as superior to past mobilizations because the content of the propaganda was scientific. In the past, commentators noted, birth planning cadres simply lectured or harangued the peasants "in a rather arbitrary and unimaginative way," producing formalistic (forced or nonexistent) results.[33] Now cadres would persuade the masses with the numbers of science, bringing them to consciousness about the necessity of birth planning and making the acceptance of one-child families a "self-conscious deed".[34]

Following the decision of the 12th Party Congress, the basic emphasis of the propaganda was to be birth planning's new status as basic state policy. To explain to the masses why birth planning and the one-child policy must be a basic state policy, campaign strategists promoted the technique of "calculating and comparing." In this technique, the masses, guided by newly numerically savvy cadres, were invited to calculate the economic costs of excessive population growth – to the nation, village, and family – and to compare the prosperity of villages and families that had many offspring with those that had few.[35] In this way, state birth planners sought to enlist the active support of the peasant masses by creating a nation of calculating, science-minded citizens. Masses who were able to figure out for themselves the steep costs they would incur by having many children, the reasoning went, would limit their births and follow the population plan with understanding, self-consciousness, and voluntarism.

Although inducing fertility decline was the explicit goal, the technique of calculate-and-compare had broader effects as well. By taking the numbers that had shaped central reasoning down to the local level and instilling a numericizing reasoning in cadres and ordinary folk at the grassroots, this technique worked to create a hierarchical network of numbers tying center to locality, leader to led, and governor to governed. Even if people were not persuaded that many children led to poverty (indeed, a venerable Chinese saying had it that "many children bring much happiness"), the technique would spread a numericizing logic, for it would get people to think about childbearing (and much more) in numerical and economic terms. People who thought numerically would be caught ever more tightly in the state's web.

Scientific surgery: using modern reproductive technology to fulfill the targets

Once the masses had the scientific facts at their fingertips and were mobilized to act, medical workers would then implement the technical measures that would ensure fulfillment of the campaign's targets. Minister Qian and the campaign's organizers were enthusiastic about the potential of new developments in contraceptive technology worldwide to guarantee the fulfillment of China's population targets.[36] Qian instructed that, "based on the principle of voluntarism," all women with one child would be required to have an IUD inserted, while one member of all couples with two or more would have to undergo sterilization.[37] All unauthorized pregnancies would be terminated by "remedial measures."

The technical centerpiece of the campaign, however, was sterilization. For China's villages, Qian wrote, sterilization was "a biological and scientific requirement" that, despite obstacles, could be promoted by allowing "scientific principles" to enter the masses' understanding.[38] Qian noted sterilization's many advantages. First, a high sterilization rate was a sign of the modern – in the U.S.A., he noted, it was the most popular contraceptive method, whereas in China the IUD was still the most common method. Second, sterilization would protect women's health and reduce their suffering by preventing contraceptive failure and thus the necessity of abortion. Yet the main benefit Qian stressed was in controlling the numbers: because sterilization represented a permanent solution, it would contribute mightily to the achievement of population control targets.[39] Qian was aware of the problems cadres would encounter trying to promote sterilization in the villages. Women were afraid of the operation. The quality of the surgery was often poor. Yet these human and health concerns were muted by the overriding necessity of reaching urgent population control targets. The association of sterilization with modern reproductive science may have made those practical concerns less salient as well.

A target obsession

While modern science was to enhance the effectiveness of certain measures, the actual conduct of the campaign was based on longstanding party practice.[40] As instructed by Minister Qian,[41] localities formed temporary propaganda-month work organizations, which in turn formed special propaganda work teams to conduct painstaking and meticulous propaganda. Masses who could not be persuaded were mobilized – that is, subjected to more and more social and political pressure until they finally agreed to comply. Special urban-based technical work teams then fanned out into the villages, where they lived and worked day and night until their work was done. The focal point of all activities was the achievement of numerical targets. Targets that were expressed in terms of population size and growth rates at higher levels were converted at the local level into surgical targets and attached to different categories of people. The number of sterilizations, abortions, and other procedures completed thus became the key measure of political performance at the grassroots level.

Because many localities failed to meet their targets during the official propaganda month, the campaign was extended into the spring months and beyond. To "push the work further," in May 1983 the SBPC held an on-the-spot national birth planning work conference in Shandong's Rongcheng County.[42] In his speech, Minister Qian noted with satisfaction that birth planning work had entered a new stage. His main emphasis, however, was on the difficulty of reaching the Sixth Five-Year Plan target of a population growth rate of 13 per 1,000. Even as he advocated shifting to less harsh methods, Qian said that shock activities were still needed several times a year and that late-term abortions, though regrettable, were necessary to fulfill the plan.[43] Qian's speech was filled with urgings to do things voluntarily and to protect women's health, but from beginning to end, his emphasis was on cadres' duties to fulfill the numerical targets. The message was, no matter what the cost – in voluntarism or surgical quality – in 1983 the population growth target must be achieved.

This added pressure produced a target obsession and numbers mania, a mentality in which population meant numbers – with no regard for the bodies or subjectivities of those targeted for sterilization, IUD insertion, and abortion. Just two weeks after the new boost given to birth planning in Shandong, nearby Liaoning Province announced a campaign to "raise birth planning work to a new level." The Liaoning campaign illustrates the heights to which the numbers frenzy went. In an article in the *Liaoning Daily*, provincial birth planners announced their success so far:

> Since the launching of a planned birth propaganda month at the beginning of this year, an unprecedentedly fine situation has taken place…Statistics for the first quarter show…the single pregnancy rate was 94.1 percent…As of the end of March, more than 216,000 male and female ligation operations [that is, sterilizations] had been performed. This was 40,000 more than the total number of ligations performed during all of 1981 and 1982.[44]

When the numbers of surgeries were reported in great detail, what was not counted was the number of accidents or complications that resulted from conducting so many procedures in so short a time. How the province would conduct the campaign must be left for future publication. What I want to emphasize here is how, through the simplifying discourse of numbers, individual surgicalized bodies were tied to provincial narratives, which were connected to national narratives that both envisioned China as a world power and sought to jumpstart its move in that direction through measures that treated people as numbers and little else.

The Attainment of Demographic Modernity and the Emergence of "Reproductive Health"

The 1983 campaign was extraordinary successful. During that year, over 58 million birth control operations were conducted, including 16 million female sterilizations and 14 million abortions.[45] That was two to three times the number of such operations conducted in any year since 1972, when such numbers were first collected. In 1983 and 1984, fertility fell to the lowest ever: the TFR was roughly 2.1, near the demographically ideal replacement level.

Meantime, however, party leaders in Beijing were getting word from the countryside about the violence against cadres, killings of baby girls, deaths of women from botched IUD removals, and other costs that had been incurred by the emphasis on controlling the numbers above all. The party had broken its own rules and engaged in "coercion and commandism" against the masses. The result was poor party–mass relations in the countryside – and political peril for the party. In December 1983, Qian was removed from his post. Four months later, an internal document prepared by the Commission's party committee revealed what had happened and took responsibility for the lapse in political judgment. With the numbers now under control, in early 1984 the leadership softened the policy and relaxed its implementation. Despite the mid-1980s relaxation, however, the nexus of urgent logics and forceful practices that emerged in the early 1980s continued to guide China's population control work through the early 1990s, when fertility fell to just under two children per woman and remained at that level.[46]

The achievement of this key measure of demographic modernity in the early 1990s gave China's population policy-makers the political space to experiment with new approaches to the state planning of births. Since the mid-1990s, a new assemblage has begun to emerge, which engages with the global in new ways. One piece of the original assemblage that persists is the nation's dream of becoming a global economic power. Today, of course, this dream is fast becoming a reality. It is sobering to realize that, by drastically reducing the "capita" in the per capita equations by which economic progress is measured, reproductive coercion played a crucial role in China's emergence as a global economic power. The new assemblage that is now coming together presents an unusual mixture of old and new, local and global.[47] The most striking change is the downplaying of the population crisis narrative in favor of (again, a Chinese version of) the new international concern with women's reproductive health, rights, and empowerment, a focus worked out at the 1994 International Conference on Population and Development, held in Cairo.[48] China has adopted its own version of this problematization that focuses on health and largely omits empowerment, and is now dismantling important parts of its target-oriented, numbers-control program, substituting programs to enhance women's health. The other parts of the original triad are also being transformed. Helped by declining child preferences, the state planning of births is shifting from mandatory to indicative and targets are increasingly being managed at higher administrative levels rather than being handed down to villages and individuals. In the area of enforcement, mobilizational campaigns and other directly coercive practices have been phased out, replaced by greater reliance on strong legal and economic measures. Although the notion of population numbers as a potential crisis continues to lurk in the background of party documents, as long as the birth rate remains low, the kinds of coercive practices seen in earlier decades should continue to fade away.

What is at Stake

Much is at stake in how we view this grim episode in China's population control history. On the surface, the 1983 campaign would seem to be an egregious example of communist coercion in practice. Yet a look at the underlying dynamics suggests that, far from the simple product of a coercive party-state, the 1983 campaign was tied to China's entry into global capitalist and scientific circuits. Behind that campaign lay a (sinified version of a) Western scientific rationale, and the nation's dreams of becoming a global economic power and ethical member of the world community of nations. The old binaries embedded in the coercion narrative – socialism/capitalism, coercion/freedom, East/West – not only obscure these strange but powerful couplings; they also stake out a claim to Western moral superiority that is problematic at best.

Although population control projects have received little attention from critical students of modernity and globalization, the Chinese case makes clear the importance of population and its control in the making of the modern world. State birth planning was crucial to the achievement of Chinese socialist modernity and to China's growing connectedness to and prominence in the world. Over the past quarter century, the emergence of population as a domain of thought and practice has been enormously productive, creating new objects and domains of administration, new forms of governance, new pedagogies of the nation, new types of docile bodies, new ethical conundrums, and even new meanings of the human. Population deserves more attention.

Building on research in science studies and governmentality studies, I have drawn out the crucial work played by numbers in the making of China's population governance project. In the hands of Chinese scientists, planners, and policy implementers, numbers proved exceptionally versatile and supple, connecting different fields of thought and practice into a gigantic network of control that tied governed to governor, locality to center, the nation to the world. Quiet and unassuming though they are, these little fractions, projections, and figures provide a productive point of entry into the politics of population governance in today's globalizing world.

Notes

1   Research for this article was supported by a grant (#0217508) from the Science and Technology Studies Program of the U.S. National Science Foundation.

2   Michel Foucault, *The History of Sexuality: An Introduction*, Vol. 1 (New York: Random House, 1978).

3   See David G. Horn, *Social Bodies: Science, Reproduction, and Italian Modernity* (Princeton, NJ: Princeton University Press, 1994); Ann Anagnost, "A Surfeit of Bodies: Population and the Rationality of the State in Post-Mao China," *Conceiving the New World Order: The Global Politics of Reproduction*, F. D. Ginsburg and R. Rapp, eds. (Berkeley: University of California Press, 1995), pp. 22–41; Susan Greenhalgh, "The Social Construction of Population Science: An Intellectual, Institutional, and Political History of Twentieth Century Demography," *Comparative Studies in Society and History* 38, 1996, pp. 26–66; Adele E. Clarke, *Disciplining Reproduction: Modernity, American Life Sciences, and the Problems of Sex* (Berkeley: University of California Press, 1998); Elizabeth L. Krause, " 'Empty Cradles' and the Quiet Revolution: Demographic Discourse and Cultural Struggles of Gender, Race and Class in Italy," *Cultural Anthropology* 16, 2001, pp. 576–611.

4   However, attentive authors include Kamran Asdar Ali, "Making 'Responsible' Men: Planning the Family in Egypt," *Fertility and the Male Life-Cycle in the Era of Fertility Decline*, C. Bledsoe, S. Lerner, and J. I. Guyer, eds. (Oxford: Oxford University Press, 2000), pp. 119–143; Nilanjana Chatterjee and Nancy E. Riley, "Planning an Indian Modernity: The Gendered Politics of Fertility Control," *Signs* 26, 2001, pp. 811–846; Susan Greenhalgh, "Controlling Births and Bodies in Village China," *American Ethnologist* 21, 1994, pp. 1–30; and Susan Greenhalgh, "Planned Births, Unplanned Persons: 'Population' in the Making of Chinese Modernity," *American Ethnologist* 30, 2003, pp. 196–215.

5   Cf., Nikolas Rose, *Powers of Freedom: Reframing Political Thought* (Cambridge: Cambridge University Press, 1999); Mitchell Dean, *Governmentality: Power and Rule in Modern Society* (London: Sage, 1999).

6   For elaboration, see Greenhalgh, "Planned Births."

7   Peter Miller, "Accounting and Objectivity: The Invention of Calculating Selves and Calculable Spaces," *Annals of Scholarship* 9, 1992, pp. 61–86; Rose, *Powers of Freedom*; Theodore M. Porter, *Trust in Numbers: The Pursuit of Objectivity in Science and Public Life* (Princeton, NJ: Princeton University Press, 1995); Joel Best, *Damned Lies and Statistics: Untangling Numbers from the Media, Politicians, and Activists* (Berkeley: University of California Press, 2001).

8   Bruno Latour, *Science in Action* (Cambridge, MA: Harvard University Press, 1987); Michael Lynch and Steve Woolgar, eds., *Representation in Scientific Practice* (Cambridge, MA: The MIT Press, 1990).

9   Ian Hacking, "Biopower and the Avalanche of Printed Numbers," *Humanities in Society* 5, 1982, p. 279.

10 Kenneth Lieberthal, *Governing China: From Revolution Through Reform* (New York: W. W. Norton, 1995).

11 Susan Greenhalgh, "Science, Modernity, and the Making of China's One-Child Policy," *Population and Development Review* 29, 2003, pp. 163–196.

12 Cf., Rose, *Powers of Freedom*, pp. 31–40.

13 Hua Shiping, *Scientism and Humanism: Two Cultures in Post-Mao China (1978–1989)* (Albany, NY: State University of New York Press, 1995).

14 Hua, *Scientism and Humanism*; H. Lyman Miller, *Science and Dissent in Post-Mao China: The Politics of Knowledge* (Seattle: University of Washington Press, 1996).

15 For example, Tian Xueyuan, "Thirty Years of Chinese Population Development" (in Chinese), in *Collected Writings of Tian Xueyuan* (Beijing: Zhongguo Jingji Chubanshe, 1991 [1981]), 79–85.

16 Anagnost, "A Surfeit of Bodies."

17 Donella H. Meadows, Dennis L. Meadows, Jorgen Randers, and William W. Behrens III, *The Limits to Growth: A Report for the Club of Rome's Project on the Predicament of Mankind*, 2nd edition (New York: Universe, 1974).

18 For example, Liu Zheng and Wu Cangping, "A Discussion with Youth on Population" (in Chinese), *Zhongguo Qingnian Bao*, August 14, 1979, p. 3; Tian Xueyuan, "The Four Modernizations and Starting from a Population of 900 Million" (in Chinese), in *Collected Writings of Tian Xueyuan* (Beijing: Zhongguo Jingji Chubanshe, 1991 [1980]), pp. 127–134.

19 Qian Xinzhong, "Chinese Delegation Leader Qian Xinzhong's Speech at the Third Asian and Pacific Population Conference" (in Chinese), *Renkou Yanjiu* 6, 1982, pp. 2–3, 6.

20 Tyrene White, "The Origins of China's Birth Planning Policy," in *Engendering China: Women, Culture, and the State*, C. K. Gilmartin, G. Hershatter, L. Rofel, and T. White, eds. (Cambridge, MA: Harvard University Press, 1994), pp. 250–278.

21 Wang Hong, "Population Planning in China," *Population and Development Planning in China*, J. Y. Wang and T. H. Hull, eds. (Sydney: Allen and Unwin, 1991), pp. 68–87.

22 Wu Cangping, "An Objective Criterion for Measuring the Conformity of Population Growth" (in Chinese), *Renkou Yanjiu* 1, 1980, pp. 32–38; Liu Zheng, "Population Planning and Demographic Theory," in *China's Population: Problems and Prospects*, Z. Liu and J. Song (Beijing: New World Press, 1981), pp. 1–24.

23 Central Committee, "Open Letter from the Central Committee of the Chinese Communist Party to all Members of the Party and the Communist Youth League

Concerning the Question of Controlling the Country's Population Growth" (in Chinese), *Zhongguo Renkou Nianjian*, 1985, Population Research Center, Chinese Academy of Social Sciences, ed. (Beijing: Zhongguo Shehui Kexue Chubanshe, 1985), pp. 27–29.

24 Peter Miller, "Accounting and Objectivity: The Invention of Calculating Selves and Calculable Spaces," *Annals of Scholarship* 9, 1992, pp. 61–86.

25 Xiao Zhenyu and Chen Shengli, "Current Birth Planning Work Viewed from the Results of the National Fertility Sample Survey" (in Chinese), *Renkou Yanjiu* 2, 1983, pp. 20–23.

26 Ibid., p. 20.

27 Liu Dizhong, "Birth Planning Ensures China's Population Target" (in Chinese), *China Daily*, November 5, 1982, p. 1.

28 Xiao and Chen, "Current Birth Planning", p. 21.

29 Hu Yaobang, "Open a New Situation in Socialist Modernization" (in Chinese), *Zhongguo Renkou Nianjian*, 1985, Population Research Center, Chinese Academy of Social Sciences, ed. (Beijing: Zhongguo Shehui Kexue Chubanshe, 1985), p. 51.

30 Tyrene White, "Postrevolutionary Mobilization in China: The One-Child Policy Reconsidered," *World Politics* 43, 1990, pp. 53–76.

31 Xinhua (New China News Agency), "Main Point of Family Planning Month Circular," radio broadcast, December 9, *FBIS, PRC National Affairs*, 1982, pp. K31–K32.

32 Qian Xinzhong, *New Articles on Population* (in Chinese) (Chengdu: Sichuan People's Press, 1989), p. 90.

33 Yan Keqing, "Problems and Prospects in Population Planning," *China Reconstructs*, June 1983, pp. 11–13.

34 Qian, *New Articles on Population*, p. 84.

35 Ibid., p. 131.

36 Ibid., pp. 66–73.

37 Ibid., p. 101.

38 Ibid., p. 72.

39 Ibid., pp. 70–73.

40 White, "Postrevolutionary Mobilization in China."

41 Qian, *New Articles on Population*, pp. 100–102.

42 Ibid., pp. 122–135.

43 Ibid., p. 125.

44 *Liaoning Ribao*, "Province to Launch Campaign of 'Three No's' and 'Five Implementations': Planned Birth Work to Reach New Level," *Liaoning Ribao*, May 21, 1983, p. 1.

45 MOPH (Ministry of Public Health), *Chinese Health Statistical Digest, 1992* (Beijing: MOPH, 1992).

46 Susan Greenhalgh, Zhu Chuzhu, and Li Nan, "Restraining Population Growth in Three Chinese Villages, 1988–93," *Population and Development Review* 20, 1994, pp. 365–395.

47 Susan Greenhalgh and Edwin A. Winckler, *Population and Power in Post-Deng China: Institutions and Biopolitics* (Stanford: Stanford University Press, forthcoming); Edwin A. Winkler, "Chinese Birth Policy at the Turn of the Millennium: Stability and Change," *Population and Development Review* 28, 2002, pp. 379–418.

48 Susan Cohen and Cory Richards, "The Cairo Consensus: Population, Development, and Women," *Family Planning Perspectives* 26, 1994, pp. 272–277.

20

BUDGETS AND BIOPOLITICS

STEPHEN J. COLLIER

In the past 30 years, neoliberal technologies have spread to ever more domains of state administration.[1] This process has reconfigured contemporary forms of what Michel Foucault called "biopolitics," understood as "the endeavour... to rationalize the problems presented to governmental practice by the phenomena characteristic of a group of living human beings constituted as a population."[2] The present chapter examines neoliberalism and biopolitics through an exemplary instance – public-sector budgetary reform in post-Soviet Russia.

In the Russian context, neoliberalism works to rationalize and reform a distinctive form of collective existence – the Soviet social[3] – composed by specific mechanisms of economic coordination and social regulation. This process of rationalization and reform is often understood as one of marketization, through which amoral mechanisms of quantitative calculation replace the Soviet moral economy of state activity and social organization.

The picture that emerges in the following analysis of budgeting is different. The central distinction between the institutions of Soviet biopolitics and the forms proposed by neoliberal reform in the budgetary sphere are not to be found on the level of *values*. Both share the basic value-orientation of biopolitics (that the state should foster life) and the basic orientation of social citizenship (that citizens are entitled to equal claims on state resources). Rather, the distinction is to be found on the level of the *technological mechanisms* through which neoliberalism seeks to rationalize and reengineer the institutions of Soviet social modernity. Reforms seek to re-inscribe existing values. Specific technical concepts are preserved but reworked, value orientations are recoded into new forms of management, as existing institutional forms are reengineered through a process of what Ulrich Beck has called "reflexive modernization."

Belaya Kalitva and Great Transformation

I begin this investigation from an industrial city, Belaya Kalitva, in which I have conducted long-term fieldwork in Russia. Belaya Kalitva is located at a picturesque confluence of rivers on the northeastern edge of the Donbass coal basin in Rostov *Oblast'* (or region), north of the Caucus Mountains in southern Russia. At first sight, Belaya Kalitva appears more an idyllic rural town than a socialist (or decaying post-socialist) industrial city. Its neat downtown faces pretty white-rock bluffs, beyond which the buildings of a former collective farm are visible. Clusters of concrete apartment blocks stop abruptly at fields. The hulking buildings of industrial enterprises stand not far from garden plots.

For the entirety of its urban and industrial history, Belaya Kalitva has been based on a single industrial enterprise – still referred to locally as "our" city-forming (*gradoobrazuyushchee*) enterprise – the Belaya Kalitva Metallurgic Factory. In the Soviet period, the factory was not just the city's most important employer and largest contributor to the local budget. It was, moreover, the organizational and financial center of a sprawling urban infrastructure and a network of social services that plugged mechanisms for meeting the daily needs of the local population into national material flows and mechanisms of regulation. Secured by the certainties of national coordination, the city of Belaya Kalitva was, thus, composed as a remarkably stable assemblage of elements that constituted a distinctive form of human community, one that is more broadly typical of Soviet social modernity.[4]

With Soviet break-up, this assemblage came undone. Industrial ministries collapsed almost immediately, destroying old mechanisms of administrative coordination. Production at Belaya Kalitva's aluminum factory sputtered along at only a fraction of Soviet levels through the late 1990s, leading not only to a precipitous decline in industrial employment but also to a steady deterioration of the social systems and urban structures that it had supported. Local economic decline led, in turn, to mounting arrears in public pensions and in wages for health and education workers, categories of payments whose importance for local households had grown dramatically through the 1990s as industrial employment collapsed.

Many observers have seen this situation in terms of a grand civilizational battle, which they cast as what Karl Polanyi called a "great transformation."[5] On one side stands the substantive reality of cities such as Belaya Kalitva: the concrete material structures, the productive apparatus, a collection of human beings, systems of social welfare, and instituted processes of social interaction. On the other side stands the market, which replaced the myriad allocative systems of Soviet socialism with a single logic: supply and demand.[6] Observers disagree, of course, on the *value* of this process. Those suspicious of neoliberalism – whether embodied in free trade agreements, structural adjustment lending, privatization programs, or welfare reform – point to the inhumanity of neoliberal reforms: people versus profits; markets versus society. Triumphalists entertain fantasies, as Polanyi once said, of "self-regulation and harmony." What these positions share is an understanding of the stakes of neoliberal reform in terms of Polanyi's characterization of the insistent *sine qua non* of market society: that *all* factors of production should be organized as commodities.[7]

And indeed, at one level the Soviet case would seem to pose this epochal tension – markets versus the existing substantive organization of society – in particularly stark terms. In no other case did state administration so deeply shape the forms of modern social life as in Soviet Russia, creating a universalistic web of social welfare for human populations concentrated in comparatively small industrial cities that were distributed over a vast territory. In no other case were these forms sustained for so long in the face of deepening systemic crisis. And in no other case is the fate of such a well-established and stable form of modern urban–industrial life so starkly in question in neoliberal times.

But do these images capture how the fabric of human communities is at stake in neoliberal reform? In the discussion that follows, I propose to answer this question by means of a detailed technical analysis. My starting point is Nikolas Rose's observation that neoliberalism has a certain *formal* character.[8] It is concerned with increasing formal rationality, which refers, following Weber, to the extent of quantitative calculation that is technically possible and actually exercised in determining the allocation of resources in a given society or social system. Neoliberal technology thus operates according to allocations that are determined not through centralized command-and-control decisions but, rather, through the autonomous choices of formally free and calculative actors, whether these are individuals, collectivities, or organizations. Neoliberalism works, in short, on a rationality of a market *type*, although this does not mean, as I argue below, that it involves marketization *per se*.

But this "formal" definition only takes us so far. Just as Weber noted that the "formal rationality of money accounting does not reveal anything about the actual distribution of goods," the formal rationality of neoliberalism tells us nothing about its relationship to the *substantive* form of human communities.[9] Thus, to restate the goal of this chapter in these technical terms, we require a clearer understanding of how the *formal rationality* of neoliberalism transforms the relationship of state administration to the *substantive forms* of human community.

Budgetary Technology

To investigate this question, I examine a technology that is in many ways exemplary of neoliberal reform – the budget – in the domain of state administration. In other words, we are concerned with the public-sector budget or the system of public-sector finance. I first became interested in public-sector budgetary reform on a field trip to Belaya Kalitva in 1999. During the obligatory pass through the offices of the regional government (where letters often have to be signed and permissions granted for fieldwork to begin), a colleague and I met with the head of the budgetary office of Rostov *Oblast'*.

The head of the budgetary office was, first of all, a woman. The circumstance was hardly exceptional. In the Soviet period, finance was a relatively unimportant secondary occupation. It was the allocation of things rather than the allocation of rubles that mattered. But this was not a typical Soviet budgetary worker. A forceful and fast-talking reformer, she described to us plans for the transformation of interbudgetary relationships in the region: the laws, regulations, and procedures that govern the system of taxation, spending, and revenue distribution between the regional budget and local budgets. From her perspective, the problems to which reform had to address itself were clear enough. The Soviet Union had accumulated social commitments in cities such as Belaya Kalitva that were massively out of proportion with the fiscal realities of post-Soviet Russia. Further, the inherited budgetary system stunted tax collection and led to distortions in decision-making by local government officials. Though the social "needs" of poor cities could not simply be ignored, it was impossible to sustain the old system through which social norms drove expenditures without regard to the fiscal capacity of the state or of local governments.

The program for reform promoted in response was not a local creation. It was, rather, the complex product of one of the new networks of technocratic knowledge and governmental activity that have emerged in post-Soviet Russia in neoliberal times. The reforms were formulated by a Georgia State University (U.S.) project on tax reform, funded by USAID.[10] The project is located in Moscow and staffed largely by Russian experts. The Russian Ministry of Finance adopted the proposals in recommendatory status, but implementation remained the prerogative of local government.

The details of the reform are discussed below. Preliminarily, it will be useful to say a bit more about the specific character of the budget as a technology, on the one hand, and, on the other, about the public-sector budget as a mechanism of modern biopolitics.

The budget is in many respects paradigmatic of neoliberal technologies of reform and, more generally, of formal rationalization.[11] A budget – whether that of an individual, a collectivity, or an organization – is a nexus of choice concerning revenues and expenditures expressed in quantitative, and thus calculable, terms. As Weber pointed out, the "budgetary" decisions of a capitalist enterprise present an ideal type of formal rationalization. *Ideal-typically,* the cost of both inputs and outputs are expressed in quantitative (money) terms. *Ideal-typically,* the value of these inputs and outputs is determined only by effective demand. *Ideal-typically,* decisions made by this special kind of actor – the enterprise – are based only on the formally free, calculated disposition of available means that yields the greatest possible return.[12]

Viewed from this ideal typic perspective, it is apparent that the public-sector budget presents a special case. Public-sector budgeting is not undertaken by wholly independent organizations. Rather, it takes place in a distinctive institutional context, namely the state apparatus, articulated both by *intra-bureaucratic* relationships and by *political* relationships (usually defined constitutionally) between different levels of government. Moreover, public-sector budgeting is not oriented toward profit and loss. Rather, it is oriented to the distinctive biopolitical goals of state administration – the health, welfare, and conditions of existence of national populations – whose historical emergence was intimately connected, in most countries, with the massive expansion of the size of the state fiscal mechanism over the course of the 20th century. As public-sector expenditures grew to a substantial percentage of the gross domestic product of national economies (between 30 and 70 percent in advanced industrial countries), public-sector budgets became – and remain – one of the central allocative mechanisms in modern societies.

Since the fiscal crises of large welfare states beginning in the early 1970s, and proceeding through successive debt crises in Latin America, Africa, and the former socialist bloc, public-sector budgets have become critical sites of neoliberal reform. Since budgetary reform involves systems that are critical to the satisfaction of human wants, fiscal reform is a critical point of contact between techniques of formal rationalization and the core institutions of modern biopolitics. The contemporary relationship between budgets and biopolitics is, therefore, a fateful one. To understand how, and in what sense, it will be necessary to add to the *formal* description of budgetary technology an understanding of the distinctive institutional setting and normative orientation of public-sector budgeting in a specific context. To do so, we will have to inquire further into the structure of Soviet social modernity through the Belo-Kalitvaen mirror.

Social Modernity in Belaya Kalitva

The industrial, though not urban, history of Belaya Kalitva began in the middle of the 19th century, when the "city" consisted of small concentrations of population in coal-mining settlements arranged around a minor Cossack *stanitsa* or administrative center. In the early years of the Soviet period, an expansion of industrial activity was planned on the basis of an aluminum factory that was to be associated with defense aviation. Construction began just before World War II, was interrupted by Nazi occupation (the foundation of the unbuilt enterprise was used as a German prison camp), and then completed after the war. Major population growth ensued, as peasants from the surrounding *khutery*, or small rural homesteads, joined a smaller number of technical experts from large cities and returnees from the front to build a new enterprise and a new city.

As in virtually all the new industrial cities of the Soviet Union, the industrial, urban, and social development of Belaya Kalitva was initially unbalanced.[13] In 1953, when the first workshops in the aluminum factory were completed the "city" was composed of a handful of barracks, some "social" facilities (two early schoolhouses and a hospital), and a small cluster of attractive residential buildings. The broader focus of postwar reconstruction efforts, however, was overwhelmingly on industrial production. Even late as the early 1960s, Belaya Kalitva remained very much a rural industrial settlement.

The situation began to change dramatically only in the mid-1960s, when the first general plan for development of the city was completed. The plan, composed by a design institute in Leningrad, was the product of the paradigm of Soviet urban planning called city-building (*gradostroitel'stvo*).[14] In contrast to urban planning in western Europe, which dealt with comparatively limited questions of land use, utility provision, and transportation planning, city-building was a comprehensive paradigm for the planning, construction, and management of every element of a socialist urban community. Given city-building's centrality as a template for Soviet biopolitics, a brief review of the planning process itself will be instructive.

The logical movement of the Belaya Kalitva plan proceeded from a series of decisions made in advance about the city's industrial base, most importantly the metallurgic factory, the coal mines, and a handful of smaller unbuilt enterprises whose profiles were initially unspecified. This industrial base, in turn, yielded a population of city-forming personnel (*gradoobrazuyushchii personal*) that included the workers at industrial and support enterprises such as inter-urban transportation facilities directly associated with industrial production.

Departing from this figure, a city plan determined all the possible substantive elements of a human community, calculated by means of what I call *biotechnical norms*.[15] These norms allowed city-builders to use a baseline figure for city-forming personnel to derive a figure for a general (laboring and non-laboring) population. The size and age structure of this population, in turn, was used to derive an integrated plan for the totality of substantive elements of a city required to satisfy local needs, including transportation and utility infrastructures, the housing stock, and education, health, and leisure facilities.

In each of these substantive areas, further hierarchies of biotechnical norms specified the details of an apparatus of service provision or material infrastructure. Thus, to take the example of education, relatively simple coefficients (literally, multipliers) made it possible for planners to move from a population of a certain size and age structure to a number of school-age children to a number of classroom units. Further norms defined the concrete components each classroom unit would require: buildings, teachers, utility services, textbooks, supplies. A general plan incorporated these complex hierarchies of norms into a single comprehensive vision that included all the possible contents of a city, including doctors, hospitals, schools, pipes, roads, public baths, parks, buses, teachers, schools, boilers, and water purification facilities. The city plan included, in short, all the possible elements of Soviet urban life.

Normed Needs and Fiscal Flows

How did budgetary institutions fit into this planning apparatus? For the most part, and particularly in smaller peripheral cities, plan implementation was the prerogative of industrial ministries. Thus, in Belaya Kalitva, the metallurgic enterprise financed construction of most of the housing stock and of most social facilities. However, a broad range of social services was financed through the system of budgetary organs organized by units of territorial administration. We can refer to these expenditures as belonging to "local" budgets.

Formally, administration of these local or territorial budgets was organized through a system of "dual subordination" (*dvoinoe podchinenie*): to the Ministry of Finance, on the one hand, and, on the other, to local soviets (the "political" organs of territorial administration). In fact, local soviets had limited control over expenditures and none over tax policy. Particularly in small cities, in which local administrative entities were weak compared to industrial enterprises, the Ministry of Finance controlled local budgets.

The structure of the Ministry of Finance formed a single "consolidated" budgetary system that included all-Union, republican, regional, and local (municipal and rural) budgets.[16] The bureaucratic logic of distribution among budgets within this system was based – ideally – on roughly the same structure of social norms that pertained in city plans. Financing norms allowed the translation or coding of normative levels of service provision (for health, education, leisure) into ruble equivalents. These ruble equivalents, in turn, were aggregated. The result was a definition of budgetary *potrebnosti* or "requirements" – a critical concept in Soviet budgeting that provided a quantitative expression of the aggregate social "needs" of the population of a given locality.

In the final step of the budgetary process, these "requirements" formed the basis for the redistribution of resources through a logic of "gap-filling." Higher-standing offices in the Ministry of Finance acted through adjustments of revenue-sharing mechanisms (tax assignments) and through interbudgetary transfers to close the gap between actual revenues for a lower-standing budget and the norm-defined "requirements" for the unit of population to which it corresponded. The logic, in theory, was straightforward: normed needs drove fiscal flows.

It was never the case that budgeting produced exactly the results that planners expected. Chronic delays in capital investment introduced myriad distortions in urban development. The imperative to provide current financing for existing facilities tended to drive expenditure decisions, thus perpetuating some imbalances in service provision across national space.[17]

Nevertheless, if we view Soviet budgeting not from the perspective of the ideality of plans but from the perspective of a comparative inquiry into the forms of social modernity, this idealized picture captures key elements of Soviet biopolitics. Through the bureaucratic concept of "requirements" (*potrebnosti*), a given human community such as Belaya Kalitva *showed up* in the budget both as a *planned future* and as an *already existing reality* of human beings, buildings, social facilities, and utilities that required wages, gas, heat, construction materials, and so on.

What is crucial for our consideration of neoliberal reforms is that this system of *budgets* was not, in Rose's sense, *budgetized*. The choices of relatively autonomous nodes of calculation had no role in public-sector finance. Calculation occurred at an aggregate level, and any given "budget" was only a *unit of account* for biotechnical norms that formed a basis for central calculation. The budgetary process was a mere adjunct of the system of substantive planning. The latter system inscribed national space materially, demographically, administratively, and institutionally, producing stable relationships among economic organization, human populations, and an apparatus of social welfare.

Despite the glaring distortions and shortcomings of the planning system, the distinctive "success" of the institutions of Soviet social modernity – ultimately Pyrrhic as it may have been – is undeniable. Belaya Kalitva can stand as an exemplary case. Over the course of the past 30 years of the Soviet period, a form of human community emerged that can only be understood in terms of the norms and forms of city-building. First brick and then concrete apartment blocks were constructed, replacing the individual houses of the early post-World War II period. Urban infrastructure was universalized. Daily life was linked to national systems of resource flow, and an increasingly uniform set of urban goods and social services was extended to the population. Through a process that continued to the onset of *perestroika*, the mechanisms involved in the material satisfaction of daily wants were systematically wrapped up in state administration. Budgeting inscribed the body biopolitic.

Adjustment

With Soviet break-up, the guaranteed need-driven financing that secured cities such as Belaya Kalitva in national systems of economic coordination collapsed. A yawning gap opened between normative levels of provisioning and the resources available to local governments. The specific novelty of this crisis is notable. What was new was not the problem of shortage *per se*. The Soviet period was far from one of abundance. Material scarcity was pervasive, whether manifest in a shortage of goods and services, or in the simple inability of public-sector employees to buy anything they wanted with wages that were paid, always in full, and always on time. The Soviet problem was not a shortage of *money* but a shortage of *things*. In the post-Soviet period as money attained real value, and all material things could be had – at a price – these material shortages became fiscal shortages.[18] The crunch was particularly acute for local governments, which were trapped between collapsing revenues and an increased expenditure burden, as many items of social provisioning that had been financed by industrial enterprises were transferred to local budgets.

Precisely this kind of imbalance led to the articulation of "adjustment" as a paradigm of social transformation. When they were initially introduced, particularly in Africa and Latin America, adjustment policies addressed the exigencies of fiscal crisis and hyperinflation, and were focused on fiscal stabilization and de-statization of mechanisms of economic allocation. As such, these policies departed dramatically from the "classic" developmentalism of the post-World War II period. Classical developmentalism was "substantive" in that it concretely planned transformation in terms of the detailed arrangement of the material, demographic, productive, and social elements of a given community. "Adjustment" policies do not envision a concrete process of substantive transformation. They are formal in the sense that they propose transformation organized not through substantive planning but through the calculative choices of formally free actors – a rationality of a market type. Thus, to take one paradigmatic general statement of the approach, in a talk on Russia in the early 1990s, Jeffrey Sachs defined neoliberal "adjustment" as the "initial allocation of productive factors after the introduction of market forces."[19]

But a closer look at actual proposals for managing post-Soviet transformation indicates that adjustment does not simply imply marketization. In fact, neoliberal technologies function in a range of domains of reform. "The market," as such, is only a special case. Thus, the World Bank's first general strategy document for Russia, issued in 1994, defined a program for *fiscal adjustment* focused on the public sector. Most generally, it sought to bring the federal budget closer to balance and to curtail inflationary spending or lending on the part of the federal government, two measures considered crucial to the emergence of market-driven growth. Beyond that, however, the report laid out a program for a broad reengineering of the state role in society, a broad reengineering, that is, of the biopolitical field.[20]

The report identified five central components of the fiscal adjustment strategy. These included taxation policy, industrial subsidies, communal services and housing, the social safety net, and interbudgetary relationships.[21] In some cases, such as the removal of industrial subsidies and the relaxation of the tax burden, the purpose of reforms was simply to replace state mechanisms of allocation with the decisions of autonomous "private" actors. In other areas – social welfare, interbudgetary finance, and communal services – reforms propose a more complex reengineering of the state role in social and economic life.

The Bank report did not articulate actionable programs for reforms in any of these areas. Stabilization and privatization were the focus in the early years of post-Soviet transformation. As the 1990s progressed, however, attention turned to these other domains of reform. In this context, the Georgia State project emerged as the most important and systematic technocratic effort to invent a new form of interbudgetary fiscal relationships.

Budgetary Reform

The Russian Ministry of Finance adopted the Georgia State program in 1999, under the auspicious title *Methodological Recommendations for the Regulation of Interbudgetary Relationships in Subjects of the Russian Federation*.[22]

Recommendations poses a series of questions that were simply unthinkable in the context of the Soviet system: Can Russia afford to support the existing level of social provisioning? What compromise between fiscal balance and the financing of social services is appropriate? What calculations or systems of value will determine which substantive ends can be sacrificed? Who will make these decisions? Do the welfare guarantees of Soviet social welfarism undermine the efficiency of public adminis-tration? Most broadly, what is the impact of the budgetary system on (market) allocative mechanisms in the economy? These questions emerged as part of a now-familiar pattern of critique and reform, which sought to wrap itself around the Soviet budgetary system, to disembed specific values, mechanisms, institutions, and routines from the broader structure of Soviet social modernity, and to rationalize and reform it.

Recommendations begins from an assessment of the system of interbudgetary relations as it stood in the latter part of the 1990s, when the project undertook detailed study of several regional budgetary systems. After ruble stabilization in 1994, the finances of most local governments in Russia collapsed, and public-sector payments and services were in crisis. Yet the basic logic of the budgetary system changed little. Following the old Soviet pattern of gap-filling, the report notes, regional budgetary offices "attempt to make up, from the regional budget, the difference between tax and nontax revenues of the local budget in a given year and its 'requirements'."[23] The reference to the old Soviet term "requirements" – *potrebnosti* – is significant. Material shortage had become fiscal shortage. The disjuncture between the fiscal capacity of the public sector and social commitments baldly confronted budgetary decision-makers at every level, no longer as a complex of particularistic shortages in this or that good or service, but as the simple quantitative difference between revenues and expenditure needs. And yet local governments did not respond by adjusting the range of goods and services they delivered. Nor, for that matter, did they adjust their understanding of expenditure need.

The consequence was that as objects of government localities continued to show up as units of accounting for biotechnical norms, as simple aggregations of needs: for heat, for medical supplies, and salaries. *Recommendations* continues:

> [T]he administrative units of the subjects of the federation [regional governments] see the local budget as lists of expenditures [*smety raskhodov*] of an administrative–territorial unit. On the regional level, they not only produce the most detailed norms for budgetary expenditures, including for the administration of local administrative organs, but they also take decisions on the types and levels of local taxes.[24]

Beyond the basic failure to confront the imbalance between expenditure commitments and revenues, *Recommendations* identifies two central problems with the inherited system of budgeting. First, it produces a number of perverse incentives in the management of the fiscal system. Lacking an incentive to increase tax collections (since any marginal increase in taxes collected locally would be effectively distributed among other localities in a given region, and since increased local collections were likely, as in the old system, to simply decrease the level of transfers), local governments do not pressure local enterprises to pay taxes in full and do not adjust expenditure commitments in line with fiscal capacities. Lacking accountability for expenditure decisions, local governments have little incentive to improve service delivery.

Second, the system as it stood in the late 1990s had broader negative implications for "adjustment" as a process of market organization of productive factors in the economy. The Soviet system of "gap-filling" supports cities that may prove to be simply nonviable in market conditions. Consequently, the system of public finances distorts the allocation of productive factors (including human beings and the concrete forms of human community) across regional and national space.

Substantive Prerequisites for Formal Rationalization

The first step proposed in *Recommendations* can be conceptualized as a move from a system in which substantive outcomes are programmed in advance to one in which allocations are driven by the decisions of calculative actors. In other words, it seeks to engineer a mechanism of *formal rationalization* of the budgetary system. Formal rationalization in this case does not involve simply removing constraints. Rather, reforms assume that situations of calculative choice are complex products of social technology that constitute what Max Weber referred to as the *substantive prerequisites* (or institutional conditions) *of formal rationalization*.

In his discussion of formal rationality, Weber noted three such prerequisites: first, the clear definition of distinct decision-making units (here, local governments, which will control local finance); second, the formal freedom of decision-making units; and, third, a system of valuation that clearly defines the costs and benefits of concrete choices made by these units.[25]

As *Recommendations* notes, though not in these terms, these prerequisites were absent in the Soviet period when local budgetary organs were not autonomous but were subordinated directly to the Ministry of Finance. In this context, the rights and responsibilities of such organs were ambiguous. The lack of competitive elections, the severe limitations on locational decisions by both enterprises and individuals, and the obligatory nature of most items of local expenditure meant that the accountability of local governments to local conditions or to the quality of local administration was limited. No system of valuation existed to assess the cost and benefits of decisions taken at the local level or in other parts of the system of substantive planning.

The task outlined in *Recommendations* is to constitute the "budgetary individual" – in this case, the local government – as an actor whose rights, responsibilities, and competencies are clearly defined, and to constitute a field of calculative choice in which the incentives of this actor will be more closely aligned with the ends of budgetary management (efficiency, fiscal balance, substantive provisioning). A number of concrete steps follow, some of which were instituted in prior legislation (the constitutional provisions on local government and subsequent national laws on local government and the fiscal bases of local government).

First, in place of the existing practice of shifting the distribution of tax revenues among different budgetary levels in response to budgetary needs, regional governments would permanently assign a certain portion of taxes to the local level. Budgetary "individuals" – local governments – would know exactly what revenues "belong" to them. One advantage is an improved basis for local budgetary planning, since most revenue would be derived from permanently assigned taxes rather than from an *ad hoc* system of transfers. Equally important, governments would know that actions to increase locally collected taxes (by promoting the development of local enterprises or simply pressuring local enterprises to pay taxes) would increase the resources available them.

Second, in contrast to the Soviet system, in which most expenditures were obligatory, local governments would be given the legal right – equally a burden in times of fiscal shortage – to make expenditure decisions.

Third, a system of accountabilities would be created by establishing principles of *valuation* of the actions of local government. In *Recommendations*, two mechanisms are to provide feedback to local governments concerning their use of budgetary resources: first, the process of democratic elections and, presumably, the mobilization of interest groups in the political sphere; and, second, the possibility of mobility on the part of both residents and enterprises who "vote with their feet." Two great modern arenas of institutionalized choice – "politics" and "the market" – are constituted as core technological mechanisms of neoliberal reform.

The implication of these changes would be a fundamental transformation of the mechanisms that govern the adjustments among economic organization, social welfare regimes, and state administration. Let us quickly summarize the essential differences between the Soviet model and the forms proposed by neoliberal rationalization.

In the Soviet period, we recall, the budgetary system was one among a number of regulatory and allocative systems that fixed enterprises, local governments, human populations, and social service regimes in given spatial and institutional relationships. Indeed, as we have seen, the reproduction of these relationships was inscribed in the very workings of the budgetary system itself, which translated normed needs directly into fiscal flows. The vision articulated in the Georgia State report places these elements in motion. They are made to interact with other social subsystems that stand to them in a relation of semi-autonomy, with dramatic though uncertain implications for the transformation of the substantive order produced by Soviet city-building. Enterprises may continue to operate, close, or move, depending in part on their economic viability in market conditions, in part on the local tax regime implemented by the local government. Residents may choose to stay or go, depending on their satisfaction with local services (education, health, and public infrastructure services in particular) and on the availability of local employment. They also may choose to re-elect or throw out local governments that are either successfully or unsuccessfully promoting their interests. Local governments, finally, may choose to adjust levels of service delivery or regimes of taxation in an effort to avoid being thrown out of office.

Thus far, the proposal *sounds* like simple marketization of the state sphere: define individual actors, impose hard constraints, and let the system work itself out through automatic adjustments that result from the autonomous choices of residents, enterprises, and local governments. If municipalities do not have sufficient resources to finance key items of expenditure – basic social services, for instance – let them be cut. If, as a result, cities become unlivable, let inhabitants and businesses move. If cities such as Belaya Kalitva are, thus, abandoned...well, the creative destruction of market adjustment is not always pretty but, reformers would argue, has proven better than other historical alternatives. Is it not the case that "marketization" – though, admittedly, a marketization that occurs not through the "freeing" of markets but, as Burchell has argued,[26] through the conscious, purposeful, creation of systems of allocation that function on a rationality of a market type – is precisely the proper description for such a vision? Do we not have to rely on the "enlightened" self-interest of actors to produce felicitous aggregate effects?

Substantive Ends of Formal Rationalization

In fact, we have only examined the first element of the Georgia State proposal. In practice, substantive outcomes are *not* left purely to automatic adjustments. Rather, neoliberal reforms will be oriented to a definite set of *values* or, to borrow another Weberian term, substantive *ends* of formal rationalization. On the most general level, *Recommendations* proposes as a basic value-orientation for the activity of the inter-budgetary system that "every inhabitant of [any given] region has roughly equal requirements for budgetary expenditures and has the right to make a claim on an equal level of services from local government,"[27] a classic value of modern social citizenship.

The difficulty, of course, is that a *guarantee* of equal budgetary expenditures as a kind of social right would reproduce precisely those characteristics of the Soviet system that *Recommendations* calls into question for their effects on efficient public-sector management, and on market allocation more generally. The question is: How can an orientation to certain substantive ends be reconciled with a system that works through a rationality of a market-type?

The mechanism proposed in *Recommendations*, typical of such fiscal reform proposals more generally, is a fund for the redistribution of resources between the regional budget and local budgets that would serve as an additional allocative mechanism beyond the system of revenue sharing. The fund proposed in the Georgia State report is constituted as a definite portion of the total revenues of the *consolidated* regional budget: the sum of revenues of all local budgets plus the regional budget in a given region.[28] Financial resources in the fund would then be divided among local governments on the basis of distribution coefficients. The rub, as we might expect, is in the technical constitution of these coefficients.

Following from *Recommendations'* most general value orientation – that all inhabitants of a region have the right to expect equal levels of public service – it would be possible for distribution coefficients to be based simply on population. The assumption would be that all inhabitants have roughly equal needs, that the "social citizen," who has "equal" rights to a claim on resources, was generic. The distribution coefficient, in this case, would simply be a ratio expressing the proportion of the regional population living on the territory governed by a local government.

In fact, the distribution coefficients reflect a much more complex understanding of "need" for social service provisioning in a given municipality, and a much more finely articulated mechanism for coding the needs of localities as collectivities of biological and social beings.

The coefficient for any given municipality is composed of a series of sub-coefficients that express normatively defined need in a given domain of social provisioning – education, health care, communal services such as heat and water, transportation services, and so on. Some equations for the calculation of sub-coefficients are quite simple. The coefficient for education is derived exclusively from the number of school-age children in a given locality. Thus, one part of any given municipality's "claim" on the distribution fund is constituted as the percentage of schoolchildren in the region that reside in that municipality. Other coefficients are much more complex. Coefficients for communal services – by far the largest category of local government expenditure in most Russian cities – incorporate a range of substantive characteristics of a locality to derive a definition of need. These include the size of the population, the amount of housing heated and maintained by a given organ of territorial administration (usually a vast majority in industrial areas), the local climate (which determines heating requirements), and various technical char-acteristics of the massive centralized boiler systems that heat Soviet cities (coal versus gas-fired boilers, for instance).

The overall distribution coefficient for a given city is then derived on the basis of these sub-coefficients. It is a composite and quantified expression of need composed of nested hierarchies of biotechnical norms. The logical movement of this technol-ogy, thus, proceeds from a certain population to a quantitative expression that captures myriad and diverse human needs. Indeed, the *entire substantive bestiary* of Soviet social modernity – heating pipes, apartment blocks, teachers, doctors, clinics, the climate, and the cost of local resources such as water – are coded into a distribution coefficient. This technical procedure bears a striking similarity to the derivation of budgetary "requirements" in the Soviet period.

Thus, in neoliberal reforms a city such as Belaya Kalitva does not "show up" *merely* as a node of calculative choice, or as a collection of calculative actors, although that is one part of the story. It also shows up as the complex integrated substantive reality that emerged from Soviet city-building. The body biopolitic is reinscribed.

But how, exactly, does this process relate to the actual distributions of resources? In the differences between the technological functioning of Soviet budgetary require-ments – *potrebnosti* – and the distribution coefficients proposed in *Recommendations* we find the key to neoliberalism as a biopolitical form. In the Soviet period, the only "technological" translation between social need and budgetary "requirements" was accomplished by means of a cost norm that expressed need in ruble terms. Although this need was not always met materially, the system accepted "requirements" as a definition of the resources to which localities were entitled.

In *Recommendations*, by contrast, the distribution coefficient corresponds not to an *actual* commitment of finances but to a multiplier that defines the *proportion* of a redistribution fund to be transferred to a given city or rural settlement. The redistri-bution fund is constituted as a clearly defined *and clearly limited* pool of resources.

Gone is the pretense of plentitude, the technological assumption (if not the material reality) that adequate resources will be available to meet normatively defined needs. The "right to make a claim on an equal level of services from local government" is not a guarantee of an adequate level of service provision; indeed, the *absence* of such a guarantee is a *sine qua non* of neoliberal reform. The crucial question is what one *does* with these proportions.

Recommendations notes a range of options for the translation of the coefficients into an actual distribution of resources. At one extreme, a vast majority of the financial resources of a consolidated regional budget may be dedicated to the distribution fund such that per capita expenditures are highly equalized across municipalities. The implication is not necessarily that needs would be met. But expenditures *relative to normatively defined need* would be roughly similar everywhere. Alternatively, a relatively small portion of regional resources can be placed in the fund, in which case expenditures relative to normatively defined need would vary substantially across localities.

Each variant, *Recommendations* notes, will have benefits and disadvantages. Increasing the level of equalization would increase the security of social provisioning. However, equalization entails corresponding "costs" in allocational efficiency of market mechanisms and in the incentives of local governments to increase revenue or to increase the efficiency of service delivery. A relatively less equalizing variant – one in which the distribution fund was composed by a relatively small portion of the consolidated regional budget – would increase the incentives of local governments to raise taxes, to make service delivery more efficient, and to adjust levels of service provision in line with the local revenue base. It would also encourage a broader process of economic "adjustment." Poor municipalities would have to cut services and public-sector employment as effective subsidies to economically nonviable communities declined.

Notably, *Recommendations* does not proscribe a "correct" path among these options. The technocratic task is to create a framework of choice that will clarify the costs and benefits of various options. Choosing among them involves questions of value – a problem of politics, not technology, that must be determined by regional governments. *Recommendations* concludes: "The concrete variation of distribution of financial resources between local budgets should be chosen by regional governments on the basis of the priorities of regional socioeconomic policy and the existing differentiation in the tax base of individual municipalities."[29]

Budgetary (Re)Assemblages: Toward an Anthropology of the Post-Social

As we have seen, reforms of the system of interbudgetary finance were proposed – at least in general form – at the very outset of the post-Soviet period. But in 1999 Rostov was one of only a few regions even considering implementing them. The Rostov proposal was revised, delayed, and, as of 2000, had not been put into practice.[30] The reasons for delay are not hard to grasp. For most of the 1990s the focus of reformers was elsewhere, on the more public battles of stabilization and privatization. Just as importantly, in the austere environment of the middle and late 1990s the choices made brutally explicit by reform proposals may have been simply impossible to swallow politically. It was more palatable, ultimately, to muddle through, to maintain a formal commitment to Soviet levels of social service delivery even as the public sector fell deeper and deeper into debt.

But situations change. The devaluation of August 1998 triggered a recovery of domestic industry in a number of sectors. Of particular local significance was the consolidation of the domestic aluminum industry, which led to a subsequent rebound in local metallurgy that revived Belaya Kalitva in the first years of the 21st century. Industrial recovery was one factor among others that substantially improved the health of public-sector finance.[31] By 2000 arrears in social payments had disappeared in Belaya Kalitva, and had become much less frequent on the national level.

An important consequence of the recovery is that, as of the first years of the 2000s, budgetary reform no longer seemed to place the future of cities such as Belaya Kalitva so starkly in the balance. Movement for reform could also be detected on the federal level, as the World Bank approved lending to support regional reform of the interbudgetary fiscal system in early 2002.

Today such reforms remain, nonetheless, more virtual than actual. But we are now in a better position to assess their potential implications for substantive transformation; to ask, in short, how human communities such as Belaya Kalitva are at stake in neoliberal reform. It should be clear from the preceding analysis that it is not my view that the implementation of further reform – either in the public sector or more broadly – will usher in a "market society" (wherever on earth one might find one of those!) any more than it will finally usher *out* the norms and forms of the Soviet social. At a level of technical detail, neoliberalism does not imply the wholesale replacement of one form of social organization with another. Indeed, the diversity of "variants" of reform outlined at the end of the Georgia State proposal underscores the *substantive* ambiguity of neoliberal reform. The extent to which values, procedures, and existing institutions are reinscribed is not simply a question of implementation versus nonimplementation of reform. It is, rather, a question of the variant of neoliberal reform in question, of the specific *technical* management of the formal rationalization of substantive provisioning by the state.

At the level of social description, then, the process of transformation that concerns us does not seem usefully described as the replacement of Soviet social modernity with a "market society." Rather, what are to be traced are the novel articulations between market-type mechanisms, old biopolitical forms, and the actual substantive fabric of existing human communities. The resulting (substantively ambiguous) reassemblage of the norms and forms of social modernity is exemplary of the process that Urlich Beck has called reflexive modernization: the disembedding of one set of modern social forms and their re-embedding in . . . another modernity.[32] Such an understanding of neoliberalism suggests one way to think about the post-social: not that which comes after the social, but the product of the reflexive modernization of the modern social.

This view of neoliberal reform also has implications for critical studies of development in neoliberal times. If neoliberal reforms incorporate values – and if at least *some* neoliberals demonstrate a carefully self-limiting attitude to the scope of strictly technological interventions – the debates around neoliberalism would have, it seems, to shift from questions of value to questions of technique. Thus, critics who are unhappy with the outcome of neoliberal reform – and the experience of the past decades suggests they should be, as should "neoliberals" – need not produce alternative values. Rather, they should seek alternative proposals for the formally rational incorporation of values in the government of human communities. In other words, critics can intervene not by humanizing neoliberal technology but by engaging in the (neoliberal) project of technologizing humanism: of finding better ways to satisfy human needs with scarce resources.

Notes

1 Elizabeth Dunn, Andrew Lakoff, and Aihwa Ong made helpful comments on this chapter.

2 Michel Foucault, "The Birth of Biopolitics," in Paul Rabinow, ed., *Ethics: Subjectivity and Truth* (New York: New Press, 1997), p. 73.

3 The term "Soviet social" is meant in the sense that Gilles Deleuze speaks of "the social", which he distinguishes from "society" – the object of sociological analysis. "The social," as Deleuze understands it, is specifically constituted by the various bio-technical forms that emerged in relationship to the human sciences and became part of governmental practice through the course of the 19th century in European cases. See Gilles Deleuze, "Foreword: The Rise of the Social," in Jacques Donzelot, *The Policing of Families* (New York: Pantheon, 1979).

4 The idea of "social modernity" is discussed in Paul Rabinow's *French Modern: Norms and Forms of the Social Environment* (Cambridge, MA: The MIT Press, 1989).

5 Karl Polanyi, *The Great Transformation* (Boston: Beacon, 1957).

6 This point is made in David Woodruff, *Money Unmade: Barter and the Fate of Russian Capitalism* (Ithaca, NY: Cornell University Press, 1999).

7 Ibid., particularly Ch. 6.

8 Nikolas Rose, "Governing 'Advanced' Liberal Democracies," in Andrew Barry, Thomas Osborne, and Nikolas Rose, eds., *Foucault and Political Reason: Liberalism, Neo-liberalism, and Rationalities of Government* (Chicago: University of Chicago Press, 1996).

9 Max Weber, *Economy and Society* (Berkeley: University of California Press, 1978), p. 108.

10 I am grateful to Andrei Timofeev and Galina Kurlyandskaya for discussing the work of the project with me in 1999–2000.

11 This point, emphasized by Rose in "Governing 'Advanced' Liberal Democracies," is a central concern in the discussion of budgeting and formal rationalization in *Economy and Society.*

12 See especially Weber's discussion of capital accounting in *Economy and Society,* pp. 90–100.

13 See, for example, William Taubman, *Governing Soviet Cities: Bureaucratic Politics and Urban Development* (New York: Praeger, 1973).

14 City-building is a central figure in Stephen J. Collier, "Post-Socialist City: The Government of Society in Neoliberal Times," Ph.D. dissertation, Department of Anthropology, University of California, Berkeley, 2001.

15 Rabinow, *French Modern*.

16 Collier, "Post-Socialist City."

17 See Peter Rutland, *The Myth of the Plan: Lessons of Soviet Planning Experience* (London: Hutchinson, 1985); Taubman, *Governing Soviet Cities*. Nonetheless, these disparities in service provision tended to diminish over the course of the Soviet period. See Donna Barry, *Outside Moscow: Power, Politics, and Budgetary Policy in the Soviet Republics* (New York: Columbia University Press, 1987).

18 Woodruff, *Money Unmade*.

19 Jeffrey D. Sachs, "Russia's Struggle with Stabilization: Conceptual Issues and Evidence," paper presented at the World Bank Annual Conference on Development Economics (Washington, DC: The World Bank, 1994).

20 *Russian Federation: Toward Medium-Term Viability* (Washington, DC: World Bank, 1996), p. ix.

21 *Toward Medium-Term Viability*, p. ix.

22 *Metodicheskie rekomendatsii po regulirovaniyu mezhbyuzhetnykh otnoshenii v sub'ektakh Rossiiskoi Federatsii.* (Ministry of Finance, Russian Federation, Department of Interbudgetary Relationships, 1999).

23 *Metodicheskie rekomendatsii*, p. 10.

24 Idem.

25 See Weber, *Economy and Society*, pp. 107–108.

26 Graham Burchell, "Liberal Government and Techniques of the Self," in Barry et al., *Foucault and Political Reason*, pp. 19–36.

27 *Metodicheskie rekomendatsii*, p. 10.

28 To be precise, the redistribution fund is a proportion of the consolidated regional budget *minus* locally instituted taxes.

29 *Metodicheskie rekomendatsii*, p. 53.

30 I thank Andrei Timofeev for keeping me updated on the situation in Rostov.

31 The others include a felicitous rise in world oil prices and the effects of the devaluation, which also devalued existing social commitments.

32 Ulrich Beck, Anthony Giddens, and Scott Lash, *Reflexive Modernization: Politics, Tradition, and Aesthetics in the Modern Social Order* (Cambridge: Polity Press, 1994).

SECURITY, LEGITIMACY, JUSTICE

21

STATE AND URBAN SPACE IN BRAZIL:
From Modernist Planning to Democratic Interventions[1]

TERESA CALDEIRA AND JAMES HOLSTON

In the last half century, the Brazilian state consolidated and then liquidated a modernist model for the production of urban space. According to this model, best crystallized in the construction of Brasília, the state produces urban space according to centralized master plans that are conceived as instruments of social change and economic development. The role of government is both to articulate these plans and to create the means for their realization. During the last two decades, however, a constellation of forces – including main elements of the state, business and industry, popular social movements, political parties, and nongovernmental organizations (NGOs) – rejected this centralized conception of state intervention. In its place, they substituted a notion of planning in which government does not produce space directly but, rather, acts as a manager of localized and often private interests in the cityscape. Moreover, whereas the modernist model entails a concept of total design, by which planners impose solutions, like demigods, the new model considers that plans should both be based on and foster the exercise of democratic citizenship.

The new planning results from a confluence of contradictory factors. On the one hand, many of its tenets were first proposed by social movements and NGOs concerned with urban reform in the 1970s and 1980s. Some of the most significant of these principles were included in the new Federal Constitution of 1988 (called the Citizens' Constitution) and developed in subsequent urban plans and legislation by these organizations. Therefore, the new model of planning is an explicit expression of the democratization process that has been transforming Brazilian society and its ways of conceiving of citizenship since the 1970s. On the other hand, the same instruments have also been used by some municipal administrations and by powerful private organizations to produce the contrary of their original intent; namely, the privatization of public space, spatial segregation, social inequality, and private real estate gain. Moreover, the redefinition of the role of the state expressed in the new planning cannot be associated with democratization alone. In addition, the collapse of the interventionist modernist mode relates to a fiscal crisis of the state, industrial restructuring, and the adoption of neoliberal policies usually justified as necessary to keep Brazil in pace with the new demands of globalization.

This chapter contrasts these two models of governmental production and management of urban space. It also addresses the consequences of each for the lives and spaces of the working-class people who inhabit both the poor peripheries of Brasília and São Paulo and the favelas and *cortiços* of their centers.[2] Since the beginning of industrialization, governmental production of space in Brazilian cities has meant the creation of a legal and regulated city for the upper classes and an illegal and unregulated city for the majority of the working poor; that is to say, for the vast majority of Brazilians. Illegality and improvisation have always been the conditions under which the urban poor have created their spaces in Brazilian (and most third-world) cities. The instruments of urban policy created during the democratic period attempt to address the problem of illegality and therefore of social injustice in Brazilian cities. Nevertheless, as powerful corporations and real estate interests engage these same instruments, they generate new forms of spatial segregation and undermine some of the paths to urban improvement and citizenship expansion that the social movements of the 1970s and 1980s achieved.

Total Planning

Owing to the need to constitute a base of radiation of a pioneering system [of development] that would bring to civilization an unrevealed universe, [Brasília] had to be, perforce, a metropolis with different characteristics that would ignore the contemporary reality and would be turned, with all of its constitutive elements, toward the future.

President Juscelino Kubitschek[3]

The apartment blocks of a superquadra [Brasília's basic residential unit] are all equal: same façade, same height, same facilities... which prevents the hateful differentiation of social classes; that is, all the families share the same life together, the upper-echelon public functionary, the middle, and the lower.

Brasília[4]

As exemplified by Brasília, total planning in Brazil cannot be separated from either modernism or developmentalism.[5] Even before the construction of Brasília, the Brazilian government had appropriated the international model of modernist architecture and planning developed by CIAM (Congrès Internationaux d'Architecture Moderne). Its intention was to use this model to create a radically new urban development as a means to overcome the nation's backwardness, as a means to bring the nation, through leaps in history, into the vanguard of modernity. Modernist total planning is an instrument of social transformation as much as of spatial production. It is conceived as a means of creating an urban environment that molds society in its image. This two-fold transformation brings progress and development. Brasília is no doubt the most complete example ever constructed of the CIAM model city – a model that dominated urban theory and policy in many countries for most of the 20th century, from the "new cities" of Eastern Europe to the "edge cities" of American suburbia. In Brazil, this conception of planning reigned supreme from the 1940s to the 1980s. As Brazil became highly urbanized and industrialized during this period, it shaped most of the state's urban and economic undertakings.[6]

Both Brasília and modern São Paulo took shape under the influence of a nationalist ideology of modernization known as developmentalism. Briefly, the idea was to use direct state intervention to promote, in a concentrated period of time, national industrialization based on import-substitution. Its main objective was to produce not only accelerated industrialization but also modern subjects; that is, rational and "domesticated" consumers for its products. The slogan of President Juscelino Kubitschek's Target Plan of development in the mid-1950s was "50 years in 5." This model of development sustained not only São Paulo's industrialization but also the construction of Brasília and other state-sponsored projects aimed at turning Brazil into a modern nation.[7] To promote progress through leaps in history, the Brazilian state took upon itself a wide range of tasks that included building cities, roads, and electric plants, sponsoring industrial production (especially of automobiles, chemicals, and steel), as well as expanding the welfare state and modernizing television programs. From factories to hospital networks, from mines to television stations, from telephone companies to universities, all materialized under the control and usually the ownership of the state.

Shared by citizens of all social classes, a strong faith in progress anchored the developmentalist project of the Brazilian state.[8] From the 1950s to the 1980s, Brazilians believed massively that Brazil was "the country of the future." Especially in the major cities, people supposed that hard work would bring individual betterment, modern urbanization to the urban peripheries where most lived, and general prosperity through industrial expansion. The sum of these achievements would produce the modernization of Brazil. Although it soon became clear that modernization would not significantly reduce the enormous inequalities that separate rich and poor, Brazilians continued to believe that progress would nevertheless benefit all.

Brasília was the most accomplished symbol of this project of progress, development, and modernization. Its founders envisioned Brasília's modernist design and construction as the means to create a new age by transforming Brazilian society. They saw it as the means to invent a new nation for a new capital – a new nation to which this radically different city would then "logically belong," as its planner Lucio Costa claimed.[9] This project of transformation redefines Brazilian society according to the assumptions of a particular narrative of the modern, that of the CIAM modernist city, most clearly expressed in Costa's Master Plan and in the architecture of Oscar Niemeyer, the city's principal architect.

As universally acknowledged, the project of Brasília is a blueprint-perfect embodiment of the CIAM model city. Moreover, its design is a brilliant reproduction of Le Corbusier's version of that model.[10] Nevertheless, Brasília is not merely a copy. Rather, as a Brazilian rendition of CIAM's global modernism, its copy is generative and original. Brasília is a CIAM city inserted into what were the margins of modernity in the 1950s, inserted into the modernist ambitions of a postcolony. In this context, the very purpose of the project was to capture the spirit of the modern by means of its likeness, its copy. It is this homeopathic relation to the model, brilliantly executed to be sure, that gives the copy its transformative power. In other words, its power resides precisely in the display of likeness. This display of an "original copy" gives the state a theatrical form, a means to construct itself by putting on spectacular public works.

As the exemplar of this stagecraft-as-statecraft, Brasília was designed to mirror to the rest of Brazil the modern nation that it would become. It was conceived as a civilizing agent, the missionary of a new sense of national space, time, and purpose, colonizing the whole into which it has been inserted. To build the city in just three and a half years, Novacap, the company in charge of the construction, instituted a regime of round-the-clock construction. This regime of hard work became known throughout Brazil as the "rhythm of Brasília." Breaking with the meters of colonialism and underdevelopment, this is a new rhythm, defined as 36 hours of nation-building a day – "12 during daylight, 12 at night, and 12 for enthusiasm." It expresses precisely the new space-time consciousness of Brasília's modernity, one that posits the possibility of accelerating time and of propelling Brazil into a radiant future.

The rhythm of Brasília thus reveals the development of a new kind of agency, confident that it can change the course of history through willful intervention, that it can abbreviate the path to the future by skipping over undesired stages of development. This modernist agency of rupture and innovation expressed itself in all domains of Brasília's construction and organization, from architecture and planning to schools, hospitals, traffic system, residential organization, property distribution, bureaucratic administration, music, theater, and more. Brasília's modernism signified Brazil's emergence as a modern nation because it simultaneously broke with the colonial legacies of underdevelopment as it posited a radiant future of industrial modernity. The new architecture and planning attacked the styles of the past that constituted especially visible symbols of a legacy the government sought to supersede. It privileged the automobile and the aesthetic of speed at a time when Brazil was industrializing. It required centralized planning and the exercise of state power that appealed to political elites.

To create a new kind of society, Brasília redefines what its Master Plan calls the key functions of urban life, namely work, residence, recreation, and traffic. It directs this redefinition according to the tenets of the CIAM model city. CIAM manifestos call for national states to assert the priority of collective interests over private. They promote state planning over what they call the "ruthless rule of capitalism," by imposing on the chaos of existing cities a new type of urbanism based on CIAM master plans. CIAM's overarching strategy for change is totalization: its model city imposes a totality of new urban conditions that dissolves any conflict between the imagined new society and the existing one in the imposed coherence of total order.

One of the principal ways by which CIAM design achieves its totalization of city life is to organize the entire cityscape in terms of a new kind of spatial logic. As we have analyzed this logic elsewhere,[11] we do not pause to examine it here – except to say that its subversive strategies have overwhelming consequences for urbanism, especially its elimination of the corridor street and related public spaces and its inversion of Baroque solid–void/figure–ground relations. Complementing its theory of spatial change, the CIAM model also proposes a subjective appropriation of the new social order inherent in its plans. It utilizes avant-garde techniques of shock to force this subjective transformation, emphasizing decontextualization, defamiliarization, and dehistoricization. Their central premise is that the new architecture/urban design creates set pieces of radically different experience that destabilize, subvert, and then regenerate the surrounding fabric of social life. It is a viral notion of revolution, a theory of decontextualization in which the radical qualities of something totally out of context infect and colonize that which surrounds it with new forms of social experience, collective association, personal habit, and perception. At the same time, this colonization is supposed to preclude those forms deemed undesirable by negating previous social and architectural expectations about urban life.

Brasília's design implements these premises of transformation by both architectural and social means. On the one hand, its Master Plan displaces institutions that were traditionally centered in a private sphere of social life to a new state-sponsored public sphere of residence and work. One of its most radical tenets in this regard was the elimination of private property altogether, in favor of state ownership – at least until 1965, when the military government created a private real estate market. On the other, Brasília's new architecture renders illegible the taken-for-granted representation of social institutions, as the buildings of work and residence receive similar massing, siting, and fenestration and thereby lose their traditional symbolic differentiation.

No one should doubt the potency of these modernist strategies of defamiliarization. In Brasília, they proved to be brutally effective, as most people who moved there experienced them with trauma. In fact, the first generation of inhabitants coined a special expression for this shock of total design: *brasilite* or "Brasília-itis." As one resident told Holston, "Everything in Brasília was different. It was a shock, an illusion, because you didn't understand where people lived, or shopped, or worked, or socialized." Another common disorientation is the sense of exposure that residents experience inside the transparent glass façades of their apartments. Thus, Brasília's modernism also works its intended subversion at an intimate scale of daily life. Harmonized in plan and elevation, Brasília's total design created a radically new world, giving it a form that possessed its own agenda of social change.

In sum, as exemplified in Brasília, modernist master planning is a comprehensive approach to restructuring urban life precisely because it advances proposals aimed at both the public and the private domains of society. Its proposals for the former focus on eliminating the street and its public, both spatial and social. Its proposals for the latter center on a new type of domestic architecture and "collective" residential unit. Its design restructures the residential not only by eliminating private property but also by reducing the social spaces of the private apartment in favor of a new type of residential collectivity in which the role of the private and the individual is symbolically minimized (by using transparent glass façades, eliminating traditional informal spaces, and so forth).[12] Together, these strategies constitute a profound estrangement of previous modes of urban life, achieving a similar kind of defamiliarization of public and private values in both the civic and the residential realms.

It is important to emphasize that the CIAM modernist model is strongly egalitarian in motivation. As the epigraph of this section indicates, its objective is to impose the means of equalization "to prevent the hateful differentiation of social classes." Hence, it develops a new type of urban environment both to eliminate previous expressions and instruments of inequality and to force people to behave in new ways that the planners envision ("the same life together"). The model's commitment to equalization is remarkably comprehensive, aimed at transforming both public and intimate relations of social life. Although committed to equalization, however, modernist planning is decidedly not democratic. Rather, it is based on an imperial imposition of its brand of panoptic equality, a "planner knows best" vision of an already scripted future. Moreover, as we shall see, as implemented means to equality, it fails perversely.

The radically new world of Brasília immediately confronted a classic utopian dilemma, one inherent in all forms of modernist planning: the necessity of having to use what exists to achieve what is imagined destroys the utopian difference between the two that is the project's premise. As Brasília's demigods – the planners – struggled to keep pace with the vitality of the city they had brought to life, their directives revealed two fundamental features of the modernist mode of governmentality: first, they maintained the priorities of the plan at all costs, not admitting any compromise with "what exists," with contingent developments, with history's engagement with the ideal. Second, their reiterations of the plan to counter contingency turned the project of Brasília into an exaggerated version of what the planners intended to preclude. In effect, they reproduced the Brazil they wanted to exclude. This Brazilianization contradicted many of the Plan's most important intentions.

One of the clearest examples of this perversion is the reproduction in the new capital of a legal center and an illegal periphery. The government planned to recruit a labor force to build the capital, but to deny it residential rights in the city that it built for civil servants transferred from Rio de Janeiro. By 1958, however, it became clear that many workers intended to remain. In fact, almost 30 percent of them had already rebelled against their planned exclusion by becoming squatters in illegal settlements. Yet the government did not incorporate the *candangos* (the pioneering construction workers) into the Plano Piloto (as the modernist city itself is called), even though it was nearly empty at inauguration. The government found this solution unacceptable because inclusion would have violated the preconceived model that Brasília's "essential purpose [was to be] an administrative city with an absolute predominance of the interests of public servants."[13] Rather, under mounting pressure of a *candango* rebellion, and in contradiction of the Master Plan, the administration decided to create legal satellite cities, in which *candangos* of modest means would have the right to acquire lots and to which Novacap would remove all squatters. In authorizing the creation of these satellite cities, the government was in each case giving legal foundation to what had in fact already been usurped; namely, the initially denied residential rights that *candangos* appropriated by forming illegal squatter settlements. Thus, Brasília's legal periphery has a subversive origin in land seizures and contingency planning.

Modernist planning attempts to overcome the contingency of experience by totalizing it; that is, by fixing the present as a totally conceived plan based on an imagined future. Holston contrasts this model with what he calls contingency planning.[14] The project of Brasília generated both modes. Although both were experimental and innovative at the time, they were (and remain) fundamentally at odds. Contingency planning improvises and experiments as a means of dealing with the uncertainty of present conditions. It works with plans that are always incomplete. Its means are suggested by present possibilities for an alternative future, not by an imagined and already scripted future. It is a mode of design based on imperfect knowledge, incomplete control, and lack of resources, which incorporates ongoing conflict and contradiction as constitutive elements. In this sense, it has a significant insurgent aspect, though it may have a regressive outcome. The built Brasília resulted from the interaction of both modes of planning, the total and the contingent. In most cases, however, the former soon overwhelmed the latter in the development of the city.

For example, to remain faithful to their modernist model, planners could not let the legal periphery of satellite cities develop autonomously. They had to counter contingency, in other words, by organizing the periphery on the governing rationality of the center. To do so, they adopted what we can call a strategy of retotalization, especially with regard to the periphery's urban planning, political–administrative structure, and recruitment of settlers. This strategy had two principal objectives: to keep civil servants in the center and others in the periphery, and to maintain a "climate of tranquility" that eliminated the turbulence of political mobilization.[15] Given these objectives, the planners had little choice but to use the mechanisms of social stratification and repression that are constitutive of the rest of Brazil they sought to exclude. First, they devised a recruitment policy that preselected who would go either to the center (Plano Piloto) or to the periphery (satellite cities), and that would give bureaucrats preferential access to the former. Second, in organizing administrative relations between center and periphery, planners denied the satellite cities political representation. Through this combination of political subordination and preferential recruitment, of disenfranchisement and disprivilege, planners created a dual social order that was both legally and spatially segregated. Ironically, it was this stratification and repression, and not the illegal actions of the squatters, that more profoundly Brazilianized Brasília.[16]

Predictably, the reiteration of the orders of the center in the periphery created similar housing problems there. These problems led, inevitably, to new land seizures and to the formation of new illegal peripheries – now in the plural because each satellite spawned its own fringe of illegal settlements. Moreover, by the same processes, some of these seizures become legalized, leading to the creation of yet more satellite cities. These cycles of rebellion and legitimation, illegal action and legalization, contingency planning and retotalization, continue to this day. A striking illustration of the perpetuation of Brasília's contradictory development is that, even today, the Plano Piloto remains more than half empty while only containing 13 percent of the Federal District's total population. This comparison strongly suggests that the government continues to expand the legal periphery rather than incorporate poor migrants into the Plano Piloto.[17] As a result, Brasília remains Brazil's most segregated city.[18]

Modernization without Substantive Citizenship

Most other Brazilian metropolitan regions have not been the product of such direct and total planning as Brasília. Nevertheless, the oppositions between legal and illegal urban areas, center and periphery, and rich and poor are equally constitutive. This is the case of São Paulo, a city that has also come to symbolize Brazil's modernity by concentrating the largest share of its industrial production, economic growth, and urbanization. São Paulo's decisive turn to industrialization dates from the 1950s, and shares with Brasília some of the same instruments and imaginaries, including the use of modernist design and the notion that the city had to be opened up for circulation.[19] The new industries were placed outside the center. As industrialization intensified and migration reached its peak in the 1950s, the local administration was busily opening avenues and removing the remaining tenement housing downtown. The modern city that emerged was disperse and organized by clear class divisions. The center received improvements in infrastructure and the most obvious symbols of modernity. It was dominated by skyscrapers (increasingly of modernist design) that multiplied in a matter of a few years from the 1950s on and gave the city its contemporary identity.

In the periphery, the rhythm of construction was no less intense than in the center. But the lack of any kind of state support, investment, and planning generated a very different type of space. On the outskirts of the city, workers bought cheap lots of land sold either illegally by outright swindlers or with some kind of irregularity by developers who failed to follow city regulations regarding infrastructure and land registration. In spite of their illegal or irregular activities, these developers received a free hand from successive generations of city administrators, who preferred to close their eyes to what was happening in the periphery and to administer only the "legal city."[20] As for the workers of Brazil – in São Paulo, Brasília, and elsewhere – they have always understood that illegality was the condition under which they could have access to land and inhabit the modern city. To them, residential illegality signifies not just material precariousness and distance from the center, but also the possibility of becoming modern and of establishing a claim to eventual property ownership. In streets without pavement and infrastructure, workers built their own houses by themselves and without financing. This could only happen through a slow and long-term process of transformation known as "autoconstruction."[21] It is also a process that perfectly represents progress, growth, and social mobility: step by step, day after day, the house is improved and people are reassured that sacrifice and hard work pay off. Thus, workers moved to the "bush" to build their houses and, through the process of autoconstruction, were the agents of the peripheral urbanization of the city. That the population density of the city decreased by half between the beginning of the century and the 1960s, in spite of remarkable population growth, indicates the enormity of this expansion.[22] As a result, the urbanized area of the city of São Paulo more than tripled between 1930 and 1954, and doubled again by the 1990s to reach its actual size of 850 km².

Thus, in both São Paulo and Brasília, governmental strategies toward modernization, industrialization, urbanization, and development were sometimes interventionist and at other times *laissez-faire*. However, they resulted in a similar structure of urban inequality. In both cities, these strategies reveal an overarching conception of how to govern society and produce its modernity. The general principle is to govern without generating social equality or turning the masses into active citizens. The split between legal and illegal symbolizes succinctly the underlying perspective of Brazilian elites on modernization: those considered nonmodern (the vast majority of the population) were incorporated into their plans as a labor force but marginalized as citizens. They were denied the right to vote, excluded from legal property in the modern cities, and violently silenced by the military dictatorship.[23]

Although developmentalist–modernist planning is quite authoritarian, for a while it had strong popular support. Indeed, both Brasília and industrial São Paulo were initially built on the basis of massive popular engagement with the project of modernization and belief in progress. This combination of authoritarianism with genuine popular support has a well-established label in Latin American politics, namely populism. It dominated Brazilian politics from the 1940s until the military coup interrupted it in 1964. The military dictatorship that ruled Brazil between 1964 and 1985 ended popular engagement by political repression. Nevertheless, development continued to be the regime's main objective. Moreover, the same planning and governmental instruments served well the developmentalist policies of the dictatorship. In fact, it was during this regime that development achieved some of its most emblematic marks. This included not only economic growth rates of up to 12 percent per year, but also the construction of roads and telecommunication infrastructure and the dissemination of social services.

In other words, intense modernization and urbanization in Brazil took place either without popular participation (military regimes) or with elite-controlled popular participation (populist regimes). Not part of any of these governmental rationalities was the project to turn Brazil's masses into modern political citizens who participate meaningfully in political and electoral decisions. As with the polity, so with the society: social inclusion was not one of the objectives of the modernization project. As the military regime often declared, it was necessary "to grow first to divide the cake later." In sum, authoritarianism and profound social inequality are marks of modern Brazil.

The Context of Change

The national-developmentalist project of modernization started to crumble in the early 1980s under the influence of contradictory forces. On the one hand, there was a deep economic crisis and the subsequent adoption of so-called neoliberal policies. Not infrequently, the justification for these policies has been the need to put Brazil in tune with the next wave of modernization; that is, the new global configurations. On the other hand, there were political transformations, especially pressures for social and political inclusion that the urban social movements articulated and that eventually led to political democracy.

Transition to democratic rule in Brazil was a long process. The so-called political opening started in the mid-1970s; the first state governors were elected in 1982; and the first election for president was in 1989. The main mark of democratization, however, was not electoral politics. Rather, it was the explosion of popular political participation and the massive engagement of citizens in debating the future of the country. In Brazil, this mobilization was known as "the rebirth of civil society." Two forms of political organization, both of which originated in São Paulo, were especially important in the transition process: independent trades unions and urban social movements. The latter were crucial for transforming the perception of urban space and including urban citizenship in the agenda of democratic consolidation.

Starting in the mid-1970s, numerous neighborhood-based social movements appeared in the poor urban peripheries, frequently with the help of the Catholic Church.[24] The movements' participants, a majority of them women, were new property owners who realized that political organization was the only way to force the city authorities to extend the urban infrastructure and services to their neighborhoods. They discovered that being taxpayers legitimated their "rights to the city"; that is, rights to the legal order and to the urbanization available in the center. At the root of their political mobilization was the illegal/irregular status of the properties that most had purchased in good faith: public authorities denied them urban services and infrastructure precisely because they considered their neighborhoods illegal. Thus, a central inspiration for these movements was an urban and collective experience of marginalization and abandonment, in spite of individual efforts of integration through work and consumption.

The urban social movements were crucial in the larger opposition that helped end the military dictatorship. The demands of these movements were summarized in the idea that Brazil had to change by becoming democratic and enforcing the rights of its citizens. Accordingly, demands included direct elections (*Diretas Já!*), amnesty for political prisoners and respect for their human rights, revocation of all "laws of exception" imposed by the military regime, and the convening of a Constitutional Assembly to write a new democratic constitution. Several of these demands were met in the first years of the democratic transition, including the promulgation of a new Constitution in 1988. It was written on the basis of ample consultation with organized popular movements and includes a full set of citizens' rights, from the right to four months of paid maternity leave to the more traditional list of rights to life, freedom of expression, and justice. The 1988 Constitution is a document that interprets citizenship rights in the broadest terms, incorporating what is sometimes called all "generations" of rights.

While the country democratized, however, the conditions that sustained developmentalism eroded. The mythology of progress started to collapse in the 1980s, in São Paulo as elsewhere in Brazil. It began with what is called the "lost decade," the deep economic recession associated with changes that significantly transformed Brazilian society and many others in Latin America and around the world. Although this is not the place to analyze these changes in more detail, it is important to mention the most important of them as they affected the metropolitan region of São Paulo in the 1980s and 1990s. They include a sharp decrease in population growth; a significant decline in immigration and increase in out-migration, especially of upper- and middle-class residents; a sharp drop in the GNP and rates of economic growth; a drop in per capita income; a deep reorganization of industrial production associated with large unemployment and instability of employment; a redefinition of the role of government in the production and management of urban space; and a significant increase in violence (both criminal and police) associated in part with the restructuring of urban segregation. As a result of the economic crisis and related changes, the distribution of wealth – which was already bad – worsened and perspectives of social mobility shrank considerably. In the periphery, important aspects of the urban inclusion achieved by the social movements eroded.[25] Many people could no longer afford a house of their own, and the reduced horizons of life chances seemed to preclude even the dream of autoconstructing one. The number of people living in favelas in the city increased from 4 percent in 1980 to 19 percent in 1993.

One of the most important consequences of this combination of economic and social crisis was that the state abandoned the model of governmentality based on protectionism, nationalism, and direct participation in production – the main elements of the modernization project. The policies adopted to deal with the economic crisis – usually indicated by agencies such as the IMF and labeled "neoliberal" – resulted in the opening of the domestic market to imported products and in the withdrawal of the state from various areas in which it had traditionally played a central role as producer. These areas included urban services, infrastructure, telecommunications, steel manufacture, and oil production.

Privatization became the order of the day, the dominant value of the new logic of governmentality that replaced the modernization project. Privatization signifies various things and affects various aspects of social life. It means selling off most of the state-owned enterprises (including those offering basic services such as telephone and electricity) to private interests and using the revenue generated to pay the foreign debt incurred under the previous economic model. It entails cutting state subsidies to national production. It signifies unmaking prerogatives and social rights created both in the corporatist labor legislation of the 1930s and 1940s and in the 1988 Constitution.[26] It also means that the state "contracts out" to private enterprise and privately funded NGOs social services that it used to provide (from the delivery of milk to schools to prison management). Moreover, the state now hires NGOs with public funds to develop policy that government agencies used to produce. In sum, privatization undermines various pillars of the developmentalist–modernist project and its type of state. In effect, it subverts the idea that the state governs the nation, and indeed creates a nation in its image, by being a direct producer of its public through state-owned and -managed industry, state-directed public works and planning, and state-provided welfare.

Privatization also affects in decisive ways the space of the city and its everyday practices. Pressured by funding cuts and new laws to balance budget, municipal governments throughout Brazil limited their range of intervention and level of investment in the urban environment. Simultaneously, they called on private citizens to invest in their own space in exchange for fiscal incentives and a flexibilization of building codes. In the periphery, citizens have always invested in their space, but as a result of minimal state investment. Now, however, private investment was becoming a matter of state policy for the whole city. Nevertheless, probably the most important forms of privatization that affect the urban environment relate to the startling increase in violent crime and fear.[27] Violence and the inability of the state to deal with it have led people to rely on private security and fortification, and to imagine city life in terms of numerous new practices of segregation.

In sum, Brazilian society experienced contradictory processes during the 1980s and 1990s: on the one hand, political democratization and the emergence of new forms of democratic citizenship; and, on the other, economic crisis, privatization, and violence that undermined the former, limited the state, closed urban spaces, and reduced possibilities of growth.[28]

Democratic Planning and the Neoliberal State

The 1988 Constitution introduced significant innovations in many areas, including urban policy. These were due to a large extent to the lobbying of organized social movements and civil organizations. During the National Constitutional Assembly of 1986–8, these grassroots forces gathered more than 12 million signatures in support of Popular Amendments, successfully pressuring the state to relinquish its jural monopoly and securing a strong presence in the new Constitution. During the next two years, state and municipal constitutional assemblies occurred throughout Brazil, with similar results. During these many constitutional assemblies, the demands of grassroots forces converged with legal assistance services. Members of the former brought their specific interests to lawyers of the latter, who rearticulated them in terms of proposals for new law. In the process, the social movements became educated in both making and using law. Thus a new conception of citizenship, grounded in the popular construction of the law and the exercise of new kinds of rights through legislation, began to take root.

One of the most significant sources of this process of innovation is popular participation in urban reform and municipal administration. Growing out of the National Movement of Struggle for Urban Reform, founded in 1986 to influence the federal constitution, this participation has rallied around the principle of "rights to the city" and around the concept of urban self-management (auto-gestão).[29] In major cities, including São Paulo, Porto Alegre, Curitiba, and Recife, it has succeeded in developing this conception of urban citizenship into innovative municipal codes, charters, and master plans.[30] In what follows we analyze two of the most important regulations that these efforts produced.

One of the Popular Amendments presented to the Assembly generated the Constitution's section on Urban Policy. Article 182 defines the objective of urban policies as "to organize the full development of the social functions of the city" and establishes that urban property has a social function. Consequently, it determines that local governments can promote the use of urban land through expropriation, forced subdivisions, and progressive taxation so that it fulfills its social function. Article 183 creates usucapião urbano (akin to adverse possession) as a means of resolving the predicament of residential illegality that affects so many of the working poor. It establishes the possibility of creating an uncontestable title of ownership for residents who have lived continuously for five years and without legitimate opposition on small lots of urban land. These two articles became the basis for a series of legislated acts, regulations, and plans that have since transformed the character of urban policy in Brazil.

The constitutional articles required enabling legislation both to define in more precise terms the concept of "social function" and to create mechanisms for its implementation. For more than a decade, the National Congress debated this legislation under pressure from the lobby of the National Forum for Urban Reform. The result is the remarkable Estatuto da Cidade (City Statute), federal law 10,257 of July 10, 2001. This legislation incorporates the language and concepts developed by the urban social movements and various local administrations since the 1970s. It is quite unusual in the history of Brazilian urban legislation for at least four reasons. First, it defines the social function of the city and of urban property in terms of a set of general guidelines that are substantive in nature. Second, on that basis, it frames its directives from the point of view of the poor, the majority of Brazil's city dwellers, and creates mechanisms to revert some of the most evident patterns of irregularity, inequality, and degradation in the production of urban space. Third, the Statute requires that local urban policies be conceived and implemented with popular participation. Thus, it takes into consideration the active collaboration and involvement of the private organizations and interests of civil society. Fourth, the Statute is not framed as a total plan but instead introduces a series of innovative legal instruments that allow local administrations to enforce the "social function." Unmistakably, the City Statute is the result of the insurgent citizenship movements of the previous decades. It is an important indication of one of the ways in which democratization has taken root in Brazilian society, and of how the grassroots experience of local administration, legal invention, and popular mobilization has made its space in federal law.

Echoing the Constitution, the City Statute establishes that the objective of urban policy is "to realize the social functions of the city and urban property."[31] Urban policy must do so by following a set of comprehensive guidelines. Among the most important, urban policy must "guarantee the right to sustainable cities, understood as the right to urban land, housing, sanitation, infrastructure, transportation and public services, work, and leisure for present and future generations";[32] use "planning . . . to avoid and correct the distortions of urban growth and its negative effects on the environment";[33] produce a "just distribution of the benefits and costs of the urbanization process";[34] allow the public administration to recuperate its investments that may have resulted in real estate gain;[35] and regularize properties and urbanize areas occupied by the low-income population.[36] By such means, the City Statute clearly establishes the production of social equality in urban space as a fundamental objective of urban planning and policy and, reciprocally, turns planning into a basic instrument for equalizing social disparities and securing social equality.

The Statute also creates powerful instruments to enforce its directives. They are of two types. First, there are instruments of management. Second, there are instruments to regulate the use of urban land. The innovations regarding management are basically two and quite substantial: those requiring popular participation in the formulation and implementation of policies, and those considering that urbanization is to be obtained by cooperation between government and private organizations. Chapter IV of the Statute is entitled "On the Democratic Management of the City," and its Article 45 presents the boldest formulation of the principle of popular participation:

> The management organizations of metropolitan regions and urban agglomerations will include mandatory and significant participation of the population and of associations representing the various segments of the community in order to guarantee the direct control of their activities and the full exercise of citizenship.

Chapter IV establishes that cities must implement a variety of mechanisms to insure this public participation in management, from debates, public audiences, and conferences to popular amendments of plans and laws to a process of participatory budget-making.[37] In these formulations, it is evident that the Statute imagines a society of citizens who are active, organized, and well informed about their interests and their government's actions.

This conception of Brazilian society could not be more different from the one that inspired the modernist–developmentalist master plans. Those plans assumed a backward society of silent and mostly ignorant citizens who needed to be brought into modernity by an illuminated and elite avant-garde.[38] Some of the modernist plans, especially Brasília's, did have social equalization as an objective. But even so, it was one to be imposed, already scripted. It would result from the plans, the values embodied in them, and the built environment they produced. Social equality would not, in other words, result from an exercise of citizenship that would generate the plans themselves. Moreover, the language of the modernist plans was one of development not citizen rights, and its principal target was underdevelopment not social inequality. The new model of planning turns this logic of development on its head. In this new formulation, the social is not imagined as something for the plan to produce but is, rather, something that already exists in organized fashion. This organization will be the basis for the creation of urban space, which will in turn confirm a more equitable and just society. The society imagined by the new model is modern, democratic, and plural, although still profoundly unequal. The new plans consider that citizens lack resources, are poor, and have their rights disrespected, but not that they are ignorant, illiterate, backward, incompetent, incapable of making good decisions, and so forth. While the old plans supposed that society's needs were modernization, progress, and development, the new ones imagine that their needs are citizenship and equality (or at least the abatement of the worst effects of social inequality). They suppose that the majority of the population that they address needs rights, not hygiene. Furthermore, whereas the modernist plans dispensed with any consideration of conflict in the imposition of solutions, the Statute and the other legislation it generated see citizens' interests as different and often contradictory. Therefore, they create mechanisms of conciliation and mediation.

In addition to enacting the principle of direct participation of citizens in managing cities, the City Statute also establishes that the government is no longer solely responsible for the process of urbanization. It thus fractures another fundament of the developmentalist model. The latter supposed that the state is the main (if not sole) producer of urban space – of the legal, admittedly, but also of the illegal, inexorably. According to the Statute, however, the process of urbanization should entail a balanced cooperation, or partnership, between public and private interests. This reconceptualization of roles is not a matter of democratic change alone. In fact, it is associated probably more with the neoliberal turn of the state, which presupposes a substantial shrinkage in the scope of its interventions, and with the exhaustion of resources to fund investments in urban infrastructure. During the developmentalist years, these resources came especially from international development banks and created an almost unmanageable foreign debt in countries such as Brazil. Today, a good deal of this funding is gone. As a result, under democracy, the Brazilian city has a huge social debt of needs with few resources to address them.

Consequently, administrators search for alternative funding, especially from private-sector investments. In addition, they develop new legislative instruments that might simultaneously tax the use of urban space and produce social justice.

For example, the City Statute introduces a series of mechanisms to tax real estate profit, force the use of underutilized urban properties, and regularize land occupied by low-income residents. The Statute also incorporates an innovative conception of property rights. It separates the right of property from the constructive potential of urban land, creating the possibility of transferring an owner's right to build. This separation allows the government to sell rights of construction beyond the coefficient (an area limit) permitted in city codes as a means to generate revenue for urbanization projects. There are a host of other innovations, including something called Urban Operations that allows a partnership of public and private interests to "bend the rules" in delimited areas of the city to achieve certain urbanization purposes, as well as provisions for both individual and collective *usucapião* (the latter in the case of favelas) to regularize land ownership among the poor.

The City Statute equips urban government with powerful tools to regulate the production of urban space. However, it conceives these measures quite differently from those of developmentalist plans. The differences are impressive. They concern the general principles that inspire the instruments (social justice and citizenship rights), the conception of how local projects will be created (through the democratic participation of organized citizens and their vigilance over governmental actions), the imagination of how projects will be implemented (the partnership between public and private initiatives), and the restricted nature of the interventions (limited urban operations, actions in "priority areas" rather than total plans). The City Statute is an instrument of democratic governance. It is based on a democratic conception of Brazilian society, as well as a democratic project for it.

It is hard, however, to predict how it will be engaged by local governments and citizens to change their cities. The legislation is still too recent for us to address the problems of its implementation and its potential to transform the patterns of inequality in Brazilian cities. Nevertheless, it is important to look for indicators of this engagement. For this, we take the case of the city of São Paulo. We will not analyze here its Master Strategic Plan (Plano Diretor Estratégico), which is the local application of the City Statute and was signed into municipal law 13,430 on September 13, 2002. The analysis of this Plan necessitates its own study, given its many innovations, such an environmentalist approach to the city's problems, and the intense process of political opposition and bargaining it generated. This process forced many changes in the version proposed by the PT (Partido dos Trabalhadores, Workers' Party) administration of the city.[39] Moreover, it is still difficult to anticipate its effects in terms of the production of social justice in urban space. Instead, we consider the use of some of the instruments adopted by the Statute even before it was approved by Congress, an implementation that already reveals paradoxical results.

Some Paradoxical Uses of the Statute

Although São Paulo has been a crucial site for the organization of political and social movements that helped to democratize Brazilian society, the city has been largely in the hands of administrations at odds with this orientation. The first democratically elected mayor, Jânio Quadros, who took office in 1986, was an old-time conservative populist. During the next term (1989–92), the city was administered by a mayor from the PT, certainly the political party connected in the most direct way with the interests of the working classes and its social movements. However, after this administration of Luiza Erundina, the city had two mayors from the PPB (Partido Progressista Brasileiro), a center-to-right and conservative party associated with the real estate and construction industries.[40] In 2001, another mayor from the PT (Marta Suplicy) took office. All these administrations used at least some of the instruments incorporated into the Statute. Following their different uses allows us to discuss some of the paradoxical ways in which democratization and neoliberalization have intertwined in the production of urban space.

During the whole democratic period, one mayor after another developed master plans for the city of São Paulo that never passed City Council because they never generated enough support.[41] These plans were intended to substitute the modernist–developmentist master plan and zoning code passed in 1971, the PDDI (Plano Diretor de Desenvolvimento Integrado). The only plan to pass City Council, in 1988, was approved by default, and its legitimacy has always been questioned. As the government retreated under the mantle of neoliberal policies, and as the City Council failed to approve one master plan after another, contingency planning ruled the city. This meant contradictory initiatives. One the one hand, various administrations were able either to introduce or to use a few instruments that are similar to those of the City Statute. On the other, organized private interests moved in to fill the space opened by the withdrawal of the state. The city of the past 15 years is one in which private investors intervened decisively, sometimes in partnership with local government, to improve the areas of their investment with the objective of increasing significantly the value of their real estate. One of the results of this action is the consolidation of a new pattern of urban segregation based on the proliferation of fortified enclaves; that is, of privatized, enclosed, and monitored spaces for residence, consumption, leisure, and work.[42]

Policies to tax real estate profits and to attract private investment in urbanization are not inventions of the City Statute. Rather, they have been practiced for some time in São Paulo and other cities. We look at two such instruments used in the past 15 years in São Paulo: the so-called paid authorization (*outorga onerosa*) and the Urban Operations. Paid authorization refers to the possibility that the government may sell rights of construction beyond the coefficient allowed in city codes, if it uses the funds thus generated for urbanization projects. Urban Operations are projects to preserve, revitalize, and/or transform specific urban areas, through partnerships of public and private investment. These operations must be defined by law, and the norms that regulate them may differ from those of the rest of the city. Paid authorization is a core instrument of Urban Operations. Both have been introduced in the administration of São Paulo as means of revising the role of the state in the production of urban space and of fulfilling the need to find new forms of investment in urbanization. In some cases, the objective was to produce social justice and allow the administration to recuperate investments that produced real estate gains; in others, it was to benefit real estate investors. The results of the latter deepened spatial segregation.

The idea of paid authorization was first introduced in São Paulo in 1976, during the administration of Olavo Setúbal.[43] Although it was not transformed into legislation at that point, it was incorporated into the discussions of the social movements and organizations addressing the urban question since the start of the democratization period.[44] What appealed to these democratic interests was the possibility of generating new sources of revenue for urban development. However, when the idea was first transformed into law during the administration of Jânio Quadros, with the name "Operações Interligadas," it had an unexpected twist.[45] It allowed the government to offer private developers the right to build beyond the limits set in zoning codes in exchange for their private investment in "popular housing." Such operations were conceived in the context of Quadros' plans of *desfavelamento* – the removal of favelas and their populations, especially in central areas. Proprietors of areas occupied by favelas could petition the city to change the rules of use and occupation in any land they owned in exchange for the construction of popular housing. This conception was at odds with the most common interpretations of paid authorization, according to which the instrument should apply only to specific areas of the city selected on the basis of urbanistic projects, such as those to increase urban density in areas of good infrastructure. In Quadros' interpretation, however, the bending of zoning rules was particularistic, for it did not follow any specific urban project but, rather, applied to any area in the city where a favela might exist. In fact, it was an instrument of social segregation. The City Statute later discarded this particularistic use of paid authorization. Instead, it adopted the conception developed by the PT administration of Luiza Erundina under the label "created soil" (*solo criado*), which required the use of urban projects to designate areas of the city eligible for paid authorization.[46] Paulo Maluf's and Celso Pitta's PPB administrations subsequently used this instrument in conjunction with Urban Operations.

In São Paulo, Urban Operations were introduced in the mid-1980s and used by the conservative administrations that followed.[47] In general, operations launched in the 1990s either failed to transform their areas or generated further social inequality, segregation, and real estate profit. Three operations – Anhangabaú, Centro, and Água Branca – were located in deteriorated downtown areas. Each resulted basically in only one private project. The third seems the most successful, but has been limited to creating the infrastructure needed by the only private project approved for the area.

Two other Operations – Faria Lima and Águas Espraiadas – are in the area of the newest business districts along the Pinheiros river. They were designed to install the kind of infrastructure required for the development of "intelligent" office complexes and accompanying commercial malls and residential units (closed condominiums) for their workers. The Faria Lima Operation is a clear example of the risks of one of the determinations of the Statute: that the funds raised by a urban operation should be used exclusively within its areas. Since Faria Lima is a region of high real estate values, further investment has only augmented its privileges.

Moreover, because the Operation encouraged the aggregation of lots, it had a strongly regressive impact in the real estate market, expelling modest investors and discouraging small-scale use. Thus, the Operation transformed a residential area of small lots into a business area of large developments. Similar effects happened in the adjacent area of Berrini/Águas Espraiadas, which received large investments in road construction and river channeling. Moreover, this area benefited from an infamous partnership between the city under the administration of Paulo Maluf and private investors. The agreement put together city agencies of social work and a pool of enterprises, the offices of which were located in the operation area of Berrini Avenue. The objective of the partnership was to remove a favela near the offices. Berrini Avenue became one of the most fashionable addresses for business in the city during the 1990s, and its poor neighbors were viewed as an eyesore. Although many favelas had been displaced in the city before, this was the first time in which representatives of the private sector participated directly in the removal. Although they used a philanthropic discourse to legitimate their initiative, they never disguised their obvious objective of obtaining real estate valorization. Similarly, the city did not disguise its interest in the partnership.[48]

In sum, the Urban Operations combining public and private investors in São Paulo have thus far increased inequality and spatial segregation. The urban areas that they requalified are emblematic of new trends in segregation transforming the city in the past two decades.[49] Clearly, once social agents engage them, instruments of planning and governmental regulation do not necessarily produce the results their formulators intended. Brasília is a clear example in this regard, as Holston demonstrated.[50] For the U.S.A., Mike Davis gives a compelling analysis of how NIMBY movements in Los Angeles have used democratic instruments to produce exclusion and segregation.[51] These examples only make us skeptical about what to expect from some of the new instruments of urban management. They also force us to consider the complex relationship between democratic and neoliberal planning.

Undoubtedly, in the past 20 years, city administrations in Brazil have reconceptualized the role of the state, the nature of planning, and the relationship between the public and private sectors in the production of urban space. The results have significantly transformed the dominant modernist–developmentalist model of planning and urban management. Undoubtedly, too, democratization alone cannot explain these innovations. Indeed, the interconnections between democratic and neoliberal rationalities of government are intricate, yet still under-investigated. Although many new instruments have been introduced in the name of an expanded role for "civil society," this role has in fact often only guaranteed specific private interests, as in São Paulo's Urban Operations, instead of a broad representation of different perspectives. To date, however, these operations have been implemented by administrations that disregarded the practices of participatory democracy and interpreted the partnership of public and private in predominantly neoliberal terms, as a means to realize market interests and not social justice. Nevertheless, as we have shown, the new planning initiatives have the potential to generate urban spaces that are less segregated and that fulfill their "social function" – spaces that are, in short, more democratic, in the sense that their resources are equitably distributed and their citizens active participants in their making and management. Therefore, one can hope that an administration committed to those ends will succeed in using the new instruments of planning to realize them. This expectation has some basis, for the democratic practices of popular social movements and local administrations have already transformed the modernist model of urban planning and government into the vastly more democratic project embodied in the City Statute. That is no small achievement.

Notes

1 The authors wish to thank the institutions supporting their research in Brazil, on which this chapter is partly based. Teresa Caldeira is grateful for support from the Núcleo de Estudos da Violência (Universidade de São Paulo and FAPESP) and from a J. William Fulbright Foreign Scholarship. James Holston gratefully acknowledges support from the Universidade de São Paulo and FAPESP and from a Fulbright–Hays Faculty Research Fellowship (U.S. Department of Education).

2 The term "favela" refers to a set of shacks built on seized land. Although people own their shacks and may transport them, they do not own the land, since it was illegally occupied. From the point of view of urban infrastructure, favelas are extremely precarious. The shacks are close together, there is no sewage service and frequently no piped water, and generally people obtain electricity by illegally tapping into existing electric lines. A *cortiço* is either an old house whose rooms have been rented to different families, or a series of rooms, usually in a row, constructed to be rented individually. In each room, a whole family sleeps, cooks, and entertains. Residents of various rooms share external or corridor bathrooms and water sources.

3 Juscelino Kubitschek, *Por Que Construí Brasília* (Rio de Janeiro: Bloch Editores, 1975), pp. 62–63.

4 *Brasília*, 65–81, 1963, p. 15 (*Brasília* is the journal of Companhia Urbanizadora da Nova Capital do Brasil – Novacap).

5 For further analyses of Brasília, see James Holston, *The Modernist City: An Anthropological Critique of Brasília* (Chicago: University of Chicago Press, 1989); and James Holston, "The spirit of Brasília: modernity as experiment and risk" in *Brazil Body & Soul*, Edward J. Sullivan, ed. (New York: The Solomon R. Guggenheim Museum, 2001), pp. 540–557.

6 Brazil's urban population represented 36 percent of the total population in 1950, 68 percent in 1980, and 81 percent in 2000 (in a total population of almost 170 million). In 1980, Brazil already had nine metropolitan regions with populations of over one million.

7 For an analysis of modernism and modernization in Brazil, as well as of the creation of Brasília and Kubitschek's Plan, see Holston, *The Modernist City*. For an analysis of the industrialization of São Paulo, see Warren Dean, *The Industrialization of São Paulo 1880–1945* (Austin: University of Texas Press, 1969); and Paul Singer, "Interpretação do Brasil: uma experiência histórica de desenvolvimento" in *História Geral da Civilização Brasileira*, Vol. 2: *O Brasil Republicano, 4 Economia e Cultura (1930–1964)*, Boris Fausto, ed. (São Paulo: Difel, 1984), pp. 211–245. For analyses of the transformations of this city during the developmentalist period, see Richard Morse, *Formação Histórica de São Paulo* (São

Paulo: Difel, 1970): Part IV; and Regina Maria Prosperi Meyer, "Metrópole e Urbanismo: São Paulo Anos 50," Ph.D. dissertation, Universidade de São Paulo, Faculdade de Arquitetura e Urbanismo, 1991.

8 For an analysis of this belief in progress and its social consequences especially for the case of São Paulo, see Teresa P. R. Caldeira, "From Modernism to 'Neo-Liberalism' in São Paulo: Reconfiguring the City and Its Citizens," a paper presented to the Sawyer Seminar "Globalizing City Cultures and Urban Imaginaries," Columbia University, 2001.

9 Lucio Costa, "Razões da nova arquitetura," *Arte em Revista* 4, 1980[1930], pp. 15–23.

10 For a discussion of the Brazilian embodiment of the CIAM model city, see Holston, *The Modernist City*, pp. 31–58.

11 Idem.

12 For a discussion of these strategies and of the residents' reaction to them, see Holston, *The Modernist City*, pp. 163–187. The reduction both of family social space and of the expression of individuality in residential architecture is consistent with modernist object-ives to reduce the role of private apartments in the lives of residents and, correspondingly, to encourage the use of collective facilities.

13 Ministry of Justice (Minister Carlos Cyrillo, Jr., Jayme de Assis Almeida et al.), *Brasília: Medidas Legislativas Sugeridas à Comissão Mista pelo Ministro da Justiça e Negócios Interiores* (Rio de Janeiro: Departamento de Imprensa Nacional, 1959), p. 9.

14 Holston, *The Spirit of Brasília*.

15 Ministry of Justice, *Brasília*, p. 9.

16 For a full account of the Brazilianization of Brasília, see Holston, *The Modernist City*.

17 The Plano Piloto was planned for a maximum population of 500,000. As of 2000, the date of the most recent findings, it has a population of 198,400. If we include the Lake districts North and South, we add another 57,600 residents, for a total that is still just half Brasília's planned population. Moreover, the demographic imbalance between center and periph-ery has only worsened with time. At inauguration, the Plano Piloto (including the lake districts) had 48 percent of the total Federal District population and the periphery (both satellite cities and rural settlements) had 52 percent. In 1970, the distribution was 29 percent to 71 percent; in 1980, 25 percent to 75 percent; in 1990, 16 percent to 84 percent; and in 2000, 13 percent to 87 percent. See IBGE-CODEPLAN 2000.

18 Edward Telles, "Structural Sources of Socioeconomic Segregation in Brazilian Metropol-itan Areas," *American Journal of Sociology* 100(5), 1995, pp. 1199–1223.

19 The urban plans for São Paulo of the 1950s to the 1970s were modernist and devel-opmentalist. These types of plans continued to be produced well into the 1970s. The clearest example is the integrated plan of development approved in 1971 (Plano Diretor de Desenvolvimento Integrado).

20 The mechanisms that created a legal/illegal city started to appear in São Paulo at the beginning of the century and were constitutive of Brazilian land occupation and legisla-tion since early colonial times: see James Holston, "The Misrule of Law: Land and Usurpation in Brazil," *Comparative Studies in Society and History* 33(4), 1991, pp. 695–725. In the case of São Paulo, legislation during the 1910s established a division of the city into four zones: central, urban, suburban, and rural. Most of the planning statutes created at that time applied only to the central and urban zones, leaving the other areas (where the poor were already starting to move) unregulated. When some legisla-tion was extended to these areas, such as requirements for registering subdivisions and rules for opening streets, it did not take long for developers to gain exemptions. The

requirements that new streets had to have infrastructure and minimum dimensions, for example, could be legally bypassed after 1923, when a new law offered the possibility of creating "private streets" in suburban and rural areas. The legal rules for the urban perimeter did not apply to these private streets. Probably the best example of this mechanism of exception relates to the required installation of infrastructure, which, starting at the beginning of the century, depended on the legal status of a street. Most of the new streets, especially in the suburban and rural areas, were either irregular or illegal, and therefore exempted from this requirement by definition. Given the intense settlement of urban migrants in these areas, this exclusion amounted to an extraordinary subvention for developers and hardship for new residents. Although the new subdivisions were progressively legalized and given urban status through various amnesties (1936, 1950, 1962, and 1968), these decrees were each ambiguous enough to leave to executive discretion the determination of which streets fit the criteria for legalization, and therefore for urban improvement, and which did not. For detailed analysis of this mechanism and its effects on São Paulo's legislation and urban space, see Holston, "The Misrule of Law"; Teresa P. R. Caldeira, *City of Walls: Crime, Segregation, and Citizenship in São Paulo* (Berkeley: University of California Press, 2000), Ch. 6; Raquel Rolnik, *A Cidade e a Lei: Legislação, Política Urbana e Territórios na Cidade de São Paulo* (São Paulo: Fapesp/Studio Nobel, 1997).

21 James Holston, "Autoconstruction in Working-Class Brazil," *Cultural Anthropology* 6(4), 1991, pp. 447–465.

22 The population of the city grew from 579,033 in 1920 to 3,781,446 in 1960, according to the census. In 2000, it was 10,405,867 in the city and around 18 million in the metropolitan region (the combined area formed by the city plus 38 surrounding municipalities). Population density in the city dropped from 11,000 inhabitants per km^2 in 1914 to 5,300 in 1963. In 2000, it was 6,823 inhabitants per km^2.

23 Until 1985, illiterate people in Brazil (all from the working classes) could not vote. Moreover, the military regime that took power in 1964 eliminated all elections for executive offices.

24 Teresa P. R. Caldeira, *A Política dos Outros: O Cotidiano dos Moradores da Periferia e o que Pensam do Poder e dos Poderosos* (São Paulo: Brasiliense, 1984).

25 Caldeira, *City of Walls*, Ch. 6.

26 Maria Célia Paoli, "Apresentação e Introdução," in *Os Sentidos da Democracia – Políticas do Dissenso e Hegemonia Global*, Maria Célia Paoli and Francisco de Oliveira, eds. (São Paulo: Nedic/Fapesp/Editora Vozes, 1999), pp. 7–23.

27 Caldeira, *City of Walls*.

28 The contradictions between an "insurgent democratic citizenship" and a "disjunctive democracy" in Brazil are the focus of a forthcoming book by Holston. It also analyzes what we discuss in the next sections of this chapter; namely, the emergence of new forms of citizenship in relation to law and its institutions, and the transformation of the insurgent notion of "rights to the city" developed by the urban social movements into new modes of urban planning.

29 This movement was later consolidated into the National Forum of Urban Reform, which congregates numerous NGOs, social movements, and trade union organizations interested in urban reform. The Forum is still quite active in promoting urban legislation at all levels of government.

30 A discussion of some of these innovations is found in: Ana Amélia da Silva, "A luta pelos direitos urbanos: novas representações de cidade e cidadania," *Espaço e Debates* 30, 1990, pp. 29–41.

31 *Estatuto da Cidade* (City Statute), federal law 10,257 of July 10, 2001, Art. 2.

32 Ibid., Art. 2, para. I.

33 Ibid., Art. 2, para. IV.

34 Ibid., Art. 2, para. IX.

35 Ibid., Art 2. para. XI.

36 Ibid., Art 2, para. XIV.

37 Most of these procedures have been used by local administrations, especially from the PT (Worker's Party) for at least 15 years. They became standard for any administration that wants to be recognized as popular. The participatory budget process is a mechanism for the formulation of the annual city budget through public audiences in which neighborhood and district representatives have the right to voice and vote.

38 It is worth remembering that one of the arguments that justified the prohibition of direct elections after the 1964 military coup was that people (meaning poor people) did not know how to choose and to vote, and should therefore be governed by those who know.

39 São Paulo's Master Plan has 308 articles dealing with not only urban policies *per se* but also with issues ranging from the rights of minorities to employment. It is a clear example of how the experience of social movements and of democratic local administrations (mostly from the PT) have framed conceptions of urban management in contemporary Brazil. This Master Plan incorporates the language and the instruments of the City Statute as well as a whole new series of concepts and initiatives developed by the social movements and Forums, such as partnerships, solidarity development, project incubators, participatory budget, and so on. The consideration of the Plan by City Council involved intense debate – as expected – and considerable opposition, especially from organized groups eager to defend their real estate interests. A number of the innovations in the 2002 Master Plan had already been introduced in previous plans that did not pass City Council, such as the Master Plans proposed by mayors Mário Covas in 1985 and Luiza Erundina in 1991.

40 The mayors were Paulo Salim Maluf, who had previously served as nonelected mayor and governor during the military dictatorship, and Celso Pitta.

41 For an analysis of the principal master plans of the city of São Paulo in the 20th century, see Nádia Somekh and Candido Malta Campos, eds., *A Cidade que Não Pode Parar: Planos Urbanísticos de São Paulo no Século XX* (São Paulo: Mack Pesquisa, 2002).

42 For a full analysis of the consolidation of this new pattern of urban segregation and of the context of increasing violent crime and fear in which it occurs, see Caldeira, *City of Walls*, chs. 6–8.

43 Câmara dos Deputados, Secretaria Especial de Desenvolvimento Urbano da Presidência da República, Caixa Econômica Federal, and Instituto Pólis, *Estatuto da Cidade – Guia para Implementação pelos Municípios e Cidadãos* (Brasília: Câmara dos Deputados, 2001), p. 68.

44 One account of the transformations of this notion, as engaged by various social movements and forums of urban reform, is given in Câmara dos Deputados et al., *Estatuto da Cidade*, pp. 68–71. See also Nádia Somekh, "Plano Diretor de São Paulo: uma aplicação das propostas de solo criado," in *Acumulação Urbana e a Cidade*, Luiz César de Queiroz Ribeiro and Luciana Corrêa do Lago, eds. (Rio de Janeiro: IPPUR/UFRJ, 1992), pp. 255–260.

45 Municipal Law 10,209 from 1986. Because changes in zoning were not authorized by City Council, these operations were later prohibited by the justice system under the allegation that they were at odds with the state Constitution.

46 The 1991 Master Plan elaborated under Erundina's administration, but not approved, was the first to follow the new Constitution's principles on urban policy. The Plan reaffirmed the social function of the city and of urban property and proposed to substitute the existing zoning code with the *"solo criado"* rule. It recommended that the whole city have the same utilization rate (*coeficiente de aproveitamento*) of one, instead of the multiple rates defined by PDDI. The utilization rate defines the relationship between the total permitted built area and the total area of the lot. The right to build above the rate of one-to-one would have to be purchased from the city. Furthermore, the Plan determined the areas and the quantities permitted for such purchases. This same principle of a single utilization rate was reintroduced in the proposal for the 2002 Master Plan. However, to get it passed by City Council, the administration had to negotiate the single rate and raise its limits.

47 The Master Plan 1985–2000 elaborated by the Mário Covas administration defined the possibility of Urban Operations.

48 The transformations of Berrini Avenue and the areas around Águas Espraiadas and Faria Lima, as well as the removal of the nearby favelas, are analyzed by Mariana Fix, *Parceiros da Exclusão* (São Paulo: Boitempo Editorial, 2001); and Heitor Frúgoli Jr., *Centralidade em São Paulo. Trajetórias, Conflitos e Negociações na Metrópole* (São Paulo: Cortez/Edusp/Fapesp, 2000).

49 For a fuller discussion of this kind of spatial segregation, see Caldeira, *City of Walls*, Chs. 6–8.

50 Holston, *The Modernist City.*

51 Mike Davis, *City of Quartz: Excavating the Future in Los Angeles* (London: Verso, 1990).

22

THE GARRISON–ENTREPÔT:

A Mode of Governing in the Chad Basin

JANET ROITMAN

A drive along the roads that link the various nation-states of the Chad Basin[1] can be a treacherous affair. One is constantly swerving and veering to avoid the craters in the few main paved roads and to negotiate the ruts and troughs that mark the secondary dirt roads. Certain regions are particularly perilous, being well-known for encounters with armed road gangs which set up roadblocks and brandish home-made rifles, and especially Kalashnikovs, in their quest for money and valuables. Limited in their scope, these road gangs, known locally as *les coupeurs de route*[2] (those who cut off the roads), are nonetheless a regional phenomenon linked to transnational flows. They are comprised of all nationals of the Chad Basin – Nigerians, Cameroonians, Chadians, and citizens of the Central African Republic and Niger (and perhaps itinerant Senegalese or Sudanese). They are connected into the regional and international markets in small arms and money counterfeiting. And they establish and participate in a network of economic exchanges and employment relations that found a significant mode of accumulation in the region. The latter extends beyond the violent forms of appropriation associated with organized gangs working the roads. It also consists of a host of unregulated economic activities that have rendered the bush and international borders spaces of big business, including the smuggling of hardware, electronics, and dry goods, as well as the trade in black market petrol, stolen four-wheel-drive vehicles, ivory, rhinoceros horns, and gold. As one ex-military man, who was discharged and imprisoned for having allegedly sold his weapon to a *coupeur de route*, put it: "Over time, I understood that even if the border zones are poor, one nonetheless makes big money there."[3]

No doubt, this realm of activity represents the only conceivable frontier of wealth creation in a region that has no viable industrial base and is not even an industrial periphery. With the severe economic hardship that was first noted in the 1980s, the application of World Bank structural adjustment programs, the contraction of bi- and multilateral aid, and the monetary devaluation of the franc CFA that occurred in 1994, the prospects for gainful employment have dwindled and purchasing power has diminished dramatically. This has been exacerbated by the demise of prices of primary products, such as cotton and groundnuts, on world markets and the recent rearrangement of industrial production, which has privileged labor markets in South-east Asia, South Asia, and Latin America. This situation has given rise to large numbers of "economic refugees," many of whom have migrated to the borders, where they serve as transporters, guards, guides, and carriers in the domain of unregulated commerce. They are accompanied by "military refugees," born out of military demobilization programs[4] and the inability of national armies to provide for their personnel. These people seek opportunities for accumulation in the emergent markets of the region. In Chad, for example, the 1992 military demobilization program, which involved approximately 27,000 men, led to the recycling of soldiers into the small arms market, for which they have contacts and expertise. Often they "enter the bush," as they say, working as road bandits with organized groups of under- and unpaid soldiers as well as the unemployed from Cameroon, Nigeria, Niger, the Central African Republic, and Sudan. They are joined by Chadian mercenaries who, after having entered Cameroon in the early 1990s to fight alongside their alleged ethnic counterparts (the "Arabe Choa"), now roam the countryside. This movement of men has transformed border regions and the peripheries of certain towns, both of which are now speckled with encampments and depots serving as warehouses, or bulking and diffusion points. While etching out spaces on the margins, these sites are not marginal. Like the activities they harbor, such spaces are dependent upon commercial and financial relations that link them to the cities. They arise from and depend upon a military–commercial link that I think is best described through the place and the metaphor of the "garrison–entrepôt."[5]

As a material effect, the garrison–entrepôt congeals and summarizes the military–commercial nexus. While surely representative of some of the most dispossessed, those who undertake its associated activities are very often financed and organized by military personnel, customs officials, gendarmes, wealthy merchants, and local chiefs (who are sometimes also well-placed political figures). Even though the problem of insecurity is recognized as the foremost challenge to governing the lands of the Chad Basin,[6] the economic activities that prevail on international borders and in far-removed areas are crucial to the urban economy, as well as to the financing of local administrations. The garrison–entrepôt is most obviously the materiality of the exercise of these relations. By allowing for certain forms of social mobility in a time of austerity and by providing rents for strapped government administrations, it is also the basis for economic redistribution. Furthermore, since the garrison–entrepôt serves to circumscribe certain forms of wealth – such as contraband associated with unregulated commerce and spoils associated with violent forms of appropriation – it is also an idiom through which certain forms of wealth are secured and authorized. In this way, illegal activities are rendered legitimate and supposedly exceptional practices become rational or normal behavior. Therefore, although the garrison–entrepôt has its historical precedents in the genealogy of slaving, *razzia*, and *jihad* in the region – and is in fact a term coined in the French colonial archives relating to northern Cameroon[7] – its resurrection on the frontiers of wealth creation in the Chad Basin involves more than the construction of new monopolies over wealth. More than that, its extension is both the result and the catalyst of transformations in the discursive field in which wealth is defined as such, spoils becoming a licit form of wealth.

In that sense, the garrison–entrepôt is significant not only because it is a site for new forms of social mobility, but also because it circumscribes the possibilities for thinking and enacting certain ways of accumulating as well as certain ways of thinking about and sanctioning wealth. Ultimately, while viewed by most living in its midst as illegal, the unregulated economic activities and violent methods of extraction associated with the garrison–entrepôt are likewise described as legitimate. Being part of the very legibility of power, these activities partake in prevailing modes of governing the economy. Thus a brief look at the garrison–entrepôt gives insight into "...how different locales are constituted as authoritative and powerful, how different agents are assembled with specific powers, and how different domains are constituted as governable and administrable."[8] While produced in the margins, the garrison–entrepôt is nonetheless at the heart of the problem – or the problematization – of power. Through its discursive domain, its constitutive relationships, its associated practices, and the teleology of its rationale emerges a particular, historical, political subject and political subjectivity. Being one domain in which power is propagated through ways and means that exceed the infrastructures of the state, those who engage in its constitutive relationships and material manifestations recognize this nexus as an intelligible site of power and governing, or as a means and mode of directing human conduct.

Unregulated Commerce and Road Banditry: A Day's Work

A short stay in the Chad Basin is enough to surmise the extent to which unregulated markets now constitute the frontiers of wealth creation.[9] Even tourists rarely have recourse to the banking system (which is eschewed by most local people), since money changing is less expensive and more easily accessed in the streets. Likewise, along roadways one is constantly passing by motorcades of trucks, motorcycles, and even bicycles filled with the goods of contraband, and especially hardware, electronics, and black-market petrol. While seemingly small-scale, the most lucrative of this unregulated commerce is based on recently revived regional and international networks of trade and finance. Although part of the economic history of trans-Saharan and east–west Sahelian economies, the resurgence of these networks since the late 1980s is in part due to the effective incorporation and novel use of resources derived from international markets. As in many parts of Africa, the demise of certain international markets, such as export crop commodities (cotton) and minerals (copper) – allegedly the foremost cause of the "marginalization" of African economies from the world economy[10] – and the proliferation of certain resources of trade and accumulation (drugs, small arms) have resulted in a drive for new forms of economic integration.[11] In the Chad Basin, these include the trade in small arms flowing through the Sudan, Libya, Chad, Cameroon, Nigeria, Niger, and Algeria; the provisioning of ongoing conflict in Niger, Chad, the Central African Republic, and the Sudan, which entails transiting petrol, hardware, electronics, grain, gold, diamonds, and (mostly stolen) cars and four-wheel-drive trucks; the ivory and rhinoceros horn trade centered around Lake Chad and the Central African Republic; the commerce in counterfeit medicines; the transfer of drugs between the Pakistani crescent, Nigeria, and western Europe; counterfeiting operations in Cameroon and Nigeria; and large-scale, highly organized highway banditry.[12]

Those who manage to assure and direct the financing, labor recruitment, and material organization required by the networks constituting these activities are a heterogeneous lot. They include the local merchant elite, political figures, high-ranking military personnel, customs officials, and leaders of factions or rebel groups that are especially active in Chad and the Central African Republic. The political and urban-based merchant class, for instance, which produced its rents through debt-financing until the late 1980s,[13] have reoriented their economic activities with the contraction of bi- and multilateral aid. Having worked as transporters and suppliers for public works projects and international development projects, the merchant elite's convoys now plow desert paths and mountain roads running through Nigeria, Cameroon, the Central African Republic, Chad, Libya, and the Sudan, being the critical links in, and financial backers of, smuggling operations. Likewise, wealthy merchants, military personnel, and local administrators (such as mayors, party delegates, and local chiefs)[14] are involved in the financing and logistical organization of regional road gangs, which is an aspect of their conversion to a newly constituted logic of accumulation. An "ex"-*coupeur de route* affirmed this point:

> *What kind of weapons did you have? Who gave them to you?*
> The leader [*le chef*] told us that we would have more sophisticated guns than those of the army, or at least the minor soldiers [*les petits soldats*] who escort vehicles, and that they [soldiers] feared our arms. I think the guns came from Chad and the Central African Republic, and even the Cameroonian army.
> *The Cameroonian army?*
> Of course.
> *Those that you grab from soldiers during attacks?*
> Oh no! I don't know how it works, but me and my comrades, we had the distinct impression that they were arms coming directly from the arsenals of the army or the police! For us, the arms came and found us in the bush, and we left them somewhere after the operation. That is how it worked with some of the operators who I collaborated with.[15]

This collaboration has given rise to hierarchies of bosses and workers that form and disband over time, creating a well-financed and yet fluid labor market that makes the garrison–entrepôt a sure source of employment and social mobility, and yet a fairly ephemeral entity.

Another "ex"-road bandit describes this as follows:

. . . Were you the head of a gang?

No, no! I played various roles in the attacks I participated in. I carried the sack of spoils [*le sac du butin*]. I assured the gang leader's security. I retrieved the arms after an operation. I participated in the planning of an attack. I never commanded. I didn't have my own group. You know, to have your own group, you have to have the means and the relations.

What means? What relations?

You have to buy arms, give something to the guys before going to the attack, pay for their food, lodge them for days somewhere, pay informers who go to the market-place to identify people who've made a lot of money, etc.

And the relations?

(sigh of aggravation) I told you that I don't know everything. The leader [*le chef*] of the team, sometimes he's someone I've never even seen before. My prison friends would take me to him and after an attack sometimes we'd never meet again, not even at the marketplace. In the Central African Republic, I had a chief [gang leader] who later became my neighbor in the [agricultural] fields! There were two guys working in his fields with whom we'd done operations.

. . .

What relations does the chief of the gang need?

Are you naïve or are you doing this on purpose? Do you think that you can do this kind of work without protection? For example, the chief who had his fields next to mine, in one operation we got a lot of money. I don't know how much exactly, but between the money we found, the jewelry, the watches, etc., the booty [*le butin*] came to something in the millions [of CFA]. We were 15 or 20 people, I can't remember. I got 150,000 CFA. Since we attacked cattle herders and cattle merchants, well, it's sure that the leader got one over on us since, for himself, he kept millions. But afterwards, when I saw him in the fields cultivating, I understood that it was the man in the car who kept most of it.

Wait a minute! Who is the man in the car? This is not the first time I've heard people talk about a man who comes in a car just after an attack.

Oh! I can't really say. In any case, we threw all the arms and the spoils into the trunk of the car. Those who had military uniforms also through them in. We dispersed and then I got my part in the evening, at the rendezvous.

. . .

And the man in the car?

I never saw him again. But I'm certain that he went back to the city.

Because he lives in the city?

Obviously! If it was someone from one of the villages around here, I would know him! A car in a rural area, that doesn't go unnoticed.

What does the man in the car who comes from the city and makes you risk your life for a pittance represent for you?

> You're the one who says that it's a pittance! Do you know what a civil servant's salary is in the Central African Republic? The 150,000 CFA that I got allowed me to spend a peaceful Ramadan and to clothe my family for the festivities. What job brings in 150,000 CFA for no more than a half-day's work?[16]

The assertion that theft is work is not unique to road gangs. While the latter surely practice perhaps the most radical or brute form of seizure, such manners of expropriation are widespread. For instance, military personnel and customs officials find rents on fraudulent commerce more attractive than, and often a necessary complement to, their official salaries. This has led to a specific denomination for them in Chad: "*les douaniers-combattants*," who are "customs officials-soldiers" or "fighting customs officials."[17] It has also led to the blurring of the lines denoting civil versus military status, and even civilians versus administrators. For instance, when arriving at Ngueli, the bridge that spans the Logone River, marking the border between Cameroon and Chad and the entry to N'djamena, the Chadian capital, one is accosted by numerous people asking for identification papers and vehicle documents. Often, someone in a uniform reviews these documents and then negotiates a fee for passage, which is formally presented as official tariffs. Shortly thereafter, a man in street clothes might appear, asking for the same documents. When you explain that you've just presented them to the government official, the "civilian" will brandish his official identity card, demonstrating that he is the "real" customs or security official. Who was the first man? Just some boy who'd borrowed his uncle's uniform or, more likely, someone who had been given the uniform and told to go out and collect the day's pay. As one customs official said, those who cross the border "can be summoned by diverse people in civilian clothes or in uniform. These people pass themselves off either for gendarmes, customs officials, police, members of the presidential special services, etc.... The problem is that there is a sort of amalgam and one doesn't know who does what. The multiplicity, the incoherence, the mix of uniforms brings on confusion. It seems that we're dealing with a blurring that is voluntarily maintained because it is part of a logic of accumulation created and maintained by the security forces who round up their monthly pay in this way."[18]

But summoning, assembling, or even supplementing – all connotations of "rounding up" – one's monthly pay is an economic strategy that is not simply the ruse of unpaid or under-paid civil servants. For the general population, smuggling activities and large-scale banditry are forms of "work," which they contrast quite explicitly to "fraud" or "theft." The start of a conversation with a well-known smuggler who works the borders between Nigeria, Cameroon, and Chad, highlights this point:

> *Thanks for having accepted to discuss your activities. To start with, what does the activity of a trafficker [traffiquant] in this region consist of?*
> To start with – as well – what do you mean by "trafficker"? Are you insinuating that we violate the law or that we take advantage of a situation, or something like that?
> *No, no! Not that you take advantage, but, after all, you aren't ordinary economic operators.*
> What is an ordinary economic operator?

It's someone who we can identify by his activity, his address, etc. He pays taxes, he has a boutique or a store at a specific place; it's someone whose life and activities obey certain norms.

If I didn't have a specific activity and a specific address, how did you know that I master the route to Nigeria, and how did you know that at this very hour I would be here, on the Ngueli bridge?

I made some inquiries and Abba Maïna led me here.

So I'm well known, or else he would have led you to someone else; there are many people who go to Nigeria, to Chad and elsewhere.

OK. You are definitely one of the oldest, most regular, and most well known in the cross-border commerce.

Voilà! Cross-border commerce is the expression that fits.[19]

Another conversation with an *"ex"-coupeur de route*, who mysteriously escaped death by execution after having been arrested following the murder and "roasting" of a prominent police officer in peculiar circumstances, reiterated this reasoning:

How do you want me to address you?

Why do you want my name? They told me that you want to write history! My name is of no use for that. And what name would I give you anyway? I've had so many; I changed my name several times. Only my mother calls me by my real name. So even if I give you a name, it's inevitably a false name, a name that I used at a given time or a certain place.

Give me a name anyway. For example, a name that you used in an instance when you were robbing.

No! I wasn't robbing; I was working.

. . .

Yes, but stealing is not working!

You don't understand anything. The thief is like the liar. The liar wastes his spit for nothing; he talks to earn nothing. The thief takes by reflex; he takes everything that passes in front of him, even useless things . . .

You seem proud to have been a different kind of thief.

Are you trying to insult me? I'm telling you for the last time that, when there is a salary at the end, you are not a thief. Me, I work the roads.[20]

The idea that theft and highway robbery constitute work is more than just a rationalization of illicit practice; it is a reflection that is grounded in particular notions about what constitutes wealth, what constitutes licit or proper manners of appropriation, and how one governs both wealth and economic relations. This is particularly influenced by the fact that the materiality of the civil link between the state and its subjects is realized through taxes and welfare services, like in many parts of the world, *as well as* through wealth produced in domains – such as private markets associated with development and public works projects – that exceed the infrastructures of the state. Since the 1980s, structural adjustment programs, down-sizing (known locally as *dégraissage*), and privatizations have pared down – or in fact displaced[21] – the sites from which the state enacts such transfers, and hence governs salaries, benefits, workers, and workdays, *as well as* economic rents, benefactors, clients, and syndicates. Hence the status of wealth, work, and state appropriations has come to the fore as a set of unstable referents.

The Intelligibility of Seizure and Tax

In the early 1990s, there was much strife over the themes of wealth, work, and state appropriations in Cameroon. This culminated in what the Biya regime dubbed *incivisme fiscal*, or "uncivil fiscal behavior." This slogan referred to the opposition-led *Opération Villes Mortes* campaign, a strategy of civil disobedience that implemented general strikes, work boycotts, economic blockades, and the use of clandestine services, such as motorcycles that served as "hidden" taxis.[22] The strategy of this campaign was fairly explicit: its aim was to deny taxation and hence to undermine the fiscal base of the regime.[23] Those who participated in the movement expressed their criticism of the regime's exactions and levies, which ultimately finance the ruling party and the political elite; the state's methods of extraction, which are often heavy-handed; and the regime's failure to provide economic opportunities and economic security to local populations. In 1993, the local government in northern Cameroon formed a special commission to investigate tax evasion and regulation of economic operators. While surely a response to the people's plaints and an effort to extinguish violent demonstrations, which included threats to burn government administrator's homes and cars, this was also an attempt by the regime to bring insurgent traders and businessmen into the fold of "civil behavior" – or tax payment. At a meeting held between high-level administrators and the merchants of the town of Maroua, Cameroon, the local Prefect reminded the merchants and their political representatives that:

> The networks are very, very complicated. The Nigerians and Chadians rent stores from you...they're in the parallel and informal circuits that you have initiated...The Commission cannot work freely...No one will reveal their profit margins. You say you have only four cartons of soap [in your store] and you're riding around in a Mercedes. We know that the command "Refuse!" [to pay tax] runs through the marketplace. But you tell me that foreigners are the ones who tell the youth to attack the people from the Ministry of Finance...Lots of activities take place in the form of traffic. Traffic was never the life of a country [*faire vivre un pays*]. And where that is the case, like in the Gambia, it was organized by the agents of the state itself. But if you have houses and cars...and the state has nothing, what can you do for Maroua? The roads must be tarred, public works are stopped; they must continue but there is no money...If you don't pay taxes, the country will die. The country is on its knees because its sons [*les fils du pays*] don't pay their taxes...It's no use to use a whip, it simply means that you are not free men.[24]

Many merchants responded that they are not opposed to the fact of state regulation of their economic activities, but that they object to the state's manners of appropriation, as well as the presupposition that they are the ultimate sources of wealth, the foundations of the state treasury.

As one merchant explained to me:

> We are not against licenses [*la patente*]; before we paid without force, without the police. They say that if you trade in the market, you need a license, at 37,000 CFA... The Prefect says it's not a political problem. They want us to pay because the civil servants don't have any money. If we pay the licenses, will that suffice to pay the civil servants? The Prefect gave 120,000 CFA to 120 policemen to come massacre the market. If we don't pay, they close down our shops.[25]

Another, somewhat elderly, man elaborated:

> Before, they came to the market to collect money; it was paid in installments and we got a receipt. They came every Monday. Even if the government sent a crazy man, we did what they asked. Now, the people who come are not children; they are big. If you say you have nothing, they close your shop... For five years now, they shut us down, chain our stores, and they leave. If they close your store and you stay in the market, they say, "Go steal!"[26]

Certain state appropriations were evidently being experienced as forms of seizure, and yet the imperative to seize was taken up by the very people who expressed this critique through the *Villes Mortes* campaign. In a very general way, the *incivisme fiscal* movement expressed – and even served to develop – interrogations about the legitimate foundations of state wealth, the forms of wealth that are to be subject to state appropriations, the distinction between licit and illicit commerce, and the integrity of the contours of the nation-state.[27] Ultimately, this debate about foundational terms such as national wealth has occasioned cross-examinations of certain established truths, such as what constitutes wealth and work. People have interrogated the status of wealth produced through seizure and raiding performed by both agents of the state and the local populace. They have also probed the status of limit zones, such as borders and the bush, where such wealth is produced. This might be thought of as a moment that has engendered supplementary definitions of licit wealth and legitimate manners of appropriation. In other words, contrary to "economic crisis" or "legitimacy crisis" readings of such moments in many parts of Africa, the destabilizing effects of this recognition of the inconsistent nature of these seemingly invariable referents has not simply led to a loss of sense and meaning in the world.[28] As a productive moment, *incivisme fiscal,* or the process of questioning it entailed, has given rise to transformations in the discursive field in which "wealth" and "work" are figured, as well as material effects of that discursive domain on contemporary practice.

Among those effects are the novel arrangements between official and unofficial forms of regulatory authority that have become institutionalized in the region. In the Chad Basin, people now find themselves implicated in relationships with numerous figures of regulatory authority of both official and nonofficial status. This pluralization of regulatory authority[29] issues from the multiplication of figures recognized as exercising legitimate authority over access to possibilities for accumulation and hence the right to employment and enrichment. This takes place at the highest levels of business through commissions on deals, right-of-entry taxes, tribute and royalty payments, protection fees, and even payment for safe delivery of goods procured through customs fraud or for their "false-legal" passage through customs.[30] Likewise, it transpires at the everyday level of business through levies on local merchants; protection and entitlement fees paid by young men engaged as guards, guides, and runners; entry taxes paid at unregulated border markets; and tolls on roads near these economically sensitive outposts.[31] These figures of authority compete with instances of national regulatory authority insofar as they become the final arbiters of enrichment and employment. Through levies and duties imposed on local populations, they establish an autonomous fiscal base. And in some respects, they have become guarantors of economic security and access to wealth for local people in spite of their association with violence. Doubtless, regional entrepôts and border settlements generate distinct regimes of violence, being highly militarized and often exercising control over residents and passers-by through arms and arbitrary attacks on villages and roadways. However, these outposts also provide access to wealth and possibilities for accumulation, as well as protection and a blueprint for action at a time of insecurity and austerity. Payments made to ensure access to international and regional markets, essential commercial and financial relationships, and protection serve to formalize various kinds of traffic, be that of small arms crossing long distances or petrol smuggled through a mountain pass. This makes such activities less unpredictable both in terms of logistics and revenues. Moreover, contributions to those who regulate access to and participation in these commercial and financial activities are not without services rendered. These include protection and a formal cadre, but they also involve the redistribution that takes place through the financing of community services, such as mosques and churches, or family demands, such as in times of illness, death, or misfortune.

However, these relationships involve more than the establishment of monopolies over new forms of wealth. They entail the normalization of particular definitions of licit wealth and manners of appropriating such wealth. Thus while recourse to unregulated commerce and road banditry, and acquiescence to their associated figures of authority, may be inspired by a contraction in material wealth and access to such wealth – the "marginalization of Africa" thesis – it also transpires from the extension of the discursive field in which wealth and value are figured. "Spoils," for instance, is now an ambivalent sign in the regional lexicon of wealth: once associated with war and asocial forms of wealth creation, it now signifies the disavowal of particular social obligations, such as tax. As with fraudulent commerce, what is seized cannot be taxed. And for those living in a web of international and local debt relations, seizure is a means of interfering in the social order implied by such obligations. Furthermore, spoils now signify a new sociability of exchange insofar as it is a new means of redistribution.[32] While tax collection was described and thus denounced during the 1990s as a from of seizure, many people – including cash-strapped customs officials, demobilized soldiers, devalued[33] merchants, local political chiefs, and the dispossessed – have inverted this power equation by seizing spoils themselves.

In the end, seizure has become generalized as a mode of enrichment: financial regulators chain merchants' stores shut, haul them to prison, confiscate goods, and exact fines. Customs officials and gendarmes skim off of trucks and travelers, usurping contraband. Game reserve wardens go poaching for ivory and rhinoceros horns. And gangs of professional road bandits hijack cars and attack road convoys. Ultimately, "tax" can be effected in sites other than within the limits of the state–citizen bind. This was affirmed by Bakaridjo – the fictitious name of the *coupeur de route* from the Central African Republic who had a decent Ramadan thanks to his "road work" – in response to the following question:

> *I want to understand better. The man in the car allowed you to have a good Ramadan. Between him and the President Ange Félix Patassé [of the Central African Republic], who is most useful to you?*
> Patassé is a good-for-nothing [*un vaurien*]. A scared man who cries over the least gunshot. I pay my taxes to Patassé. The man in the city gives me the means to pay Patasse's tax. Patassé sabotages the state; he steals from the Central African Republic, which is already very poor, and starves the people. My employer [gang leader] both fills in and rectifies [*combler*] the theft created by Patassé.
> *With 150,000 CFA? [earnings]*
> Patassé never gave me 15 CFA! In all of Patassé's offices [state administration], you have to pay for services! In any case, I don't give a damn about what you think. I deplore the deaths, of course. I've never killed anyone. In fact, once when a companion killed a passenger in cold blood because he didn't like the sight of him, the gang leader shot him after the operation and we split his part [*son butin*] amongst ourselves.
> *So, in conclusion, you are unconditionally devoted to the man who allows you to take care of your family, whatever the provenance of the resources?*
> I was. I stopped now. I told you before; I paid by going to prison. Anyway, money has no color, no odor. A man should be ashamed of hunger. When one has all his limbs and all his senses intact, one must work. Me, I never attacked a poor man. What would I take from a poor man? I am sure that the merchants and others who fall into our attacks are people who earn their money illicitly.
> *Illicitly?*
> Yes.
> *Why?*
> They buy cheaply; they sell at very high prices, without respect for Islamic rules of commerce. They don't pay the charity tax. And we pray to Allah that we will fall upon such people [during attacks]. Moreover, when they negotiate cattle all day at the market, when do they have the time to pray? We see them at the market; they don't pray.
> *And you pray before going to work the road?*
> What do you think?
> *What prayers do you do? Which verses?*

You also want to work the road? Allah exercises everyone's prayers. Those who don't
want to pay the *zakkat* [Islamic charity tax], we take up the responsibility to take it
from them. It's a charity payment on their fortune, a revenue tax.

So you replace the state tax services! Is that legal? Is it legitimate?[34]

Legal? Surely not! As for legitimacy, it is not for you nor anyone else to tell me how
I should assure my survival. You, the civil servants, you have your "benefits" on the
side. Is that legitimate? When people are named to a position of responsibility they
bring along their close relations, members of their tribe. What happens to those who
don't have relations in high places? In any case, for me, the ends justify the means and
long live the man with the car.[35]

For many, seizure is more than a brute means of accumulation. In the Chad Basin,
as in many parts of the world, violent appropriation is a modality not only of
social mobility, but also social welfare, being intrinsic to the nexus of relationships
that provides and ensures economic security. The commercial–military bind is a site
of transfers and redistribution; it is the realm in which forms of protection are
founded and guaranteed; and it is a mode of sociability in remote and supposedly
marginal areas that etch out specific forms of productivity. Today, seizure is a means
for both reversing and participating in the social order implied by certain obligations,
such as tax and debt. It is a manner of exercising power that partakes of practices of
both freedom and domination. This makes sense when one considers, following
Michel Foucault,[36] that power relations are modified, strengthened, and weakened
in their very exercise, such that practices of resistance are "never in a position of
exteriority in relation to power."[37] That is, practices of freedom and resistance
are inherent to and devised out of power situations; they are not something constructed from outside the bounds of the epistemological grounds of power or its
forms of knowledge.

Practices of Government on the Margins and in the Norm

The ongoing cycle of theft and seizure is often construed as a marginal condition that
is in fact the norm, a perspective put forth by a young man who works the
unregulated border trade:

The government's latest policy is the struggle against poverty. In order to get money
from the whites, Cameroon says that it is now a Highly Indebted Poor Income
Country [HIPIC], while we know that in our region we are a great power. People of
all nationalities come here every day, to Mbaimboum . . . Cameroon is a HIPIC by
cheating, by demagogy, in order to have the white man's money. So Cameroonians
follow the example of the state!

Meaning?

The state steals from the whites, the civil servants steal from the state, the merchants
steal from the civil servants by selling them products at prices incompatible with their
standard of living or by making them pay exorbitant rents on housing, and the

bandits steal from the merchants and the civil servants, who, together, transformed the state into a criminal entity. In fact, me, I don't condemn Cameroon for having really become a HIPIC because, if Cameroon steals from the whites it's due to the fact that the whites always stole from Africa.[38]

In the late 1980s, mechanisms for the exchange of debt, or the emergence of debt markets that dominated international financial markets (the Baker and Brady Plans),[39] became a crucial element of African political economies. This engendered what Olivier Vallée calls "political economies of debt," which involve not only the debt trade, but also the displacement of public law in favor of commercial law.[40] This system is based on various modalities for the conversion of debt into investment credits, funds for development projects, stock options in newly privatized companies (electricity, telephone), rights to natural resources (gas and oil), and promissory notes that become objects of speculation and exchange. Such conversions – or the selling of debt – involve value transformations, or the reformulation of distinctions between public wealth and the private domain. This phenomenon has allowed strapped public treasuries to access hard currency and, more typically, has ensured the enrichment of public personalities, who have placed such currency in offshore accounts and bought into, via their rights constituted in debt, recently privatized companies. Public debt has been converted into private wealth,[41] making the state of liability a resource in itself.[42]

Thus the assertion that theft and violent appropriations are illegal and yet licit modalities – as noted by Bakaridjo, above – is based on specific understandings about manners of rendering illegality a form of licit practice, habits of straddling the fine line between criteria that denote public versus private wealth, and ways of remaining both marginal and indispensable to productive systems. These statements extend beyond the circumscribed sphere of road banditry and smuggling insofar as they refer to a larger realm of knowledge that includes practices of government, such as the debt trade. Such practices are often dependent upon or generated out of the very ambivalence of certain statuses – such as "public," "private," "governed," and "governors." As was noted on a recent cover of a widely read African news magazine: "Cameroon: cop or hoodlum?"[43]

Statements and interpretations about how illegality is licit practice are also widespread with regards to unregulated economic activities, such as those pursued by the taxi-motorcyclists, the original clandestine operators of the *Villes Mortes* campaign. In the late 1990s, and in an effort to quell *incivisme fiscal* and to capture this lucrative domain, the taxi-motorcycles were legalized through a series of regulations. These include a new tax (the *impôt libératoire*), a driver's license, vehicle registration, vehicle insurance, a vehicle inspection sticker, a permit to carry passengers, a parking permit, and a custom's receipt for imported motorcycles. Drivers are now supposed to paint the motorcycles yellow, and wear helmets and gloves, none of which I have ever seen. Most young taxi-men do not pay these myriad impositions, which might be described as a host of mini-seizures. But this is not because they do not have the means, since most taxi fleets are financed by merchants, gendarmes, police, prefects, and even governors. The motorcycle-taximen – who are often referred to as *les attaquants* (the attackers) or *les casquadeurs* (the cascaders) – simply refer to a different register of appropriations which, ironically, often involves the very same people who perceive official taxes. In response to criticism for not having paid his official taxes, one young motorcycle-taximan, a member of the *Association des moto-taximen* in Ngaoundéré, declared:

> We pay our taxes every day! Whether we have the all the right papers for the motorcycle or not, we pay taxes to the police and gendarmes. In fact, it's become a reflex. The policemen of Ngaoundéré don't stop me anymore. I'm an old hand in the moto-taxi business. I've driven moto-taxis for people in high places, for men in uniform [who are owners of fleets of clandestine motorcycles]. Furthermore, often even when the police don't stop me, I go to them to pay the tribute [in a monetary sense]. My older brother initiated me. He is a *djo*, someone who knows all the secrets, all the strings. He told me that, with the police, it's not enough to go tell them that they are big men [*grands*]; you have to show them. It's like with the traditional chief, the *lamido*. The *lamido* doesn't work but he has a lot of money because people come to give it to him. The *lamido* doesn't ask anything of his subjects. His subjects come to give him envelopes out of respect... Since the policeman is also a chief – in fact, we call him "chief" [*chef*] – you have to go towards him even when your papers are in order, especially when you are in order.[44]

During the same conversation, another moto-taxi driver added:

> The police and the moto-taximen, we're partners. We know that if we are disposed to giving them a bit of money from time to time, we can work together. Together – that is the police and the moto-taximen – we exploit illegality. Even when you have all your papers in order, you're in illegality because the motorcycle is illegal. Not even 15 percent of the motorcycles are painted yellow. We have imposed our vision of things on the authorities. The police themselves close their eyes; they can always find an infraction to ticket. That way, they have money for beer. Today, we have representatives at each crossroads, leaders who negotiate with the adminis-tration when there are problems. We parade in front of the authorities during national festivities, they solicit us during election campaigns. We've become an integral part of society through the force of resistance. That's power. So that the system can continue to function properly, it's important that there are people in violation because, if everyone was in line with the law, the authorities – the police – wouldn't gain their share and then they would suppress the motorcycles on the pretext that they cause accidents, that we are hoodlums, etc. Today, maybe we are hoodlums, but we are hoodlums who help sustain families and contribute to the well-being of agents of the force of law. Long live the tolerant police [*la police compréhensive*]![45]

When asked whether they considered their activities licit or illicit, there was general agreement among the moto-taximen that "anything that can move a poor man from hunger and begging is licit." But one young man argued:

We struggle in domains that force you to circumvent the law – with all the risks. For example, we sell contraband petrol and medicines, etc., which are officially forbidden. But what do you expect? Often those who are supposed to see that people respect the law are our sponsors; they give us our original financing. A customs official who finances a petrol smuggler is not going to attack him [the smuggler] or the protégés of his colleagues! And without us, the work of the policeman, the customs official, the taxman, the head of the gendarmes, would have no interest for those who do it. Thanks to us, they have no financial problems.

But that's corruption!

That's not corruption. When you give 10,000 or 20,000 CFA to a policeman or a customs official to get your merchandise through, what does that change for the national economy? Corruption is when one sells the *Régie Nationale des Chemins de Fer* [rail company], the SNEC [water company], the SONEL [electric company], etc. Everyone knows that that's negotiated; there are big commissions. One single person can earn in a privatization more than all of Touboro [a local town known for contraband] can produce, save in a decade. Us, we give with pleasure and the police receive with pleasure, just like the customs official. They've become family.[46]

An older and well-known smuggler – who, above, insisted on his status as an "ordinary economic operator" – corroborated:

The civil servants are people who always have financial problems. They have needs that are not covered by their salaries, and so they become indebted to those who have money. In the end, needy civil servants and us, we have the same bosses [*patrons*] and this is not the government, but rather the merchants. Look! Since we have been here [on the Ngueli bridge], have you seen a single man or woman stopped by the Cameroonian customs agents or the gendarmes? All these hundreds of people who pass by here have their papers in order? The customs agents or the gendarmes who come here [to work] don't seek to be transferred elsewhere unless they have problems with the big merchants, or if they've amassed enough wealth. The passport for all that you want to do here, it's the franc CFA. Instead of paying for official documents at 200,000 CFA, it's better to just give 50,000 CFA with your own hands. That way, you have papers and protection.

Corruption?

What do you call corruption? They say that Cameroon is the world champion of corruption. How can a poor country be the world champion of corruption? They say that in Arab countries, in France, and in the United States, there are people who have more money than the Cameroonian government. I imagine that those countries have several times over what Cameroon possesses! Giving 5,000 CFA, 10,000 CFA, or 50,000 CFA, what does that represent in the Cameroonian economy?

Someone else recently said the same thing to me. Explain what you mean by corruption. Giving 5,000 CFA to a gendarme or a customs official is illegal!

I told you that every profession, like every religion, has its codes. Giving 5,000 is not giving 15 million. It's part of the code of trafficking: giving to continue to have.[47]

The code of trafficking, or the code of the route, was explained as follows:

> The Koran governs the Islamic religion, the Bible governs Christianity, the Torah is for
> the Jews, the road manual is for those who drive... You cannot take the Koran to
> adore Jesus, you can't go to church with the road manual. If you take the Torah to fix
> your motorcycle, you will soon end up with a carcass in its place... I say that a
> trafficker who wants to respect the law of the government cannot succeed because
> trafficking is not governed by the law of the government. It is governed by the law of
> the roads. If, when leaving Nigeria with petrol, you go see the customs officials to give
> them some money so that you can get through, they are going to arrest you. They'll
> say that you're suspicious, that you're not an ordinary trafficker, you want to tempt
> them, you're a spy. But if, while you're trying to evade them, they find you in the bush,
> then you can negotiate because you're in the normal order of the law of trafficking.[48]

These arguments all present the rationality of illegality, a disposition that is both
economically strategic and socially productive. But, more than that, the practice of
illegality with respect to economic regulation is inscribed in extant power relations.
That is, it is a means of reading the nature of power relations, of discerning its
legibility, and thus of participating in the productivity of power. In this case, it is a
mode for establishing and authenticating the exercise of power over economic
relations and forms of wealth. Thus, as was just explained, the code of trafficking
refers to and engages with a larger code of power relations. As participants in the
world of trafficking and road banditry recognize, this code may be illegal, since it
departs from the codes and regulations of official law, but it is neither illicit nor
illegible. It must be understood from within its own script which, while circumvent-
ing government, partakes in modes of governing the economy that are fundamental
to the workings of the various national states of the Chad Basin.

One might argue that this poses the problem of the efficacy of modes of governing,
since it would seem that the various nation-states of the Chad Basin are not producing self-governing citizens, or people who enact the spontaneous payment of official
taxes. But the problem of efficacy depends, of course, on the criteria upon which it is
judged, or the register to which one refers. Government law and the "law of the
roads" – or the code of officialdom and the code of trafficking – are deployed
simultaneously, their conditions of emergence being both mutually constituted and
yet in ceaseless autonomization. Their logics propagate certain forms of state power,
being the *raison d'être* of security forces and customs officials, and specific practices of
governing, being sources of the scripts by which forms of wealth are recognized and
circumscribed as such. In that sense, the garrison–entrepôt, which generates and
harbors unregulated commerce and organized highway crime, delimits the boundaries for modes of accumulation, social welfare, and security that represent both forms
of dissension and manners of engaging in practices of government. As a realm in
which one evaluates the nature of licit practices, as well as representations of the self
and self-conduct, the garrison–entrepôt is a space of ethics. It makes possible certain
kinds of resistance. And yet, because evaluations of what constitutes licit practice and
licit self-conduct are not derived out of a set of ethical standards that are distinct

from those that make power legible, such resistance is necessarily generated out of states of domination. It is an example of the ways in which states of power are constantly engendered at the multiple points of its exercise. And it gives insight into the ways in which power situations are apprehended as such according to specific, historical codifications of the rationality of power, of which the state is one, incontrovertible, locus.[49]

Evidently, a particular, historical political subject is produced in the realm of the garrison–entrepôt and in the midst of new forms of regulatory authority. And yet this political subject, or subjectivity, is not produced primarily through the forms of rationalization and individuation associated with modern liberalism and bureaucratization. Nor does it result from a seemingly autonomous and oppositional "moral economy"[50] that has emerged in the margins of state failure. Insofar as the generalization and intensification of unregulated economic activities and violent modes of appropriation has led to the process of questioning the status of effective legality and licit practice, it is surely the basis for the reconfiguration of governmental relationships. And yet these processes do not establish the bases for new forms of sovereign power, understood as a condition of unqualified power. For one, the possibility of such forms of power is, as Michel Foucault argued, nonsensical, or at least an irrelevant question, since such totalizing, coherent, and unitary situations do not obtain.[51] But more significantly, it is not at all clear that the domain inscribed by the garrison–entrepôt challenges this juridical representation of power: To what extent is the intelligibility of the very idea of sovereignty destabilized? To what extent can we discern changes in the production of valid statements about what the sovereign *is*, or is not? The definition and circumscription of new realms of thought and action, such as the garrison–entrepôt, give rise to unprecedented possibilities for the organization of economic and political life, leading, in the Chad Basin today, to the pluralization of regulatory authority. But the ultimate question is whether such changes result from transformations in the organization of knowledge, or in the prevailing manner of producing valid statements, such as "this is (legitimate) regulatory authority" or "this is a (legitimate) sovereign."

Notes

1   While the Chad Basin is a somewhat vague geographic concept, I use it here to refer to what are today northern Nigeria, northern Cameroon, Chad, and the Central African Republic. I lived in this region during various extended periods from 1992 to 2002. I thank the SSRC-MacArthur Foundation Program on Peace and Security Fellowship; the Ciriacy-Wantrup Fellowship of the University of California, Berkeley; and the MacArthur Foundation Program on Global Security and Sustainability for their kind support. I also thank Professor Saïbou Issa of the University of Ngaoundéré, who conducted some of the interviews cited herein and collaborated closely with me in this research, and Tobias Rees, Stephen Collier, and Aihwa Ong for their engaging thoughts. Language translations from Fulfulde were done by Hamidou Bouba, Saïbou Issa, and myself; all language translations to English are my own.

2 This phenomenon became most intense in the 1990s, being labeled as a "war" by the press. See F. Soudan, "La guerre secrète," *Jeune Afrique* 1871, November 1996, pp. 13–19; F. Dorce, "Cameroun: cette guerre qui cache son nom", *Jeune Afrique économie* 229, November 18, 1996, pp. 54–56; *N'djamena Hebdo*, "L'insécurité dans le nord Cameroun," January 1997; K. Pideu, "Une province abandonnée aux coupeurs de route," *La Nouvelle Expression* 243, March 28–31, 1995, p. 6; "Extrême-Nord: Demain la Guerre?" special issue of *Le Messager*, March 10, 1994, pp. 5–13.

3 November 17, 2001, Ngahoui, Cameroon.

4 Between 1992 and 1997, 27,000 Chadian military personnel were to be demobilized and disarmed. See *Jeune Afrique*, November 19, 1992, pp. 28–30; *Le Progrès* (N'djamena), "Armée: lumière sur la démobilisation et la réinsertion," May 13, 1997, pp. 10–11; *N'djamena Hebdo* 281, May 15, 1997, pp. 6–7; M. B. Teiga, "Une armée, certes, mais combien de divisions," *L'Autre Afrique*, December 17–23, 1997, pp. 14–15.

5 Janet Roitman, "The Garrison–Entrepôt," *Cahiers d'études africaines* 150–152, XXXVIII(2–4), 1998, pp. 297–329.

6 Cf., Jean-Baptiste Zoua (Lieutenant-Colonel), "Phénomène des coupeurs de route dans le nord-Cameroun: une épine dans la plante des pieds des responsables du maintien de l'ordre," unpublished MS, Chef d'état-major de la région militaire no. 4, Garoua, 1997; C. Seignobos and J. Weber, *Elements d'une stratégie de développement rural pour le Grand Nord du Cameroun*, vol. 1, *Rapport principal* (Montpellier: CIRAD, 2002).

7 The multiple histories that make up the trajectory of the garrison–entrepôt will not be treated herein. For that perspective, see Roitman, "The Garrison–Entrepôt."

8 M. Dean, *Governmentality: Power and Rule in Modern Society* (London: Sage, 1999), p. 29.

9 A point developed in Janet Roitman, "Productivity in the Margins: The Reconstitution of State Power in the Chad Basin," in *Anthropology at the Margins of the State*, V. Das and D. Poole, eds. (Santa Fe, School for American Research, forthcoming). On the productive and generative capacities of unregulated markets, see J. F. Bayart, ed., *La réinvention du capitalisme* (Paris, Karthala, 1994).

10 On the marginalization thesis, see T. Callaghy and J. Ravenhill, eds., *Hemmed In: Responses to Africa's Economic Decline* (New York: Columbia University Press, 1993) and Castells' depiction of "The Rise of the Fourth World," in M. Castells, *End of Millennium*, vol. 3 (Oxford: Blackwell, 1998), pp. 70–165.

11 Cf., J.-F. Bayart, S. Ellis, and B. Hibou, *La criminalisation de l'Etat en Afrique* (Brussels: Editions Complexe, 1997).

12 This information is from my own fieldwork. Some sources include the following: on Kalashnikovs, *Jeune Afrique*, November 19, 1992, pp. 28–30; on the continental drug economy, Observatoire géopolitique des drogues, *Géopolitique des drogues 1995* (Paris: La Découverte, 1995); and on petrol smuggling, X. Herrera, "Du 'fédéral' et des 'Koweï-tiens': la fraude de l'essence nigériane au Cameroun," *Autrepart* 6, 1998, pp. 181–202. More generally, see K. Bennafla, "Rapport sur les échanges transfrontaliers informels au Tchad," unpublished MS, 1996; and E. Grégoire, "Sahara nigérien: terre d'échangess," *Autrepart* 6, 1998, pp. 91–104.

13 J.-F. Bayart, *L'État en Afrique* (Paris, Fayard, 1989).

14 All of which were recently accused by *coupeurs de route* before a military tribunal in Cameroon. Cf., R. Guivanda, "Des coupeurs de route accusent" *L'œil du Sahel* (Cameroon) 75, February 21, 2002, p. 3. Discussions with judicial authorities, police,

and gendarmes confirmed the financing and organization of the road-gang industry by local chiefs and leaders of political party cells.

15 December 2001, Blangoua, Cameroon.

16 November 14, 2001, Meiganga, Cameroon.

17 Scant references include the following. On the military's rent-seeking activities, see A. Abba Kaka, "Cette fraude qui tue!" *Le Temps* (N'djamena) 69, April 9–15, 1997, p. 8; and S. Ngarngoune, "Alerte au Sud," *N'djamena Hebdo* 280, May 8, 1997, p. 4. On the guerilla movement around Lake Chad, see F. Faes, "Le dernier maquis," *L'Autre Afrique* 1, May 21–27, 1997, pp. 64–69.

18 December 8, 2001, Kousseri, Cameroon.

19 December 2001, Kousseri, Cameroon.

20 November 14, 2001, Meiganga, Cameroon.

21 On this process, which Hibou calls the "privatization of the state," see B. Hibou, ed., *La privatisation des états* (Paris: Karthala, 1999).

22 J. Champaud, "Cameroun: au Bord de l'Affrontement," *Politique africaine* 44, 1991, pp. 115–120; K. Noble, "Strike Aims to Bleed Cameroon's Economy to Force President Biya's Fall," *The New York Times*, August 5, 1991; *Africa Confidential*, "Cameroon: Crisis or Compromise?" October 25, 1991; *Africa Confidential*, "Cameroon: Biya Besieged," July 26, 1991; C. Monga, "Les dernières cartes de Paul Biya," *Jeune Afrique Économique* 165, March 1993, pp. 116–121; A. Kom, "Trahison d'une intelligentsia," *Jeune Afrique Économique* 165, March 1993, pp. 122–123.

23 *Opération Villes Mortes* certainly crippled the Cameroonian economy, and thus to a large extent achieved its goal of depriving the regime of its fiscal base. It is estimated that it resulted in a 40 percent decrease in economic activity, which represented 4 billion CFA per day for the state, including collection of taxes and fees, or the previous year's revenues. See M. Diallo, "Qui gouverne le Cameroun?," *Jeune Afrique* 1595, July 24–30, 1991, p. 18; N. van de Walle, "The politics of non-reform in Cameroon," in Callaghy and Ravenhill, eds., *Hemmed In*, p. 381.

24 Prefect, Departement du Diamare, Cameroon, April 15, 1993.

25 April 21, 1993, Maroua, Cameroon.

26 April 21, 1993, Maroua, Cameroon.

27 Janet Roitman, "Unsanctioned Wealth, or the Productivity of Debt in Northern Cameroon," *Public Culture* 15(2), 2003, pp. 211–237; Janet Roitman, "Productivity in the Margins"; Janet Roitman, *Fiscal Disobedience: An Anthropology of Economic Regulation in Central Africa* (Princeton, NJ: Princeton University Press, forthcoming, October 2004).

28 As is implied by James Ferguson's recent and otherwise interesting reading of the situation in the Zambian copperbelt: see J. Ferguson, *Expectations of Modernity* (Berkeley: University of California Press, 1999).

29 Janet Roitman, "New Sovereigns? Regulatory Authority in the Chad Basin", in *Intervention and Transnationalism in Africa: Global–Local Networks of Power*, T. Callaghy, R. Kassimir, and R. Latham, eds. (Cambridge: Cambridge University Press, 2001), pp. 240–266; Janet Roitman, "Productivity in the Margins."

30 Cf., Hibou, *La privatisation des états*.

31 Cf., K. Bennafla, "Mbaiboum: un marché au carrefour de frontières multiples," *Autrepart* 6, 1998, pp. 53–72; E. Grégoire, "Sahara nigérien: terre d'échanges," *Autrepart*, 6 (1998), pp. 91–104.

32 See Roitman, *Incivisme Fiscale*, Ch. 5, on how this situation is reminiscent of practice during the 19th-century *jihad*, when spoils were articulated from within the discourse on legitimate property and wealth.

33 Referring to the 1994 devaluation of the franc CFA, which rendered imports – such as spare parts for the merchants' fleets of trucks – considerably more expensive and led to a decrease in local purchasing power.

34 This question, like those that follow regarding corruption, was intended to provoke conversation and is in keeping with manners of exchange practiced in the region. Such questions are not accusations.

35 November 14, 2001, Meiganga, Cameroon.

36 Michel Foucault, *The History of Sexuality*, Vol. I: *An Introduction* (New York: Vintage - Books, 1990 [1978]); Michel Foucault, "The ethic of the care of the self as a practice of freedom," in *Technologies of the Self: A Seminar with Michel Foucault*, J. Bernauer and D. Rasmussen, eds. (London, Tavistock, 1988), pp. 145–162.

37 Foucault, *The History of Sexuality*, p. 95.

38 November 15, 2001, Meiganga, Cameroon.

39 James Baker, the former U.S. Secretary of State, was behind the initiative that established a list of middle-income countries, which were slated as of high strategic interest due to their very high levels of debt outstanding with commercial banks. In 1989, Nicholas Brady put forth an official program for "voluntary debt reduction," which would absorb these debts through market mechanisms.

40 O. Vallée, "La dette privée est-elle publique? Traites, traitement, traite: modes de la dette africaine," *Politique africaine* 73, March 1999, pp. 50–67.

41 Idem.

42 Roitman, "Unsanctioned Wealth."

43 *Jeune Afrique economie* 337, January 14 – February 17, 2002.

44 December 2001, Ngaoundéré, Cameroon.

45 December 2001, Ngaoundéré, Cameroon.

46 November 23, 2001, Touboro, Cameroon.

47 December 2001, Kousseri, Cameroon.

48 November 2001, Mbang Mboum, Cameroon.

49 See Michel Foucault, "The Subject and Power," in *Michel Foucault: Beyond Structuralism and Hermeneutics*, H. Dreyfus and P. Rabinow, eds. (Brighton: Harvester, 1982), p. 224; Michel Foucault, "The Ethic of the Care of the Self as a Practice of Freedom," in Bernauer and Rasmussen, eds., *Technologies of the Self*, pp. 145–162; Michel Foucault, "Questions of Method," in *The Foucault Effect: Studies in Governmentality*, G. Burchell, G. Gordon, and P. Miller, eds. (London, Harvester Wheatsheaf, 1991), pp. 73–86.

50 For critique of the concept of the moral economy, see Janet Roitman, "Économie morale, subjectivité et politique," *Critique internationale*, 6, Winter 2000, pp. 48–56.

51 Foucault, *The History of Sexuality*, esp. pp. 93–97; Michel Foucault, "Two Lectures," in *Power/Knowledge: Selected Interviews and Other Writings 1972–1977*, C. Gordon, ed. (New York, Routledge, 1981), pp. 82–102.

CITIZENSHIP AND ETHICS

23

BIOLOGICAL CITIZENSHIP

NIKOLAS ROSE AND CARLOS NOVAS

Introduction

A new kind of citizenship is taking shape in the age of biomedicine, biotechnology, and genomics. We term this "biological citizenship."[1] Since Marshall's classic essay, it is conventional to think of a kind of evolution of citizenship since the 18th century in Europe, North America, and Australia: the civil rights granted in the 18th century necessitated the extension of political citizenship in the 19th century and of social citizenship in the 20th century.[2,3] This perspective is useful, to the extent that it breaks with political–philosophical considerations of citizenship and locates citizenship within the political history of "citizenship projects." By citizenship projects, we mean the ways in which authorities thought about (some) individuals as potential citizens, and the ways in which they tried to act upon them. Examples include: defining those who were entitled to participate in the political affairs of a city or region; imposing a single legal system across a national territory; obliging citizens to speak a single national language; establishing a national system of universal compulsory education; designing and planning buildings and public spaces in the hope that they would encourage certain ways of thinking, feeling, or acting; and developing social insurance systems to bind national subjects together in the sharing of risks. Such citizenship projects were central both to the idea of the national state, and to the practical techniques of the formation of such states. Citizenship was fundamentally national.

Many events and forces are placing such a national form of citizenship in question. The nation can no longer be seen as, really or ideally, a cultural or religious unity, with a single bounded national economy; and economic and political migration challenge the capacity of states to delimit citizens in terms of place of birth or lineage or race. Discussions of these challenges have rarely touched on issues of biology, bioscience, or biomedicine. But we want to argue that developments in these areas also challenge existing conceptions of national citizenship and that they intersect with all these other challenges in significant ways. And we make a more general claim: specific biological presuppositions, explicitly or implicitly, have underlain many citizenship projects, shaped conceptions of what it means to be a citizen, and underpinned distinctions between actual, potential, troublesome, and impossible citizens.

Of course, there have been many discussions of the importance of biological beliefs for the politics and history of the 19th and 20th centuries. But the biologization of politics has rarely been explored from the perspective of citizenship. Yet histories of the idea of race, degeneracy, and eugenics, and those of demography and the census, show how many citizenship projects were framed in biological terms; in terms of race, blood lines, stock, intelligence, and so forth. Thus we use the term "biological citizenship" descriptively, to encompass all those citizenship projects that have linked their conceptions of citizens to beliefs about the biological existence of human beings, as individuals, as families and lineages, as communities, as population and races, and as a species. And like other dimensions of citizenship, biological citizenship is undergoing transformation and re-territorializing itself along national, local, and transnational dimensions.

Inevitably, in discussing these issues, the specter of racialized national politics, eugenics, and racial hygiene is summoned from its sleep. Such biological understanding of human beings clearly related to notions of citizenship and projects of citizen-building both at the level of the individual and of the nation-state. Nonetheless, contemporary biological citizenship does not, in the main, take this racialized and nationalized form. Of course, these forms of biological citizenship that we discuss here are differentially territorialized – as analyses of bio-prospecting and bio-piracy show, not all have equal citizenship in this new biological age. Nonetheless, the links of biology and human worth and human defects today differ significantly from those of the eugenic age. Different ideas about the role of biology in human worth are entailed in practices of selective abortion, pre-implantation genetic diagnosis, and embryo selection. Different ideas about the biological responsibilities of the citizen are embodied in contemporary norms of health and practices of health education. Different citizenship practices can be seen in the increasing importance of corporeality to practices of identity, and in new technologies that intervene upon the body at levels ranging from the superficial (cosmetic surgery) to the molecular (gene therapy).[4] A different sense of the importance of the "bare life" of human beings as the basis of citizenship claims and protections is bound up in contemporary transnational practices of human rights.[5] And while it is true that many states are once more regarding the specific hereditary stock of their population as a resource to be managed, these endeavors are not driven by a search for racial purity. Instead, they are grounded in the hope that certain specific characteristics of the genes of groups of their citizens may potentially provide a valuable resource for the generation of intellectual property rights, for biotechnological innovation and the creation of what we will term, following Catherine Waldby, *biovalue*.[6]

However, an analysis of biological citizenship cannot merely focus upon strategies for "making up citizens" that are imposed from above. The languages and aspirations of citizenship have shaped the ways in which individuals understand themselves and relate to themselves and to others. Projects of biological citizenship in the 19th and 20th centuries produced citizens who understood their nationality, allegiances, and distinctions, at least in part, in biological terms. They linked themselves to their fellow citizens and distinguished themselves from others, noncitizens, partly in biological terms. These biological senses of identification and affiliation made certain kinds of ethical demands possible: demands on oneself; on ones' kin, community, and society; on those who exercised authority. It is this sense of biological citizenship that is most clearly developed by Adriana Petryna in her study of post-Chernobyl Ukraine.[7] The government of the newly independent Ukraine based its claims to a right to govern on the democratically expressed will of its citizens. And those citizens who have, or who claim to have, been exposed to the radiation effects of the nuclear explosion at the Chernobyl reactor believed that they had rights to health services and social support which they could claim from that government in the name of their damaged biological bodies. In this context, she argues, "the very idea of citizenship is now charged with the superadded burden of survival ... a large and largely impoverished segment of the population has learned to negotiate the terms of its economic and social inclusion using the very constituent matter of life."[8] Biological citizenship can thus embody a demand for particular protections, for the enactment or cessation or particular policies or actions, or, as in this case, access to special resources – here, "to a form of social welfare based on medical, scientific, and legal criteria that both acknowledge biological injury and compensate for it."[9] Life acquires a new potential value, to be negotiated in a whole range of practices of regulation and compensation. This is not a unique situation. We can see something similar in campaigns for redress for the victims of Bhopal, and in numerous American examples of fights for compensation for biomedical damage, portrayed in semi-fictionalized accounts in films such as *Erin Brockovich* and *A Civil Action*. Of course, there are very different political, legal, and ethical framings in these different locales. But in each case, we can see that claims on political and non-political authorities are being made in terms of the vital damage and suffering of individuals or groups and their "vital" rights as citizens.

Biological citizenship is both individualizing and collectivizing. It is individualized to the extent that individuals shape their relations with themselves in terms of knowledge of their somatic individuality. Biological images, explanations, values, and judgments thus get entangled with a more general contemporary "regime of the self" as a prudent yet enterprising individual, actively shaping his or her life course through acts of choice.[10] The responsibility for the self now implicates both "corporeal" and "genetic" responsibility: one has long been responsible for the health and illness of the body, but now one must also know and manage the implications of one's own genome. The responsibility for the self to manage its present in the light of knowledge of its own future can be termed "genetic prudence."[11] Such a prudential norm introduces new distinctions between good and bad subjects of ethical choice and biological susceptibility. This contemporary biological citizenship operates within what we term a "political economy of hope." Biology is no longer blind destiny, or even a foreseen but implacable fate. It is knowable, mutable, improvable, eminently manipulable. Of course, the other side of hope is undoubtedly anxiety, fear, and even dread at what one's biological future, or that of those one cares for, might hold. But whilst this may engender despair or fortitude, it frequently also generates a moral economy of hope, in which ignorance, resignation, and hopelessness in the face of the future is deprecated. This is simultaneously an economy in the more traditional sense, for the hope for the innovation that will treat or cure stimulates the circuits of investment and the creation of biovalue.

Biological citizenship also has a collectivizing moment. As Paul Rabinow has shown, new forms of "biosociality" and new ethical technologies are being assembled around the proliferating categories of corporeal vulnerability, somatic suffering, and genetic risk and susceptibility.[12] Biosocial groupings – collectivities formed around a biological conception of a shared identity – have a long history, and medical activism by those who refuse the status of mere "patients" long predates recent developments in biomedicine and genomics. Many of these earlier activist groupings were fiercely opposed to the powers and claims of medical expertise. Some remain implacably anti-medical; others operate in a manner which, whilst not explicitly "opposed" to established medical knowledge, prefers to remain "complementary" to it. Nonetheless, we suggest, collectivities organized around specific biomedical classifications are increasingly significant. The forms of citizenship entailed here often involve quite specialized scientific and medical knowledge of one's condition: we might term this "informational bio-citizenship." They involve the usual forms of activism such as campaigning for better treatment, ending stigma, gaining access to services, and the like: we might term this "rights bio-citizenship." But they also involve new ways of making citizenship by incorporation into communities linked electronically by e-mail lists and websites: we might term this "digital bio-citizenship."

Thus, as Heath, Rapp, and Taussig have pointed out,[13] citizenship in the contemporary age of biomedicine is manifested in a range of struggles over individual identities, forms of collectivization, demands for recognition, access to knowledge, and claims to expertise. It is creating new spaces of public dispute about the minutiae of bodily experiences and their ethical implications – a politics of embodied or somatic individuals. It is generating new objects of contestation, not least those concerning the respective powers and responsibilities of public bodies, private corporations, health providers and insurers, and individuals themselves. It is creating novel forums for political debate, new questions for democracy, and new styles of activism. In each case, the forms that these are taking are shaped by many factors that vary in different national contexts, notably their differing biopolitical histories and modes of government, their traditions of activism, and their presuppositions about persons and their rights and obligations. In the remainder of this chapter, we explore these issues in relation to some empirical examples from a number of different configurations: bipolar affective disorder, Huntington's disease, and PXE. Our aim is largely descriptive – to begin to map the new territory of biological citizenship and to develop some conceptual tools for its analysis.

Making up the Nation

Paul Gilroy has suggested that gene-oriented constructions of "race" are very different from "the older versions of race-thinking that were produced in the eighteenth and nineteenth century."[14] As the relations between human beings and nature are transformed by genomics, the meaning of racial difference is changed and this provides the possibility of challenging the tainted logic of raciology. His assessment may be optimistic, but it points to the way in which certain presuppositions about biology bound together thinking about nation, people, race, population, and territory from the 18th century onward. To think of individual and collective subjects of European nations was to think in terms of blood, stock, physiognomy, and inbuilt moral capacities. Those over whom Europeans would exercise colonial dominion were also thought of in these terms. In short, citizenship was grounded on what, from the early 19th century onward, would be termed "biology." Distinctions within nations as to those more or less worthy of, or capable of, citizenship, and distinctions between peoples, as to their respective capacities to rule and be ruled, were built on an explicit or implicit biological taxonomy inscribed in the soma of both individual and collective and passed down through a lineage.

This is not the place to review the various ways in which people, race, nation, history, and spirit were linked in the blood, divided and placed into hierarchies and patterns of descent. These can be traced from the philosophers of 18th-century liberalism, such as Locke and Mill, through 18th- and 19th-century raciology, into the political debates about racial deterioration and degeneracy in the second half of the 19th century, and concerns about the consequences of the size and fitness of the population for the fate of nation-states in imperial rivalry. Ideas of character and constitution, of blood, race, and nation, remained inextricably intertwined in the eugenic arguments of the first half of the 20th century, which shaped the political imagination of the nation-states of North America, the Nordic countries, Australasia, South America, and elsewhere. Such ideas were translated into many different strategies to preserve the biological make-up of the populations of states. Some focused on outside threats, such as those posed by immigration from lower races. Others focused on threats from within, such as the dangers posed by the breeding of defective, insane, sick, or criminal individuals and their kin. Conceptions of the biological basis of national identity and national unity underlay many legal definitions of nationhood and citizenship in terms of descent. In Germany the citizenship law of 1913, which was framed in these terms and defined citizenship in terms of the line of descent, survived the Nazi experience and remained in force until 1999.[15] In the 1920s, Chinese citizenship was built on a myth of a single lineage of blood of the yellow race.[16] In the same period in Mexico, some attempted to argue that it was the fusion of blood that gave the Mexican race its defining characteristics.[17] The nation was not only a political entity; it was a biological one. It could be strengthened only by attention to the individual and collective biological bodies of those who constituted it.

Within these 20th-century projects of biological citizenship, there were clear differences between those who felt that their objectives could only be reached by strategies involving compulsion and those who opposed compulsion in the name of liberty. But this distinction did not map onto a simple division between strategies of reproductive control and strategies of health education and public health. An emphasis on the need to educate individuals so that they will take personal responsibility for the genetic implications of their reproductive decisions is not new: the genetic education of the citizen was a constant theme in the eugenic period. Early eugenicists developed all sorts of events to encourage individuals and families to reflect on themselves, their marriage partners, and their past and future lineage in eugenic terms, with a view to enhancing healthy procreation. Through education, the genetic citizen was to be enabled to take responsibility for his or her own heredity. We shall return to this question presently.

What, then, of the present? It would be too simple to believe that such concerns with the biological and/or genetic make-up of the population and the individual citizen have ceased to be matters of national political concern. The very existence of state-supported public health measures indicates that the vital biological existence of the citizen remains an issue within the political rationalities of the present. The very existence of certain practices that have now become routine in medical care – ultrasound, amniocentesis, chorionic villus sampling, and more – shows that judgments of value concerning certain features of the bodies and capacities of citizens have become inescapable – even if it is the individual citizen and his or her family who must carry the responsibility for the choice now rendered calculable for them. And successive state-funded health promotion programs show how the biological education of the citizen remains a national priority, although it is now supplemented by a host of other forces that seek to shape the reflexive gaze though which the citizen views his or her past, present, and future biological corporeality.

And, from another perspective, national genetic peculiarities became a key resource for genetics over this period. This involved the search for lineages with a high incidence of particular diseases and the belief that the study of such pedigrees would provide the key to unraveling the genetics of disease. We can take Finland as our initial example.[18] It has long been recognized by geneticists that sectors of the Finnish population are attractive for gene hunting, because of a combination of low geographic mobility, relatively high rates of "inbreeding," good genealogical and health records, and high rates of prevalence of certain diseases. For example, many claims about the discovery of genes linked with schizophrenia, manic depression, alcoholism, and other disorders were based on genetic research in Finland. In the age of genomics, such conditions, which were once seen as burdens on the national population and its health service, have become potentially valuable resources: hence, they are included in the Finnish proclamation of biotechnology as a national impera-tive. As we discuss in detail later, the national population has become a resource not only for understanding particular pathologies, but also for profitable biomedical exploitation.

Making Biological Citizens: From Public Value to *Biovalue*

Over the past decade, campaigns of popular education have been undertaken in the belief that it is crucial to increase the ability of citizens to understand the complex ethical and democratic dilemmas brought about by scientific and technological progress. Increasing the "public understanding of science" is seen as a means of regaining the confidence and trust of lay members of the public in the regulatory mechanisms that govern science, and in biomedical expertise more generally. It is additionally seen as a mechanism for redressing a kind of "democratic deficit" that is said to exist when citizens do not actively participate in shaping scientific and technological futures. Such arguments concerning the need to enhance the scientific – in this case, the biological – understanding of citizens have a long history. We have already commented on the attempts by eugenicists and similarly minded educators in the 1920s and 1930s to inculcate a particular version of scientific literacy – in this case, the capacity to reflect in a eugenically informed manner on reproductive and marital choices. These attempts were one of a number of ways in which the capacities of the individual for citizenship have been linked to his or her understanding of "advances in science."[19]

We can view such endeavors to educate the public about science and technology as aspects of strategies for "making up" the biological citizen.[20] By "making up citizens," we mean, in part, the reshaping of the way in which persons are understood by authorities – be they political authorities, medical personnel, legal and penal professionals, potential employers, or insurance companies – in terms of categories such as the chronically sick, the disabled, the blind, the deaf, the child abuser, or the psychopath. These categories organize the diagnostic, forensic, and interpretive gaze of different groups of professionals and experts. Classification of this sort is both "dividing" and "unifying." It delimits the boundaries of those who get treated in a certain way – in punishment, therapy, employment, security, benefit, or reward. And it unifies those within the category, overriding their specific differences. Here, we can point to the way in which new biological and biomedical languages are beginning to "make up citizens" in new ways in the deliberations, calculations, and strategies of experts and authorities: for example, the emergence of categories such as the child with attention deficit hyperactivity disorder, the woman with pre-menstrual dysphoric disorder, or the person who is pre-symptomatically ill because of genetic susceptibilities.

By making up biological citizens, we also mean the creation of persons with a certain kind of relation to themselves. Such citizens use biologically colored languages to describe aspects of themselves or their identities, and to articulate their feelings of unhappiness, ailments, or predicaments. For example, they describe themselves as having high levels of blood cholesterol, as being vulnerable to stress, as being immuno-compromised, or as having an hereditary predisposition to breast cancer or schizophrenia. Such persons use those languages, and the types of calculation to which they are attached, to make judgments as to how they could or should act, the kinds of things they fear, and the kind of lives for which they can hope. In part, of course, the languages that shape citizens' self-understandings and self-techniques are disseminated through authoritative channels – health education, medical advice, books written by doctors about particular conditions, and documentaries on television that chart individuals coping with particular conditions. Whatever may be said about their general level of scientific literacy, in these areas, individuals are actively engaging with biological explanations and are forming novel relations with figures of scientific or medical authority in the process of caring for, and about, health. But the contemporary biological citizen sits at the intersection between these more or less authoritative endeavors and a variety of other flows of information and forms of intervention. Or perhaps, "sits" is the wrong term – for even while sitting, an active scientific citizenship is increasingly enacted, in which individuals themselves are taking a dynamic role in enhancing their own scientific – especially biomedical – literacy. They are doing this using a variety of media, but most notably through linking up with support groups – often now through the use of the Internet. The active search for scientific knowledge is particularly marked in the field with which we are concerned – that of health and illness, of medicine, genetics, and pharmacology – in what Rabinow has termed "the third culture,"[21] where an individual's own vitality is at stake, or that of those for whom they care. In engaging with such issues, the language with which citizens are coming to understand and describe themselves is increasingly biological.

For those suffering directly or indirectly from illness or disability, reading and immersing oneself in the scientific literature of the illness that oneself or a loved one suffers from can be a key technique. This knowledge can be used to gain a better understanding of the disease process, to provide better levels of care to those suffering from an illness, and to discuss and negotiate with the doctor a range of therapeutic possibilities. Over the past decade, the Internet has come to provide a powerful new way in which those who have access to it, and who are curious about their health or illness, can engage in this process of biomedical self-shaping. But a key feature of the Internet is that it does not only give access to material disseminated by professionals; it also links an individual to self-narratives written by patients or carers. These accounts usually offer a different narrative of life with an illness, setting out practical ways of managing a body that is ill, the effect and harms of particular therapeutic regimes, ways of negotiating access to the health care system, and so forth. That is to say, these narratives provide techniques for the leading of a life in the face of illness. They have a further distinctive feature, which relates to truth itself. Strategies for making up biological citizens "from above" tend to represent the science itself as unproblematic: they problematize the ways in which citizens misunderstand it. But these vectors "from below" pluralize biological and biomedical truth, introduce doubt and controversy, and relocate science in the fields of experience, politics, and capitalism.[22]

In response to the perceived power of such problematizations from below, those whose investment in biomedicine is measured in terms of capital returns and shareholder value – the biotech, biomedicine, and pharmaceutical companies – now actively engage in these processes of self-education of active biological citizens. They set up and sponsor many of the consumer support groups that have sprung up around disorders from attention deficit hyperactivity disorder (ADHD) to epidermolysis bullosa (EB). In doing so, they seek to represent their activities and their products as beneficial, to counter the claims of the critics, and to educate actual or potential consumers of their products. In the United States, recent legal changes allow pharmaceutical companies to engage in "direct to consumer advertising," and television advertisements for the benefits of different brands of psychiatric drug are now widespread. But, across all jurisdictions, such companies are now using the Internet for this purpose. It is thus worth considering one example from this domain in some detail.

The Prozac website maintained by Eli Lilly (http://www.prozac.com) is emblematic of techniques to promote a particular version of scientific or biological literacy. The home page of this site is titled "Your Guide to Evaluating and Recovering from Depression." Prozac.com thus represents itself as a resource center where individuals can learn more about depression, its treatments, and ways to securing a recovery. It claims – characteristic of all such "direct to consumer" practices – that the information and knowledge provided on this website is not intended to supplant the authority of the health professional, but rather to encourage the person suffering from depression to form an "active" alliance with the medic in the realization of a program of care. But, of course, this activity is to take a specific, brand-related, form: a form supported through the provision of information on how Prozac can aid in recovery from depression.

In part, this is a matter of forming the problem in a particular manner. The Prozac.com website uses a biological explanation of depression, couched in terms of the action of neurotransmitters. Text and animated images are used to provide a way for individuals to understand their depression at a molecular level, in terms of chemical imbalances and the action of neurotransmitters, and to imagine the ways in which Prozac can directly target and correct these molecular imbalances. It is, it seems, important to learn about the action of Prozac. This is not because taking the drug is all that is required of the individual. On the contrary, it is because the individual should know "what to expect while you work toward your recovery."[23] The process of recovering from depression does not simply require compliance with a drug regime: "You can and should be an active participant in your recovery from depression."[24] This process of recovery enlists a whole range of techniques of the self: practicing self-discovery, liking yourself, being kind to oneself, reducing stress, engaging in physical exercise, eating well, writing lists and keeping diaries, building self-esteem, joining a support group, or reading the Prozac.com newsletter. This website is thus an element in what we term "the political economy of hope" (of which more later), in that it sutures together, first, hopeful beliefs that one can recover from depression if one knows how to recognize and deal with it and, second, the marketing of the drug Prozac itself.

The role of biomedical authority here is not to encourage the passive and compliant patienthood of a previous form of medical citizenship. Citizenship, here as elsewhere, is to be active. Thus the actual or potential patient must try to understand his or her depression, to work with his or her doctor to obtain the best program of medical care, to engage in self-techniques to speed the process of recovery – and, of course, to ask his or her doctor to prescribe Prozac by name. Indeed, as the daily form of Prozac is now out of patent, the website seeks to maintain market share. On every single web page, a banner advertises a free trial of Prozac® Weekly™ – which is in patent – and tells patients that they can ask their doctor about this new formulation. Another page suggests that their may be differences between brand-name Prozac and its generic equivalent, fluoxetine hydrochloride, explaining to potential customers that there is no such thing as "generic Prozac" – for example, they come in different packaging – and that if they feel uncomfortable about changing to a generic, they should ask their doctor to prescribe brand-name Prozac.[25] What kind of scientific literacy is being promoted here? What kinds of active biological citizens are being shaped, and to what ends? This is the citizenship of brand culture, where trust in brands appears capable of supplanting trust in neutral scientific expertise. The weaving together of Eli Lilly's commitment to education and brand marketing gives us the title of this section of our paper – from public value to biovalue – for this is just one example of the way in which biovalue is supplanting public value in the biological education of citizens-consumers.

Biosociality: Active Biological Citizens

Perhaps we have given the impression that biological citizens are individualized, required to understand their nature and cope with their fate alone or with their own family, accompanied only by the ministrations and advice of experts, the solitary reading of informative material, or seated alone at their computer searching the Web. Undoubtedly such isolation is the condition of many. But it is not the destiny of the biological citizen to be an isolated atom, at least in circumstances where the forms of life, ethical assumptions, types of politics, and communication technology make new forms of collectivism possible. Perhaps the templates for these new forms of biological and biomedical activism were the campaigning groups that arose around AIDS, especially in the English-speaking world. AIDS activists organized themselves into groups, and through a variety of means constituted those who were actual or potential sufferers from the condition as "communities" for which they would speak and to which they were responsible. These groups had a number of functions: to spread information about the condition; to campaign for rights and combat stigma; to support those affected by the illness; to develop a set of techniques for the everyday management of the condition; to seek alternative forms of treatment; and to demand their own say in the development and deployment of medical expertise.

The case of HIV and AIDS activism is exemplary for another reason: whilst initially relations between the activists and the conventional biomedical community were antagonistic, gradually an alliance developed. For the community, and the identifications it fostered, came to provide key elements for the government of HIV and AIDS. That is to say, it was through their identification as members of this community, that those in "high-risk groups" were recruited to their responsibilities as biological citizens, and health educators came to realize that it was only by means of the translation mechanism provided by AIDS activists that they would be able to gain the allegiance of the active gay men who were their primary target. In allying itself with the health establishment in promoting the message of safe(r) sex, AIDS activists, in return, would have their say in the organization and deployment of social resources, and indeed gain the resources necessary for their activities. This was not a matter of co-option, although some saw it as such, but of alliances and translations. And "governing through community" produced its own problems: most notably, that of shaping the conduct of a younger generation of gay men who did not identify themselves in the same terms as the previous generation, and that of governing the conduct of "men who had sex with men" but who did not identify themselves as part of any gay community.

Since the 1980s, biosocial communities following a roughly similar form have proliferated, and, since the advent of the World Wide Web, they have found the Internet a congenial host territory. Take, for example, the issue of manic depression. Until quite recently, in the U.K. at least, in addition to physicians and medics, those with such a diagnosis or their families (if they were not amongst the very few actively allied to the anti-psychiatry movement) could access only one other organized source of information and support: the National Association for Mental Health (MIND). Things began to change in the 1980s. In 1983, the Manic Depression Fellowship (MDF) was founded, which described itself as a "user-led" organization whose aims are to "enable people affected by manic depression (bipolar) to take control of their lives" through the services that this organization offers.[26] These services include MDF self-help groups, information and publications, employment advice, the MDF Self Management Training Programme, a 24-hour Legal Advice Line for employment, legal, benefits, and debt issues, and a travel insurance scheme. MDF also seeks to combat the stigma and prejudice experienced by those affected by manic depression, raise awareness of the disease, and develop partnerships with other organizations concerned with mental health.[27]

Over the 1980s, the MDF was joined by a host of other user- and survivor-led organizations, some local and some national. And 20 years later, these sources of biosociality have proliferated, especially on the World Wide Web. It is true that those based in the U.K. are somewhat few and far between. But outside the U.K. the resources are manifold. For example, Pendulum Resources is a website that presents itself as a "Bipolar Disorders Portal," a gateway to comprehensive quasi-medical and other information. It urges people with bipolar disorder to participate in the

NIMH-funded Bipolar Genome Study at the Washington University School of Medicine, and in other similar projects, in the hope that "this kind of study will enable medical researchers to find safer, more effective treatments for Mental Illness and brain disorders."[28] Pendulum also provides links to at least 24 homepages of people diagnosed with, or living with, bipolar disorder, who describe, in very different ways, their modes of living with the condition. These include, for example, "A Better Place to Be," which contains – amongst other things – a diary of the website author's "personal struggle with bipolar disorder," a journal, and a link that enables readers to ask questions.[29]

These new forms of citizenship are not always premised on genetics. Many of these biosocial communities do indeed refer to genetics, but its significance varies. Whilst in single-gene or single-substitution disorders such as Huntington's, PXE, or Canavan's disease, genetics clearly plays an organizing role, in the biosociality forming around other conditions, genetics is not dominant. In the case of bipolar disorder, for example, visitors to the Pendulum website are urged, as we have mentioned, to consider participating in genomic research. In the case of "A Better Place To Be," on the page entitled "Sources of My Depression" the author writes, under the heading "serious reasons": "a genetic heritage that comes from being half Finnish" and "other genes in my DNA that tend toward improper chemical balance," but also cites her "need for more vocational satisfaction and personal fulfilment," her "lack of recovery from a dysfunctional childhood," and what she terms "whiney reasons," such as "nobody loves me," "everyone hates me," "tendency at times to identify any negative feeling as depression," and "lack of disposable income to purchase all the fun and necessary things I must have!"[30,31] What can be learned of biosociality from such sites?

Rayna Rapp, writing about women and men facing complex reproductive decisions brought about by the technology of amniocentesis, designates them as "moral pioneers."[32] Her argument – which would include AIDS activists[33] – captures something crucial. These women and men are pioneers because, in their relation with their bodies, with their choices, with experts, with others in analogous situations, and with their destiny, they must shape new ways of understanding, judging, and acting on themselves, and must also engage in a kind of re-imagining of those to whom they owe responsibilities – their progeny, their kin, their medical helpers, their co-citizens, their community, their society. We think, in a comparable way, that the new biosocial communities forming on the Web and outside it are moral pioneers – we would prefer to say "ethical pioneers" – of a new kind of active biomedical citizenship. They are pioneering a new informed ethics of the self – a set of techniques for managing everyday life in relation to a condition, and in relation to expert knowledge. Whilst some might deride these techniques of the biomedical self as a kind of narcissistic self-absorption, we think that they show an admirable ethical seriousness. Like those techniques that Foucault found amongst the Greeks,[34] they identify an aspect of the person to be worked upon, they problematize that field or territory in certain ways, they elaborate a set of techniques for managing it, and they set out certain objectives or forms of life to be aimed for.

Of course, in a certain political, cultural, and moral milieu, this idea of activism in relation to one's biomedical condition becomes a norm. Activism and responsibility have now become not only desirable but virtually obligatory – part of the obligation of the active biological citizen, to live his or her life though acts of calculation and choice. Such a citizen is obliged to inform him- or herself not only about current illness, but also about susceptibilities and predispositions. Once so informed, such an active biological citizen is obliged to take appropriate steps, such as adjusting diet, lifestyle, and habits in the name of the minimization of illness and the maximization of health. And he or she is obliged to conduct life responsibly in relation to others, to modulate decisions about jobs, marriage, and reproduction in the light of knowledge of his or her present and future biomedical make-up. The enactment of such responsible behaviors has become routine and expected, built in to public health measures, producing new types of problematic persons – those who refuse to identify themselves with this responsible community of biological citizens.[35]

Of course, these obligations, and the forms of biosociality with which they are linked, are specific to certain times and spaces. Despite the much-vaunted global span of the Internet, Manuel Castells has documented the national and regional variations in access to the Internet, which is dependent on the availability of telephone lines and other basic communication technology, as well as the penetration of the computer hardware and software necessary to access it.[36] Whilst young travelers of the world may be able to dial up their Internet connection from almost anywhere, the same is hardly true of those who are the prime potential subjects of biosociality. The kinds of biosociality we have documented in the United States, Europe, and Australia are not merely a product of the availability of certain technological means of communication, but of conceptions of citizenship and personhood. In particular, they connect up, in various ways, with the history of previous forms of activism in the feminist, gay, and AIDS movements, with the varieties of identity politics and the existence of a vociferous politics of rights and recompense. Hence the forms of biosociality that we have documented have no visible presence in whole geographic regions. AIDS biosociality in sub-Saharan Africa is very different from that in Paris, San Francisco, or London.[37] Biological citizenship in the Ukraine is not a matter of contesting the power of medical expertise, nor of sculpting an autonomous life in which collectively shaped self-understandings are a pathway to self-fulfillment: it takes the form of demanding redress from the state for certain ills, in the form of benefits, and activism is oriented toward demanding medical recognition for a condition and obtaining expert judgment as a credential to obtain state benefit.[38]

Political Economies of Hope: Science, Citizenship, and the Future

Citizenship has long associations with forms of local political activism: involvement with the local work of political parties, working in charitable organizations, and for causes such as reducing inner-city poverty or improving literacy, as well as small-scale activities such as charity bake sales, car washes, or raffles in order to support the local church, school, or community center. These aspects of citizenship are constantly reshaped in relation to new causes, and are often inventive in their styles of organizing and activism. We have already discussed the ways in which, since the 1980s, there has been an upsurge in citizen activism and political inventiveness around issues of health and illness. But while patients' organizations and support groups have been around for many years, today we see one notable innovation: the formation of direct alliances with scientists. Patients' organizations increasingly are not content with merely raising funds for biomedical research, but are seeking an active role in shaping the direction of science in the hope that they can speed the process by which cures or treatments are developed. Recent discoveries in the fields of genetics and the neurosciences have given rise to the hope that cures and treatments for many human diseases will be found in the near future. This has intensified a particular form of the capitalization of life and its investment with significant social meaning that we have termed "a political economy of hope."[39] This phrase tries to capture the forms of political activism and fundraising by citizens themselves, and the patients' groups that represent them, as they seek to act upon the world of science. It also tries to encapsulate the ways in which life itself is increasingly locked into an economy for the generation of wealth, the production of health and vitality, and the creation of social norms and values. Contemporary biological citizenship, that is to say, is a hopeful domain of activity, one that depends upon and intensifies the hope that the science of the present will bring about cures or treatments in the near future.

This economy of hope is not eschatological; rather, it comprises a domain of possibility, anticipation, and expectation that requires action and awareness of the present in order to realize a range of potential futures. Hope, as it is manifested in contemporary patients' organizations, is not passive: rather, it requires an active stance toward the future, and it involves a certain degree of commitment, in addition to a willingness to take chances in order to bring about the outcomes that are individually and collectively hoped for. Hope thus ties together personal biographies, the aspirations that patients share for better treatments or a cure, and the campaigns of patients' groups to achieve particular goals. Lastly, of course, this political economy of hope often takes place under conditions of suffering, privation, and inequity: it is contoured by the shortcomings of the social security system, the lost earnings and personal difficulties of having to care for a loved one, the lack of funding for scientific research on rare diseases, and the discrimination meted out by insurance companies and employers to those affected by a range of human illnesses.

Within this political economy of hope, a key role is often played by the personal advocacy efforts of creative individuals. Carmen Leal is one such person. Her ex-husband Dave suffers from Huntington's disease and she is still actively involved in his care. She also plays an important role in providing support to other carers through an online mailing list called Hunt-Dis.[40] Carmen Leal also advocates on behalf of those with the disease through such activities as editing a collection of stories and poems about persons' experiences with the disease,[41] using her speaking and singing skills to provide inspiration to others,[42] and maintaining a website alongside others called the Huntington's Disease Advocacy Center.[43] In an article published on this website, entitled "The Last Generation," Carmen refers to how "various members of the HD family point out the desire for this to be the last generation to have to worry about Huntington's disease. Thanks to researchers, there is now tremendous hope that this will definitely be the last generation."[44] However, she does not believe that it is the exclusive task of scientists to find a cure for the disease: she asks, "So what can you do in this fight?"[45] Her ten-point list of the ways in which individuals can personally contribute to this endeavor serves as a useful starting point to examine the forms of citizen activism and ethical self-formation that are constitutive of a political economy of hope.

Carmen's ten-point program includes the suggestion that persons educate themselves and read about various aspects of disease – the Internet providing a useful starting point for this education and literacy project. She urges individuals to express themselves with whatever talents they possess and to communicate with others, a process which may have therapeutic effects upon themselves and possibly help others in a similar situation. She highlights the importance of saving and giving: Carmen suggests that, "We all have spendable income that we can squirrel away and donate for the cure." In very practical terms, Carmen asks "Do you drink at least one soda from a machine every day? At seventy-five cents a can, that's $273.75 a year for the cure."[46] She suggests that visitors to the website participate in fundraisers, which not only contributes to the cure, but also helps to raise awareness of the disease. In this political economy of hope, citizenship is enacted through ethical self-formation, through personal economizing, and through activism. It thus tries to constitute a public arena in which responsibility for the cure is not merely attributed to scientists and doctors, but is embraced by those who have a stake in the suffering wrought by a disease such as Huntington's. Hence this exemplifies the formation of new public arenas in which the hopes and responsibilities of citizens become tied more closely to their biology.

We can explore these links between the hopes of citizens and their biology a little further by pursuing the example of the Huntington's Disease Advocacy Center website. The right-hand frame of this site contains links to a whole range of scientific articles written on Huntington's disease. Biological citizens, that is to say, are encouraged to read and to understand their condition in particular, and their biological existence in general, in the languages and rhetorics of contemporary bioscience and biomedicine. Citizenship takes on new biological colorations and hope becomes bound up with scientific truth. Marsha L. Miller, Ph.D., one of the contributing editors of the Huntington's Disease Advocacy Center, in an article entitled "Reasons for Hope," illustrates how the advances made in understanding Huntington's disease provide a rationale to look toward the future with expect-ation.[47] One reason why individuals affected by this disease should be hopeful can be found in the "exceptionally dedicated researchers" whose willingness to collabor-ate, share ideas, and collegiality has "undoubtedly shortened the time to the cure."[48] A second reason for hope is that researchers have discovered that a number of other neurodegenerative diseases are caused by excessive polyglutamine repeats, and that research in these other diseases may aid in the quest to find a cure for Huntington's.

A third reason consists of the creation of transgenic HD mice, which not only opens pathways to understanding the pathogenic process, but provides an experimental site in which to test potential therapies. The seed money provided by the Hereditary Disease Foundation and the Huntington's Disease Society of America constitutes a fourth reason for hope, as they play a "critical role in funding more speculative studies that might not get funded if the researchers had to compete for funds with researchers addressing a spectrum of diseases."[49] Thus we can see that bioscience is not only about the production of truth: it can become invested with hope and optimism by citizens who have an active stake in their health and that of others. In such a political economy of hope, this investment in bioscience by patients and patients' organizations is made through directing energy to political activism, donating parts of ones' earnings, gifting blood and tissues samples, providing care to others, and participating in clinical trials. These forms of political activism and biosociality, created through the experience and suffering wrought by a disease such as Huntington's, potentially at least extend beyond it to shape the field occupied by other diseases and those who suffer from them and research into them.

Biological citizenship in a political economy of hope requires active political engagement – it is a matter of *becoming* political. A certain amount of education and technical administration is required in order to make ones' individual and collective voice heard. The Political Activist section of the Huntington's Disease Advocacy Center website provides a range of tips on how to make biological citizenship effective. Using hypertext links, this section provides information on how to lobby elected officials, how to prepare for a meeting with a political representative, how to build coalitions, a list of who to contact, and samples of correspondence written to political officials. One topic of concern to members of this coalition and other patients' groups in 2001 was President George W. Bush's ban on stem cell cloning. Stem cell research is thought to provide a promising avenue for research on Huntington's disease, in addition to a number of other neurological disorders. As such, it provides opportunities for coalition building with other patients' organizations. The policy-related sections of patients' groups' websites show an active engagement with the new terms of inclusion of life itself into the body politic. Politics, as it is enacted by biological citizens in a political economy of hope, involves profoundly normative judgments about values and ethics concerning the uses and ends of life itself.

Producing *Biovalue*: Materializing Ethics, Health, and Wealth

As politics begins to take on more "vital" qualities, and as life itself becomes invested with both social meaning and capital, the vitality of each and every one of us becomes a potential source of *biovalue*. The bodies and vitality of individual and collective subjects have long had a value that is as much economic as political – or, rather, that is both economic and political. As for citizenship itself, however, from the 19th century onward, the preservation of this value and its enhancement became a matter of state: political authorities took on the obligation and responsibility for preserving, safeguarding, and enhancing the biological capital of their population. Along this dimension we can place a whole sequence of developments, from clean water and sewage to registration of births and deaths, child welfare and maternity services, medical inspection of schoolchildren, and indeed the development of state-organized national health services. Of course, private enterprises played a key role in producing the food, services, and pharmaceuticals that would simultaneously generate private profit and public good. A market economy of health came into being. Over the 20th century, this market was increasingly shaped by the activities of the "social" state – regulating the purity and hygiene of foodstuffs and the production and marketing of pharmaceuticals. But the regulated political economy of health – consisting of relations between the state apparatus, scientific and medical knowledge, the activities of commercial enterprises, and the health-related consumption of individuals – is being reshaped.

Recent advances in the fields of genetics and the neurosciences transform the potentialities embodied in life itself into a source of value creation. We have used the term biovalue for this – a term introduced by Catherine Waldby in her study of the Visible Human Project.[50] For Waldby, biovalue refers to the ways in which the bodies and tissues derived from the dead are redeployed for the preservation and enhancement of the health and vitality of the living. We suggest that one can analyze three dimensions of biovalue. Along the first, we see how life is productive of economic value. Along the second, we see that the manipulation of life generates a value accorded to the enhancement of health. Along the third, we see that the production of both wealth and health is bound up with ethical values.

Let us begin with the consideration of biovalue and the creation of wealth. Contemporary biomedicine, by rendering the depths of the body visible, intelligible, calculable, and capable of intervention at a molecular level, makes it amenable to the production of economic value. In many ways, what is being accomplished through the life sciences is a kind of "flattening" of the vital processes of the body. This not only enables these "surfaces" to become equivalent with one another at the most basic biological level, but also allows them to be enfolded within processes of capital or social accumulation. They contain the potential to transform the vitality of each and every one of us into a standing reserve for the creation of biovalue. One area in which this is occurring draws on the health technologies of social citizenship and redeploys them in the service of biovalue. Two examples of this logic can be found in Sweden and Iceland.

A recent article in *Science* begins with the memorable lines: "Sweden and some other Nordic countries are sitting on a genomic gold mine. Their long-standing public health care systems have been quietly stockpiling unique collections of human tissue, some going back for decades ... The samples were originally stored for possible therapeutic or diagnostic uses for the patients themselves, but researchers now realize that they could contain valuable information about inherited traits that may make people susceptible to a variety of diseases."[51] In many Nordic countries, census data, patient records, and tissues samples maintained in the process of providing health care in the past – through a heritage which runs from the pastoral government of the Church, through that of the strong state, to that of the social state – have been combined with large-scale genomic analysis in order to transform their citizenry into a resource for the production of wealth and health.[52] Thus, in Iceland, deCode genetics, who were given an exclusive license to create and operate such a database by an Act of the Icelandic parliament in 1998, declare in their mission statement that they are "Making the Map of Life ... a Blueprint for Health."[53] The Swedish firm UmanGenomics describes the "unique resources" that are available to it, including a "unique collection of blood samples and data in the Medical Biobank of Umeå," derived from records of health examinations of the local population amalgamated in an 1985 epidemiological study of the population combined with samples from state-supported medical examination and blood donation.[54,55] Despite the origins of these samples in public health, "UmanGenomics has the exclusive rights to commercialise information derived from these samples."[56] In these and other cases, then, the state plays an active role in transforming their citizens into a potential resource for the generation of wealth and health.

However, this transformation need not come from above – from the state and private enterprise. It can also come from below, from patients' organizations themselves. Take the example of a patients' organization called PXE International. This group was founded by Patrick and Sharon Terry in 1995, after their two children, Elizabeth and Ian, were diagnosed with pseudoxanthoma elasticum (PXE). They played an important role in forming networks of support amongst affected families, getting researchers interested in studying the disease, organizing conferences for scientists and patients, and lobbying the U.S. government for more funding to be directed toward the study of PXE, but also of skin diseases more generally. PXE International also established a blood and tissue registry in order to create a central repository, and to avoid the need for patients suffering from the disease to donate multiple samples. By maintaining this registry, PXE International is able to exert an influence on how this material is used and also a share of intellectual property rights that arise from it.

The productivity of this blood and tissue registry for the generation of biovalue was demonstrated in 1997, when the gene for PXE was discovered by researchers at the University of Hawaii. This discovery not only generated new insights into the pathology of the disease, but also the potential for property rights. The technology transfer unit at University of Hawaii was initially reluctant to yield patent rights to PXE International, but as they had previously negotiated the terms and conditions of access to the registry, in addition to Sharon Terry being named as a co-inventor, they were able to work out a process of sharing royalties with the university and a stake in deciding on licensing deals: from their perspective, this is a vehicle for ensuring that any resulting medical treatments be affordable and accessible.[57] As can be seen, the ownership of this gene by PXE International is not driven by a logic of commercialization, but rather by a desire to serve the values and interests of persons suffering from genetic diseases. Patrick Terry defends the potential of patient-controlled patents, asserting that, "We're not interested in lining our pockets. We just want a cure."[58]

A further dimension of contemporary biovalue can be seen in attempts to produce health and vitality from blood and tissues samples extracted from the living and the deceased. We will focus here on the ways in which knowledge of a single condition such as PXE can lead to the production of health and vitality not just for those affected by a particular disorder but, potentially, for all of us. For the discovery of the genetic basis of PXE not only offers hope that a treatment may some day be available to those who suffer from this illness, but also holds out a promise to others who suffer from apparently unrelated disorders. It is suggested that the opening of this particular genetic pathway on chromosome 16 may shed light on hypertension and cardiovascular research, since the mineralization of the mid-size arteries in PXE mimics the general ageing of the arteries.[59] PXE may also provide clues to macular degeneration; this affects the eyesight of many individuals suffering from this dis- order, but another 60 million Americans are thought to be at risk for this condition due to ordinary ageing.[60] As PXE International owns a share of the patent for the gene, they have the potential to gain significantly if a broader use for the gene is found. However, Sharon Terry says that PXE International will resist the temptation of patient profiteering: she claims in an article in *The American Lawyer*, "It's been suggested that we could make a killing because who cares if we're making the cost of cardiovascular treatment huge. We always say, we don't just represent people with PXE, we represent anybody, who has anything."[61]

The visualization of the body at the molecular level not only creates new possibil- ities for the generation of wealth, but also generates new ethical values that spill over into market interactions. The co-production of health and wealth is a profoundly ethical endeavor. The vital life processes of the citizenry are increasingly being penetrated by market relations and are becoming productive of wealth, and as such, the morality governing the very nature of economic exchange is being recon- figured. In an economy in which the vitality of biological processes can be bought and sold, ethics becomes both a marketable commodity and a service industry in its own right. UmanGenomics in Sweden, for example, trades on the fact that all the blood samples contained in its collection are drawn on the principle of informed consent.[62] It proclaims that "Correct ethical handling of human tissue and medical data is essential" and highlights how it has been "... internationally recognized for its ethical stance and procedures."[63] Ethics, in this instance, is not only a means of access to a valued resource, but is also a marketable asset that the firm can trade upon in establishing relationships with other enterprises.[64]

The growing importance of ethics in the commerce of extracting value from life can be seen in a recent start-up biotechnology firm in Redwood City, California, called Genomic Health. This firm is a good example of how ethics is becoming central to the production of health and wealth, as well as how citizens are being made up as consumers of the potential range of goods that genomics has to offer. Genomic Health's wish to be seen as committed to consumer concerns was manifested in the recruitment of Patrick Terry as the director of consumer advocacy, in addition to the firm's goal of trying to develop affordable genetic technologies. In bringing affordable genomics to the consumer, the chief executive officer, Dr. Randy Scott, insists that the future of the genomics industry rests on the "education, trust and support of the consumer" and that the uptake of these new products will only take place on "a foundation built on bioethics" – a foundation "critical to engaging consumers ... whether for research, for medical treatment, or for business."[65] Ethics, in this sense, is both a means of increasing the commercial value of products and a means of satisfying the values necessary to gain the trust and confidence of the citizen-consumer.

The enterprising forces behind Genomic Health compel us once again to consider the relation between public value and biovalue – for the values embedded in new genomic artifacts are polyvalent.[66] The multifaceted nature of biovalue complicates the entry of genomics products into the world of consumer goods and services. As the huge amount of literature generated in the name of the public understanding of science suggests, the process of bringing science to citizens and consumers requires that they be educated and are enabled to trust those who seek to reduce their suffering and enhance their quality of life. The chief executive officer at Genomic Health intermixes public and private value through his suggestion that it is critical "for industry to begin to create an open public dialogue with all stakeholders in order to facilitate understanding and to build trust."[67] This dialogue, he claims, will be both difficult and complex, but "Our quest to cure disease and prolong life will ultimately lead to much deeper questions – the very definition of what it means to be human." At stake here is not merely how one should act in an age in which our biology is open to remediation and modification through the forces of the market: the process of generating biovalue transforms our conception of human life itself.

Conclusion

We have argued that, while citizenship has long had a biological dimension, a new kind of biological citizenship is taking shape in the age of rapid biological discovery, genomics, biotechnological fabrication, and biomedicine. New subjectivities, new politics, and new ethics are shaping today's biological citizens. As aspects of life once placed on the side of fate become subjects of deliberation and decision, a new space of hope and fear is being established around genetic and somatic individuality. In Western nations – Europe, Australia and the United States – this is not taking the form of fatalism and passivity, and nor are we seeing a revival of genetic or biological determinism. Whilst in the residual social states in the post-Soviet era, biological citizenship may focus on the demand for financial support from state authorities, in the West novel practices of biological choice are taking place within a "regime of the self" as a prudent yet enterprising individual, actively shaping his or her life course through acts of choice. In this regime, a "political economy of hope" is taking shape – both a moral economy and an economy in the more traditional sense, of a space involving the creation and circulation of (bio)value. We have tried to describe some of the new forms of "biosociality" – patients' groups – and new ethical technologies that are being assembled around genetic risk and susceptibility. The new biological values that are taking shape are simultaneously ethical and commercial: life is productive of economic value, the manipulation of life embodies and incites the increasing value accorded to health; and new ethical dilemmas and possibilities arise in the links between virtue, vitality, and biovalue. Those who operate in these complex dilemmas, whether they be medics, patients, support groups, or entrepreneurs, are ethical pioneers. In tracing out, experimenting with, and contesting the new relations between truth, power, and commerce that traverse our living, suffering, mortal bodies and challenging their vital limits, they are redefining what it means to be human today.

Notes

1   We have discovered that others have used this term, although with different resonances. In particular, N.R. has learned a great deal from Adriana Petryna's *Biological Citizenship: Science and the Politics of Health after Chernobyl* (Princeton NJ: Princeton University Press, 2002), and thanks her for generously letting him see this in manuscript. We draw on her use of the term here, as will become clear, although we place her specific usages of it in a more general context. A web search picked up a paper by Chris Latiolais called "The Body Politic: Naturalizing Biological Citizenship and Philosophical Reservations," delivered at a University of Chicago Midwest Seminar, in March 1998, but the author tells us in an e-mail that "I don't take the term seriously at all. The term 'biological citizenship' is patently oxymoronic, the conflation of theoretical, natural-scientific categories with the quite different practical, moral-political categories of elective allegiance. The 'naturalizing' qualifier ambiguously hints at the requisite process that might span the gap between organism and political identity, and the thrust of my paper consists in (1) just mentioning that gender classification as a biological concept is extremely confused (particularly binary sex classifications) and, more importantly, (2) that such classifications are wholly irrelevant to legal standing."

The idea of genetic citizenship is more widely used – see A. Peterson and R. Bunton, *The New Genetics and the Public's Health* (London: Routledge, 2002) – and we have benefited in particular from the work of Deborah Heath, Rayna Rapp, and Karen-Sue Taussig on this theme and thank them for allowing us to see some of their work in draft: D. Heath, R. Rapp, and K.-S. Taussig, "Genetic Citizenship," in *Companion to the Handbook of Political Anthropology*, D. Nugent and J. Vincent, eds. (Oxford: Blackwell, forthcoming, 2004). However, from our perspective, genetic citizenship is only one possible articulation of a longer, and more diverse, array of ways in which citizenship has been linked to or articulated in biological terms. Similarly, others have sought to apply the distinction between passive and active citizenship to an analysis of various aspects of health provision: our analysis clearly shares something with the view that contemporary citizens are obliged to be "active," but we find the simple distinction of passive and active, and its mapping onto different stages of late capitalism, rather too crude a device to capture the complexity of the forms of biological citizenship we are seeking to describe. See, for example, J. Abraham and G. Lewis, "Citizenship, Medical Expertise and the Capitalist Regulatory State in Europe," *Sociology* 36(1), 2002, pp. 67–88.

In addition, we would like to acknowledge initial guidance from Chetan Bhatt of Goldsmiths College, University of London, and Engin Isin of York University, Toronto, comments from participants at the Prague conference on Global Anthropology, where the original version of this chapter was first given, especially Aihwa Ong and Stephen Collier, and comments from participants in a CRICT Seminar at Brunel University in November 2002. Particular thanks are due to Amaya Carmen Novas-Peña, who introduced us to some very contemporary aspects of biological citizenship.

2　T. H. Marshall, *Citizenship and Social Class: and Other Essays* (Cambridge: Cambridge University Press, 1950).

3　We will not discuss conceptions of citizenship, and projects of citizen-building, in earlier periods. For this, see Engin Isin, *Being Political: Genealogies of Citizenship* (Minneapolis: University of Minnesota Press, 2002).

4　Cf., P. Gilroy, *Between Camps: Race, Identity and Nationalism at the End of the Colour Line* (London: Allen Lane, 2000).

5　Cf., G. Agamben, *Homo Sacer: Sovereign Power and Bare Life* (Stanford: Stanford University Press, 1998).

6　C. Waldby, *The Visible Human Project: Informatic Bodies and Posthuman Medicine* (London and New York: Routledge, 2000).

7　A. Petryna, *Biological Citizenship: Science and the Politics of Health after Chernobyl* (Princeton, NJ: Princeton University Press, 2002).

8　Ibid., p. 5.

9　Ibid., p. 4.

10　C. Novas and N. Rose, "Genetic Risk and the Birth of the Somatic Individual," *Economy and Society* 29(4), 2000, pp. 485–513.

11　Cf., P. O'Malley, "Risk and Responsibility," in *Foucault and Political Reason*, A. Osborne, T. Barry, and N. Rose, eds. (London: UCL Press, 1996).

12　P. Rabinow, "Artificiality and Enlightenment: from Sociobiology to Biosociality," *Essays on the Anthropology of Reason* (Princeton, NJ: Princeton University Press, 1996).

13　Heath et al., "Genetic Citizenship."

14　Gilroy, *Between Camps*, p. 15.

15　C. Joppke, "Mobilization of Culture and the Reform of Citizenship Law: Germany and the United States," paper presented at the Twelfth International Conference of Europeanists, Chicago, March 30 – April 1, 2000; available at http://www.europanet.org/conference2000/papers/a-2_joppke1.doc

16　F. Dikötter, *Imperfect Conceptions: Medical Knowledge, Birth Defects, and Eugenics in China* (New York: Columbia University Press, 1998).

17　N. Leys-Stepan, *The Hour of Eugenics: Race, Gender and Nation in Latin America* (New York: Cornell University Press, 1991).

18　See E. Bergelund, "Biotechnology as a Finnish National Imperative," paper presented at BIOS Research Group, Goldsmiths College, February 28, 2002.

19　Notably, of course, Lancelot Hogben's *Science for the Citizen* (London: George Allen & Unwin, 1938).

20　Our use of this phrase, obviously, derives from the work of Ian Hacking; see, for example, I. Hacking, *Historical Ontology* (Cambridge, MA: Harvard University Press, 2002).

21　P. Rabinow, "The Third Culture," *History of the Human Sciences* 7(2), 1994, pp. 53–64.

22　Cf., B. Claeson, E. Martin, W. Richardson, M. Schoch-Spana, and K. S. Taussig, "Scientific Literacy, What it is, Why it's Important, and Why Scientists Think We Don't Have it? The

Case of Immunology and the Immune System," in *Naked Science: Anthropological Inquiry into Boundaries, Power, and Knowledge*, L. Nader, ed. (New York: Routledge, 1996).

23   See http://www.prozac.com/HowProzacCanHelp.jsp

24   See http://www.prozac.com/DiseaseInformation/Recovery.jsp

25   See http://www.prozac.com/generic_info.jsp

26   See http://www.mdf. org.uk/about/

27   Idem.

28   See http://www.pendulum. org/

29   See http://www.searchingwithin.com/bipolar/

30   These range from antique wooden boxes, through art supplies and computer hardware and software, to music CDs, a big house, and a weekly maid.

31   See http://www.searchingwithin.com/bipolar/notes/reasons.html

32   R. Rapp, *Testing Women, Testing the Fetus: the Social Impact of Amniocentesis in America* (New York: Routledge, 1999).

33   E. Martin, *Flexible Bodies: Tracking Immunity in American Culture from the Days of Polio to the Age of AIDS* (Boston: Beacon Press, 1994); S. Epstein, *Impure Science: AIDS, Activism, and the Politics of Knowledge* (Berkeley: University of California Press, 1996).

34   M. Foucault, *The History of Sexuality*, vol. 2: *The Use of Pleasure* (London: Penguin, 1985); M. Foucault, *The History of Sexuality*, vol. 3: *The Care of the Self* (London: Penguin, 1986).

35   Cf., M. Callon and V. Rabeharisoa, "Gino's Lesson on Humanity," paper presented at the 4S/EASST Joint Meeting, Session on Disabilities, Subjectivities, Politics, Vienna, September 27–30, 2000.

36   M. Castells, *The Rise of the Network Society* (Cambridge, MA: Blackwell, 1996).

37   V.-K. Nguyen, "Antiretrovirals, Globalism, Biopolitics and Therapeutic Citizenship," Chapter 8, this volume.

38   Petryna, *Biological Citizenship*.

39   C. Novas, "The Political Economy of Hope: Patients' Organisations, Science and Biovalue," paper presented at the Postgraduate Forum on Genetics and Society, University of Nottingham, June 21–22, 2001.

40   Hunt-Dis is an electronic mailing list where persons affected by HD, those at risk, and carers can discuss any topic relating to Huntington's disease.

41   C. Leal-Pock, ed., *Faces of Huntington's* (Belleville, ON: Essence Publishing, 1998).

42   Carmen Leal also maintains a website called writerspeaker.com, which aims to help aspiring writers and speakers to learn how to use the Internet for research and bring their products to market. See http://www.writerspeaker.com/

43   This coalition was formed on April 1, 2000, and is designed to provide support for HD families by HD families, in addition to providing a range of information and answers to those affected by this disease. Source: http://www.hdac.org/about.html

44   C. Leal, "The Last Generation," Huntington's Disease Advocacy Center, April 8, 2001; http://www.hdac.org/features/article.php?p_articleNumber=13

45   Idem.

46   Idem.

47   M. L. Miller, "Reasons for Hope," Huntington's Disease Advocacy Center, April 8, 2001; http://www.hdac.org/features/article.php?p_articleNumber=23

48   Idem.

49   Idem.

50 Waldby, *The Visible Human Project*; see also C. Waldby, "Stem Cells, Tissue Cultures and the Production of Biovalue," *Health: An Interdisciplinary Journal for the Social Study of Health, Illness and Medicine* 6(3), 2002, pp. 305–323; for analogous concepts, see S. Franklin, "Stem Cells R Us: Emergent Life Forms and the Global Biological," Chapter 4, this volume; Nguyen, "Therapeutic Citizenship."

51 A. Nilsson and J. Rose, "Sweden Takes Steps to Protect Tissue Banks," *Science* 286, 1999, p. 894.

52 For an account of the developments in Iceland, see G. Pálsson and P. Rabinow, "Iceland: The Case of a National Human Genome Project," *Anthropology Today* 15(5), 1999, pp. 14–18.

53 Source: http://www.decode.com/. The company website further states that "Iceland makes an ideal home for the company, as the Icelandic population is, genetically speaking, relatively homogeneous. The country has a sophisticated, high-quality health-care system and extensive genealogical records. Through these, resources can be generated to identify genes associated with a multitude of diseases. Research based on this unique population provides distinctive insights into the pathogenesis of these diseases, and the depth and comprehensiveness of deCODE's genealogical database are unrivalled worldwide": see http://www.decode.com/company/profile/

54 Source: http://www.umangenomics.com/index2.asp. The recognition of the potential of the Medical Biobank of Umeå for the production of biovalue was made by the technology transfer unit at the University of Umeå called the Technology Bridge Foundation. See A. Abbott, "Sweden Sets Ethical Standards for the Use of Genetic 'Biobanks,'" *Nature* 400, July 1999, p. 3.

55 K. Høyer, "Conflicting Notions of Personhood in Genetic Research," *Anthropology Today* 18(5), 2002, pp. 9–13; K. Høyer, "'Science is Really Needed –That's All I Know.' Informed Consent and the Non-Verbal Practices of Collecting Blood for Genetic Research in Northern Sweden," *New Genetics and Society* 22(3), 2003, pp. 229–244.

56 Source: http://www.umangenomics.com/index2.asp

57 M. Fleischer, "Patent Thyself (online version)," *The American Lawyer*, June 21, 2001; http://www.americanlawyer.com/newcontents06.html

58 A. Coghlan, "Patient Power," *New Scientist*, February 24, 2001, p. 4.

59 Fleischer, "Patent Thyself."

60 Idem.

61 Idem.

62 Høyer, "Conflicting Notions"; Høyer, "Science is Really Needed."

63 Source: http://www.umangenomics.com/index2.asp. Apart from gaining the informed consent of research participants, novel uses of the tissue and information stored in UmanGenomics' database require approval from a regional ethics committee, in addition to the Swedish Medical Research Council. Source: http://www.umangenomics.com/index2.asp. Sune Rosell, temporary chairman of UmanGenomics, in an article in *Science*, states that the company created a unique model for the handling of ethical issues: "There is control at the individual level through informed consent, at the social level through the regional ethics committee which screens all research proposals, and at the population level, since local politicians sit as non-voting members on the boards of both the company and the Medical Bank" (quoted in Abbott, "Sweden Sets Ethical Standards"). Klaus Høyer's ethnographic fieldwork indicates how many participants in UmanGenomics database do not actually read the informed consent sheet that is provided to them, tacitly

consenting to participate in this study, and only engaging in the public arena of informed consent when confronted in the context of the anthropological interview. See Høyer, "Science is Really Needed."

64 S. Rosell, "Sweden's Answer to Genomics Ethics (letter)," *Nature* 401, 1991, p. 208.

65 R. Scott, "The Forces of Acceleration are Upon Us," *Genomic Health*, April 8, 2001; http://www.genomichealth.com/message_article.htm

66 N. Rose, "Do Psychiatric Drugs Have Ethics?" paper presented at Brunel University, workshop on "Do Bio Artefacts Have Ethics?" February 15, 2002.

67 Scott, "The Forces of Acceleration."

24

ROBUST KNOWLEDGE AND FRAGILE FUTURES[1]

MARILYN STRATHERN

Daniel Miller anticipated beginning a paper thus: "While anthropology often proceeds by developing generalisations on the basis of detailed ethnography, this paper represents an attempt to locate a phenomenon through ethnography having predicted its existence in theory." The theory addressed virtualism as "the successive replacement of actual consumers as the beneficiary of welfare and provision by abstracted models that come to stand in their stead."[2]

An example from public service delivery made the point. New statutory provisions imposed on local government councils in the U.K. render them regularly subject to what is called Best Value inspection, demanding a competitive and modernizing self-consciousness as to how and why the service is provided. Local councils cannot be seen just to have grown through administrative evolution; they must spell out their goals and specify reasons for them. The five-yearly Best Value (BV) report uses performance indicators to measure how they have implemented the continuous improvement that is part of the same policy. Above all, evidence must be given of consultation with the public. One effect, Miller argued, is that an apparent commitment to consumers and taxpayers as the population at large becomes encompassed by institutions of accountability (such as BV inspection) that aggregate moral authority to themselves. This is paralleled in the private-sector rise of management consultancy: "companies increasingly listen to consultants who come to 'stand for' the voices of consumers and users," or where "the knowledge of workers and management about their own customers tends to be replaced by abstract consultancy models such as 'category management.'"[3] It is no accident that he found an exemplar for his ethnographic phenomenon in audit.

Traditional financial audit checks accounts. Public-sector audit, which in the U.K. over the past 25 years has transformed people's expectations of the state through the state's expectations of them, checks the delivery of services. That checking is premised on making certain social processes explicit, especially monitoring how aims and objectives have been achieved. The purpose is to show that organizations are managing their affairs properly, and this elision of propriety and efficiency requires proof that they are acting as proper organizations. Thus Miller's councils were increasingly concerned "with the active representation of a performance of consult-ation." Organizations are mobilized to perform *as* organizations.[4] Making "organiza-tion" explicit comes with the further presumption that information an organization obtains about itself is information to be acted on – knowledge about its achievements becomes constitutive of its aims and objectives. When knowledge is pressed into the service of enhancement, the admonition to be explicit turns (self-) description into grounds for improvement. Hence the rise of management audit.[5]

One consequence is that the future is forecast as fragile. *Unless* the organization strives to improve, it will fail to meet its (new) targets. What makes the future fragile is not just the chronic "uncertainty" that drives competition, but the need to translate abstract models into working practices, and back again. Miller's anticipation, locating an ethnographic phenomenon after its prediction in theory, is in a sense what audit promises organizations: management today, institutional practices tomorrow. Yet the ethnographer's model is robust in a way that the auditor's or manager's is not. The ethnographer creates a model for description, and the unpredictable can be taken in its stride, for that only gives reason to improve the model. By contrast, a model for improvement is vulnerable to the unpredictable, for sufficient measurements must be held in place to allow for repeated description. Performance indicators are supposed to register changes in performance, not lead to changes in the indicators, even though this may happen over the long term. Fragility inheres, then, in having to rely on conditions that are stable enough for new practices to be translated back into the *same* models. (Miller wrote that the job of BV inspection "is to ensure that the service is creating improvements that would be acknowledged by the users of that service"; while he deployed this to observe that "the authority of the inspectorate is that they possess the authority of the consumer," displacing consumer fickleness by its own assurances. He goes on to note that the service-provider also has to find people to consume its services – and register the improvement in terms that are translatable into the appropriate indicators.) This is where audit takes a tiny pre-emptive step. Carrying out an audit is itself an enactment of procedures of improvement. One is on the way to achieving BV objectives in submitting to a BV inspection. Meanwhile, the next inspection is always on the horizon.

Corinne Hayden's investigation of "ethical engineering" in the biosciences is germane.[6] Ethical engineering tries to anticipate public objections. The phrase "built-in ethics" comes from Sarah Franklin's observations of cell line research in genetics, where the issue is how "to build a degree of management of public opinion into [the] product" itself.[7] An "ethically sensitive biotechnology" is based on a projection of future public opinion. Although my own examples are stimulated by policy concerns in the U.K., they belong to a globally dispersed mode of accountability that runs alongside just such anticipation of questions about public consultation and ethical practice. There is a particular interest in considering the public service sector, because of the nature of its commitment to "society" as at once consumer and ethical arbiter. That sector's fragile future includes not just untoward events and as yet unborn interest groups, but the changing nature of society itself.[8] For if impact on society is to be the register of an accountable project, enough features of society must be held stable to provide continuing measures of the project's self-improvement.

While one might choose any of several arenas bound up in local government (as Miller does) – welfare, health, education – I focus instead on certain directions being given to national research policy. For these imagine it is possible to "build into" particular projects not just future demands of public or customers, society in a weak sense, but an authority that lies beyond service provision or beyond the market, in the name of "society" in a strong sense. Almost a decade on from Arturo Escobar's alignment of anthropology and technoscience lie new issues for the social anthropologist.[9]

Science and Society: Imagined Communications

Society emerges in a strong sense as a foil to "science." A widespread consensus that we live in an "age of uncertainty" has become the newly explicit environment to this relationship. The phrase is from Nowotny et al.'s sequel[10] to *The New Production of Knowledge*,[11] that explored the difference between two modes (1 and 2) of knowledge production. Uncertainty is not a passive state – as a precondition for innovation,[12] it is animated, among other things, by society's internalization of science:

> In traditional [modern] society science was 'external'... and scientists saw their task as the benign reconstitution of society according to 'modern' principles [Mode 1]... In contemporary [modern] society, in contrast, science is 'internal'; as a result science and research are no longer terminal or authoritative projects... but instead, by creating new knowledge, they add fresh elements of uncertainty and instability [Mode 2].[13]

Now Mode 2 knowledge production accompanies "an important shift in the regime of control...[whereby] control is now exercised indirectly and from the 'inside'... [through] ever more elaborate systems of peer review, more formal quality control systems, and other forms of audit, assessment and evaluation."[14] Audit gets globally dispersed (across sectors of society and across societies) through its appeal as an internal mechanism of self-improvement. In the U.K., it accompanies an institutionalized uncertainty as to how far one can trust public service agencies (as well as company directors), which creates and is created by ever more attempts to check up on them.[15]

The academy continues to have a major role in the production of science, and in the U.K. alongside audit of the institution has come a kind of knowledge audit (my phrase). Checks on the delivery of knowledge, as through the four-yearly national Research Assessment Exercise, are one thing; input (research funding) and output (publications, patents) offer indicators that the academic community is delivering. Checks on the nature of knowledge are another. For here, monitoring reaches beyond the point of production to consumption, to the point at which information about something becomes knowledge for someone. Partly because of the scale of public investment, science has come under particular scrutiny. For decades its effectiveness was mediated through products, as when technology was harnessed to engineering or pharmaceuticals. But the past 25 years has seen an increasing supposition that the public should *understand* [absorb knowledge of] science, or at least understand the science agenda; that is, its aims and objectives. While Nowotny et al. relegate need for the "public understanding of science" to traditional (Mode 1) aims,[16] their following comment is germane to the Mode 2 model: the realization that more information does not necessarily lead to more empathy – rather, education encourages critical questioning, for example on the traditional distinction between experts and lay people. In this context, "science and society" burgeons as a rubric for research funding programmes,[17] the title a House of Lords enquiry into public perceptions of science gave to their report.[18]

But expectations continue to move: from science demonstrating its effectiveness by reaching toward potential consumers through the promise of (say) medical advancement to requiring from "society" something akin to endorsement. Consumption now becomes part of the production process. In research policy rhetoric, the switch away from "public understanding" of science to "public engagement" switches from society as the passive consumer to society as an active consumer–participant in knowledge production. The science that was once robust through its own validation procedures (Mode 1) must now acquire an (other) efficacy from beyond itself (Mode 2). Insofar as society can confer acceptability, can take on an auditing role, scientific knowledge makes itself robust in being seen to be "socially robust."[19] In effect, science incorporates society into its aims and objectives in order to anticipate or pre-empt society's verdict. Yet, I wonder, will it be audit itself that renders the future of science fragile? Uncertainties over the kind of social reception given to new knowledge may well pale beside the institutional requirement to demonstrate robustness. That will require, among other things, keeping stable what counts as "society." And society will need to be kept visible.

The British government has initiated forums to make social verdict at once possible and visible, or rather to simulate it. To the extent that it is prepared to stand in the stead of society, the government can – through commissions of enquiry and such – produce abstract models of what a future social verdict would be like. It also mobilizes (parts of) society to this end:

> One of the historic roles of government has been to facilitate investment in the infrastructure of communication or transportation: canals...telecommunications...The new challenge for government, in the global circumstances of the 21st

century, is to find ways of encouraging the capacities of individuals to communicate (of investing in the "human capital" infrastructure of communication).[20]

This comes from a report, supported by the Department of Trade and Industry (DTI), on the arts and humanities in relation to science and technology. Arts and humanities have an important role in preparing people for future challenges, and the report notes the significance of understanding the social and ethical consequences of new medical technologies. The appeal to join forces occurs, I would add, in the presence of their shared need for public accountability.

If communication can be an end, it is indubitably a means. Society appears as an entity with which communication can take place. How is such an entity performed? It is consulted – that is, questions can be asked in such a way that it seems society is "answering back."[21] Now what consultation with society yields is a source of information about society. So relayed back to science as "social implications" is precisely that – society's knowledge of itself. Such knowledge may involve quite complex understanding of the ways in which different interests engage one another, but it is also the case that an abstract model of responsiveness can come to stand for response. As Miller said, if British local government workers knew one thing about BV it was that they were supposed to consult with the public, since much of the preparation for BV consists of questionnaire surveys to demonstrate awareness of the public's preoccupations:

> A modern democratic society is also one in which all citizens are expected to have opinions about major political, social and economic choices, and in which public participation in these choices and discussions is itself a major source of social responsiveness, and resilience.[22]

Robust itself, society can confer robustness. Let me give an example.

Real-Time Protocols for Imagined Consultations

A baseline assumption is that science itself is changing "at an accelerating rate," becoming more "multidisciplinary" and "complex at the same time": "Accordingly, we have identified a set of key strategic steps which will empower the Research Councils . . . to meet future challenges and deliver a science portfolio which promotes excellence."[23] This is from the DTI's *Quinquennial Review* of publicly funded Research Councils in the U.K.

Critical areas concern the delivery of science; that is, how research funded by the government should be seen to have an impact. Needed is a "clearer strategic framework for delivering science," "to 'join up' with stake holders so as to work with them in a more collegiate fashion," and "to apply principles of public service delivery . . . [in] dealings with users."[24] Principles of public service delivery, notably to be sure to consult and involve, were mobilized in the very production of the report itself, at least in its references to identifiable individuals and organizations. "The public" is there by implication. However, in the chapter on stakeholders, "the public" is explicitly identified *as* stakeholder, its interest in knowing how its taxes are spent being spelled out. Public accountability is evoked, and then given a use for science:

> In addition to highlighting the importance of public accountability and the involvement of the public in decision-making, the science and society agenda identifies an important role for the Research Councils . . . in helping to promote an awareness of science as part of the fabric of society and an understanding of science and new technologies.[25]

A science that describes itself as internal to society also allows society within its own practices. Internalization is likely to take a particular cultural form (notably as "views and opinions," or "social implications"). So an admonition to address the science and society agenda through "consultation, engagement and dialogue" carries the warning that this must not be a passive matter of dissemination: the views of the concerned public should be actively sought.[26] For modernizing (improving) government itself means that "*engagement* with stakeholders at strategic level is of key importance, not just consultation: the aim should be to get mutual understanding, support, participation."[27] This does indeed mean "the involvement of the public in decision-making," co-evolution in Nowotny et al.'s Mode 2 paradigm.

Monitoring and evaluation procedures affect the Councils across the board. Critical of the way performance indicators have been used in the past, the report identified "responsibility, ownership and accountability" as the basis of a revised management system.[28] It proposed a new social body that would have oversight of all the Councils (subsequently, "Research Councils UK" [RCUK]). Its nine key tasks include developing a collective voice for the Research Councils in order to increase their influence; encouraging systematic and regular dialogue for the Research Councils as a group with other science funders; developing a single point of focus for stakeholders to interact with Research Councils together; and managing the boundaries between the Research Councils, to avoid duplication or gaps.

The nine tasks engage two axes of social identity, the collective and the individual. The text given above reads in full: "Accordingly, we have identified a set of key strategic steps which will empower the Research Councils, *collectively and individually*, to meet future challenges and deliver a science portfolio which promotes excellence *in individual researchers and in research teams*." Now "the simultaneous assertion and management of difference as core functions of central institutions" is in Greenhouse's eyes diagnostic of the modern political institution "whose self-defined mandate rests . . . on successfully defending its claims to stewardship in the transformation of difference into participation in the state, and vice versa."[29] We should be alert, then, to the report's mix of equations/elisions and separations – to what are subsumed within the Research Councils as a body (common aims, influence) and what is regarded as apart from them (other funders, stakeholders). These are fairly easy to identify for a single-purpose, and thus sociologically simple, institution.

We see emerging in microcosm a community recognizable to stakeholders, through a social form in which interests are simultaneously elided (it will offer itself as a single point of focus) and distinguished (it will manage the boundaries between its internal concerns). The Research Councils communicating among themselves might, if not actually standing in the stead of communication with the public, at least be a kind of first step.

But what if the single focus of a collective voice is problematic and boundaries are not amenable to management? As elsewhere, I draw on a report of a public consultation that turns crucially on the difference between a collective voice and individual interests. It uncannily presages many of the issues that this account has already raised. In counterpoint to the real-life protocols for the anticipated activities of RCUK, here are some imaginary protocols derived from a real-life exercise; the exercise had to create a "society" that could be consulted, and I trace in retrospect some of the steps it might have taken in order to produce the report that emerged. My imagined ten steps only begin to touch on the complications.

Imaginary Protocols for a Real-Time Consultation

The intention of the exercise was to give robustness to scientific endeavor embodied in late-1980s/early-1990s technologies of reproductive medicine. The Canadian Royal Commission on New Reproductive Technologies (NRT) was charged with finding out what people thought, interpreting its mandate as speaking on behalf of "Canadian society as a whole." It did not just imagine what this society might be; it set in motion social processes that would yield information attributable to society precisely to the extent that society had been mobilized.[30] And it did so through at once channeling and celebrating diversity. Aside from differences of language and culture, sections of the population – women's lobbies, religious groups – had issue-specific interests. Crucially, an unpredictable future was part of it. Society was assumed to be changing: greater cultural diversity, new attitudes toward family and parenthood, and so forth. "The trend towards diversity... has significant implications for society's response to new reproductive technologies... [E]thical questions... will not be resolved by referring to an unchanging common set of social beliefs, assumptions, and values. Nor can we assume that established ways of setting priorities... will be adequate to the task of accommodating Canadians' diverse aspirations and goals. Yet this is precisely what more and more Canadians expect of their systems and institutions."[31]

With its enlightened view on making fertility treatment available everyone, the Commission will want to endorse the legitimacy of individually held wishes; given the values of pluralism written into the Canadian constitution, it will want to give voice to minority as well as majority views; finally, it will want to convey the depth of people's feeling. Now it has to hand a particular exemplar of agency, the individual as a decision-making bearer of views and attitudes. The one thing that it can do is to make clear how widely the Commissioners have consulted.

Step one: separate society from technology. This renders society a distinct entity. The report asks how NRT will change people's understanding of society. While the number of users is small, a minority can affect "broader societal values and norms." The example of adoption takes it into an area where public understanding has changed (how "society's views and values" have been "affected by the collective experience of those involved in it"). Depicting the technologies as having implications for society renders them notionally beyond it: technology is "outside" society. *In vitro* fertilization and embryo transfer may be understood as medical solutions to biological impairment without evoking new social elements. Technology having been separated from society, the Commission can specify different family forms as a matter of social variation. "Social" factors, with their own trajectory of change, are in turn seen to have implications for NRT: society is "outside" technology.

Step two: separate society from the individual. This renders the individual a distinct entity. Society and individual can be translated as Canada and Canadians: their separation has a concrete form. One can bring them together again as the "collective principles and values of Canadians."[32] But this can only be done through first establishing the views of individual Canadians. Surveys target a population (by phone) controlled for factors such as age, ethnicity, and region, alongside ten focus groups for Aboriginal peoples, representatives from ethnocultural communities being sought for their unique attitudes.

Step three: put both society and individuals alongside (numerous) other social entities. This naturalizes the concept of diversity. The report talks about the impact of NRT on individuals, on identifiable social groups, and on society as whole. "The increasing diversity of Canadian society means that we cannot make assumptions about the impact of new reproductive technologies on society as a whole. Different groups will be affected in different ways by the technologies,"[33] and the special needs of "women" come to stand for many "groups." Visible groups can be put alongside individuals.

Step four: equate social groups with individuals. This separates "Canada"/"society" from the social entities that constitute it. The report sets up the general public ("Canadians") as a mass, with minority groups and interests to be separately consulted. At the same time, as Canada "becomes more heterogeneous, it will become increasingly important to make core values transparent and to ensure that consensus on technologies takes into account the diverse nature of the country."[34] Advocacy groups are a facet of empowerment to ensure that the interests and expectations of different constituencies are taken into account. Diversity reiterates the need for regulation.

Step five: equate society with government. This separates government from those to whom it is responsible. On the one hand, a vision of one society is rendered through the possibility of consensus, collective values (including access to public resources and protection from harm) defining the moral community. On the other hand, implementing collectivity becomes the specific duty of the state. An equation between government and society seems implied in statements such as "Government should act as guardian of public interest to set limits"[35] and "It is society's responsibility to see to it that knowledge gained from science develops in a way that is beneficent."[36]

Society is in turn depicted as a part accountable to a wider whole. Society has a right and responsibility (to those to whom it is accountable) to ensure that research is circumscribed by appropriate ethical boundaries.

Step six: put both state and community alongside personal needs. This naturalizes the need for government. A central goal of the Commission's recommendations is to enable individual Canadians to make personal decisions about their involvement with the technologies. This views society as a provider of services and individuals as consumers of them. But what if the actions of some individuals interfere with those of others, personal interests pursued at others' expense? The Commissioners give as examples individuals demanding equal partnership of information with medical practitioners; individuals claiming rights to medical treatment without regard to the social implications of financial consequences for the health care system, and the state having to provide counseling to assist individuals to make informed decisions.

Step seven: put personal differences alongside a difference of interests. This naturalizes the individuality of interests. Under the heading, "Where individual and collective interests may differ," it is observed that there need be no conflict between individual and *collective* interests, that a *community* flourishes when its members flourish, and that it is important for *society* to care for its members.[37] This slides from a sense of a community of interests to a definition of society as a state charged with care of its individual members. But, in some situations, protecting certain individuals might harm "the rest of society." This step imagines a society at risk, victim of people's decisions. Thus surrogacy could "create broad social harms by diminishing the dignity of reproduction and undermining society's commitment to the inherent value of children."[38] But if society can be harmed, what entities harm it? It can only be entities that it has it separated from itself: Technology? The individual? Its constituent social units? The individual emerges as most significant. When certain individuals – such as those entering into commercial surrogate arrangements – stamp their own values on childbirth, their actions can lead to a perversion of the general value that society puts on having children. Finally, if society is at risk, what does this mean for state or government? Two procedures convert individual interests into diversity.

Step eight: encompass diversity through quantification. This sets the scene for an elective approach to difference and choice. The report points to statistics collected in research reports and produces summary percentages. Opinions can be counted and differences enumerated. Social and cultural diversity, then, is like the quantity-dependent consumerist's choice (choice between a multiplicity of items). Views and attitudes themselves divide people into majorities and minorities.

Step nine: encompass diversity through presenting dissenting opinion. This sets the scene for dealing with dissent as a minority view. A dissenting Commissioner spells out her disquiet over the new kinds of family ties that a liberal, choice-rich approach to regulation would produce. The Commission's use of majority opinion turns out to have been highly selective:[39] the dissenter takes to task the Commission's self-portrayal as representing the views of Canada when, by its own statistics, its recommendations go in the face of strong opposition to certain family forms. For the statistics uncover solidly conservative views. The majority consulted on the question are against single, homosexual, or welfare-supported parents receiving treatment (nearly three-quarters opposed to NRT provision for homosexual couples, and nearly two-thirds for couples on welfare). Yet the dissenting opinion is itself presented as a minority one, indicating a "respectful difference of opinion."

Step ten: encompass diversity through the fact of inquiry itself. What prevails in the end is the reasoning of those with oversight of all aspects of the inquiry: "Where there was divergence on specific policy questions, we decided that our moral reasoning should have greater weight if it was in line with fundamental values endorsed by Canadians, because we had spent much time weighing the evidence and thinking through the implications of different policies on such specific questions."[40] The Commissioners are liberal persons who, in the name of government, must ultimately depend on their own expertise: "There were a few occasions... when our moral reasoning led us to conclusions that were not strongly supported by the responses to some specific questions in our surveys of Canadians. This kind of situation usually arose when a value that Canadians strongly endorsed... such as equality, was not upheld in answer to a question on a specific situation, such as whether single women should access to donor insemination."[41] The Commissioners' own consultation among themselves epitomizes, abstracts, subsumes – stands in the stead of – consultation with others.

Offering a "regulative" approach to "choice" and a "consensus" about "difference," the report thus dealt at once with Canadians as individuals and with Canada as a society. However, the very process of drawing out the ethical and social implications of NRT modified the CRC's model of technology's "impact" on society. Each is obviously implicated each in the other. Society is already committed to a description of itself as caught up in technological change; technology is already defined as assisting institutional solutions to problems, including those created by social change. The enactment of "society" orchestrated by the enquiry suggests a comparison with audit inspections that have organizations act out being (efficient) organizations. Could one then imagine an enactment of the very way in which *science and society* are implicated in one another? In other words, could one imagine an enactment of the science and society agenda itself, a performance that made explicit the processes by which it becomes possible to produce "socially robust" science? I would not ask the question if there were not a potential ethnographic exemplar to hand.

Science with Society: Relations in Real Time

The CRC exercise mobilized interest groups of various kinds, but to momentary effect. Suppose that one mounted a semi-permanent consultative exercise, bringing together diverse people over a period of time. It would hardly be feasible to do so with sections of "the public," but a quasi-virtual solution would be to stimulate a flow of information among professionals with the public very much in mind.

A government vision for creating Knowledge Parks that would channel and communicate genetic information has been taken in exactly this direction by a proposal from Cambridge.[42]

In the Cambridge Genetics Knowledge Park (CGKP), as it gets working over a five-year period, we shall see the unfolding of an experiment. It originates in the need articulated by the Department of Health to support research in clinical genetics by bringing together multiple aspects of emerging developments, from test methods to the requirement for counseling patients, and to ensure their acceptability to the public. The outcome is premised on interdisciplinarity, between several sciences, between scientific and clinical applications, between academic and nonacademic users, and between Cambridge and the commercial community. Of bids put into the Department of Health (with DTI support), the Cambridge proposal goes furthest in explicitly responding to the invitation to "develop appropriate economic, ethical, legal and social frameworks for the effective delivery of genetic services."[43] Society must be taken into science before, so to speak, it leaves the laboratories: new research will have implications beyond the field of human genetics, and (with regard to accountability) it has become irresponsible not to anticipate that. But among these "implications," the joker in the pack is "social." While ethical and legal issues draw in professional expertise, that has hardly been true for society. Society belongs to all, not just to social scientists. Exploring ethical and legal issues may take one into areas that only an expert can elucidate, whereas society – as we have seen – can be consulted directly! As we have also seen, this may be understood as eliciting the opinions, values, and attitudes, individual and collective, to which people give voice. (Hence the endless quest for "what people think"; it would be an unusual ethics committee or commission of enquiry that did not attempt some representation of "public" opinion.) Here, government is stimulating a situation in which, in the conduct of scientific research itself, the public contributes a judgment about the nature of knowledge.

At the core of the CGKP is the concept of genetic knowledge. Enabling the outcome of genetic research to be exploited for the benefit of both personal and population health is the first aim; successful commercial exploitation, which I do not consider further, is the second. Exploitation for medical benefit means dissemination to health professionals, policy-makers, and so forth: CGKP's objectives are both to undertake secondary research and to "create knowledge" of a rather special kind. This is knowledge

> which we define as information that has been validated through critical appraisal of research findings, and integrated with an ethical, legal and social analysis and the input of consumer views.[44]

In short, it is a vision of co-produced knowledge. The Cambridge proposal does not shrink from complexity. The way in which diagnostic techniques are developed alongside strides in communication technologies and policies of data protection is an obvious example of complex ("Mode 2") knowledge production. It is precisely the co-evolutionary nature of research and policy on numerous fronts, the simultaneity of developments, that the CGKP invites us to grasp.

To realize that things are all happening together is less a totalizing vision than a tracery of the complex inter-folding of issues as they cross seemingly separate domains; sometimes concerns hardly touch, while at others they seem deeply embedded in one another. Complexity is particularly apparent at moments when a fragile future is suddenly actualized in the present – measurements cannot be held stable, precipitating what we colloquially call crises, and it is an ongoing crisis in public confidence that called forth the Knowledge Parks in the first place. Thus Callon compares reactions to disaster, where experts are called in with their instruments of measurement [Mode 1], to the [Mode 2] perception that one does not know which of many instruments is crucial.[45] Here, the scientist cannot remain in the laboratory but must engage with other specialists and nonspecialists alike, for "society as a whole must agree to take action."[46] A network of diverse interests, policies, and research outcomes somehow have to be combined, for as fast as calculations are required, the very instruments of measurement must be created and agreed upon. Such situations are becoming increasingly prevalent, he argues, as controversies cross disciplines and it gets harder to produce consensus on how to measure, say, what is safe.

It is this kind of complex interlocking that the CGKP will make explicit. But it will add another ingredient. More than a model of connections we know about, it will be putting into place connections we do not (yet) know about. Some of these will lie in the local society that, if only by default, it will create. For I see it not just as anticipating the co-presence of diverse factors in the way clinical genetics develops as an intervention in people's lives, but as activating relations of its own. It will not just be anticipatory; it will also produce, in real time, on its own scale, un-looked-for effects. And here it will, importantly, lay itself open to the unpredictable – a fascinating ethnographic object, though as yet hardly in existence.

The remainder of the chapter reflects, then, on a kind of report in prospect, the CGKP funding proposal, though less in terms of documentary process[47] than in terms of its aims and objectives. Knowledge Parks were conceived with the aim of helping to restore an authority to science, specifically genetics – in the Cambridge case through two overlapping objectives. One is to bring together the best of scientific expertise in the area, across disciplines, which will require common measurements of usefulness or applicability. The other is to bring about a new robustness in Gibbons' terms,[48] by building into the very concept of knowledge a mix of scientific and nonscientific expertise. (The Cambridge proposal uses the phrase "socially robust science," recognizing that the institutions of society must deal with "dispersed knowledge" and "mixed expertise.") We saw that "knowledge" is defined as information validated through critical appraisal of research findings that are integrated with ethical, legal, and social analysis and the input of consumer views. Scientists will combine with avowedly nonscientists to produce validated knowledge. This will require some common measurements, at the very least compatibility in the languages of intention. It will also require social tools, but these tools will have to handle incompatibility as well.

I have in mind Harvey and Green's account of an inter-system network of communications that was meant to turn Manchester into a virtual city.[49] A basic requirement of electronic technological systems is that they must be compatible (made into a single system, inhabiting the same circuit) before they interact. Interaction is an outcome or effect of their compatibility. Between people in their social life, to the contrary, interactions may or may not lead to compatibility. Social interactions are inherently open-ended – can encompass diverse aims and intentions – because relations between persons do not require compatibility between them in advance. We live in a world of numerous worlds, homepages, untold imaginings of communities; people follow through complex traceries of experience, and their compatibility need not be an issue. Simply, Tsoukas says from a management perspective, "it is impossible to know in advance the entire range of responses an individual is capable of."[50] From this comes much of the creativity and energy of social life. Might the mobilization of personnel, resources, and communications networks turn the CGKP into a social world in which stimulating the flow of knowledge would be the very animation of the world itself? If so, requirements for common measures would interact with situations that dispensed with them. The CGKP proposal talks of a dissemination strategy, of networking, in relation to the genetic knowledge; that is, transactions in such knowledge. Transactions often work on very partial compatibilities. It will be interesting to see what transactions emerge.

In this context, we would do well to be wary of the kind of co-production of knowledge that hypothecates *society* as a partner, the political and policy climate in which the CGKP is conceived. If it is scientific to be in doubt, it is good social science to be at once open-minded to the potential social implications of particular practices and suspicious of abstractions. This brings us back to Miller's point about audit. "Social implications" point to the need to find out what practices, institutions, and so forth may be caught up as effects of scientific effort, what transactions emerge. An abstract notion of "society," on the other hand, is pre-emptive. It demands demonstration rather than investigation; it will require performance, representatives, and evidence of its presence in people's calculations. For the CGKP, the difference between these could be the difference between a novel experiment with an unpredictable outcome and the banal validation of validation procedures.

Some of the banal consequences of abstraction (an abstract notion of "society") are obvious. It produces the concept of "science" (or technology, or academia) in contradistinction to itself; this de-socializes "science and technology" as somehow less part of society than arts and humanities, while de-professionalizing social science. It encourages the idea that all "science" need show is that it does useful things "for society." It could even prompt people to equate ethics committees and government commissions with society's studied opinion. But, above all, the invocation of "society" summons the fragility of measurement: What will count as "society"? Whose views will figure? Society's future satisfaction could not be a more unstable performance indicator. We live alongside creationists who say that scientific evidence proves their belief that the world is 6,000 years old, citing a Cambridge geologist who said that evolution gives no answers (he apparently said no such thing).[51] We live alongside proposals to set up religion-based schools in the U.K.[52] Perhaps I am willfully too elaborate about what is no more than a shorthand ("society") for numerous interests. But, and I take my cue from Born,[53] searching for the representatives of "society" would obscure just how knowledge is going to become (re)formed in the CGKP project, and how social interests will indubitably change in the process. Here lie interesting questions, and I sketch one.

If stimulation of the flow of knowledge is the very animation of social interactions in the CGKP, to whom will it belong? Ownership may include a sense of attachment or belonging or identity, including outcomes of participatory efforts, but it also points to property rights. IPR will no doubt deal with narrow definitions of ownership where rights to profits are at stake, but along the lines of current debates in relation to scientific authorship[54] the whole process of social/ethical validation will become part of what is transacted. (The value of the commodity will include its certification.) The proposal refers to nationally validated science. Is this a new localization of scientific knowledge? The validation procedures could almost lead into issues that have come up in other arenas, in relation to cultural property and indigenous expertise. "Collective" ownership and "the commons" will take on interesting meanings.

Scientifically validated knowledge rested on methods being universally accepted: definitive yardsticks and practices of measurement in Nowotny et al.'s Mode 1 format, such as auditing methods that depend on repeatable correlations. The instruments of measurement have to be held stable. But ethically and socially validated knowledge (in Mode 2 style) will be the outcome of internal negotiations between interest groups in a pluralistic population where one may not be able to, and may not want to, invoke a moral consensus. So what are the presumptions of a validation procedure here – a presumption of a common culture? And what of social life if it is not always built on debate, conflict, pluralism?

It is important in this regard that the CGKP is an ethnographic object that has not yet been fully assembled, although we could say it was "predicted" by Nowotny et al.[55] What is so interesting about the CGKP conception is that it will encompass both kinds of knowledge production, Mode 1 and Mode 2, scientific *and* social, if I can put it like that. This is not because it will bring about an "interaction" between science and society, but because the exercise is to be embedded within social structures that will have something of a life of their own. It will be put down in a context where the production of genetic knowledge is already embedded in its own routines; it will also be put down in (near to) a preexisting community of scientists with its own conventions. And the users (consumers, stakeholders, co-participants) will be of a special kind: not the public at large, but primarily an already committed nursing profession. These dimensions will complicate the social possibilities for the new venture. With any luck, the diversity of social trajectories will defy attempts to abstract "society" from them.

Afterword

In 2001, the University of Cambridge circulated a draft for a new Strategic Plan. There is a new orientation to the opening Mission Statement:

> The mission of the University of Cambridge is to contribute to society through the pursuit of education, learning and research at the highest international levels of excellence.

Its core values are defined by two bullet points: freedom of thought and expression; and freedom from discrimination. The new element here is *writing in* its wish to "to contribute to society." It cannot mean that the university was not doing that before, just that now it will be explicit about it. But this bow to a fragile future denies the university power to describe a rather robust position that it could occupy: as a part of a society that does not for ever refer back to itself.[56]

Notes

1 Principal thanks are owed to Ronald Zimmern, for his encouragement of social critique. The chapter draws on "Elsie and the Problem of Believing in Everything," presented to the Cambridge Bioethics Forum, King's College, 2001, and I thank Corinne Hayden for juxtaposing ELSI and the section on Canadian Royal Commission; the latter was first presented at, "Reproductive Values: The Individual and Society," Dublin 1997, Manchester University and the EC BIOMED-2 Programme, *Reproductive Choice and Control of Fertility,* led by Margaret Brazier. Daniel Miller's "The Virtual Moment" is published in the *Journal of the Royal Anthropological Institute,* NS 9(1), 2003, pp. 57–75, but not in the form I cite; permission to quote from the draft is gratefully acknowledged. Many have had creative put input, if unknowingly, including Andrew Barry, Georgina Born, Ann-Louise Kinmonth, Monica Konrad, Maryon McDonald, Frances Nieduszynska Bronwyn Parry, Pat Spallone, and James Leach.

2 Daniel Miller, personal communication with author.

3 Daniel Miller, "The Unintended Political Economy," in *Cultural Economy in Cultural Analysis and Commercial Life,* P. Du Gay and M. Pryke, eds. (London: Sage, 2002, p. 176).

4 R. Munro, "The Cultural Performance of Control," *Organization Studies* 20, 1999, pp. 619–640.

5 R. Harper, "The Social Organization of the IMF's Mission Work: An Examination of International Auditing," in *Audit Culture,* M. Strathern, ed. (London: Routledge, 2000).

6 Corinne Hayden, "Towards an ethnography of the adverse effect," paper delivered at EASA conference, for panel "Genes, Genomes, and Genetics," convenor G. Pálsson, Copenhagen, 2002.

7 S. Franklin, "Culturing Biology: Cell Lines for the Second Millennium," *Health* 5, 2001, p. 342.

8 Ibid., p. 337.

9 A. Escobar, "Welcome to Cyberia: Notes on the Anthropology of Cyberculture," *Current Anthropology* 35, 1994, pp. 211–231.

10 H. Nowotny, P. Scott, and M. Gibbons, *Re-Thinking Science: Knowledge and the Public in an Age of Uncertainty* (Oxford: Polity Press, 2001).

11 M. Gibbons, *The New Production of Knowledge: The Dynamics of Science and Research in Contemporary Societies* (London: Sage, 1994).

12 R. Barnett, *Realizing the University in an Age of Supercomplexity* (Buckingham: Society for Research into Higher Education & Open University Press, 2000).

13 Nowotny et al., *Re-Thinking Science,* p. 2.

14 Ibid., p. 115.

15 O. O'Neill, *A Question of Trust [The BBC Reith Lectures, 2002]* (Cambridge: Cambridge University Press, 2002).

16 Nowotny et al., *Re-Thinking Science,* p. 240.

17 An example is the Wellcome Trust's *Medicine in Society* program, and its change of ethos from "public understanding of science" to "science and society." The British government initiative has been fuelled by crises over food and technology, and by apparently plummeting public respect accorded to "science," much played up by the media; its motive is to anticipate and thereby obviate public objection. A European example: the new *Society in Science* international fellowship program at the Swiss Federal Institute of Technology, Zurich.

18 Franklin, "Culturing Biology," pp. 339–340.

19 M. Gibbons, "Science's New Social Contract with Society," *Nature* 402 (Supplement), 1999, pp. C81–C84.

20 CST (Council for Science and Technology), *Imagination and Understanding: Report on the Arts and Humanities in Relation to Science and Technology* (London: Department of Trade and Industry, 2001), p. 14.

21 Nowtony et al.'s phrase.

22 CST, *Report on the Arts,* p. 9.

23 DTI (Department of Trade and Industry), *Quinquennial Review of the Grant-Awarding Research Councils* (London: Office of Science and Technology, 2001), p. 2.

24 CST, *Report on the Arts,* pp. 1–2.

25 DTI, *Quinquennial Review,* p. 61.

26 The full warning reads: "The views of the concerned public should be actively sought . . . and then subjected to the normal process [!] of analysis. Seeking the views of the public in this way will assist better decision-making." Later, on page 72, in a chapter on monitoring, we read: "The OST [Office of Science & Technology] and the Research Councils should devise a new performance measurement system that integrates output and performance indicators [OPIs] and benchmarking and facilitates the development of a set of critical management performance tools." This mixes Mode 2 aspirations with Mode 1 practices.

27 CST, *Report on the Arts,* p. 53; original emphasis.

28 DTI, *Quinquennial Review,* p. 72.

29 C. Greenhouse, *A Moment's Notice: Time Politics across Culture* (Ithaca, NY: Cornell University Press, 1996), p. 218.

30 This public inquiry (1989–93) tackled heterogeneity and the multiplicity of interests that ethical issues call up. The final report (Canada 1993) of 1,275 pages states that over 300 scholars participated in the exercise, across 70 disciplines, involving more than 40,000 Canadians, with a newsletter, research studies, public hearings, symposia, written submissions, and 6,000 individuals leaving their views on toll-free telephone lines. Over 250,000 "pieces of information," such as brochures and press releases, were distributed;

the report acknowledges the reciprocal process of having to inform the people whose are sought.

31 Canada, Minister of Government Services, *Proceed with Care: Final Report,* 2 vols. (Ottawa: Royal Commission on New Reproductive Technologies, 1993), p. 20.

32 Ibid., p. 11.

33 Ibid., p. 35.

34 Ibid., pp. 29–30; emphasis removed.

35 Ibid., p. xxxvi.

36 Ibid., p. 47.

37 Ibid., p. 63; emphases added.

38 Ibid., p. 686.

39 Ibid., p. 1088ff.

40 Ibid., pp. 430–431.

41 Ibid., p. 431.

42 The Secretary of State for Health tendered for what turned out to be six parks across the U.K. The Cambridge Park was set up by a consortium of public health, university, and commercial interests, under the direction of Dr. R. Zimmern, Director of the Public Health Genetics Unit, Cambridge. Among the interests of the University is its Centre for Medical Genetics and Policy [on whose management committee I sat], with a remit to focus on the ethical, legal, and social component of the CGKP. The project intends to build not only on the huge interdisciplinary expertise that exists in Cambridge's medical and genetics-related institutions, but specifically looks to Philosophy, HPS, Law, Social and Political Science, and Social Anthropology. This is the orientation from which I write, although the entire enterprise is very much larger. Starting in 2002–3, it is due on present funding to run for five years. I keep ethnographic tryst with other documents cited in this chapter, and restrict my observations to the proposal (Zimmern, pers. comm.); I am most grateful for permission to draw on it.

43 Implemented specifically in the U.S.A. in tandem with the Human Genome Project, ELSI ["Ethical, Legal, and Social Implications"] stands for scrutiny of science in the name of public accountability. Over the past quarter century, there has been a general consensus that creativity and innovation are to be found in interdisciplinarity: an image for cutting-edge stuff was disparate disciplines brought together, now thoroughly sedimented in academic expectations. So it seems unremarkable that bodies of experts can be composed of representatives from different disciplines – honoring a long tradition of consulting people "from different walks of life." ELSI condenses the assumption that it is particularly vital to bundle together the "ethical, legal, and social implication" of particular policy measures or research ventures, most explicitly in relation to biotechnology.

44 Zimmern, pers. comm.

45 M. Callon, ed., *The Laws of the Market* (Oxford: Blackwell / The Sociological Review, 1998).

46 Ibid., p. 262.

47 D. Brenneis, "Reforming Promise," presented at *Documents: Artifacts of Modern Knowledge,* a conference convened by A. Riles, Center for Law, Culture and Social Thought, Northwestern University, November 1999.

48 Gibbons, *Science's New Social Contract.*

49 P. Harvey and S. Green, "Scaling places and networks: an ethnography of ICT 'innovation' in Manchester," presented at the Internet & Ethnography Conference, Hull, 1999.

50   H. Tsoukas, "Introduction: From Social Engineering to Reflective Action, in Organiza-
     tional Behaviour," in *New Thinking in Organizational Behaviour: From Social Engineering to
     Reflective Action*, H. Tsoukas, ed. (Oxford: Butterworth–Heinemann, 1994), pp. 15, 16.

51   *Times Higher Education Supplement*, March 22, 2002.

52   *The Guardian*, April 9, 2002.

53   G. Born, "Public Museums, Museum Photography, and the Limits of Reflexivity," *Journal
     of Material Culture* 2, 1998, p. 249.

54   M. Biagioli and P. Galison, eds., *Scientific Authorship: Credit and Intellectual Property in
     Science* (New York: Routledge, 2003).

55   Nowotny et al., *Re-Thinking Science*.

56   For further reading on these topics, please see O. O'Neill, *Autonomy and Trust in Bioethics*
     (Cambridge: Cambridge University Press, 2002); M. Power, *The Audit Society: Rituals of
     Verification* (Oxford: Oxford University Press, 1997); P. Rabinow, *French DNA: Trouble in
     Purgatory* (Chicago: University of Chicago Press, 1999); M. Strathern, ed., *Audit Cultures:
     Anthropological Studies in Accountability, Ethics and the Academy* (London; Routledge, 2000).

INDEX